"Although written from a Wicca perspective, most of the content in Covencraft *generalizes beautifully to other Pagan groups such as groves, circles, or steadings; the quality and detail of content, especially [the material on] group dynamics, make it relevant to most traditions. It is also suitable for all experience levels, though of most use to intermediate or advanced practitioners who wish to found a coven or tune up an existing one."*

— Elizabeth Barrette
"Reviews from Hypatia's Hoard," *PagaNet News*

"Amber K has long been recognized as a respected High Priestess, author, artist and teacher of Wicca. [She is] one of a few authentic visionaries in the Wiccan community today.

"Whatever form the practice of contemporary Witchcraft takes in the future millennia, this book will go far to preserve the role of the coven as a primary living and ever-evolving community structure and vehicles for spiritual teaching, transformation, improvement, and healing of the human community and of the Earth. Covencraft *is one very important and helpful guide to that goal."*

— Reverend Gary Lingen, a.k.a Earthkin
Founder and Elder High Priest of New Earth Circle Coven

"Despite the volume of information covered, Covencraft *does not come across as some dreary association manual; rather, it's infused with an easy readability and ethical sensibility that does honor to the Craft it promotes. ... Anyone interested in Wicca should read this book."*

— *NAPRA ReView*

About the Author

Amber K is an ordained High Priestess of Wicca. She was initiated and received her early training at the Temple of the Pagan Way in Chicago. Later, she and Catelaine founded the Coven of Our Lady of the Woods in Wisconsin, and when she moved to New Mexico she reorganized the coven there.

She has served as National First Officer and National Publications Officer of the Covenant of the Goddess, a federation of more than one hundred covens and many solitaries in the United States, Canada, and overseas. She has also been associated with the Re-formed Congregation of the Goddess' Cella priestess training program, and Of A Like Mind women's spirituality network.

She is a former editrix of *Circle Network News* and *The COG Newsletter*, and her writings on the Craft have been widely circulated in the United States and beyond. Her publications include *True Magick: A Beginner's Guide*; *Moonrise: Welcome to Dianic Wicca*; *The Pagan Kids' Activity Book*; and others.

Amber has traveled widely throughout the United States teaching the Craft, and has been a guest speaker at Heartland, Dragonfest, United Earth Assembly, and many other gatherings.

Presently she lives in Los Alamos, New Mexico, with her partner Azrael Arynn K, her son Starfire, and their dog Kitsune.

Amber says, "We are at a pivotal point in human history; with wisdom, love, and power, we can influence the course of humanity and its relationship with the Earth. Let us begin a great ingathering of our people, to join our strengths in service to the Lady and make the Craft a force on this planet."

To Write to the Author

If you wish to contact the author or would like more information about this book, please write to the author in care of Llewellyn Worldwide and we will forward your request. Both the author and publisher appreciate hearing from you and learning of your enjoyment of this book and how it has helped you. Llewellyn Worldwide cannot guarantee that every letter written to the author can be answered, but all will be forwarded. Please write to:

Amber K
℅ Llewellyn Worldwide
P. O. Box 64383, Dept. K018-3
St. Paul, MN 55164-0383, U.S.A.

Please enclose a self-addressed, stamped envelope for reply, or $1.00 to cover costs. If outside U.S.A., enclose international postal reply coupon.

Amber K

1998
Llewellyn Publications
Saint Paul, Minnesota 55164-0383, U.S.A.

FIRST EDITION
First Printing, 1998

Cover illustration: Paul Mason
Cover design: Anne Marie Garrison
Cover calligraphy: Amber K
Interior illustrations: Amber K
Editing and interior design: Astrid Sandell

Library of Congress Cataloguing-in-Publication Data
K, Amber, 1947–
Covencraft : witchcraft for three or more / Amber K. -- 1st ed.
p. cm.
Includes bibliographical references and index
ISBN 1-57618-018-3
1. Witchcraft. 2. Covens. I. Title.
BF1572.C68K19 1998
133.4'3--dc21 9830547
CIP

Publisher's Note: Llewellyn Worldwide does not participate in, endorse, or have any authority or responsibility concerning private business transactions between our authors and the public. All mail addressed to the author is forwarded but the publisher cannot, unless specifically instructed by the author, give out an address or phone number.

Llewellyn Publications
A Division of Llewellyn Worldwide, Ltd.
P.O. Box 64383, Dept. K018-3
St. Paul, MN 55164-0383, U.S.A.

Printed in the United States of America

Other Books by Amber K

True Magick: A Beginner's Guide

Moonrise: Welcome to Dianic Wicca (Re-Formed Congregation of the Goddess)

The Pagan Kids' Activity Book (Horned Owl)

Dedication

This book is lovingly dedicated to my partner, Azrael Arynn K . . .
and of course, to Trixie.

Acknowledgments

No book is written without the cooperation of many people, and I would like to thank the following people for their direct or indirect assistance with this one:

Dave Norman and Ginny Brubaker, who showed me from Day One how a good teaching coven works;

Catelaine, who was my partner in founding the first incarnation of Our Lady of the Woods;

Amber-Isis and Ur, Rowan and Sparrow, Merlyn, Tehom, Brother Wolf, Cedar, Cernos, Gaia Morgana, and the others who read part or all of the manuscript and offered their wisdom to improve it;

Alane Crowomyn, who provided the material for the chapter on the life cycles of a coven;

Nancy Mostad, Astrid Sandell, and the other folks at Llewellyn Worldwide who offered their help and encouragement;

All my coven sisters and brothers, past and present, who taught me more than I could ever have taught them;

Flo, my high desert dolphin who swims with me always;

And most of all, my partner Azrael Arynn K, who was supportive in precisely all the right ways as I put it all together.

To all these and all those I have not named, thank you.

Blessed be,

Amber K

Contents

Preface

Witchcraft Yesterday and Today

Witchcraft! To most people in Western society the word conjures up images of a ragged figure on a broom silhouetted against a full moon, or cackling hags bent over a steaming cauldron. Many recall the villainesses of childhood fairy tales: the woman in the gingerbread house who tried to eat Hansel and Gretel, or the "Wicked Witch of the West" in the Land of Oz.

Yet there are people living today who claim the name "Witch"—in the United States and Canada, Europe and Australia. We do not curse people or praise Satan, much less fly on brooms or threaten children. The truth concerning our beliefs and practices is a far cry from the ugly stereotype of Halloween masks and ghost stories. We are for the most part gentle and friendly people, no different in appearance from our neighbors. We are good citizens who happen to practice a minority religion.

For Witchcraft—also called Wicca or the Craft—is a religion, as surely as Christianity, Buddhism, or Islam. In fact, it may be the world's oldest religion. Cave paintings, sculptures, and burials dating back 15,000 to perhaps 200,000 years (the approximate date of an Acheulian "Earth Mother" statuette discovered recently in the Golan Heights) suggest that many of the traditions important to Witches today are identical to the religious practices of Paleolithic times. In a way this is not surprising, since the Craft is largely based on natural processes and cycles that change little over the course of millennia.

So what do Witches believe and do? Why are they so often portrayed as malefic hags in folklore? And does this very ancient spiritual tradition have any relevance for people in today's technologically sophisticated society?

To begin with, true Wiccans are ethical and caring people. They follow a guideline called the Wiccan Rede: "An ye harm none, do as ye will." A rough paraphrase might be, "Follow your own destiny and live as you choose, as long as you don't hurt yourself or others." They believe that harming others results in a natural, inevitable backlash—not necessarily from the victim—so that the original nastiness returns multiplied to the perpetrator. This process is called "The Law of Return," among other names.

Rather than cursing folks, in fact, many Witches are active in herbal and psychic healing.

Witches feel a strong connection with the world of Nature. They celebrate natural cycles of birth, death, and renewal: the changing of the seasons and the cycles of the moon and sun. Generally they enjoy animals, gardening, and outdoor life and are strong supporters of conservation and environmental protection. To Witches, the Earth and Her creatures are sacred.

Many Witches believe that all goddesses and gods of all cultures are reflections of some facet of the Supreme Being, and therefore should be respected. But the favorite deities of the Craft are the Triple Moon Goddess, Whose changing face represents Maiden, Mother, and Crone; and the Horned God of wildlife, death, and rebirth. They have many names.

Some Witches practice their religion alone or among their immediate family. Others meet in small groups called covens, at the Full Moon and other times. All practice magick—not the illusions of stage magicians, or the supernatural feats of fantasy-novel wizards, but magick as practical psychic techniques to effect change in themselves and their world. Their meetings include invocations and spells, singing and dancing, food and laughter: they are by turns very serious and very merry.

To understand how this benevolent religion received the negative image it has among some today, one must know a little religious history. When Christianity began to move into Pagan Europe, it was at first able to coexist peacefully with the indigenous religions, including Wicca. But as the power of the Roman Church grew, it began to treat the Pagan spiritual traditions more and more as rivals rather than neighbors. In 1207, Pope Innocent III began a war of extermination against the Cathari of France, which began a campaign of violence and terror against "heresy" throughout Europe—that is, against anyone accused of holding beliefs different from Church dogma. The Inquisition reached full flood in the 1480s, with Innocent VIII's bull against Witchcraft, then the publication of the *Malleus Malificarum*, a Witch-hunting manual. Several hundred thousand people at least, and perhaps as many as nine million, were tortured and killed over a period of about five hundred years. Sometimes the motivation was religious fanaticism, and sometimes heresy was an excuse for cold-blooded political machinations to amass land, wealth, and power.

In order to mobilize public opinion against Wicca, the Church levied the most extreme charges against the Craft, most of them patently absurd to educated and thoughtful people of the time, but believable to the superstitious bulk of the population. Witches were accused of sacrificing Christian babies, holding Black Masses, worshipping Satan, and more. False "confessions" were extracted by torture and used as further fuel for anti-Witch propaganda.

Of course the practitioners of the Old Religion went underground, forming small groups later called "covens," and over centuries the horror stories promulgated by the medieval Church found their way into fairy tales and folk legends. For a long, long time, none dared speak out and set the record straight.

In the twentieth century, scholars such as Margaret Murray began to unravel the truth of the matter. Gerald Gardner and Sybil Leek, both initiated into surviving Craft traditions, wrote of their experiences. In some more liberal communities it became possible to discuss the Craft openly. Covens came into the open and new ones were formed.

People who love Nature, want to explore their psychic abilities, or need to reclaim the female aspect of divinity become curious, then involved. Today the Craft is undergoing a renaissance. The ancient traditions have been injected with a great deal of spontaneity and creativity, and now Wicca shows a vitality and exuberance it has not seen in a thousand years.

Many questions about the Craft must occur to modern observers, and some of the more common ones can be touched on here.

Why call this re-emerging religion "Witchcraft" at all? Hasn't that word been hopelessly twisted, and wouldn't it be better to present this faith under a new name?
Many in the Craft would agree, and they use "Wiccan" instead of "Witch" to refer to themselves, at least in public. Others consider the word "Witch" to be part of their heritage, to be reclaimed and restored to its ancient connotations of wisdom, healing, attunement to Nature, and the power to shape one's own destiny. After all, we would not suggest that people stop calling themselves "Jews" or "Mormons" simply because they have been persecuted under those names.

Why speak of a "Moon Goddess" and "Horned God?" Can educated people seriously believe that such beings exist?
How do you feel seeing a full moon rise over the sea or mountains? Does this not evoke in you a sense of wonder? The moon exists, and is an old and powerful symbol for natural powers and processes that all women experience. She changes, as we do, from young to mature to old. She affects the tides and rhythms of our bodies, as She raises and lowers the tides of the seas. She is visible at night when covens meet to practice magick—and so symbolizes the magickal or psychic part of our personalities. She is sometimes depicted as a woman to remind us that women share Her divine qualities.

The Horned God symbolizes the creative male energy as expressed in wild Nature, as well as the process of death followed by new life. All this could be assigned to some abstract symbol, but that would not express the idea that human beings embody these qualities and processes. Gods and goddesses in human form remind us of our own divinity, actual and potential. This is not to deny that Spirit also resides in animals, plants, stones, and stars.

How Witches experience the Goddess and the God varies from person to person. To some They are Jungian archetypes, mythic constructs that express realities deep in the human psyche. To others They are personal deities: wise counselors, friends, or lovers. To others They are the Spirit that animates the Earth and all creation. But to all Witches, They are real.

Do Witches claim to have unusual powers? Why do you write about "magick," with that unusual spelling, instead of "magic"?
To most people, "magic" suggests tricks and illusions for the purpose of entertainment. To others it is a quite unreal ability to perform miracles through supernatural power stored in a wand or incantation: for example, the spurious "magic" of sword-and-sorcery novels or fantasy role-playing games.

Many Witches write "magick-with-a-k" to differentiate it from illusions or miracles. The techniques of true magick produce real effects through natural means. Because changes caused by magickal or psychic means are often subjective and hard to measure, or haven't been strictly researched, some scientists equate magick with superstition or delusion. It would be more accurate to say that magick employs means and achieves results not yet fully confirmed by the scientific tools so far available. But Witches are generally down-to-Earth people, whose main concern is that magick works for them.

Why all the emphasis on Nature and the Earth? Are Witches opposed to technology?
Most Witches very much approve of science and technology—when intelligently used. Many are computer owners or electronics buffs, or support the space program. It is only when technology threatens the delicate balance of the ecosphere that Witches oppose it, which is why so many are ardent conservationists and opponents of nuclear arms technology.

Craft folk see the Earth as the source and shelter of life, and humankind as one part of the web of life that covers her. They feel a sacred obligation to protect the Earth as the Mother of life, and to share Her resources with other life forms as we would with sisters and brothers.

What is the point of joining a coven? Why not practice the Craft alone?
Some Witches do practice alone, either because they have some intensely personal inner work to do or just because no suitable coven exists nearby.

For others the coven system allows each Witch to share the energy and creativity of others in practicing magick. It becomes a sort of "magickal cooperative" where joint efforts benefit everyone.

Simple companionship is important as well. Celebrating a sabbat as a group is far more fun than trying to sing, dance, and feast by yourself.

Perhaps most important is the caring support of one another. A coven is usually a very close-knit group of friends, virtually an extended family, all sharing many of the same values and all committed to spiritual growth within the same tradition. As coveners work and play together, they form emotional and psychic bonds that make it possible to share dreams and fears, explore hidden parts of themselves, and take those risks so necessary for growth that are so difficult to do with casual friends or acquaintances.

Though this closeness and intensity is valuable in itself, it also certainly serves to enhance magick. When a well-established coven practices ritual magick together, usually all proceeds smoothly and powerfully toward a climax—without the awkwardness and miscommunication that occur when strangers try to work together.

All this only touches the surface of Wicca's rich traditions and long history. A reading list is included among the appendices for those who wish to study its goddesses and gods, history, and magickal practices in more depth. In this book the focus is on the coven—what it is, how it works, and how you can make your coven experience more effective, enjoyable, and exciting.

Terminology and Grammar

Writing about Witchcraft in the modern age is a challenge, entirely apart from the fact that my spellchecker thinks I've gone daft. I would like to clarify some of the ways I have used the English language in this volume.

First, I have capitalized "Witch," "Witchcraft," "Wiccan," and "Wicca." Proper nouns relating to other religions are capitalized but some journalists haven't got the picture yet, and I want to make it clear that Wicca deserves the same respect as any other faith in this regard.

Second, I have used "Witchcraft" and "Wicca" interchangeably, as well as "Witch" and "Wiccan." I am well aware that some in our faith consider these to be different phenomena, but as I have never heard an explanation of that bias that makes sense to me, I will draw no distinction. With all these "W-words" I refer to "a Pagan nature religion having its roots in pre-Christian western Europe and undergoing a twentieth-century revival, especially in the United States and Great Britain," to quote the *American Heritage Dictionary*—which also defines a Wiccan as "a follower of Wicca; a Witch."

It has always seemed unfortunate to me that some want to call every kind of magick-worker, shaman, healer, or nature-oriented priest/ess a "Witch," no matter what their culture or religion. There are perfectly good terms out there to specify these other types of people: a bruja, an herbalist, a skinwalker, a sorceress, a rune master, or whatever. But not everyone who practices magick is a Witch.

Third, I have used "God/dess" or "Goddess and God" to refer to the Ultimate Divine Source, and "god/dess," "goddess," or "god" to refer to certain facets or aspects of the Divine, such as Athena, Odin, or Cerridwen.

Fourth, I do not believe in the "generic masculine" (the sexist notion that "he" refers to people of both sexes) and have tried to avoid it. Unfortunately, it is awkward to include both genders in every sentence, such as "He or she is fortunate if he or she can find a coven to his or her liking." Instead, I have often used "they" and "their" to indicate the indeterminate singular as well as the plural. For example, "If a Witch wants to learn magick, they had better be prepared to work hard."

I know perfectly well that this is ungrammatical by conservative standards, but it is becoming increasingly commonplace in actual usage—and it's not sexist.

Those who disagree with my choices are certainly entitled to their opinions, and they are free to employ other usages in the books they write.

Introduction

If you are a seeker hoping to learn more about the ancient spiritual path of Witchcraft . . . if you are a coven member wanting more rewarding experiences in your group . . . if you are looking for a coven to join, or thinking of starting one . . . if you are an experienced High Priestess or High Priest gathering proven techniques and fresh ideas . . . this book is for you.

It is for anyone who hopes to practice Witchcraft in a caring, challenging, well-organized spiritual support group: a coven.

It is emphatically NOT ONLY for the titled leaders within a coven. It is for every member and potential member, because each covener shares responsibility for whatever happens in the group. In the best kind of coven, we are all "coven leaders" to the fullest extent of our individual skills, knowledge, and energy. We need not watch passively while a High Priestess or other Grand Poobah runs the entire show. In the emerging Aquarian Age, there may be a place for titles, offices, and honors—but the keynotes will be mutual responsibility and cooperative endeavor.

Every member helps to guide and maintain the coven because each of us is "Priest/ess and Witch," or aspiring to be, and empowered to create whatever destiny we will. That responsibility begins with shaping ourselves and our covens.

We come to the coven to cast the circle, celebrate the Mysteries, work magick, change reality. We act. Because we choose to act with and through covens, we need tools to make covens work. We need training and skills in group work, and these are hard to come by. Even basic group process skills are not usually taught in public schools, and the course titled Coven Management 101 hums quietly to itself on some astral plane, waiting for a Wiccan seminary to manifest. True, much can be learned simply by participating in a solid, well-organized coven, but many Wiccans have never had that opportunity; and even those of us who have had it often want to expand our knowledge and sharpen our skills further.

To help meet this need I offer this book, so that I may share with you what I have learned (so far) about covens, in nearly twenty years as a Wiccan priestess. Some of the material here derives from my associations with various covens and magickal groups: Temple of the Pagan Way,

WomanScouts, New Earth Circle, The Pool of Bast, Our Lady of the Woods, The Covenant of the Goddess, and the Re-formed Congregation of the Goddess. Some of the small-group information is based on my university training and professional experience. Before becoming a priestess, I worked in the fields of organization development, group process, volunteer management, and leadership training. To all who have been my teachers, both within the Craft and outside it, I am grateful.

If occasional suggestions I have offered seem unusual from the perspective of your tradition, it may be because I believe in borrowing techniques from other organizations and disciplines, as long as they fit the spirit of the Craft. There is great value in both tradition and innovation, and wisdom lies in keeping them balanced.

Naturally, not every Witch will care for all the ideas presented in this book. That is as it should be: diversity enriches us. It is the spirit of the Craft that unites us, not details of coven practice. Throughout this book, I have tried to offer a range of possibilities to accommodate differing needs and styles. When I make a suggestion, it is not a dictum but a friendship offering for you to adopt, change, or set aside as your inner voice guides you. There is no "One, True, Right and Only Way," thank the Goddess.

One more word about this book: it covers a lot of territory, so do not try to use all the ideas at once. A massive "Coven Reorganization Program" consisting of 397 proposals tends to leave the coven sisters and brothers glassy-eyed. Take one step at a time . . . .

. . . and may the Triple Goddess of the Moon and the Horned God walk with you.

Blessed be,

Amber K

July 1997
Los Alamos, New Mexico

1 To Be a Witch

A Witch is a priestess or priest of the Old Religion of Europe: Wiccacraeft or Wicca. The word comes from an Anglo-Saxon root that meant wisdom, divination, or "to bend or shape." Witches shape reality with their magick.

What Witches are NOT: we are not devil-worshippers, celebrants at Black Masses, workers of evil magick, or sacrificers of children or animals. We are not ugly old hags with green skin and warts on our noses.

What Witches ARE: people. People who are a lot like everyone else in many ways. We smile, laugh, or kid around when we're happy. We stomp around and maybe cuss when we're mad. Some of us like bowling, pizza, and television; some don't. Some of us enjoy ballet, quiche, and Shakespeare; some don't.

Well, something makes us different, makes us Witches. Partly it's what we believe. We believe the divine Spirit is present in all creatures and all things: people, animals, plants, stones, you name it.

Because the Earth and all of Nature are divine, we treat them with reverence and respect.

We believe the ultimate creative force manifests as both feminine and masculine; so we often symbolize "It" as The Goddess and The God. In some covens, both are celebrated equally. In others, the Goddess is given precedence or even celebrated without reference to the God.

Most of us believe that all goddesses and gods that have ever been created, imagined, or discovered are aspects of The Goddess and The God. Some of our favorites are the Triple Goddess of the Moon (Maiden, Mother, and Crone); the Horned God of wildlife, death, and rebirth; the Earth Mother; and the Green Man.

Most of us think that we evolve spiritually over the course of many lifetimes. Upon death we go to the Summerland, a state of rest and reflection, and eventually we choose where and when we will be reborn.

We also believe that every individual has access to the divine. Nobody needs an intermediary to get to God/dess. Every initiate is regarded as priest/ess. We have no revealed scripture, prophet, or messiah.

We believe in a rule called the Wiccan Rede: "An ye harm none, do as ye will." This is reinforced by The Law of Return, the understanding that whatever energy you send out returns to you multiplied. More on these later.

We do not believe that race, ethnic heritage, gender, or sexual orientation matter when it comes to spiritual worth. So we welcome all those whose hearts are drawn to the Old Religion.

Last but not least, we think people should be free to choose the religion that best fits their needs. Wicca is not the only valid spiritual path, and we try to respect and learn from other religions.

But Witchcraft isn't only about what we believe. It's mostly about what we do, how we live.

We see the world differently from most, with what some have called "starlight vision." Partly, that means that we see the web of energy that connects all things and the auras of each creature. Partly it means that we see the truth of dreams and imagination: we see signs in the stars, omens in the sudden appearance of a mountain lion, portents in the wind-driven branches of the trees. Partly it means that for us the world is a place of infinite possibility, filled with the promise of magick and the certainty of transformation.

And so we work magick, real magick, which is not like the hocus-pocus in movies or fantasy novels. But magick only for positive purposes: spiritual development, healing, guidance, safety, and so forth. With magick we visit realms unseen by other eyes, make our visions manifest, and re-create our lives.

We work our magick according to the phases of the Moon. We also gather at sabbat festivals to celebrate the change of the seasons. Witches prefer to meet outdoors when possible; mostly we don't have church buildings. Small groups don't require them and generally cannot afford them, anyway.

Witches work, study, and celebrate in small groups, usually three to thirteen in number, called covens; and sometimes in larger congregations or "groves." These may be associated with a tradition or federation, but are usually autonomous—there is no central church authority. That's why we have dozens of diverse traditions with somewhat differing beliefs.

Witches take responsibility. This is so very important that I'm going to say it again: Witches take responsibility. We are God/dess, integral parts of the Divinity that surrounds us; and it would be very unbecoming for a deity to shirk responsibility. No whining, no denial, no shrinking from the huge, complex problems of human society, or from the difficult choices in our individual lives. As entities we are divine; as humans we are possibly the most imaginative, capable species on this planet; as Witches we are magick-workers. Don't like your life? Change it. Don't like what's happening to the planet? Make a different reality. Be responsible for yourself, and for your world.

Witches learn to face the darkness within and without. We move through the night in the forest, knowing the terrain with other senses; and this is a metaphor for that inner journey where we meet our pain, grief, and anger—and heal them. We believe that healing and growth must be never-ending.

Because this world is sacred, we celebrate it with laughter and song, dancing and making love, feasting and play. Our bodies are good; life is good, and we meet it head-on, with whole hearts: like lovers clasping, like bears wrestling, like a great goblet of wine to be quaffed in a single draught. We love festivals and games and bright, dramatic costumes (at least when we're away from the office).

Healing is an ancient part of our heritage, from the days of the herb women and cunning men of the villages of Europe. So it is no surprise that many modern Witches follow professions within the healing arts as nurses, physician's assistants, health aides, nutritionists, chiropractors, and the like. Witches with other kinds of jobs still tend to have a keen interest in alternative medicine; many are unpaid herbalists, masseurs and masseuses, counselors, psychic healers, and so on.

Another field Witches are deeply involved in is computers. We see no conflict between magick and technology, and it is not at all strange for a Witch to come in from her herb garden, hang up the St. John's wort and feverfew she has harvested, and plunk down in front of her PC to surf the internet. Those Witches who are not computer professionals still, in large numbers, find desktop publishing, e-mail, and many other applications useful. However, other media are by no means abandoned: most Witches are voracious readers, with three or twelve books going at a time; and some have private libraries of impressive size and variety.

Because we represent not only ourselves, but also an often-misunderstood community, we have a responsibility to dress and act in ways that will give credence to the Wiccan community. There are Witches who dress always in black, with tons of eye makeup, exuding drama and mystery with every word and gesture. But others feel that such accouterments speak so loudly that people may not be able to hear our words or discern the person beneath the trappings. Still others believe that we should choose to be either completely private or completely open; and if open, that we need to show ourselves to be responsible, approachable friends and neighbors. Certainly this is one way of educating the public and protecting the Wiccan community.

Because all of Nature is a wonder to us, you will find many of us outside every weekend, hiking, picnicking, camping, gardening, skiing, swimming, caving, and enjoying a multitude of different forms of outdoor recreation. Because Nature is sacred to us—is the Goddess Herself—few of us can sit by when She is threatened by pollution and commercialism run rampant. So you will find many Witches working as environmental activists, either on local coven projects or with organizations like Greenpeace, the National Wildlife Federation, and the Nature Conservancy.

Witches sense a wider world than most people imagine; part of our calling is to explore the tiny nooks of wildness, the astral planes of existence, the realms of the honored dead, the kingdoms of imagination, the ancient past and the possible futures, and to discover God/dess and our own wholeness in the quest.

And part of our calling, our mission if you will, is to know the sacredness of All-That-Is: to respect the Earth, protect other species, foster wisdom among our own, celebrate the turning of the seasons, affirm the beneficence of the Universe, and honor God and Goddess in all Their glorious and diverse manifestations.

On Wiccan Ethics

Being a Witch is understanding and living a certain code of ethics. An eight-line poem sums it up:

Bide the Wiccan Law ye must,
In perfect love, in perfect trust.
Eight words the Wiccan Rede fulfill:
An ye harm none, do what ye will.
Ever mind the Rule of Three:
What ye send out, comes back to thee.
Follow this with mind and heart,
And merry ye meet, and merry ye part.[1]

The first line speaks of the Law, which may refer to the body of rules called the "Ardaynes" (*ordains*), honored by several traditions. The Ardaynes govern personal behavior and coven operation, and offer advice for protecting oneself from the Inquisition. There are several versions in print, including an older version with 162 laws, and a modernized version with eighty-eight. Most are written in archaic (or pseudo-archaic) language; whether they are genuinely from the Burning Times, or partially so, or a modern creation is uncertain (and really doesn't matter anyway). An updated version, *A New Wiccan Book of the Law,*[2] is a worthy set of guidelines.

"Perfect love and perfect trust" is an important ideal of the Craft. This is not an exhortation to trust everyone in a gullible way, but to constantly strive within the coven (and the world) to create love and trust. The primary way we do this is to be worthy of the love and trust of our covenmates (and everyone else). Yet we recognize that, being human, each of us will sometimes make mistakes. When this happens, rather than simply withdrawing love and trust, we trust that the individual was doing their best, and try to help them balance their error and grow from it. The individual who stumbled should not focus on feelings of guilt or unworthiness, but work intelligently to avoid similar errors in the future.

The third and fourth lines speak of the Wiccan Rede, the keystone of Wiccan ethics. "Rede" is an old Anglo-Saxon word meaning "wise counsel"—and it is wise advice, whether it is genuinely ancient wording or, as some believe, relatively modern. The first part of the Rede, "An ye harm none" means "If you harm none" or "As long as you harm none." What constitutes harm is sometimes crystal-clear, and sometimes not clear at all. Within Wicca, a great deal of respect is given to each individual's perception of what means "harm" to them. So for example, we would not do healing work for someone without permission, in case they would regard it (on any level) as interference rather than assistance. Working magick against someone's wishes but "for his own good" is contrary to Wiccan ethical practice. Often we will preface or end a magickal spell with "With harm toward none, and for the greatest good of all," which effectively nullifies the work if it would unintentionally engineer a negative result.

"None" means *no one*—the ethics of the Craft apply to non-human beings as well as human. For example, most Wiccans consider it wrong to compel a spirit to manifest, to kill baby seals for fashionable fur coats, or to disrupt a biological community unnecessarily. "No one" also includes the Witch him- or herself. That's why, even though most of us like a glass of wine or mead, very few Witches are alcoholics and addictive drug use is very rare.

"Do as ye will" means to act in accord with our True Will, our "Higher Self's" understanding of what is most wise and loving. (To put it another way, the Rede does not say "Do as ye whim.") Finding our True Will is not always easy; often it takes hard work to discern the best path: meditation, dreamwork, divination, and discussion with respected friends and teachers. Sometimes it springs clearly from the heart in an instant.

"Ever mind the Rule of Three: What ye send out, comes back to thee." The Rule of Three is sometimes called the Law of Return or the Threefold Law, and simply says that whatever energy we put into the world comes back to us multiplied by three. It is as though the Universe is a great echo chamber, and if we call out a word, it bounces back repeatedly and more loudly. This is not orchestrated by some Big Judge in the sky; it is a natural law. The effects may happen instantly, or be delayed or mitigated for a little while, but ultimately the Law is fulfilled. So of course it only makes sense to put good into the world, so that we receive good back.

"Follow this with mind and heart" suggests that we should follow the Wiccan ethical path wholeheartedly and without mental reservations. If we have either intellectual doubts or emotional reluctance, we will wander from the Rede and find ourselves in trouble. This comes down to a gut-level, intuitive trust that this is right for us, and a better personal guide for us than, say, the Christian ten commandments or Islamic religious law. The Wiccan Rede cannot be adopted through persuasion or argument: it either feels right, or it doesn't—it is a knowledge of the heart.

"And merry ye meet, and merry ye part." There are a couple of messages here. It emphasizes merriment as an important mode of being, that joy is to be sought and embraced. It suggests that beginnings and endings are both important, and celebration should happen at both times. No sad faces when it's time to say farewell because, of course, no parting is forever; when the wheel turns we will meet again.

Ethics are central to magick. It is not simply that some things are "not nice" to do: your spiritual growth, the effectiveness of your rituals, your happiness and even safety depend on using power correctly.

Wiccan ethics are for those who want to live mindfully. The Rede sounds so simple, but is actually challenging to live. It requires deep thought, exploration, investigation, discussion, divination, and reliance on intuition, logic, experience, and the wisdom of our communities. It is for those who realize that responsibility for ethical action can never be delegated or gifted to religious gurus or civil authorities. It is ours alone.

I Am A Witch

In deepest night, in forest deep,
In broad daylight, awake, asleep.
I am a Witch at every hour,
Touching magick, wielding power.

I am God/dess, Neverborn;
I wear the crescent, wear the horn.
I cast the circle, raise the cone,
And pour the wine when power's flown.

"An ye harm none, do as ye will"
Heal always, never kill,
Work your will but Earth revere,
And every creature living here.

Celebrate as the Wheel turns,
Dance and leap as balefire burns.
Sing to Goddess, Moon times three,
Drink to God, stag-horned He.

Soar upon the astral planes,
Visit woodland fairy fanes,
Swim with dolphins in the sea,
Say to all things, "I am Thee."

Live in peace with cowan folk,
Touch with magick, give them hope;
Live with kindness, die with peace,
In Summerland to find surcease.

—Amber K

NOTES

1. Original author unknown. The original version reads "Lest in thy self-defense it be, ever mind the Rule of Three." I have changed this to read "Ever mind the Rule of Three: What ye send out comes back to thee," in the belief that self-defense is possible without the use of negative energy.
2. Lady Galadriel, *A New Wiccan Book of the Law: A Manual for the Guidance of Groves, Covens, and Individuals*. Grove of the Unicorn: Moonstone Publications, rev. 1992.

2 A Short History of the Coven

Much of the history of Witchcraft is shrouded in mystery, in part because its traditions were oral, and partly because "history is written by the winners," and Christian rulers and clerics were extremely biased against the religions they were trying to supplant.

It would appear that ancient Europe and much of Asia practiced a nature-oriented religion focused on the Earth Mother Goddess and a Horned God of wildlife. Magick was practiced, and the cycles of the seasons were celebrated. Spirituality revolved around these basics for millennia.

By the rise of the Roman civilization (500 B.C.E. and after), Europe had several variants on the Old Religion. In parts of the south there was the Greek pantheon, which heavily influenced the Roman state religion; and also various mystery religions with roots in Egypt, Anatolia, and the Near East. In the north, the pantheons of the Vanir, and later the Aesir, were venerated. In the British Isles the religious practices of the Picts and other early inhabitants were swept aside by the Celts, but doubtless left their influence. The Celtic folk religion was at least part of the basis for Wicca and for Druidism, the faith of scholars, bards, historians, and leaders. Then as Angles, Saxons, and Jutes migrated westward into England, the Celts accepted a layer of Teutonic beliefs.

When Rome began the conquest of Europe, the Roman religion naturally mingled with local faiths; the Celtic moon goddess came to be worshipped under the name Diana, and Roman cavalry adopted the worship of Epona, the Celtic horse goddess. Roman influence was naturally stronger in the towns where legions were posted; people from the rural areas were rather contemptuously referred to as *pagani*, the Roman word for "country-dwellers," with the connotation that they were unenlightened hicks who would not adopt Roman culture.

In time, Christianity moved north and west, at first independently and later under Rome's sponsorship once it became the official religion of the empire. Early Christian churches very often co-existed or even blended with the indigenous religions; for example, members of the Culdee Church of Ireland lived in harmony with local Pagans, until the Culdees were exterminated by the Roman Church.

Throughout this period, there were no covens. There were the common folk and there were the wise women, cunning men, priests, priestesses, healers, oracles, and shamans who served their spiritual and health needs.

By the Middle Ages, the Roman Church had gained political power over most of Europe. The native faiths were on the wane in urban areas, but still practiced vigorously (sometimes right along with Christian practices) in the rural villages. But Rome faced problems: the Crusades were, for the most part, bloody disasters; plagues swept the burgeoning cities; a growing merchant class threatened a nexus of economic and political power not under the Church's control; and the corruption and excesses of the princes of the Church led to discontent and planted the seeds of the Reformation.

Faced with threats to its domination, the Church reacted with increasing harshness. It denounced heretics of all kinds and launched the Inquisition to wipe out those who would not acknowledge Rome's supremacy. The Church savagely attacked the Cathars, the Waldenses, the Albigensians, the Knights Templar, the Gnostics, the Jews—and the Witches.

As affiliation with the Pagan faiths became more dangerous, meetings of the Old Religionists became more and more secretive. Finally they went completely underground. The coven was born: a small, close-knit society of people who refused to give up their traditions and their faith. In some places, tiny congregations composed mostly of priests and priestesses struggled to preserve the old knowledge. In other areas, families privately practiced the Old Religion and publicly attended mass.

As the Inquisition gained power, it spread the most incredible propaganda against other faiths, branding them as sorcerers, perverts, and child-sacrificing devil-worshippers. It was asserted that they worshipped Satan, a "prince of evil" cobbled together from Lucifer (a god of light remodeled into a rebellious archangel), the Horned God of the woodlands, and the Hebrew *shaitan* (minor spirits of temptation). Until the Church invented Satan no one had ever heard of him, much less worshipped him; once he was publicized a few people actually did worship him on the theory that anything the Church was against must be all right.

The Burning Times had been launched.

Over a span of five centuries or so, roughly between 1200 and 1700 C.E., huge numbers of people were executed on charges of Witchcraft. Estimates range from a very conservative sixty thousand to as many as nine million killed. Anyone could begin the accusations—a jealous lover, a land-hungry neighbor, a hired "Witch-finder" paid by the head. The accused were then "put to the question," tortured until they confessed to all manner of gruesome acts. The *Malleus Malificarum*, the Inquisitor's handbook published in 1486, provided a standard confession of crimes for the accused to confess to. In England they were usually hanged, and on the continent often burned. Occasionally they were drowned. Sometimes the families of the accused were made to watch; sometimes they were put to death at the same time—children included. If some homosexuals had been rounded up in the same campaign, they became the "faggots" burned at the "Witches'" feet.

Almost certainly most of those murdered were not Witches. They were people of land and wealth, or political rivals, or young women who were extraordinarily beautiful or exceptionally ugly, old women living alone, and the mentally retarded or emotionally disturbed of all ages. It is little wonder that the real Witches went underground. Some were undoubtedly unmasked and killed, but many survived, especially those who were too powerful to be attacked without retribution and those who lived in remote rural communities sympathetic to the old ways.

The surviving small groups, or covens, became more and more closely knit and secretive as the centuries wore on. Although there were attempts to keep in touch through a network of special messengers, many covens gradually lost all communication with their co-religionists. Within each tradition, coven, and Witch family, parts of the old lore were preserved and parts were forgotten. Sometimes only a few fragments of herb lore or a handful of corrupted spells were remembered.

According to legend, an ideal Witches' coven consisted of thirteen members led by either a High Priestess, who embodied the Goddess, or a Magister or Man in Black, who was the Horned God incarnate. Groups of thirteen have been part of religious history for a very long time. A prehistoric cave in Spain revealed a group of thirteen bodies seated in a circle and surrounded by poppies; we may never know their story, but it seems likely that they were a religious gathering. Much later, Jesus had his twelve disciples, making thirteen at the Last Supper. Some legends say that there were thirteen places at King Arthur's Round Table in Camelot. Robin Hood and Maid Marian had a band of eleven outlaws in Sherwood, making thirteen in all. So it is possible that some covens, seeking connection with the spiritual power of the number, did admit thirteen members and no more.

Opinions diverge as to what happened next. One school of thought says that the Old Religion was completely lost and that the Witchcraft described by Gerald Gardner in the 1950s was pure invention, made up of pasted-together fragments of Masonic lore, ceremonial magician Aleister Crowley's writings, simplified rituals from the Order of the Golden Dawn, southeast Asian magick, and Rosicrucian bits, with the gaps filled in by the creativity of Gardner and his High Priestess, Doreen Valiente.

Though undoubtedly Gardner and Valiente were very creative people, there seems to be considerable evidence that the Old Religion did survive to modern times in several lines. Even if one assumes that Gardner invented the existence of the New Forest coven (doubtful, since Valiente has proven that Gardner's initiating priestess, Dorothy Clutterbuck, was a historical personage), there were the covens of George Pickingill in the nineteenth century, the covens of the Shield tradition, the Village Craft entrusted to Dolores Ashcroft-Nowicki, the colonial American lineages, *la vecchia religione* of Italy, and the Pecti-wica discovered by Ray Buckland. One could argue that any one of these were fabricated, but all of them? It seems more likely that the old faiths of Europe were more durable than historians guessed, and that Christianity's triumph there was never complete.

And entirely apart from any formal, organized traditions, at least some of the beliefs, lore, and attitudes survived within families. Sometimes it was a special love of nature, or a knack for herbal healing, or tales of the old gods and heroes. It might be passed on as stories about the faerie folk, or as various methods of divination, or little rhymes and remnants of spells "for luck." It is said, however, that some of the noble families of England perpetuated the Craft as a conscious, proud heritage, and kept lines of communication open with other such families into recent times. There is a persistent legend that the royal Plantagenets were all of the Old Religion, as well as certain other noble families better left unnamed.

Be it history or mythology, many modern Witches believe that the Craft survived. Covens met for the sabbats on deserted moors or deep in the forests where few good Christians would venture at night. They spread the stories of faerie folk and dangerous creatures of the night to improve their chances of privacy. They wore black to blend into the night and hooded cloaks to hide their faces. They sometimes carried hollowed turnip jack-o-lanterns on sticks, which looked like disembodied goblin faces bobbing through the darkness.

In their homes they disguised their ritual staffs as brooms and made pentacles of wax, which could be cast into the hearthfire in an emergency. They avoided fancy ritual tools, which were expensive and difficult to obtain, and used ordinary kitchen tools in their ceremonies. They held to their ancient traditions like the stubborn pagani they were, and faded from the view of society.

The Church of Rome, which during the height of the Inquisition had declared it heresy not to believe in the existence of Witches, in time did an about-face and declared that to believe in them was rankest superstition. As science and rationalism gained ground in Europe, educated men agreed that Witchcraft had never been anything more than delusion, and that the Witch hunts of the Middle Ages were a bizarre form of mass hysteria that swept the continent. By the twentieth century, Witches were firmly ensconced in the pages of fairy-tale books.

Then, in 1921, a distinguished archaeologist, Margaret Murray, wrote a book called *The Witch Cult in Western Europe,*[1] later followed by *The God of the Witches.*[2] In these she presented the startling hypothesis that Witchcraft had existed and was actually the survival of an old folk religion of Western Europe. Her scientific colleagues, who had been loud in their praise of her Egyptological studies, suddenly decided that her new crackpot theories should be dismissed without serious examination. And the Witches weren't talking.

In 1951, the English Witchcraft Act was replaced by the Fraudulent Mediums Act and for the first time in centuries it became legal to practice Witchcraft. In 1949, Gerald Gardner, a former civil servant, had published a novel about magick and Witchcraft under the pen name Scire.[3] Five years later he published *Witchcraft Today*,[4] describing the rites of a surviving Witch coven based in the New Forest of England. This seemed to unleash a tremendous flood of interest in the Craft: the "Gardnerian" tradition of Witchcraft (a mix of New Forest lore and the creativity of Gardner and Doreen Valiente) expanded and soon came to the U.S., where it encountered other traditions, some claiming to have been here since colonial times, coming out of the broom closet. An explosion of new traditions and covens followed, including Alexandrian, Georgian, Old Dianic, Dianic, New Reformed Order of the Golden Dawn, Pagan Way, and a host of others. Many were offshoots of Gardnerian Craft, others took their inspiration mostly from feminism, the environmental movement, or ceremonial magick. A few appear to be genuine survivals from centuries ago; other supposed "ancient traditions passed down from my grandmother" have all the hallmarks of something cobbled together on someone's kitchen table last month.

At this point, the precise origins of modern Witchcraft are moot. It may well be equal parts ancient religion and recent inspiration, with a strong tendency to borrow anything that doesn't run away. It may be a modern religion springing from the same sources of inspiration as the old Pagan faiths. It is certainly a decentralized folk religion with no prophet, messiah, head guru, or holy scripture. It is an earthy nature religion co-existing happily with science and technology, a working blend of the ecstatic Dionysian and the rational Apollonian. For those who care, it is officially recognized by the U.S. Armed Forces, the Internal Revenue Service, and other government agencies as a legitimate religion. It is cropping up in modern dictionaries, interfaith conferences, and college curricula. But what's really important is that Wicca is a vital, living, growing religion that meets the spiritual needs of many, many people.

As a living, growing religion it is already changing form once again. The Goddess and the Horned God, the seasonal celebrations, the magick and reverence for nature live on as the spiritual essence of the faith; but the structures, some attitudes, and the relationship to the outside world are changing. Even the coven as primary unit is different: it may have been created as a means of survival in the time of the Inquisition, but now it is increasingly a family of priest/esses serving a wider Pagan community. It is likely that the Craft will continue to revere those things our distant ancestors honored, and equally likely that it will continue to adapt to a changing world. The Craft has proven one thing beyond doubt: among religions, it is a survivor.

NOTES

1. Margaret Murray, *The Witch Cult in Western Europe* (London: Oxford University Press, 1921, 1971).
2. Margaret Murray, *The God of the Witches* (London: Oxford University Press, 1931, 1970).
3. Scire, *High Magic's Aid* (n.p., n.d.).
4. Gerald Gardner, *Witchcraft Today* (1954; reprint New York: Magickal Childe Publishing, Inc., 1991).

3 The Gods and the Universe

This chapter is about cosmology and thealogy—our beliefs about the universe and the gods. (I use the feminine "thealogy" rather than the masculine "theology" to add some balance to a field of study that has focused solely on male divinity for too long.) Because Witchcraft has no central authority, no dogma, no "Apostle's Creed," it is difficult to say anything universal about Wiccan cosmology and thealogy. It is an issue of concern for your coven, however, for two reasons. First, you will eventually be faced with applicants who share some beliefs but not enough for you to be comfortable calling them Witches. It would be nice to have some definition of "who you are and what you believe" in place before then. And, at the opposite extreme, if your coven's beliefs are too narrow you may exclude some great potential Witches over a relatively trivial point.

If you live in a huge city, perhaps you can find a covenful of folks who share very strictly defined beliefs: that the Universe is shaped like a '57 Chevy, that the Goddess gave birth to the God 4.739 thousand years after She became self-aware, and that He first appeared in a plaid sportcoat and a Panama hat with a purple band. But if you live in a small town or rural area, you had better be prepared to accept a broader range of beliefs.

The following discussion is designed to provoke thought and discussion within your coven, not to present some Ultimate Truth About the Big Questions. Toss the ideas around in your coven, incorporate them into your rituals when it feels right; but think carefully before you start dividing people into the "spiritually correct" and the "heretics." We probably don't need Wiccan Fundamentalists enforcing their notions of "The Truth." What matters is that we agree on a few basics: the immanent Goddess, the sacred Earth, the Wiccan Rede.

Reality, the Cosmos, and Everything

The scope of reality is vast beyond imagining. On the physical level, we can see—so far—a hundred billion galaxies in space, each with an average of a hundred billion stars in it. In terms of the "fourth dimension," time, scientists think the present cosmos was launched as long as seventeen billion years ago. No one knows how long it will continue or whether its present incarnation is one of an endless series of expanding and contracting universes. Consider also macrocosmic and microcosmic levels: perhaps every atom of matter contains within it countless galaxies too small for us to perceive; and perhaps our whole universe of a hundred billion galaxies is but a grain of sand on the beach of a far greater world. But even beyond all this, there is the concept of vibrational levels, interpenetrating planes of existence that occupy the same space and time as we do, but vibrate on an energy level that is usually invisible to our senses.

Space and time, microcosm and macrocosm, planes of . . . it is all too huge and strange for human comprehension. The British scientist J. B. S. Haldane said that "The universe is not only stranger than we perceive it to be, it is stranger than we can perceive it to be." But perhaps a model will help. Join me in a short journey as we visit Indra's Web, which is just one way to begin to visualize this reality of ours.

You float silently in the deep, velvet blackness of infinite space. Before you and behind you, receding forever, is a line of glowing crystal spheres. You are aware that they continue endlessly into the farthest reaches of the universe. To your left and your right, you can see more illuminated spheres punctuating the darkness into infinity. As you look up, then down, you can see that yet a third dimension is filled with the globes of light, layer upon layer upon layer, so that it seems that all of space and time, all the vast, unimaginable scope of the cosmos, is filled with the crystal spheres.

Every one of these countless spheres reflects within it the image and light of each other sphere; and every reflection in turn shines with all the reflections of the reflected spheres, so that their light is magnified again and again and again into infinity, and the universe blazes with the glory of their radiance.

This is the Web of all that is. Each object, each person, tree, stone, and star is connected with every other by the light. This is Indra's Web.

That's one model or analogy for the universe. Your coven may come up with one you like better. Try having a discussion where every covener completes the sentence, "The universe is like . . ." or "Reality is like . . ." and go from there. Is reality like a bowl of cherries? An onion? A complicated mechanical toy with missing directions? A dream of the Goddess? The dance of the Lady and Lord? You decide.

The Original Source

Some covens begin their cosmology with an Ultimate Source, similar to what is called the Tao or the Atman in other faiths. It is the Prime Mover, the Creator of all things. I'd like to share *The Blessing of the Cosmic One*[1] from the Temple of the Pagan Way that expresses this concept about as well as words can:

> In the Name of the Cosmic One, the Ancient Providence, Which Was from the beginning and Is for eternity male and female; the

> Original Source of All Things: All-Knowing, All-Pervading, All-Powerful, Changeless, Eternal; In the Name of the Lady of the Moon and the Lord of Death and Resurrection; In the Name of the Mighty Ones of the Four Quarters, the Kings of the Elements; Blessed Be this place, and this time, and they who are now with us.

An invocation from Starhawk's *The Spiral Dance*, "Invocation to the Ground of Being,"[2] has much the same feeling.

> In this model, the Original Source is formless Spirit, which gives rise to the Goddess and the God, Who mate and create all the diverse elements of the Universe. The Chinese equivalent can be summed up: "First there is the Tao; then there is the Yin and Yang; then there is the world of Ten Thousand Things." In Witchcraft, we have the subdivisions of Earth, Air, Fire and Water—matter, thought, energy, and emotion.

In another thealogical model, the Goddess is identified with the source, and the God is Her first creation and consort. In other words, the original Creator-as-birthgiver is seen as the Great Mother of all. She divides into the two polarities and mates with Her other self, the God, to create the cosmos. The story "Creation" from *The Spiral Dance* illustrates this idea:

> Alone, awesome, complete within Herself, the Goddess . . . floated in the abyss . . . . She drew . . . forth . . . and made love to Herself, and called Her 'Miria, the Wonderful.' . . . Miria was swept away, and . . . became the Blue God . . . . Then She became the Green One . . . . At last She became the Horned God . . . .[3]

In a third model, Goddess and God, Yin and Yang, are seen as co-equal and eternally co-existent. In other words, in the beginning there were two primal forces, not one. Who knows?

Polarity

Regardless of how we conceive of the original source, the issue of polarity soon arises. We are used to thinking of things in terms of either dualities or linear spectra with "opposite" ends: darkness and light, cold and warmth, Moon and Sun, substance and form, structure and energy, positive and negative. In some Eastern cultures there are the two great polarities of Yin and Yang. Yin, form or structure, is considered to be feminine, dark, and cold. Yang, energy, is thought to be masculine, active, light, and warm. One analogy says that Yin is the banks of a river, and Yang is the water rushing between the banks: form and energy. The polarities on the Tree of Life (a glyph or diagram that is a kind of map of spiritual reality in the Jewish mystical tradition) are called Binah and Chokmah. In Wicca, we personify them as the Goddess and the God.

This polarity-consciousness has huge social implications: we bring the whole notion into our lives in many ways. We have sexual roles and stereotyping: girl babies wear pink, boy babies wear blue. Women aren't mechanically talented, men aren't emotionally sensitive. These are oppressive simplifications or even perversions of the polarity concept, but that doesn't stop us from using the stereotypes. We sometimes carry the polarity idea into our thealogy by having sex-stereotyped goddesses and gods. That is, the Goddess is presented as pretty, loving, and tender while the God is handsome, rugged, and athletic. "Barbie goddesses" and "hunk gods." The Goddess is the Moon, emotion, and intuition; the God is the Sun, light, and rationality. Fortunately, the more you study deities of various times and cultures, the more you discover examples that break the stereotypes: warrior-goddesses and love-gods, and so on. And there are plenty of Sun-goddesses (Arinna, Bast, Sekhmet, Amaterasu, Grainne) and Moon-gods (Sin, Khonsu, Varuna, Ptah, Chandra). Polarity can be preserved in thealogy/theology without contributing to social stereotypes.

C.G. Jung provided a liberating idea: that both women and men have qualities of the other polarity within them. In women, the masculine soul-component is called the *animus*; in men, the feminine soul-component is the *anima*. To achieve psychological wholeness, one must recognize, accept, and embrace the other polarity within. This process is called the *hieros gamos* or Sacred Marriage.

The polarity that is not part of Wicca is the division between a Good Deity (Yahweh?) and an Evil Deity ("the Devil"). Some religions make the universe a battleground between these forces, with everyone taking sides—or being assigned a side. Thus, in the Middle Ages, darkness, magick, and women were consigned to the evil polarity, while light, logic, and men were automatically placed on the good side. We see this theme played out in our stories ad nauseam: the Westerns where the heroes wore white hats and the villains wore black; or "Star Wars" with Obi-wan Kenobi and Darth Vader. This whole concept comes from Zoroastrianism, a fairly late Persian tradition; our roots in Paleolithic times show no trace of it.

In Wicca, the God and Goddess are ultimate Reality incorporating both the Light and the Darkness, and their relationship is not a conflict but a dance of love and creation. It is basically an abundant and beneficent universe when we live in harmony with it. This has profound implications for living: though we do not embrace pain, hatred, or violence, we face them, learn from them, and seek whatever healing and blessing we can bring forth from them. We believe that in the long run nothing is lost and all can work out for the best. We are not pawns on a spiritual battlefield but partners in a great dance.

Thealogy/Theology

To most Wiccans, all historical deities are facets of the Divine. Each god or goddess represents someone's understanding of divinity, and all are valid in their own way. Gray explains it this way:

> So-called civilized Man makes a terrible mistake in supposing Divine or other Telesmic Images to be nothing more than worthless figments of immature imagination, having no more behind them than purely human origins. Half a truth is worse than a whole lie. Man may formalize Divinities or Devils, but he cannot energize them. Their force must come from the Entities they represent, and These are real enough in Their own realm. Everyone formulates according to their own ideas. Whether we make up Father-Gods, Mother-Gods, Savior-Gods, Nature-Gods, or the likenesses of our deceased ancestors, we shall provide some kind of Form for the God that in us lies. There is nothing wrong, inaccurate, or undesirable in the fundamental idea of constructing formalized expressions for the forces of Entities beyond and behind our ordinary human state of being . . . .[4]

God/dess thought-forms are a conceptual bridge between humanity and the unknowable Ultimate. It helps us to put a human face on the Divine, making it easier to relate to, and easier to see the divinity within ourselves. But of course divinity resides everywhere, not just in people. I once saw a cartoon that depicted a woodland scene with several animals each thinking about God. The stag was thinking, *And God created deer in His own image*. The vixen was thinking, *And God created foxes in Her own image*. The squirrel was thinking, *And God created squirrels in His own image*, and so on. It made perfect sense that a squirrel could relate better to a Squirrel-God than to some deity in human form, or pure Spirit or whatever. And as long as we don't limit Deity, and say that She or He exists *only* in human form, it's all right to see Deity in that form . . . or whatever form is most useful for our present purpose.

Wiccans understand God/dess to be in all things, not "Out There" somewhere apart from Nature. We talk about an immanent Deity rather than a transcendent one. This theme runs through one of our most beloved pieces of literature, "The Charge of the Goddess":

> . . . if that which you seek, you find not within yourself, you will never find it without. For behold, I have been with you from the beginning. . . .

A famous ceremonial magician of our time, W. E. Butler, expressed the same idea in different words:

> The ignorant man gazeth upon the face of Nature, and it is to him darkness of darkness. But the initiated and illumined man gazeth thereon and seeth the features of God.[5]

In what sense are the Gods "real?" An immanent Deity is not a matter of abstract belief, but something we experience and relate to in a thousand different ways every day. Starhawk explained it very well:

> People often ask me if I believe in the Goddess. I reply 'Do you believe in rocks?' It is extremely difficult for most Westerners to grasp the concept of a manifest deity. The phrase 'believe in' itself implies that we cannot know the Goddess, that She is somehow intangible, incomprehensible. But we do not believe in rocks—we may see them, touch them, dig them out of our gardens, or stop small children from throwing them at each other. We know them; we connect with them. In the Craft, we do not believe in the Goddess—we connect with Her; through the moon, the stars, the ocean, the earth, through trees, animals, through other human beings, through ourselves. She is here. She is within us all. She is the full circle: earth, air, fire, water, and essence—body, mind, spirit, emotions, change.[6]

Although all goddesses and gods may be valid in their own way—they may offer a glimpse of divinity—Witches have our own favorite deities, from the European cultures where Wicca flourished so long. One of the most ancient is the Earth Mother. We don't know what She was called thirty thousand years ago by the people who sculpted her in Paleolithic clay. Perhaps Danu or Doni, perhaps something else. Today we often borrow the Greek name Gaia.

The Horned God of wild things is also very ancient. We have seen His likeness painted on the walls of ancient caves. As Cernunnos, He was known and celebrated throughout Europe and beyond; He is also called Herne and is related to Pan.

The Triple Goddess of the Moon has many names: She is Maiden, Mother, and Crone at different points in Her cycle. She has been called Flidais, Diana, and Artemis. She is also Arianrhod of the Silver Wheel. As the crone, She is the Morrigan or Hecate. She is Mistress of Magick and the night, of the seas and tides.

The process of describing, understanding, and connecting with Divinity is never-ending. The tools we use for this immense task are the names, images and stories of goddesses and gods from many cultures and eras. For Witches, no single image can convey the vastness and wonder of Deity: God is too large to fit in so small a box. Therefore monotheism does not work for us in the day-to-day practice of our spirituality. A blend of animism, pantheism, and polytheism does. Who is God/dess? S/he is All. Where shall we look for God/dess? Anywhere and Everywhere.

Planes and Levels of Reality

Realities co-exist on different vibrational levels. We potentially can exist on any of the planes, and even while existing on this one can become aware of others through a change in consciousness. An analogy would be the guy with a beer sitting in front of the TV who is totally immersed in a football game. His consciousness is focused on the game, and he is unaware of his surroundings. When the commercial comes on, he sits back and becomes aware of the other people in the living room: he is suddenly in a different world. Then someone asks if he feels OK, and his consciousness refocuses inward, to yet another reality: his own feelings. He becomes self-aware, self-conscious. That night he falls asleep and dreams, and finds himself in yet another reality. All these different experiences are real, just as all the planes are real, even though they are not solid or material.

In order to try to understand different levels of reality, we create models, sometimes called planes of reality. Marion Weinstein says:

> In the occult, when we talk about 'coexisting space' we are usually referring specifically to coexisting planes, or dimensions, also known as 'astral planes.' I believe that these are the same dimensions which science refers to as 'alternate universes.' Here reside spirits, ghosts, invisible beings, and thought forms. Here also are the human auras and astral bodies, invisible counterparts of the physical human bodies.[7]

Many occultists believe there are seven Planes of Existence, each divided into seven sub-planes, which are likewise subdivided, and so on. The seven major planes are the:

Divine or Adi
Monadic or Anutadaka or Angelic
Spiritual or Nirvana
Intuitional or Buddhi
Mental, Causal, or Manas
Astral or Kama
Physical, Material, or Sthula

Weinstein, among others, has little use for this rigid approach to a very fluid realm: "This is a . . . simplistic linear view of nonlinear space."[8] True, but it works for some, and Witches are very pragmatic.

A person can gain access to other planes with techniques such as astral travel, either through conscious intention or in a dream state (your astral body still remains attached to your body by the "silver cord"). There are also dimensional gateways, as shown by mysterious appearances and disappearances of people and objects which are documented from time to time. Some of the legends of people going underground into the land of the fairies or the sidhe may be experiences of this sort.

The astral plane is non-material, fluid, and responsive to thought and emotion. Some of its inhabitants are much like us, some are not. Weinstein talks about spirits and the astral:

> Spirits are living beings composed entirely of invisible essence. Our own invisible essences are enclosed in physical form (our bodies) . . . . Some spirits were in human form in other lifetimes, and some will be

> again. Some were never human, and some will never be . . . . Rarely, some entities manifesting as 'spirits' may also be aspects of the self, in another time/space dimension.
>
> All spirits exist in the Unseen Realm. Some spirits do reside on the astral planes . . . . By choice, others come closer to the World of Form; these may coexist in the same room with us, ready to be perceived if we choose to become aware of their presence . . . .[9]

She goes on to remind us that spirits may be tricksters and cranks as easily as wise spiritual guides. They do not have all the answers; or to put it another way, "Being dead don't necessarily make you smart." Or ethical.

Wicca is a spiritual path that explores a wider reality and our connections with it all. We cannot as yet understand the whole, and can only seek to experience fragments of it directly or understand the big picture by analogy or models. Your coven or tradition will have its favorite creation myths and your own ways to understand divinity. And that is as it should be, as long as you honor others' right to their own perceptions, and have a healthy respect for the Unknown—which is still vaster than the total sum of human "knowledge."

RECOMMENDED BOOKS

The Spiral Dance and Dreaming the Dark, by Starhawk
Positive Magic, by Marion Weinstein
The Crack in the Cosmic Egg, by Joseph Chilton Pearce
The Tao of Physics, by Fritjof Capra
The Dancing Wu Li Masters, by Gary Zukav

NOTES

1. Book of Shadows, Temple of the Pagan Way (no longer in existence).
2. Starhawk, "Invocation to the Ground of Being," *The Spiral Dance: A Rebirth of the Ancient Religion of the Great Goddess* (New York: Harper & Row, 1979), p. 105.
3. Ibid, p. 17.
4. William Gray, *Inner Traditions of Magic* (York Beach, ME: Weiser, 1970), pp. 119–120.
5. William Butler, *The Magician: His Training and Work* (York Beach, ME: Samuel Weiser, n.d.), p. 29.
6. Starhawk pp. 77–78.
7. Marion Weinstein, *Positive Magick* (New York: Pocket Books, 1978), p. 27.
8. Ibid.
9. Ibid, pp. 29–30.

4 Finding a Coven

You may have to be quite persistent and patient as you seek to establish your first contact with a coven. For obvious reasons, few advertise their presence to the surrounding community; but there are ways to get in touch.

If you live in or near a city with an occult or New Age bookstore, the staff may be able to give you leads or may have a bulletin board that offers possibilities.

Watch the newspapers, especially in university towns, for announcements of lectures on Witchcraft at the local library or student union (lectures by Witches, needless to say, not right-wing religious extremists; you can usually tell from the publicity). These often occur around Halloween, when some Witches use the opportunity to try to educate the public. If you attend such a lecture, and the speaker seems genuinely well informed, you can speak to her or him afterwards and make your interest known.

Another place to look for contacts is at Pagan festivals. There are now many open gatherings across the country each summer, and a few in the spring and fall. In some cities you can find open sabbats celebrated throughout the year. Pagan newsletters and occasionally "alternative" or "New Age" periodicals publish notices for these events. There is likely to be one in your state or region. (See also the appendices on "Festivals" and "Pagan Periodicals.")

Once you get there, be friendly and talk to lots of people. Mention that you would like to find a coven and give your post office box address to a select few who strike you very favorably. It is usually all right to ask whether a coven is open to new members and pose general questions about their tradition and program. It is not all right to ask people for their legal names, phone numbers, or meeting locations (unless they have public meetings); they will share this information if and when they are ready to consider you as a potential member.

If you attend a festival and don't find any red-hot leads, don't worry about it. You can still learn a lot and have a good time.

Wiccan and Pagan periodicals offer leads through their classified advertisements. If you don't already subscribe to some, then see Appendix A-19 in the back of this book for a list. Sometimes covens that are open to members will place ads; more often, individuals place them, and you may want to put in your own. Keep it simple, as in the following example:

> Sincere student of the Craft desires coven contacts in southern Michigan. Offers skills in drama, woodworking, typing. Write Arianrhod, Box 333, Your Town, State, Zip Code.

List your geographical area rather than a specific town or city: there might be a coven a short drive away that is worth commuting to. Mentioning magickal or mundane skills you can share is an incentive for covens to respond: too many hopeful neophytes focus only on what they want, rather than what they can also contribute. Of course if you have specific and non-negotiable needs, these should be included: "seeks Dianic coven," "must include Qabalistic teaching," or whatever. Such restrictions will naturally reduce your chances of a reply, but there is no point in getting involved with a group that doesn't offer what you want.

There is always the possibility that an ad will draw some odd responses, either from fundamentalist missionaries or generic oddballs. To insulate yourself from such folk, you would be wise to list a post office box rather than your home address or telephone number. It is much easier to deal with a strange letter than a phone call or visit to your home some evening.

If you take out the box under your Craft name and have all your Pagan correspondence directed there, your chances of maintaining some privacy are improved. This works best in large towns or cities; if you live in a tiny village where the postmistress knows every face in the village, you may want to get a box in the nearest large town.

Another approach is to join a Wiccan or Pagan correspondence network. These publish newsletters and facilitate correspondence and contacts among people nationally or in a particular region of the country. Don't hesitate to write to "pen pals" elsewhere in the country just because your immediate goal is to find a coven locally. The Craft being what it is, someone two thousand miles away might know of a group in your own backyard. The networks often sponsor festivals and workshops as well, and some sell publications and products in order to finance their activities. Some of the major organizations or networks are listed in the appendices.

One more important source is *The Guide to Wiccan/Pagan Resources,*[1] published by Circle Publications (the address is in appendix on networks, page 412). Some covens place listings in it; though many of them are quickly outdated because of address changes, it is still worth exploring.

Then there is the internet. There are many web sites, forums, and "chat rooms" where you can make contact with other Witches (see the internet appendix, page 415). Even if you don't meet someone who happens to know of a coven down the street from you, then you will meet someone who knows someone who knows. If you are not on the internet, then find a trusted friend who is and ask them to make inquiries for you.

One last resort would be to place a classified ad in the largest regular newspaper nearby, of course using your Craft or magickal name and post office box number. It is not advisable to mention the words "Witch" or "Witchcraft" in your ad, since that could draw attention from unenlightened evangelists bent on saving your soul. A reference to "The Craft" or "the Old Religion" will alert the people you want to reach, and is more likely to slip right by the fundamentalist crusaders.

The hard part to accept is this: your best efforts may result in nothing. If so, do not be discouraged. It is simply a sign that the time is not yet right for you to be involved in a coven. Keep studying, practice rituals, and celebrate sabbats on your own, read the periodicals, and correspond with pen friends as you feel inclined. When all is ready within and without, you will either find a coven—or create one.

What to Watch For

Suppose you make contact and are invited to meet with members, or attend a ritual. How can you tell if it is really the kind of group you would be proud to join? Here are some positive clues to watch for:

- A friendly but cautious approach toward visitors or prospective members. Most covens will not initiate anyone until the candidate has been around for the traditional year and a day, so that everyone concerned can feel sure it's appropriate.
- Candor and willingness to explain. Certain rituals and advanced magickal techniques may be reserved for initiates; but the basic organization, beliefs, and activities should be no secret to a serious seeker.
- Wiccan thealogy and ethics. Do rituals, teaching, and discussion emphasize the God/dess within, the Wiccan Rede, individual responsibility, caring for the Earth and one another, and ethical magick?
- Mutual caring and respect. Do participants seem to like and respect each other? Is there courtesy, friendliness, open warmth, and affection?
- Spirituality. Do people seem to be "in touch" with their best qualities, their Higher Selves? Are their auras bright and clear? Do they discuss spiritual growth?
- Knowledge. Do coveners seem to know what they're talking about? Can they answer questions in a clear and sensible way? Do they draw information from a variety of sources? Have they apparently tried magickal techniques they talk about?
- Health. Do coveners seem vital, healthy, and alert? Is there interest in wholesome food, self-healing techniques, and outdoor activity?
- Fun. Is there laughter, lively conversation, singing, and dancing? Do people obviously enjoy each other's company?

- Organization and efficiency. Do meetings and rituals show evidence of careful preparation and run fairly smoothly? Are meeting schedules planned in advance? Is there a working system for teaching new people? Do coveners care about quality and punctuality and take assigned tasks seriously?
- Shared responsibility. Does everyone have a voice in making coven decisions? Are leadership and teaching roles spread around or rotated?
- Mental stimulation. Do they ask intelligent questions of each other, explain things well, and make perceptive and thoughtful comments on magick and the Craft? Are they curious?
- Physical surroundings. Are the ritual area and altar clean and neat, and carefully set up? Are ritual tools well cared for? If indoors, are there plants and fresh flowers? Do the coven symbols and tools radiate an aura of benevolence and quiet power? If books are in evidence, are there titles by Gardner, Starhawk, Weinstein, and other positive practitioners? Are there books about the Goddess, healing, and personal growth?
- Sharing outside of coven activities. Do members discuss interests and activities they share apart from rituals and coven events? Do their friendships extend into their mundane lives?

Intuition is your best guide. Do you feel relaxed, open and accepted? What does the God/dess within say: is this right for you? If you are reasonably healthy and sensitive to your "inner voice," you can trust your instincts.

What to Beware Of

On the other side of the coin, there are warning signals. If you observe any of the following signs, beware.

- Evangelism. Are they overeager to recruit you? If so, they may not be considering your best interests, but only how many "disciples" they can amass.
- A shroud of mystery. Is everything cloaked in secrecy and mumbo-jumbo? You can hardly expect them to share all their coven secrets on your first visit, but if you are troubled by things no one seems willing to talk about, then back away.
- Questionable beliefs. Does their philosophy seem narrow, intolerant or sexist in any way? Are there ideas you can't agree with, and are they closed to serious discussion of these?
- Disrespect for each other. Do criticism, sarcasm, and verbal "jabs" in the guise of humor dominate the conversation? Do members criticize one another openly or behind each others' backs?

- Authoritarian leadership. Do the leaders seem to exercise complete control over coven activities, or worse, over the personal lives of members? Do they take themselves too seriously? Is there a "Great Guru" mentality with blind obedience expected? Do they change the rules erratically and verbally abuse or guilt-trip members?
- Grim solemnity. Does every ritual have a deep, dark, "heavy" emotional atmosphere? Do they ignore the playful side of the Goddess and God, frown on merriment, and find it impossible to laugh at themselves?
- Dissipation or intemperance. Are drunkenness and drug use considered normal behavior? A couple of glasses of wine are one thing, but alcoholism is another. A lack of self-discipline is not characteristic of any skilled priestess or magician. As far as drugs go, a few native religions use mushrooms or peyote as part of their spiritual practice; but these are not part of modern Wiccan rituals, much less casual use of hard drugs! If addictions and poor health are common in a group you visit, this is a danger signal.
- Chronic disorganization. Are members consistently sloppy, unprepared, or indifferent about rituals or classes? Are they overly casual about individual responsibilities, ignoring or laughing off their forgetfulness or inefficiency?
- "True Believer" attitudes. Do participants seem to accept everything they hear from an "authority," without question? Do they believe in hollow-earth theories, messages from "Space Brothers," Illuminati conspiracies, and the like without intelligent discussion?
- Spiritual immaturity. Do members have shallow or childish attitudes toward life and the Craft? Do they participate in hexes, curses, or "psychic wars" with other groups? Are their auras muddy, dim, or angry? Is there an assumption that they have a monopoly on truth and that other paths are somehow inferior? Do they speak disparagingly of other religious beliefs?
- Ignorance. When members discuss ritual and magick, do they parrot phrases which they can't explain clearly? Are they unable to compare their system of magick to others? Do they talk glibly about magickal techniques they have never actually used?
- Profiteering. Are there hefty fees for training or initiation? Are there muddy financial relationships between the leaders and the members?
- Lack of teaching. Is there no clear system for instructing new members? Or is there a system on paper—but when you ask about specific dates and details, no one can supply them?

- Lack of connections outside coven activities. Does it seem that they never see each other outside of rituals? Or are there cliques that do things together but exclude certain members?
- Isolation. Are members uncomfortable with you visiting other covens or taking classes outside the coven? Do they avoid working with other covens on public sabbats or large projects? Do they seem unfamiliar with, or contemptuous of, the larger Pagan community around them?
- Physical surroundings. Is the altar area messy or shabby? Are ritual tools dirty or cheap? Are there tacky props in evidence—plastic skulls, gruesome sculptures? Do you get feelings of vague distaste near the coven's ritual objects? Does the library lean toward negativity or sensationalism, with books on psychic control, demonology, or magick of the "how to get power and riches" variety?

Again, trust your "inner bell." If something is wrong, you will feel it. Are you uncomfortable, even though you can't consciously pinpoint any problem? Is your breathing shallow, your chest tight? Is it hard to think clearly? If you experience any of these, to a degree beyond the normal nervousness of meeting new people, then thank your hosts and move on.

Checking Out Compatibility

Very few covens are likely to either meet your highest expectations or be completely without value. Like other human characteristics, they tend to be a mix of good and not so good, and to organically grow, change and wither as people come and go and the energies shift. Because they are small and are the focus of intense magickal energies, they can shift "personality" and direction much more rapidly than, say, a church with a congregation of three hundred. The addition or loss of one person can make a crucial difference in the life of a coven—which means that you can make a crucial difference.

Let us suppose that you find a coven not too far away that seems congenial. Even if everything seems perfectly fine, there is still the compatibility factor to be considered.

It is entirely possible that two or more decent, friendly, intelligent folks with similar interests and goals will not be able to work together. In fact, close contact may drive both of them wild, as many formerly married people can certify. There is no blame attached to either party, but the "chemistry" is wrong. Perhaps their styles of communication are different, so that neither ever really quite understands the other. Perhaps their goals are similar but they have different approaches to achieving them. Perhaps they are alike in too many ways, so that instead of complementing each other's strengths they duplicate efforts and crowd each other. Or perhaps their body chemistries are producing scents which are slightly irritating on a subliminal level—who knows?

It is important that the whole coven's energy field be comfortable and harmonious, which is why most covens wait at least a year and a day before initiating someone. Ordinarily any potential disharmony will become apparent over that length of time.

However, there are ways that you can speed up the get-acquainted process and discover whether there's a problem in a shorter time. And if it isn't going to work out, it's to everyone's advantage to find out as soon as possible.

On the mundane level, spend lots of time with each covener—not just the leaders and extroverts—in a variety of activities. Invite them to dinner, go on a picnic, see a movie, help clean a garage. The time and energy you invest will be amply repaid as your friendships ripen—or you learn that they're not going to.

In the realm of magick, as you participate in rituals with the coven you should be very open and sensitive to the energies within and around you. If you soon feel that your power blends smoothly with the others', and you can sense the ebb and flow almost before it happens, that is a very good sign indeed. But if you attend several rituals and still feel awkward and off balance, like an observer rather than an integral part of the circle, then it may be that you are not meant to join forces.

Divination may help. Using meditation, a pendulum, or other divinatory tools, consult your inner self and/or spirit guides. Ask lots of questions. Would I enjoy being part of this coven? Would I learn a great deal from them? Would I contribute something important? Would I be able to work well with Diana? Moss Agate? Thoth? (Name each covener.) All in all, would joining this coven be the best thing I could do at present for my spiritual growth?

You can use any other form of divination as well, as long as you or one of the coveners is skilled in it. Astrologers can compare natal charts; a karmic astrologer can see whether your spiritual goals dovetail well and possibly check for past-life relationships you may have had with anyone in the coven. Don't neglect Tarot, I Ching, runestones, and scrying if you have access to any of these. Look for guidance in dreams after casting a circle around your bed before you retire. Fast and meditate, or even do a vision quest outdoors. Compare your readings, insights, and discoveries with those of the coven members. When the time is right, hopefully you will be able to mutually decide whether your joining this particular coven is best for all concerned.

If it doesn't feel right to you or to some of the coven members, do your best to part on good terms, without disappointment or hard feelings. Remember that a decision not to invite you is no reflection on your personality, character, or skills. A puzzle piece that does not fit a particular hole is not a "bad" puzzle piece; it simply has not yet found the niche where it will fit perfectly and help complete the pattern. You will find your place in the pattern. Nor should you blame or belittle the coven; it may not be right for you, but for someone else it could be perfect. If you part, make it a "no-fault" parting.

If all the divination and meditation and delay seem excessive, bear in mind that initiation into a coven is an extremely important step—in some ways like being adopted into a family. In a good coven, the members are sisters and brothers to one another; they care deeply about each other, play together, heal one another, and help each other make their dreams come true. They grow together intellectually, emotionally, and spiritually. They teach, counsel, and feed each other, dance and sing together, and perform ritual together until their psychic energies flow and blend and peak together.

More than this, they are karmically linked. Their destinies are intertwined even if their paths part and circumstances decree that some members live thousands of miles apart. The happiness of one brings joy to all; adversity for one demands that they all rally to cope with it. If one covener achieves shining success in her chosen field, the accomplishment reflects credit on the entire coven. If another commits some reprehensible act, all are shamed. Thus initiation into a coven is no light matter.

Relocating

We have not yet considered the possibility of relocating in order to become part of a particular coven. Such a decision depends on how much it means to you to have the support of that particular community in your spiritual growth, and how deep your roots are in your present location.

In the past few years many Wiccans have chosen to move closer to a favored group or Pagan-friendly community, especially young couples and single people. Often the seed of such a pilgrimage is planted at a large Pagan festival, where solitaries meet and "click" with a group from another area.

If you have a good job, a home, and friends and family where you are now—but no coven—it may be a tough choice. But if you are attracted to the idea of moving, consider it well with both magickal and mundane techniques before you decide.

On a mundane level, visit your prospective new community several times. Check the housing situation and job market, as well as factors like weather, schools, or anything else that is important to you about the place you live. See what you can learn about the religious climate and tolerance for different lifestyles and beliefs.

Magickally speaking, you may want to visit natural landmarks such as lakes, mountains, or caves, and spend time in quiet meditation allowing the land to speak to you. There may be power points and ley lines that are worth exploring. If the landscape feels conducive to magick—or conversely, torn and polluted by the hand of man—this may be a factor in your decision.

Each time you visit, take the opportunity to spend some social time and if possible do ritual work with the coven that interests you. You can also invest in an astro-cartography analysis, which outlines the kind of energies awaiting you in every area of the world based on your natal horoscope.

If the coven invites you, and the move feels right to the point of inevitability, then do a private ritual to mark the decision. Thank the Powers for Their participation and guidance; meditate on the chapter of your life that is drawing to a close, and on what you have learned; and raise power for a smooth transition, invoking Hermes and Iris or other appropriate aspects of Deity. It is important to affirm at this time that the decision and the responsibility for its consequences are yours alone. You are in charge of your life, and should the move not immediately work out as you hope, it would not be fair or constructive to blame the coven, the people of the new community, or anyone else. (Or yourself, for that matter: responsibility is one thing, blame is quite another!)

Having done the ritual, channel your best energies into making it work out. If you have a new coven waiting, enlist their aid in finding a home and a job, and actually unpacking once you arrive. Invite them to a housewarming party, including a ritual of purification, blessing, and consecration of your new residence. The Law of Return applies as always: whatever energy you invest in getting off to a good start will come back to you threefold. Enjoy the adventure.

NOTES

1. *The Guide to Wiccan/Pagan Resources* (Circle Publications, biannual).

5 Organizing a Coven

Perhaps you have explored the idea of joining an existing coven and rejected it, either because the people are not a congenial match, they are on a different path, or because your own growth requires that you assume leadership responsibilities in a new group. Or maybe there's no coven within driving distance, and you choose not to relocate. It's time to think about organizing a coven.

Founding a coven can be immensely challenging and rewarding. But in doing so, you take on a great responsibility not only to the new coveners but also Witches present and past—to all who have followed this ancient spiritual path in life and even held fast to their beliefs under threat of death. Wicca is a proud and beautiful way of life, and if you would honor the Gods and yourself, you should not use its name or call your group a Wiccan coven unless you can commit yourself to live in its spirit of love, wisdom, and strength.

Looking at Yourself as a Coven Leader

Ideally one should have experience as an initiate in an established coven, as well as training in the specialized skills required of a High Priest/ess, before attempting to found a new coven. Initiation can refer to two different experiences. The first is a spiritual transformation not easily described; in part it involves an ecstatic realization of oneness with the universe (which is to say God/dess), the opposite of alienation, and the certain recognition of the spiritual path one is destined to follow. But "initiation" can also refer to the ritual that marks full acceptance of a candidate into a coven. Usually the aspirant must master certain basic skills and knowledge before the ritual is scheduled, and there is a waiting period to make sure that candidate and coven are a good match.

If you have never been initiated into a Wiccan coven, yet still feel called upon to organize one, then you have a decision to make. Only you can decide whether to seek out coven membership and training (which may take a long time and require relocating) and set aside thoughts of a new coven until you have more experience; to glean what you can from correspondence courses and occasional workshops; or to plunge ahead, learning by doing. If you have past-life experiences in the Craft, and the relevant skills are not too deeply buried, you may do a wonderful job with a minimum of training. You may also fall on your face and disappoint all the people who join you. There are no guarantees except perhaps one: however well you might do without prior coven experience, you will probably do better if you wait and get experience as a member first.

The same considerations apply to High Priest/ess training and ordination (third degree initiation in most traditions). The quality and depth of such training vary greatly from coven to coven, and ordination in itself is no guarantee of leadership ability. Ordination in one group may mean years of study and proving competence in key areas. In another, it may simply mean that someone sent in $5 for a mail-order certificate.

All in all, lack of formal ordination or a third degree should not necessarily deter you. But lack of skills and experience should. To some degree, the skills of teaching, counseling, ritual leadership, group process, and administration are transferable: experience in other organizations can be of some use in a coven. But none of these work quite the same in a coven of Witches as they would in, say, a service club or professional society. So before you assume that "Hey, I was President of the PTO, I can lead a coven," you would be wise to observe one or more experienced coven leaders in action.

Before you go further, take a good hard look at your desires, motivation, and skills. What role do you see yourself playing once this new coven is organized? "Ordinary" member? Democratic facilitator? High Priestess or Priest? And if the latter—what does that mean to you, and why do you want the job?

The title of High Priest/ess is seductive, conjuring dramatic images of yourself in embroidered robes, silver crescent (or horned helm) on your noble brow, adoring coveners hanging on every pearl of wisdom which drops from your lips . . . .

REALITY CHECK! The robes will be stained with wine and candle wax soon enough, and the coven members may give you as much grief as joy. A coven leader's job is mostly hard work between rituals and behind the scenes. It is not always a good place to act out your fantasies. The lives and well-being of others are involved, and what is flattering or enjoyable to you may not be in their best interests. So consider carefully.

If your prime motive in establishing a coven is to gain status and ego gratification, other people will quickly sense that. If they are intelligent, independent individuals, they will refuse to play Adoring Disciple to your Witch Queen impressions. They will disappear, and that vanishing act will be the last magick they do with you.

And if you do attract a group ready to be subservient Spear Carriers in your fantasy drama—well, do you really want to associate with that kind of personality? What are you going to do when you want someone strong around to teach you or help you, and at the next New Moon you look out on a roomful (optimistically speaking) of Henry Milquetoasts and Frieda Handmaidens? If a person is willing to become your unpaid servant, then they will also become dependent on you, drain your energy, and become disillusioned if you ever let down the Infallible Witch Queen or King mask for even a moment.

Some other not-so-good reasons for starting a coven are because it seems glamorous, exotic, and a little wicked; because it will shock your mother; or because you can endure your boring, flunky job more easily if you get to go home and play Witch at night.

Some better reasons for setting up a coven, and even nominating yourself as High Priest/ess (if your coven uses the title), include feeling you will be doing useful work in helping yourself and others grow spiritually; having enjoyed leadership roles in the past and have proven yourself capable of putting the members first; or looking forward to learning and growing in that role more than you could in any other. Last, but most important, you may feel yourself called to help create a coven on a deep level of the heart that has nothing to do with reason. When the God/dess Within calls, you answer.

Whatever your motivation, you will need to have or quickly develop a whole range of group process skills, such as the following.

- **Gatekeeping, or guiding discussion in such a way that everyone gets a chance to express their ideas and opinions.**
- **Clarifying and summarizing points of discussion.**
- **Conflict resolution, or helping participants understand points of disagreement and find potential solutions that respect everyone's interests.**
- **Recognizing when differences are irreconcilable, and helping the group learn to live with them or part amicably.**
- **Moving the discussion toward consensus, or at any rate decision, by identifying diversions and refocusing attention on goals and priorities.**
- **Achieving closure smoothly when the essential work is completed or an appropriate stopping place is reached.**

In addition to these skills in group facilitation, four other competencies necessary to the functioning of a coven are: ritual leadership, administration, teaching, and counseling. Hopefully these responsibilities will be shared or delegated frequently, but a coven leader will still be expected to be reasonably capable at all of them. Let us look briefly at each.

Ritual leadership involves much more than reading invocations by candlelight. Leaders must understand the powers they intend to manipulate: how they are raised, channeled, and earthed. They must have clarity of purpose and firm ethics. They must be adept at designing rituals that involve all the sensory modes. They should have a repertoire of songs and chants, dances and *mudras* (gestures), oils and incenses, invocations and spells, visual symbols and effects, meditations and mantras, and the skill to combine these in a powerful, focused pattern. They must understand timing: where a given ritual should fit in the cycle of the Moon, the Wheel of the Year, and the dance of the spheres. They must be able to pace the ritual once begun, so that the energy peaks and is released at the perfect moment. And they must understand the laws of magick and the language of correspondences, as well as knowing when magick is ethical and appropriate and when it is not.

Administration includes basic management practices necessary to any organization. These include apportioning work fairly and following up on its progress; locating and obtaining resources (information, supplies, money); fostering communications (by telephone, printed schedules, newsletters, etc.); and keeping records (minutes, accounts, ritual logbook, Book of Shadows). Someone has to collect the dues if any, buy the candles, chill the wine, and so forth.

Teaching is vitally important. If only one person has any formal training or experience in the Craft, that individual should transmit the knowledge—but in a way which respects the intuitions, re-emerging past life skills, and creativity of the others. If several participants all have knowledge in different areas, they can all act as teachers.

If no one in the group has solid training and you are unsure where to begin, then you may need to call on outside resources: informed and ethical priest/esses and magicians who can act as visiting faculty, or who are at least willing to offer some guidance by telephone, correspondence, or e-mail. Much can be gleaned from books, of course—assuming you know which books are trustworthy and at the appropriate level—but there is no substitute for personal instruction. Magick can be dangerous if misused, and an experienced practitioner can help you avoid pitfalls as well as offer hints and techniques not found in the literature.

Counseling is a special responsibility of coven leadership. It is assumed that all members of a coven share concern for one another's physical, mental, emotional, and spiritual welfare and are willing to help out in practical ways. In covens without designated leaders, this may include peer counseling or co-counseling one another. In covens with a traditional structure, however, High Priest/esses are expected to have special skills in helping coveners explore the roots of their personal problems and choose strategies to deal with them. This is not to suggest that one must be a trained psychoanalyst; but at the very least, good listening skills, clear thinking, and some insight into human nature are helpful. Magickal skills such as guided visualization, trancework, Tarot counseling, and radiesthesia (pendulum) are valuable tools as well.

Think carefully about your skills in these areas as you have demonstrated them in other settings. Ask acquaintances or co-workers who can be trusted to give you a candid opinion about how they see you in these roles (hopefully you are mature enough to really hear constructive criticism). Meditate and decide what role you really want for yourself in the new coven. Will you be content with being a catalyst and contact person, simply bringing people with a common interest together, then letting the group guide its destiny from then on? Would you rather be a facilitator, either for the first few months or permanently: a low-key discussion leader who enables the group to move in the direction they choose with a minimum of misunderstanding and wasted energy?

Do you really want to be High Priest/ess—whatever that means to you—and serve as the guiding force and acknowledged leader of a coven? If you want that job, exactly how much authority and work do you see as part of it? Some coven leaders want a good deal of power and control, others simply take an extra share of responsibility for setting up the rituals (whether or not they actually conduct the rites), and act as teacher and "magickal advisor" to less experienced members. The High Priest/ess can be the center around which the program of the coven revolves, or essentially an honorary title, or anything in between.

That is one area that you will need to have crystal-clear in your mind before the first meeting. There is nothing to be gained—and much to be lost—by modestly withdrawing yourself as a candidate for leadership, then envying the person chosen and backseat driving. Nor should you let yourself get drafted into a job for which you aren't ready.

You must also be clear as to your personal preferences on other points: program emphasis, size, meeting schedule, finances, degree of secrecy, and affiliation with a tradition or network. You owe it to prospective members and to yourself to make your minimum requirements known from the outset: it can be disastrous to a group to discover that members have irreconcilable differences on these points after you have been meeting for several months.

First Steps

When the vision is clear to you, or as clear as it is going to get until other people add their ideas, you may wish to hold a ritual to celebrate the conception of the coven and prepare for its successful birth (see the appendices, which include a suggested outline that you can adapt to your needs). For this ritual, as in all magick, you will need to follow the steps on the following list.

- **Create a vivid vision of the new coven-to-be.**
- **Raise energy and channel it into a driving sense of purpose.**
- **Know that you shall accomplish your will: "An it harm none," nothing can stop you.**
- **Keep your plans and progress quiet, except to potential members; do not invite opposition or dissipate your energy in idle talk with those who are not likely to help.**

Give your curiosity full rein, learn all you can from books, periodicals, workshops, Pagan festivals, experienced priest/esses, past life recall, dreamwork, divination, and so on. Then be discriminating in choosing what to use: discard the dubious; hold on to the wise and sacred. Then open the gates of your heart and let your love of Nature, the God/dess within, the Craft, and your future sisters and brothers flow forth, sweeping away obstacles with joy.

When you have completed your initial ritual, you should feel refreshed and exhilarated, your body coursing with controlled energy, your mind clear and alert.

If you feel at all uncertain or frustrated, do some divination or deep meditation to discover where the obstacle lies: deep within you or outside? On this plane or another? Depending on what you learn, you may need to reconsider your plan. Perhaps the timing is not right, and you should wait a few months or longer, until you reach a more appropriate stage in your personal growth. Perhaps you have doubts or fears that must be resolved before you can proceed. Maybe there is opposition, not necessarily conscious, from family, acquaintances, or even non-material entities. And just possibly this is not the right path for you at all, at least for this lifetime. Dig deep, until you discover the truth. Have the courage to accept it and face the implications. If it is not time for your desires to be realized, if you are swimming against the currents of your karma, it may be that nothing you can do will cause the coven to manifest successfully, at least for now.

But know this also: if the time, place, people and energy are right, then all will proceed smoothly to the birth of a new entity, your coven.

If your instincts and divination tell you that it is time to move ahead, then start thinking about setting up an organizational meeting. But whom should you invite?

Finding the Right People

The people who attend your first meeting may very well set the tone and direction of the coven for a long time to come; therefore it is important that you be very selective. You have a responsibility to Wicca, to yourself, and to those whom you start on the path. On no account should you simply open the meeting to anyone who walks through the door: that is an excellent way to meet some very strange and inappropriate personalities, and the Craft is no place for psychologically fragile or borderline personalities. Offering a Wicca 101 class, and later privately contacting participants you were impressed by, is one good method of screening candidates.

The surest and safest way to begin is to invite only a handful of people whom you already know and trust, friends who want to grow spiritually, who feel deeply connected to Nature and the feminine aspect of the divine, but have not yet found a religious path that answers their needs. If you have a friend whom you would enjoy working with, but who does not know about your interest in Wicca, then you will need to bring up the topic casually in conversation to test the reaction. If it is positive or at least open-minded, invite her or him to the initial gathering.

You may not know many people who are potential candidates for the coven; but then, you don't need many to get started. In fact, a large group can be unwieldy in the crucial first stages. Better three reliable, committed people at the core than a dozen assorted folks with different degrees of interest and commitment. Start small, then build slowly and carefully to the size that feels right—and stop. The American tradition that "bigger is better" has nothing to do with natural law or the quality of magick your coven will perform.

However, if your coven starts very small and stays that way, it will be in a precarious position. For one thing, if you have eight members and two can't attend an activity, the show can go on. But if you have three members and two can't make it, there goes your coven ritual. The average coven in the United States seems to include about seven or eight adults; this is probably a good working size to shoot for. The traditional maximum size is thirteen, after which you should consider dividing or "hiving." The reasons for this are discussed in Chapter 18, "Group Dynamics."

If you don't know anyone who might be interested, do not press your friends to get involved just so you will have company. There is a powerful tradition in the Craft that we do not proselytize. If someone is ready for this path, they will seek it on their own, without cajoling or repeated invitations. If they are not ready, then it is a disservice to drag them to meetings. There are countless other lifestyles and spiritual paths that are perfectly valid for their adherents, and each individual must be free to choose their own path.

So you may need to seek farther afield than your immediate circle of acquaintances. To make connections, you could:

- **Put up a notice in a metaphysical, feminist or New Age bookstore nearby.**
- **Place a classified ad in a national or regional Pagan periodical such as *Circle Network News*, or others listed in Circle's *Guide to Pagan Resources*.**
- **Put up notices on university bulletin boards, or place an ad in the campus newspaper.**

It is wise to be reasonably clear about your goals in public notices, so as to discourage responses from those on divergent paths. The challenge is to let those with some understanding and interest know what's happening without drawing the attention of religious bigots and other neurotics. An example might read something like this:

> Group forming to explore the nature-oriented, feminist religions of ancient Europe, especially Wicca. Women and men seriously interested in study and ethical practice are welcome. Ongoing meetings, 2 to 4 times a month. Organizational meeting April 13. Come and get acquainted, no obligation. Write Sybil, Box 333, Covenstead, CA ZIP CODE.

Depending on your locale, it may be all right to include the word "Wicca," or you may need to be more vague. It is often useful in public, since it does not have the same baggage that "Witchcraft" does.

You may also want to list other parameters: perhaps you want a women-only or men-only group; or you may want to emphasize herbal healing, ecological activism, a Scots-heritage tradition, or whatever.

Notice again that the example mentioned only the organizer's first (or magickal) name and post office box number. With a box number your privacy is protected, and the worst you will have to deal with are some odd letters. However, some covens have decided that they will be completely open as a matter of policy, and for them elaborate precautions may be unnecessary.

Once some replies have come in, screen them carefully to weed out those whose interests are not compatible, or whose motivations seem suspect. Trust your instincts and psychic sensitivity; if a given letter "feels" bad when you touch it or look at it, pass that person by. Out of courtesy, you may wish to send notes to those who won't be invited; simply explain that you don't feel your group is what they are seeking, and thank them for their interest. Do not sign your legal name or include a return address, unless you are completely "out of the broom closet." If they persist in writing to the post office box, ignore further letters.

All this is not to imply that you will be deluged with cranks; our experience is that the vast majority of those who show interest are sincere seekers. Nonetheless, it pays to be prepared for the occasional unbalanced personality.

Assuming you have some replies that sound straightforward and compatible, and feel right, call the people and chat with them a little. Ask what they know about Wicca, why they are interested, what books they have read on the subject, and so on. If your impressions continue to be favorable, only then should you invite them to the organizational meeting and provide the address. Please note: if you are uneasy about an individual for any reason, remember that you have no obligation to invite that person into the group. You have every right to limit it to people you are comfortable with, and indeed it is necessary if your magick is to be effective.

One more cautionary note for those concerned about privacy: remember that if you call an interested party on the telephone, they can trace your number, name, and address through "Caller ID" and the reverse telephone directory. Unless you have blocked caller ID, don't call anyone you are unsure about; communicate in writing through your post office box, or use a public telephone.

The First Organizational Meeting

Choose a date and hour that are appropriate from an astrological point of view; if you are not knowledgeable in that field, either consult someone who is, or use these guidelines:

Season: Late winter, spring, or early fall are best. Avoid late fall and early winter if possible, especially the period between Samhain and Yule (October 31 until about December 21), which is more appropriate to reflection and rest than new beginnings. Summer is difficult simply because so many people have vacation or travel plans.

Lunar Phase: A new moon is best, or any time up to and including the full moon. Do not schedule it during a moon void-of-course, however; these are marked in the popular astrological calendars published by Llewellyn. New projects launched during a void-of-course tend to flop spectacularly.

Day: Wednesday is fine, because it is the day of Mercury, Who rules communications. Sunday is good. Monday is also fine, especially for a Dianic coven. Other days can work if the planetary aspects are good, but you may want to avoid Tuesday (sacred to Mars, God of war) and Saturday (Saturn, God of limitation, etc.).

Hour: Choose an appropriate hour from a table of planetary hours. Hours correspond to the Sun (enlightenment), the Moon (magick and emotion), Mars (conflict), Mercury (communications), Jupiter (increase), Venus (love), or Saturn (limitation).

The initial meeting could take place at your home or a friend's, especially if you know all the invitees. However, if there are people coming whom you don't know well, it might be best to hold it at a community center, library meeting room, or a park. Gathering on "neutral ground" protects the privacy of your home address a little longer. Besides, it is often easier to find and more comfortable for folks who are a little nervous about the whole thing.

Once everyone is present, begin by introducing yourself, explaining the purpose of the meeting, and saying something about Wicca. Answer any burning questions before you move on to decision-making. Once the questions are answered, you might announce a short break for refreshments. Tell everyone that if they are definitely *not* interested given what they have heard so far, this would be an appropriate time for farewells. Thank them for attending, and announce that the meeting will reconvene in fifteen minutes, so that those remaining can get down to specifics.

When everyone has reassembled, speak candidly about your vision for the coven and what you hope participants will gain from participating. Be very clear about what aspects are non-negotiable "givens" as far as you are concerned, and what things are still open questions. For example, "It is important to me that the coven draw material from several branches of Wicca, rather than getting tied to any single tradition. However, I don't have any rigid ideas about how we should structure the group or how often we should meet." Encourage the others to do the same; the more clarity you have at the beginning, the fewer problems will arise later. If you have two or three core people as organizers, each of them should have a short prepared statement.

Make it clear from the beginning that divergent opinions will be respected, and that if people have very different needs or interests, then some may wish to form a second group with a different kind of program.

After all have spoken, then you can outline an agenda for the rest of the evening. It is not crucial that everything be decided in one evening; much will be decided later or as you go along. Mainly you want to get a beginning sense of whether people are "of a like mind" in their visions for the coven. This cannot be determined in any great depth in one meeting, of course; time and interaction will show whether you can work together.

Major Decisions: The Agenda

If you have kept your "non-negotiable" points few and clear, then everyone should understand how much latitude they have in making decisions about the coven. With most American groups, people will assume that anything not specified already may be open to discussion and democratic decision. But in certain subcultures or other cultures, participants may assume that every decision will be made by a leader or elders, except where they are specifically invited to help decide something.

The agenda for the rest of the meeting could include the following topics:

I. Program Emphasis: Some potential foci are:

- Celebration of life and its mysteries
- Magick for spiritual growth and insight (theurgy)
- Magick to cope with day-to-day life (thaumaturgy)
- Healing
- Ecology, protecting the Earth and Her creatures
- Feminist spirituality
- Research into ancient religions or specialized areas of magick
- Political and social action
- Community service
- Public education regarding Wicca, Paganism, and Nature religions generally
- Socializing and fun

Of course many of these overlap, and a coven will typically work in several areas, devoting more time to its favorites. Try having your initial group do a "rank ordering" exercise with these, listing the program foci from the one they like best (1) to the one they like least (11). Then compare lists and see if you're mostly on the same wavelength. Another useful exercise is to come up with a motto for the coven. Summing up their priorities in a couple of words really makes people think about what is important to them. As an example, the motto of Our Lady of the Woods is "Teaching Wicca—Healing the Earth."

II. Type of Activities: Will you primarily be performing rituals? Holding classes? Doing exercises designed to strengthen magickal and psychic abilities? Will you set up field trips to sacred places and museums? Attend Pagan festivals as a group? Plant trees or set up a wildlife refuge? Collect food for low-income families? All of these?

III. Cultural Context: Many cultures and eras had magickal traditions. Most serious practitioners choose one system and immerse themselves in it, at least in the first years of their study. To hop from one to another can load your mind with a confusing welter of names, symbols, and models of reality. This is all right if your main interest is comparative cultural anthropology, but for practical magick, focus on one at first. After you have a foundation in one system, then you can explore others and gradually, carefully incorporate compatible techniques or symbols.

Some systems of magick include:

Wiccan (from Anglo-Saxon, Celtic and pre-Celtic European sources)
Norse (Scandinavian)
Shamanic (overlapping concepts and techniques mainly from the Celts, Native Americans, Norse, Germanic, Siberian and indigenous South American cultures)
Egyptian
Middle Eastern (Sumerian, Babylonian, Assyrian)
Greek or Greek/Roman
African and Caribbean
Qabalistic (Hebrew)
Thelemic (Western ceremonial magick)

There are many others you can explore as well. Though Wicca is more or less Eurasian in origin, its structure and ethics can be blended with the mythology, pantheons, and magick of many different cultures.

IV. Decision Making: Who sets up the program schedule, assigns duties and so forth? You, as High Priest/ess? A council of elders? All initiates, either by consensus or voting democratically? Elected leaders? Individuals on a rotating basis? Everyone present, by consensus?

V. Organizational Structure: Will the coven have an Outer Court or congregation (loosely affiliated members, friends, and visitors) and an Inner Circle (initiates)? Will the coven have a hierarchy with candidates, initiates and degrees of attainment? Will there be offices and titles (Summoner, Scribe, etc.)? Many Witches have an independent nature, and are leery of any kind of formal structure. As Phil Agre wrote in another context, they believe that "structure means constraint means domination." He correctly points out that "Lots of people believe that, but it's not true . . . . structure imposed from the outside may imply constraint . . . . but structure agreed from within a group through a legitimate consensus-building process should not."

VI. Size: How many people are the right number? More people may mean more energy in magickal operations, but with fewer it is easier to psychically attune with one another. Traditionally a coven consists of no more than thirteen members, and some groups of adepts limit their number to eight. You may wish to start small and add people until intuition or divination tells you to stop, or until a newer coven hives off from the parent body. Coven size is discussed further in Chapter 18, "Group Dynamics."

VII. Finances: Will you need funds to purchase candles, incense, books and so on? If so, will you set dues, ask for donations, or run a fundraising project? Some covens get by fine with informal contributions, others raise hundreds or thousands annually for temple renovation, libraries, travel, precious metals for ritual tools, donations to environmental organizations, and so on.

VIII. Meeting Schedule: How often will you meet and when? Virtually every coven meets on the night of the Full Moon for ritual, and often the New Moon as well, and of course at the eight sabbats. Classes, business meetings, work parties, and field trips may be set for other dates.

IX. Attendance: What will your policy be? Do people show up as they please, or is attendance expected except in case of emergency? For effective teaching and magick, a firm policy is often best; if different people attend every time, you will spend a lot more time back-tracking, repeating explanations, and re-developing attunement.

X. Meeting Places: Many groups, especially in the beginning, will rotate among members' homes or meet in the living room of one of the organizers. However, if one member has an extra room in the house you may want to set it up as a temple or ritual chamber, and hold most indoor meetings there. You will need to discuss roommates' feelings, privacy from neighbors, allergies to pets, and other issues, before deciding. Of course during warm weather you may hold most meetings outside; even urban covens can occasionally take a field trip to hold an outdoor sabbat.

XI. Communications: Will you rely on participants' memories regarding dates, locations, and what to bring? This is not a good idea unless your meeting schedule is very regular. Or will you have a Summoner call coveners before each meeting, or set up a phone web among all the members? Will you print schedules and reminders? How about establishing a bulletin board for announcements and schedules at your covenstead?

XII. Affiliation/Networking: Will you attempt to share information and activities with other groups, or even formally affiliate with like-minded Craft folk? Covens of many traditions join the Covenant of the Goddess, a Wiccan federation based in the United States with some members in other countries. Within Wicca there are many traditions (like denominations), such as Gardnerian, Alexandrian, Georgian, Dianic, and Faerie, to name a few. Some are more formally organized than others. Given time and patience you can usually connect with people from each one through Pagan publications or at the festivals. If your approach is eclectic, then the Covenant of the Goddess, independent regional associations, the Pagan Spirit Alliance (a friendship network sponsored by Circle), or the Covenant of Unitarian Universalist Pagans (CUUPS) may be good ways to connect with others.

XIII. Group Privacy and Security: Can you reach agreement as to what may be shared with non-members and what must be kept secret? In some areas, practicing magick or the Craft openly can lead to harassment or even danger. Trust your most conservative instincts and make sure everyone is clear and unified on your policy.

As the coven evolves and important decisions are made over the months ahead, it is wise to put them clearly in writing. This can prevent much misunderstanding at the time and later on. These policies can be organized as formal by-laws and amended from time to time as necessary, or they can be written in a special section of the Book of Shadows. When new people consider joining the coven, they can be given a copy of the by-laws or allowed to copy that part of the Book, so they know what the rules are. This becomes a contract between coveners as each point is agreed upon.

Expressing Your Coven's Identity

A coven's true identity is the pattern created by the interaction of its coveners' spirits. On this plane, however, it is expressed by the name, symbols, and traditions which members adopt. In time, these shared symbols and practices help to strengthen the group's sense of identity and feelings of community.

An early concern will be the name. How can you find the right one? Use your magick. For example, you can hold a group dreamworking and in the morning compare notes to find out if a common image appeared in many of your dreams. Or do a Tarot reading and see if a particular image or card suggests possibilities. Consider naming the coven after an animal, tree or herb native to your area, checking with that species' spirit or deva before you make a final decision. Or brainstorm a list, narrow it down to a few favorites, and choose with a pendulum.

Appendix A-4 (page 366) lists possible elements for coven names. Of course these are simply suggestions. Try combining them in different ways: Coven of the Silver Unicorn, Ring of Sacred Fire, and so on. If your coven intends to do public education and community service, be careful not to choose a name that is whimsical, obscure, or difficult to spell or pronounce.

Many groups are able to find a particular deity or aspect of nature that is precious to all or symbolizes the kind of energy they will create. For example, Our Lady of the Woods refers to the forest goddess known as Artemis in Greek culture. A women's group I belonged to was called The Pool of Bast, Who is the Egyptian goddess of joy, celebration, birth, music, and the sun's warmth. But before you adopt a deity's name for your coven, learn everything you can about that goddess or god: most deities have much more to Them than a single myth or paragraph in an encyclopedia would suggest. Naming your coven is an act of magick as well as common sense, and it is a rule of magick that you know what names mean before you call upon their power.

Some covens prefer to use the name of an animal, plant, or natural phenomenon: something like Grove of the Living Oak, Daughters of the Crescent Moon, The Nightingale Assembly, The Emerald Circle, or the Coven of the Four Winds. (As far as I know these are made-up names and do not refer to actual groups. However, there is no central registry of coven names, so one can never be certain that one hasn't re-invented a name already in use.)

Many covens also adopt a sigil or pictograph to represent them. This should be simple enough that any coven member can sketch it after their signature. It can also be put on your stationery, ritual tools, coven banner, and the silver bracelet of each covener (if this is part of your tradition). See the examples in the appendices.

Probably you will wish to adopt or create rituals or ritual elements that will become part of your coven's traditions. While much of your ritual magick will be created to serve a particular need on only one occasion, in other cases repetition and continuity increase the power you can raise and direct. Develop your own special touches on ways to: ground and center, attune to one another, cast the circle, call the quarters, initiate or welcome new members, celebrate new and full moon esbats, and observe the sabbats. Some resource books to get you started are listed in the appendices; use their rituals intact until you get the feeling for the flow and pattern, then change them according to your needs. You are limited only by the laws of magick and your own ingenuity.

Your selection, design, and use of magickal tools will reflect the group's identity. Will you use wands or athames most often to channel energy? Will they be made of similar materials for all coveners? For example, perhaps everyone will make a willow wand from the same tree by the coven's outdoor circle (after obtaining the tree spirit's permission). During one period in the Temple of the Pagan Way, every covener made an athame with a copper blade; copper is the metal of Venus, and reminded us to use our magick only for loving purposes. Will you symbolize the element of Air with a sword, a wand, incense, or a feather? Will the Water symbol on your altar be a bowl of sea water, a chalice of wine, or a seashell? Will you put a great deal of care and effort into your tools as a magickal discipline, or will you try to develop magickal and psychic skills with minimal reliance on tools? It helps to have agreement on such issues if you are going to work as a magickal team—it can be quite distracting to have people doing different things with different tools at a given point in the ritual.

Ritual clothing is another issue to consider. You have several options:

- Work skyclad (nude). Many traditional covens do this—not to emphasize sexuality, but to let psychic energy flow unhindered, to help members accept their own bodies as natural and good, and to point up the fact that all are social equals in the circle.
- Work in any robes or magickal clothing individuals select. This approach certainly respects individuality and freedom of choice, but can be a subtle hindrance to building the group mind because it emphasizes differences more than commonalities.
- Work in robes of the same color (or general range of color, as in any shade of green), but in varying designs selected by individuals: a compromise approach.
- Work in robes of the same design, color and fabric, possibly with the coven sigil embroidered or appliquéd on each.
- Work in robes of varying colors according to the magickal degree or rank each has attained or according to individual magickal specialties (green for an herbalist, blue for a bard, and so on). Vary the color of the robes according to the type of magick in progress or the season of the year.

Robes need not be fancy or expensive. A simple T-shaped design in a cotton-blend fabric is easy to make. If you have someone with sewing experience in the coven, then you can have hoods and more elaborate patterns. Just be sure that the seamster or seamstress is reimbursed for their labor (either with money or an exchange of skills) unless they explicitly want to donate their services to the coven.

In many groups it is traditional for each member to choose, or be given, a "Craft name" or "magickal name" upon initiation. These can reflect the cultural orientation of your group: if you work with Egyptian magick, use Egyptian names. Most Wiccan covens draw from either British or Celtic (Irish, Welsh, Scots) sources. In some circles, it is considered all right to name yourselves after gods and goddesses; in others, it is considered presumptuous. Naming oneself after natural objects or creatures is popular: there are Pagans named Falcon, Willow, Jade, Morning Glory, Otter, and so on. Try not to choose anything too obvious, or you will be tripping over your namesakes at festivals. For example, Diana is very popular and common; Diana Halfmoon or Diana Silverglow is more distinctive. It is up to you whether you use your special name only within your coven, or at Pagan events generally, or even in daily life.

You will probably emphasize a particular aspect of the Goddess, and perhaps the God as well, in your rituals. The Triple Goddess of the Moon is central in very many covens: Diana, Selene, and Hecate representing Maiden, Mother, and Crone. The Horned God of the woodlands, Cernunnos, is probably the most popular god among Witches. But depending on your cultural slant, you might choose Cerridwen and Lugh, Freya and Frey, Hera and Zeus, Isis and Osiris, or others. Many women's groups just focus on a goddess, and focus less or not at all on the male principle in their magick. I am not aware of any covens that focus only on god-energy; this is not to say they don't exist.

Do a lot of reading and research before choosing; when you call upon a deity, you are invoking a thought form/energy source/archetype that has a great deal of specialized power invested in it over millennia of time. Know Who you are inviting to your circle.

Building the Group

One of the first tasks of a new coven is for the members to get better acquainted, creating a community feeling and "group mind" so that you will be attuned to one another in ritual workings. Some magickal approaches to group-building include the following.

- Comparing your natal horoscopes (astrological charts); if none of you are experienced astrologers, invite one in for an evening. (Give them your birth information well in advance.
- Doing Tarot card readings for one another.
- Reading each other's auras.
- Doing a guided group meditation or tranceworking in which, for example, participants meet a spirit guide or receive counsel from an aspect of the Goddess, then discussing your experiences afterwards.
- Doing a dreamworking together one night, and discussing your dreams in the morning.
- Doing a simultaneous past-life regression and comparing experiences.

You can accelerate group-building on a more mundane level, as well.

- Spending time with each other outside of coven meetings and rituals; for example, getting together in pairs or trios for lunch, movies, hikes, or other social and recreational activities.
- Sharing your individual experiences at the beginning of each regular meeting: "what I've been up to in the past week," sometimes called a "check-in" or "weather report." Is someone going back to college? Does someone have a cold? Has someone made a special new friend? The bad news should be shared as well as the good, so that the coven

can be supportive (although reports must be reasonably brief or they will eat up the whole evening).

- Going on occasional trips together: to museums, to see the magickal artifacts of other cultures; to ancient sacred sites such as mounds or stone circles; to visit covens or magicians in other towns; or to open sabbat celebrations or festivals.

You may be wondering about all this effort to create strong social bonds among the group—how necessary is it? Well, it is possible to learn a good deal about magick without personal ties, but it is very difficult to actually do powerful group magick unless you are close to the other participants. This is one reason why many covens have inner circles to which visitors are not invited. If a non-attuned person is present, no matter how friendly, it becomes hard to raise and channel power. Hopefully, the time will come when you realize that you no longer have merely a collection of individuals; a new entity exists, a genuine group mind. It is good to recognize this fact with either a group initiation or a coven birthing ritual.

Initiation and Birthing

If you want to do a formal initiation, but none of you have received initiation in another coven, you might consider asking a High Priest/ess from outside to lead this ritual. Be aware that there are initiation practices important to many Wiccan traditions, such as:

- "Only a Witch can make a Witch." This refers to the idea that only one who has been trained and initiated can initiate another. But many Wiccan traditions respect self-initiated Witches if they are sincere, knowledgeable, and exemplify the Craft in their lives.
- "A year and a day . . ." is the shortest allowable training period before initiation. This gives the candidate time to learn Craft basics and be sure this is the right spiritual path for them.
- "A priestess initiates a male candidate, and a priest initiates a female." This is important to covens where male-female polarity magick is central. Obviously it is not followed in single-sex covens, and many eclectic covens are flexible on this point.

Not all covens follow these practices, and there is no "central authority" to revoke your Witch license if your coven does something different. But if you want to follow the old customs, you may be able to locate a helpful priest/ess though the Covenant of the Goddess, Circle Network, or a regional Pagan association. If you find one who knows their stuff, be prepared—they will want to interview each of you to be satisfied that you are informed, serious, and aware of the implications of becoming initiates. Don't be surprised if they require additional work, or if they are unwilling to initiate anyone they have not worked with for a year and a day.

Of course, you also have the option of performing a self-initiation. If so, you will need to do a lot of research and reading to understand what initiation means and various ways it can be commemorated with ritual. Then you will need to create a ritual that is powerful and focused. Some books designed for solitary practitioners have suggested self-initiation rituals that could be adapted to your needs.

Whether or not you set up an initiation, a birthing ritual can solidify coven spirit and be fun as well. Be creative—discuss what the ritual signifies to each of you and plan to express your hopes and dreams in symbolic form. Include music and dance, candles and ribbons, oils and incenses. Give gifts to one another and to the coven altar and library. Hold a great potluck feast afterwards, and let the wine flow. Celebrate!

Continuing . . .

As the coven continues, planning your program and education will become more challenging. At first, it may be sufficient to read good books and discuss them. Soon you will want to begin actively practicing magick—preparing ritual tools, setting up an altar, casting the circle, calling the Quarters. A helpful resource at this stage is my book *True Magick: A Beginner's Guide*.[1]

As coven members develop their individual specialties, you can teach one another. But continue to invite priest/esses in for classes and discussion whenever the opportunity arises. Visit workshops at Pagan festivals and bring back lore and techniques to share with the coven. Visit events sponsored by other religious and magickal traditions and see if their approaches are compatible with your path. Correspond with other covens and solitary Witches and trade information. Subscribe to Pagan and magickal publications and study them carefully. Never stop learning.

And if you proceed slowly and carefully, listen more than you speak, and allow your higher self to guide you—then together, you will create a unique, beautiful, and life-transforming experience.

NOTES

1. Amber K, *True Magick: A Beginner's Guide* (St. Paul: Llewellyn, 1991).

6 The Covenstead

Where we meet to perform magick and celebrate can be as important as the content of the ritual itself. There are two broad classes of ritual environments: natural and constructed. Often these have different purposes in Witchcraft.

We gather in natural outdoor settings in order to celebrate the powers of Nature, to connect with our roots and attune to the seasons of the Earth and the cycles of the moon and sun. Fields, seashores, hilltops, forest groves, mountain valleys, desert mesas—all are sacred places where we may feel Her presence and dance to the music of His pipes in the wind.

Yet a constructed ritual area, usually indoors, can be immensely valuable in other ways. We can arrange it so as to focus on one aspect of reality, or a certain combination of aspects, rather than the complex and vital interplay of forces in the wild. We can plan each element of the ritual environment, creating an atmosphere conducive to working magick for a specific goal.

Indoor Ritual Space

As an example, suppose you find your goals thwarted by a lack of willpower and vital energy. As part of a magickal strategy to remedy this problem, you decide to create a "fire shrine" in your home and draw more "fire-energy" into your life.

Now, it would also be quite possible to go outside and focus on the fire-energies present there: the sun's steady heat, the vital energy, and the inexorable growth of plants. Such outdoor work may be an important element in your strategy. Yet the elements of earth, air, and often water are also abundantly present outside, and may interfere with the narrow focus you desire; it is hard to concentrate on fire-energies in a pouring rainstorm or with ants crawling on your leg.

Indoors, in your home or the coven's temple area, you can create a kind of "one-dimensional" fire-space. Cover the walls with red hangings, light a dozen candles. Put up a big golden sun-disc over the altar, burn olibanum and cinnamon incense. Perhaps you have a brass dragon or salamander for the altar, or a fireplace, or red clothing to wear. All this helps your deep mind to focus on the work at hand.

Of course a coven's members have diverse needs, so a permanent shrine dedicated to one element would not do (unless you want to create an altar for each element). In general, a flexible ritual environment is necessary, which the group can transform at will. At the New Moon it may become a temple consecrated to Diana; a week later it may change into a Cernunnos Shrine as a covener designs a training ritual, an Air Circle for someone who needs intellectual stimulation for a graduate exam, or the somber gathering place for Samhain sabbat.

For this kind of adaptability, you need a facility that can be changed without great effort or expense. Heavy furniture, built-in fixtures, or walls and carpets in bold colors all make it difficult to create different moods. The perfect indoor temple would begin as a quiet, empty space of indeterminate size, shape, and color. It's worth keeping in mind, even if none of us has a room that quite meets those specifications.

Rotating the Meeting Space

One option for indoor meetings is to rotate them among coveners' homes. Many newer covens do this. It means that you will have limitations on what you can do with the space, aside from shifting some furniture or covering up the more distracting objects in the room (no, not Willow's children), but you can work around the difficulties.

To minimize visual distractions, set up a central altar with the appropriate colors, tools, and symbols on it, and illuminate it with a few candles. The rest of the room will be too dim to intrude on your attention. If coveners are dressed according to the evening's theme—with appropriate colors, jewelry, masks, or whatever—this will help to keep all eyes focused on the ritual instead of the mundane surroundings.

Outside noises can be a nuisance, especially in an apartment house or city. The "white noise" of an electric fan or humidifier can help screen these out, as well as making your chants or invocations less audible to neighbors. Naturally, recorded background music helps as well.

Don't neglect the olfactory environment: noses deserve equal time. Cooking smells, new paint or perfumed "air fresheners" can be very distracting. Fresh air if possible, and an incense corresponding to the energies being invoked, can eliminate the problem. Of course if you live in an apartment house, you may need to be very sparing with the incense: you don't want a smoke alarm going off in the middle of the ritual.

So it is possible to work around the inconveniences of rotational meetings, and there are advantages to the system as well. Most coveners will enjoy hosting an occasional ritual, partly because the energy raised will linger and bestow a subtle blessing on the home. In addition, coveners can learn a great deal about each other by experiencing one another's homes, and this strengthens the bonds within the group ("Hey, Robin! I didn't know you made frog sculptures from Barry Manilow LPs; me too!"). It also gives the coven a chance to see personal altars, sacred objects, artwork, and the like in the host/ess' home.

These are all good reasons for even an established coven with a permanent meeting place to go afield into members' homes a few times a year for esbats, sabbats, or specialized classes.

A Permanent Covenstead

Many covens have the exclusive use of one room, usually in the home of the High Priest/ess or a founding member. Such a permanent temple area has several benefits:

- **It gives coveners a more stable, settled feeling about the coven experience: the coven has a "home."**
- **Material resources can be collected and stored: a library, wall hangings, musical instruments, candles, herbs, and so forth. These are useful both in the coven training program and increasing the scope and variety of rituals.**
- **It simplifies life, eliminating the confusion and mix-ups possible when the meeting is never at the same place twice in a row.**
- **The magickal energies raised accumulate over many rituals and are available as a sort of "psychic storage battery" for all succeeding work done there.**

The familiarity and special energies of the place make it easier for the coveners to make the transition into sacred space: the deep mind associates the room with magick. Rather than transforming mundane space into sacred, you almost slide into it. The circle almost casts itself.

Over time, the space can be improved and shielded to the point where it is nearly ideal: lighting, temperature, access, storage, and so on can be changed to fit the coven's needs.

If there is direct access to the outside, initiates or elders may be given keys so that they can use the ritual space, library, and other resources for personal magickal work, teaching classes, or decorating for sabbats without disturbing the homeowners.

These are powerful reasons for setting up such an arrangement, but there are challenges as well. For one thing, the privacy of the owners is compromised. Several times each month they will have people trekking in and out, borrowing their utensils at potlucks, using up toilet paper, subtly disarranging things and so on. This creates a certain amount of stress no matter how courteous and careful the coveners are.

And of course, there are the inevitable candle drippings and wine spills on the rug. Our coven jokes that we could start a winery just by wringing out the living room carpet into bottles. Burgundy-colored carpets are highly recommended for any Pagan gathering place.

Another consideration is that increased traffic can cause curiosity and comment among the neighbors; one might just peek in a window at the wrong moment or overhear careless conversation outside as coveners leave. Further, if the owners ever need to move away, there can be a powerful sense of loss when the temple room is no longer available to those who have become attached to that space. If that should become necessary, create a ritual to gather the energies and formally transfer them to the new meeting place.

Still, the advantages probably outweigh the potential problems. Provided that you have a settled, committed coven member with a large extra room—or a convertible living room or family room, plus some storage space—it is worthwhile to create a permanent covenstead. But set up some ground rules along the lines of those which follow, and make sure everyone understands and accepts them.

Ground Rules for Creating a Covenstead in a Home

1. Schedule in Advance. Once a meeting schedule has been established—in writing, well in advance—stick to it so that the residents know exactly when to expect the coven. The only exception would be if the coven has a separate room reserved for it, with a private entrance.
2. Schedule Additions or Changes. Any additional meetings should be cleared with the residents with as much advance notice as possible; and they should be informed of any cancelations. If a proposed last-minute meeting is inconvenient for the owners, hold it in another covener's home or outdoors.
3. Renovation Costs. All renovation or redecoration necessary to create a workable ritual and class space should be financed by the coven treasury, after approval by the Coven Council (meeting of all members), or whatever is the governing body of your coven.
4. Boundaries. The temple area should be clearly demarcated from the rest of the house if practical. Coven supplies should not encroach on the owner's living space or vice versa. If it is a shared ritual/living space, at least try to keep coven materials in their own closet, drawers, or cupboards.
5. Incidental Expenses. It would be a courtesy for the coven to offer a small monthly or yearly stipend to the owner, to cover the costs of

extra toilet paper, dish detergent, electricity, heat, and so on. Alternatively, the coven might schedule a work party once or twice a year to help the owners with a thorough "spring cleaning."

6. Mail. Coven mail should go to a post office box rather than the covenstead address. Your host/ess could be in for trouble if a copy of *Pagan Revels* magazine, addressed to "Coven of the Bubbling Cauldron," accidentally winds up in a neighbor's mailbox.
7. Discreet Behavior. Coveners should probably arrive and leave in street clothes, changing into robes behind closed drapes. Everyone should be sensitive about what they say outdoors: merry cries of "Blessed be, Witches!" and "The Horned One Lives" are not appropriate outside the covenstead door, unless it is a very liberal neighborhood and your host/ess is quite out of the broom closet.
8. Order and Cleanliness. When members arrive, they should find a reasonably neat and clean household—at least the parts the coven will be using. Before they leave, coveners should clean up any mess, wash their dishes or wine goblets, and leave the premises as nice as they found them.
9. Liability. It should be noted that the owner is not liable for theft or vandalism of coven items stored on the property. Of course if the coven has set up strong wards, backed by solid locks, you won't have a problem. If you are not sure of your warding skills, you can always insure valuable ritual tools or rare books. In this regard, you may want to mark temple goods for identification and keep an itemized inventory of temple property.
10. Punctuality. If the ritual and living space is shared, there should be an understanding as to when coven activities begin and end, so that coveners don't traipse through the dining room while the resident owners are eating supper, or stay so late that they wear out their welcome. After sabbat festivities, the host/ess should not have to wait up until dawn entertaining diehard celebrants who won't go home. Once the ending time is set, the coven Summoner—not the homeowner—should gently, but oh so firmly, send incorrigible merrymakers on their way.

If the ritual area is well separated from the living space, this last item may not be an issue. In our coven, the hostesses/homeowners go upstairs to bed when we feel like it: our parting admonition to the remaining coveners is, "Stay as long as you want; turn off the lights and lock the door when you go; good night and blessed be."

Given such guidelines, a permanent covenstead in someone's home can work out very nicely.

Making It Cozy and Functional

Often the same room will function as a temple, classroom, and conference room when it is not being someone's living room, family room, or den. You can make it a better gathering space by following a few simple tips.

- Have several large cushions available for people to sit on or lean against during meetings. Even if the room has enough chairs and couches for everyone, they're handy for doing meditation or trancework on the floor.
- Keep a supply of inexpensive clipboards with tablets of lined paper nearby, and a box of pens and pencils, for taking notes during classes and business meetings. If your members keep their Books of Shadows in looseleaf notebooks, have prepunched tablets so the notes can be saved directly into their books.
- Create a flexible lighting system with several table lamps or track lights and perhaps a rheostat switch controlling the main light source. You want to be able to provide bright light for taking notes in class, or dim light for rituals or trancework.
- Make beverages available during meetings; perhaps herb teas, coffee, and hot chocolate in cool weather, and iced drinks in the warm season. If the kitchen isn't right next to your meeting room, then you can set up a beverage table or cooler in one corner. Some groups have a set of identical coven goblets or chalices that they keep by the beverages, and every covener is responsible for washing their own cup at the end of the evening.
- Have the altar supplies either stored in the altar or in a chest or cupboard nearby. It's a good idea to sew up altar cloths in several basic colors for different seasons or magickal purposes. If you want to keep them free of candlewax and wine stains, cut a sheet of thin, flexible, transparent acrylic to cover your altar top; but keep flames away.
- Keep the coven library in the meeting room if convenient. In any case make sure you have a card system or list to keep track of books checked in and out.
- Do make sure that the room has locks, and curtains or drapes, and preferably is reasonably soundproof, at least if your neighbors live close by.

Renting Coven Space

Sometimes it is simply unworkable to have the covenstead in someone's home. Perhaps some coveners have non-Pagan roommates, others live in tiny apartments, and so forth. If this is your situation, you may want to consider renting or leasing space commercially. This may be an option in a city but very risky in small towns.

The first step is to gain consensus as to whether the idea is worth exploring. It will mean a financial commitment, after all. If there is real interest, then price some different facilities in a central location. You might be able to rent basic meeting space in a church (Unitarian, Society of Friends, or another tolerant religion), a community building, a public library, school, or service club. The local Chamber of Commerce may also have a list of meeting rooms available for rent.

If you prefer someplace where you can store things and decorate, then offices, artists' lofts, apartments, or unused garages or outbuildings are possibilities. Check out:

Costs: not only the rent, but utilities, damage deposits, and any costs for repair and renovation.

Terms: monthly rental or long-term lease, special rules, decorating allowance or resources, etc.

Privacy: is it soundproof, and can your people enter and leave without being scrutinized by curious neighbors or the landlord?

Zoning: can you get in trouble for operating a church in a residential neighborhood? (At least one coven did!)

The owner or manager: what kind of personality and prejudices would you have to deal with?

Some owners and managers have no interest in what happens on the property as long as the rent is paid, nothing is damaged, and nobody complains. Others are extremely inquisitive or opinionated. Best of all, naturally, would be a Pagan landlord.

What do you tell a potential landlord if he or she is not Pagan? There may be some temptation to fudge the truth, or create some story likely to be acceptable to non-Wiccan ears. Don't. Falsehoods destroy trust and can only harm you and the reputation of the Craft. If you were to imply to some landlord that your coven was a prayer group, or a bird-watching club, you can be sure that the truth will come out and you will get a spectacular demonstration of the Law of Return in action.

Of course you don't have to instantly blurt: "We're Witches and we need a place for the coven to meet!" You can ask, "How do you feel about renting to alternative religious groups? We are part of a nature-based religion, similar in ways to Native American spirituality but with roots in Europe. We need a place for classes and small-group ceremonies or services, and we plan to take very good care of the place . . . oh, it's called Wicca. We have been meeting at the Unitarian Church on Green Street but their schedule is so busy it's hard to get the dates we want . . . ."

Your coven should delegate two members to look at prospective facilities. Owners and managers can be bewildered and even threatened if a crowd shows up to view an office or apartment. Of course you must be honest about the fact that the space will be used for group activities, but avoid confusion by giving the manager only one or two names and faces to deal with. The coven representatives can take notes and even snapshots of the space to share with the whole group later.

During the discussion with the landlord or manager, be sure to ask about evening access, whether it is all right to have potlucks and play music, how much redecorating you will be allowed to do (and who pays for it), and any other details.

If the facilities, price, and terms are agreeable to everyone in the coven, and the landlord seems comfortable with you, then the same representatives can close the deal. Be sure the coven agrees on the following details, and put it all in writing (e.g., a lease).

- Whose name will be on the papers (who is legally liable?).
- How long a trial period should be after which the coven can review the arrangement and decide whether it's working out well.
- Exactly where the funds are coming from, and which coven member will coordinate all financial arrangements.
- How you will jointly handle any legal or financial obligations (subletting, rent due, damage repair) if the coven must pull out for any reason.

Since the arrangement is bound to be somewhat experimental at first, it may be best to look for a month-by-month rental with a modest deposit. You want to be able to get free of the arrangement quickly and with minimal expense if it doesn't work out.

If you do find the right space, clean it thoroughly, decorate to the extent you are allowed, and then hold a full-scale blessing rite, celebration, and potluck feast. Post a sign-up sheet or calendar, so you can schedule classes, rituals, and meetings. Whenever there is not a group event scheduled, individual coveners should be able to use the space for private ritual, study, construction of ritual tools, and other spiritual or magickal work.

A word about security: it is wise to establish and charge wards at the doors and windows to discourage thievery and vandalism. Large, natural quartz crystals or Saturnian stones (obsidian, black onyx, black jade) are useful for this purpose. You may want to set them into small carved wooden masks representing guardian spirits. The charges should be renewed regularly, perhaps as part of your Full Moon esbats. Then act in accord by checking all window latches and door locks, installing heavy bolts, and even shutters if need be.

Consider locking all your Craft books, pentacles, and other Witchy-looking paraphernalia into a sturdy cabinet when not in use. Obtain a fire extinguisher and keep it fully charged, if there is not already one on the premises. The coven Watcher should have charge of all safety and security precautions, with the active cooperation of all the members. It remains only to agree on "house rules," hand out keys, and enjoy your new coven home! Oh, and maybe put up a plaque:

Blessed be this place, and those who enter here
in perfect love and perfect trust.

Sky Roofed Temples: Gathering Outdoors

The temple of the Lady and Lord is all outdoors. In ancient times our forebears mapped the currents of power flowing through the Earth, and marked the places these converged. There the great sabbats were held: high on a windswept tor, deep in a sacred grove, near the diamond-clear waters of a holy spring, or on a rolling moor under the curious gaze of wild ponies. Today many of the stones which mark such gathering places still stand; and many a Christian church is built on the site of a Pagan meeting ground, though few remember why.

The best place for a sabbat is still outdoors—weather permitting—so that we can refresh ourselves and renew our connections with Mother Earth.

Many covens, however, are city-based and find it difficult to locate a good site for outdoor rituals. Some city parks are notoriously unsafe. If delinquents don't harass you, the police may do so—especially after dark. Nevertheless, a public park ritual is possible if safeguards are set up. I recall one Lughnassad feast at a public beach, where we set especially strong wards and an invisibility spell: people strolling by a few yards away did not appear to notice as we chanted and offered a very large corn dolly to the flames, sending sparks showering through the dusk.

In another occasion, at Samhain, our black-robed group stood quietly meditating within a circle marked by carved jack-o-lanterns, in a city park partially screened by trees. A passer-by, not very sensitive to the presence of a religious rite, wandered toward us and cheerily inquired what we were doing. With one accord we all swiveled and stared silently at him from beneath our hoods. He left.

But other groups have encountered problems in public parks, and it will always be a judgment call as to whether your coven can risk it. Unless you can instantly shapeshift into an empty beer can, it is best to err on the side of caution.

If you do decide to use a public park, consider these guidelines:

- Check local regulations and obtain any necessary permits for your gathering.
- Notify the police department in advance, especially if it will be a fairly large gathering. If the police are forewarned, then they are less likely to interrupt the ritual asking questions, and more likely to be supportive if someone harasses you.

- Have Watchers assigned to protect the circle from outside it. If any stranger approaches, the Watcher(s) should intercept them and quietly explain that a religious service is in progress.
- Coven members should discuss other possible contingencies, and have plans ready just in case. This should be done calmly and do not belabor it; you don't want to infuse the group mind with paranoia.

The park should of course be treated with extreme respect. Do not use open flames if the area is dry, and pick up every scrap of litter before you leave.

Afterward, send a note to the park district thanking them for use of the facility and offering to assist in future clean-up or landscaping projects.

County and state recreation areas and national forests usually offer more space and privacy. However, they are good places to avoid during hunting season. Also, the privacy is a two-edged sword: intolerant folks are less likely to see you, but if they do, then the police are usually not available to intervene if you are harassed. You may be able to cover yourself a little by writing to the area ranger in advance, and asking if religious services are permissible there. Usually they are, and the ranger's letter can be produced if anyone questions your right to hold a ritual there. But paper or no paper, be very cautious about loud or skyclad celebrations on public land, and work hard at setting your wards and casting a strong circle.

Buying Coven Land

It's no wonder that so many urban Witches dream of moving to country places, where they can simply walk out the kitchen door and up the hill to a private grove.

One possible course of action for city, suburban, or small-town covens is to buy land for the group. Then it can be used jointly or individually by coveners for ritual magick, sabbat celebrations, classes on herbcraft and nature lore, vision quests, saunas, retreats, camping, picnics, and more. This is a project for a strong, well-established coven: it takes time, energy, and lots of money.

Much depends on finding the right land at the right price (map dowsing with a pendulum may save gas) and getting consensus as to who holds title and what happens if the coven ever hives or parts company.

If the land is secluded, it need not be a large acreage. A couple of acres may do quite nicely if there are no close neighbors and it is far from suburban sprawl, or is terrain considered unsuitable for development. A woody, rocky area at the back of a large farm might do the trick, or land adjacent to a park, national forest, wildlife refuge, or BLM land. Topographical maps, available from the U.S. Geological Survey or through bookstores, can provide possibilities since they show which areas are steep, hilly terrain unsuitable for farming or housing tracts. Your local county seat will have plat maps showing who owns what land, should you wish to approach a private owner directly instead of working through a realtor. In any case, be sure it is far from prying eyes and curious ears. In addition, discreetly check out the neighbors to make sure they are not members of some intolerant church or political group.

If you have any thoughts of building a cabin, yurt, pavilion, or kiva on the land, you will need to research county and state zoning laws. You may have to own a minimum number of acres before you build. You may need to drill a well for water, and percolation tests may be required before you can establish a septic field. Can you hook up to public electric power, or will you need to explore solar or wind energy? Taxes on the property must be considered as well, unless your coven is recognized as a tax-exempt organization and will hold title to the land.

The owner of the land may be able to answer questions about zoning and so forth, or direct you to the appropriate agencies. In discussing your needs, you should not have to go into much depth about your plans for the property; it is enough to say that it will be a primitive retreat area for your church, unless of course you have more grandiose plans.

Once you find land that seems to meet your requirements and feels welcoming, then it is time for some more divination. Get out your Tarot cards, yarrow stalks or coins, runestones, showstone, or whatever you use, and check the probable future for the project as a whole, the particular land you are considering, and the best strategy for acquiring and using it in harmony with its ecology and energies.

Be sure to make contact with resident nature spirits or devas and begin to build rapport. It should be evident very soon whether they are well disposed toward your coven.

Once you have title to the property, set up wards against anyone who would behave irresponsibly on the land, perform a cleansing ritual to remove any negative energies from the property, and fence and post it if you are in hunting country. (Even with these precautions, hunting season is a good time to stay indoors—not all hunters respect "NO TRESPASSING" signs.) If there is erosion or other conservation problems, deal with them promptly—the County Extension Agent can provide valuable expertise.

If dowsing or intuition tells you that one spot is especially powerful or congenial, you may want to give it extra attention in preparing it for use as a ritual site. You can simply remove branches and rocks, or set up a stone circle, or even plant a ring of trees as a sacred grove.

If your members are all closet *dryads* (tree spirits), you can either buy seedlings from a local nursery, or transplant them from a heavily wooded area that needs thinning anyway. Don't do this without professional advice unless you are an expert: the nursery people or County Extension office can advise you as to correct transplanting techniques and follow-up care. The trees you choose should be suited to the terrain, altitude, and climate, and if possible correspond to the energies you want to share or emphasize.

birch: Beginnings and blessings; Cerridwen and rebirth

rowan or mountain ash: magick, protection, initiation; sacred to Brigid, triple goddess of inspiration, healing and smithcraft

ash: guardian-tree; water energy; the World-tree of Norse mythology

alder: tree of the fairies and the minstrel's pipes

willow: sacred to Diana; Moon-magick and enchantment

hawthorn: special to Cardea, mistress of all crafts; ripening and fullness; discourages unwanted visitors

oak: strength and endurance; Druid's groves; Dagda, the Good Father

holly: foresight and defense; sacred to Lugh, the Celtic fire god, and to Habondia, goddess of plenty

hazel: wisdom, healing, positive magick, divination; sacred to housekeepers

elder: the dwelling-place of spirits; completion; special to the Crone

pine: Cernunnos, horned god of the woodlands and wild animals

Should you wish to work with stones, you can make a ritual/astronomical calendar by placing large stones to mark sunrise on the solstices and equinoxes, moonrise and moonset points, and so on. Books about Stonehenge and the Native American calendar wheels of the West will give you useful information, as will astronomy texts.

Or if you just want to mark a circle permanently, you can space thirteen large stones evenly around the perimeter. Of course tall menhir-type stones of a size to be impressive weigh a lot; there is no question of bundling a couple of them into the trunk of your subcompact and driving into the circle. Better to hire someone with a tractor to snake them to the area, then very carefully lever them into prepared base holes. If you are moving stones weighing even a couple of hundred pounds, you cannot stress safety too much: it is dangerous work and requires patience, foresight, and lots of heavy-duty restraining ropes. Do not overextend yourselves by trying to create a stone circle in a weekend or two. If you place one stone at each sabbat outing, or even have an annual stone-setting party and finish in thirteen years, you will be doing just fine.

A far simpler approach to outdoor circles is to mark the four cardinal points with flat altar stones, tree seedlings, or log posts with the carved faces of the Guardians. Other quarter-markers include staves with magickal talismans hanging from them, or colorful banners that can be taken down and stored between rituals.

If you mark the quarters, be sure to align them to true north, which may be many degrees away from the magnetic North to which your compass points. The amount of discrepancy depends on where you live. Check out a book on orienteering or science from your library; the *Orienteering Merit Badge* booklet published by the Boy Scouts of America has relevant information.

Yet another project: plant a magickal herb garden bordering the area, or four small stone-bordered herb gardens, one at each quarter. Plant appropriate herbs or flowers in each, such as the following (abstracted from Starhawk's tables in *The Spiral Dance*[1]):

east (air): vervain, yarrow, pansies, primroses, violets

south (fire): garlic, red poppies, nettles, onions, red peppers, mustard

west (water): ferns, mosses, rushes, or (fancy!) a pond with water lilies

north (earth): comfrey, ivy, grains (wheat, barley, oats, and the like)

Unless the land already has a cabin or barn you can fix up, you may want to supplement your outdoor circle with a structure for rainy-weather meetings. Even a 15'x20' cabin will hold a group of ten or so, plus a few cupboards for supplies; or consider a geodesic dome or wooden yurt, which is easy to build and provides a lovely circular space perfect for ritual work. A round pavilion or gazebo would also be fine. Think about constructing something of wood, stone, or adobe that blends with the terrain. You may also need to build an outhouse, unless you have a great deal of land and very few people. If so, plan on regular cleaning and servicing.

Is all this tinkering and building really necessary? Of course not. The land is equally sacred whether you plant gardens or add human structures or not, and for many kinds of celebration and ritual, an untouched wild area is preferable to an "improved" site.

Yet, most of us have an instinct to somehow mark the places that are special to us, to make them recognizably our own in a way that no legal paper can. We feel better in a motel when our belongings are spread around; we enjoy walking in the woods and seeing the log we moved to bridge a stream. This is not a bad thing in itself. Every creature changes its environment in some way: gophers dig burrows, bees spread wildflowers through pollination. We have some right to affect our world, provided it is done intelligently and with love. The problem is that most people have no idea how their building projects will affect the soil, the ground water, or the ecology of "their" land. As Pagans we have a sacred responsibility to approach environmental change carefully, and to seek the counsel of those wise in these matters.

We all know how hugely our species has changed this planet, and continues to. In those corners of the Earth where we have influence, let us set an example for sustainable land use and living in harmony with other creatures.

One last piece of advice regarding coven land: once you hold title, be there. There is not much use having it if you don't visit it. Schedule coven activities there regularly and encourage individual coveners and families to visit for ritual work or recreation. This is part of creating a relationship with the land—keeping in close touch, not only to enjoy it but to understand it, and to be able to intervene if danger threatens. It is a great responsibility, but there is satisfaction in knowing that one little part of Mother Earth is protected from exploitation.

Creating an Astral Temple

Does your coven have a beautiful place all its own, surrounded by grass and trees, where you can go anytime to rest, work magick, swim in shimmering pools or listen to nightingales sing in the moonlight? A place with deep, soft carpets, libraries full of ancient lore, rustling silken curtains, and radiant stained-glass windows?

If not, it's time to create one—on the astral plane. Material-plane meeting places are fine and necessary, but we must not end the discussion there. Much of the coven's work takes place on or through the astral planes and it is helpful to have a temple there, too. As its name implies, an astral temple is a sacred place constructed on another plane of reality by the power of the mind—or, in this case, the combined faith, imagination, and will of your coveners.

Once created, it is a place of gathering, rest, re-creation, and learning. A covener who is far from the covenstead on a sabbat night can, by the power of mind, visit the astral temple and connect with their Craft sisters and brothers. One who is weary, upset, or ill can find peace and a chance to become centered. Facing difficult situations or tough choices, a covener can go there and meditate or seek guidance from the gods and spirits.

Here also, the covener can come to find safety from nightmare creatures (though often it is important to confront them); from psychic attack by another magician (though a strong and ethical Witch has little to fear); or from inimical astral entities accidentally aroused (though almost all are benign or neutral). Rarely, if ever, will you need the astral temple as a refuge—but it's nice to know it's there!

The very process of creating the temple helps the coveners connect and grow as a group. As co-creators, we learn to understand, respect, and cherish one another more. The creation becomes a living, growing symbol of our unity and love, and a reservoir of power for the group mind and spirit.

The creation may begin on a night when the Moon is new, waxing or full, and when the planetary aspects are right for dreaming and creativity. The span of time between Yule and Imbolc is an especially appropriate season to start, though it can be done at any time. If you have a coven astrologer, they can help you choose an auspicious time. If not, at least check an astrological calendar to make sure that Mercury is not retrograde (impedes communications), and that the Moon is not void-of-course. Then use divination to double-check, making sure that the proposed time is appropriate.

The coven gathers, each member relaxes and centers, then all attune. The circle is cast. Play soft music as you sink into delightful reverie, each imagining the perfect temple. What follows may go something like this:

Leona: "We are gathered this night to create an astral temple for the Coven of the Evening Star, a sacred place of sanctuary, re-creation, and learning for all our initiates. Join hands and let the vision grow, then speak as the sprit moves you." (Silence for a time.)

Forest: "It is a place of safety. Its very existence is known only to us. Going there, we shed our fears and self-consciousness. We may be wholly ourselves, free, sharing our deepest thoughts and feelings."

Moonbird: "It is a place of rest and renewal. When our troubles and burdens pile up, we go there and become refreshed in spirit, heart, mind, and body."

Arinna: "It is a place of insight. There we learn new magicks, discover new facets of ourselves, and divine the answers to our questions."

Will: "It is a place of joy. There we can laugh, play, dance, sing, feast, and delight ourselves and each other in a thousand ways."

Leona: "It is all these and more . . . and we can reach it at any time, from any place. To find it, we need only visualize this sign, the key to the astral temple of the Coven of the Evening Star." (She traces a sigil in the air, and it lingers for a moment, blue light against the darkness. There is a long pause while each covener commits the symbol to memory.)

Foxfire: "Entering the temple grounds, we see a sacred grove, a ring of ancient oaks and willows. The soft grass within is sprinkled with flowers of white and gold."

Bel: "A gentle breeze flows through their branches, and touches our skin."

Arinna: "The soft rustling of leaves is the only sound . . ."

Forest: ". . . except for the tinkling of wind chimes in the air."

Leona: "Behind the grove is the temple, a sprawling structure of wood and stone, Earth-sheltered, blending with the contours of the land."

Will: "Now we can hear the sounds of laughter and flute music coming from the open doors."

Foxfire: "There are always companions, playmates, or teachers if we need them—but also places of solitude and stillness."

Moonbird: "The path from the grove to the temple is bordered by gardens full of herbs and flowers. I recognize chamomile, rosemary, and angelica."

Bel: "The great doors of the temple have unicorns and dragons carved upon them. We pass through and into the great hall."

Arinna: "Sunlight floods the room through stained-glass windows, so that the thick, gold carpets are splashed with jewel-like colors . . . ."

And so on, until one silence stretches longer and the High Priestess or trance guide gently brings you back.

It is very helpful if someone suggests a "key" to the temple early on, which allows access and is shared with each new member at their initiation ritual. The key can be the coven sigil, glowing in a certain color; a mantra, chanted just so; an actual key-image of a special material and design; or any combination of visual, auditory, and kinesthetic cues. Whenever the key is recalled, it will automatically bring the covener to the outskirts of the temple grounds, or to the inner sanctum of the temple—whichever the coven agrees on.

Before the initial session closes, raise power to charge the creation, while each person holds the image firmly in mind. Then link it strongly to natural sources of energy (such as the moon, the sun, or starlight) so that the pattern of its reality will be maintained even when the coven is not present to energize it.

An excellent tradition to establish is that of visiting the astral temple every time a new member is initiated, so they can be introduced to it in the company of their sisters and brothers. Other group visits can be arranged either at regular intervals or whenever the coven feels the need. Generally, it is a good idea to share the temple only with full-fledged members who are bonded in love and trust with the rest of the coven.

Each time you go to the temple you will discover new facets: a hidden shrine in some nook, a delightful carving or frieze unnoticed before, a passage leading to a deep cave filled with glowing crystals. Your astral temple can be a place of endless fascination, which grows in vividness with each passing year.

If your coven creates magickal places to meet indoors, outdoors, and on the astral, you will feel blessed indeed. Ultimately, though, the coven "home" exists wherever you gather in love and trust.

NOTES

1. Starhawk, *The Spiral Dance: A Rebirth of the Ancient Religion of the Great Goddess* (New York: Harper & Row, 1979), pp. 201–204.

7 Ritual Tools and Coven Supplies

The Craft doesn't require tools and materials but most Witches have them because it's traditional and fun, and because props can make magick easier—they are aids to focusing magickal will. In most covens, each new dedicant is expected to make, find, or buy certain basic ritual tools. The four basic tools are:

1. The athame
2. The wand
3. The chalice
4. The pentacle

The athame (pronounced ah-THAY-mee) usually looks like a double-edged dagger with a black handle. The blade may be of steel, silver, bronze, copper, or iron, depending on coven tradition or individual preference; it need not be sharp, since the athame is used only to cut lines of energy, not material objects. The handle may be of wood, metal, bone, stone, or ceramic. Often the athame will have the owner's Craft name and a pentagram inscribed upon it, and other symbols explained later. The athame is used to cast the circle and open it, to invoke and banish certain energies, and to cut energy cords. It is considered to be a tool of the element Air in most traditions, Fire in others.

The wand is traditionally a cubit in length, or the distance from your elbow to the tip of your middle finger. It is most often cut from a fruitwood, or one of the sacred trees and plants of Celtic tradition:

birch	rowan	ash
alder	willow	hawthorn
oak	holly	hazel
vine	ivy	reed
elder	silver fir	aspen
yew	furze	heather

Wands have a "female" end, carved with a hole or cleft into which energy flows, and a "male" end, carved with an acorn-shape or pine cone (fertility symbols) or set with a quartz crystal, from which energy is projected. Meaningful runes or the owner's name may be carved along the length. The wand is used to attract various energies (healing, prosperity, etc.) or repel others (illness, fear, etc.). Most think of it as a tool of Fire; some say Air.

The chalice is a goblet traditionally of silver (or silver-plated), though it can be of ceramic, crystal, glass, clay, or other material. Again, it may have runes or other symbols on it. It is a symbol of the womb, and may be used to share wine or other beverages; to mix herbal potions; or for divination, scrying in the water within. It is the tool of Water and the Moon.

The pentacle is a disc of wood, glass, stone, ceramic or wax, upon which is inscribed a pentagram and various magickal symbols. It may be used as a platter to serve the cakes, or as a protective magickal shield. It is a tool of Earth.

In addition, Witches use many other magickal tools, some of which are listed below. See the Glossary in the appendices for brief descriptions of these terms.

Amulets
Asperger
Bell
Bolline
Book of Shadows
Candles
Casting Stones
Cauldron
Cord
Drum
I Ching Coins or Yarrow Stalks
Lamps of Art
Magick Mirror
Mortar and Pestle
Pen of Art
Runestones
Salt Bowl
Show Stone
Staff
Sword
Stang
Talismans
Tarot Cards
Thurible
Water Bowl

Coven Tools

Some tools may well be owned jointly by the coven. A sword, a large thurible or incense burner, and a coven-sized chalice are examples. You may want two cauldrons—one medium-sized one for ritual purposes (such as burning parchment spells), and one larger one suitable for cooking soups, stews and chili at sabbat feasts.

The coven may also own several musical instruments that are kept handy and passed around whenever spells or celebration call for a joyful noise. Drums, tambourines, and rattles are ideal. A few covens use a solemn gong or ethereal chimes to accent important moments in ritual.

Such items are in addition to coven banners and wall hangings, altar cloths, paintings, statuary, tapestries, large candlesticks, candelabras, and the altar.

Creating Your Tools

It is wonderful to make your own tools because they are then filled with your energy and intimately connected with you emotionally and psychically. The first step is to design the tool, and make a full-sized drawing of it. If you don't draw well, ask a friend or fellow covener to draw while you describe it. Some aspects of the design may be traditional—for example, the double-edged blade and black handle of the athame. But there is still room for creativity in shapes and materials. Plus you may want to inscribe your magickal name, personal symbols, or Craft runes on each tool. Some possibilities are shown in the illustrations at the end of this chapter.

When you use metals, remember that each metal has a planetary and energy correspondence and choose accordingly.

Silver: Moon—Magick, psychic skills, Woman, the night

Gold: Sun—Brilliance, intellect, success, healing, Man, the day

Copper: Venus—Love, sensuality, harmony, femaleness

Iron: Mars—Assertiveness, aggressiveness, drive, maleness

Tin: Jupiter-Expansion, success, higher education, science

Bronze: Combination of copper and tin energies

Lead: Saturn—Discipline, structure, authority, higher learning (Note: Lead is poisonous and requires following certain precautions to work with.)

Woods, too, have their own sacred meanings.

Birch: Birth, beginnings, encouragement

Rowan (Quickbeam, Mountain Ash): Magick, quickening, initiation, protection

Ash: Knowledge, rebirth, health, prosperity

Alder: Strength, life-force, light, sisterhood, music, Faeries

Willow: Enchantment, Moon-magick, fertility

Hawthorn: Fullness, ripening, skill at crafts

Oak: Power, endurance, strength, triumph of life, fatherhood

Holly: Abundance; heroism, foresight, defense

Hazel: Positive magick, healing, wisdom, poetry, art, science, knowledge, divination

Vine: Joy, mirth, dance, resurrection, thanksgiving, exaltation

Ivy: Attachment, fidelity, eternal friendship

Reed: Established power, wisdom, protection, night, death

Elder: Completion, fullness, Witchcraft

Also keep in mind Silver Fir, Aspen, Yew, Furze, and Heather, sacred Celtic trees whose traditional meanings are obscure.

A covener's workshop may be all you need to create pentacles, wands, and athames. A "hobby tool" with interchangeable points might be all you need for some projects. You can cut athame blades from sheet metal (bronze, copper, or silver) with a hacksaw, or order a blade from a knifemaker's supply catalog and make the handle yourself. You can make chalices on a potter's wheel and fire them in a personal or school kiln. If necessary you can take crafts courses at a local community college, adult evening school, or recreation department, individually or as a group.

Other Sources of Ritual Tools

You do not have to make all your tools. Some can be ordered from occult supply catalogs or found at occult or New Age shops. Most of the summer festivals feature Pagan artisans selling their wares or accepting custom orders to your design. Antique and curio shops are good sources, as are pawnshops, estate sales, auctions, and even garage and yard sales.

One Craft tradition states that you should never haggle over the price of an item for ritual use. Presumably if it is the perfect thing, it is worth whatever is asked for it. If it is not perfect, then don't buy it—unless you have the skills to modify it so it is just right.

Some tools come as gifts of Nature. A stick just right for a wand or staff; a seashell to serve as chalice or water bowl; a water-smoothed, round, flat stone to be your pentacle; a twig with pine cone to asperge the circle. These may be more precious to some than the most ornate tools crafted by artisans.

Cleaning, Consecration, and Care

Tools should be ritually cleansed from time to time, especially when you first get them, if they were pre-owned, or if others have handled them. Some books suggest that you bury a tool in the earth for a full cycle of the Moon. You may also place the tool in running water, such as a stream, or simply expose it to the light of the noonday Sun or full Moon for a while. You can also cast a circle and ritually purify it with Earth (salt), Air (incense), Fire (candle flame) and Water (water or wine), and then bless it with Spirit (an aromatic oil).

In a consecration ritual, you state the purpose of the tool, name it if you wish, dedicate it to the service of the Lady and Lord, charge it with energy for good, and use it for the first time. An example:

> I call upon the Gods and this coven to witness the consecration of this, our coven sword. May it cast many strong circles to contain the power of our spells and protect us from outside influences; and may it well perform all other magicks we may ask of it for years to come.

> I name this sword Blue Fire, and dedicate him to the service of the Triple Goddess of the Moon, and the Horned One, Her Consort. As I cast the circle with Blue Fire for the first time, let us all chant his name and charge him with the power, that he may ever harm none, but act for the greatest good of all. So mote it be!

Tools should always be kept clean and polished (or in the case of wood, occasionally oiled). For coven tools, this task may be given to one of the coven officers, such as the Maiden, or to the dedicants, or rotated among the group. When you are not using the tools, place them on the altar or in bags, boxes, or sheaths. You may wish to wrap a tool in silk and lay it in a box with fresh herbs or charged crystals.

Coven tools may be especially well cleaned and re-consecrated each year at Imbolc, which is, among other themes, a festival of purification.

It is a point of ritual etiquette, by the way, that no one touch or handle another's tools without permission.

Coven Supplies and Materials

It is very useful to keep on hand whatever supplies you might use during rituals. These would include candles, incenses, oils, herbs, parchment, pens, charcoal, and wood. Stones, shells, and feathers may also be helpful for making amulets and talismans. A suggested list is shown at the end of this chapter. Keep such supplies neatly labeled and stored, if possible someplace convenient to the altar. One of your coveners should be responsible for all supplies.

Candles can often be purchased on sale after the holidays. While beeswax candles are ideal and should be used in important magick, the cheaper paraffin ones will do for most rituals.

A rock shop or wholesale supplier can sell you semi precious gemstones such as those listed: if you buy polished, baroque (odd-shaped) stones, they should not be expensive and will work fine for most talismans and spells. Cabochons (domed, usually oval) and faceted stones cost more, and should be reserved for ritual tools and jewelry.

Scraps of wood can be obtained in the wild or from a lumberyard, cabinet-maker, or woodworkers' specialty store. You can also order exotic hardwoods in small quantities by mail—for example, farm-grown ebony for athame handles (wild ebony is clear-cut and endangered in the Amazon).

Herbs may be grown in your garden or harvested in the wild and dried. They may also be obtained by mail order or you may be lucky enough to have a botanica, herb shop, or health food store nearby. Don't buy herbs just to be Witchy: at least one covener should receive extensive training in herbal medicine from a qualified herbalist and know how to make teas, extracts, tinctures, poultices, and so on.

What about major items? Should the coven own things like tents and pavilions; a van; or power saws, grinders, and kilns for crafting ritual tools? For most covens, this is not practical: fundraising and maintenance use up precious coven time. Plus, covens grow, hive and dissolve, and questions of ownership or stewardship can then get very sticky.

It is usually simplest to rely on the resources and generosity of coven members for such things. If the coven wants a van for a special outing, and no one owns one, you may consider renting one. The same goes for an awning or pavilion for an outdoor sabbat celebration, or a power grinder for making athame blades. It is usually far simpler to borrow or rent such occasional-use items than to worry about ownership, insurance, storage, and maintenance.

A Coven Library

Books can be expensive, and there are many good books on the Craft that are out of print or otherwise hard to find. Most local libraries don't have very good holdings on Witchcraft and magick. So your members may want to pool resources and set up a coven library.

Your library can consist of books purchased using the coven treasury, given as gifts when a covener is initiated, or donated from individual collections. It is important that you set up a sign-out/sign-in system, to be supervised by the coven Scribe or Archivist. This officer can jog the memories of library "patrons" who keep a book out too long, recommend new books for acquisition, and mark each book "PROPERTY OF WILDWOOD COVEN" or whatever. Include the coven's post office box address and a telephone number if possible.

A list of recommended books is included in the appendices. This list will do for a start, but remember that new books are being published all the time. Read the book reviews in various Pagan periodicals to get an idea what might be worth acquiring. Areas to focus on include:

Wicca/Witchcraft	Neo-Paganism
Nature Religions	Magick
Divination	Ancient History
The Goddess	The God
Feminist Spirituality	Ancient Religions
Counseling	Personal Growth
Animal Lore	Ecology/Environment
Myths/Folklore	Plants, Herbs, Trees
Men's Spirituality	Healing Arts

And how about a small library of videotapes and movies on these topics?

And, you will certainly want a library of Pagan music—cassette tapes and compact discs—for ritual and meditation. The number of Pagan artists is growing rapidly, and you may want some Renaissance/baroque music, flute or panpipe solos, Celtic folk music and ballads (perhaps with Irish harp or pipes), drums, and New Age meditation music. Also, some of the "sounds of nature" tapes such as thunderstorms or ocean surf are excellent.

RESOURCE

Eleanor and Philip Harris. *The Crafting and Use of Ritual Tools: Step-by-Step Instructions for Woodcrafting Religious and Magical Implements* (St. Paul, MN: Llewellyn, 1998).

Divinatory Tools

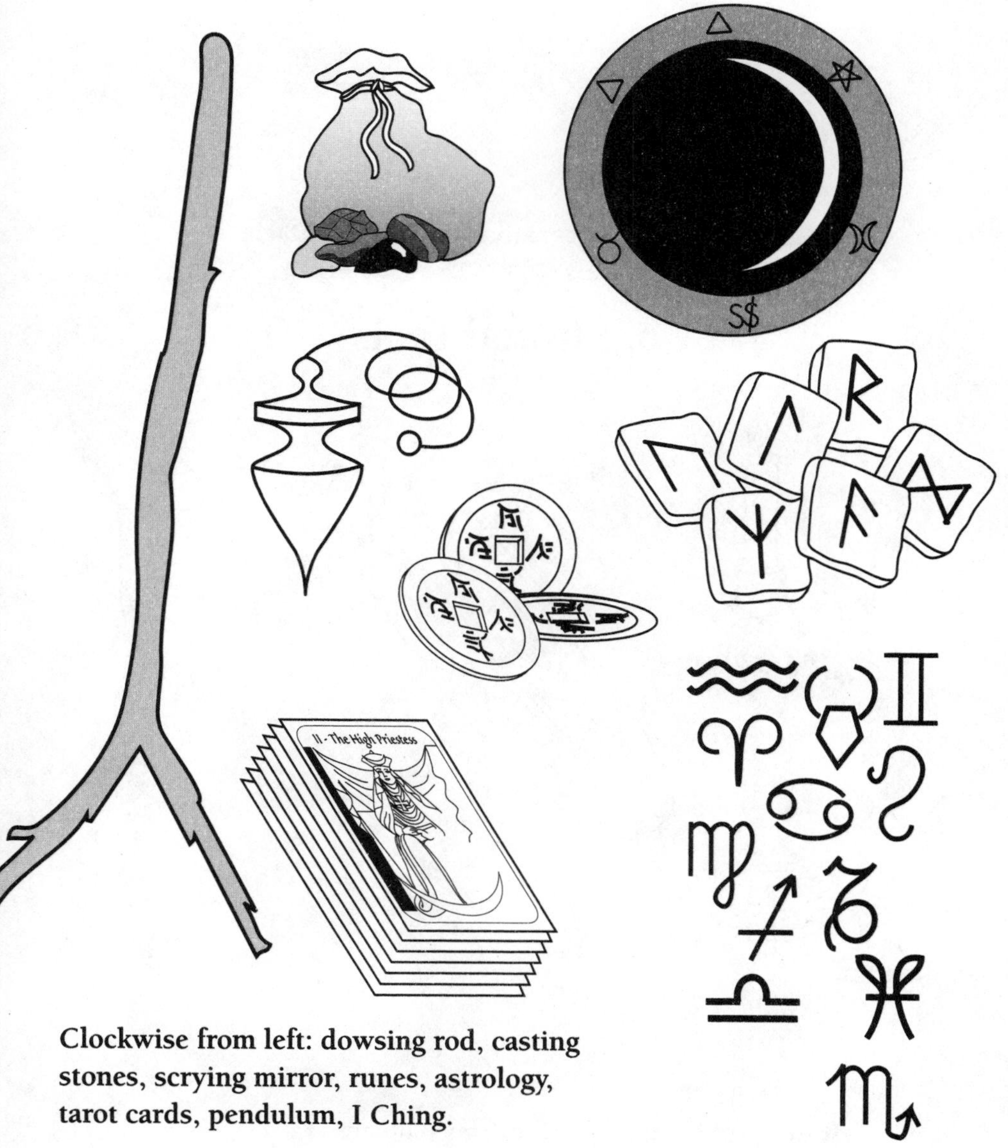

Clockwise from left: dowsing rod, casting stones, scrying mirror, runes, astrology, tarot cards, pendulum, I Ching.

Basic Ritual Tools

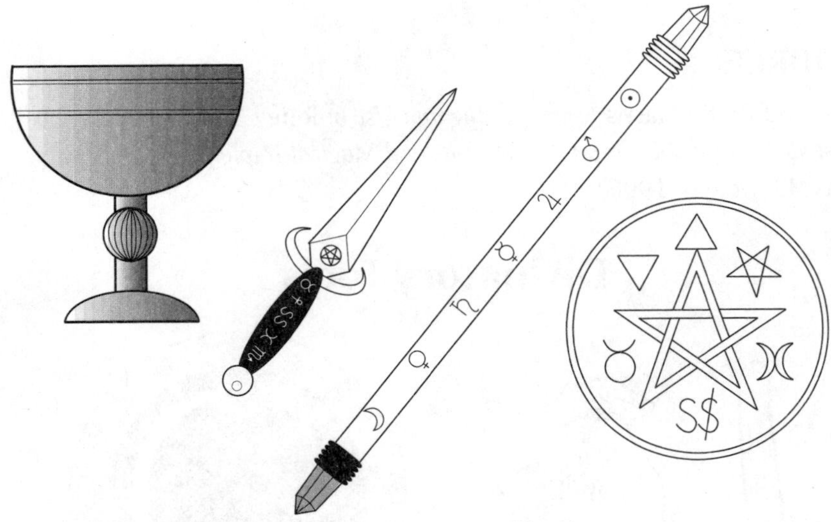

Left to right: Chalice, athame, wand, pentacle.

More Ritual Tools

Left to right: Lamps of Art, drum, shamanic rattle, stang.

Clockwise from top left: bolline; sword; Book of Shadows and pen of art; staff; thurible; cord, girdle, or cingulum; cauldron.

Coven Supplies

Altar candles:
- white (all-purpose)
- dark green (wilderness)
- light green (growth, fertility)
- red (fire, life, warrior energy)
- silver (lunar qualities)
- gold (solar qualities, prosperity)
- yellow (air, intellect)
- violet (higher spirituality)
- dark blue (discipline, order)
- light blue (protection, blessing, water)
- black (limitation, banishing)
- brown (earth)
- orange (energy)
- rose or pink (blessing, love)

Pillar candles (white)
Votive candles (white)
small individual candles (white)
Thin taper candles
Incenses:
- amber (healing, light)
- cedar (beauty, prosperity)
- frankincense (Spirit)
- galbanum (Air)
- myrrh (Water)
- Olibanum (Fire)
- pine (the Horned God)
- Sandalwood (celebration)
- Storax (Earth)

Oils: your choice
Self-igniting charcoal
Tongs to handle charcoal
Parchment, pens, and ink
Small seashells
Stones, especially:
- quartz crystals (energy)
- rose quartz (blessing, healing)
- holy stones (fertility, luck)
- obsidian (cutting through obstacles)
- black onyx (protection, sealing)
- bloodstone (warrior energy, healing)
- moonstone (psychic abilities)
- carnelian (warmth, healing)
- amethyst (temperance, spirituality)
- citrine (illumination, solar)
- malachite (safe travel)
- moss agate (growth, plants)
- lapis lazuli (psychic abilities, spirituality)
- turquoise (health, good cheer)

Scraps of wood:
- birch (beginnings, encouragement)
- rowan (initiation, protection)
- ash (knowledge, rebirth)
- alder (strength, life, light)
- willow (enchantment, fertility, moon magick)
- hawthorn (fullness, sexuality)
- oak (power, endurance)
- holly (increase, foresight, defense)
- hazel (healing, inspiration, wisdom)
- elder (completion, night, spirits)
- apple, cherry (magick wands)
- cedar (beauty, prosperity)
- pine (the Horned God)
- walnut (fertility, the gods)

Model paints (all basic colors)
Small paintbrushes
Workshop tools
- (multipurpose hobby tool, e.g. Dremel)
- small drill
- whittling knife
- sandpaper
- wood oil or wax
- strong glue
- assorted beads
- assorted feathers
- cord, thongs, "rattail"
- wooden matches

Modeling clay (the kind that can be baked in an oven to harden it)
Metal poles
Cleaning rags
Small bags or pouches
Dried herbs, especially:
- catnip (relaxation)
- cayenne pepper (bleeding, ulcers, heart attack, stroke)
- chamomile (sedative, inflammations)
- coltsfoot (heals coughs, colds, asthma)
- comfrey (healing skin, bones)
- garlic cloves (antibiotic)
- ginger (relaxes cramps, stimulates internal organs)
- ginseng root (energy, tonic)
- lobelia (convulsions, spasm, cramps, headaches)
- mugwort (enhances psychic abilities and dreaming)
- peppermint (soothes tummy)
- plantain (blood detoxifier; stings, bites)
- rose hips (against colds)
- valerian (stress, headaches)

Magickal Symbols for the Athame

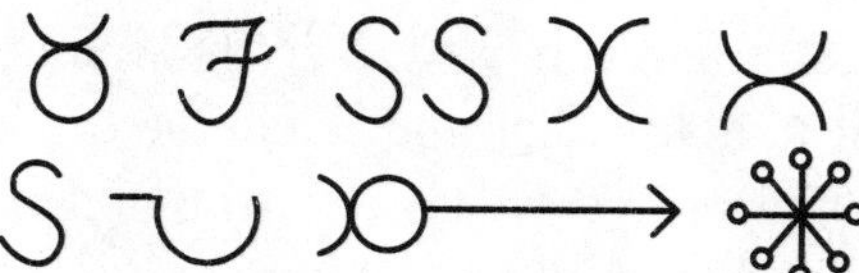

From *The Key of Solomon*, as described in *The Witches Way* by Janet and Stewart Farrar: (*Top row, left to right*) The Horned God, initial of His Name, Kiss and Scourge, Goddess as Waxing and Waning Moon, stylized initial (*Aleph*) of Her Name in Hebrew. (*Bottom row, left to right*) the serpent (life, rebirth), the Sickle (death), power flowing from the Horned God, eight rituals, eight kinds of magic.

From Doreen Valiente, quoted in *The Witches Way* by Janet and Stewart Farrar: (*Top row, left to right*) The Horned God, fertility, May Eve, the "light" half of the year; the ankh cross, life; Salute and Scourge; Goddess as Waxing and Waning Moon; Scorpio, death and beyond, Lord of the Underworld, Hallowe'en, the "dark" half of the year. (*Bottom row, left to right*) the perfect couple; power flowing from the Horned God, or the "conjunction of Sun and Moon"; The Eight Ritual Occasions, Eight Ways of Making Magick.

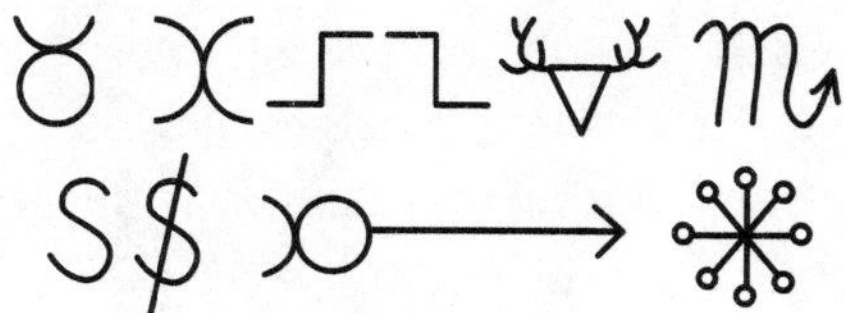

A suggested variation by the author: (*Top row, left to right*) Taurus, May Eve, the light half of the year, Life; Goddess as Waxing and Waning Moon; the perfect couple; The Horned God; Scorpio, Hallowe'en, the dark half of the year, Death and Beyond. (*Bottom row, left to right*) Salute (kiss) and Scourge; power flowing from the conjunction of Sun and Moon; the eight Sabbats, the Wheel of the Year.

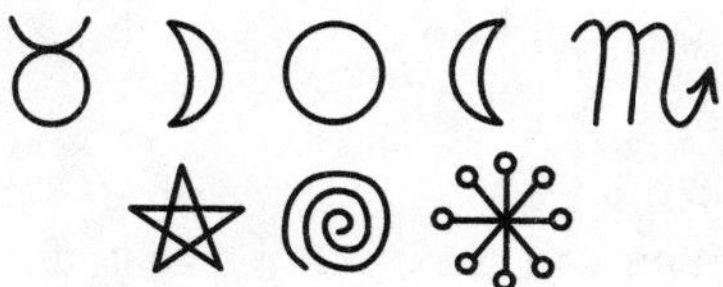

A suggested sequence for Dianic Witches by the author: (*Top row, left to right*) Taurus, May Eve, the light half of the year, Life; Goddess as Waxing, Full, and Waning Moons (Maiden, Mother, and Crone); Scorpio, Hallowe'en, the dark half of the year, Death and Beyond. (*Bottom row, left to right*) the Pentagram; the Spiral Dance; the eight Sabbats, the Wheel of the Year.

The Purposes of Ritual Tools: A Quiz

The purpose of the pentacle is:

A. To spin and watch when you want to go into trance.
B. To represent Earth, hold cakes, and shield the Circle.
C. To flip when you want to decide whose turn it is to clean the temple.
D. To serve as the national headquarters for the Pagan armed services.

The purpose of the chalice is:

A. To hold wine or juice, or to scry (divine) with.
B. To keep sacred goldfish in.
C. To keep little dinner mints in, which people can take as they leave.
D. To put out fires if somebody knocks over the candles.

The purpose of the athame is:

A. To fight off weird spooky things in a ritual.
B. To cast the Circle and invoke or banish.
C. To carve meat and slice bread at a feast.
D. To open official letters from the Witch Queen of the Cosmos.

The purpose of the wand is:

A. To point to people's places in the Circle.
B. To send or draw energy, especially that of Fire.
C. To stir-fry bats' eyeballs, newts' tongues, etc. in a cauldron.
D. To conjure up spirits or riches by waving it and chanting stuff.

The purpose of the Book of Shadows is:

A. To keep shadows in.
B. To explain about curtains and venetian blinds.
C. To write down rituals and magical things you learn.
D. To amuse yourself if the ritual gets boring.

The purpose of the cord or cingulum is:

A. To bind (tie up) or release things in magick.
B. To hang naughty coveners upside down from the ceiling of the temple.
C. To keep your robe closed and preserve modesty in a high wind.
D. To tie a watchdog outside circle.

The purpose of the candles, or lamps of art, is:

A. To drip hot wax into cold water, and read the future from the interesting blobs.
B. To give light for rituals.
C. To cook small quantities of popcorn to eat after a ritual.
D. To goose the ritual leader when she or he messes up a reading.

Answers: B, A, B, B, C, A, B

8 Coven Business and Finances

It might be nice if religion were totally a matter of shared spiritual experience, and the planning, organizing, scheduling, accounting and such took care of themselves. They don't. The business end of religion may be simple or complex, pleasant or agonizing, but it needs to be done because to some extent the spiritual part depends on it. Imagine holding your Yule celebration in a blizzard because nobody remembered to reserve the hall and pick up the key; doing a shamanic trance without drumming because a covener wasn't asked to bring his drum; finding out on the morning of the coven retreat that no one has directions to the campground. This is Earth-plane stuff that must be dealt with, and unlike some religions, we do not denigrate things because they are practical, "worldly," or material.

The Coven Council

You may call it the Coven Council or the Elders or the Supreme Mystical Pooh-bahs of the Galaxy, but there is a governing group in your coven and it should meet regularly to transact coven business. Some covens hold business meetings monthly, for example, on the first Wednesday of the month; some have them every other month or quarterly. The rule of thumb is this: if you can't get through your business in two hours, you're either running a sloppy meeting or you need to meet more often.

There are some simple tips that will help you run a smooth, efficient meeting:

- Make sure business meetings are announced verbally and in writing, well in advance. Having business meetings on a regular day (i.e., first Wednesday of each month) helps prevent confusion.
- Avoid the temptation to make coven decisions at informal, unannounced times, unless the entire coven is present and willing. A member who hears that "Oh, most of us were at the workshop Saturday and decided to . . . " is going to feel left out at best, and quite possibly angry.
- A few days before the meeting, ask people what business they have and write up the agenda. Set priorities, with the most important or urgent items first.

- Ask yourself what information the group will require in order to discuss each item; make sure someone commits to bringing that information. On important decisions, make sure that everyone has necessary information in advance so they have time to think about the issues.
- If possible, get copies of the agenda to everyone in advance.
- Start the meeting on time. Have a short attunement exercise, such as chanting or breathing together. Ask the blessing of the gods on your work.
- Choose or confirm roles for the meeting (see the section after this on facilitating meetings).
- Ask participants to speak only if they have something new to add; people who simply want to agree with the last speaker can "twinkle" (see below).
- Make sure you have an effective chairperson. A good meeting facilitator insists on courtesy and encourages everyone to participate. They state the proposal or define the problem, keep track of alternative suggestions, re-focus discussion on the issues when it wanders off topic, and remind the group of its standards for a "good solution."
- If you have a break partway through, make it short. This is for stretching and the toilet, not refreshments and socializing.
- If a discussion is dragging because people can't agree or don't have enough information, refer it to a committee of those who care most about the issue.
- Use a talking stick if necessary.
- Impose a time limit on comments if necessary. If things really start to drag, hold the meeting standing up.
- Record your decisions and read them aloud at the time to make sure there is no misunderstanding.
- Briefly evaluate the meeting at the end.
- Close on time, even if you have to delegate authority or schedule a follow-up meeting. Closure can be as simple as "That finishes our business; you're all welcome to stay for refreshments," or you can stand in a circle and give thanks for what you have accomplished.

Some explanation is in order. Twinkling is a technique borrowed from the Grand Council of the Covenant of the Goddess. It means holding your hands in front of you, palms forward, and wiggling your fingers. It quickly and quietly tells people that you agree with the current speaker, and saves endless repetition: "I would just like to say that I agree with the last speaker blah de blah blah . . . ." It also gives the chair an idea whether the group is approaching agreement; if everyone twinkles, there is not much point continuing discussion and the matter can be wrapped up.

The talking stick is an important tool. The rules are simple. Only the person holding the stick may speak. When they have finished, they pass it to whoever has raised their hand next for it, in order. If you want to make sure that the quieter members can express their views, then pass it round-robin instead; a covener who really has nothing to add may say "pass" and send the stick on. The talking stick can be any object that can be lifted by the smallest covener; an engine block or sacred boulder won't work in most covens. Some groups create an elaborate carved wand with feathers and beads on it. Some use a candle, a stuffed animal, or a sofa pillow.

You may remind everyone that finishing on time means there will be more time for refreshments and socializing afterwards, or an early bedtime for those who still indulge in sleep. And remember, every time you have a concise, productive meeting you encourage people to attend the next one.

Chairing or Facilitating Meetings

Having a skilled chairperson is half the battle. Note that your High Priestess or official leader does not have to chair the meetings; that job can be delegated to whoever is good at it. Recruit a chairperson who can say, for example:

> "This sounds like it's going to be a good story, Feather; can you share it during the social hour afterwards?" (Cut off diversions.)
>
> "Perhaps that's a detail that we can delegate to Mugwort. I'm sure we can trust him to decide what kind of salsa to bring." (Delegate small decisions.)
>
> "It seems we can't decide this without knowing how much each plan will cost. Thistle, will you work up some figures for next Monday, and we'll meet quickly after the ritual to decide?" (Postpone until information is obtained.)
>
> "We're not getting to consensus so far; how about if you three meet later to hash it out, and come back to the Council with a proposal?" (Refer to committee.)

What are the qualities and skills of an effective facilitator? Look for:

- Active listening skills.
- The ability to recognize participants' feelings, moods, and intentions, whether expressed verbally or silently.
- The sensitivity to "read" silence (tension? boredom? repose? disapproval?), and accept or even impose it when necessary.
- The skill to ask constructive, focused questions.
- Respect for everyone's needs and opinions, and the ability to evaluate an idea on its merits instead of its source.

- Determination to focus on the goals of the group and decisions that have to be made
- The strength to "call" participants on disruptive behavior
- The ability to see similarities in viewpoints, identify crucial differences, and suggest creative solutions that address them
- The ability to summarize and review clearly and concisely
- Self-restraint in voicing one's own opinions
- Patience with useful process, but not with diversion or disruption
- The clarity to remind members of their common values and standards
- Courtesy, and insistence on courtesy from participants
- Humor, used as a tool to break tension, refocus, and build community
- Discipline to follow up on decisions made, as well as items postponed or referred to committee

Facilitation Jobs

The jobs involved in chairing a meeting can be handled by one person, if they are very skilled, or parceled out to several individuals. Starhawk suggests having a "facilitator, vibeswatcher, timekeeper, and notetaker," and there are other possibilities. Here some are described:

Gatekeeper

Gatekeeping is controlling access to "the floor" so that a few members don't dominate the discussion while the quieter ones have no chance to express an opinion. You can gatekeep with general techniques or specific. A couple of general approaches:

> "Let's go round-robin so that everyone gets a chance to contribute. Starbird, why don't you start?"
>
> "How about if we each write down two or three ideas for a coven fundraiser, then put them all on a big chart and discuss them?"

Or you can be specific and target individuals:

> "Pardon me, Sequoia, I want to hear the rest of your ideas but there are several folks who haven't spoken yet. Could you hold that thought for a moment?"
>
> "Grey Mouse, we haven't heard from you on this issue. What do you think?"

Or you can combine approaches by nominally addressing a suggestion to the whole group (even if it's actually aimed at one or two folks), and then immediately refocusing on members who have been left out.

"Okay, if you've already spoken to this, please hold off until we've heard everyone's input. Chipmunk, were you wanting to say something?"

Focuser

We've all been part of discussions that wandered everywhere and arrived nowhere. You can courteously re-focus an individual or the whole group.

"Excuse me, Sequoia, those are some very good ideas but we're getting a bit off the subject. Can we come back to those thoughts later in the agenda, when we get to the fall program?"

"All right, folks, let's refocus and take the agenda items in order. We can't determine the cost of the retreat until we know where we're staying. Earlier someone suggested Crazed Weasel Lodge, and Feather offered the use of her family's summer cabin. Are there other ideas?"

It helps if everyone has a written agenda, and everyone agrees on the order of business at the beginning of the meeting.

Parliamentarian

That is, someone who reminds the group of the rules and processes that are part of the coven contract. Usually this role is taken by a founder, elder, or current leader of the group. Some examples:

"Excuse me, Cybele, but we promised everyone could speak and you just interrupted Flower. Please let her finish her comments."

"You've all heard that Trailwalker has resigned as Summoner. Our by-laws provide that a new candidate for the office will be recommended by the High Priest and High Priestess and voted on by the whole coven."

"If we take this issue to court, we would be violating the Ordains. Wiccan law in our tradition states that we should submit the issue to an Elder or High Priestess for judgment, not a secular court."

Peacekeeper/Conflict Resolver

There are whole books on the subject, so we will just cover the highlights here. First, you need a process in place or in mind:

"Jonquil, we have a way to deal with these problems: the by-laws provide that if you and Moonray have a dispute, and you can't settle it on your own, then you go to the High Priestess and High Priest and they will help you work it out."

Or:

"I know you're pretty angry at Touchwood; what if both of you asked Granite to hear you out and mediate? I know you both respect him."

Or:

> "Would you both agree that mediation hasn't worked? I'm wondering if you would be willing to accept arbitration from a neutral third party." (In mediation, the facilitator attempts to find a solution agreeable to both parties. In arbitration, both parties agree in advance to accept whatever decision the arbitrator imposes.)

Assuming you get both parties to agree to the process, the mediator or arbitrator meets with both parties and hears their stories. Adept questioning may reveal hidden issues beneath the ostensible problem. The ideal solution is usually a "win-win" situation, in which both parties get what they want. For example:

Yellowstone: "Look, the coven treasury can't front the money for the local Interfaith Conference AND put a down payment on the wetlands acreage for a wildlife sanctuary. At least, not at the same time. And the conference is getting close."

Ermine: "Well, we can't wait on the wildlife sanctuary. If we don't put money on the table now, the Megalopolis Development Corporation is going to gobble up the land."

Prairie Fire: "Maybe we can do both. After all, the Interfaith Conference should break even—we'll get our 'front money' back. Could we find some people who would be willing to loan the coven the money for the land, just for a few weeks?"

Yellowstone: "Well, we could try for a bank loan. Or we could ask coven members for short-term loans. I've been saving for a car, but I could loan that money for a little while."

Ermine: "My husband knows the loan officer at the bank. And for that matter, we could defer our car loan payment for a month. Maybe we could get a combination of a small bank loan and some individual loans."

Prairie Fire: "And suppose we include some information on the Wetlands Wildlife Sanctuary in the conference mailings, then do a presentation at the conference and take up a collection for the land. Make the sanctuary an interfaith project!"

Doing some creative thinking, pooling ideas, and looking for a "win-win" solution can often resolve conflicts.

Emotional Monitor

This job has also been called the "Vibeswatcher." This person keeps track of the psychic and emotional flavor of the people participating in a meeting and suggests remedies when the group is getting tired, angry, bored, or otherwise functioning at less than peak capacity. Examples:

> "Excuse me, this is your friendly local Vibeswatcher. It's hot and stuffy in here and half the folks are falling asleep. Can we break for five minutes, get some air, and bring in some cold drinks?"

Or:

> "Whoa, whoa, I know some of us are upset, but let's pause here before the discussion gets ugly. Would you join me in a grounding exercise, then perhaps we can take a short break? Please close your eyes and take a deep breath...."

Or

> "I just want to mention that it's past eleven and some of us are really tired. We're going around in circles. Can we refer this to a committee and ask them to bring back a recommendation next week? Then we can wrap up the meeting. If anybody wants some coffee before they drive home, or even wants to sleep on the sofa tonight, you're welcome."

Timekeeper

Often this function is handled by the chairperson. It can be as simple as glancing at a watch and informing the group, "It's 8:30 now and we're only halfway through the agenda. We may need to move faster or schedule another meeting to finish up." In a large or complicated meeting, the group may impose time limits on individual speakers (perhaps one or two minutes each) or on the time a given topic will be discussed (perhaps fifteen–twenty minutes).

Note-Taker/Scribe

It's essential that everyone be clear as to what is decided, who takes responsibility for a given project, what the deadlines are, and so on. Having someone take notes tends to ensure that there is clarity during the meeting and afterward, and that important pieces are not overlooked ("Now that we've planned out the Fall Festival, did we ever choose a date for it?").

Elemental Roles

Another way to divide up these facilitation jobs is to appoint Lords or Ladies of Air, Fire, Water, Earth for the duration of the meeting.

The Lord or Lady of Air does necessary information-gathering before the meeting and makes sure decisions are clear and detailed. They also imagine creative solutions to problems (or encourage the group to do so), and may act as Scribe. QUALITIES: intelligence, organization, imagination.

The Lady or Lord of Fire keeps the energy flowing and moves the group toward decision and action. They resist rambling and redirect the group attention when it gets off topic. They also suggest resources to make projects or events possible. QUALITIES: focus, purposefulness, energy.

The Lord or Lady of Water is the vibeswatcher, or emotional monitor. They detect and address tension, anger, conflict, and help individuals and groups flow toward a more harmonious and loving space. QUALITIES: empathy, sensitivity, mediation, healing, love.

The Lady or Lord of Earth handles practical, "down-to-Earth," material matters. They sets up the room, make sure materials are on hand, organize snacks and beverages, and assure that the environment is comfortable during the meeting. They also make sure that practical logistics are covered during the discussion: supplies, transportation, finances, etc. QUALITIES: practicality, pragmatism, physical awareness, detail-mindedness.

These roles within a group interaction are not offices; they don't have to be permanent or year-long titles. In many groups, whoever is chairing a meeting will automatically handle all these functions. However, sometimes some of these important tasks will "slip between the cracks" and get lost, either because the chairperson is preoccupied with something else or because they are not very skilled at a certain task.

Then it makes sense to delegate tasks to others to take some of the pressure off the leader. The tasks can be rotated among members at different meetings, so that everyone gets the opportunity to grow, to increase their self-confidence, and gain fresh perspectives. And why not have a workshop based on this chapter, making sure that everyone is aware of the different roles of a group facilitator?

And remember: no matter who has the official title or assigned responsibility, if we care about the coven then we had better ALL be facilitators.

A Variation From Starhawk

Starhawk, author of *The Spiral Dance* and an experienced teacher and priestess, suggests another approach to facilitation and leadership. She offers the following roles:

Crows: "Keep an overview. Goals, plans, directions, details, what needs to be done, by whom? Make alliances, anticipate problems, strategize." Crows are the creatures of East and Air.

Graces: "Help group expand, make people welcome, provide energy and enthusiasm, mediate conflicts." Graces are the people of South and Fire.

Snakes: "Keep an underview of the group's mood, emotions, conflicts, sexual liaisons, secrets, and gossip. Bring up conflict." Snakes represent the West and Water.

Dragons: "Guard the group's boundaries, remind the group of its limits, keep it from expanding too fast, make possible a nurturing environment." Dragons embody North and Earth.

Spiders: "Hold the center, link people together, coordinate information, connect the group." Spiders represent the Center.

In each case, the people holding these roles would have to offer their particular perspectives without getting fanatical about it or hoarding authority in their realms. For example, a Dragon might "remind the group of its limits" when an ambitious new project is suggested; but having done that, must be open to the possibility that the group should challenge itself and stretch its limits by tackling the project anyway.

The Snakes have to be especially skilled and sensitive; they must know when a conflict is trivial and when it requires the whole group's attention; how to intervene constructively when the group's mood is negative; when to keep silent and when to speak up (and to whom) about gossip and liaisons. Although any of the roles could be abused, the Snake's role could be extremely destructive in the wrong hands.

Of course a coven could adopt the same roles and just as easily call them Eagles, Lizards, Dolphins, Bears, and Queen Bees; or Sylphs, Salamanders, Undines, Gnomes, and Unicorns. If the model appeals to your coven, you might try it on an experimental basis. Consider rotating the roles so that individuals don't get locked in to a particular mindset.

Ground Rules for Discussion

Consider setting up ground rules for your meetings, which the entire coven creates or agrees to as a group. Review them at the beginning of each meeting. One such set, via Rowan Fairgrove, includes the following:

Say what you think
Feelings count
No hidden agendas
No personal attacks
One meeting at a time (use a "parking lot," which is a list of items deferred for later discussion.)
Look after your needs
It's OK to disagree

Another set comes from the children of the Unitarian Church of Los Alamos in New Mexico (with their spelling reproduced intact; comments in italics are mine):

Listen when others talking
Listen to conslers *(listen to coven elders?)*
Respect each other
Behave or get a time out *(or know when to take one voluntarily)*
Use inside voices inside
Help each other out
Don't critize
Be polite, no hitting
No monking around

No name-calling
Stay in boundries *(and stay on topic)*
No swear words
Always make sure the conslers know where you are
(call if you can't be at the meeting)
Clean up meses (even if it isn't yours!)
(including emotional messes)
HAVE FUN!

Not a bad list. If every coven discussion followed these rules, we would be doing well.

Money and the Coven

Why does a coven need money?

Actually, it doesn't. Some covens operate entirely on in-kind donations: "Who wants to bring red and white candles for the Imbolc sabbat celebration?" Meetings are held in someone's home or on public land, shared meals are potluck, incense and wine are donated. This is the simplest way to operate, and it works for any basic coven program.

One step up the ladder of fiscal complexity: have a small bowl, pot, or cauldron out at each meeting and accept free-will donations. If everybody puts in a couple of dollars each time you meet, then pretty soon you have enough for ritual supplies or an occasional book for the coven library.

Some covens have modest monthly dues. Traditionally these are only high enough to cover expenses, not "payment" for learning the Craft. The Goddess says, ". . . nor do I demand aught in sacrifice." But once you have dues, then it is advisable to have a Pursewarden to keep track of the funds.

Other covens have more ambitious plans and feel a need to raise larger amounts of money to accomplish them. A coven might want to:

- Build a large coven library for all to use;
- Purchase land and building materials for a covenstead or coven retreat;
- Contribute funds to a worthy cause, such as legal fees for a Wiccan group under attack, a Pagan land project, or an environmental cause dear to the hearts of members;
- Sponsor an event or campaign to educate the public about environmental issues in its local community;
- Travel as a group to a large summer festival in another part of the country;
- Have "seed money" to sponsor its own local or regional festival; or
- Travel as a group to the British Isles to visit sacred sites like Avebury, Stonehenge, Silbury Hill, Glastonbury, and Newgrange.

For projects like these, your coven will probably want to do some fundraising events or projects. You may wish to:

- Sell something at Pagan festivals, Renaissance faires, or arts and crafts shows. Possibilities include t-shirts, robes and cloaks, ceramics (chalices, pentacles, salt and water bowls), food and beverages, incenses, candles, books, God/dess statuary, jewelry, tiaras and wreaths, ritual tools, carved staves, buttons and bumper stickers, drums and rattles, and services such as massage or tarot readings. (Unless you are officially tax-exempt, you may be asked to pay sales taxes to the state.)
- Hold yard and garage sales once or twice a year or participate in a flea market. If several coven families work together, you can easily make a few hundred dollars.
- Sponsor an event such as a talent show, seminar weekend, Renaissance faire, or local festival.

You can probably think of other ideas as well. Check the talents, resources, and connections your coven members have—someone may have a hobby that could be turned into a fundraiser, have special tools and equipment, or know an inexpensive source for salable items. Whatever you do, keep careful track of the expenses and income associated with the project; only then can you tell what your "profit" was, and whether it was worth the effort.

If your coven is strictly a "shoebox operation," financially speaking, you may not need a budget. But if you're going to be handling more than a few hundred dollars in a year, you can get organized and have your Pursewarden draft a budget. A sample appears on page 88.

Your coven will probably want a bank account. You should have printed on your checks the full name of the church (coven), followed by "a California (or whatever) Not-for-Profit Religious Corporation," and your Employer Identification Number, as discussed in the next section. It is wise to have two signators on the account, both board members and/or officers of the coven. Make certain that the account is used only for coven business, and never personal use. If you reimburse an individual for a coven-related expenditure, make sure the Pursewarden has an annotated receipt.

Incorporation and Tax-Exempt Status

Many covens wonder about incorporation and tax-exempt status as a church. For most covens with a small budget, there is little point to going through the process, which does take an investment of time and money. But if you have a largish budget of several thousand dollars, to the point where sales tax amounts to a respectable sum, or major plans for the coven which involve significant donations and cash flow, then it may be worth the effort. And yes, your coven can make money even though it becomes a non-profit corporation. As long as the money goes to church programs (potentially including paid staff) and not to the pockets of shareholders, you are legal.

Scarlet Oak Coven-Annual Budget

CARRIED OVER FROM LAST YEAR:	$ 68
INCOME:	
Donations	372
T-shirt sales (Summer festivals)	516
Tarot readings (Renn. Faire)	85
Coven garage sale	329
TOTAL INCOME	$ 1302
EXPENSES:	
T-shirts and silkscreen materials	$ 319
Garage sale advertising	15
Altar Supplies (Candles, incense, flowers, etc.)	132
Books for Coven Library	186
Gas, cabin rental for Coven Retreat	223
Open Beltane costs (flowers, ribbons, flyers, paper plates, etc.)	96
Open Yule costs (decorations, gifts, hall rental, etc.)	127
TOTAL EXPENSES	$1,098
REMAINING IN TREASURY AT YEAR'S END:	$ 272

First, you should be aware that any church in the United States is automatically tax-exempt. But—and it's a big one—most merchants won't take your word for it. If you want to avoid paying sales tax, you must show them a "Nontaxable Transaction Certificate" from your State Department of Revenue. If you do business regularly with a merchant, they will probably want to have a copy of your Certificate on file.

The other catch is that donations to your coven treasury are tax-exempt—*but* for the donor to deduct them from her income taxes, she may want or need your tax-exempt number. The IRS can disallow such donations if they are not convinced your "church" is legitimate. And what convinces the IRS that you are legitimately tax-exempt? Why, an IRS Letter of Exemption granting 501(c)(3) status, of course.

The initial step in becoming officially tax-exempt (as opposed to merely Constitutionally tax-exempt) is to become a non-profit corporation in your state. This is actually pretty simple: call your State Capitol, get a copy of the application from your Secretary of State or whoever handles such things, and fill it out. Elect officers; usually three are required. For this purpose your High Priest and High Priestess may become President and Vice-President, your Pursewarden becomes Treasurer, and your Scribe becomes the Secretary. Attach a copy of your Articles of Incorporation and By-laws, attach the fee, and send it in. Most states are not terribly picky, and will process your application without question. They may ask you to fill out a short form once a year, updating your address and list of officers, and return it with a small filing fee.

The articles of incorporation can be fairly simple, and in many states you simply follow the outline the state gives you. Usually the document will include:

The name of your organization;
How long it is intended to exist (Say "perpetual");
Its purpose;
Where the "office" is (your home, a P.O. Box won't do);
The name and address of your "registered agent"
(you or any coven leader);
How the articles will be amended;
The size of your board (at least three),
and their names and addresses;
How people can become members; and
Your name and address as incorporator.

Sample articles of incorporation are included in the appendices; if you wish, borrow any of the language which seems to fit your coven. But look at your state's form before you write anything.

You will also need by-laws, which are a more detailed document explaining how your coven operates. Your by-laws provide the practical, day-to-day "working rules" for your group: when will you have meetings, how will you make decisions, how will you choose officers, and so on. By-laws are traditionally easier to change than articles of incorporation. Again, see the appendices for an example.

You may wonder whether you should hire a lawyer to handle your incorporation. It is not necessary if you are willing to do paperwork. However, if you do decide to get a lawyer, make sure you find one who is experienced in setting up non-profit corporations (most are not) and who is sympathetic to the Craft.

Now it gets a little more challenging. Call your local or regional IRS office, and get the forms to apply for an Employer Identification Number, which is like a Social Security number for your group. The coven doesn't actually have to employ anyone. Also get an application for tax-exempt status as a 501(c)(3) organization. The application is long and detailed, and requires information on your finances for the past couple of years (if you have existed that long). They will want you to attach your Articles of Incorporation, by-laws, newsletters, schedule of worship services, religious education classes, and the like—any documents confirming that your group is organized and active in religious activities. And then there is the filing fee—at this writing, $150 for organizations with less than $10,000 annual revenues.

The IRS uses fourteen criteria in deciding whether a group is a legitimate church. Your coven doesn't have to meet all fourteen to qualify, but obviously it helps if you meet most of them. Here are the points:

1. A distinct legal existence.
2. A recognized creed and form of worship.
3. A definite and distinct ecclesiastical government.
4. A formal code of doctrine and discipline.
5. A distinct religious history.
6. A membership not associated with any other church or denomination.
7. A complete organization of ordained ministers ministering to their congregations.
8. Ordained ministers selected after completing prescribed courses of study.
9. A literature of its own.
10. Established places of worship.
11. Regular congregations.
13. Sunday schools for the religious instruction of the young.
14. Schools for the preparation of its ministers.

You can satisfy the first point by incorporating. Numbers 2 to 9 are not a problem for most covens, even if your answers won't look "mainstream." Your "established places of worship" are your covenstead and your favorite outdoor circle. Your "regular congregation" is simply your coven membership. For number 13, you may have to explain that children are tutored in our faith by their parents, with help from the "ministers" as needed. And for the last point, most covens will explain that ministerial candidates are prepared through a mentoring system by ordained and experienced priests and priestesses.

All this may seem daunting, but remember that many Wiccan organizations have successfully completed the process. In fact, one of the questions the IRS staffer may ask is, "Why don't you just work under an umbrella Wiccan organization that's already tax-exempt, like Covenant of the Goddess or Re-formed Congregation of the Goddess?"

For many groups, that would be appropriate. For others, it is not useful. For one thing, most tax-exempt Wiccan organizations do not have "Group Letters," meaning that the central body is tax-exempt, but affiliated covens are not. In addition, your coven may be planning programs or projects that don't necessarily dovetail with another organization's, even if you are a member. But not to worry—your coven can join a national group like COG or RCG and still qualify for your own, separate, tax-exempt status if you need it.

You may be asked if you can't apply as a "religious organization," a "charitable foundation," or some other tax-exempt category. There is no reason for a coven to accept such a status; a coven meets the legal definition of a "church" and is entitled to all of the protections that any other church has.

The IRS will ask you many reasonable questions, and some that are startling. When Our Lady of the Woods applied, we were asked if we sacrificed children or animals. When we answered—making our outrage very clear—the IRS representative apologized. Soon afterwards we received our 501(c)(3) status. For us this status will be useful, since we plan to create a Wiccan teaching center and the tax savings will be significant. A copy of the questions we were asked is in Appendix A-8, page 380.

If you need help incorporating your coven or getting federal tax-exempt status, you may wish to talk to covens who have successfully completed the process. Or contact the staff of any non-profit organization in your state, including local churches even if they are not Wiccan. Ask where they went for the applications, and see if they will show you a copy of their articles and so forth. Most groups will be friendly and willing to help.

Once you are incorporated and officially tax-exempt, check your local, county, and state laws to see if you need to register the coven as a church, or register your "ministers" so they can legally perform marriages and such. These agencies will ask for information but cannot legally refuse to register you; if someone gives you trouble, they are acting illegally. Contact the Covenant of the Goddess or other Wiccan umbrella organization for help if you encounter discrimination.

Paid Clergy, Teaching Fees, and the Craft

A perennial topic of debate in the Craft is whether we should have paid clergy. Most traditions believe it is unacceptable to take money for teaching the Craft, at least in the coven setting. There is a strong feeling that if money changes hands, it could corrupt the learning process. The teacher may be tempted to give students what they want rather than what they need. And the student may be inclined to expect certain privileges, such as initiations, whether or not they have been truly earned.

All this may be moot as long as most Witches are in small covens. Very few covens would be willing or able to tithe a sufficient amount to provide a salary for their leaders. Of course, there are covens experimenting with large outer groves or congregations, and if this becomes a successful movement then salaries might become possible. But would making the size of the priest/ess' salary dependent on the size of the congregation be a temptation to proselytize?

Many would argue that the whole idea of paid clergy is too risky; that priest/esses should hold mundane jobs like everyone else, and thereby keep in touch with the day-to-day realities of the wage-earners they serve.

Some Witches, myself included, do not accept fees from our regular students within the coven, but do accept fees or honoraria when we travel long distances to give seminars on Craft-related topics. This is work "above and beyond" the normal, already numerous responsibilities of a priestess or priest, and sometimes requires taking time off from our mundane jobs as well. One other instance where priest/esses may receive fees for teaching is those few individuals who offer correspondence courses in Witchcraft. (There has been very little criticism of this practice from an ethical standpoint, but some experienced elders wonder whether the Craft can really be taught effectively without face-to-face contact. Still, for those in isolated areas with no other training opportunities, it is better than nothing.)

Then there is the question of charging fees for classes open to the general public. Many Wiccans seem to agree that:

- **Some subjects may not be taught to the public at all, such as advanced magick which could potentially be used for harm (as opposed to self-healing spells or other "harmless" magick);**
- **Wicca 101 classes are the beginning of instruction in the Craft for some, and are generally offered free of charge or for a small materials donation; and**
- **Many other subjects are all right to charge for, in order to reimburse the instructor's time and expenses. These might include topics such as herbal healing, reading the tarot, or meditation techniques.**

Clearly there is ambivalence in the Craft about money. Some believe that we are more spiritually pure if we avoid it altogether, at least in the context of Craft programs. Others say that money is just another form of energy and that Witches should never be afraid to use energy as long as it is done in accord with the Rede. To those with generosity of spirit, the right course of action in each situation will be apparent.

RESOURCES

Jade, *How to Incorporate a Non-Profit Religious Organization* (P.O. Box 6091, Madison, WI 53716: Triple Crescent Press).

Pete Pathfinder, "Magick and the Law; or, The Proper Way to Obtain Legal Recognition of Your Church" (Aquarian Tabernacle Church, P.O. Box 57, Index, WA 98256).

9 Coven Offices

There are covens with no jobs, titles, or officers. They run task-to-task by volunteer effort: "Everyone wants to learn tarot? Well then, who knows enough to teach it? Who wants to bring refreshments next week?"

Even in these groups, there is usually leadership happening. It is simply not acknowledged with titles or specific responsibilities and authority. Let us say that a woman named Cathryn gathers some of her friends, and they begin celebrating Full Moons together, and perhaps reading and discussing books on the Goddess. It is all very informal, with jobs shared around as convenient; Cathryn is never recognized as a High Priestess, or even Chairperson or Facilitator.

Nonetheless it is Cathryn who brought everyone together, and it is she who suggests many of the program ideas and puts the most energy into the group. Other members instinctively turn to her if they have a question or need resources. She is the *de facto* leader by virtue of her organizational skills and her commitment. Possibly she is a quiet one who leads by example and excellence. Possibly she is loud and aggressive and leads by force of personality and a dominant will.

This arrangement works for many covens, at least for a time. It sometimes has the virtues of anarchy: lots of room for creativity, spontaneity, and individual freedom. It also has the problems of anarchy: inefficiency in accomplishing group goals, occasional mass confusion, and a leadership that is hard to deal with if anything goes wrong, because it is not only unstructured but officially nonexistent.

Let us say that Jan doesn't like the direction Cathryn is taking the group. Jan can't say, "Hey, I don't like the way you're doing your job." Cathryn doesn't have a job, officially; she's just the leader. Jan can't suggest another candidate at the next election; there are no elections. Jan can't even criticize Cathryn openly, because, after all, Cathryn's a volunteer who puts a lot of time and energy into the group without asking for recognition or reward.

The problem is, Cathryn also has no specific responsibilities and no clear limits on her authority. A strong leader acting without any structure can become a loose cannon. A strong leader who has a contract with the group—what she's to do, when she's to consult with others, when she can make decisions on her own—can be a wonderful resource.

All of which brings us to the point: any group that is not dead has leadership. If the leadership is informal, it may also be sporadic, weak, disorganized, authoritarian, and/or erratic—and it may stay that way until the group dissolves. If the leadership is recognized and defined, it becomes easier to look at it clearly, talk about it, and make it effective.

Formal leadership is not a panacea and much can still go wrong. But it avoids one problem: the covert tyranny of the unacknowledged leader.

Offices, Traditional and Additional

The four officers of a traditional coven are the High Priestess, the High Priest, the Maiden and the Summoner, sometimes called the Fetch or the Red Priest. Each is discussed in more detail on the pages that follow.

An all-female coven would of course leave out the High Priest position, and allot certain of his duties to the Maiden and Summoner. Or, a women's coven might adopt the three faces of the Goddess—Maiden, Mother, and Crone—as coven offices.

I have added other offices as possibilities; they are:

The Scribe (secretary)
The Pursewarden (treasurer)
The Bard or Minstrel (lore-keeper and musician)
The Watcher (security officer)
The Ranger (environmental officer)
The Guide (youth advisor)
The Archivist (librarian)
The Merchant (fund-raiser)
The Herald (public information)
The Wayfarer (trip organizer)
The Training Coordinator (supervisor of dedicants)
The Congregational Coordinator (outer-grove organizer)

That's a lot of jobs. I list so many on the theory that every coven member should hold an office, thus sharing responsibility for the coven's operation. In a large coven, that means you need a lot of jobs. Depending on the size and interests of the coven, not all these offices may be filled; some may be combined or new ones may be created. The duties of each office are listed in detail below, and in concise form in the appendices.

I also considered adding "Healer" to the list, but did not because every Witch should be in training as a healer of one sort or another. We might be herbalists or counselors or Earth healers, but healing has been part of our religious heritage since the times of the village midwives and cunning men.

Filling the Offices

There is no single, traditional method of matching people with jobs. Basically it can happen through consensus (volunteers), election, or appointment. In the first case, one of the existing officers describes all the jobs, and then people volunteer for the job they like best. If two or more people want a given job and consensus can't be reached, you can have co-chairs or resort to appointment by the High Priestess. If no one wants a given job, perhaps it can be restructured or divided up to make it more popular.

Elections appeal to many people because they are "democratic" and familiar. They also have shortcomings. People may run for an office because it looks comfortable or because they like "power-over," and not because they would grow in the position or do the best job for the coven. Further, the votes may go to the best campaigner, not necessarily the best candidate. And last but not least, the process may polarize the coven in unhealthy ways.

Appointment after consultation often works well. An open discussion on all the offices may be held, after which the High Priestess talks over options with the High Priest and other elders. They take into consideration the individual desires of the coveners, as well as the needs of the coven overall, and reach consensus on the appointments. If consensus is not reached fairly quickly, the decision is left to the High Priestess who may wish to consult the Tarot, Runes, I Ching, or pendulum before announcing her decision.

Training the New Officers

Ideally, a new officer should apprentice with the outgoing officer for a couple of months or more before taking over the job. This is not always possible, in which case the High Priestess or someone she designates might do the training.

Suppose a new coven appoints a Bard or Minstrel, an inexperienced but enthusiastic Witch named Songbird. But she has no predecessor to teach her, and the High Priestess can't carry a tune in a basket, nor can anyone else in the fledgling group. The new Bard will have to look farther afield for resources. For example, she could collect Pagan music tapes, find songs and chants in books, and jam with Pagan musicians and attend workshops at summer festivals.

Each officer in the coven should compile a written guide to that job for the benefit of any successors. In the example of Songbird, she should put together a collection of songs and chants, and even better, photocopy a simple songbook for each coven member. The Pursewarden must have up-to-date financial records, the Summoner an accurate phone and address list, and so on.

Term of Office

Some covens renew or change part of their officers yearly. Just before Samhain is a good time for this, so that new officers can learn their duties over the next two months and take charge at Yule.

However, there is no rule that says officers must have a limited term. Usually a High Priestess holds her office until she chooses to pass it on, and the High Priest keeps his as long as he and the Priestess are a working team. Other officers may keep their jobs until they desire a change, can no longer perform their duties, or leave the coven. Some will achieve second or third degree and hive off to found new covens. At that point a trainee or apprentice can take over their former position.

Successful Performance

The High Priestess and High Priest must do all in their power to help coveners succeed. When a member assumes a new office, they should immediately have all the training, guidance, encouragement, and resources they need to do well in the job.

In part, this means giving them responsibility and letting them "run with it." A High Priestess who nit-picks, watches over one's shoulder, or does part of the job for them is discouraging individual responsibility and empowerment. Accept this from the beginning: the coven officers will never do things exactly the way you would—and that's okay. As long as the job gets done and done well, that's what counts.

But what if an officer really messes up? First, work with them to repair the damage. Second, help her or him find ways to do better next time. Third, if the situation is hopeless, and they absolutely are not capable or willing to improve, then get them out of the job. You do them no favors by keeping them in a place where they are bound to fail. Besides which, the coven's needs must be considered.

Nobody likes to fire people; but when it must be done, it can be done with courtesy and tact. For example: "Blue Moon, I've noticed that you're still having trouble keeping the coven correspondence up to date. We've talked about this before, but it looks like there's still a problem. I wonder if you wouldn't rather help us out as Assistant Bard—I know you love music, and Gwenhyfar could sure use your help with the new songbook. No, don't worry about the Scribe job; it turns out that Chalice used to be an administrative assistant, and I'm pretty sure she'd be willing to take it on."

This gives the covener a chance to make a fresh start in a job they might enjoy more and succeed with. Note that it is a job, not several. Occasionally you will encounter an enthusiastic new dedicant who volunteers for every position: "We need a Ranger? Sure, I'll do it! No problem, I can handle that and Pursewarden and Minstrel and teach some more classes and. . . ." Then you must gently explain that it's important to share the work and give everyone responsibilities; and besides, every member should have some time for a life outside the coven.

Matching people to tasks, developing a pattern of interacting human energies that is complete, efficient, and growth-enhancing—that is an important part of leadership.

Recognition

It is to be hoped that each officer will perform to the best of their ability because that helps the coven, and they believe in excellence. Still, everyone appreciates recognition, and Witches are no exception.

Illustrated at the end of this chapter are some suggested symbols that can be used as badges of office. Some, like the High Priestess triple Moon, are traditional. Others were invented or adapted by the author, and of course your coven can design your own. If you wish, these symbols can be made into pendants and worn by the officers. They could be carved of wood, cast in metal, or molded of clay and fired. You need not have a ceramic kiln to do the latter: hobby stores sell durable clay that can be "fired" in an ordinary oven, then painted; two brand names are Femo and Super Sculpy.

Officers should also be addressed by their titles occasionally—certainly on formal occasions—and thanked for their work in front of the coven.

The High Priestess

The High Priestess is the spiritual mother of the coven, an example to her coveners of the Goddess incarnate. Her duties include (but are not limited to) the following.

1. To teach the insights and skills of the Craft to the coven, or oversee the teaching program, so that each member grows in wisdom, love, and power.
2. To lead the coven in ritual magick and celebration or to serve as a guide and resource to other coveners who may do so.
3. To know and guide the emotional, social, and psychic dynamics of the coven, so that a healthy balance of power and flow of energy is maintained.
4. To counsel coveners in their personal challenges or refer them to resources that may help them.
5. To speak for the coven before other Pagan groups and the community, always placing the best interests of the Lady, the Lord, and the Craft first.
6. To see that the coven's programs are well organized and administered by guiding and inspiring the officers of the coven.

The High Priest

The High Priest, as chief representative of the God incarnate, has similar responsibilities to those of the High Priestess in many ways. The High Priest assists the High Priestess as a leader of the coven, being an example to his coveners of the God incarnate. His duties include (but are not limited to) the following.

1. To help teach the insights and skills of the Craft to the coven, so that each member grows in wisdom, love, and power.
2. To help lead the coven in ritual magick and celebration or to serve as a guide and resource to other coveners who may do so.
3. To support the High Priestess in guiding the emotional, social, and psychic dynamics of the coven, so that a healthy balance of power and flow of energy is maintained.
4. To counsel coveners in their personal challenges or refer them to resources which may help them.
5. When requested by the High Priestess, to speak for the coven before other Pagan groups and the community, always placing the best interests of the Lady, the Lord, and the Craft first.
6. To see that the coven's programs are well organized and administered by guiding and inspiring the officers of the coven.
7. To support the High Priestess with the strength of his hands, the wisdom of his counsel, and the love of his heart, in all that she may do for the honor of the Lady and the Lord.

Note that the division of duties between the Priestess and Priest will depend in part on the strengths and skills each one brings to the coven. One theory has it that women are more active on the Inner Planes and men on the Outer, so the High Priestess should lead in the areas of magick, ritual, and the bonding of the group; while the High Priest leads in matters of organization, administration, and community relations. This arrangement may work well in many covens. However, you must not ignore individual talents and variations, and wise Witches will each allow the other to lead in the areas they are strongest.

The High Priestess/High Priest relationship is a partnership. As long as each person places the needs of the coven first, and doesn't worry about their own authority, prestige, or prerogatives, it will work. Performing these offices is a service to Goddess, God, Craft, and coven, not an exercise in ego.

The Maiden

If the High Priestess is the spiritual mother of the coven, and the Mother-Goddess incarnate, then the Maiden is the Young Goddess Who works at Her side to gain knowledge and wisdom so that She may one day fulfill that role. The specific duties of the Maiden may include the following:

1. To receive additional training to prepare her for the office of High Priestess, especially in the following areas:

   Ritual design and leadership
   Teaching

Counseling
Group process
Administration
Advanced magick

2. To serve as an example to the rest of the coven in her participation, learning, appearance, and ethics.
3. To be a resource to the coven especially in her knowledge of the lore, mythology, attributes, and aspects of the Goddess.
4. To take special care that the temple be appropriately decorated, attractive and well supplied with necessities (candles, incense, altar cloths in various colors, etc.). She may enlist the energy of the Dedicants to help her in this.
5. To assist the High Priestess in ritual and in projects designed to strengthen and harmonize the coven community.
6. To act as High Priestess when the High Priestess is absent, or occasionally as a training experience.

The Summoner

The Summoner is responsible for communication of accurate and timely information to coveners and is the chief assistant to the High Priest. He must be well-organized, a good communicator, and extremely dependable. In addition, he must be very accessible to coven members. His duties are as follows.

1. To keep in his possession an up-to-date list of coven members, their residential addresses, their e-mail addresses, and their telephone numbers, and a schedule of the coven program a year in advance or as far ahead as is known.
2. To disseminate this information to coveners and notify them of changes in the coven membership or program.
3. To provide all coveners with information necessary for full participation in the program (i.e., the location of events, what tools or apparel are appropriate, or whether a potluck is to be held).
4. To serve as courier to other covens or Pagan organizations when requested by the High Priestess.
5. To serve as an example to the rest of the coven in his participation, learning, ethics, and appearance.
6. To be a resource to the coven, especially in his knowledge of the lore, mythology, attributes, and aspects of the God.
7. To receive additional training to prepare him for the office of High Priest, especially in the following areas:

Ritual design and leadership
Teaching
Counseling
Group process
Administration
Advanced magick

8. To assist the High Priest in ritual and coven projects as requested.
9. To act as High Priest when the High Priest is absent, or occasionally as a training exercise.

In a small coven, he may also assume the duties of Watcher. In certain traditions, these positions are combined as the Red Priest.

The Pursewarden

The Pursewarden keeps track of the coven treasury and accounts. They must be highly accurate and careful with money. Their duties are detailed here.

1. To establish and monitor coven bank accounts.
2. To collect and deposit dues, contributions, and the proceeds of fundraising projects.
3. To issue checks and make purchases as requested by the governing body of the coven.
4. To present accurate reports on the state of the treasury at regular coven business meetings.
5. To coordinate fundraising projects, unless the coven appoints a Merchant or Fundraiser with that responsibility.
6. To be knowledgeable about the coven's tax-exempt status, tax rules and reporting requirements.

The Bard or Minstrel

The Bard keeps the history and lore of the coven intact and transmits it though words and music. They are responsible for the musical resources and program of the coven. They must have a good singing voice and be able to drum and play at least one other portable instrument, such as a guitar or flute. It is also very helpful if they can read and write musical notation. This position can be divided into Bard (storyteller and keeper of the ancient lore) and Minstrel (musician and song leader). Their duties are:

1. To teach the knowledge and lore of the Craft through story, verse, and song.
2. To keep a file of songs, chants, and instrumental music suitable for sabbats, esbats, and other coven rituals.
3. To share these materials with coveners in the form of a coven songbook with the songs and chants most often used.
4. To teach coveners the music to be used in upcoming rituals, and when necessary to lead them during the ritual.
5. To maintain a supply of simple coven instruments on hand, such as drums, rattles, tambourines, and bells.
6. To study the uses of music in magick and share what they learn with the coven.
7. To compose new poems, stories, songs, chants, and instrumental music as the occasion warrants, including music for teaching and for spells.

The Scribe

The Scribe is responsible for the written records of the coven and most correspondence. They must be clear and accurate in written communications; word-processing and computer skills are very useful. The Scribe's duties are:

1. To keep the coven Book of Shadows, including all rituals and other new material devised by the coven (though this may be in the form of a File of Shadows or a Diskette of Shadows);
2. To keep a record of attendance at classes and rituals, initiation dates, and other individual covener information;
3. To keep minutes of coven business meetings;
4. To handle most routine correspondence for the coven; and
5. To take charge of the coven library, unless a separate Archivist is appointed for this purpose.

The Archivist

The Archivist is responsible for the coven library. This may include books, magazines, articles, a scrapbook or photo album, and audio resources such as tapes and discs (unless the Bard takes charge of these). They must be well organized and enjoy research and detail work. The Archivist's duties are:

1. To keep an inventory of all printed and audio materials owned by the coven;

2. To care for the materials, keeping them safe and organized, and repairing bindings, etc. as needed;
3. To assist coveners to find appropriate information and resources for their Craft work;
4. To keep track of materials, checking them in and out to coveners;
5. To recommend new materials for acquisition by the coven; and
6. To create and maintain recommended reading lists on various relevant topics.

The Guide

The Guide coordinates youth programs, with the help of the rest of the coven. These might include religious education classes; participation in sabbats, esbats, and summer festivals; field trips to sacred places; and parties and camping trips just for fun. They must be dependable, imaginative, and energetic, and enjoy working with young people. The Guide's duties are:

1. To meet regularly with the young people of the coven, encouraging their input and responsibility for their own programs whenever feasible;
2. To find and mobilize the resources necessary for the youth program to succeed, including but not limited to the energies of parents;
3. To facilitate the growth of young people in the spirit of Wiccan ethics and ideals;
4. To make sure that appropriate standards of conduct and safety are enforced at youth events;
5. To obtain and file signed permission slips from both parents or guardians of participating youth; and
6. To work with the High Priestess and High Priest to integrate youth activities into the overall coven program, and the Summoner to keep coveners informed of youth plans and needs.

The Ranger

The Ranger helps coveners keep informed about humanity's relationship to the Earth and take appropriate action to protect and heal Her. They must be well informed, assertive, and able to inspire and organize others. The Ranger's duties are:

1. To guide the coven in developing ecologically sound lifestyles that are gentle on our Mother;

2. To keep abreast of developments in ecology, environmental law and related issues—locally, nationally, and globally;
3. To share such information with the coven;
4. To assist the coven in developing action priorities that will maximize the impact of coven efforts;
5. To recommend specific projects for the coven in areas such as habitat protection and restoration, wildlife shelters, pollution control, recycling, conservation, or public education; and
6. To coordinate and lead such projects.

The Watcher

The Watcher is responsible for the immediate safety and security of members at coven events and, in coordination with the High Priest, the long-term safety and defense of the coven. The ideal Watcher is self-assured, calm, strong, foresighted, and quick-thinking. They must always work toward peace and harmony with the community, but be instantly prepared to deal with violence if it is unavoidable. Protection of the coven with minimal or no damage to the assailant is the goal. The Watcher's duties are to:

1. Be knowledgeable about laws regarding religious freedom, freedom of assembly, trespass, citizen's arrest, and related matters;
2. Develop contacts and resources within law enforcement agencies and organizations devoted to the defense of religious freedom, civil liberties, and Pagan rights;
3. Become skilled in conflict resolution, magickal/psychic self-defense, and some form of defensive martial arts;
4. Share his/her knowledge and skills with the other coveners and help them learn self-defense techniques;
5. Maintain security at coven events. When indoors: checking locks, closing curtains, setting wards, etc. When outdoors: finding safe places for events, setting wards, posting sentries if need be, etc.;
6. Have contingency plans ready for possible emergency situations at each coven event and for long-range situations; and train and rehearse coveners in them; and
7. Keep track of organizations, proposed laws, individuals or trends that may threaten the coven or the Craft as a whole, and keep coveners informed of these.

The Merchant

The Merchant coordinates coven fundraising projects unless the Pursewarden handles this responsibility. Projects might include garage sales; selling handcrafts, literature or refreshments at Pagan festivals; or bake sales. They must be organized and energetic, and their duties are:

1. To research and recommend project ideas to the coven;
2. To manage each project, allocating jobs, supervising progress, and keeping records; and
3. To work with the Pursewarden, making sure that all moneys spent and received are handled properly.

The Wayfarer

The Wayfarer coordinates coven field trips. These might include retreats, expeditions to summer festivals, visits to sacred places, workshops in other cities, or camping trips just for fun, or even major pilgrimages to sacred sites overseas. They must be organized, foresighted, and a good communicator. The Wayfarer's duties are:

1. To keep informed about places the coven may want to visit, such as historical or sacred sites, Pagan festivals, workshops and seminars on topics of interest to Witches, and potential sites for coven retreats such as campgrounds and conference centers;
2. To research special coven events or excursions so that they have on hand maps and routes, lodging information, weather forecasts, local resources and points of interest, and so on;
3. To recommend such activities or programs to the coven at coven planning meetings;
4. To work with the High Priestess and High Priest to integrate the trip into the overall coven program, and with the Summoner to keep coveners informed of the plan;
5. To manage or delegate preparations for each journey such as reservations, transportation, equipment, food, lodging, registrations and permits. For a camping trip, the Wayfarer might coordinate menu planning, food buying, and major equipment such as tents and campstoves; and then distribute a list of recommended personal camping gear to each covener.

The Herald

The Herald deals with the media and any sort of communications beyond the coven membership. Of course this office would have been impossible during the Burning Times, and some covens will find no use for it even today. But covens in more tolerant and accepting communities, or those with an interest in outreach and public education, will probably want to fill this position. The Herald should be diplomatic, patient, and good with both oral and written communications. The Herald's duties are:

1. To maintain working relationships with local newspaper, radio, and television station staff;
2. To create and distribute news releases, "church news" updates and public service announcements, to the area media and possibly to the Internet;
3. To participate in occasional interviews with the media or make arrangements for other coven leaders to do so;
4. To create and distribute flyers, posters, or banners for open coven events; and
5. To edit the coven newsletter, if there is one, and maintain the mailing list. Note that the whole coven can help with folding, addressing, stamping and other tasks if the newsletter goes to a large readership.

The Training Coordinator

The Training Coordinator keeps track of new students or dedicants of the coven, especially in regard to their learning needs. If a coven has a list of twenty subjects that new people are expected to learn before initiation, the Training Coordinator would keep attendance lists and arrange special training or make-up classes as needed, so that each student gets the full array. In a small coven, this function could easily be handled by the High Priestess, Maiden, or Summoner; but a large coven focused on outreach and teaching may find it useful to have a separate officer for this job. (In our coven we call this position "Quail Mother," partly because it is a New Mexican bird and partly because our Dedicants tend to come in groups.) Their responsibilities are:

1. To get to know each of the new students or dedicants and have an idea of the progress they are making and what their special needs are;
2. If you have a mentor or apprentice system, to help match trainees to mentors and facilitate changes if any pairing doesn't work out;
3. To serve as a resource for mentors, suggesting ways to work more effectively with their students;
4. To keep written records as to who has taken what training and to help arrange make-up work if a dedicant misses a class or workshop;

5. To work with the Archivist and others in creating or updating a Recommended/Required Reading List, getting the books stocked in the coven library, and encouraging the dedicants to do the necessary reading; and
6. To make recommendations for improving the coven training system.

The Congregation Coordinator

This officer is the administrator for the congregation or outer grove—those people who wish to be part of the wider coven community, to celebrate the sabbats, socialize, take an occasional workshop, and make use of priest/ess services such as counseling or rites of passage, but who do not desire the more intensive training of a coven priest/ess. Their duties are:

1. To work with the Coven Council in scheduling congregational or open events: sabbat celebrations, selected workshops and classes, festival trips, and Full Moon esbats as appropriate;
2. To keep a contact list for mailings or phone calls and notify congregation members/area Pagans of events and activities;
3. To mobilize people outside the coven proper to help with such events (phone trees, set-up, clean-up, program assistance, refreshments, car pools); and
4. To make sure, in general, that there are open communications and a harmonious relationship between the coven and the congregation or outer grove.

Ritual Leaders, Trip Organizers, and Special Event Coordinators

Not all jobs within the coven require regular officers. If you rotate ritual leadership, then the assigned priest/esses are responsible for a single ritual at a time. Someone might volunteer to coordinate a coven outing to a summer festival (food, transportation, registration etc.) without necessarily becoming the Wayfarer for the year. Another member—better yet, a team—might organize an intercoven potluck, a field trip to a sacred place, a workshop with an outside herbalist, a park clean-up project, or a community bardic circle.

In summary, an active coven has plenty of work to do. If one or two coven leaders shoulder all the burden, they will burn out quickly, and, more importantly, they deny the other coven members the chance to contribute their skills and grow as priest/esses. Smaller covens do not require such an ambitious program or all these officers. But large or small, the responsibility for the coven must be shared if the coven is to belong to all its members.

10 Merry Meet! New Members

Do you want more people in your coven? How many Witches is the "right number" for a coven? Technically, a coven consists of anything from three to thirteen members. At the lower end of that range, a triad is difficult to sustain as a working group—if anyone is unavailable, there goes your group mind. Four to five members works better, and according to a survey taken by the Covenant of the Goddess, the average size nationally seems to be about seven.

As we will see in the chapter on group dynamics (Chapter 18), a full coven of thirteen has a very complex web of relationships, and is quite challenging to handle. Except in rare circumstances, covens usually split, or hive off a daughter coven, if they get any larger.

Unlike some religions, we have no imperative call to "save" as many souls as possible. There is a positive tradition in the Craft that we do not proselytize or evangelize. This is probably a reaction to the historical recruiting practices of many Christian monarchs, who offered neighboring tribes a choice between conversion or death. Many missionaries drew the line at murder, but were happy to desecrate or commandeer Pagan sacred places and then bribe the natives with food and health clinics.

Deciding Whether to Expand

So for Wiccans, the question is, what works? What feels right to you and the other coveners?

The addition of even one new member changes the entire energy pattern.

You may have a group that is closely attuned, a working team that you don't want to disrupt with new energies. That's fine.

Or you may welcome the excitement, growth, and challenge of new members. Or perhaps your coven is lopsided with males or with females, and you would like to work with a better balance of the sexes. Or perhaps your coven is the only one in the area, and you feel a responsibility to offer religious community to more Wiccans.

Whatever the reason, you may choose to expand. Witches do this without proselytizing or conversion. It is a matter of making your presence known to those who are already Pagan at heart, and then getting acquainted well enough to learn whether Wicca is truly the right spiritual path for them, and if they can work harmoniously with this particular coven.

Be clear in this: Wicca is always freely chosen. You must never pressure anyone to join—not because you think they are one of us, not because you would like to work with them, not because "Mother Earth needs help"—not for any reason. You may inform, you may invite, and if the answer is "No," there's an end to it.

The other side of the coin is this: if someone wants to join your coven but is clearly unsuitable, you should turn them away—kindly, but firmly. What would prompt you to do this? Possibly:

- **The applicant is underage and does not have their parents' support (they should wait until they are older or living independently);**
- **The applicant has doubtful ethics and wants to learn magick for negative purposes (they should first get counseling or education about ethics);**
- **The applicant is excited by the mystery and romance of Witchcraft alone, and has no particular interest in Wiccan spiritual growth (they may join the Society for Creative Anachronism or play Dungeons and Dragons);**
- **The applicant is in the midst of a life crisis and is grasping for straws to cope with it (they may ask for the coven's help, but not join); or**
- **The applicant is genuinely drawn to Wicca as a spiritual path but has a personality conflict with one or more members of the coven (they must work out their differences outside the coven, or seek another group).**

Open Classes and Other Ways to Meet

How do you make contact with potential members? One excellent method for those who are "out of the broom closet" is to offer a series of "Wicca 101" classes, open to the public.

The positive side of such classes is that you can educate many people in the community about the true nature of Wicca while connecting with like-minded people who may wish to join you. Organizing and teaching the class will also reinforce and extend the knowledge of the instructors.

The negative side is that someone must identify publicly as a Witch, and thus expose herself or himself to potential harassment by the intolerant. Further, there is the possibility that a public class will catalyze fundamentalists into a "witch hunt" in one form or another. While unthinkable in many areas, there are still places where it could happen.

Our coven's experience is that careful preparation and a strong, assertive attitude will carry you over any fundamentalist bumps in the path. But you will need to decide how your community will react—with positive interest, indifference, or suspicion and fear.

One reason that our classes are well received (barring a few letters to the editor from fundamentalists) is that our teachers are already known to the town in other capacities, through our jobs, civic activities, and so forth. We already had a network of non-Pagan friendships and reputations as community-minded citizens. This inclines people to think twice before they judge us.

Also, our attitude is important: we are strong, clear, and matter-of-fact: "Yes, we're Wiccan. So what? Yes, we're holding public classes. So does your church. We're Americans. That's our right."

In addition to open classes, you can post notices in magickal or New Age bookstores if any are in your area. Sometimes a friendly journalist will do a feature article on your coven; this may bring inquiries if a contact point is included, such as a post office box number.

Then there is magick. Magick to draw new members is ethical if it does not seek to draw anyone against their will. An example: "We ask you, Mercury and Iris, to let our presence be known to those who are seeking a coven like ours. Smooth their path that they may find us, if doing so would be to their benefit and ours. With harm toward none, and for the greatest good of all, so mote it be." Of course you would also raise power and charge the vision of new friends finding you.

If—and *only* if—you have experienced magickians in your coven, your group can create a fetch or artificial elemental—a living thought-form capable of independent action within the guidelines you set. Its first job is to guide seekers to you, and it can also help as an astral guardian and Watcher. Or your coven may create an astral beacon, for example, a glowing pentagram in the sky above your community, anchored to the Earth and drawing power from Her. After our coven tried this approach, we held a public class that had the largest attendance we have ever enjoyed, and fifteen members of the class later asked about becoming Dedicants with us.

First Impressions

When interested folks do contact you, they may be a little wary and nervous at first. Someone who is brand-new to Paganism has very little idea what to expect: Will you be burning-eyed fanatics out to steal their brains? Will you want large sums of money? Will you seem pleasant and normal at first, then suddenly announce that their pet beagle must be sacrificed to demons at the dark of the moon?

So, it is your job to set them at ease and dispel all the nonsense they may have seen at the movies. Your friendly attitude and willingness to answer questions freely will go a long way toward helping them past that first tension. Also, you may wish to go easy on the black robes, make-up, and occult paraphernalia when you are first meeting people at a class or in your living room—save it for rituals. New people need to know first that you are "folks" who talk rationally, pay your taxes, and like furry animals. Then they will be better able to handle the sight of you in a cloak the size of Manhattan and twelve pounds of eye shadow, or whatever your ritual persona may encompass.

Suppose Joe Seeker comes to a Wicca 101 series, then gets invited to a couple of rituals. Everyone in the coven likes him and believes he might do well with the group. Maybe you'll want to meet him socially and do some get-acquainted exercises. Some activities have already been discussed in the chapter on organizing a coven; the following are more games you can use to get better acquainted with potential Dedicants, or to strengthen coven ties at any time.

Coven Get-Acquainted Games and Activities

When introducing these games, it is important to create an atmosphere of fun and cooperation even if the game is nominally "competitive." Make it clear that the point is not to establish a winner, but to have fun and get to know one another.

Correspondence "You-Sheets": Give each person in the coven a large sheet of newsprint and place a good supply of crayons or markers in the center. Put each person's name on a slip of paper, and have everyone choose one at random from a chalice or cauldron. Each person then writes the selected name at the top of their sheet, then writes or draws things that seem to "correspond" to that individual's personality. For example: animals, herbs, colors, trees, time of day, celestial objects, season, piece of furniture, vehicle, food, geological formation, or god/dess. When all are done, have each person explain their sheet to the whole coven, then present it to the person depicted. You may wish to have music playing and snacks available while coveners are working.

Jam Session: Ask everyone to bring over any musical instruments they own, including lots of simple ones like rhythm sticks, bells, and drums. If some of your coven are skilled songbirds or musicians, wonderful—but it's not required. Start with some songs or chants that everyone knows, just to get warmed up, then get original! If someone feels inspired to sing an impromptu chant, or say a poem over the evolving music, so much the better. Feel free to record, listen, and modify, or to jam with recordings. The keynotes are spontaneity, experimentation, and fun!

Kim's Games: Did you ever play these as a child? They're still fun! Collect a bunch of unrelated small objects (a candle stub, spoon, small doll, firecracker, and others), spill them on a blanket in front of everyone, then cover them after ten seconds—and see who can remember the most. Variants: have different substances with strong odors in capped jars, and see who can identify and remember the most. Make mysterious noises behind a screen or blanket (lighting a match, clicking a ballpoint pen, rolling a marble, etc.) and see who can identify the greatest number. Or put strange objects in a "feelie bag" to identify by touch.

Face and Body Painting: Find the nearest theatrical supply shop and obtain some washable face or body paints. Then gather one day, get skyclad (or at least down to minimal coverage), and turn coveners into canvasses. There are several ways to organize this:

Each person can describe what colors and designs they want on themselves, and volunteers can begin; or each covener may "gift" another with symbols representing blessings and wishes (e.g., "I give you inner serenity, as represented by this seascape I'm painting on your tummy"); or the coven may choose a theme for the event (e.g., Power Animals, Runes, Goddesses, etc.) that all adhere to.

When everyone is suitably gorgeous, the coven photographer can shoot some Polaroid keepsakes for those who are not camera-shy. You can conclude with a ritual, including lots of music and dance.

Computer Fun: Assuming that one or several of your members have personal computers, there are many programs the whole group can enjoy—such as the one that writes "poetry" from a word list supplied by the coven, or some of the fantasy-quest games that require ingenuity rather than ultra-fast reflexes. Of course you can also make a "Disc of Shadows" by inputting the coven's Book of Shadows, or organize a coven songbook. There is also software available to do astrological charts and interpretations, and even Tarot "readings." Or you can surf the Net together, looking at the Pagan Web sites or visiting the chat rooms.

Swap Meet: Ask each covener to sort through the odd corners of their home and bring an array of interesting goodies they no longer want—and let the trading begin. Clothes, books, jewelry, ritual supplies, knick-knacks; it's more fun than a yard sale, because every object has a story and you may learn surprising new facets of your coven siblings ("Tell me again why that boomerang has a picture of Betty Boop decoupaged on it?"). When every member has had a turn at the goodies, donate the extra things to a charity or have a coven yard sale. If you like, make it an ongoing thing by having a permanent "Swap Box" at the covenstead. Then at any meeting, coveners can drop off unneeded goodies and pick out what they can use. If you want to keep it simpler, focus only on books or clothes.

Resource Sharing: Of course your coven has classes in divination, ritual, spell-casting, and so forth; but for a change of pace, why not have each covener lead a workshop or demonstration in their "non-magickal" field of expertise? Your members may have skills and talents you never dreamed of, and it's fun to share them! Our coven has had members who were expert in chiropractic, plumbing, calligraphy, gerontological social work, early childhood education, rock music, animal rights, woodworking, fantasy games, horse management, baking, camping, yoga, sex education, and more. Probably some discussion would turn up an equally impressive variety of skills in your coven. And asking members to share their skills (especially new members, whose magickal knowledge may be limited) can do wonders for boosting self-confidence and strengthening friendships. Besides, it makes a welcome change sometimes from "heavy" spiritual topics.

Get Acquainted Garbage: On a lighter note, you can ask each member to prepare a box of "your own personal trash" for the scrutiny of the Coven Archaeological Survey Expedition—the other members. You might include old photos, odd food containers, a page from your monthly appointment calendar, torn tickets, a broken ritual tool, outworn clothing, an empty matchbook from an unusual place, cryptic notes from friends and relatives. "By their garbage ye shall know them." What better way to reveal unsuspected facets of your personality?

Name Tag Mixer: Give 5"x7" cards to each covener, and fine-tip markers. Ask them to print their names in the middle; around the outside or in the corners, ask them to write short answers to certain questions. You can choose some of these or make up your own:

What historical person do you admire most?
What is your favorite book or music?
What exciting sport have you always been secretly attracted to?
What is your best physical feature?
Name three things you really, really enjoy doing.
What mammal (or bird or fish) would you most like to be?

Then sit in a circle and share your responses in more detail, going round-robin, one question at a time. If this proves to be fun—and revealing—you can do it on a regular basis, changing the questions each time. In fact, let a different covener come up with the questions each time.

Question Circle: So simple, but surprisingly effective at building group feeling. Sit in a circle, perhaps with beverages and munchies at hand. One at a time, round-robin, each covener asks a question and all the others respond. The questions might include something like these:

When you were little, what did you dream of growing up to be?
What is the most embarrassing thing that ever happened to you?
What is the most important thing you have accomplished so far?
What is your favorite fantasy?

. . . and so on. People can say "pass" if they really need to, but usually very few do that.

Psychodrama/Role Reversal: Handled sensitively, this can be educational. It involves pairs of coveners switching roles, with each acting in the character of the other as they perceive it. The "scenario" can be a ritual planning session, or a class, or a discussion about the last sabbat. What's important is that each participant try to "climb inside the skin" of the other and interact from there.

The potential catch is this: some people may feel misunderstood or even mocked by the way the other person presents them. Unless yours is a *very* mellow group, it might be tried in pairs, privately, then perhaps discussed in the group. If it is acted out a pair at a time before the whole coven, be sure you have a skilled facilitator on hand. You may wish to suggest that everyone focus on mimicking only the positive traits of their partner, at least until you can judge the level of tension. In any case keep discussing, and keep working from your heart chakras (loving energy), until you're sure that everyone's okay.

Human Sculpture: One covener becomes the "sculptor," the rest are the raw material. The sculptor takes each person by the hand and places them in the location and position that best reflects their relationship to each of the other people. When completed, the sculpture is a model of all the major relationships in the group as seen by one person. Take a while for the sculptor to explain his or her perceptions, then disband the sculpture, stretch, and let someone else become the "sculptor."

Tarot Visions: Spread an entire tarot deck face up on a blanket with all the coveners around it. Select one person and ask all the others to choose one card that best represents that individual. When all have made their selections, then go round-robin and have each covener show the card they picked and explain why they feel this card describes something important about the focus person. The selected cards are then handed to that person, who has a few moments to study them and think about what's been said. Then move deosil to the next person and repeat the process. Listen carefully and you'll learn a lot about how members see each other. In a well-bonded coven, people will come away from this exercise feeling very warm, empowered, and understood by their coven sisters and brothers. In a new group, people will begin to learn how they come across to others.

Note: Depending on the size of your coven, you may need two or three sessions to complete the activity. Do not push on until people are tired and bored, or the last "chosen people" will get short shrift.

Biobooklets: Each covener prepares a booklet introducing their personal history, skills, likes and dislikes, dreams, guiding principles, and so forth. The booklets are photocopied so that each covener has a copy of every booklet, and they are presented at a sabbat or special ritual.

Only the author can decide what should be put in or left out. Possibilities include a short autobiography, college transcript, poetry, lists of "favorites" (foods, colors, animals, plants, clothes, books, art, and so on), or a vision of your ideal life ten years from now.

Fantasy Sharing: Tell your most fun daydream/fantasy. Or, make up a fantasy for someone else in the circle and share it with the group!

Potlatch: Spread out in the woods for a few minutes, looking for a "sacred object" (feather, neat stone, leaf, wand, etc.). Gather and present your gift to another in the circle with a short speech as to its significance.

Psychic Guessing Game: Focusing on one person at a time, everyone guesses her or his: favorite color, animal, food, game, TV show, period in history, sport or hobby, place to vacation, and "type" of romantic partner.

Trust Exercises: Try the Trust Fall (where one person topples off a kitchen chair and is gently caught by everyone else), or the Trust Walk (lead one another blindfolded), or Face Trust (explore each other's faces with eyes closed).

First Reactions: As the following words are read, write down the first word or phrase that comes to mind. Discuss.

Conjure	Snake	Ritual	Witch	Cool
Love	Wild	Midnight	Hope	Book of Shadows
New Age	Potion	Goddess	Spirit	Horned God
Magick	Pot	Drugs	Hot	Sexy
Party	Circle	Mother	Dangerous	Hunter
Healing	Sabbat	Priest	Priestess	Holy
Parent	Father	Child		

Charades: Play charades with either book titles, movie titles, fairy tales, goddesses and gods, animals, or other categories.

Team Poetry: Choose a subject and each write three lines of poetry about it (blank verse). Then pool your efforts and try to arrange or adapt the lines into one coherent poem. Or go round-robin, each person adding a line to a total of thirteen lines (a form of poem called a "haiwitchku"). Be sure to have someone write down the finished product for sharing with the whole coven later.

At some point, when and if the whole group feels it appropriate, you can offer Joe formal affiliation as a dedicant (candidate). Here are some suggestions for what your coven might require of potential members.

Dedicant Requirements

Potential Dedicants must:

1. Have a strong desire to explore Wicca as a potential personal spiritual path, and this coven as a potential spiritual family;
2. Agree that neither the identities of the members, nor any coven business, nor any covener's personal business, shall be shared outside the coven without the express permission of those involved;
3. Have lives that are settled enough to have room, psychically and emotionally, for powerful new experiences and personal growth;
4. Have the support of significant others in the decision to become a Dedicant;
5. Have attended all Wicca 101 classes;
6. Have schedules which allow participation in most coven activities (classes, esbats, sabbats, etc.);
7. Agree to use all knowledge shared by the coven teachers in the spirit of the Wiccan Rede;
8. Make a serious, good-faith effort to get to know all the other coven members and build good relationships with them;
9. Support the coven program on the material plane through contributions of money, goods, or work (if there are no set "dues");
10. Make or obtain a robe for rituals, in the traditional color or pattern of the coven;
11. Begin to create or obtain basic ritual tools (athame, wand or staff, chalice, pentacle, candlesticks, salt and water bowls) and set up a personal altar at home;
12. Agree to abide by the attendance requirements and by-laws of this coven; and
13. Understand that participation in the coven as a Dedicant does not guarantee eventual initiation into the Craft or the coven.

You may need to adapt this to your group. For example, if you practice skyclad, then the robe requirement might be unnecessary. Or you might have monthly dues, a small amount sufficient to cover candles and photocopies of class handouts.

The Dedication ritual need not be elaborate (a suggested outline is included in the appendices). Its main purpose is to formally welcome the new Dedicant as a working member of the coven. We repeat our expectations of Dedicants, learn their Craft name if they've chosen one, present a white cord, hug and welcome them, do a short divination to suggest a direction for personal growth in the coming months, and have a potluck or refreshments.

Organizing a Good Beginning

The first weeks are very important for new people. They will be filled with expectation, excitement, and energy. Make sure that they have every opportunity to get better acquainted and bond with other coveners, and have easy access to more experienced members whenever they have questions or concerns. You may wish to assign each new dedicant to an initiate who will act as guide and advisor (see the section on mentoring in "Education and Training"). In a large coven, divide into working teams of two or more Witches and mix them up frequently. These teams will prepare and lead sabbats, esbats, or classes, or are given special tasks such as starting a coven library, creating a coven ritual tool, decorating the "temple" (ritual meeting place), organizing a community service project, planning a field trip, and so on. One coven called these teams "pods," after the highly social and cooperative families of dolphins and whales.

A friendly coven where all the coveners care about one another and that has a well-organized program of classes, celebrations, and magickal work will not only attract like-minded people but keep them around for a long time.

11 The Coven Calendar

Sabbats, esbats, classes. Initiation rituals, rites of passage, public education programs. Community service projects, field trips, festivals. Potluck dinners, business meetings, work parties. A busy coven's program calendar can fill up fast—to the point of overstressing and burning out your members. A not-so-busy coven can drift along, getting little done, until members grow bored and leave. How do you strike the right balance, one where coveners are active and enthusiastic about the program and can maintain the pace over the long run?

To begin with, resolve to plan your coven program a full year at a time and have next year's schedule in the hands of coveners well before the end of each year. Planning a month ahead, or even three or six months, does not work well. People are busy, and have other commitments and interests outside the coven. They need to plan ahead, and if the coven calendar is blank, they will fill in all the spaces with conferences, vacations, sports, youth programs, and everything else. Then you are left scrambling to find acceptable dates for coven activities in the nooks and crannies of several different and well-filled personal calendars.

Participation will be much higher if your members have information in their hands far in advance. This doesn't mean the program is carved in stone: flexibility is good and plans will change. But it is much easier to change an existing schedule than to cobble one together at the last minute.

Before you start marking up a calendar, the coven membership must answer some policy questions:

- What are our program priorities? Ritual? Education? Community service? Networking? If we run short of time, what must stay and what can go?
- What sabbats will we celebrate? Most traditions celebrate the four Greater Sabbats (cross-quarters) and the four Lesser Sabbats (solstices and equinoxes). However, some observe only the Greater Sabbats, or those plus the solstices.
- Is it important to us to celebrate moons and sabbats on the traditional or actual dates, or will

we "fudge" in order to have more weekend events and fewer weeknight events?

- Will we celebrate only Full Moon esbats, or New Moons as well? Or will we substitute Diana's Bow for New Moons? (Diana's Bow occurs when the first slender crescent is visible after the New Moon; some covens prefer the waxing energy of the young moon for ritual, rather than the dark-moon energy, which is best for divination.)
- Will rituals normally be led by the coven leaders, or will this responsibility be shared around as equally as possible?
- If you are a mixed coven, will rituals always be led by a priest-and-priestess team, or will you also have rituals sometimes led by two priestesses or two priests?
- How often will we have classes each month? Will we try to have short classes before esbats or devote a whole evening to each class?
- Will initiations and rites of passage be worked into our esbat and sabbat rituals or be scheduled as separate events?
- Does the coven want to attend a big regional or national festival as a group or will we leave it to individuals as to what festivals they attend?
- Do we want to schedule in some fun social activities, like dinners, film nights, picnics, and camping trips? Or shall we leave such events for members to do informally as the mood strikes them?
- If your coven is fairly democratic in nature, then you will also need to discuss class topics. What do coveners want to learn? Do you want to survey a great number of things (one class on spellcasting, one on drumming, one on tarot, etc.) or would you rather focus on a few topics (three months on runes, three on ritual design, etc.)? What kind of teaching resources are available in your coven and community? And if seven members want to learn about astrology and two want to become herbalists, is there any way you can accommodate everyone?

Once you have guidelines in place and your class topics, then a couple of the coven leaders can sit down and pencil in dates. Don't forget to consider competing community events and secular holidays: you may want to avoid scheduling an open sabbat on the same day as the local county fair, and you may not want to plan a coven camping trip on the Fourth of July weekend. Major personal commitments also have to be taken into account: if a member serves as a volunteer Scout leader every Thursday evening, don't schedule regular classes on that night.

Start with the sabbats and esbats. Once these are scheduled, look to see if any of them fall very close together: if your September New Moon esbat falls on the day before the Mabon sabbat, you can combine them in one ritual.

Add in your classes for coven members. Some covens have a regular "class night" each week, but will skip class if an esbat or a sabbat occurs too close to the class. Some have class nights but may add short "mini-classes" before each esbat, and occasionally schedule a longer workshop on a weekend. The most important thing is to have some clear pattern that members can count on and remember easily.

Now add in your other activities:

Business meetings/Coven Councils
Community service
Wicca 101/public classes
Social/fun events
Field trips
Work parties

Rites of passage and initiations will probably be added to the schedule occasionally throughout the year. For more activity ideas, see Chapter 15, "Special Activities."

Let's suppose the Blessed Bee Coven has decided that they will focus on teaching and ritual. They will celebrate all eight sabbats, Full Moons, and Diana's Bow rather than the New Moon. They will hold classes on Mondays, and Coven Councils (business meetings) on the first Wednesday of each month. They want to celebrate rites of passage at the nearest esbat, and will schedule initiation rituals separately as they come up. The coven wants to attend a fall regional festival as a group, though individuals will attend some summer festivals on their own. They will schedule a couple of social events, and will add others informally later on. Overall, they want to average about six coven events a month. The following draft calendar incorporates all of these considerations.

DATE	ACTIVITY	PLACE	LED BY
JANUARY			
Wed. 1/3	Coven Council	Covenstead	High Priestess
Fri. 1/5	Full Moon Esbat	Covenstead	Emerald, Staghorn
Mon. 1/8	Movie Night	Willow's	Willow
Sat. 1/13	Regional Workshop	Metropolis	COG Local Council
Mon. 1/22	Diana's Bow Esbat	Pendragon's	Crescent, Pendragon
Mon. 1/29	Class: Animal Mgk	Covenstead	Staghorn
FEBRUARY			
Fri. 2/2	Imbolc Sabbat	UU Church	Chamomile, Longbow
Wed. 2/7	Coven Council	Covenstead	High Priest
Mon. 2/12	Class: Tarot	Covenstead	Willow
Mon. 2/19	Diana's Bow Esbat	Starlight's	Willow, Starlight
Mon. 2/26	Class: Communic.	Covenstead	Crescent
Wed. 2/28	Wicca 101	Pub. Library	Emerald

MARCH			
Mon. 3/4	Full Moon Esbat	Covenstead	Staghorn, Pendragon
Wed. 3/6	Wicca 101	Pub. Library	Longbow
Mon. 3/11	Class: Tarot	Covenstead	Willow
Wed. 3/13	Wicca 101	Pub. Library	Crescent
Sun. 3/17	Ostara Sabbat	Hilltop Park	Starlight, Chamomile
Wed. 3/20	Wicca 101	Pub. Library	Pendragon
Mon. 3/25	Class: Tarot	Covenstead	Willow
Wed. 3/27	Wicca 101	Pub. Library	Chamomile
APRIL			
Mon. 4/1	"Fool Moon" Esbat	Holywood	Emerald, Pendragon
Wed. 4/3	Wicca 101	Pub. Library	Starlight
Mon. 4/8	Class:Past Lives	Covenstead	Longbow
Mon. 4/15	Class: Shamanism	Covenstead	Pendragon
Fri. 4/19	Diana's Bow Esbat	Chamomile's	Crescent, Chamomile
Tues. 4/30	Beltane Sabbat	Holywood	Willow, Staghorn
MAY			
Fri. 5/3	Full Moon Esbat	Holywood	Starlight, Longbow
Mon. 5/6	Class: Shamanism	Holywood	Pendragon
Wed. 5/8	Coven Council	Covenstead	High Priestess
Mon. 5/13	Class: Astral Travel	Covenstead	Starlight
Sun. 5/19	Diana's Bow Esbat	Emerald's	Chamomile, Emerald
Mon. 5/27	Class: Shamanism	Holywood	Pendragon
JUNE			
Sat. 6/3	Full Moon Esbat	Holywood	Willow, Pendragon
Wed. 6/5	Coven Council	Covenstead	High Priest
Mon. 6/10	Class: Rites of Pass.	Covenstead	Emerald
Mon. 6/17	Diana's Bow Esbat	Staghorn's	Crescent, Staghorn
Fri. 6/21	Litha Sabbat	Holywood	Starlight, Pendragon
Mon. 6/24	Class: Herbcraft	Covenstead	Chamomile
Sun. 6/30	Full Moon Esbat	Holywood	Willow, Emerald
JULY			
Wed. 7/3	Coven Council	Covenstead	High Priestess
Mon. 7/8	Class: Meditation	Covenstead	Starlight
SS 7/13-14	Coven Retreat	River Falls	All
Mon. 7/15	Class: Huna Magick	Holywood	Staghorn
Thu. 7/18	Diana's Bow Esbat	Chamomile's	Chamomile, Pendrgn.
Mon. 7/22	Class: Meditation	Covenstead	Starlight
Sun. 6/30	Full Moon Esbat	Holywood	Willow, Emerald
AUGUST			
Thu. 8/1	Lughnassad Sabbat	Holywood	Emerald, Staghorn
Wed. 8/7	Coven Council	Covenstead	High Priest

Mon. 8/12	Class: Circle Dance	Holywood	Longbow
Fri. 8/16	Diana's Bow Esbat	Crescent's	Willow, Crescent
Mon. 8/19	Class: Meditation	Covenstead	Starlight
Wed. 8/28	Full Moon Esbat	Holywood	Starlight, Longbow
SEPTEMBER			
Wed. 9/4	Coven Council	Covenstead	High Priestess
Mon. 9/9	Class: Astrology	Covenstead	Emerald
Sun. 9/16	Diana's Bow Esbat	Holywood	Chamomile, Staghorn
FS 9/19-22	Mabon Festival	Pines St. Pk.	COG Local Council
Thu. 9/26	Full Moon Esbat	Holywood	Crescent, Emerald
Mon. 9/30	Class: Astrology	Covenstead	Emerald
OCTOBER			
Wed. 10/2	Coven Council	Covenstead	High Priest
Mon. 10/7	Class: Shapeshifting	Holywood	Chamomile
Wed. 10/16	Diana's Bow Esbat	Starlight's	Starlight, Staghorn
Mon.10/21	Class: Astrology	Covenstead	Emerald
Sat. 10/26	Full Moon Esbat	Holywood	Willow, Chamomile
Thu. 10/31	Samhain Sabbat	UU Church	Crescent, Longbow
NOVEMBER			
Mon. 11/4	Class: Stone Magick	Covenstead	Longbow
Wed. 11/6	Coven Council	Covenstead	High Priestess
Mon.11/11	Class: Palmistry	Covenstead	Crescent
Wed.11/13	Diana's Bow Esbat	Emerald's	Starlight, Emerald
Mon.11/18	Class: Dprtd Spirits	Field Trip	Chamomile
Sun.11/24	Full Moon Esbat	Covenstead	Staghorn, Longbow
DECEMBER			
Mon.12/2	Class: NLP&Magick	Covenstead	Crescent
Wed. 12/4	Coven Council	Covenstead	High Priest
Mon. 12/9	Community Service	Comm.Cntr.	Emerald
Fri. 12/13	Diana's Bow Esbat	Crescent's	Starlight, Crescent
Mon.12/16	Community Service	Comm.Cntr.	Emerald
Sat. 12/21	Yule Sabbat	UU Church	Willow, Pendragon
Tues.12/24	Full Moon Esbat	Covenstead	Chamomile, Staghorn

How did the Blessed Bee Coven do? Well, they managed to schedule about six coven events a month; the big exception is March, which has eight because of the Wicca 101 class series. The coven isn't too worried about that, because they've spread out the responsibility for those classes, and only one or two coveners will be at each class (though the High Priest and High Priestess may be present at all.)

Some class topics have been scheduled for a single evening, others cover three sessions. The coveners wanted a mix of quick, simple introductory classes, and others that would be more in depth.

They worked hard to make sure that ritual leadership was shared pretty equally, so everyone has a chance to learn and grow as ritual leaders. Because this coven has five women and three men, that meant there would be a fair number of rituals led by a team of priestesses. This doesn't bother Blessed Bee too much, because gender-polarity magick is not crucial to them; in another coven it could be a major issue. There is no "right" or "wrong" way for everyone: traditions and covens make the choices that work for them.

Blessed Bee also wants to make sure that every covener leads ritual with every other one, again for the learning experience. So they did not focus on teams of "magickal partners," but made new pairings for each ritual. Again, a different coven might make different choices, if it was important to them to work with established, ongoing magickal partnerships (usually, but not always, committed life partners). Since it's important to Blessed Bee to have as many combinations as possible, they will often have female-female teams, and occasionally—because there are fewer men—male-male teams.

Another interesting choice this coven has made is to meet in different places from time to time. Classes, Coven Councils, and Full Moon esbats (in cold weather) are held at the Covenstead, which happens to be the High Priestess' home. But in warm weather they move their Full Moon esbats outside, to a place in the National Forest they have named Holywood. Some classes may be held there as well. Their Diana's Bow esbats move around to the homes of the people leading those rituals; this gives everyone a chance to play host/ess once in a while and takes some pressure off the High Priestess since her home is used less often. For their sabbats, which are open to the community, they rent a room in the local Unitarian Church.

Having leadership assignments made in advance for the entire year means that there are fewer last-minute scrambles to get an event ready. Members who need lots of time to prepare will have it. When an event is going to be led by a team, they have opportunity to meet and plan as often as they need to. It should be noted that every ritual on the schedule is a team effort. What isn't as apparent is that most classes are really team efforts as well. One person may volunteer to be the "Lead Teacher," but they are encouraged to find a helper or co-teacher. This makes teaching easier and more fun, and gives the second person valuable experience.

No schedule is going to be perfect. Inevitably someone will be disappointed that they can't lead the ritual at their favorite sabbat or that their suggestion for a class just didn't fit in. A flexible coven will try to make accommodations. Maybe Longbow doesn't get to lead the Yule sabbat this year, but he's first in line for next year. Perhaps Starlight won't get the class in Enochian Magick she wanted, but Emerald is interested and wants to study it with her on their own time. You make the best choices you can and hope that the things you left out this year can get included next time around.

All this may seem like *a lot* of organization and effort for a rather small group of people. It is. But it is one thing that makes the Craft different from some other religions: each individual is valuable and worth the energy. Besides, spiritual growth and religious community aren't cheap. They require commitment and investment. To priestesses and priests of the Craft, the result is worth it.

Attendance

Most people have busy lives and do not find it easy to work in a full schedule of coven events. However, if attendance is sporadic then your coven is not going to be able to accomplish its goals effectively.

Suppose training people as priests and priestesses is important to you, and you come up with a program of classes that cover all the skills you believe are important for Wiccan clergy to have. If three people miss a class, either their education is incomplete, or someone has to organize a make-up session for them, or they have to wait until that class comes around again, perhaps in a year's time. Worse yet, if that class is part of a series where each builds on the last one, then those people aren't going to get much out of the succeeding classes.

In ritual your coven is gradually creating a magickal "group mind" as you work together and get to know one another's energies and styles. If people are erratic in their participation, this process becomes much harder and your magick suffers.

Consistent attendance is important no matter how you define the mission of your coven, yet members have other responsibilities in their lives. What priority should they place on coven activities, and what should your coven's attendance policy be?

A general recommendation is this: family and job responsibilities come first, then the coven, then everything else. No one should be expected to neglect their loved ones or their economic needs for their religious activities; in fact, most would be very suspicious of a religion that suggested such priorities, and rightly so. At times when your family or job needs extra attention, it may even be necessary to take a sabbatical from coven work. On the other hand, if one is training for the priesthood, one's religious and spiritual life should take precedence over a sports event, a hobby, or any single social event.

You may want to state this in your coven by-laws. You may even want to set an attendance standard for members. A good rule is that members should participate in at least 75% of the classes and rituals, and call the program leader anytime they will be unable to make it. If this is not possible, they should discuss the situation with a mentor, the High Priestess, or the High Priest. Possibly they will need a leave of absence until such time that they can participate regularly; or they could join the congregation that has a lighter schedule and no attendance requirements.

There might reasonably be a different standard for elders who have already been through all the basic classes. Hopefully they will still be happy to participate in most of the rituals, but they might be excused from classes unless the subject is new to them or they are teaching it. This assumes that all elders will be continuing their education in solitary or small groups, mentoring others, and taking an active role in the community, all of which take a great deal of time. So the elders are not just "getting time off."

Joining a coven means making a commitment to your coven sisters and brothers. It should not be a greater commitment than you make to your partner or children, but it is important nonetheless, and the coven has a right to expect regular participation. If the coven schedule is planned and communicated well in advance, and does not include more than one or two events in the average week, it should be possible for every member to balance the needs of their families, jobs, and covens.

12 About Ritual

At the Full Moon and sabbats, or whenever there is need, Witches do structured rituals. The style may vary tremendously from Witch to Witch, coven to coven, and occasion to occasion. From light and joyous, with lots of singing and dancing, to heavy and somber, with more spoken invocation, chanting, or silent meditation.

The centerpiece of any sabbat gathering is the ritual. There may be a class or workshop before the ritual, and doubtless there will be a potluck and social hour afterwards; but a good teacher will take care of the workshop, and Pagans have never needed much help with eating and socializing. The ritual is the challenge.

What Is Ritual?

For some people the word "ritual" has the connotation of meaningless repetition: something done over and over the same way each time, habitual and uninspiring. Wiccan ritual, done well, is anything but boring. It should be creative, transformative, awakening, and energizing.

A ritual is an exercise in the "technology of the sacred." On one level it is a logical series of actions designed to use energy for change: preparation, attunement, cleansing, creating sacred space, drawing various kinds of energies, raising power, directing it, grounding the excess, and restoring the space to something like its previous state.

Ritual is usually planned and intentional—to a point. For a couple of reasons it cannot be wholly controlled and still have power: first, because it is aimed at transformation and no one can predict exactly how each individual will respond and change; second, because a good ritual takes on a life of its own and can flow in directions not imagined by its designers. Ritual leaders who know their craft will flow with this spontaneous permutation and encourage it, as long as the energy is positive, and not try to force the ritual to stay in a preconceived pattern if it needs to break free.

But it is not that cut-and-dried. On a spiritual level, other things are happening. First, it must be experiential: people do not merely observe, they participate: with their bodies, their voices, their emotions, their energy. The people are wholly present and involved; they all become co-creators of the ritual experience.

They experience connection with each other in the circle, with the past and the future, with forces and spirits normally beyond the threshold of consciousness. They become part of something greater: the coven, the group mind, the Earth, the God/dess.

They experience transformation. But not without fear, pain, and a sense of loss. No matter how necessary, or how desired, change is scary. We release the limitations and delusions that formed our old, comfortable (or at least familiar) realities, and move into unknown territories of the soul, knowing that we can never go back.

What Is Ritual For?

In an article in the journal *Heresies*,[1] Kay Turner suggests certain core purposes for ritual, which can be summarized as follows.

- To envision and create the future of the self: achieve symbolic, therefore psychic and spiritual change; and support one another in personal transition.
- To envision and create the future of the group: achieve shared meaning, resolution, emotion, goals; reaffirm relationship, belonging, identity; connect individuals to the group and strengthen group loyalty.
- To envision and create the future of society and the world: promote and sanction social change; renew commitment to transforming society; know what a different world might feel like.
- To communicate images that identify personal and collective power: embody and activate images of the archetypal God/dess' wisdom, love, power, and transformation.
- To perpetuate knowledge essential to the survival of the culture.
- To name, gain and transfer power; to share and exchange insight, understanding, energy.
- To affirm, cherish, uplift and sacralize an individual by her/his peers; to heal and nurture.
- To establish a spiritual and emotional center to which one can return for support and comfort.
- To connect with different realms of reality and facilitate change by experiencing them.

In short, ritual is a process of:

- envisioning/imagining
- communicating
- embodying/empowering/identifying

- supporting/affirming
- linking/connecting/creating a center

The Outline of Ritual

A Wiccan ritual for any purpose usually includes the following steps.

1. Preparation of the space and any materials you will need.
2. Preparing yourself (bathing, centering, meditating).
3. Asperging the area (cleansing with a broom, sprinkled salt water, or incense).
4. Casting the circle (drawing a circle with the athame or sword to create sacred space).
5. Calling the quarters (powers of Air, Fire, Water and Earth).
6. Invoking Goddess and God (into/from yourself).
7. Stating your purpose.
8. Raising power (through chanting, dance, song, drumming, etc.), channeling it toward your goal, and grounding it.
9. Relaxing with "cakes and wine" (refreshments).
10. Saying farewell to the quarters and thank you to God/dess.
11. Opening the circle.

Sabbats are celebratory in nature, and may include more songs, dances, games, and a potluck feast. There may also be special activities such as candle-making (at Imbolc), gift-giving and tree decoration (at Yule), or making daisy wreaths (at Beltane).

Suggestions for Ritual

Have a very clear opening and closing. The opening might include a procession to the ritual site, or the ringing of a gong and the cry of a herald: "Oyez, oyez! Come to the circle!" A good way to focus attention once all are gathered is to ask everyone to clasp hands. For the closing, the farewells to Goddess and God, plus the releasing of the elements, serves to let people know the ritual is ending. A final declaration is useful, such as: "Merry meet, merry part, and merry meet again!" or "The circle is open but never broken—blessed be!" or "May the peace of the Goddess go in your hearts."

Keep the ritual simple and not too long, particularly if there are children or inexperienced people in the circle or the physical conditions are uncomfortable (very hot or cold, for example). An hour is a good maximum for most groups of mixed age and experience.

Most of the ritual should be experiential: participants can sing and chant; do a simple circle dance; share thoughts or feelings round-robin (if it's a small circle; and even then, briefly!); symbolically place things on a Yule tree or in a cauldron or Ostara basket; share cakes and wine; play drums and rattles; choose a tarot card; join a guided meditation—the possibilities are endless.

Conversely, it is fine for people to be passive observers at times—particularly at the beginning of the ritual when they're grounding or catching their breath, or any time they have just finished being active. These are the times when an invocation, poem, solo song, instrumental, dance performance, or mystery play are perfect.

Assign a Keeper of the Gate to let people in and out of the circle as required, and make sure everyone knows where the Keeper is. Most traditions prefer the gate to be in the northeast when possible, and you may want to mark it somehow. When outdoors, lashed poles entwined with flowers or greenery work well.

If you are going to use chants or songs that most people don't know, teach them before the ritual starts. Simple ones are good.

Do not plan dancing (except in place) unless the indoor area is large, or the outdoor area has smooth, flat ground. Hurdling furniture and tripping on rocks are not part of normal Wiccan liturgy.

If you do "cakes and wine," let everyone know in advance that they may either sip, salute with the chalice but not drink, or pour a tiny libation on the ground if you are outdoors. Some people may have (or want to avoid) communicable diseases, and others may not drink alcohol, so they need alternatives.

Remember that the most powerful and effective rituals use all the sensory modes to communicate: visual, auditory, and kinesthetic. Visual elements include lighting, the altar, costumes, wall hangings, symbols, fires, and scenery. Auditory elements might include invocations, poetry, stories, parables, chants, singing, drumming, bells, animal sounds, or recorded music. The kinesthetic realm includes dance, mudras, touch, processionals, incense (smell), "cakes and wine" (taste), gestures (such as drawing pentagrams), and temperature. Be creative.

Appropriate Ritual

An otherwise fine ritual can be spoiled for some or all of the participants by oversight or carelessness. The following guidelines can help ensure that everyone benefits.

- The ritual is held in a place accessible to all those invited to participate.
- Participants are informed in advance as to the nature of the ritual. Will participants be skyclad? Is physical contact expected (holding hands? kissing? massage?)? Will alcoholic beverages be passed?
- Have a place and a role for those who are differently abled. People who are physically challenged and cannot dance or move about freely may be invited to sit with the drummers, for example, near a central fire or

on the north side of the circle. Perhaps they will wish to drum, use rattles or zills, or assist with the preparation of cakes and wine. It is sometimes necessary to have an interpreter to sign for the hearing impaired and perhaps guides to assist the visually impaired.

- Any songs or chants which may be unfamiliar to participants are practiced in advance.
- The ritual space is free of hazards such as poison ivy, nettles, sharp rocks and stinging insects.
- The ritual space is located where there is privacy for participants and where neighbors will not be disturbed.
- The leaders are well prepared, both for the ritual and also for unexpected emergencies or intrusions.
- Magick is performed ethically in accord with the Wiccan Rede, and influences only those individuals who have given their informed consent.
- Participants are informed in advance of the ingredients of any food or beverage served (as cakes and wine), in case of food allergies or other concerns. Mind-altering drugs or pharmaceuticals of any kind are never served without advance discussion and the freedom to refuse without prejudice.
- Participants are not expected to share a common chalice unless they wish. Other options should be discussed beforehand, as mentioned earlier.
- An attitude of respect is maintained among members within the circle, regardless of a participant's degree, tradition, race, nationality, ethnic origin, age, or sexual orientation.
- Participants should be clean and neatly dressed.

Rites of Passage

Sabbats and esbats or "moon rituals" are each discussed in their own chapter, but there is a third kind of ritual that you will be involved in, or leading if you haven't already done so. Rites of passage are rituals that mark great transitions in our lives: child blessings or "Wiccanings," coming-of-age rituals, handfastings, handpartings, the recognition of crone- or sagehood, and funeral or memorial services.

Outlines for such rituals are given in Appendix B, along with other transition rites for initiations and for changes in the coven. You should adapt these to fit your needs and desires, and—very importantly—you should personalize them, especially the ones that recognize changes in an individual's life. Nobody being recognized on a special occasion wants some canned, off-the-shelf ritual exactly like everyone else's handfasting or croning.

How can you personalize a ritual? Look at each piece of it. Hold it in a place the honoree enjoys: their home or yard, their favorite hiking trail, at the beach, or in a cave. Choose a time they feel is magickal: dawn, midnight, whenever they want. Decorate the temple site in a way they will like, and put special things on the altar: photographs and personal mementos, sculptures of animal allies, their ritual tools, or favorite stones and herbs. During the ritual invoke the god- and goddess-aspects most significant to them, and sing the songs and chants they enjoy. Later, serve their favorite foods and beverages, and give them little presents from the participants. Depending on the occasion, it may also be appropriate to recognize them by a new Craft or magickal name, celebrating their new status.

It may even be appropriate to structure the whole ritual according to the honoree's personality, life events, and spiritual challenges. You could choose a myth which reflects their life, and enact it: the descent of Inanna, the voyage of Odysseus, Theseus and Ariadne in the Labyrinth, Gilgamesh's struggle with Enki, Isis' search for Osiris, Amaterasu's emergence from the cave, Spider Grandmother's journey to find fire, and so on.

Just make sure that the ritual celebrates not just a transition, but their unique and personal transition. This will give your rites of passage meaning and power.

Ritual Critique

At some time after the ritual, it is helpful to evaluate what happened and even make notes for the future. In some covens, the High Priestess and High Priest draw the ritual leaders aside shortly afterwards, and in a positive, constructive way lead a critique of the ritual. It is more useful to ask questions and let the ritual leaders do a self-critique than it is to simply criticize.

Others believe that the evaluation should wait at least a couple of days, to allow reflection and a chance for the effects of the ritual to sink in. This is fine if someone makes sure that it really happens; there is a risk that the critique will simply be put off and then forgotten.

In either case, participants owe it to the leaders of the ritual to give them some feedback. An outline you can use for discussion and critique is given at the end of this chapter on page 134.

A Sample Ritual for World Peace

Materials

- White altar cloth
- Blue cloth for sand painting
- World map to draw from
- Rose quartz chips
- Dried rosemary and chamomile
- Glitter

Sand in various colors
Drum
Large white chalice
Rose water
Rose petals
Small plastic bags
Dove/peace poster or sculpture
Peace cards to hand out
Pens or pencils

Ritual

Begin with a chanting attunement:

I am the Goddess, and the Goddess is me;
I am the white dove and the world's harmony.

Bless rose water and asperge the area.

Cast the circle: one at a time, moving deosil, clasp the hand of the person to your left and say:

Hand to hand, the circle is cast. Hand to hand, peace is born.

Call the quarters, with a formula such as:

Guardians of the Watchtowers, Powers of Air, I summon thee!
Let there be peace in the East, and in our minds and thoughts.

Invoke the God in His aspect of Erh-Lang, Lord of Protection.

Invoke the Goddess as Kwan Yin, Lady of Compassion and Mercy.

State the purpose:

We are gathered here in the cause of peace, to work magick so that we shall live in harmony with our sisters, brothers, and all the creatures of the Earth. So mote it be.

On the blue cloth, draw a large sand painting of the Earth while visualizing peace and harmony throughout the world. Play soft background music as the map is drawn. Fill a large white chalice with the herbs, glitter, and rose quartz chips and place it in the center of the map. Have everyone fill out a "peace card" pledging specific actions to work for peace. Share the cards aloud then place them around the chalice.

Meditate silently for a few minutes on bringing peace to your own mind and the minds of those in your life.

Holding hands, move around the map in a simple round dance step to raise power. At the climax, charge the chalice, then sprinkle the mixture on the map, concentrating on those places that most need peace right now.

Earth the extra power.

Lift the corners of the sand painting cloth so that the mixture flows to the center. Scoop the magickal mixture into the small bags; distribute it and ask that each participant mail one or several bags to places all over the Earth.

Hold hands. Deep abdominal breathing. Chant:

I am the Power in everyone.
I am the dance in the Moon and Sun.
I am the hope that will not hide.
I am the turning of the tide.

Say farewell to Goddess and God, and the Guardians of the Watchtowers. Open the circle:

By the Earth that is Her body,
By the Air that is Her breath,
By the Fires of Her passion,
By the Waters of Her living womb,
May the peace of the Goddess go in your hearts. Blessed be.

Distribute peace cards to those who wrote them as a reminder.

Potential Ritual Themes

Rituals for a Better World

Save the Wildlife (specific species)
Save the Rivers
Johnny Appleseed Ritual
Protecting the Soil
Never Again the Burning
Emergency Weather Magick
Neighborhood Safety
Save the Rain Forests
Save the Seas
A Rite for Clean Air
World Peace
A Rite for Protecting Children
Interfaith Harmony

Rituals for Daily Life

Safe Travel
House Blessing
Prosperity Ritual
To Find Employment
Personal Protection
A Rite for Justice in Court
Garden Blessing
Car Blessing
Family Understanding
Coven Harmony
Psychic Self-defense
Invitation to a Child-Spirit

Rituals for Magickal Learning

Aspecting the Goddess
Power of the Runes
Earth Connections
Fire Connections
Invite a Dragon
Meeting the Plant Devas
Meeting the Faery Folk
Aspecting the God
A Tarot Circle
Air Connections
Water Connections
Qabalistic Pathworking
Meeting the Tree Spirits
Consecration of Ritual Tools

The Dumb Supper
Astral Travel
Past Life Regression
Mental Shapeshifting
Communication with the Dead
Connecting with the Ancient Ones of this Land

Rituals for Personal Growth and Healing

Healing Your Heart
Honoring Our Ancestors
Discover the Lover Within
Hail Eris/Hi Coyote
Mental Clarity
A Funeral for Fear
A Celtic Bragfest
Connecting with the Female Within
Hieros Gamos: The Sacred Marriage Within
Exploring Your Dark Side
Honoring Our Pagan Forebears
Discover the Warrior Within
Explore Younger Self
The Middle Pillar
Taking a New Name
Finding Your Animal Ally
Connecting with the Male Within
Personal Growth
To Revamp Eating Habits

Rites of Passage (see sample rites in Appendix B)

Birthing
Wiccaning
Womanhood
Manhood
Handfasting
Dedication
First Degree Initiation
Second Degree Initiation
Third Degree Initiation
Croning
Becoming a Sage
Handparting
Passing/Memorial

NOTES

1. Article on Ritual in *Heresies*, by Kay Turner (n.p., n.d.).

A Ritual Critique Checklist

1. Was the necessary information communicated to everyone involved well beforehand? (When, where, what to bring, who has what responsibilities during the ritual.)
2. Was the purpose of the ritual clear?
3. Were the ritual leaders prepared and rehearsed, and the altar setup and all materials on hand in advance? (Did the ritual begin essentially on time?)
4. Were all the necessary steps of the ritual included and well done? (For example, remembering to cleanse the area, or ground the energy after the cone of power was released.)
5. Were lunar, planetary, and other cyclical influences considered in scheduling? (Avoid a moon void-of-course, Mercury retrograde, or any difficult conjunctions.)
6. Was it stimulating:

   Visually (colors, costumes, props, decorations, lighting)?
   Auditorally (music, singing, chanting, invocations, sound effects)?
   Kinesthetically (dancing, asanas, mudras; smell, touch, taste)?
   (Make sure it's not only a "head" ritual, or an "eye" ritual, or an "ear" or "body" ritual.)
7. Were the Elements invoked in the participants?

   Earth: Was the body stretched?
   Air: Was the mind stimulated?
   Fire: Was the will engaged and energy raised?
   Water: Were the emotions aroused?
   Spirit: Was it spiritually powerful?
8. Did the ritual move at a good pace and build to a climax of intensity? (More rituals move too slowly and "drag" than move too quickly.)
9. Did all parts contribute to the main theme or purpose? (Did any part feel extraneous or irrelevant?)
10. Was everything done ethically, in accord with the Rede?
11. Was the purpose achieved?
12. Did "action in accord" flow naturally from the ritual and complement it? (Does everyone have a clear idea "what to do next" in support of the magick?)

Altar Layout Diagrams

There is considerable flexibility as to how the altar is laid out, and what symbols you use for the elements—so be creative! Instead of a pentacle to represent Earth, you may use a rock or crystal. Replace the censer with a feather or a picture of a hot-air balloon if you wish. Use a cauldron instead of the chalice, or a brass dragon or fire wand rather than a red candle. If you can, make the altar's colors and objects reflect the theme of the ritual. For sabbats, you will want seasonal items such as evergreen boughs for Yule, flowers for Beltane, a cornucopia for Mabon, a few ears of corn for Lughnassad, and so on.

Here are two examples of basic altar set-up. It is most common to put the altar in the East, the direction of dawn and beginnings; or in the center, especially if the circle is large or there is to be dancing around the edge of the circle. But for special purposes you might put the altar anywhere in the circle.

A Round Altar in the Center.

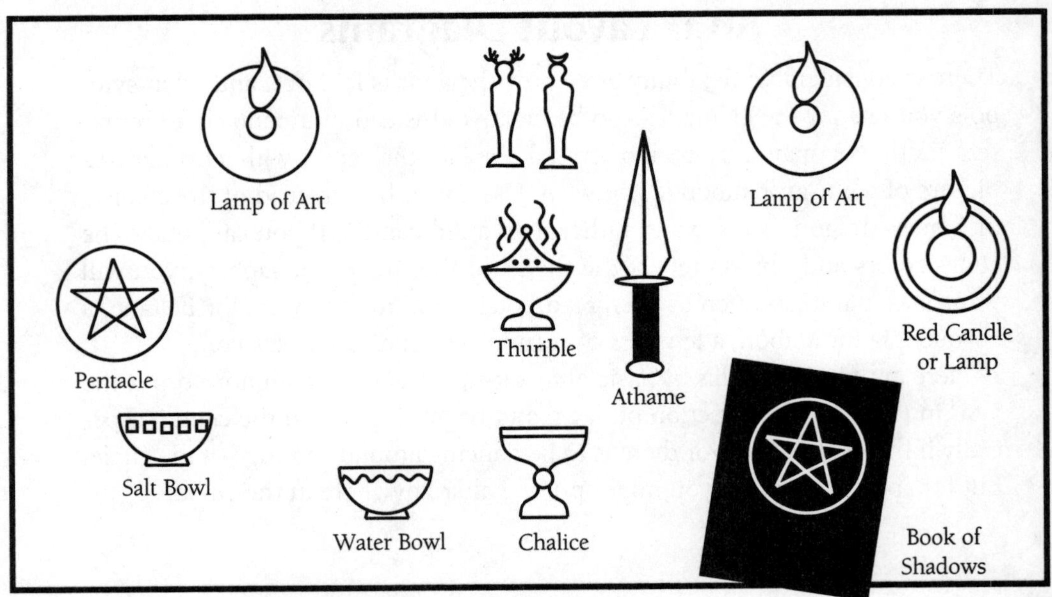

A Rectangular Altar in the East.

13 The Esbats

An esbat is a gathering of Witches at a certain phase of the moon. The word "esbat" comes from the French *esbattiere*, meaning "to frolic." It may be a medieval word, though historians disagree how long it has been in use. It hardly matters; Witches and our spiritual forebears have been meeting under the light of the moon for thousands of years, no matter what the name.

The moon, a powerful aspect of the Goddess, controls not only the great tides of the ocean, but also the internal rhythms of women's menstrual cycles. As the moon waxes, reaches full, and wanes, She represents the three stages of woman's life: Maiden, Mother, and Crone. Studies of the moon's effect by law enforcement agencies and hospital emergency rooms show that the moon affects more than female cycles, but seems to intensify human emotion generally. Both the lunar month and the solar year are woven into our calendars, and their different powers are recognized and used in every spiritual system from alchemy to Zoroastrianism.

As far as is known, all Witches gather on the night of the full moon, as suggested by the Charge of the Goddess: ". . . once in the month, and better it be when the moon is full, you shall assemble in some secret place and adore the spirit of Me Who is Queen of all the Wise . . . ." This meeting is in part worship—or celebration, as some Witches prefer to say—but it is primarily the best time for most magickal work. At this time the priestess draws down the moon, that is, draws the energy of the Moon Goddess into her, and speaks with Her voice. This is also an opportunity to use the full lunar power for both thaumaturgy (practical magick for healing, prosperity, safe travel, etc.) and theurgy (magick to evolve spiritually).

Many covens also gather at the time of the New Moon, which is to say when the moon is dark and about to begin Her cycle back to full. Magickally speaking, this is a good time for divination of all kinds (tarot, scrying, runes, casting stones, I Ching, and so on) and for banishing. One might want to banish an illness, or an unworkable relationship, or a bad habit.

Instead of the new moon, some covens celebrate Diana's Bow: this occurs about three days after the new moon, when She is just beginning to show a slender crescent. This is an opportunity to bless new projects and to do gentle magicks that require a gradual building of energy. One might bless a new garden, home, business, or learning venture.

The influence of both new and full moons is apparently spread out over two or three days. It is not essential to hold your ritual at the precise time of the full or new moon, and indeed that could be very awkward since She may well enter the desired phase in the middle of the workday or at some early hour in the morning. Most covens check the exact time in an astrological calendar or ephemeris, then meet on the evening closest to the desired phase, say at 7:00 P.M. or whatever is convenient for most members. Some studies suggest that the energy actually peaks about twenty-four hours before the "official" times of the new and full moons, so if you are planning an esbat and cannot gather at the exact time, it is better to meet earlier rather than later.

Location may vary according to the season. It is the Summoner's job to make sure everyone knows where to meet.

Sample ritual outlines are included in the appendices. If your tradition has certain established rituals, then these may not be useful for you; but if you are an eclectic coven, then feel free to use them as is or adapt them to your needs.

The two parts common to most esbats are Drawing Down the Moon and magickal work requested by the coven members. The "drawing down" is a form of "aspecting" or "assuming the god form." That is, the High Priestess changes consciousness and *becomes* the Moon Goddess. (In some traditions, the High Priest is considered essential to helping her do this; in others, she may do it on her own.)

"Drawing down" the Goddess is not the same as simply calling Her. You can simply request that the Lady join the circle and bless its work, but when She is drawn down, She becomes incarnate in the priestess. A proper drawing is immediately apparent and quite impressive: everyone in the circle can feel Her energy, and the appearance, voice, and mannerisms of the priestess change dramatically. She may speak voluntarily to the coven or be willing to answer questions. There will be no doubt that your coven sister Susie has stepped aside for the moment, and that the goddess Diana is fully present. However, this is not the place to go into more detail.

Preparing For the Esbat

The magickal work of the esbat will be different at each meeting, but we can explore a sort of typical gathering of the Mockingbird Coven. Imagine now an esbat evening, and the coven preparing for ritual.

Candles glow with a pure, warm light, though not enough to illuminate the dark silhouettes of the surrounding oaks and maples. The sweet smells of cedar and frankincense drift through the circle. This is a good time for coveners with magickal needs to discuss them with the ritual leaders before the circle is gathered, and the ritual leader asks: "Is there work to be done tonight?"

With these familiar words, the coven begins the most creative phase of its ritual work. Now members will come forth to state their most pressing needs, knowing that the coven stands ready to raise the Cone of Power on their behalf.

Each request is a challenge to all assembled, for they may need to design a spell on the spot to serve that specific need. Only rarely is a ready-made spell at hand in some old grimoire or magickal text. Usually the magick succeeds or fails according to the knowledge, imagination, will, and ingenuity of the coveners present.

Here the coven shines most brightly, for each covener can experience the energy and support of all the others. They are bound together not only by the stimulation of cooperative creative endeavor, but by a glowing web of love and trust. Each knows in her or his heart, "Here I have friends. Here are those who care, who will bend their skills to help me create the reality I desire."

The requests are as varied as the personalities within the circle. Sirius asks for healing energy for an obstinate pain in her ankle, while Wayland needs a job. Rhianna asks the coven to exert its power on behalf of nuclear disarmament. Aengus wants an energy boost to get through his graduate exams. When these have spoken, there is a moment of silence. The ritual leader's careful observation has not missed Moriath: though asking nothing, she seems troubled and withdrawn.

"Is that all?" the leader asks. And then, "Moriath, can we help?"

Moriath hesitantly admits that she is confused about a relationship outside the circle that is not going well. She wonders whether to break it off, but is a little shy about discussing it in front of the group. She is not sure whether to ask for help or how the coven might help her.

Now the ritual leader's skill and judgment are put to the test. They must guide the coven in deciding which needs should be addressed tonight, and which would be better postponed or dealt with outside the circle.

The leader turns first to Moriath: clearly she is hurting right now, and compassion demands that she be given priority. Further, until her pain and confusion are (at least temporarily) soothed, her energies will not be fully available for the other work ahead.

"Moriath, there's no need for you to discuss the situation in front of the whole group tonight in order for us to help. Perhaps for tonight we can help you find your calm center, and then sometime very soon one of us could do some divination or co-counseling with you."

"I could meet with you tomorrow," adds Argante, who is known for her gentle wisdom and skill with tarot.

"Thank you," replies Moriath. "I tried the pendulum, but I guess I'm too tense about this to do it for myself. I appreciate both offers. Argante, I'll talk to you later about when we can meet, if that's okay. For now I guess I'll just ask for clarity." Argante nods.

"Sirius, what have you been doing about that ankle?" inquires Willowithy, who is the coven's most experienced healer.

"Soaking it in hot water. Trying to stay off it—without much luck!"

"And getting mad at it?"

Sirius grins sheepishly. "That too."

"Are you sure you're ready to be healed?"

"Oh, yes!"

Willowithy looks around the group. "I'd suggest that we invoke Brigit as goddess of healing, and then after the circle I can look at it, maybe do some acupressure for the immediate pain. Then it really needs a poultice. I can explain that to her later, and some herbs she can take."

"You need to stop being mad at it, too," puts in Frey. "Maybe if you ask yourself why you got this injury, and then forgive yourself."

The leader rejoins the discussion. "Sounds good. However, she can do that after the circle, and tonight we'll simply give her healing energy. Is that all right, Sirius?"

"Sure."

The focus shifts to Wayland. Soon it becomes clear that he has just started to think about looking for another job, isn't very clear on what he wants, and has not yet taken steps on his own to deal with the situation. Someone suggests that he meditate at home on precisely what kind of work he wants, possibly visit a career counseling center, and outline a job search plan. Wayland agrees.

"Let us know by the full moon how it's going," adds the ritual leader. "If you run into problems, we can work together then." She feels relieved. If the coven had tried to deal with Wayland's problem as it stood, they could have spent the whole evening on it. Now the coven's time need not be spent doing something that one person may be able to accomplish.

She turns to Rhianna. "You're suggesting that we raise power to help get the nuclear disarmament treaty ratified. Do you have a specific spell in mind?"

"No," says Rhianna. "I just think it's awfully important."

Better be sure we're all in accord, thinks the ritual leader. Someone might think the treaty doesn't go far enough or that it has some problem that could end up undermining peace. "Is everyone here in favor of the treaty?"

All nod or voice approval.

"Then let's do it," says Wayland. "But I don't want to do anything vague or general. How about if we focus on energizing the people in the local anti-nuke organization?"

"That's using magick directly on individuals without their consent," objects Sirius. "We can't ethically do that unless they ask for energy; and I know those people—most of them don't even believe in magick."

"Anyway, it's an international issue," adds Bel. "We should deal with it as a world problem, not a local thing."

Chalcedony speaks for the first time. "Isn't that a little ambitious for one coven? Let's start locally, with what we can do right here. What if we all declared our homes to be nuclear-free zones, and encourage our friends to do the same?"

The ritual leader breaks in: "It's clear that we've opened a can of worms here, and are not going to get consensus on a strategy very soon. Can we refer this to a smaller group, a committee, and ask them to thrash it out and bring back a proposal next moon? Including, of course, what we can do to act in accord."

Everyone likes this idea. Rhianna, Bel, and Sirius agree to work out a proposal. The rest are invited to share their ideas with these three later, during the potluck.

That leaves Aengus' request. "Energy for your exams?" asks the ritual leader. "How about this: when we send energy to Moriath and Sirius, we'll channel through you. That will focus the energy better and help clear and energize you as well."

"Okay," says Aengus. "But, well, could we do something more? I'm not sure what, but I need to keep my energy really strong for a couple of days at least."

"Let's charge a crystal while we're at it," suggests Chalcedony, who is heavily into gemstone magick. "You could wear it at the exams." Aengus likes the idea, and Chalcedony produces a quartz crystal from a little pouch hanging on her cord.

"And lay off the caffeine and junk food," says Willowithy sternly. "You can't ace a test if your blood sugar's bouncing around like a yo-yo." Everyone knows that Aengus is susceptible to fast-food binges, and he blushes a little. Nutrition is taken seriously in the coven, as an important adjunct to psychic development.

"And," adds Sirius, "I can show you some pranayama exercises after the ritual." Aengus looks puzzled.

"Yogic breathing exercises," explains Sirius. "Some are great for energy and for concentration."

"Then are we ready to begin the work?" asks the ritual leader.

"I just remembered," interjects Bel, "my uncle's sick with a cold. Can we send him some healing energy?"

"He's not Pagan, is he?" inquires Argante. "Has he requested our help or agreed to it?"

"Well, no . . . ."

"You know the rules," says the ritual leader. "We don't know if he's ready for healing, open to it, or willing to accept help from Witches. Do you want to ask him?"

Bel hesitates. "Guess not," he finally says. "I'm not ready to come out of the broom closet with Uncle Jack. Maybe if he was seriously sick."

"There is an alternative," Willowithy reminds the group. "We can place some healing energy in a reservoir on the astral for Bel's uncle to use or not, as he wishes. Bel, that means some astral work for you, to contact your uncle's higher self and let him know the energy's there."

"That would be good," says Bel.

"Then let it be done," says the ritual leader. "Now we've also decided to work with Moriath and Sirius tonight, and to charge a crystal for Aengus. If everyone is ready, let's circle up and begin the ritual."

The details are imaginary, but the scenario described above is the kind of thing that happens in many covens at each New Moon and Full Moon esbat. Coveners help one another with healing and guidance, finding apartments, spells for safe travel, and many other needs. Often it's helpful just to clearly define a problem, briefly talking it out with the coven. Some work needs an entire evening: magick for social or political change, house blessings, major healings, and so on. But much can be accomplished in an hour or two, after the invocations and before cakes and wine are brought out.

Organizing Your Magick

It should be mentioned that there is a simpler alternative to individual spells, for use when you have many requests and none of them are life-and-death matters. You can write each request on a scrap of parchment (or draw a little sketch, or mold a wax figure representing the need), and put them all in a pot at the center of the circle. Then the coven raises power and charges all the tokens at the same time. Each covener can take their token home and place it on a personal altar for occasional recharging. Alternatively, charge the tokens and then cast them into a fire; as they burn, they are translated "onto the astral plane" to materialize later in complete form.

Is this as effective as doing individual spells for each need? No. But it can be effective enough, and if the coven has seventeen requests for magick it may be your only practical choice.

Before the coven begins to raise the Cone of Power, some sifting is required to determine what needs should be met with magick, what magick should be done immediately, and what must be delayed or denied. Some guidelines follow.

First, it must be recognized that each covener has the primary responsibility for managing his or her life effectively. The coven acts only when individual effort is not enough to get the job done in a reasonable length of time. If an individual has done nothing mundane or magickal to get results, no one really knows what kind of coven energies might be needed. Therefore, the coven should agree to help an individual only when they have made serious efforts to work out the problem, and have not succeeded, or when the problem is obviously so challenging that it is beyond the capacity of any one person to cope with alone.

Occasionally a covener will try a magickal approach to the situation but neglect to try certain material-plane or "mundane" remedies. Often other coven members can suggest resources they have overlooked: techniques, people, places, books, and so forth. There is no point in raising the Cone if an ounce of chamomile, a better resume, or a toll-free telephone number will do the trick.

Power should normally be raised only for those who ask for help. Even sending healing energy unasked can be a mistake. Illness always occurs for a reason, and to try to heal someone before they are done cleansing, resting, or learning from the experience is to meddle unwisely in another's karma. The ethical exception to this, as mentioned in the example of Bel's uncle, is to send energy not to the person directly but to an astral reservoir where they can tap it if they wish.

Likewise, sending energy to someone of another faith, who may not believe in magick or may fear the occult, is unwise unless the individual can overcome their reservations enough to request it.

In healing a covener, they must not only request it but be ready for it; that is, be psychically and emotionally "finished" with the symptoms and consequences. If someone unwisely asks for healing before the illness has achieved its purpose, and the purpose is not addressed in some other way, then magick can only repress the symptoms for a time. True healing does not merely repress symptoms, but explores causes and fosters growth and transformation at the level where the illness began.

Requests that seem frivolous to most coveners may be legitimately denied or attempted by volunteers outside of coven meetings. There may be nothing inherently wrong about doing magick to obtain a hang glider for Joe, as long as the proviso "an it harm none" is included in the spell; but the coven ordinarily has more important priorities, and besides there is the risk that the group's power will be impaired if the deep mind begins to associate the circle with requests for unnecessary luxuries.

If Joe works on his own, say for a Cadillac, that is primarily his business. He might be wiser to "work for the essence," calling for "reliable transportation" or "a vehicle I feel good about driving," but there has to be some latitude for individual discretion and experimentation in such matters.

The coven must always be "in accord" or "of a like mind" to do its best work: that is, in tune and in agreement with one another. If coveners do not agree on a given request, or agree that action is necessary but can't get together on a strategy, then the magick should be postponed. It is better to do no magick than hasty and ill-considered magick.

In some cases, such as social issues, the entire coven may never reach consensus. The coveners who share a common desire can work their magick as a "special interest group" outside the coven meetings.

When only the strategy or tactics are at issue, the request can be referred to a committee who will think it out, perform divination if necessary, and bring a specific proposal back to the coven later.

In all magickal work the Wiccan Rede should be observed. Curses are not legitimate requests, and even binding should be used only in grave emergencies when no other avenue is open. If someone wrongs or hurts a covener, the temptation to punish the perpetrator can be very strong. But doing this means that you have appointed yourself judge, jury, and enforcer, and this is a dangerous path to travel. A few covens have tried to sanction this approach by modifying the Rede to state, "An ye harm none innocent, do as ye will." But this puts us right back in the judge's seat; and even if we are certain of the offense and the offender, who are we to choose a specific punishment, to decide what will deter or enlighten the offender? A better magick is to ask that justice be served for all involved.

This does not imply that harmful acts should be ignored. On the contrary—we reject the role of victim as well as judge! Magick for protection, self-defense, shielding—fine. And if your shield is wrought so well that an attacker's force instantly rebounds on him, so be it.

Whatever may be done regarding the offender, it is always appropriate to work with the covener who is the injured party. Divination and meditation can show us what is to be learned from the situation. Healing and catharsis are usually needed. One may ask the coven to help her or him empower and shield so that it need not happen again. If the coven enables their sister or brother to emerge from the experience as a stronger and wiser person, they have done well. And if that person is motivated to help others in the community to prevent similar crimes or heal their effects, so much the better.

To sum up, there are several things a coven needs to know before working magick on request:

- Exactly what outcome will you be working for?
- If the work is for someone who is not present, have they specifically asked for help, or at least given permission for the coven to act on their behalf?
- Is the recipient truly ready for results; are they sure this is what is wanted and that the timing is appropriate?
- What have they attempted on their own, either on a mundane or magickal level?
- Is the goal important enough to justify calling on the powers of the whole coven?
- Will the proposed action harm no one, as far as you can tell?
- Is the coven in accord as to what should be done?

The Art of Spellcasting

If all is well, then the fun begins: designing the spells. Follow the rules of brainstorming. Share any idea that comes to mind, no matter how far-fetched it seems. It just might work or spark another idea that will. Build on each other's ideas. Don't criticize any idea in the early stages: the first priority is just to generate lots of possibilities.

What you are seeking are ways to focus on the desired goal, ways to raise power, and ways to send or store the power.

Depending on the talents in your coven, you might focus on the goal by invoking specialized god/desses or spirits, storytelling, drawing runes or symbols, guided trancework, ritual drama, simple visualization, speaking words of power, or writing out the goal.

You might raise power by singing, chanting, dancing, drumming, clapping, breathing, visualizing energy flowing, or even pounding stones together.

The power can be stored by charging a talisman, amulet, stone, crystal, herb, beverage, or ritual tool; and it can be released by pointing, touching, inhaling, exhaling, relaxing, burning a paper, cutting a cord, throwing a stone into the sea, and so on.

It is very helpful to have a variety of tools, materials and "props" on hand. These might include colored candles, incenses, wall hangings, shells, stones, herbs, ink and parchment, oils, pictures, and altar cloths. These are discussed in more detail in the chapter on ritual tools.

Once you have a variety of ideas, choose the best one and do it. Some ideas might better be attempted by individuals at home; others may simply not feel powerful or focused enough. Soon one or two approaches will emerge which seem just right. These guidelines can help your coven design and cast spells:

- The most urgent magick should be done first—usually healing, especially if a covener is incapacitated by pain.
- Ordinarily, it is far better to work for essence rather than form: "safe and reliable transportation" rather than "the green Chevy I saw in the lot today," or "the perfect job for me (and for which I am the perfect worker)" rather than "the position as Manager at Whitney's." You get what you ask for, and that green Chevy might have a transmission that's ready to fall out.
- At the same time, avoid huge or vague goals, such as "healing the Earth" or "having a happy life." These are too amorphous to focus on.
- Keep it reasonably simple, unless you are willing to spend a lot of time rehearsing. Don't attempt to use a guided trance, a complicated dance, cord magick, crystal healing, plus Enochian invocations all on the same person in the same evening. If you are trying to remember the next step on a long list, it becomes difficult to focus on your goal and raising power.
- Requests can sometimes be combined: two people in stressful situations may both need centering and wisdom, for example. Even though the situations are very different, the need may be the same, so the kind of energy required will be the same.

- If an idea will require unusual props or a great deal of time, it might best be postponed or discarded in favor of a simpler approach.
- Coveners should be reminded to channel energy from outside sources (such as the Earth, sun, or moon), not from their bodies' own reserves; otherwise they will quickly feel exhausted and depleted.
- Everyone should agree in advance what variety of power they will be raising and sending. Having a common set of symbols or correspondences is crucial here, so that everyone knows what is meant by "lunar energy," "solar energy," "earth energy," and so on.

It may be helpful to have a few books from your magickal library on hand for quick reference. Of course you don't want to research a whole new magickal system while a dozen people stand waiting in the circle. However, quickly checking a color correspondence, astrological conjunction, or goddess' name will not be much of an interruption. Some suggestions:

- The current *Astrological Calendar* (Llewellyn, annually). For checking the energies at any give time: conjunctions, trines, moon voids-of-course, Mercury retrogrades and other factors influencing your magick.
- The current *Witches' Calendar*, also annually by Llewellyn.
- *True Magick*, Amber K (Llewellyn, 1991). Includes simple spells for a variety of common needs, and a chart of correspondences.
- *The Spiral Dance*, Starhawk (HarperSanFrancisco, 1979, 1989). Includes some excellent invocations and a chart of correspondences.
- *The New Book of Goddesses and Heroines*, Patricia Monaghan (Llewellyn, 1998). A quick reference to goddesses from many cultures; alphabetical by name.
- *The Ancient and Shining Ones*, D. J. Conway (Llewellyn, 1994). A good quick reference to gods and goddesses with a cross-reference by type (healing, fire, agriculture, etc.).

See also the reference chart at the end of this chapter, "The Names of the Full Moons." You will also want good books on herbs, runes, tarot, and the magickal uses of gemstones.

Above all, trust your intuition and "inner voice." The techniques chosen should feel focused and powerful to everyone present, but most especially the covener who asked for help. If several ideas seem good, let his or her wishes be the deciding factor.

The Esbat Ritual

Among covens there is a sort of spectrum of ritual practice, ranging from one extreme where the ritual is the same every time (except that magickal goals change), to those where every ritual is unique and wildly different from the one before. Your coven will have to find its own place on the lines from stability to creativity, and planning to spontaneity. Hopefully you will land somewhere toward the center. Too much sameness becomes rote and boring, while too much experimentation can lead to confusion, lack of groundedness, and leaving out necessary ritual elements.

Sample esbats are outlined in the appendices, for use in case you are an eclectic coven without a format specified by your tradition. Feel free to use them as templates, and add your coven's special touches.

After the Esbat: Acting in Accord

Working magick is only half the answer to any situation. "As above, so below" is a two-part model. Ritual magick creates a new reality "above" on the astral and is the first step toward manifestation "below" on the material plane. To complete the work, the magickian or recipient must "act in accord" with the magickal intention on a material level.

For example, after a healing ritual, the covener who is ill may rest, meditate, drink herbal teas, visit a chiropractor, and do whatever else feels appropriate and is recommended by a healer. After working magick for a new job, one must contact potential employers. After you charge an amulet of malachite or comfrey root for safe travel, check the tires and brakes on your car.

So when the coven works together, no act of magick is complete until follow-up action in accord has been planned and performed; and your brothers and sisters in the coven may have many helpful, down-to-earth suggestions along these lines.

When the coven acts creatively to help one another survive and grow, we forge ties of love and trust which are not easily broken. In easy times or hard, the coven sustains and empowers each of us.

The Names of the Full Moons

Month	Wheel of the Year[1]	Village Craft[2]	Odinist[3]	Old Farmers Almanac	Christian and Recent American[3]	Goddesses[4]	Native American[5]	Celtic Trees
January	Wolf	Snow	Snow	Wolf	Winter	Inanna	Frost in the Tipi, Little Winter, Snow	Beth (birch)
February	Chaste	Death	Horning	Snow	Trapper's	Februa	Crow, Sore Eye, Snowblind	Luis (Rowan)
March	Seed	Awakening	Lenting	Worm	Fisherman's	Persephone	Red Grass appearing, Green Grass, Planting	Nion (Ash)
April	Hare	Grass	Ostara	Pink, Fish Sprouting, Grass, Egg	Easter, Planter's	Isis	Wait Until I Come, When Ponies Shed, Planting	Fearn (Alder)
May	Dyad	Planting	Merry	Flower, Corn Planting	Mother's, Spring	Sappha	Rose, Making Fat	Saille (Willow)
June	Mead	Rose	Fallow	Strawberry, Hot	Stickman's, Mid-Year	Hera	Thunder	Uath (Hawthorn)
July	Wort	Lightning	Hay	Buck, Thunder	Summer	Cybele	When the Cherries Turn Black	Duir (Oak)
August	Barley	Harvest	Harvest	Sturgeon, Red, Green Corn	Dog Days, Woodcutter's	Selene	Hunting When Deer Paw the Earth	Tinne (Holly)
September	Wine	Hunter's	Shedding	Harvest	Fall	Demeter	Changing Season, Falling Leaf, Ten Colds	Coll (Hazel)
October	Blood	Falling Leaf	Hunting	Hunter's	Harvest	Artemis	Wait Until I Come, Mad Storms, Deer Antlers	Muni (Vine)
November	Snow	Tree	Fog	Beaver	Hunter's	Hecate	Long Night, Popping Trees, Big Winter, Sweathouse	Gort (Ivy)
December	Oak	Long Night	Wolf	Cold	Christ's Christmas	Minerva	Hunger	Ngetal (Reed)
13th Moon		Ice		Blue				Ruis (Elder)

1. Pauline Campanelli, *The Wheel of the Year*. St. Paul: Llewellyn, 1990.
2. Via Dolores Ashcroft-Nowicki's workshop of "The Village Craft."
3. Amber K files: original sources unknown.
4. Mari Bianca in *Moon, Moon* by Anne Kent Rush, Random House, New York and Moon Books, Berkeley, CA, 1976.
5. Teton Sioux, Oglala Sioux, Cheyenne, Kiowa, Omaha in *Moon, Moon* by Anne Kent Rush.

14 The Sabbats

The sabbats are the high holy days of Witchcraft, marking the changes of the seasons as the wheel of the year turns. They have been celebrated since before most people were literate, so there are several spellings for each one (i.e., Imbolc, Immolg; Beltane, Beltaine; Ostara, Eostre).

Your coven may celebrate the four Greater Sabbats (Imbolc, Beltane, Lughnassad, and Samhain), or these plus the summer and winter solstices (Litha and Yule), or all eight possible sabbats including the spring and fall equinoxes (Ostara and Mabon). The Greater Sabbats, the cross-quarter sabbats, are the older holidays based on the Celts' pastoral culture (the first sabbats in Europe may have been Beltane and Samhain—the times when the herds of cattle were moved from winter to summer pastures and back again). The Lesser Sabbats, the solstices and equinoxes, were apparently imported at a later time, possibly by Romans, Angles, and Saxons.

The sabbats keep us attuned to the seasonal changes in the natural world. Most of us don't experience these changes in the ways that a herder or farmer would; yet our physiologies are still intimately connected to the cycle, and our lives are richer and healthier when we stay attuned in some fashion.

Unlike the esbats, sabbats are primarily celebratory in nature. However, there may be an appropriate teaching about the meaning of the sabbat, often in the form of a "mystery play" or re-enactment of a myth. Instead of a coven of priests and priestesses who are an experienced magickal working team, you may have an "open" sabbat with a throng of happy Pagans. One of the first things you must decide as a coven is whether to have closed sabbats for only coven members, family sabbats where coveners can bring relatives and significant others, or open sabbats for the local Pagan community. Or, you can have a combination. Some covens even double up on certain sabbats: for example, they might have two Samhains—one open event, say on the weekend closest to the thirty-first, and one on the night of the thirty-first for coven members only. Similarly, you could have an open Yule celebration, and later a dinner for the coven where gifts are exchanged.

A word of warning: don't try to double up on all the sabbats, with a public and a private one each time. Eight sabbats are plenty for most people: even the most rabid party animal will soon burn out on all sixteen.

Sabbat celebrations may be scheduled on the actual date, which is traditional for most Witches, or within a few days for convenience. If you cannot celebrate on the exact calendar date, it is recommended that cross-quarter sabbats (the "Great Sabbats") be celebrated a few days later rather than earlier; this makes them closer to the original dates. But some Witches are very precision-minded, and do not like to be even a day "off" in their celebrations. Among other reasons, they like to tap into the "group consciousness" of thousands of people who are celebrating on the same day or evening.

However, there is some evidence that our ancestors in small farming communities were not always so strict. They may have celebrated not when the calendar declared a holiday, but when the weather changed or when the local wise woman said it "felt right." In modern society, many covens choose a weekend date so that everyone can "party hearty" and not worry about getting to the office the next morning.

Mythological Cycles

All the sabbats can be understood to fit into cycles of myth. Because Witchcraft combines many influences and cultures, it does not have one clear "storyline" to the wheel of the year. We can identify at least four among various traditions.

The Oak King and the Holly King: The Oak King, representing rebirth, rules the warm half of the year, and at Litha his crown is taken by the Holly King, the God in His aspect as Lord of Death, who rules until Yule when the Oak King returns. This seems to be the Druid myth. A variant has the Holly Boy struggling with the Ivy Girl, represented as the last sheaf of grain from the harvest, tied up with twining ivy.

The Summer Queen and the Winter King: Another cycle has the Goddess ruling the warm season (Imbolc to Lughnassad or Beltane to Samhain) and the God ruling the cold season.

The Sun God's Life Cycle: The infant Sun God is born at Yule, grows to young manhood by Beltane, reaches the height of his power at Litha, and pours his energy into the crops, becoming a willing sacrifice at Lughnassad. The Goddess is His mother at Yule, his lover at Beltane, and the crone by Lughnassad.

The Goddess Life Cycle: The Goddess is born at Yule, becomes a young woman by Beltane, grows into the bountiful Earth Mother by Mabon, and then the wise crone at Samhain.

Your tradition may have a clearly established myth cycle, or you may wish to choose one as a framework in which to design your sabbat rituals. Or you may use whatever feels appropriate at the time.

Practical Notes

As with most celebrations, it is good to have a team planning and organizing each sabbat. If you are sponsoring a large public sabbat, you may want to have the whole coven on the team. For such an event, you can divide up areas of responsibility as follows:

- **Ritual design and leadership:** This includes costumes and props, music, and altar set-up, unless these are delegated to the Maiden, the Bard, the Minstrel, or other officer. More on the ritual itself later.
- **Facilities arrangements:** You may need to borrow or rent a hall, unless the weather is fair and you can hold the sabbat outdoors in someone's yard, a park pavilion, or a National Forest site. Indoor sites can include community centers, library meeting rooms, park fieldhouses, liberal churches, village halls, and private enterprises such as dance studios or service clubs. Be clear about the rules for usage (for example, are candles all right? What about alcoholic beverages?). Be sure you have the key well in advance and have a backup plan in case you can't get access at the last minute.
- **Room set-up and decoration:** Allow at least an hour. It is useful to have some tables as well as a few chairs on hand. There may be elderly or disabled participants who cannot stand or sit on the floor, and during the potluck/social hour many people would be more comfortable in chairs. Make sure you know where to find water, restrooms, brooms, a fire extinguisher, and the thermostat. Also make sure that you know where the cardinal directions are; bring a small compass with your altar supplies. You can decorate nicely without spending a fortune on crepe streamers. If your lighting is focused on a few spots (entry door, altar, and food table), you can embellish these areas lavishly and largely ignore the rest of the space. The visual impact will be as good as if you had decorated every corner.
- **Publicity:** You may want to send announcements to any Pagan periodicals that serve your area, and perhaps to the leaders of other Pagan groups. You can post an e-mail announcement on Pagan lists on the Internet. News releases can be sent to the local newspapers and radio and television stations. You can post flyers on community bulletin boards (at bookstores, libraries, supermarkets, community centers, etc.). If any of your members are public and also comfortable in front of a camera, you can arrange an interview on the local Public Access Channel (cable TV). Some covens even put up banners in public places such as street overpasses, if permitted by the local government. And of course, all your coven members can mention the event to Pagans they know or friends who might be interested.

- **Potluck dinner or refreshments:** If you serve refreshments, go for quality and put out a donation basket to cover your expenses. Don't assume that everyone likes coffee and cookies, or wine and cheese. It is good to have a variety of items, including fruit juices and herb teas as well as wine or mead, and fruits or vegetables with dips for those who don't eat junk food. It's also a good idea to have a coven "picnic basket" with paper plates, napkins, cups, paper towels, serving spoons and flatware, which you can bring to every potluck and replenish in between.

For potlucks, simplest by far is to just let everyone bring whatever they want, and not attempt to organize a balance of dishes. You may get all desserts one night and seven veggie platters the next time, but that's not a crisis. If you are compulsively organized, you can try the zodiac approach: ask the Water signs to bring beverages, the Earth signs to bring breads and salads, the Fire signs to bring cooked main dishes, and the Air signs to bring desserts. Better yet, mix them around so that the Water signs bring cooked main dishes, etc. If you are even more compulsive and have no life beyond potlucks, then you can make a detailed list for a perfectly balanced banquet and have each individual or family sign up for a specific item.

- **Host/ess:** Someone should welcome folks at the door, show them the information table, give them name tags, and introduce them around. This is an essential kindness for people who are new to the Pagan community.
- **Information table:** Here is where you can put brochures about Wicca and your coven, newsletters if you have them, sign-up sheets ("Contact me about future open events . . ."), and a donation container; our coven uses a shiny copper cauldron. Sabbats should not be profit-making events, but it is nice to break even on your expenses.
- **Clean-up crew:** Whether you are renting or even if you're not, leave the place in better shape than you found it. If everyone pitches in, it will take only a little while to sweep, wash, and replace furniture where you found it. This is not only karmically correct but means you have a good shot at getting invited back.

Every sabbat has its own special meaning, character and traditional ways to celebrate; some of these follow.

Yule

Yule means "wheel" in reference to "the wheel of the year," and is also called the Winter Solstice, or Alban Arthuran by the Celts. It marks the longest night of the year and the point when the days slowly begin to lengthen. In Pagan theology it may mark the rebirth of the sun and the first promise that light and warmth will return to the world.

It is therefore sacred to all infant Sun/Son gods—Horus, Apollo, Bel, Baldur, Shamash—as well as to the Horned God as Winter King. In many Dianic circles, however, the birth of Lucina or other Sun Goddesses (Arinna, Amaterasu, Bast, and so on) is celebrated instead.

As the Sun is reborn, our time of quiet reflection and meditation, the rest following the harvest, draws to a close. New ideas, dreams, hopes, and projects are born, and our thoughts and energies turn to the new season of life ahead. True, there are months of cold ahead for many of us, but the light grows and warmth will follow.

The newborn Sun is the Great Mother's gift to the world, and this is reflected in our gifts to friends and family. Giving is a statement of faith in the abundance to come and in the love that survives the coldest winter.

It is not hard to see a Pagan element in Santa Claus or "Old St. Nick," but in many European countries a Goddess figure brings presents to everyone. She is La Befana or Santa Lucia in Italy; La Vecchia di Natali in Sicily; sometimes Strina (from Strenia, a Roman Goddess), Frau Holda, or colorful Mother Berchta in Germany, and Lucia in Sweden.

In Alsace, Kristkindl ("Christ Child") and Hans Trapp bring the presents. Kristkindl, interestingly, is represented as a woman in a white gown and gold sash, with a crown of candles. Hans wears a bearskin and long beard and carries a rod; it appears that He represents severity, and She is mercy.

Evergreens, holly (for the Lord of Death), ivy, and mistletoe (which grows in the sacred oak) are plants considered special to Yule. The decorated tree is a symbol of life continuing through the bleakness of winter, and it is also the World Tree or Tree of Life that is the framework of the universe. The Celts called sacred trees "Bele-Trees" or "Billy-Glas," sacred to Bel, according to Campanelli. In Greece the fir was sacred to the Moon Goddess Artemis.

Here are some ways you can celebrate Yule:

- Decorate your temple in gold, white, green, and red. Put up Sun symbols, or Winter King symbols such as stag horns, pine cones, and evergreen boughs.
- Hang mistletoe over your door—with berries, if you want fertility (the white berries represent the God's semen)—and kiss beneath it. Or hang a "Green Branch" over the door to symbolize hospitality, as the old wayside inns used to do.
- Decorate an oak Yule Log (ideally a large root) with ribbons, fir, yew, ivy, birch and holly; light it using an unburned piece of last year's Yule log, to symbolize the blazing of the reborn sun. Spread the ashes in your garden for fertility and save a small unburnt piece to start next year's fire.
- You might enact a mystery play about the birth of the Sun. Begin your ritual in darkness and end it in a blaze of light.

- As an alternative, draw lots for two coveners to represent the Holly King and the Oak King, and reenact the "changing of the guard" as the Oak King comes to power.
- Burn a pair of bayberry candles, as Pauline Campanelli suggests,[3] anointed with "magnetic oil" (soak a lodestone in oil, new moon to full) and carved with the Feoh (cattle) rune for prosperity.
- Share your hopes and desires for the coming year with others in the circle.
- Sing carols: "Deck the Halls," "Jingle Bells," or reclaimed Christmas tunes with Pagan lyrics. These may be available from another coven in your area, or over the Internet. You may even want to carol up and down the streets in your neighborhood.
- Go wassailing: take a bowl of cider to your fruit trees (or one in an orchard) and dip the tips of the branches in, place a piece of soaked cake in the limbs, and pour a libation on the roots to encourage abundance.
- Have a gift exchange of magickal goodies crafted by each covener. This is a way to control gift-giving so that it doesn't get out of hand: put all the coveners' names in a cauldron and each draw one to make or buy a gift for. No one is expected to have gifts for all eight or eleven or whatever members. (In practice, coveners who are especially close will exchange other gifts privately later—but nobody is obligated to gift everybody.) Official exchange gifts are opened in front of the whole coven, by the way, so that everyone can admire them and share the pleasure. Then unveil special gifts from individuals to the whole coven or from the coven to the Earth.
- Since the Yule Tree is an ancient Pagan symbol for the Goddess, the world, and everlasting life, why not decorate it as part of your Yule ritual? Have your storyteller explain about the Tree of Life, the sacred groves, the great ash tree Yggdrasil of Norse mythology, and so on. Then play music and cover the tree with homemade ornaments: strings of popcorn and cranberries, stars and suns, pentagrams and crescents, snowflakes and animals, harps and white horses, fruits and vegetables, wrens and robins, miniature torcs and talismans, little goddess and god images, and other sacred symbols.

  After the holidays, replant the tree outside if it is live; or give it to a recycling program to be chipped or mulched; or place it reverently in the woods with a supply of seeds and grains for the wildings, so it can continue to shelter life.
- Perform a "Mumming Play" with traditional characters like the Hobby Horse, the Fool, King George, and the Black Knight, just to celebrate success over adversity. This will take some research into British folklore!

- Enjoy a visit from Santa or Mother Berchta! Do you know Her? Each Yule She rides her scraggly giant goat, Gnasher Skeggi, all over the world and brings toys (or rocks or sticks or used cat litter) to children of all ages. She's a no-nonsense crone with a sharp tongue—and a kind heart beneath the prickles. She wears long woolen skirts and about seventeen shawls and Her hair is as wild as Skeggi's beard. She could visit your Yule celebration this year, if you invited Her.

  If you have bardic talent in your coven, hold a contest for the "Wildest Mother Berchta Tale."
- Have a Pagan sleigh ride! You may have to ask around to find out who owns a sleigh or "cutter"—and then either determine that the owner is open-minded or find an experienced Pagan to drive it. But if it all comes together, what fun you'll have! You'll need warm clothes, especially headgear, and wool blankets. You'll need song sheets for your Pagan carols (some reclaimed: "Hark! The nature spirits sing . . . . ."). And you'll need hot mulled ale or spiced apple cider and home-baked cookies when you gather afterwards at the covenstead.
- Celebrate with an old-fashioned feast of plum pudding, roast pig, duck, kolcannon (layered potatoes, mushrooms, onions, and cheese), home-baked breads, pies, and tarts. Or hold a feast of hearty "Earth" foods: baked potatoes, chili, and fruitcakes; and drink hot mulled cider spiced with cloves, cinnamon, and ginger; and finish off with cakes shaped like suns and stars.

Imbolc

Imbolc means "in the belly," because this is the time of year when the flocks begin to give birth. Other names for the sabbat are Oimelc ("ewe's milk"), Candlemas, The Feast of Waxing Light, The Feast of Flames, Laa'l Breeshey, Brigid, Brigantia, and La Feill Bhride.

At Yule the days begin to lengthen, but by Imbolc we can clearly see the change. Truly the sun's light is with us longer each day. This is the first harbinger of spring, our assurance that the Wheel is turning and the long, warm days of summer will return. Kore, the divine Daughter, has begun Her journey of return from Hades' dark realm: in the time ahead She will embrace Mother Demeter and the world will grow green again.

Thus, this sabbat has long been considered an especially appropriate time for initiation—for transformation, rebirth, new beginnings.

Imbolc is particularly sacred to women and to Brigid, the goddess of healing, inspiration, and smithcraft. Too often we remember only the goddesses of spring and summer, of flowers and warm sunlight. Brigid reminds us that the strength of women is also manifest as the invincible fire that burns steadily through the heart of winter, no matter how dark and cold the world. She is special not only to women generally, but also to all poets and artists, healers and midwives, and craftspeople of all kinds.

The sabbat is a turning point, when we lift our eyes from inner remembrance and reflection and begin to envision the season of growth that lies ahead. Now is the time for cleansing and purification, for discarding the outworn things of the year past so that we may create room in our lives for the Goddess' new bounty.

How to mark the sabbat? Here are some ways.

- Hold a ritual where coveners recite their own poetry, with the sound of a hammer softly striking an anvil as a rhythmic background accompaniment. When the readings are finished, the hammering continues more softly, and in silent meditation each member seeks within for any negative feelings they are ready to release. Then feelings of grief, anger, pain, and the like are put on slips of parchment and cast into the Cauldron of Transformation and Rebirth, where they are burned. Grounding and celebration follow.
- In the sabbat fire, burn the evergreen boughs that decorated your house.
- Clean your house, and discard all useless or unnecessary possessions (recycle where possible, or take them to a charity or neighborhood thrift store).
- Cleanse your body with a ritual bath, or make a sauna or sweat lodge.
- Cleanse your body inside by eating foods with fiber, and using a mild herbal laxative. Then wise fasting: drink plenty of juice and pure water.
- Cleanse your heart of old anger, pain, and fear; make peace with those you quarreled with.
- Meditate to cleanse your mind of old limitations; welcome new challenges.
- Have a Candlemas "candle bee." After a workshop on candle magick, let coveners design and create their own unique magickal candles for special purposes. You will need wax (beeswax is best, paraffin will do), color dyes or broken crayons, essential oils for scent, wicking, molds (waxed-cardboard juice containers work), potholders or gloves, a double-boiler, and a sharp knife for carving symbols in the candles. If you make them during the afternoon, they can be cool and ready for consecration at the evening sabbat ritual.

  NOTE: For safety's sake, melt the candle wax in a double boiler, improvised if necessary. Young children should not be involved in the hot-wax part of the process, through they can decorate their own candles later.

- Clean your altar and ritual tools and reconsecrate them.
- Have a "God/dess in Art" night. Come together and let Brigid inspire you to create god/dess images in clay or wood, photo montages, paintings, poetry, papier mâché, or any other medium. Or create the artworks individually at home and bring them to share with the coven at this sabbat. Each artist may tell the story of their chosen deity, and then they may all grace the altar.
- At the nearest well or spring, tie tiny strips of brightly colored cloth to the bushes, invoking Brigid's help in your life. Use cotton and tie it loosely; birds can use it for nests, and it will biodegrade.
- Create "Brigid's Crosses" of woven rushes or straw; hang them in your home as protective charms, and burn the old ones from last year.
- Make a Corn Bride with corn, a sheaf of wheat or other grain, and dress Her in a little white bridal gown. Place Her in a "Bride's Bed," perhaps made from a basket by the hearth, with a phallic pinecone-tipped wand beside Her. Then light red and white candles and invite the spirit of Brigid in.
- Go skyclad or in white during purification rituals. Wear brilliant red the rest of the time—red robes, red jewelry, or red ribbons.
- In ritual, have your priestess wear a "Crown of Lights." The Farrars suggest that this can be a band of actual small candles (over a tin-foil skullcap), which is practical if you are outdoors. Indoors use a battery-powered electric version or simply a tiara of shiny tinsel. Or, you may have three priestesses representing inspiration, healing, and smithcraft.
- Play the "Candle Game," where the men stand in a circle and pass a lighted candle around, while the women stand outside the circle and try to blow it out (or vice versa). The one who succeeds gets to claim a kiss. This is just for fun, and has no deep religious symbolism.
- Light the new fire in your hearth.

Ostara

The sabbat that celebrates the arrival of spring was named for the Saxon Goddess Ostara, Eostar, or Eostre. She is identified with Astarte of Phoenicia, Ishtar of Babylon, Hathor of Egypt, Demeter of Mycenae, and Aphrodite of Cyprus. She is Venus, the morning star and evening star; She is the goddess of desire Who descends to the underworld to reclaim Her lover; the Moon, Astroarche, "Queen of the Stars" and Heavenly Virgin; and the Warrior Maiden as well, robed in flames, with sword and arrows. Skyclad, She rides the lioness, with mirror and lotus in one hand and two snakes in the other.

The Christian holy day of Easter is named for Her, and is observed on the first Sunday after the first full moon following the vernal equinox—when the pregnant Goddess enters the season of fertility.

For Pagans, Ostara marks spring's return; the fertility of animals, crops, and humans; the balance of darkness and light, and therefore female and male energies in Nature; and the astrological passage from Pisces to Aries. It is the time when the Daughter Kore returns from the Land of the Dead, and becomes reunited with Mother Demeter: thus it stands for the bond between mother and daughter and their perpetuation of life.

The "Easter Bunny" derives from the hare, which is sacred to the Moon Goddess. Eggs, colored red in ancient times, are a symbol both of fertility and resurrection. In some myths, the Goddess lays the "Golden Egg of the Sun."

It is a good time to:

- Decorate your temple in green, with silver candles.
- Bake "Hot Crossed Buns," spicy roundcakes with fruit in them and the equal-armed equinoctial cross marked on the top.
- Put a moon hare on your altar to symbolize fertility. Obtain little stuffed bunnies (stuffed animals from resale shops and yard sales can be washed and recycled) and share them with each covener.
- Place a big wheel symbol over the altar, either of gilded plywood or cardboard covered with foil, glitter, or tinsel. Also, the Farrars[1] describe a "Wheel Dance," where coveners are connected by holding knotted cords.
- Choose a Spring Queen, who gets to take all the flowers home after the celebration.
- Share baskets filled with spring treats: chocolate bunnies, decorated eggs, marshmallow chicks.
- Bless the seeds for your garden, visualizing the large and healthy plants they will become.
- Make Ostara divination eggs. Take a white crayon and draw magickal symbols on a bunch of hard-boiled eggs. They can be astrological symbols, Norse runes, alchemy signs, or simple drawings of plants, trees, animals, and mythological beasts.

  When the coven gathers for the sabbat, have an egg hunt. Have pots of colored dye waiting (natural dyes include boiled onionskins, turmeric, beet juice and vinegar, red cabbage and vinegar). As the colors come on the eggs, the symbols will stand out in white. Help each other interpret the meaning of the symbols for the recipient's life.

  Or as a variation, let each covener use their egg to gift another within the coven. For example, if Freyakin gets an egg with a dragon symbol, she might decorate it by gluing on colored yarn and sequins, and then at the ritual present it to the covener who she believes can use more dragon energy.

- Bless your ovaries or testicles.
- Celebrate the Eleusinian Mysteries. One evening the circle forms on a bluff over the ocean. Torches are lit, and the people line a path down to the sea. Demeter comes wailing between them, lamenting Her loss, and plunges into the sea. She emerges, and leads everyone to a deep cave, where the torches are extinguished. In the darkness, the moaning of lost souls is heard from the Underworld. Suddenly there is a flash of light—and Persephone leaps out! She is dressed in red, and dances a dance of life—the belly dance. Then She leads the procession back up to the original circle, singing "We all come from the Goddess, and to Her we shall return . . . ." (Obviously you need a fairly warm body of water for this ritual, lest "Demeter" get hypothermia.)
- Launch projects to be completed or harvested in the fall.
- Gather wood to dry for the Beltane Fire; ideally, three pieces each of nine different woods. Select dead branches still on the trees, rather than live wood or rotting ground wood.

Beltane

Beltane is also called May Eve, Walpurgis Night, Beltaine, or Baltein. At this time Pagans celebrate the blossoming of spring and the powers of sexuality and fertility. As Starhawk says, this is the eve when "Sweet desire weds wild delight . . . ."

It is one of the Great Sabbats, perhaps the most ancient, recognized by the early pastoral peoples of Europe. In celebrating the waxing of life, it stands directly opposite the more somber sabbat of Samhain in the Wheel of the Year, which explores the theme of death and beyond.

The aspect of the Goddess paramount at Beltane is the Virgin—called Maya, Maia, Mai, or May (for Whom the month is named) in northern Europe, Flora in Rome, or Kore in Greece. She is of course "virgin" in the old Pagan sense—a woman who belongs to herself—not in the later meaning of "presexual."

The festival is also sacred to the God Bel, Baldur, or Baal, for Whom it is named. He is a god of fire and light, "the Bright One." "Bel fires" or "balefires" blaze on the hilltops of Europe to mark the night, and sometimes the God is burned in effigy to symbolize His "love-death" in the fires of passion. The more recent custom in which celebrants leap through the flames or over them is an echo of ancient practices.

The maypole represents the divine lingam planted in the Earth's womb, and may also be called a herm or hermes. In India, phallic pillars directly related to the maypole are still venerated. Centuries ago in England, after the all-night revels of May Eve, teams of oxen would be hitched to the pole, which was gaily decorated with flowers, green boughs, paint, and ribbons. Then it would be transported back to the village in a grand processional followed by the laughing, singing people. Once it was erected and "summer halls, bowers, and arbors" created nearby, the traditional dance would take place, and ribbons be woven about its length as the villagers danced in and out in opposite directions (the Maypole Dance), after which the Great Rite was enacted in harmony with the fertile energies of the season. In some locales, all marriage vows were suspended for the night and all who wished would make love in plowed fields or forest glades. More formally, the rite might involve only the High Priestess and High Priest enacting the parts of the young Goddess and God, or in its most abstract form, the dipping of an athame into the sacred chalice.

You may wish to celebrate by:

- Weaving a garland of flowers to wear in your hair.
- Wearing green all day (and nothing all night).
- Rising before dawn (assuming you ever went to bed) and washing your face in the dew, whereupon you will have beauty all year. Your coven can adapt this old custom by washing your faces, then sitting in a circle. As the sun rises over the horizon, let coveners share aloud what they already find beautiful in one another.
- Hanging fruits and baked goodies from trees for later feasting.
- Building a Beltane fire of your nine different woods. Leap over it to cleanse yourself, leaving unwanted things behind in the purifying flames, or state your desires and let the energy of the fire carry them upwards.
- Choosing a May Queen and May King (or Beltane Maid and Jack-o-the-Green) to preside over the festivities—preferably partners or lovers.
- Ritually enacting the "Love Chase," a dance where the God pursues the elusive, beckoning Goddess and finally wins Her.
- Blending a May Bowl of white wine, strawberry wine or liqueur, fresh strawberries, and sprigs of woodruff. Pour a libation and toast the Gods.
- Leaping over your garden rows (or house plants), sharing joyous energy.
- Holding a contest for the "Most Unusual Aphrodisiac" or "Most Enchanting Endearment."
- Making "May gads" or Bacchanalian *thrysi* (wands) to carry in procession. Find slender rods of willow, hopefully without cutting live ones unless the deva grants permission. Decorate each one with bells and ribbons, and twine cowslips or other flowers about them. Carry them as wands in your Beltane procession and ritual.

Each covener should choose the colors of ribbon that best symbolize his or her hopes for the coming season. Later they can be put on the fire to transform the thought to energy, taken home, or exchanged.

- Erecting a maypole. Choose a bright color of ribbon to symbolize your desire and dance the weave.
- Watching Morris dancers sing and dance in the dawn, ribboned and belled, on May 1.
- Creating a "Hobby Horse" costume or a Green Man bedecked with leaves, flowers, and ribbons. Lead a serpentine dance to celebrate the death of winter and the return of spring.
- Making Beltane bowers. Indoors or out, part of your celebration can be beautiful isolated "bowers" where couples can slip away to celebrate. Outdoors, a tent or pavilion will do, with candles, incense, recorded music, and soft pillows, or screen off a small area between three trees with fabric hangings. Indoors, any room can be transformed into a miniature Temple of Aphrodite.

  It should be made clear at the outset that touching and sensuality are for the singles in your coven as well as the married or partnered folk. So if two people want to use the space for a foot massage, or aura combing, or hair brushing or whatever, that's fine too. This idea works best if you have a long, loosely scheduled Beltane celebration planned—like all afternoon and evening.
- Holding a sensuality workshop. After a very light snack, each covener dresses up (or down) in her or his most sensual outfit. Personal preferences will vary: at ours, the attire included loincloths, a beautifully embroidered folk dress, a soft cotton tunic with pants, a favorite nightgown, and a few wisps of silky, translucent fabric.

  When all are dressed, do an attunement (chanting, breathing, dancing, or whatever), then ask each covener to write down two sensual experiences they would enjoy that evening. They might include hair brushing; aura combing; back, face, foot or hand massage; or yoga or tai chi (we ruled out explicitly sexual activity).

  Then divide the group into threes. Each triad gathers in a different part of the room. Meanwhile soft music is playing, the room is decorated with soft fabrics and lit by colored votive lights, and a light incense is burning (sandalwood?). Massage oils and aromatic essences are available on a central tray.

  Within each triad, one covener enjoys the attentions of his or her covenmates: one might brush hair and the other give a hand massage, according to the preferences expressed earlier. If the recipient has special needs (e.g., "Please don't touch my neck"), these are respected. After 15 minutes, those within the triads change places, so that someone else receives the attention. When all have had a turn, enjoy a short group hug, then move on to serious feasting. Note: you can preface these activities with a short demonstration of proper massage techniques if anyone in your coven is an expert in the field.

Litha

Litha is the sabbat of Midsummer's Eve or the Summer Solstice. It is the longest day and shortest night of the year, when the sun is at the height of its power. The solstice was a sacred day to many ancient peoples. It was marked by the alignment of the sun and stones at Stonehenge and other circles throughout Western Europe, at the Medicine Wheels of the Plains tribes in North America, and at the observatories of the Sumerians, the Maya, and others.

In many traditions the sun is a masculine God-symbol: he is the Divine Son, born at Yule and now at the peak of His splendor. Bel, Shamash, Ra, Apollo, and Helios are a few of His names.

However, there are many sun Goddesses (and fire Goddesses) as well: Ushas, Eos, and Aurora of the dawn; Celtic Etainne and Grainne; Akewa, Arinna, and Amaterasu; loving Bast and destructive Sekhmet of Egypt; Spider Grandmother in North America; and once, even Diana. In some traditions the Lady rules the warm half of the year, and Her power is greatest now.

Some say the solstice represents the wedding of heaven and Earth, as the sun's full strength is poured into the growing crops. Though the light begins to diminish after Litha, it is not destroyed but only transmuted: we see it again in the ripened grains, fruits, and vegetables gathered at harvest—Earth and sunlight blended in Life.

It is a festival both of triumph and of sadness: we share the sun's radiance and glory, yet know it must fade as the summer wanes.

Here are some appropriate ways to mark this sabbat:

- Wear the sun's colors: crimson, orange, gold, or white.
- Decorate your altar and cauldron with yellow and white summer flowers, gold ribbons, and a big solar disc or solar wheel (equal-armed cross in a circle).
- Build a great fire in the evening (with proper precautions), and dance around it. Or, build two fires, sprinkle on magickal and medicinal herbs, pass between them, and make your wishes for the blessings of health and prosperity. Later, scatter the ashes on your fields, garden, lawn or house plants.
- Have the High Priestess or Summer Queen make a bouquet of nine herbs or flowers, and nine weeds; she should bind it with five ribbons (one each of red, blue, green, yellow, and white), and cast it in the fire,

calling a blessing on the valuable plants and fiery destruction (or at least a home elsewhere than the garden) upon the weeds.

- Raise power to perform magick of will and transformation; remember your goals and strive toward them.
- Hold a ritual at high noon. Let the sun's rays enter an amber chalice of brandy or chamomile tea, and then drink of the sun's energy.
- Celebrate the height of the sun's power with a grand display of coven fireworks—possibly worked into the design of a ritual about sun gods and goddesses. Fireworks are on sale well before Litha, for Independence Day festivities. Check state and local laws about the kind you can use, check potential fire danger, and be very safety-conscious.
- Starhawk suggests making a God-figure of sticks with a foil-wrapped loaf in the center, entwining flowers in it, and casting it into the fire; the Sun-God "dies" in the flames, yet is reborn in the grain and the baked bread.[4]
- Enact the death of the Oak King and the coming-to-power of the Holly King.
- The High Priestess, or her chosen representative, may perform a special Midsummer Dance.
- Make a Catherine Wheel, or frame of sticks and withies (slender, flexible branches) with flammable material among the spokes. At the climax of your ritual, light it and send it plunging down a hillside into a pond or lake. Obviously the hillside must be stone, bare earth, or covered with moist vegetation—no dry grass or underbrush!
- Perform fire divination. See what you can read of will, purpose, and transformation in the leaping flames.

Lughnassad

Lughnassad is named after the Celtic solar God Lugh, or "Lugh of the Long Arm," Who is skilled in many crafts. It is also known as Lunasa, or August Eve. It is an extremely ancient Celtic fire festival, and one of the Great Sabbats, when Pagans mark the shortening days and celebrate the first harvest.

It is the Feast of Bread. In ages past, the divine priest-king was sacrificed willingly in the fields that the harvest might be abundant and the people might survive through the winter. Some Christians celebrate in their own manner with a harvest blessing or "loaf-mass," later called Lammas.

The priest-king's death was a reflection of the dying of Lugh, the sun God. The waning light heralded the coming of darkness and winter. Now the Goddess becomes the Reaper, and attends the God in His passing. It is a sober time, but not tragic, as the God says in "The Lord of the Dance":[5]

I sleep in the kernel and I dance in the rain;
I dance in the wind and in the waving grain;
And when you cut me down I care nothing for the pain:
In the spring I'm the Lord of the Dance once again!

Nowadays, we attune to the events of the season by sacrificing whatever is inappropriate in our own lives, fear or unrealistic expectations; by completing the major projects and goals we have been working on since spring; and by tasting the rewards of these as well as the harvest from our fields and gardens.

You may wish to commemorate Lughnassad by:

- Decorating your altar with a yellow cloth and candles, as well as corn and sheaves of grain.
- Holding your own "Tailltean Games" (the Irish contests in honor of Lugh or His foster-mother Tailte), when coveners or local Pagans compete in athletic games, poetry reading, and any other contest that would be fun.
- Baking and sharing a special "Lammas-loaf" with family and coveners, using whatever grains are native to your area.
- Making a god-figure which is whole ears of corn wired together with sticks, and covered with gold foil. During the ritual this sun god image is cast into the fire—later to emerge transformed into the corn god. We eat Him along with other ears of corn which have been roasting around the fire's edge, and of course other potluck goodies. Thus the power of the sunlight is transformed into the harvest which sustains us, and we give thanks for His willing sacrifice by feasting on corn and wine.
- Doing magick to help you finish long-standing projects by the fall.
- Ritually sacrificing negative emotions, outworn habits, etc.
- Blessing your garden, where Lugh's vitality has transformed into the sustenance of ripe vegetables, fruits, and grains.

Mabon

Mabon is named for the Sacred Son of Celtic lore. It is also the Fall (or Autumnal) Equinox, and marks the halfway point between the zenith of the sun's power at Litha and its nadir at Yule. It is a time of balance between day and night, light and darkness, summer and winter; between the domains of the Lady of Life and the Lord of Death and Resurrection.

It is also the Second Harvest, the end of the grain harvest and beginning of the hunt, a time of rejoicing as we reap what we have tended all summer. Some harvest crops of vegetables and grains, others harvest new relationships or the completion of a cherished project. Yet a few weeks remain before Samhain, the Third Harvest—what crops still stand in the fields; what projects remain unfinished?

Now is the time to complete the season's business, celebrate all you have accomplished in the warm season, and prepare for a time of rest and reflection following the last harvest which is soon to come. The season is sacred to Demeter, Goddess of the Earth's bounty, and to Tammuz, God of the dying vegetation.

To mark this holy day:

- Decorate your temple and altar with yellow, orange, and brown; with sheaves of corn and grain, and cornucopia overflowing with fruit, squash, or whatever vegetables are native to your area.
- Harvest herbs and vegetables from your own garden, giving thanks to the plant devas and the Lady for the gifts of the Earth. Gather seeds and bless them for next year's garden.
- Select ears of corn or a bundle of wheat to be the Bride at Imbolc, and welcome Her into the house.
- Harvest gourds, then dry and paint them to make shamanic rattles. Some gourds have seeds that rattle; or you can fill them with dried corn, beans or pebbles.
- Meditate on that which you have achieved so far this year; appreciate yourself, your energy and skills; bask in the glow of your accomplishments.
- Perform ritual magick to give yourself the power, love, and wisdom to finish projects which are near completion. Make your endings as enthusiastic and adept as your beginnings.
- Create "bellarmine jugs" with the image of Bel (or Dionysius) on them—you can use oven-fired clay for the God-face—and make your own wine or mead in them. Be sure you use non-toxic glazes.
- Play the "Squash Game" with your coven or family. Sit in a circle and roll a squash back and forth to each person; the recipient shares their plans for finishing their personal "harvest" in the next few weeks and asks for any help they may need.
- Say farewell to the sun as His (or Her) power wanes. Hold a Spiral Dance at your ritual.
- Celebrate the harvest with a great feast of wholesome, natural foods—all the gourmet specialties you and your friends have prepared with love and attractively served. Some of us are vegetarian, and yes, you can make a very hearty and satisfying feast without meat or dairy products. Vegetarian chili, a spicy grain loaf that tastes like sausage, mashed potatoes and onion gravy, baked squash, thick split pea soup, chunky salads with homemade dressing, fresh bread, wild rice with mushrooms, cheesecake, soy-milk "ice cream," and sunflower-seed fudge are among the treats we've enjoyed—thoroughly. After the feast, sing, dance, and make merry far into the night.

Samhain

Samhain is the Irish Gaelic name for the month of November, and may mean "summer's end." It is also sometimes called Hallows, November Eve, the Third Harvest, Feile na Marbh, or the Feast of the Dead. It is sacred to the Goddess in Her crone aspect, and to the Horned God as Lord of Death.

To the ancient Celts, it was the time when the fattened summer cattle were slaughtered and the meat preserved, leaving only the breeding stock alive. Everyone wondered if there would be food and fodder enough for the village and its animals to survive the winter.

Although this is the Celtic "New Year's Eve," in some Wiccan traditions it is seen only as the end of one year—not as the beginning of the next. The period from November 1 until Yule is regarded as an appropriate time for rest and deep reflection, not belonging to the old year or the new—a time out of time. Then the new year begins with the Winter Solstice, the sun's rebirth.

Samhain is a very, very ancient holy day: on the wheel of the year it is opposite Beltane, and these festivals of death and life are the oldest and most sacred of the Great Sabbats.

On this night, the veil between the worlds is thinnest; according to lore, the spirits of the departed return to this plane to be with their loved ones among the living. In some regions, places are set at the table for such spirit folk, in a rite called "The Dumb Supper" (in the sense of mute or silent).

This is a propitious time to communicate with anyone who has passed on, and to perform divination through scrying, tarot, I Ching, pyromancy, and the like.

Though solemn, the occasion was not generally regarded as frightening until the popular view of death and the dead changed from respect to fear. The Roman Church attempted to change the meaning of the event by renaming it "All Saints' Day," to recognize otherwise unknown Christian martyrs and heroes. The connection with death and rebirth lingers on, however, in the children's activities of Halloween. Among Hispanic Catholics, Dia de los Muertos (the "Day of the Dead") on November 2 continues to be very popular.

In the Greek classical tradition, Persephone goes to the Underworld with Hades about this time; as Demeter mourns Her daughter, the Earth grows cold and barren. In some Wiccan traditions, the season ruled by the Horned One begins with Samhain, and continues until the Lady's power blossoms again (and Persephone returns) at Beltane.

Though much of the focus of Samhain is on death, the Farrars remind us that it is also "an uninhibited feast of eating, drinking and the defiant affirmation of life and fertility in the very face of the closing dark."[6] Practically speaking, everyone wanted to eat the last of the perishable food and fatten up while they still could.

Here are some ways you may wish to mark this holy time:

- Do some public education. Talk to the media (if you are public), merchants who sell "ugly witch costumes," and community groups that run "haunted houses" for local children. As always, simply be courteous and informative: pushing hard invites resistance. For an extra community service, distribute "Halloween Safety Tips" leaflets door to door, with "Courtesy of (your coven's name)" printed at the bottom.

- Choose and enthrone a Winter Queen and Winter King, the counterparts of the May Queen and King.
- Wear black clothing and jewelry, and decorate your altar, shrine, or temple in black.
- Make masks and costumes representing the different aspects of the Goddess and God, and wear them to ritual; or, simply make masks and use them to decorate your temple.
- Have each covener carve a jack-o-lantern. When all are ready, hold them alight on top of your heads and process slowly to the ritual site. This is done in remembrance of the Burning Times and our Craft sisters and brothers and all the others who lost their lives. In those times Craft folk could frighten away superstitious people and get safely to the sabbat meeting places by carrying jack-o-lanterns carved from hollowed-out turnips (before New World pumpkins were available).

  At the ritual, let the lanterns become Spirits of Nature, and have each in turn speak for them, giving wise counsel to the coven. Continue the ritual with scrying, mystery plays, chanting, meditation, and communion with the spirits of the departed; then return to the covenstead for the feast.
- Toll "Lost in the Dark" bells, as some old English villages did, to guide travelers who may be lost in the forest or on the moors.
- Whenever possible, pay your debts and settle your quarrels.
- Symbolically extinguish the "hearthfire" of your home, and relight it from the Samhain sabbat fire (or cauldron).
- Meditate on what you have accomplished during the season of growth just past; accept it, and release that which is finished and harvested.
- Visit your coven or personal astral temple. Center yourself and prepare for a quiet time of rest, reflection, and evaluation over the next few weeks.
- Set your life in order on the material plane, and arrange your schedule so that you have the time and space necessary for reflection (and mark some quiet time on your calendar, or it won't happen!).
- Enact a mystery play about death, perhaps "The Descent of Inanna" or the story of Persephone and Demeter.
- Perform important divination by scrying in a dark mirror or using tarot, runes, or flames. Or drip candle wax into cold water, or egg whites into hot, and read what you may.

- Place an apple and a pomegranate on the altar. Slice the apple horizontally, display the star inside, saying "This is the fruit of life—which is death." Slice the pomegranate and display the seeds, saying "This is the fruit of death—which is life."
- In your ritual, place family memorabilia on the altar and invite the spirits of departed loved ones to come, visit, and hear news of the family. This part of the ritual may take the form of a widdershins processional led by the Maiden, with the veiled High Priestess welcoming the dead and leading the meditation or communion.
- Connect with the spirits of the discarnate by holding a Dumb Supper. Set places for a meal within the circle, including an extra place and chair for the spirit of one you would like to invite. Have "witnesses" or "object links" to that person on hand. When all is prepared, speak aloud, inviting the spirit to join you. Everyone should concentrate on their memories of the departed or on the object links. Raise power quietly with breathing or visualization . . . and if the spirit chooses, it will begin to manifest in the open chair—usually as a light in the shape of a human figure. You may then communicate with a pendulum, automatic writing, or by other means. After a little while, thank your guest and say good-bye.
- Visit a cemetery and meditate on your ancestors or relations buried there. If there are none, then choose an obscure or isolated grave and try to visualize that person's life. Offer blessings before you leave.
- If you have unresolved issues with people who have passed over, communicate with them and finish what needs finishing.
- Write or update your will and put instructions in writing for your Wiccan funeral or memorial service.
- Perform the symbolic Great Rite as an affirmation of life in the season of approaching darkness.
- Have the coven or High Priestess choose a Lord of Misrule, and present him with a wand of office (traditionally either a pig's bladder—a balloon will do—or a doll's head with bells and ribbons, on a stick). He becomes the coven jester or "Sacred Fool" for the evening.
- Drink a toast to the Crone and the Lord of Death and Rebirth!

During this period it is appropriate to rest, reflect and meditate more than usual, and indulge in quiet activities such as reading and writing, or handicrafts. Of course everyone's life is likely to become busy as they get closer to Yule, which marks the rebirth of the sun and the beginning of a new turn of the wheel.

The Sabbats

Name	Other Names	Date	Theme, Deities, and Symbols	Colors
Yule "YOOL"	Winter Solstice	Dec. 20–23 (varies)	Longest night of the year. Rebirth of the Sun. Death of Holly King, birth of Oak King, Sun/Son Gods, Sun Goddesses. Yule tree or log, holly, mistletoe.	gold, white, red, green
Imbolc "IM-bolc"	Oimelc, Brigid, Candlemas, Feast of Flames La Feill Bhride	Feb. 2	Growing light promises spring. Purification, Initiation. Brigid, goddess of inspiration, healing, and smithcraft. Invincible flame burning forever. New fire in hearth, candles, crown of light, Brigid's bed.	red, white
Ostara "o-STAR-ah"	Spring Equinox, Eostre	Mar. 20–23 (varies)	Equal balance of day and night. The arrival of Spring. Fertility. Ostara, goddess of dawn and fertility. Moon hares, colored eggs, baskets.	silver, green, lavender
Beltane "BEL-tayne"	May Eve, Walpurgis Night	April 30	The Sacred Marriage. Desire, Sensuality. Passion. Bel and Maia, Flora, Kore. Balefires, May poles, May gads (wands), flower garlands.	green, rainbow
Litha "LEE-tha"	Summer Solstice, Midsummer's Eve	June 20–23 (varies)	Longest day of the year. Sun at height of power. Oak Kind dies, Holly King is born. Arinna, Bast, Grainne; Shamash, Ra, Helios. Sun symbols, fireworks, Catherine wheels.	gold, green
Lughnassad "LOO-nus-uh"	Lunasa, Lammas, August Eve First Harvest	August 1	Harvest. Willing sacrifice of the Sun. Transformation of Sun's energy into food. Lugh. Loaves of bread, "corn dollies."	yellow, dark green
Mabon "MAY-bon"	Fall Equinox, Second Harvest	Sept. 20–30 (varies)	Balance of light and darkness. Abundance. Thanksgiving. Demeter, Tammuz. Feasting, cornucopia.	yellow, orange, brown
Samhain "SAH-win" or "sah-VEEN"	Hallows, Hallowmas, November Eve, Third Harvest	Oct. 31	Final Harvest. Death. End of the year. Contact with the dear departed. Divination. Rest and reflection. Dark Lord and Lady. Scythes, bones, jack-o-lantern, dark mirror.	black, flame

RESOURCES

Campanelli, Pauline and Dan. *Ancient Ways: Reclaiming Pagan Traditions* (St. Paul, MN: Llewellyn, 1991).

———. *Wheel of the Year: Living the Magical Life* (St. Paul, MN: Llewellyn, 1989).

Farrar, Janet, and Stewart Farrar. *Eight Sabbats for Witches* (London: Robert Hale, 1981).

Green, Marian. *A Calendar of Festivals: Traditional Celebrations, Songs, Seasonal Recipes and Things to Make* (Dorset: Element, 1991).

McCoy, Edain. *The Sabbats: A New Approach to Living the Old Ways.* (St. Paul, MN: Llewellyn, 1994).

Starhawk. *The Spiral Dance: A Rebirth of the Ancient Religion of the Great Goddess* (New York: Harper & Row, 1979, rev. 1989).

NOTES

1. Janet and Stewart Farrar, *Eight Sabbats for Witches* (London: Robert Hale, 1981).
2. Ibid.
3. Pauline and Dan Campanelli, *Ancient Ways: Reclaiming Pagan Traditions* (St. Paul, MN: Llewellyn, 1991).
4. Starhawk, *The Spiral Dance: A Rebirth of the Ancient Religion of the Great Goddess* (New York: Harper & Row, 1979), p.177.
5. Author unknown, "The Lord of the Dance."
6. Farrar.

15 Special Activities

A coven should not survive strictly on rituals, educational activities, and community service projects. A balanced program should also have social and recreational activities—pure fun! Following is a potpourri of ideas for your coven to try.

Coven-Building Activities

Coven Calendar

After you schedule the year's events at your annual planning meeting, get together and create a custom-made calendar. It's simplest to start with a very simple 8½"x11" desk calendar from your local office supply store, then type in your events on the appropriate days; or if one of your members has "calendar creator" software for their computer, use that. Add pentagrams, stars, moons, coven sigils and astrological notations. If you want, have each covener do a drawing (in black ink) to be printed on the backs of the monthly sheets. You might also do a cover with a large coven sigil and your coven's name. When all is prepared, take it to a copy shop and make a set for each member. You can go simple or fancy: our coven calendar had a cardstock cover, and the whole thing was spiral-bound. They cost us less than we would have paid for a commercial calendar with pictures of scenery or kittens.

Coven Book of Shadows

If your coven doesn't yet have a Book, it's time! If it does—why not add to and refurbish it? Have every covener bring the rituals, spells, incantations, poetry, and herbal recipes they like best, and combine and organize them, together with any materials that are part of your tradition. Each person can hand-copy it all in the old way, it can be on a covener's computer, or find another way to discreetly print a few copies. Perhaps you have coveners with calligraphy, illustration, or bookbinding skills to make the finished products look beautiful.

Coven Scrapbook

Why not keep a permanent record of your most special activities? Appoint a Coven Archivist to coordinate the project, and let coven members take turns making snapshots of coven sabbat celebrations, outings, and feasts. You probably won't want to interrupt actual rituals with photography, but at least you can capture the altar and costumes afterward. Ideally, photos should be kept in a nice album, with a sentence or two of explanation with each. Our coven has photos of a caving trip, a mask-making workshop, our beribboned may pole, the altar at Yule, and so forth. Your "archives" will bring back fond memories for the old-timers, and give new folks an idea of your program and traditions. One caution: take photos only with permission; those who wish can step out of the picture or turn their backs.

Covenstead Spring Cleaning

Chances are your coven has one place where you meet most often: "The Covenstead," otherwise known as the basement or living room of your High Priestess. Why not gather for a major cleaning/organizing/redecorating party sometime between Imbolc and Ostara? Clean floors, paint, panel walls, install new carpeting, add shelving, rewire light fixtures if you have a skilled electrician (Indirect? Rheostats? Colored lights?), paint murals, polish brass candlesticks, clean votive lights, put in a new sound system, dust, organize the coven library . . . the list goes on. All done? Time for pizza or a potluck feast!

Coven Songbook

Collect songs and chants on tape at every festival or visit to another coven, then transcribe them into your coven's own songbook. As with the coven calendar mentioned earlier, you can add artwork, calligraphy, computer graphics or whatever, then print several copies at your local copy shop. Don't forget to use a fairly large font—14 point bold type is good—so that you can read the lyrics by candlelight!

Coven Land Sanctuary

Especially if yours is a city coven, consider buying a few acres in the country for a coven retreat. See Chapter Six for more details.

Outdoor Activities

Create a Sacred Mound

If your covenstead is owned rather than rented property, and includes enough land (at least a large backyard), you might build a small mound in the shape of a Mother Goddess, Horned God, or coven totem animal. But first do some divination to find out whether the idea is acceptable to the land spirits and devas in the area. If so, then you will need to come up with a design, via books or your coven artist; then you can lay it out on the ground with stakes and string, oriented in the proper direction. If you are not sure which way to orient it, then put the head toward the north—the direction of the element of Earth, and "homeland of the Lady and Lord," as one song puts it. Don't be overambitious in planning the size: even a mound ten to fifteen feet long and two to three feet high represents a great deal of hard work.

You'll need to bring a truckload of earth or stone in, possibly from a quarry in the area. Talk to a landscape architect or sand-and-gravel dealer about sources. Carefully remove the topsoil and set it aside on plastic sheets. Unload the earth or stone into the center of your design, then start shoveling. When you have a mound in the appropriate shape, replace the turf on top and extra topsoil on the sloping sides.

Seed the sides with a hardy, fast-growing grass or cover plant. A local nursery or county agricultural extension agent can advise you. Water well. Invoke blessings and protection, and nurture the turf and new growth until everybody is settled in. The mound may become a focal point for outdoor ritual and meditation.

Note: Don't build a mound if you are in an area of thin topsoil or fragile ecology; a rock shrine or stone circle might be a good alternative.

Adopt a Park

This is especially nice if your coveners are scattered over a large area. Find a large park, probably a state or county one, which is more or less central to all of you. Hold some coven outings there, such as picnics and hikes, and get to know the feeling of the park. If you like it, then begin meeting there more often. If there are secluded areas or campsites, you may be able to hold occasional esbats or sabbats in the park. (We have done so in various parks over the years, even reserving a large cave for our "church services" once.)

If you are on friendly terms with the rangers or caretakers, and put up strong wards, you should be fine. In time your "church group" will become a familiar sight to the custodians, and you may want to offer help in cleaning up or improving the area. Pick up trash even if it wasn't yours, and always leave the park in better shape than you found it. The more energy you invest, and the more you get to know the geology, history, flora, and fauna, the more it will become special to your coven.

Earth Walk

Walking meditations are part of Australian aboriginal and Japanese cultures, and we might do well to learn from them. They can be simple: let the rhythm of your pace help ease you into a trance state, at one with the land. Or you may want to have each covener visit the route in advance, and learn about one part of the whole, like trees, or herbs, or rocks, or wildlife. When the whole coven goes there together, you can pause at each interesting feature and learn a bit about it from your resident specialist. Then take a few silent moments to meditate on it, sense the God/dess within, and offer a biodegradable present of love and appreciation.

Diana's Bow Tournament

Find a weekend that is two or three days after the new moon, when Her crescent is a slender sliver in the sky. Gather the coven in a large park or on rural land with clear visibility and lots of privacy. Bring out your bows and arrows, and let the contests begin!

You may preface the event with instruction from a skilled archer; if you don't have one in the coven, import one from an archery club. Your events can have differing degrees of difficulty, with a wide variety of targets: hoops, balloons, pendulums, staves, cardboard shapes, bells, etc. Design and name the events after the famous archers of myth and legend: Robin Hood, William Tell, Cupid, Apollo, Odysseus, I the Excellent Archer (Who shot nine of the ancient ten suns from the sky and saved the earth from burning up, according to Japanese legend), and, of course, Diana. If you have children in the coven, be sure they have a special and colorful event. Focus on safety, give lots of creative prizes, and wrap it up with a feast.

Sunrise Vigil

On a coven camping trip, ask everyone to turn in early. An hour or two before dawn, all silently arise, dress, and scatter into the woods to meditate silently alone . . . to reach into the dark places in their hearts and ask the Goddess of the dawn, Aurora, for strength and guidance. Then as dawn approaches, all gather on a nearby hill or at the shore to celebrate the sunrise. You might perform the series of yogic asanas called Surya Namaskar, the "Salute to the Sun." You may wish to chant or sing together. When the solar disc has cleared the horizon, offer a prayer of thanks to all the goddesses and gods of the sun: Bast, Arinna, Amaterasu Omikami, Akewa, Etain, Ushas, Apollo, Helios, Mithras, Ra, Horus, Lugh, Aten . . . . After a further moment of silence, return to camp for a hearty breakfast.

Photography Expedition

There's nothing like a camera to make you really look at the world. Why not go out with the whole group and try your skill? If you don't have enough cameras to go around, buddy up and share. Let the more skilled folks teach the rest. A couple of weeks later, have an exhibition at the covenstead, where each covener brings matted, framed enlargements of his or her favorite shots. If you're really, really proud of your efforts, offer to lend the whole exhibit to the local library or bank for temporary display. This is an especially fine teaching activity for the younger set, who can find out how much fun it is to shoot wildlife with a camera instead of a gun, and who will be extremely proud when their photos are displayed right alongside those of the grown-ups.

Note: If you really get caught up in the excitement, have several photo expeditions throughout the year, each concentrating on a single theme: trees, wildlife, landforms, flowers, and so on.

Caving

To experience Mother Earth's energies from within is a rare privilege. The dark silences of womblike caverns can be very powerful for meditation, trance or ritual. Research the possibilities for your coven: there are caves in parks (we enjoyed Maquoketa Caves State Park in Iowa), caves which are used as commercial enterprises with guided tours, caves on national forest or Bureau of Land Management land, and privately owned caves that are not normally open to the public. Many of the caves in county, state, or federal parks are great ritual sites, but you may have to ask permission. for your "church" to use them.

Council of All Beings

Assign each covener to speak for a different species of animal—possibly an endangered species, or that individual's power animal—and gather in a great council to discuss wildlife's current situation as humanity affects it. If each representative researched her or his animal, and can speak authoritatively about its habitat, food supply, and other concerns, this can be very powerful. If you wish, hold the council in the circle, include drumming and chants, and wear costumes or masks. End with a magick working for wildlife, and pass the hat for the National Wildlife Federation, Audubon Society, or the like. You may be able to tie this event in with a conservation project, such as creating or restoring a wildlife habitat in a state or county park.

Rock-Climbing

If you live in a state with hills or mountains, you have rocks to climb. And if you have a college or university nearby, there is probably a rock-climbing club where you can get expert guidance. If your coven would like an eagle's eye view of the world, be prepared to invest time and energy doing it right. It's risky unless you have training by qualified experts, proper equipment, teamwork, and strict attention to safety rules. But once you get it together, there's nothing like an air ritual perched high above the earth with only wind and sky around you.

Outdoor Shrines

Every Pagan has little shrines or altars indoors at home; but after all, nature gods and goddesses do prefer the outdoors. Help each other create little shrines in your yards or on rural land, if any of you are fortunate enough to own country acreage. A hollow tree, a rock cairn, or a stone or wooden hutch can shelter a sturdy carving or casting of your favorite deity, or S/he might prefer a simple stone circle or a tiny grove with wind chimes and amulets hanging from the branches. There is much you can do with shells, stones, carved and painted wooden posts, wickerwork, and appropriate herbs, flowers, or trees. Naturally you will wish to have a dedication ritual and celebration feast when it's done! Then remember to visit the shrine often to clean it, bring offerings, do magick or just meditate.

Canoeing with the Undines

Pagan canoeing means that you remember the water spirits whose home you are skimming, communicate with them, and enjoy their presence. If you have your own canoes (and a body of calm water), you can paint water symbols on the bows and paddle blades, and name them for a goddess, god, or spirit of the element. Invoke Them and ask a blessing before you set out, sing water chants ("Like a drop of rain, flowing to the ocean"), and around the campfire at night, tell legends of the Rhine Maidens, the Sirens, the great river goddesses of Europe and Asia, and so on.

Meet the Stars

If someone in your coven has an astronomical telescope or can borrow one, you can have a wonderful evening visiting the Moon, Mars, the satellites of Jupiter, and several prominent stars. It takes patience to set up and get focused, and make frequent adjustments while everyone gets a turn (the first thing you notice in astronomy is that everything moves; and the more powerful your scope, the more quickly things move out of the field of vision). But even if you stick with the Moon on your first expedition, you can have a fine time viewing the mountains, seas, craters and rills; and telling stories about moon goddesses (Fleachta, Shing Moo, Iemanja, Artemis) and moon gods (Sin, Thoth, Chandra). If you do this on the night of the full moon, you can finish the evening with ritual: with crescent cakes and white wine or apple juice, toast the Queen of Heaven in all Her glory.

Coven Camping

Does your coven go camping together? Hope so! It can bring your group closer together—especially if it rains, and only one tent doesn't leak. Find a secluded nook in some lesser-known park, national forest, or Bureau of Land Management area: the more famous parks may be mobbed when you want to camp. Be sure to drink enough water and eat healthy most of the weekend. Camping can be stressful, and your body doesn't need a whole lot of sugar and caffeine on top of that. Dress appropriately for the weather. And try this idea for dividing up camp chores: Make badges with the names or pictures of various sprites or creatures on them: *Podlings* cook, *Raccoons* wash up, *Mermaids* fetch water, *Brownies* keep the campsite tidy, *Salamanders* tend the fire, *Elves* gather wood, and the *Unicorn* keeps track of everybody's kids. Put up a chore chart with these names along one side, and time periods along the top; then fill in the coveners' names. Suddenly the camp chores seem a lot lighter. You may even hear things like "Great! I get to be a salamander tonight!"

Winter Carnival

If you live in a snowy region, celebrate winter Pagan-style. Build snow sculptures of the Horned God (with tree-branch horns), the goddess Brigit, and "mythological" beasts. Re-enact Norse myths or make up new ones. Celebrate Ull and Skoohi, the god and goddess of snow and skis. Set out food for the wildings. Ski, skate, and sled as you sing reclaimed Pagan carols. And finish up with hot mulled cider and home-baked spicecakes around the fire!

Make Friends with the Night

Sure, we're all Witchy and like the moon and wolves and owls and such, but are you sure you don't feel just a tiny bit spooked when you're all alone outdoors at night and it's very quiet and you hear—something—moving in the woods behind you? Well, we've all been raised as day animals, and we have little encouragement to become night creatures unless we work the "graveyard shift" at a job. Now's your chance to remedy that.

As a group, go to a quiet place away from people, roads, and buildings. Sit and talk quietly about your feelings: childhood fears or safe spaces, how your senses work differently in the dark and how that makes you feel, what you fantasize about in the night. Then drift apart and spend some time out of sight and hearing of each other. After half an hour or an hour, let one covener signal with a light and a whistle. Reconvene and share the results of your solitary meditation. In time, you may like the night so well that you begin to take long night walks by yourself. You'll be fine as long as you use your senses, don't hurry, and avoid that occasionally dangerous predator with two legs.

"Goddess of the Earth"

This is the title of one of the shows in the *Nova* television series, and it explains the Gaia Hypothesis—the "theory" that the entire Earth and Her biosphere amounts to one huge, interdependent organism. Clever, these scientists. Anyway, it's worth viewing before your next outdoor excursion. You can probably obtain a copy through your local library, community access television channel, or public television station.

Tree Planting

You can plant trees to mark a birth, celebrate a new initiate, commemorate a coven success of any kind, or simply in gratitude to the Mother. Talk to a county extension agent from your State Department of Agriculture for advice in choosing and planting trees, or ask a local nursery. Reforest an eroded hillside. Create a windbreak. Plant a sacred grove. Of course you will need permission from the landowner or responsible government agency.

Orchard Harvest

Does someone in the coven know how to put up fruit—or have a mother or aunt who does? Maybe you know someone with fruit trees on their land, or a "pick-your-own" commercial orchard that hopefully uses a minimum of chemical sprays on the trees. Take the whole gang out, pick like mad, stop for a picnic lunch in the shade, then pick some more. Back home—perhaps on another day—move into the largest kitchen available in the coven and go to work. You'll be enjoying your harvest in preserves, jellies, and fruit leathers all winter long. You might be moved to sing: "Give thanks to Mother Gaia, give thanks to Father Sun, give thanks to the trees in the orchard where the Mother and the Father are one."

Note: Remember that you don't have to use refined sugar in putting up fruit. A little honey works fine, or just let the natural sweetness be.

A Coven Herb Garden

Someone in your coven has a nice area in their yard just begging to be planted with herbs, and you've got the whole coven to help tend it and share the harvest. Start by reading a lot and talking to experienced gardeners, if you're not one.

Some herbs will grow fine in your climate and soil, others won't. Some need shade, others don't. Some want lots of moisture, others want it drier. Consider raised beds and companion planting. Think it out before you lay it out. Then organize a schedule of garden chores, and begin. Do start small. You can always expand next year if everyone's enthusiastic. This is a particularly fine project if some of your folks are training as herbal healers, though it's also fun even if all you want are some fresh, delicious salads, teas, and culinary spices.

A Tree Ritual

Next full moon, why not climb a tree? Our coven did it, and we liked it a lot. First we located a huge, ancient willow in a state park nearby on a path that was deserted in the evenings. Once we chose the tree (or were chosen?), most of us went up and found nooks, forks or hollows where we could be comfortable. Two coveners chose to stay on the ground, and one of them cast the circle.

We called the elements: Earth, for the body of the tree and the ground in which it is rooted; Air, for the wind in her branches; Fire, for the sunlight on her leaves; and Water, for the sap running through her. We meditated there in the light of the full moon, and she gave us insight and counsel. We thanked her, and Her, and shared our cakes and wine at the base of her trunk, pouring Her a libation.

Creating a Labyrinth

Build a labyrinth of string, stones, corn meal markings or snow, and walk it in and out as a spiral meditation on life.

Elvish Chess, Perhaps

I don't remember the rules of Elvish Chess. I am not sure there are rules. Here is how we play it. We gather twigs, stones, seeds, shells, pine cones, and other natural objects, in a little cleared space on the ground. One of us places an object just so. The other puts something nearby. The first may move it, or add another. A pattern begins to form, and grow, and change. It is our pattern, and we discover what it means as we create it. We talk about it. It grows more. After a while, we both discover at once that we like the pattern as it is, and want it to stay that way for a time. The game is over. We win.

Party Themes

Gourmet Potluck Dinner

This is a surprise party for your appetite! Each covener brings the prepared dish which is his or her absolute masterpiece—without telling anyone else what to expect. No coordination of dishes at all: you could wind up with nine different soups, or a meal that's all appetizers and desserts. But they'll be great appetizers and desserts, because everyone's bringing the foods they're best at preparing. Of course if you have non-cooks in the coven, they'll need enough advance notice to practice and get really good at—something. This occasion calls for candlelight, white linen, soft music, and formal wear, and a fine wine for those who indulge. Hey, maybe that non-cook could just bring the wine. Something more than three months old, please.

Movie Night

These used to be complicated to organize, and then the projector usually broke. Now we have VCRs, so it's just a matter of reserving or borrowing the videotapes well in advance. Then bring together the most comfortable living room in the coven, the biggest TV, and the best VCR available.

You can choose more serious movies with a Pagan theme, such as *The Wicker Man*; *The Witches and the Grinnigog* (British, aired on Nickelodeon); or the mostly excellent British *Robin Hood* series; complete with appearances by Herne Himself. Or you can go for comedy—*Bell, Book and Candle*; *I Married a Witch*; and *The Witches of Eastwick*. Then there's *The Craft*. Rude comments and hurling of peanut shells are okay, if you vacuum the rug afterwards. A potluck beforehand and popcorn later in the evening are recommended. If you show serious films, by all means discuss them afterwards; half the fun is good conversation.

Sandwitch Contest

That's right, see who can create the best sandwitches. Award silly prizes in categories: Tallest, Most Ingredients, Heaviest, Most Magickal, Most Beautiful, Greenest, Spiciest, Messiest, Most Unlikely, Most Alien in Appearance, Most Suggestive, Tiniest, etc. Get religious if you want: Most Godlike, Most Goddesslike, Most Earthy, Airy, Fiery, Watery, Least Resembling a Unicorn, Best Pagan Overall. (Pagan overalls in a sandwitch? Oog.) After the hilarity, divide them up with sharp knives and share them.

Blessed Bee Sewing Bee

You have sewing machines in your coven, yes? You have maybe one or two competent seamstresses in your coven, yes? You have eighty-three sewing projects you haven't gotten around to, yes? Well, yes. So bring all the machines, fabric, thread, patterns and people to one place on a Saturday or Sunday, use the experts as teachers, and go to work on those robes, altar cloths, cloaks, amulet bags, ritual tool pouches, tabards, and banners. You, too, can actually finish a project.

The Great Moosemas Celebration

No compendium would be complete (well, maybe sort of complete) without mentioning Moosemas, the moveable sabbat invented a few years ago by very strange people of highly questionable taste, who shall remain blameless. It is an event devoted to loafing, eating, lounging about in odd attire like tawdry lingerie and furry bathrobes, and playing such absurd party games as "Weremoose" and "Pin the _____ on the Moose." Its patron is the divine Bullwinkle, and details may be had in *The Complete Discordian Guide to Moosemas*,[1] available hardly anywhere. Thank you. I feel much better now.

Hot Tub Tonight

Thanks to recent liberalization of federal law, people other than Californians are now permitted to sit about in hot tubs sipping wine coolers. Has your coven done so? Why not? Won't you be embarrassed when your whole coven goes to California to visit the Reagan library and none of you knows hot tub etiquette?

Let's get going. One of you knows someone who knows someone who has a hot tub and might be willing to rent it for an evening, no questions asked. Or you could build one from candle stubs, but that's a major project. You will need candlelight, incense, towels, and fragrant oils for the massages afterwards. Yes, we're talking unbridled Pagan sensuality here, with actual touching of human skin. (With permission of touchee, naturally.) Music? Hors d'oeuvres? Light beverages? Why not? Deep down inside, aren't we all a little Californian?

Word Party

For those who like word play, an evening of Scrabble, the dictionary game, and oxymorons. In the dictionary game, one person finds a very unusual word in the dictionary, and everyone secretly makes up an official-sounding definition. One person reads them all, including the true definition, and everybody guesses which one is correct. So, does "tunicate" refer to a family of fish, a Roman fortification, spherical layers, or that floating ball that stops the toilet flushing? Oxymorons are contradictory combinations such as "jumbo shrimp," "thunderous silence," or "airplane food." Can you invent some?

A Pagan Songfest

So you've gone to fourteen Pagan festivals this summer and have 1,397 new chants and songs written on scraps of paper toweling, or taped on cassettes over workshops on "Astral Moneylending" or "Handling Flirtation by Non-human Entities in the Seance." What to do now? Why, get a friend or six to help type them up, and have the coven over for an old-fashioned songfest some winter's eve. Intersperse old favorites with teaching new songs, have snacks and beverages on hand, and have a real foot-stomper.

Eris/Eros Festival

That cultural center of the Midwest, the Temple of the Pagan Way, was responsible for this inspiration (honest, this one's not my fault). Yes, it's an Erisian Pagan Valentine's party. First, you get those little cardboard cupid decorations from a card shop or variety store, add any overlooked organs with scissors and construction paper, and put them up on the walls in compromising positions. Then you find some tapes or CDs with really smarmy love songs. Then you prepare lots of really sensual foods ("Peel me a grape, Beulah").

Then you all put on sexy or romantic costumes—Frederick's of Hollywood is the couturier of choice. Then you play silly games, like seeing who can make up the most passionate and turgid love letters (draw names at random to see who you're writing to, and read them out loud to the lucky objects of desire).

Or invent variations on "spin the bottle." We're not talking orgy here, just having fun with the humorous side of romance. Who's got their hand on my knee!? Oh well, if it's your hand. . . .

International Cuisine Potlucks

Food again? Why not! Each person in the coven brings a dish-to-pass from the same culture, such as:

Chinese	Hawaiian	Mexican	German
Greek	Mid-Eastern	Slavic	Vietnamese
French	Jewish	Italian	British
Danish	East Indian	West African	Native American
Southern U.S.	Barbarian	Martian	Northeastern U.S.
Middle Earth	Ozish		

Or try color-coded cuisine, where you forget about the ethnic origin and all bring, say, red foods or purple, or black and orange. Whatever your theme, you can just focus on fine dining or you can organize costumes, music, and decor to match. Nothing like a little piñata action after a big Mexican feast!

NOTE: Announce this event well beforehand—at least a month or two.

Stone Soup Party

The emphasis is on cooperative effort: for the meal, each person drops an ingredient into a big pot, which simmers all afternoon, producing a strange and rich soup by the evening (agree in advance whether it is to be vegetarian). Other activities follow the same pattern. Make a mural for the temple wall, where everybody adds to it. Create a song, with everyone cooperating on music and lyrics. Tell a story round-robin, where each covener adds the next part—and a surprising twist. See what you can make together.

Costume Party with Dish to Match

So if you come dressed as a Roman goddess, bring Italian food. If you're a dragon for the evening, a Chinese dish would suit your scalewear. Conversely, you can choose the food and then the costume. A bowl of mixed nuts might call for a straitjacket. A heavy noodle dish—how about Einstein? A simple bowl of apples—well, you're either Eve or a snake for the evening.

Wine or Juice Tasting Party

If your coveners are all okay with alcoholic beverages, and you can locate a knowledgeable guide, you may want to spend an evening sampling fine vintages. Some wine distributors have staff people trained to lead such events in private homes, though of course their goal is to have everyone order wine from their companies before the event is done.

If the sales pitch doesn't bother you, you can enjoy and learn from these company representatives. The alternative is to ask around until you find an acquaintance, wine shop owner, or winery worker who will do it for fun or goodwill. Your best bet is someone who understands the process of wine-making thoroughly and is filled with the lore of the vineyards.

This sounds like an expensive event at first, even if no one is selling you anything. But remember that you are tasting wine, not swilling mead after an ancient Irish cattle raid. A few bottles of moderately good wine, carefully chosen by your guide, are all you need to teach the whole coven some essentials.

And for coveners who do not imbibe, how about some exotic juices and juice blends to taste? Papaya, mango, blackberry, raspberry with pear, pineapple-cranberry—the possibilities are endless. And if anyone in the coven has not tasted fresh cold carrot juice—you're in for a treat!

Last but not least, there are herbal brews to taste, simple or blended, hot or iced.

Fantasy Role Party

For the aficionados of fantasy role-playing games, come dressed as your favorite elf, mage, warrior, cleric, heroine, hero, troll, orc, werebeast, gnome, hobbit, dwarf, sprite, steed, healer, or mutant. You can either play the games in full regalia, or focus on story-telling, swapping yarns about your impossible quests, mind-boggling journeys, and hairsbreadth escapes. Since you're not in your usual persona, you can set modesty aside for the evening and celebrate yourself in epic prose.

A Potpourri of Costume Parties

After all, we are otherwise engaged on October 31, and it doesn't seem fair that everyone else gets to dress up and we don't.

You can have a basic free-form party with no restrictions on costumes: come as a ballerina, or Mr. Spock, or a zucchini—whatever you like. Or, narrow the theme. Everyone can come as their favorite deity, an elemental, a magickal creature (no basilisks, please—they're the ones that turn you to stone when you look at them), a famous mage, or, perhaps most intriguingly, as an actual past-life persona (for a party-leaning-toward-group-therapy-session).

Be sure there's an opportunity for each costume to be the center of attention, as its creator explains its significance. If we are dealing with deities, a myth or story about each would be wonderful.

Field Trips

Religious Networking

As more and more Wiccans "come out of the broom closet," it is important that we communicate with people of other faiths and explore our commonalities. Most of us are pretty familiar with the mainstream Christian faiths, but how many of us have any firsthand knowledge or experience of Zen Buddhism? The Hopi religion? Santeria? The Black gospel churches? Shinto? The faith of the Brujeria?

Chances are there are people practicing several minority faiths within driving distance. Think about sending a representative to discuss the possibility of a group visit to their temple or meeting place—if not for a religious service, then perhaps for a lecture-presentation or even just a social hour. Emphasize that you don't want to convert anyone (or be converted), but to learn and share perspectives. Invite them to an open ritual, class, and social hour in return. For the present, such exchanges are pleasant and educational. Someday we may need to work together to maintain our religious freedom.

Renaissance Excursion

On a lighter note, is there a medieval or renaissance fair near you? Some areas have huge summer festivals with several weekends of music, jousting, bazaars, mime shows, tournaments and the like, while other cities may hold a winter "boar's head" feast and baroque concert. In either case, your coven can attend as a group and carouse together, or help stage the event, or even sponsor a miniature one yourself, just for friends and family.

Imagine a savory Yule feast of stuffed Cornish game hen, Yorkshire pudding, steaming kolcannon (layered white and sweet potatoes, with onions, mushrooms, and grated cheese), home-baked rye bread all crusty and fragrant, sweetmeats and fruit trifles, and flagons of ale to wash it down while flute music plays in the background and candlelight gleams off the satins and jewels of the royal diners (you).

Pilgrimages to Sacred Places

Not far from you may be places considered sacred by native or ancient peoples—special lakes, mountains, islands, mounds, or shrines. Your coven may, with permission of the tribal council or stewards (or spirits of the old ones, if there are no living guardians), be able to visit such a place to meditate and learn. Talk to those who keep the traditions alive, or, if necessary, the area historical society. And do read relevant books about the culture beforehand.

Visit and Expert

Just for fun, take the coven for a talk or demonstration by a calligrapher, martial artist, masseuse, silversmith, yogi, baker, weaver, potter, forester, herbalist, drum-maker, or whomever you choose. Many experts are willing to share their knowledge for free, although it is courteous to assume otherwise and offer some recompense for their time.

Activities in the Arts

Life Masks

Using plaster-impregnated gauze bandage, such as is used to set broken limbs, you can make wonderful ritual masks. You must pull the hair back and put Vaseline on the face. Cut the bandage into wide strips, narrow ones, and triangles, so you can contour over the facial planes. Moisten and apply, leaving breathing holes for the nostrils (use plastic straws). You'll need three or four layers. After half an hour, when the mask is partly dry, gently lift it off. A day later it will be fully dry, and you can sand it, paint it, and glue on feathers, horns, bangles, or shells. Violà!

Painting with Sand

Some rock shops carry colored sand, or you can start your own collection as you travel, or write to friends in other parts of the country and ask them to send you sand. Then make god/dess images on glued boards to decorate your temple.

Personal Tarot Trumps

Design new Major Arcana cards, with you as the primary figures—in your god/dess aspects, of course. Paint or color them, and use them in ritual—for ideas, read *Nine Princes in Amber* by Roger Zelazny. In coven rituals, you might all bring your cards and put them in patterns on the altar or in the center of the circle.

Silk-Screening the Coven Sigil

Have your coven artist draw your sigil or logo about eight to ten inches high, then get a photographic silk screen made at a t-shirt emporium or photo studio. With a good how-to book from the library and a little practice, you can put your symbol on banners, tabards, altar cloths, plaques, t-shirts, jackets, ritual tool pouches, and more.

Creating a Coven Banner

Making a large banner will keep all your coven artists and seamstresses busy for a while. Be sure to use fabric that can stand rain and don't be stingy with the fringe, feathers, bells, and amulets. If somebody is adept with wood, they can make a sturdy portable stand—or just sew a sleeve at the top and slide a dowel through for hanging. You will look so fine at open rituals and festivals!

Mural Painting

If your temple or covenstead has a spare wall that is not doing anything important, maybe it would like to become a mural. Find some Pagan-oriented painting or drawing you like (or create your own design), make a transparency or color slide of it, project it on the wall, trace it with a soft pencil, and paint. Keep it simple, unless you have some really skilled painters on hand.

Bookbinding Party

If one of you takes a course at a local college, they can teach all of you how to make and bind your own Books of Shadows.

Poetry Party

There is lots of poetry around which is Pagan in spirit or you can share your own work. Wine and hors d'oeuvres?

And so much more: Sculpting and firing ceramic god/desses for your altars. Impromptu drumming jam sessions. Woodcarving. Weaving. Origami. Macramé wall hangings. Kites with mythological themes. Blessed be!

NOTES

1. Andalusia, called "The Heretic," *The Complete Discordian Guide to Moosemas,* (Nine Candles Publications, 1983).

16 Education and Training

Imagine yourself as a young person living in Britain sixteen centuries ago, aspiring to become a priestess or priest. Perhaps you are chosen to work with the village Wise Woman or Cunning Man as an apprentice, and become part of an unbroken lineage of knowledge and experience reaching back untold generations to a legendary past.

Or perhaps one day you find yourself on the crest of a hill looking down at a Druidic college, which you have traveled weeks to find. In your leather pack is a crust of bread, a bit of baked rabbit, another homespun tunic and a crude harp you made yourself. In your head are all the songs you could learn and dreams of becoming a great bard.

Those days are gone. The events of the past millennium shattered our traditions and scattered most of our knowledge, and we are left to remember and re-create as best we can. Today, Wiccan covens and traditions each teach what they know, often with radically different levels of expertise in various areas. One coven may excel in the creation of transformative rituals, while another focuses on Tarot. One may work deeply with Nature devas and herbalism, while yet another explores the astral. It becomes difficult for a seeker to get a complete education without becoming a pilgrim, wandering from coven to coven every couple of years.

But there is good news. In the last few decades, especially in the United States, great seasonal festivals have blossomed in most regions. At these, workshops are offered on a great variety of subjects. They have become a means of information-sharing and cross-fertilization, where Witches can gather knowledge and skills new to them, and return to share it with their home covens.

At the same time, the number and quality of Pagan periodicals continues to increase (see list in the appendices). Many of these offer articles on magick and mythology, discussion of practical issues affecting groups, herbal recipes, ritual outlines, contact information for individuals and covens, book and music reviews, event information (seminars, festivals, open sabbats and moons), and ads for occult suppliers.

The number of books on the Craft has jumped astronomically in the last several years. Once our written resources were limited to the coven Book of Shadows plus the works of Leland, Murray, and Gardner. Then we saw books by Sybil Leek, Starhawk, and Margot Adler, and then it seemed as though the floodgates opened. Publishers such as Llewellyn and Samuel Weiser do a brisk business in Craft as well as New Age titles, and other major publishers are taking a keen interest. We no longer have to scrape to find books on the Craft; now we have to sort through mounds of them to find the really good ones. Unfortunately there will always be some that are superficial or sloppily researched; and there are still some of the coffee-table shocker variety, the "Witchcraft and Demonology" sort replete with medieval woodcuts of devils and recipes for icky and improbable spells. Luckily there are also a lot of good books on the Craft. A recommended reading list is included as an appendix, though it will already need updating by the time you read this. But for those getting started, here is a short list of highly rated introductory books.

Recommended Basic Reading

Adler, Margot. *Drawing Down the Moon: Witches, Druids, Goddess-Worshippers and Other Pagans in America Today.* 2nd ed. Boston: Beacon, 1997.

Buckland, Raymond. *Buckland's Complete Book of Witchcraft.* St. Paul, MN: Llewellyn, 1990.

Crowley, Vivian. *The Phoenix and the Flame.* London: Aquarian Press, 1994.

Crowley, Vivian. *Wicca: The Old Religion in the New Age.* London: Aquarian Press, 1989.

Ehrenreich, Barbara, and Deirdre English. *Witches, Midwives and Nurses: A History of Woman Healers.* The Feminist Press, 1973.

Eisler, Riane. *The Chalice and the Blade.* New York: Harper & Row, 1987.

Farrar, Janet, and Stewart Farrar. *Eight Sabbats for Witches.* London: Robert Hale, 1981.

Gardner, Gerald. *Witchcraft Today.* New York: Citadel, 1954.

Gardner, Gerald. *The Meaning of Witchcraft.* London: Aquarian Press, 1959.

K, Amber. *True Magick: A Beginner's Guide.* St. Paul: Llewellyn, 1990.

Starhawk. *The Spiral Dance: A Rebirth of the Ancient Religion of the Great Goddess.* New York: Harper & Row, 1979.

Valiente, Doreen. *Witchcraft for Tomorrow.* London: Robert Hale, 1978.

Weinstein, Marion. *Positive Magic.* New York: Pocket Book, 1978.

Yet another source of information is the Internet. If you are online and have a question, there is someone on the Net who has the answer, or knows where to find the answer. If you have a search program it may get you close, or you can ask in one of the appropriate folders or forums, or begin by looking at related World Wide Web pages (see the appendices for Net resources).

Festival workshops, periodicals, books and Net conversations are no substitute for a well-organized program of learning within a coven, but they can certainly supplement the coven training.

The Mentoring System

When a new student joins the coven, it can be difficult for them to integrate into the group and also learn all the things that the more experienced coveners take for granted. The first few weeks or months are critical, and having a special person to guide and encourage the new person can make an enormous difference in their coven experience. Such a person is sometimes called a mentor.

The mentor is actually a combination advisor, teacher, and big brother/big sister. It is their responsibility to stay in close touch with an assigned student, to answer questions, keep an eye on attendance, help them find or make a robe and ritual tools if necessary, make sure they are getting the classes they need, and facilitate a smooth integration into the coven.

Mentors are generally recruited by the High Priestess and/or High Priest in close consultation with the coven elders and coven council. In matching a mentor with a student, you will need to consider common interests (are they both interested in herbalism or whatever?), personalities, where they live (hopefully not too far from one another), history/background (are they from similar cultures so they "talk the same language"?), and possibly variables such as age, sex, sexual orientation, and scheduling conflicts. Mainly, they have to be comfortable with each other and both want to work together.

Mentors and "mentees" should get together at least once a month to discuss the student's progress, work out any problems, and perhaps do some tutoring on topics the student is having trouble with. Teaching basics is not necessarily the mentor's main duty—presumably the student is taking classes taught by other coveners—but the mentor can reinforce the classes and fill in any gaps. The mentor/mentee meetings can take place on an evening or weekend, or over lunch occasionally. In addition to these special meetings, the mentor should check in with their assignee at regular coven events, even if it's only a moment's chat after a ritual. A list of questions to help the mentor keep track of the student's progress is given at the end of the chapter.

Perhaps once every three months the mentors can gather together and discuss their work with the students. They can share resources, brainstorm to solve problems, and inspire one another. Such meetings are a good time to see if the various matches are working out, or whether it would be best in some cases to switch assignments. You don't want to change a student's mentor very often or they will begin to feel unwanted; but occasionally it's necessary. If so, handle it tactfully and explain the change in positive terms.

It is probably a good idea to formally end the mentor assignment when the student is ready for first-degree initiation. Then the new initiate can be allowed to work more independently, assigned a new mentor, reassigned the same one if appropriate, or possibly even be assigned as mentor to a brand-new student. It is up to the coven whether to extend the formal mentor program past first degree.

It should be emphasized that every covener is a resource to every other covener, and the mentor program exists simply to make sure that no new member gets "lost between the cracks." No mentor should ever get territorial about "their" mentee, and every coven member should connect with every new student.

A Coven Training Program

What might a coven curriculum look like? There is a great deal of variation, but some topics appear in almost any coven's program. A fairly typical one might begin with "Wicca 101" introductory classes, such as this six-week series:

Class One: The Goddess and The God

- Goddess and God as "The Humanized Face of Divinity"
- Immanent vs. Transcendant Deities
- Monotheism vs. Polytheism vs. Animism vs. Pantheism
- The Great Goddess Archetypes
  - The Earth Mother
  - The Maiden/Virgin
  - The Wise Crone/Healer/Magician
  - The Bringer of Civilization/Artisan
  - Moon and Sun Goddesses
  - The Queen of Heaven/Sky Goddesses
  - Warrior Goddesses
  - Goddesses of Love and Fertility
- The Great God Archetypes
  - The Horned God
  - The Green Man/Earth Gods
  - The Hero
  - Sun and Moon Gods
  - Father Gods/The Wise Sage
  - Warrior Gods of Sky and Mountains

Class Two: The History/Herstory of Witchcraft

- Religion in Paleolithic Times
- The Pagan Religions of Old Europe
  - Wiccecraeft
  - Druidism
  - The Norse Pantheons
  - Influences from East, South, and West
- The Roman Religion and Culture
- Early Christianity and Paganism
- Medieval Europe: The Burning Times
- The Craft Underground

The Witchcraft Act Repealed and Gerald Gardner
The Renaissance of the Craft

Class Three: Cosmology and Thealogy

Creation Myths in Wicca
Goddess and God
Deities as Facets of Ultimate Reality
  The Birth of All Things
  The Scope of the Universe
Levels of Reality
All Things are Energy
Consensual Reality vs. Starlight Vision (magickal, intuitive perspective)

Class Four: The Wheel of the Year

The Lunar Calendar
Esbats: Celebrating the Phases of the Moon
The Great Sabbats: Imbolc, Beltane, Lughnassad, and Samhain
The Solar Calendar
The Lesser Sabbats: Yule, Ostara, Litha, and Mabon
Seasonal Celebrations and Modern Society

Class Five: Magick and Ethics

Magick in Brief
The Wiccan Rede
The Law of Return ("Threefold Law")
Psychic Self-Defense vs. Negative Magick
Working with Permission
Ethics Scenarios for Discussion

Class Six: Living Pagan

Manifesting the God/dess Within
Honoring the Goddess in One Another
Living with Younger Self
Celebrating the Wheel of the Year
Magick: Theurgy and Thaumaturgy
Protecting and Healing the Earth
Working with Animals and Plants
Divination in Daily Life

Some covens teach basic magick as part of their Wicca 101 series. Ours does not, because our Wicca 101 is open to the public and our vows do not permit us to share potentially powerful magickal techniques with people who might not use them in accordance with the Wiccan Rede. Instead, we teach a second series to "Dedicants," those who are seriously exploring Wicca as their spiritual path and have sworn to live by the Rede. Let's call this series "Wicca 102."

Class One: Elements and Correspondences

Earth: Foundation, Body, Prosperity, the Material World
Air: Mind, Intellect, Imagination
Fire: Energy, Will, Purpose, Passion
Water: Emotion, Feelings, Intuition
Spirit: Balance, Creation, the All

Class Two: Beginning Ritual Magick

Ritual Etiquette
Ritual Leadership
Overview (Components of Ritual)
Self-Preparation
Setting Up the Altar
Attunement/Centering
Asperging
Casting the Circle

Class Three: Inviting the Powers

Review of Part 1
Calling the Quarters
Invoking the Goddess and God

Class Four: Using Energy and Closure

Stating the Purpose
Raising Power
Sending the Power
Earthing the Extra Energy
Cakes and Wine
Farewell to God and Goddess
Farewell to the Quarters
Opening the Circle
Acting in Accord

Class Five: Review and Planning

Review and Practice—all major elements of ritual
Planning a Full Moon Esbat

Class Six: The Witches' Pyramid

Making of a Magickian
The Foundation: Knowledge
The Inner Structure: Love
The North Face: Faith
The East Face: Imagination

Class Seven: The Witches' Pyramid, Continued

The South Face: Will
The West Face: Silence
Guided Mediation
Make Your Own Mini-Pyramid

Class Eight: Ritual Tools

Why Use Ritual Tools?
Your Book of Shadows
Athame
Wand
Chalice
Pentacle
Other Miscellaneous Tools

With this foundation, and under the guidance of experienced elders, the dedicants then proceed to carry out the ritual they have planned. After this, they are free to join the rest of the coven in planning and leading esbats and sabbats, and to attend more advanced classes.

Not all covens emphasize teaching their advanced students—for those who do, there is an endless supply of potential topics. Here are some possible subjects:

Divination

Tarot	Runes	Lithomancy (casting stones)
Astrology	I Ching	Radiesthesia (pendulum)
Geomancy	Scrying	Palmistry

Psychic Skills

Psychometry	Telepathy	Precognition
Levitation	Clairvoyance	Clairaudience
Telekinesis	Teleportation	Channeling
Remote Healing	Research	

Basic Magick

Spell-casting	Trancework	Psychic Self-Defense
Candle Magick	Cord Magick	Amulets and Talismans
Magickal Names	Theban Script	Affirmations/Words of Power
Chanting	Drumming	Circle Dancing

More Advanced Magick

Chakra Work	Aspecting Deity	Past Life Regressions
The Middle Pillar	Astral Travel	Shamanic Journeys
Invisibility	Shapeshifting	Artificial Elementals

Nature Magick

Power Animals	Plant Devas	Herb Magick
Weather Magick	Tree Magick	Stone Magick
Ley Lines		

Other Magickal Systems

Kabbalah	Golden Dawn	Huna
Feng Shui	Taoist	Santeria
Vodoun	Bruja	Norse
Native American	Egyptian	Enochian
Alchemy		

Mythology

Celtic	British	Gaelic
Middle Eastern	Teutonic	Norse
Egyptian	Roman	Greek
Hindu	Asian	African
Australian	Polynesian	Inca
Native American	Finnish	Mayan

Healing Arts (Some Possibilities)

Herbal Healing	Nutrition	Chakras, Energy Work
Psychic Healing	Remote Healing	Co-Counseling
Flower Remedies	Visualization	Affirmations
Massage	Reiki	Gem Stone Healing

History/Herstory of Witchcraft

Paleolithic Roots	Celtic Culture
The Basque Connection	The Connection with India
The Gypsy Connection	Paganism and the Culdee Church
Fairies, Picts and Elves	The Burning Times
The Craft and Royalty	The Craft Underground
The Grimoires	Salem: A Case Study
Margaret Murray's Theories	Charles Leland's Works
The Laws or Ardaynes	Gerald Gardner and Doreen Valiente

Issues in Modern Wicca

Networking Organizations	Clergy Role and Credentials
Wicca and the Law	Pagan Congregations/Lay Wiccans
Pagan Publications	Centers and Land
Witches and Technology	Public Education
Witchcraft and Feminism	The Religious Right
Witches and the Environment	Witches in the Military
Rites of Passage	Pagans in Prison
The Festivals	Wicca and Community Service

This is by no means an exhaustive list, but it gives some idea of the possible scope of a priest/ess' education. Practically speaking, most Witches will learn the basics, specialize in a few areas of magick, healing, and psychic work, and continue their educations all their lives.

How does a coven set up its teaching program? First, define your coven's tradition (unless you are completely eclectic). Then list the basics that everyone "should" learn according to your tradition or understanding of the Craft. Add the topics that your members are most interested in; the lists above should help.

Then find resource people to teach them. As mentioned above, some things you can pick up at festivals, though not every festival workshop leader is as expert as we might wish. Sometimes guest speakers, such as nationally known authors, will come to your area and give workshops. If you are in touch with other covens in your area, see about a teaching exchange program: their herbalist can come teach your coven, and your tarot expert can visit them. Local non-Wiccan experts, say in drumming or meditation, may be willing to visit your coven and teach for a modest fee. Various universities and centers in your community may offer classes and workshops of interest to Witches: our not-very-large town has had programs on circle dancing, feng shui, neuro-linguistic programming, and "Making a Beaded Amulet Pouch," among many other topics, within the past year.

Many of your teachers will come from within your coven: be sure to poll members to find out what they can teach. Don't fall into the trap of having one or two members do all the teaching, no matter how experienced they are. First, even the best teacher can get a little boring and repetitive eventually. Second, your other members need practice teaching; some of them will be leading covens one day. If you can arrange team-teaching it's often more fun for teachers and students alike.

Most covens like to schedule classes on a regular basis. Some try to hold a short class at the beginning of each esbat, but more prefer to have a separate class night every week or every other week. Make sure your teachers know the date well in advance, so they can prepare properly. Record attendance, so you know who's learning what, and who will need make-up classes later. Make sure the setting is fairly comfortable, whether indoors or out. Start and end on time. There is a running joke that Pagans operate on "Pagan Standard Time"—always late—but it's not that amusing to people with outside lives and responsibilities.

How to teach? Maybe you're an old hand or even a professional teacher; if so, don't get too relaxed—you can always improve even a good class. Maybe you feel new to teaching and very unsure of yourself. Don't worry; first of all, you probably have more experience than you think. Every time you teach your child to tie her shoelaces, or explain a procedure at work, you're teaching. With preparation, you can teach in the coven just fine. And these are your friends; they're going to be attentive and supportive, yet hopefully provide honest feedback.

Let's suppose that you have been asked to teach a beginning class in tarot. Organize your class step by step:

1. Confirm the date, time and location.
2. Be sure you know who is going to be attending—unless it's an open class, in which case you just try to be ready for anyone from rank beginner to expert.
3. If possible, find out in advance how much your students know about the subject, if anything. You don't want to make the class too simple or too advanced.
4. Outline the information and skills you would like your students to learn; that is, set specific goals for the class (and share them with the students). For example:

   I. History of Tarot
   II. Variety of Decks Available
   III. What Comprises a Traditional Deck
      A. 78 cards
      B. 22 Major Arcana
      C. 4 Suits: Wands, Swords, Cups, and Pentacles
      D. Within each suit: Ace, 2–10, Page, Knight, Queen, King
   IV. Different Techniques for Reading the Tarot
      A. Traditional Interpretations (see books)
      B. Psychic Interpretation
      C. Gestalt Interpretation (elicit what cards mean to querent)
   V. A Sample Spread: The Celtic Cross

5. Since a lecture can get boring and a technique is more clear when you show people how it's done, add another part:

   VI. Demonstration

6. So far so good, but students can't begin to master a skill until they try it. So add:

   VII. Practice in Pairs

7. The practice will mean more if students can process it afterwards, sharing their experiences, insights, and questions. So we add:

   VIII. Discussion: How Did It Go?

8. What if they want to keep learning on their own, after the class is over? Add:

   IX. Resources for Further Learning (book list, decks, sources, etc.)

9. Now you can go back and add detail to the first parts. Do all the reading and research you need to, and ask for help if you get stuck.
10. Check your outline for variety. All that talk at the beginning could get dull. Maybe you want to break it up with a game or exercise. How about

something simple with the major arcana? Show everyone the major arcana in order, but cover their numbers with scraps of Post-It Notes. Then scramble them up and have the group try to put them back in order. Discuss mnemonic tricks to help you remember their order. This little game begins to get your students familiar with the major arcana, whether or not they actually memorize the order.

11. Ask yourself whether there are visual, auditory, and kinesthetic elements in your plan. Different individuals learn best in different sensory modes, and everyone learns most easily when all modes are used. Let's consider the visual mode: we've got the decks to look at and a sample spread. For auditory, we have the lecture at the beginning and discussion later. For kinesthetic, there is the chance to handle different decks, put major arcana in order, and place the cards in a spread. Seems pretty varied and balanced.
12. Go through and allocate how much time you'll give to each part. See if it all fits in your time bloc or if you'll need to add or cut activities, or extend into a second class or a series of classes.
13. Decide if you want handouts. How about a list of all the major arcana and suits, a diagram of the Celtic Cross spread, a recommended reading list, and brief descriptions of some popular decks with the addresses of area stores that sell them.
14. Rehearsal time. Run through the whole class in your mind or aloud. See if it flows well or if you want to switch some parts around. As you go make a list of all the materials you'll need.
15. Gather your materials: sample decks (borrow some if necessary), tarot books from the coven library to show, handouts, and Post-It Notes for the game.
16. Before class starts, look over your "classroom." Is it comfortable, well lighted, roomy enough, with a good temperature and ventilation?
17. Do the class.
18. Afterwards, ask for feedback. If you like, you can even get fancy and ask for written evaluations—see the sample "Teaching Assessment Tool" at the end of the chapter. On your class outline, make notes to help improve the class the next time you teach it.
19. Bask in your well-deserved praise and enjoy the feeling of accomplishment!

Your teaching can be lively and fascinating if you remember a few points. First, get your students involved, not just passively listening (or not listening) to a lecture. There are lots of different participatory, experiential learning techniques you can use to add variety and interest: see the list at the end of the chapter for ideas. In general, learning happens more from thinking and doing than from listening or watching.

Second, teaching's not about teaching, it's about learning. Don't just focus on what you're doing when you teach—notice how the students are responding. If they're attentive, alert and focused, you're doing something right. If their attention is elsewhere, change your tactics in a hurry. The point of the exercise is not to pour words into the ether, it is to trigger changes in human beings.

Third, be open to the resources your students have to share with one another. A class where everyone is trading stories, asking questions, and offering ideas is much richer than one which is silently spoon-fed by The Teacher. Even if you do not share one iota of information with the group, a class can be wildly successful—if you encourage people to share with one another.

And lastly, remember that the opportunity to teach is a privilege. The more you teach, the more you learn; every class is a wonderful chance for you to expand your knowledge and skills. And your students honor you by coming to your class, investing their precious time in an event which they trust will be rewarding. So teach with gratitude and joy.

Some Sample Classes and Learning Experiences in Magick and Psychic Development

Dancing Your Power Animal

First each covener must discover his or her power animal. This is usually done through a shamanic trance journey (see *The Way of the Shaman*[1] by Michael Harner). Then coveners should work individually to get to know their animal better—by visiting it in the wild, dreamwork, meditating on photographs, reading, or making amulets or fetishes using a bit of fur, a tooth, or a claw (though most Pagans would never harm the animal just to obtain these, or patronize a dealer who did).

When you are ready, find a drummer or a good shamanic drumming tape and dance your animal, letting its spirit guide your movements. You may or may not choose to wear a costume representing the animal. The longer you dance, the easier it may be to release your conscious mind and flow with the animal spirit. You may dance alone, before the coven, or the coven may be able to dance their animals simultaneously. Remember always that "your" power animal is an ally, not a servant. It is a symbiotic relationship: you provide access to this world, and they share their power.

Tool and Talisman Workshop

You can gather tools, materials, books, and yourselves and work on ritual tools and talismans together. Music, good company, and a potluck partway through can infuse new tools with something of the coven spirit and energy. (Of course, with some tools you need to be alone when you create them, as they require intense concentration on the purpose and design.)

A group workshop requires careful planning to make sure you have everything you need, otherwise people will be running home or to the hardware store every little while. X-acto knives, small woodworking tools, moto-tools, paintbrushes, and hand drills may be useful. Reference books are useful for some projects: try *Amulets, Charms and Talismans*[2] by Lippmann and Colin and *Amulets and Talismans*[3] by E. A. Wallis Budge.

Then go to it. Create your own wands, athames, jewelry, talismans, salt holders, wards, incense burners, cords, magick mirrors, runestones, or whatever else your magickal hearts desire.

Elemental Evenings

Dedicate an evening's ritual each to Earth, Air, Fire, Water, and Spirit. For newer folks, this is a great learning series; for experienced Witches, it can be quite pleasurable to reconnect with the pure forms of these energies.

Fire, for example. Perhaps you will have wall hangings and altar cloth of red or gold, or red-orange-yellow prints. Perhaps a blazing fireplace is your altar. The gleam of brass is everywhere, and a brass salamander or dragon winks at you in the flickering light. "Fire of Azrael" incense fills the air, and spirited music plays—perhaps baroque trumpets. In the chalice is brandy or tomato juice spiked with cayenne pepper, and spicecakes with cinnamon fill the platter. Fire Goddesses and Gods are invoked: Vesta, Brigit, Hertha, Pele, Agni, Apollo, Vulcan. The High Priest takes you to the country of dragons or the smithy of Wayland in guided meditation, and you reconnect with your life's energy, your will, purpose, and power. Dance a fiery dance, then carefully earth the excess energy.

You get the idea: create your own variation, and work likewise with the other elements. And for Spirit—how do you plumb the heart of the Goddess and the God? Perhaps with song and poetry, art and dance . . . and by reliving, in silent trance, those moments in your life when you felt Her touch your heart and fill you.

Crone and Sage Day

The Crone and the Sage are archetypes; we each have them within us, but we vary greatly in how well we accept and express them. In this culture, many of us have little contact with the elderly, who are often segregated in retirement homes instead of staying in the extended-family household once common. It is worthwhile making connections with older people, if you do not already have such relationships . . . and considering carefully how you feel about aging and your own elder years. For many of us this means confronting fears about powerlessness and death, fears which must be worked through lest they poison our lives and lead us to further isolate the elderly.

So visit older relatives, or elderly people who have few visitors. If they are willing, tape their stories and take their photographs. Share these in the coven circle and discuss your feelings. Do magick to accept aging and the rewards it brings, and resolve to keep your health, power, and community. Plan specific strategies. And if they have been absent, ask how you can welcome elderfolk back into your life.

Note: at least one tradition uses the term "Sennex," a Latin equivalent of "Sage."

Casting the Stones

Lithomancy is the art of divination by casting stones on a prepared cloth or board, or directly on the earth. One system is explained in Doreen Valiente's *Witchcraft for Tomorrow*.[4] You can gather your stones from streambed, beach, and roadside, or from the nearest rock shop. Stones have an earthy strength, simplicity and beauty different from any other divination tool. If your coven has not used them, then set aside an evening to explore different systems and read for one another.

Dream Circle

First you study dreamcraft with some good books like *Dream Work*[5] and other reliable sources—forget the "gypsy lore" booklets that tell you that dreaming about tuna means you will marry a wealthy shoe factory owner.

Then, individually begin to record your dreams, practice lucid dreaming, and use self-hypnosis to help guide your dreams. Then one night the coven gathers to drink herbal teas (chamomile, mugwort, and skullcap), cast the circle, listen to a guided meditation, and fall asleep lying like the spokes of a wheel, with heads toward the center. In the morning, share and record your dreams.

Note: It may take more than one try before you are attuned enough on this level to connect in your dreams. Persevere.

Exploring the I Ching

Most who have worked extensively with the I Ching seem impressed by the depth and accuracy of its counsel. However, until recently there was really only one form of the oracle to work with. Now at least we have two new versions, Barbara Walker's *I Ching of the Goddess*[6] and Diane Stein's *Kwan Yin Book of Changes*.[7] The old Wilhelm/Baynes translation[8] was grating to read, at least for feminist women and men; but Walker and Stein are a pleasure. You will need yarrow stalks or coins. Three Chinese coins are often preferred, in order to connect with the culture of origin; however, any three coins will do. It is educational to cast the coins and then read the appropriate passages from different books and compare.

Good-Bye to Guilt

Most of us recognize that guilt is a self-destructive emotion, though very useful for authoritarian religious systems interested in controlling large numbers of people. Since Wiccans are not intrigued by such games, it can only help us if we release our feelings of guilt and act from more positive motivations such as love and understanding.

It can be very healing to have a coven "Guiltfest" where you each talk about the things that make you feel guilty and devise magickal strategies to let go of the guilt. One person suggests that you assume a push-up position over a mirror, and hold it until you're willing to release the guilt or have figured out a way to expiate it. Sounds a bit like the Marines, but who knows?

A Visit from Darth Vader

Apart from the Disney-Wicca Total-Sweetness-and-Light crowd, most Witches agree that we need to confront the "dark side" of human nature and learn to cope with it honestly and fearlessly.

One way to work on this is to have a "Darth Vader Night" for the coven, where you talk out such issues as: Does evil really exist? What is it? What motivates people to do good or evil? What can I do with feelings like hatred, anger, or envy? Can I have such feelings and still be a good person? If I have done bad things, how can I balance the scales and be forgiven?

And so on. Having grown up in a society where we often get the message that we are weak and sinful, we have a lot of inner healing and reorientation to do, to help our feelings catch up with our Pagan philosophies. But we don't have to do it alone; let's help each other do it, in the coven.

Once Upon a Time

The story of your life is a fascinating one, full of great challenges and adventures, with exotic landscapes and a host of strange characters. But we don't usually see it that way, because it's not presented in the dramatic language of myth, legend, and fairy tale

Well, guess what? It's time that you got the same kind of respect as Odysseus, Queen Guinevere, or Sleeping Beauty. So write your story: you are the God/dess or hero/ine at the center, and the people or animals in your life become Faithful Companions, Nasty Orc Warriors, or Winged Steeds. The suburb where you grew up might be the Deadly Gray Waste, and the company you first worked for is in the bustling, teeming Merchants' Bazaar. The conflicts and successes of your life, in this story, assume the heroic proportions they deserve, because they are huge and important in your life—and your life counts for a lot.

When you've written it up to the present moment, then write some possible future scenarios, and how the hero/ine (you) might get there. If you like, each of you in the coven can share your story with the others in an atmosphere of interest, love and respect.

Note: Share only one story a night, perhaps after a regular coven event. They each deserve special attention.

Sensory Extension Ritual

In other words, you are all blindfolded at a moon ritual or sabbat. Let your visual abilities rest while you focus on auditory and kinesthetic ritual: on sounds, smells, touch, taste, and body movement. Once you relax you'll learn a lot. And don't just focus on yourself; hear the voices of your beloved covenmates with fresh ears; touch their faces and hands, if they permit it.

Tarot Games and Exercises

Sure, everyone reads tarot, but how about playing with tarot? Go round-robin: the first person lays out a card "at random," and begins to make up a story. After a few sentences, the next person puts out a card and continues the storyline based on that image. And so on.

Or, each assumes the persona of a tarot figure, and then you discuss world affairs. How would the Queen of Swords and the Fool express themselves about the latest scandal in Washington or the national crime rate?

Or, each covener draws one of the Major Arcana and assumes that persona, and then you all play poker using the Minor Arcana. It will be educational. And—irreverent? Well, if the Goddess and God have a sense of humor, certainly the Tarot does too. Relax and enjoy.

Erisian Slapstick Ritual

Yes, humor mixes very nicely with spirituality. Sometimes. And humor can certainly be healing. So gather your clown noses, face paints, funny costumes, rubber fish, squirt guns, Nerf balls, hand puppets, and big balloons and design a ritual.

Of course plain clowning around is fun, but it's nice to have a purpose to the ritual: humor is most delicious with a serious counterpoint for contrast. Write satire and parody into the ceremony, some outrageous puns and ribald mockery. If you can flow back and forth between solemnity and silliness, you will raise power. Also, you can learn much from the humor of other traditions—especially Coyote, Raven, the *koshare*, and the contraries in Native American religion, and Hare in African mythology.

Incense Potpourri

The whole coven brings all their collected incenses and has a party lighting one at a time and passing it around the circle. Make notes in your Book of Shadows on the impressions you get from each, and mark your favorites so that you can get a supply. You may find your nose giving up after eight or nine different incenses, so don't try to cover too many in one session. After a couple of sniffing sessions you may want to have an incense-making workshop, and trade recipes you've invented or discovered in books. Also, homemade incense is a wonderful Yule gift.

Dealing with Death

What deaths can you remember from past lives? How would you prefer to die this time around? How would you choose not to die? Is your will prepared? What kind of funeral or memorial service would you like? What should be done with your body? What epitaph would you want on your marker? Would a wake be a good idea? What do you suppose Summerland is like? What do you think you might want to do next life, that you probably won't get to in this one? Such questions make for fascinating conversation and help you deal with these important issues.

Making Magick Mirrors

Who needs a crystal ball when you can make a mirror for scrying? Obtain a clock glass (the lens that goes over the face) and paint it solid black on the inside (concave) surface. Then glue it inside a flat wooden box with a hinged cover, or on a plywood backing in a picture frame. If you choose the latter design, you will need a heavy cloth or quilted bag to protect it when not in use. The dark of the moon is the best time to scry: work in a quiet space, dimly lit by one candle. You will be seeing with your Third Eye, so relax and let the images flow. Thoughtful questions from covenmates can help you interpret what you have seen.

Past Life Exploration

First read *Reliving Past Lives*[9] by Helen Wambach, then develop your own trance techniques to begin to experience your own previous incarnations. If you are weak in trancework and no one in the coven can teach you self-hypnosis, take a seminar in clinical hypnosis from a psychologist. You may not find much fame or glory in your past lives, but you will find clues to your present psyche and old connections with people important to you today.

Bragfest

A certain amount of humility is useful sometimes, but when your self-esteem lies gasping on the sidewalk, then it's time to dump humility and get larger-than-life about your abilities, exploits, and accomplishments.

Gather the coven and pretend you're ancient Celtic warriors telling your adventures to a horde of admiring clanspeople. Here it's not only okay to boast, it's required. These folks are looking for a great yarn and as long as it's got a nugget of truth in it, they aren't going to get picky about adjectives.

So tell about your adventures—at work, on the street, at home, at the Pagan festival you went to. At first you may feel self-conscious, but as the coven cheers and applauds you'll get into it. You were brave. You were strong. You were eloquent. You were magnificent. You accomplished incredible feats, overcame huge obstacles, vanquished mighty foes, and lived to tell the tale. So tell it.

Gyromancy and Other Pleasures

The Encyclopedia of Ancient and Forbidden Knowledge[10] has a lovely appendix explaining unusual forms of divination. When the tarot cards wilt and the runestones stick together, try gyromancy: walk in a circle of letters until you get dizzy, and mark the letters where you stumble. After a while—a message! "PZXGRKLFOT." How occult.

Or try cromniomancy: finding signs in onion sprouts. Ceroscopy is fun: pour melted wax into cold water and read the shapes. If you happen to be a law enforcement officer, try margaritomancy: pearls under an inverted pot will bounce upward if a guilty person approaches, or so we are told. Saves time selecting juries. There's alectryomancy: recite the alphabet and note when the cock crows. Critomancy is for quieter Witches: find omens by studying barley cakes.

So why not invent your own methods—can they be any stranger than these? (Personally, I think the patterns of mold on last week's oatmeal in the refrigerator hold arcane secrets.)

Sweat Lodge or Sauna

Anyone who has attended many Pagan festivals has at least seen a sweat lodge, but has your coven ever built one for its own use? A framework of poles, some tarps and blankets, a fire pit and the right sort of rocks will set you up. Then it's one thing to just sit and sweat; to make it into a purification ritual is something else. Don't try to copy Native American techniques, unless of course you have Native blood and are trained in them. Create your own in a Wiccan mode. If you have a sauna available, you can also do purification rituals there. Imbolc (Candlemas) is a great time of year to do this, but it can't hurt in any season.

In Praise of One Another

"Thou art God/dess." We believe it, but do we show it well enough? Plan ahead to invoke each other as Gods or Goddesses at a major sabbat. First, draw one another's names from a cauldron to learn who you will invoke. Then interview that covener to learn what divine qualities should be emphasized in the invocation. For example, suppose you have an accountant named Woodshadow who loves animals:

> I call upon the Divine Protectress of Animals, Whose love is poured upon the creatures of field and forest, hearth and home . . . She who is the bountiful Mother to pets, familiars and wildings alike . . . and in Her other aspect, She who is the Great Balancer, Mistress of the Power of the Pure Realms of Numbers. Great Lady Woodshadow, I call upon You to join and bless our circle this night!

Write it carefully, memorize it if you can, arrange for drums, props, or background music. At the ritual, invoke your covenmate as a God/dess by her or his usual Craft name, while the rest of the coven adds psychic energy. Very simple, very powerful.

Experiential Learning Techniques for Any Class

Milling

Everyone circulates at random and makes individual contacts, often as part of a get-acquainted exercise. Each person may have a question they must ask, or a list to complete.

Discussion

In larger gatherings, break into pairs, triads, or small groups; then later report conclusions or results back to the larger group.

Observer Triads

Two people try a skill, such as focus listening, while a third observes and later critiques their performance. Rotate roles within the triad twice.

Fishbowl

Two or more people do an exercise or a role-play while everyone else observes silently, perhaps taking notes. Later, all the observers provide feedback to the "performers."

Sensory Exercises

These are games or exercises designed to improve listening, observation, and concentration skills and sometimes, the senses of touch, taste, or smell. The "Kim's Games" explained earlier are an example.

Role-Play or Psychodrama

Participants act out roles in hypothetical situations, then discuss the interaction and how different behaviors might have changed the outcome. Sometimes all participants are given role cards to act out, and sometimes one or more will simply "play" themselves.

Guided Meditation

A narrator or "guide" describes a fantasy setting or situation, and participants imagine themselves there. These are often preceded by relaxation, breathing, or trance induction exercises.

Anonymous Sharing

Participants write down a question, comment, or experience, and put the unsigned notes in a pile. Everyone takes one at random and reads it in turn, and discussion follows. This is useful for sensitive topics.

Concentric Circles

An inner circle of chairs is set up, facing outward. Another larger circle faces inward, so that chairs are matched in facing pairs. Participants quietly discuss a given question in these pairs, then, on signal, one circle rotates one chair right or left. After a time, the other circle rotates a chair in the opposite direction, and so on. You can bring in a new question with each change if you wish.

Written Exercises

Participants write down their answers to thought-provoking questions, then share their responses in discussion. The group's answers can also be written on the large sheets of newsprint beloved by corporate trainers.

Consensus Building

A problem or question is presented to pairs or small groups, and each group tries to reach agreement on a solution. Their solutions are reported back to the larger group.

Group Problem Solving

Groups respond to a puzzle, scenario, or real-life problem, without necessarily trying to reach consensus.

Brainstorming

Participants are encouraged to toss out ideas, alternatives, or solutions as fast as possible, without any criticism or evaluation during the process.

Priority Lists

Individually or in groups, participants "rank order" items on a list—from Most Important to Least Important, Most Practical to Least Practical, etc. Final lists are shared and discussed.

Ceremony and Ritual

Symbolism, readings, music, candlelight, chanting or singing, movement—all can be part of a class as well as events in their own right.

Values Clarification

These are written or discussion exercises designed to help participants understand their most cherished values, needs, and desires. Sometimes an open-ended scenario is presented, and participants must weigh moral questions in deciding how they would respond in such a situation.

Resource Sharing

Participants with skills or knowledge are put in contact with others who need such resources and are given time to learn from each other.

Active Games

Relays, ball games, circles, scavenger hunts, and so forth can be adapted for educational purposes or just included as a break from lectures.

Quiz Contests

Participants compete to see how many questions on a topic can be answered correctly. This can be used to assess knowledge levels before a class, or to review and evaluate afterwards.

Meditation

There are several forms that can be used to enhance understanding, work out problems, or simply clear and focus the mind prior to an exercise requiring concentration.

Interview Whip

An interviewer moves rapidly ("whips") among seated participants, soliciting responses to provocative questions.

Power Games

Teams or individuals attempt to accumulate "power" (play money, Monopoly properties, poker chips, colored beads) through alliances, trade, theft, subterfuge, political processes, or whatever.

Round-Robin

Participants sit or stand in a circle and respond in turn to a question, add on to a mnemonic, share a feeling, and so on.

Continuum

Participants rank themselves on a continuum (for example, from "totally ignorant about runes" to "a complete master," or from "Maiden to Mother to Crone Goddess," etc.) and then physically place themselves in a line.

Mentor Discussion Questions

At least once every month or two, each mentor should meet with their assigned dedicant or student to check their progress. The mentor can ask questions like these as well as more specific questions about the student's life and Wiccan studies. It is a good idea for the mentor to take notes so that they can ask follow-up questions at the next meeting.

1. How is your life going?
2. What are the most important things you need to work on right now—either life issues (job, studies, housing, relationships) or personal growth issues (self-esteem, addictions, health)?
3. Can you think of ways the coven could help you with these issues?
4. What do you like best about our coven?
5. Is there anything about the coven that you don't like, or could use improvement?
6. Are there people in the coven you feel a special bond with? Do you get to see them outside coven activities?
7. Are there people in the coven whom you don't know very well yet? How could you get to know them better?
8. Is there anyone in the coven whom you have problems with, or feel uncomfortable with? (Your answer is confidential.)
9. What area have you learned the most about since you joined the coven? Do you want to pursue it further?
10. What other area of magick or priest/essing would you like to study further? How can you do that in the coming months?
11. There are a lot of different ways to be a Wiccan priest/ess. Specialized ministries, if you will. What do you see as your special ministry? Coven leadership, healing, organizing and networking, public education, Craft training, ritualist, scholar/writer, artist . . . ?
12. How do you plan to continue training for your specialty in the year ahead? What resources might you find within the coven? In the wider Pagan community? Outside the community?
13. How are you feeling about your progress toward your next degree? When do you think you will be ready for that degree?
14. How are your family and friends feeling about your involvement in the Craft? Is there anything you need to be doing to educate them?
15. What Craft-related books have you been reading? What do you think of them? What have you learned from them? What would you like to read next?
16. What can I do, as your mentor, to help you have the best possible experience in the coven?
17. Do you have any more questions or comments for me?

Thank you for your time. I feel privileged to work with you, and I've enjoyed our time together.

Teaching Assessment Tool

1. Were you given clear and complete information on the class in advance? (Content, who the class was designed for, dates, times, location, fees, and what you should bring, etc.)
2. Was the environment comfortable? (Temperature, ventilation, furniture, visibility of teacher and materials, audibility, restrooms, and water nearby.)
3. Was the teacher already there, or did s/he arrive punctually?
4. Did the teacher have necessary notes and materials well organized and ready to go?
5. Did the teacher speak clearly, loudly enough, and at an appropriate pace?
6. Did the teacher give you the feeling that you were warmly welcomed to the class?
7. Did the teacher introduce him or herself and share information about their background in the class subject?
8. Did the teacher attempt to learn students' level of knowledge and/or skill before proceeding?
9. Did the teacher give you an overview of the class material to be covered, and the methods that would be used? (Lecture, discussion, exercises, projects, lab work.)
10. Was the order of presentation smooth and logical?
11. Was the material appropriate to your level of understanding? (Not too simple, not too advanced.)
12. Did the teacher make it clear when you could ask questions? (OK to interrupt lecture? At a defined "question and answer" period afterwards? In her office between classes?)
13. Did the teacher make it clear what would be required of you between classes? (Reading, practicing skills, research, making something.)
14. Did the teacher include visual aids in the presentation? (Posters, charts, diagrams, blackboard outlines and diagrams, examples to show, slides, transparencies, videos.)
15. Did the teacher include auditory aids in e presentation? (Music, taped audio supplements, sound effects.)
16. Did the teacher include kinesthetic elements in the presentation? (Movement, things to touch and feel, smells, tastes.)
17. Did the program involve experiential activities where you could try things, do things, be actively involved?
18. Was there time allowed for breaks as needed?

19. Did the teacher answer questions clearly and completely, admit when s/he didn't know the answer, and/or suggest where the answer (or additional information) might be found?
20. Were additional resources suggested at the end, in case you wanted to continue your studies in this field? (Books, more classes, resource people, Net sources.)
21. Did the class begin and end on time?
22. Did you come away from the class feeling more knowledgeable or skilled and pleased with the experience overall?

Comments:

NOTES

1. Michael Harner, *The Way of the Shaman* (San Francisco: HarperSanFrancisco, 1990).
2. Lippman and Colin, *Amulets, Charms and Talismans* (Evans Press, 1974).
3. E. A. Wallis Budge, *Amulets and Talismans* (University Books, 1961).
4. Doreen Valiente, *Witchcraft for Tomorrow* (London: Robert Hale, 1978).
5. Jeremy Taylor, *Dream Work: Techniques for Discovering the Creative Power in Dreams* (Paulist Press, 1983).
6. Barbara Walker, *I Ching of the Goddess* (San Francisco: HarperSanFrancisco, 1986).
7. Diane Stein. *Kwan Yin Book of Changes: Goddess of Mercy and Knowledge* (St. Paul, MN: Llewellyn, 1993).
8. Richard Wilhelm, trans., *The I Ching or Book of Changes*, Cary Baynes (Princeton, NJ: Princeton University Press, 1977).
9. Helen Wambach, *Reliving Past Lives: The Evidence Under Hypnosis* (New York: Bantam Books, 1978).
10. Zolar, *The Encyclopedia of Ancient and Forbidden Knowledge* (Nash, 1970).

17 On Initiation

According to tradition, after at least a year and a day of learning the dedicant may be considered for an initiation ceremony; in many Wiccan traditions, the first of three. A first degree Initiate must be able to act as a priest/ess for oneself, and is recognized by covenmates as a priestess or priest of Wicca and a full member of the coven.

Actually there are two kinds of initiation. Spiritual initiation occurs when an individual comes to a powerful realization and experience of their own divinity: when they partake of the God/dess energies that are manifest in all things. This may be an ecstatic feeling of oneness with the universe; an exalted feeling of boundless power, love, and responsibility; and heightened sensitivity to the rhythm and cycles of the natural world, combined with deep serenity.

It is not suggested that one must live in such a state constantly in order to be considered an initiate; but if one has not experienced it at all, then the second form of initiation may not yet be appropriate.

The experience of spiritual initiation may come gradually or suddenly to consciousness, depending on the individual. Interwoven with it may be a growing conviction that the Craft is the most natural vehicle in which to continue developing spiritually. There may be past-life connections with the Craft, and a warm and glowing feeling of "coming home." Or, this may be the first incarnation in which the candidate is ready for what the Craft has to teach.

The second type of initiation is an Earth-plane event where one's Wiccan sisters and brothers recognize the candidate as one of their own, and welcome them into the Craft and usually their coven. The ritual also recognizes a certain degree of magickal skill and knowledge of Craft tradition.

The year-and-a-day rule allows the candidate time to be certain of their feelings toward the Craft, and to get to know other coveners, and be sure that they can all work in harmony. During this period, the candidate may attend most rituals and classes offered by the coven, but may be restricted from participating in certain events which are reserved for initiates (such as initiation rituals and advanced classes).

Another tradition says that "Only a Witch can make a Witch." That is, an Earth-plane initiation might not be recognized as valid by the Craft community unless a properly trained and initiated priest/ess performs it. The intent is to preserve continuity and high standards, not to pretend to "insider status." In ancient times, however, an apprenticeship system was probably used, and no one knows whether there was some sort of initiation ceremony at the completion of the apprenticeship.

Given the shortage of qualified Wiccan teachers, there is growing acceptance of self-initiation. Anyone who has studied faithfully and feels in their heart that they are a Witch may proclaim that fact to the guardians and the gods in a personally designed ritual.

Yet the fact remains that many Wiccans are more likely to welcome someone as a Craft sister or brother if they have been initiated by an acknowledged priestess or priest.

A third tradition states that female candidates should have their initiation ritual conducted by a priest, and male candidates by a priestess. This is always the case in Gardnerian and certain other traditions. With the rapid growth of the Craft, the shortage of clergy in some areas, and the emergence of single-sex covens, this custom is ignored by many. In any case, another tradition says that a priestess may act in the stead of a priest when necessary, though not the other way around.

The custom of cross-sex initiation stems from the traditional emphasis on duality and polarity—the perceived need for the energies of the Goddess and God to interact for change or creation to occur. Many present-day Witches, however, are comfortable with the concept of androgyny—the presence of both polarities within every individual. This concept makes it appear less important to have both females and males present in order to perform creative magick, because the group can draw on many forms of energy regardless of their physical sex. This is not to discourage mixed covens, but just to point out that there are many kinds of magick beyond physically bipolar ritual.

To these traditions we would add the thought that Earth-plane initiation should be offered only to candidates whose lives are reasonably stable and in good order at the time. Someone who is going through a major emotional crisis or illness may not be able to clearly consider the ramifications of this act. Hopefully the coven would support such a candidate through the crisis before mutually deciding whether it is time for initiation. If the candidate seems to encounter a constant stream of crises, they should consider getting some long-term counseling before making any major religious decisions.

The effects of Earth-plane initiation are primarily social and psychological. In joining a coven, the new initiate is welcomed as a full-fledged member, with additional opportunities and responsibilities. They may be invited to more advanced classes; they should take a more active role in planning and leading rituals; they may have a greater voice in planning coven policies and programs; they may be asked to take charge of projects for the coven's benefit, and may well help to teach new candidates.

If they are to practice as a solitary, at least they have an entree to events and Craft contacts if needed. Mentioning the name of one's teacher will often bring a delighted response: "Really? You worked with Nightingale? I know her. How is she?"

Apart from all this, initiation may bring a sense of re-connection and new energy. It helps you to affirm your values and define your identity, allowing new strengths and talents to emerge. To say "I am a Witch" is to lay claim to great powers, challenges and responsibilities, and to add a rich and deep understanding to your knowledge of who you are and where you are headed.

Sample Requirements for Initiation

Although the requirements will vary from one tradition to another, these represent some common ones:

The candidate or dedicant must:

1. Have experienced initiation on a spiritual level (how this is experienced varies from individual to individual);
2. Find the common beliefs, traditions, practices, and ethics of the Craft completely compatible with their inner experience;
3. Have chosen Wicca as their spiritual path for this lifetime;
4. Have been actively exploring the Craft with your coven for at least a year and a day;
5. Know certain skills and terms basic to the Craft (see below);
6. Have read certain books;
7. Be willing to take an oath to honor and serve the Goddess and God within, in daily life as well as in ritual; and to aid and defend sisters and brothers of the Craft;
8. Create a personal oath, declaring their spiritual and magickal goals;
9. Work to develop and maintain strong, wise, caring relationships with each coven sister, brother and child; and to clearly communicate her or his needs, expectations and resources to other coveners;
10. Actively participate in coven activities, and take a fair share of responsibility for planning, organization, and leadership;
11. Choose a Craft name to mark a new stage of spiritual growth and explain to the coven what you will manifest in your life thereby, and when and where it may be appropriately used (Note: magickal names may be changed later, as the individual's work and needs change);

12. Support the material needs of the coven through modest dues or financial contributions, donations of supplies, and/or time and energy toward coven projects;
13. Arrange a suitable altar and space at home for doing personal ritual work; and
14. Create or obtain the basic garb and tools of the Craft and this coven: a long, hooded robe; an athame; a chalice; a wand; a pentacle; and a Book of Shadows.

Terms the Candidate Should Understand

There are some important concepts in Wicca which should be understood by every candidate before initiation. Different traditions might emphasize different terms, but the following would probably be on most lists:

Animism	Elements	Polarity
Aspects of Deity	Esbats	Polytheism
Attunement	Evocation, Invocation	Priest
Aura	Familiar	Priestess
Blessed Be	God, god	Quarters
Book of Shadows	Goddess, goddess	Reincarnation
Burning Times	Healing	Ritual
Centering	High Priest	Ritual Tools
Chakras	High Priestess	Sabbats
Charge of the Goddess	Immanence	Skyclad
Circle	Initiate	Spell
Cone of Power	Law of Return/Threefold Law	Summerland
Correspondences	Lunar Cycle	Three Levels of Self
Coven	Magick	Traditions
Cowan	Pagan and Heathen	Wheel of the Year
Degrees	Pantheism/Divination	Wiccan Rede
Earthing or Grounding	Pentagram	Witch, Wicce, Wicca
Elder	Perfect Love and Perfect Trust	Witches' Pyramid

These terms are defined in the glossary of this book (page 481).

Skills the Candidate Should Have

An initiate is a priestess or priest, and while they do not require vast knowledge or advanced skills in coven leadership, they should be able to minister to their own spiritual needs on a basic level. Some skills in which basic competence is suggested follow.

- Progressive physical relaxation techniques.
- The ability to center oneself emotionally, ground, concentrate, and meditate.
- The ability to enter a trance state; i.e., self-hypnosis.
- Simple self-purification or cleansing, including the Middle Pillar exercise.
- One form of divination: Tarot, I Ching, runes, astrology, pendulum, etc.
- Ritual design and leadership.
- Creating sacred space: cleansing an area, casting the circle, calling the quarters, and invoking the gods.
- Drawing power from the ambient field, or specifically from lunar, solar, or Earth sources.
- Channeling energy to a specific target or purpose.
- Earthing or grounding excess energy.

And of course, any candidate must use the Wiccan Rede as their ethical standard (see Chapter 1). Knowledge and skill, however impressive, are not sufficient for initiation.

A Personal Oath

Though not all traditions require it, we have found it valuable to ask each candidate to create a personal oath to be read at the initiation ritual. This is very helpful in making candidates think seriously about their direction, and set clear goals. The oath might include the following.

- Personal ideals
- Personal resolutions: goals for spiritual and magickal development
- Requests to The Lady and Lord (or specific aspects) for energy to meet these goals

An example follows:

Great Diana and Lord Pan, I am Artemis Earthshield. In your presence, I dedicate myself to sensitivity, wisdom, courage, and harmony among living creatures.

I shall be strong in the defense of our Mother, the Earth, and Her creatures. My special goals are to educate other Pagans about the human threat to endangered species and to mobilize our people on behalf of this planet's wildlife.

To this end, I ask your aid as I work to develop my rapport and communications with wild creatures and with people; work

> magickally with familiars, animal allies, and totem spirits; improve my skills as a leader and organizer; and sustain my energy at a high level.
>
> For all your help granted thus far, and for that which is to come, I give you thanks.
>
> So mote it be!

Depending on the individual, the oath might focus instead on healing, achieving a balanced personality, developing skills as a priest/ess, bringing magick and spirituality into one's job, or other needs.

The oath should be typed or clearly written, and shown to the priest/esses conducting the rite sometime before the date it happens, for clarification and revisions if necessary.

Steps to Initiation

As dedicants near the time when they will have been with the coven for a year and a day, they should meditate in solitude to decide whether they are ready for initiation. Doubtless, a dedicant will discuss this step with other members of their coven and their immediate family, yet ultimately it is a very personal decision.

If the dedicant feels essentially ready and desires to proceed, they review the requirements for initiation and finish any additional study or other preparation, with guidance from their High Priestess, High Priest, and mentor if they have one.

The dedicant should also think about her or his relationships with each of the Initiates in the coven. Is there a strong sense of compatibility with each one? In any case where a good connection has not been made, it may be wise to give some special attention to that individual and clarify whether they can work together as covenmates. Phone calls, letters, social and recreational activities, and working together on coven projects can all be helpful in exploring the relationship. This can be time-consuming in a large coven, yet is worth the effort.

Each dedicant should feel free to talk about initiation with any of the coveners and to ask as many questions as necessary. The details of your coven's ritual should be kept secret so that the impact is not diminished, but in general it should be made clear just what initiation does and does not involve. Probably no two coveners will explain initiation in exactly the same way, but it should be generally consistent. If there should ever seem to be important contradictions or confusion, it is important that the dedicant speak up and ask questions.

Coven leaders may need to make it clear that initiation does NOT include: sexual activity, sacrifices, the use of drugs, "surprise" oaths, or physical pain. You might be surprised at how hidden, irrational fears continue to lurk in candidates' minds even after a year of participation. These must be dispelled, so that the candidate may approach initiation with anticipation and joy.

Whenever the dedicant feels the time is right, they may ask for an initiation interview with those who will make the decision—usually the initiates of the coven, sometimes the High Priestess and High Priest. The High Priestess and Priest may then ask the dedicant why they want initiation, how they feel about the coven, and about Craft knowledge and magickal skills (see "Some Sample Questions" further on).

In some careful covens, the leaders will do a confidential poll of all the members, either orally or in writing, to determine the "sense of the coven" as to the candidate's readiness. If problems surface during this poll, then they can be addressed quietly with the affected parties rather than in a formal interview. The interview should never be scheduled until the coven leaders have a strong sense that all is well and the candidate will be approved unanimously.

"Initiation interview" sounds rather formal and frightening, so it is wise to put the candidate at ease early on by reminding them that it is just a conversation with the same people they have worked, learned, and played with for months. No one expects a candidate to have a huge amount of magickal lore at their fingertips, or to have the same kind or depth of relationship with every person in the coven, or to be a Spiritual-Adept-Bordering-On-Ascended-Master. So they can relax a little.

Together they will discuss whether it feels like the right time to recognize the candidate as "Priest/ess and Witch" and to formally welcome them into full membership in the coven or whether additional learning and growth are needed. If coven communications have been good all along, there should be no great surprises. Everyone involved should arrive at the interview with rather clear answers to the questions: is this candidate a Witch, and are they in harmony with the whole coven?

If there is additional work to be done, this is the time to recommend it. The candidate may say something like, "I guess I feel weak in my knowledge of ritual design. I'd like to help plan a couple of esbats, and the next sabbat, and see how that goes before I go for initiation." Or the High Priestess may say, "I sense that there is some tension between you and Marten, and I'd like to help resolve that before we set a date for initiation. Can you speak to that?" It is important to offer specific help and support to remedy any deficiencies.

Or, a dedicant may be qualified in every way, except that there are simply personality differences that make it difficult for them to work in this particular coven. If the differences cannot be resolved, then the candidate should be gently but firmly advised to seek another coven.

Strive to be as objective as possible; if a dedicant is otherwise qualified but "pushes some of your buttons," ask whether it is the candidate's issue that needs work—or yours. Having explored your own issues, nonetheless listen to your instincts; a "gut-level," uneasy feeling which persists must be respected.

Don't rush, or impose or accept artificial deadlines. This does not mean that you can keep a candidate dangling indefinitely without clear cause. It does mean that if they have work to do, they must do the work before the initiation ceremony is scheduled; and it is the responsibility of the initiators to explain what is required and help find or provide resources so the candidate can meet the requirements; or to explain clearly that they are unable to do so, and that the candidate should seek elsewhere.

If there are serious problems, such as a stubborn lack of ethics or some strong beliefs that are really antithetical to Craft tradition, then the individual should be steered away from the coven and Wicca long before any talk of initiation arises. (This is one reason for the "year-and-a-day" custom.) Initiating a candidate is a solemn responsibility. In many traditions, the initiator is karmically and magickally responsible for a new initiate until they attain their "majority" (i.e., third degree). Be careful whom you initiate!

But if an interview is appropriate, and all goes well, then a date can be set for the ritual. It should, of course, be fortunate in astrological terms—consult an almanac—and when the moon is waxing or full, and preferably not in the dark period between Samhain and Yule.

Then the candidate can review the oaths they will be asked to take and should be told how to prepare (fasting, ritual bathing, etc.).

Those who will participate in the ritual must meet separately to choose a location and review the ritual (see the appendices for a suggested initiation ritual outline) and perhaps personalize it for this candidate. Although indoor initiations are often held, especially in bad weather, an outdoor site is preferable. If you can, find a place with drama and power: a deep forest, a high peak, an ocean shore, or a cavern.

The other dedicants will not attend the ritual—it would spoil it when their own turn comes—but they can occupy themselves setting out a meal or refreshments near the site or at the covenstead. When the rite is over, the whole coven can come together to sing, feast, offer toasts and gifts to the new Witch, and generally make merry.

The New Initiate

First-degree initiation is not an end, but a beginning—the beginning of a career as a priestess or priest of the Old Religion. It is a vocation for the very few, people of great dedication, courage, and will. It is for those who would find the God/dess within, who would dance to the rhythms of nature, who would accept with open eyes their heritage of wisdom, love, and power. It is for the healers, the teachers, the counselors, the magickians, the seers. It is also a way of life that has led many to persecution and hardship, to torture, to gallows or the pyre. May each new priestess and priest live an exemplary life, in honor of those who died in the service of the Lady and Lord.

Continuing the Journey

In many covens, an initiate who continues in study and service may receive second- and third-degree initiations in time. By tradition there is a minimum period of at least a year and a day between initiations, and the time may be much longer depending on the candidate and the circumstances. Definitions of the degrees vary, but in general a second-degree initiate is a more experienced Witch who takes on more responsibility within the coven or community, and serves as a teacher, counselor, and spiritual resource to others. A third-degree Witch is considered fully qualified to found and lead a coven, and pass on the complete teachings of their tradition. They may not choose to do so, but instead pursue another form of ministry such as healing, networking, public education, art, or community organizing.

Sample Questions for the Initiation Interview

1. Have you chosen Wicca as your spiritual path for this lifetime? Why?
2. An initiation could be defined as a "powerful and ecstatic realization of oneness with the God/dess." Have you had such an experience? Can you tell us about it?
3. Who is the Goddess to you? And the God?
4. When one becomes a priest/ess, the gods may make many demands of you. You may be presented with challenges requiring great wisdom, strength, and self-sacrifice. Are you prepared to face the responsibilities of priesthood?
5. There are individuals and groups within our society who have declared themselves enemies to Paganism. If they achieve more power, they could bring back the times of persecution and inquisition. By formally becoming priest/ess and Witch, you could risk a great deal. Are you willing to put your home, your career, your life, and perhaps the safety of your family and friends on the line?
6. Much of the Craft is about healing and spiritual growth. What are your personal goals for healing and growth? How might the coven support you in achieving them?
7. What is it about our coven that especially attracts you?
8. Do you feel that you can work in harmony with each of our coveners? Discuss your relationships and communications with each member. Can you share your thoughts, feelings, and dreams freely? Do the coveners feel like spiritual family to you?

9. The Craft depends on the sharing of responsibility. Are you willing to share the work of the coven, including teaching and leadership? Give some examples of how you have already done this during your time with us. What additional knowledge and skills could you still share with the coven?
10. What do you think this coven needs most in the year ahead? What does the Craft as a whole need? What role do you see yourself playing in order to help accomplish this?
11. The initiation ritual will recognize you as a priest/ess of Wicca—a Witch—and as a full member of our coven. What to you expect to gain from the ritual? How will your feelings about yourself, the coven and the Craft be changed?
12. What questions do you have about initiation in general or the ritual in particular?
13. Are you ready to be recognized as priest/ess and Witch? If not, what further preparation, knowledge or experience do you need?

18 Group Dynamics in the Coven

Welcome to the Mockingbird Coven ("Mock Coven" for short). This is a fictitious coven that we have invented in order to demonstrate some aspects of group dynamics; any resemblance to actual covens, living or dead, is purely coincidental.

Group Identity

What defines the group identity of Mock Coven? Well, all the members agree that they are Witches, and most of them have the same definition of "Witch." So they share a religious bond. Their name sets them apart: they chose it to commemorate an incident involving a birdhouse and an unfortunate precipitation on the High Priestess' forehead at the high point of a ritual. For Mock Coven, it is a reminder that humor and the unexpected are important elements of the universe.

The members of Mock Coven are linked by a shared history, shared beliefs, and a common goal. Their coven's purpose is summed up by their motto: "Sisters and Brothers All." In addition to perpetuating the Craft and celebrating the esbats and sabbats, they have a strong interest in promoting tolerance among people of all faiths and respect for the other creatures who share the planet. Therefore, their priorities are interfaith work and wildlife preservation. Every year they participate in interfaith conferences, arrange joint projects and social activities with other local religious groups, and work to protect wildlife habitats and monitor laws and events that might affect them.

They have other, outward symbols of their group. Their coven sigil shows two human hands, a paw, a wing, and a flipper all touching in the center of a pentagram; their coven artist has painted it on a coven banner, which they take with them to Pagan events. Their robes are all soft gray, with white down the front and on the backs of the sleeves, mimicking the colors of the common mockingbird. Every covener also wears a symbol or token of their individual power animal: an owl talon, a bit of shed wolf fur in an amulet bag, a silver dolphin pendant, and so on. All this, say the members, is "just part of who we are." And it all helps satisfy important needs for them.

Human Needs

People join groups because it serves their needs. Some years ago psychologist Abraham Maslow mapped the "hierarchy of human needs." Physiological needs (air, water, food) are the highest priority, followed by safety, love or belonging, esteem or status, and self-actualization. Because of these needs, it makes sense to remind your coveners that job and family come first. A job satisfies the basic needs for shelter, food, and clothing, and to some degree safety, and possibly the others. The family is a primary source of love and acceptance. Coven membership ideally provides another source of acceptance, plus esteem, self-actualization, and personal growth.

Any coven leader who demands that coven responsibilities come first has their priorities scrambled. Coven activities come after family and job responsibilities are taken care of. Conversely, if a potential member comes to you and does not have their life together—is jobless, homeless, not taking care of their health, or in the midst of a messy divorce—the wise answer is: "Not now. You have more urgent things to deal with than training as a Wiccan priest/ess. The coven will lend you a hand in getting your life together, and then we'll talk about possible membership."

If the individual is unable or unwilling to feed themselves, or find a place to live, or support their family, they are certainly not prepared to take on the responsibilities of a priest/ess.

Within the coven, every member should help the others keep their priorities in order. If you see a covener getting so immersed in coven activities that job, family or health are slipping, it is time for some friendly but firm counseling. They must learn to share or delegate their coven duties, to skip an occasional activity, and to rechannel some time and energy to the first priorities. In short, they must find a balance.

Balancing Individual Needs and Group Needs

Every organization is a balancing act between the needs of its members and the needs of the group as an entity. Some people have a need to serve in ways that strengthen the group: Thistle wants to be useful, so she volunteers to coordinate a series of "Wicca 101" classes open to the public. The classes bring in some enthusiastic new members and help change the image of Witchcraft in town. Meanwhile Thistle improves her skills as an organizer and teacher and feels more self-confidence. Her individual needs dovetail nicely with the needs of the group for membership and public acceptance.

Sometimes a member's needs do not harmonize with those of the group. Perhaps Mock Coven wants to do a tree-planting project, but Birdwing is allergic to plant pollens. Several things could happen. Birdwing could loudly disparage the project and perhaps derail it. She could remain silent and simply not show up on the appointed day. Or she could support the project by volunteering to find a source for seedlings, order them, and pick them up. While the rest of the group is outside planting, she could prepare a dinner for the hungry workers. So an apparent conflict of interest is turned into a successful project.

It isn't always that easy. Some people have a need to be the center of attention constantly, to be embroiled in dramatic conflict, or to belittle anyone who doesn't agree with them. Such needs are pretty much impossible to reconcile with the needs of a healthy group. Then it is up to the coven leadership to see what's happening, confront the individual, and offer support to them in changing those needs or finding a more positive way to satisfy the underlying needs. Counseling and behavior modification may be called for, and possibly a sabbatical from the coven until the problem is resolved. If the rest of the membership is in agreement that a problem exists, but the individual refuses to "own" the problem and work on it, then there is no choice but to ask them to leave the group. This should be done as quickly, cleanly, and courteously as possible under the circumstances. It's not pleasant, but it's better than watching the coven dissolve slowly and painfully while everyone waits for a miracle.

Achieving Goals vs. Maintaining the Group

A group can be totally goal-oriented, ignoring the needs of the individual members; or it can be totally member-oriented, forgetting its long-range goals; or it may be anywhere in between on the spectrum.

An example of the first extreme is a Roman slave galley. Its officers are very goal-oriented: they want to get their ship from Piraeus to Alexandria. They will spend minimal energy on "group maintenance"—chain the slaves to the oars, feed them slop twice a day. Bingo, the group is maintained. No team-building, consensus process, or individual career planning here.

The other extreme might be represented by the Society for the Prevention of Cruelty to Galley Slaves. Centuries after the galleys and slaves are gone, the organization continues to meet monthly, elect officers, issue a newsletter, and recruit new members. Of course the original goal is pointless, but all the members keep busy doing group things, because—well, it's there, and it's habit.

Normally a group devotes balanced energies to each type of activity. Examples of goal-oriented activities in the Mock Coven are attending interfaith conferences, preparing educational literature about Wicca for other churches, sponsoring a Community Interfaith Day, planting trees, giving educational programs about endangered species at the schools, and so forth. Examples of maintenance activities are welcoming and training new members, collecting dues, issuing a coven newsletter, social activities, cleaning the covenstead before a meeting or ritual, and the like.

There are times when it is entirely appropriate to focus wholly on goals or on maintenance. If Interfaith Day is happening tomorrow and your coven is a sponsor, that's all you deal with. If there's a breach in the membership or one of your leaders vanishes, you focus on internal matters until the crisis is resolved. But a coven that habitually forgets their goals or ignores the internal needs of the group is either not going to be effective or not even going to survive.

Work, Process, and Combat Modes

Another way of looking at groups is that they operate in one of three modes: work, process, or combat. A "working mode" means that the group is either accomplishing its goals or doing the tasks required to maintain the group, as discussed above. A "process mode" indicates that the group is examining the way it does its work. A "combat mode" means that the group is fighting for its survival, health or reputation. Here are some examples:

Work Mode

Firelight: "So, the Community Church has agreed to host the Interfaith Day, and we have seven churches tentatively involved. Any word on the synagogue yet?"

Prydana: "Rabbi Moser is favorable, but he's got to check with some of his people. We should know by Sunday."

Firelight: "Good. We probably have enough information to start writing a news release and designing a flyer. Albion, can you do that?"

Process Mode

Albion: "Well, I guess you've all heard that our High Priestess has to move to Colorado for job reasons. But I'm sure that Sunflower will do a wonderful job when she takes over."

Pinebough: "Uh . . . just a second. Shouldn't we have an election to fill the High Priestess job?"

Albion: "Well, Sunflower has been Maiden of the coven for over a year. I just assumed that she would move up . . . ."

Persephone: "Nothing against Sunflower, but I think we should discuss the possibilities and see if we can come to consensus. We usually work by consensus."

Pinebough: "You can't do elections that way. We should have a secret ballot, majority rules."

Combat Mode

Butterfly: "I just found out that we may not be able to use the Community Center for our Yule sabbat. What's going on?"

Talltree: "It seems that a local fundamentalist group is pressuring the city not to rent space to Witches. This bunch has a big 'spiritual warfare' thing going, and we're the target."

Badger: "Yeah, I hear we've actually been denounced from the pulpit. What do we do?"

Talltree: "I think first we call a Coven Council for tonight. Badger, you're Summoner, will you call everyone? Butterfly, will you find a copy of the city's non-discrimination policies? And I'll call our friend Reverend Cupton, and see what he's heard from the other ministers in town. We may need to mobilize the state Pagan Association to write letters . . . ."

Obviously a coven spending most of its time in work mode is healthier than one which is always processing or fighting. Too much processing may mean that there is a lack of trust in the coven, and some members want everything spelled out in detail so their interests are protected. Too much "combat" may mean that you're out of the closet in an area where you shouldn't be, or need to disengage from a combative personality, or somebody in your group enjoys drama too much. Remember that coven members do have control over the coven's time and energies. On any given day, you can decide not to fight and not to process—by doing something else.

Membership and Boundary Issues

One of the most fundamental issues which any coven must decide is: who are members? This can be structured several ways.

Membership can be free-flowing and undefined. Whoever shows up for a given meeting acts as a member. There is no difference between a member and a visitor. This approach gives enormous freedom to the participants, since they don't make any commitment. However, there are disadvantages. It is difficult to organize anything since you don't know who is interested and active at any given time. Also, it is hard to create any sense of group mind or esprit d' corps: many people want a feeling of belonging, of specialness, even of family, and that doesn't happen if the group has no boundaries.

Membership can be self-defined. That is, you become a member by saying you're a member and perhaps by signing a list. This becomes easier to work with, since you have a finite group. But what if someone chooses to become a member and has very different goals and values from the rest of the group? What if they don't mind working negative magick? What if they're immature, emotionally draining, or a loudmouth? Most covens want some way to screen out people who are disruptive or just on a different wavelength.

Membership may be leader-defined. Perhaps a candidate applies to the High Priestess and High Priest (or a Council of Elders), and they grant or withhold membership. This model assumes that their combined experience and wisdom will enable the leaders to recognize a serious candidate who will fit in with the rest of the coven and who has priest/ess potential. This model is becoming less common as time goes on.

Membership can be group-defined. That is, the whole group of current members sets membership standards and decides who may join. The standards might be pretty basic, as in "Prospective members must be at least eighteen, avow that they are Witches, agree to follow the Wiccan Rede, and not be involved in any criminal activity." Or they could be more complex. In either case, the membership usually reserves the right to disallow anyone on any grounds, specific or not. In a democratic group, the members would all get acquainted with a candidate and then a vote would be taken. In a consensus group, the candidate would be discussed until everyone was in agreement.

Then there are degrees or types of membership. Some covens are divided into an Outer Grove and an Inner Circle (terminology may vary). The Grove members attend sabbats and esbats and take some classes, but are usually barred from the advanced classes and certain rituals. A grove participant must prove themselves to be admitted to the Inner Circle. Of course, this can lead to major problems since the Inner Circle presumably has more status and prestige, and the Outer Grove folks may resent the cliquishness of the system.

Some covens are replacing this with a Coven/Congregation system. Those who want to invest more time and energy and train as priest/esses join the coven. Those who want to be part of a Pagan community and take the occasional class, but don't define themselves as priest/ess candidates, join the congregation. Many activities are joint events, but the coven members have additional classes, rituals, and responsibilities. The chapter on "Congregations and Covens" explores this system in more depth.

Within the coven, there may be gradual degrees of membership. A visitor may attend an open sabbat and begin to get acquainted with the coveners. After a few more visits they decide they would like to study with the group. If the coven agrees, there is a simple ceremony and they are invested as a dedicant (or candidate, or novice—terminology varies). This is a sort of provisional membership: the dedicant has a year and a day (or more) to explore Wicca and get to know the coven members much better. The coven has time to decide whether the dedicant has the necessary qualities to become a Wiccan priest/ess, and whether they want to forge karmic ties by admitting the dedicant to their coven. At the point when the coven agrees to initiate the dedicant, they become a full-fledged member and may begin working toward the higher degrees of initiation.

The Size of the Coven

What size "should" a coven be? Whatever size works for the members. There is an old Craft joke that a Gardnerian coven is "thirteen Witches, evenly divided between males and females" but most covens today do not have thirteen members and don't expect to be balanced between the sexes. The survey done by the Covenant of the Goddess and mentioned earlier showed that the average coven had about seven adult members, and that nearly two-thirds of modern Witches are female.

Let's look at a hypothetical coven of seven members. The first diagram shows lines to represent all the possible relationships between two members. As you can see, even this modestly sized group has twenty one one-on-one relationships, and is therefore a rather complex organism. Of course, all the relationships are not of the same type or intensity. The second diagram shows four different general kinds of relationships: friends, friendly acquaintances, partners, and parents with adult children in the coven. This is a crude breakdown—a coven might also include lovers who are not life partners, aunts and nephews, friendly rivals, or other flavors of relationship. But the diagram at least hints that not only are there twenty-one dyadic relationships, but that every one is unique.

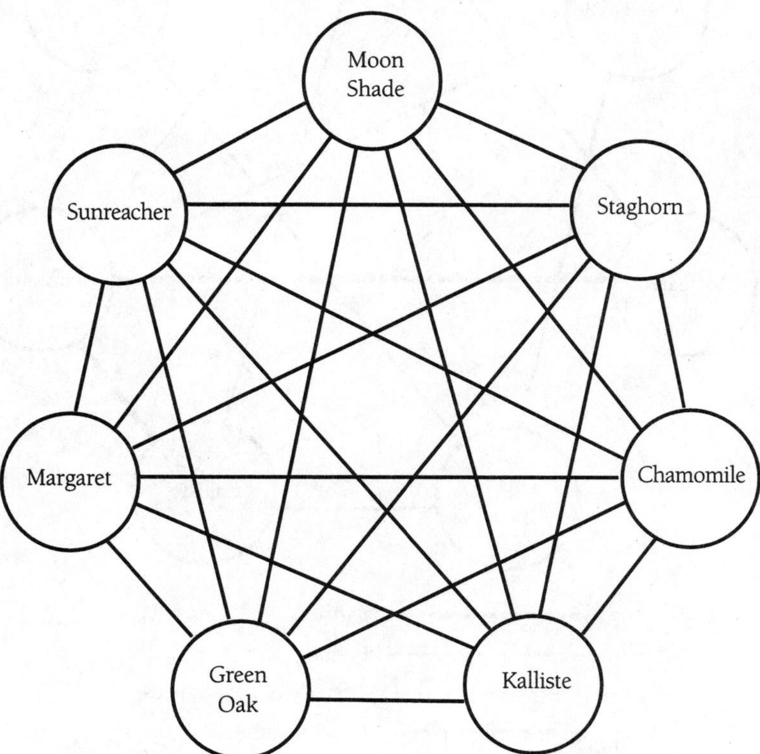

Relationships in a Coven of Seven.

That's a lot for coven leaders to keep track of; and keep track you must, if the coven is to develop into a working magickal team. A single sour relationship can distort the entire coven, and has the potential to destroy it.

Now let's look at a big coven of fourteen, twice the size of our earlier model (and one more than a "full-size traditional" coven of thirteen members). The third diagram shows a surprising fact: it is not just twice as complex as a coven of seven. There are eighty-eight different relationships, making this coven more than four times as complex. And this is still a crude measurement that understates the complexity—we are not even considering the relationships between subgroups, cliques, or factions of three or more.

So it is no wonder that covens average about seven people. More than that gets really complicated and requires very sensitive, skilled, and capable leadership to keep it functioning well.

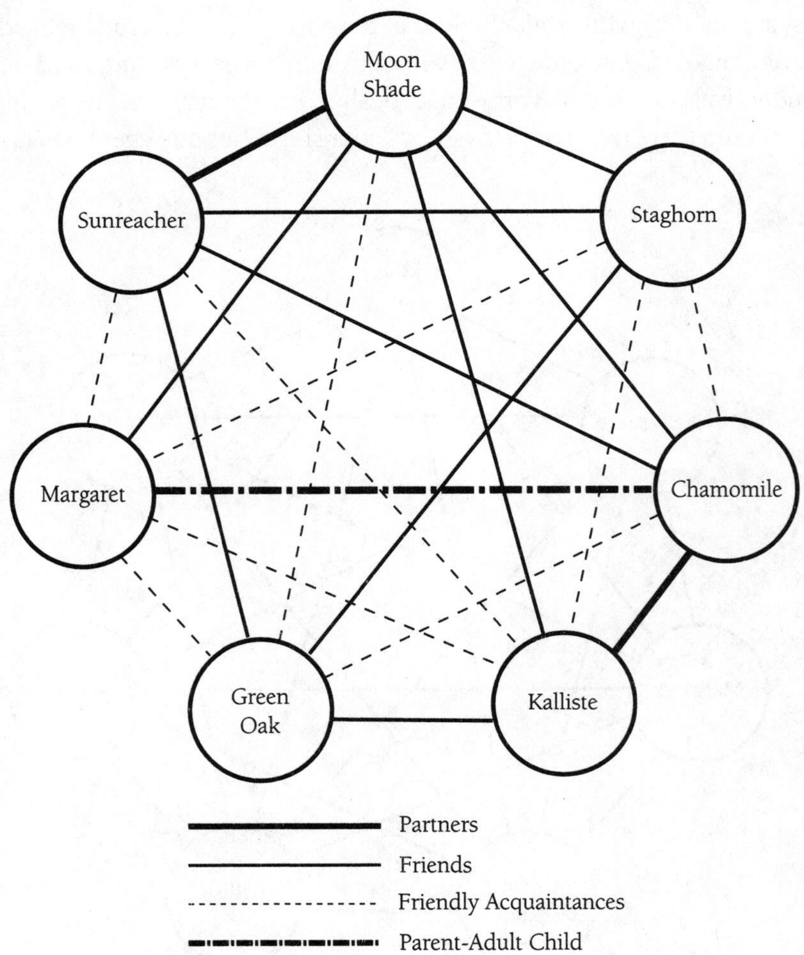

Interpersonal Relationships in a Coven of Seven.

An intriguing sidebar: when Sir Robert Baden-Powell founded the Boy Scouts, he suggested in the leaders' manual that troops should be no larger than thirty-two members. When someone asked why he had chosen that number, Baden-Powell answered in effect that "I have learned by experience that I can work effectively with up to sixteen boys; and I figure someone out there might be twice as capable as I am."

So if your coven is "only" six or seven members, don't be discouraged: there may be someone out there who feels twice as capable as you, but most High Priest/esses are doing well to maintain a coven of seven.

Incidentally, the recommended maximum for a Boy Scout patrol (one part of a troop) is eight. So perhaps the "normal" effective size limit for a primary group is in this range.

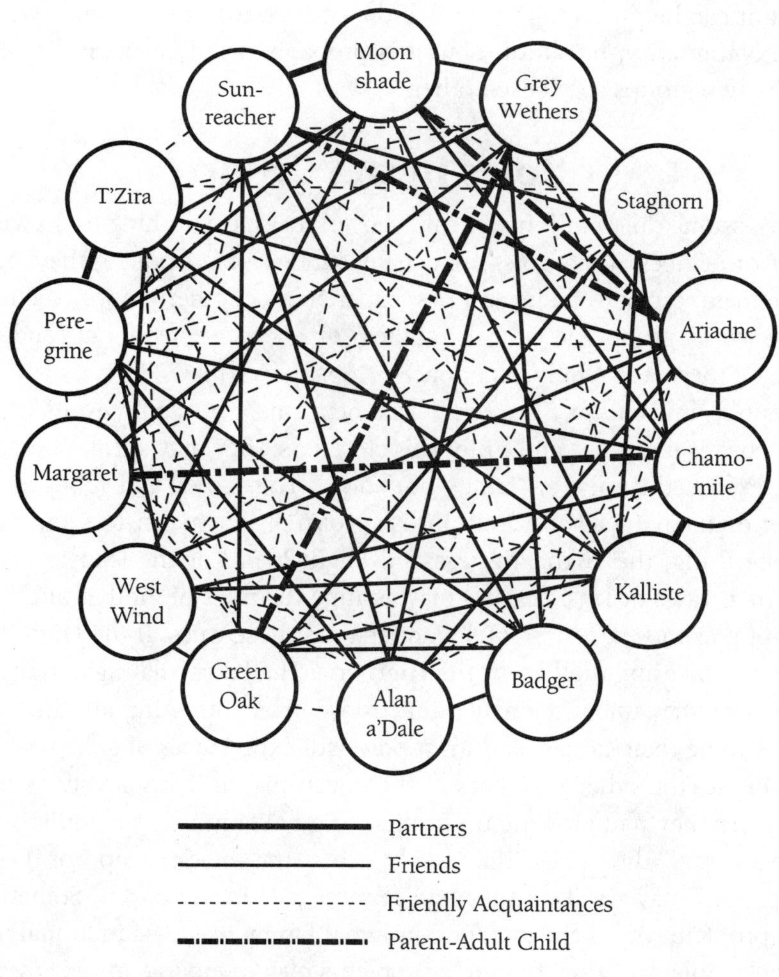

Relationships in a Coven of Fourteen.

Should your coven grow to thirteen members, it is traditional to consider "hiving" or dividing the group. Typically a priest and priestess who have reached second or third degree will strike out on their own with as many members as wish to join them. The old rule was that a new coven should "void the coven" it hived from; that is, have no contact for a year or more, so that it could develop its own identity and establish the authority of the leaders. In a friendly hiving today, however, it is common for the mother coven and hived coven to celebrate sabbats together occasionally, trade teachers, and maintain bonds of friendship. The new leaders may even continue studying for a third degree under the supervision of their old leaders. No one should have dual membership, however; it is very difficult to be a contributing, active member of two busy covens, and schedule conflicts are inevitable. What about an "unfriendly" hiving, when members leave because of disagreements with the old coven leadership? It cannot always be avoided. Perhaps in time a neutral mediator can help heal the rift so that the two covens can cooperate within the Pagan community; but until then, it is probably best that the old rule stand, and the two groups avoid each other.

Roles in the Group

People assume different functions in a coven that have nothing to do with their offices or degrees. These roles are usually subtle and unspoken; they are based on the member's personality and past experiences in other groups, such as their family, work group, previous churches, or social, recreational, and service clubs. Of these, the family experience is most powerful.

It is not unusual for a coven to become a surrogate family to its members. Some covens recognize and foster this closeness: they may speak of themselves as an "extended family" or "family-of-choice." This is well and good, but it goes deeper than having a warm, supportive group of spiritual sisters and brothers. For one thing, the High Priestess and High Priest (or the leaders no matter what their titles or lack thereof) may assume the roles of mother and father to the group as they subconsciously understand those roles. If the High Priestess had a domineering mother, or the High Priest had a vacillating and indecisive father, they may unconsciously mimic those behaviors. After all, their original families were their earliest and most powerful experiences of group behavior.

Likewise, the other members of the coven may unconsciously assume the same roles they had growing up in their original families. A member who was the "good son," the "rebel," the "family jester," the "black sheep," or the "surrogate parent" may wind up playing the same role in the coven. Sometimes it's not a problem. But if the member's original family was dysfunctional, or their particular role was, then the same problems may re-emerge in the coven. Or if there is a mismatch in the roles (a member is unconsciously reenacting their role, but the High Priestess is not responding as their mother did), that can lead to problems.

Similarly, people can come to the coven and use the same behavior that worked (or didn't work) for them at the office, their old church, or in their soccer team. These behaviors are rarely conscious—they're just the way we are used to behaving in groups, and out of habit we do some of the same things in a new setting. And when our behaviors turn out to be inappropriate in a coven, and problems result, people have no clue as to why. It would not occur to most people that their anger against an abusive parent, for example, is getting projected onto the High Priest because he is acting in a "father role."

When unexplained conflicts crop up in the coven they must be worked through, or else someone must leave. In talking about them, you need to deal with the initial catalyst or rationalization, then get past it to the issues underneath. An example:

Daria: "Well, there's obviously some friction between you two, and the High Priestess has asked me to sit down with you and see if we can understand what's happening. Thornbush, how are you feeling?"

Thornbush: "Uncomfortable. Angry, I guess. I don't like it that this is happening, but I really get tired of being asked to do so much more than the other dedicants. And now I'm supposed to do the pool party. I just want Old Oak to ease up on me!"

Old Oak: "I'm sorry if you feel that I've been asking too much. I have come to rely on you a lot. Some of the other dedicants are too new to handle these projects, and Heather and Buck are tied up painting the ritual room. I wish you'd just told me how you felt when I first asked you to organize the pool party."

Daria: "Is it just the pool party, Thornbush?"

Thornbush: "No. It's everything. Sometimes it's like I was back home and my dad would never let up on me—always one more chore to do."

Daria: "Didn't you have brothers and sisters to help?"

Thornbush: "Not really. I mean, Joey and Michelle were too little to do much, and Peter was always tied up with high school activities. I had to do a lot more than my share, and Dad was always on my case."

Daria: "So, does Old Oak remind you of your father? And the other dedicants are like—"

Thornbush: "Like my brothers and sister! But Old Oak's not at all like my dad. Well, a little . . . . I guess maybe I've been reacting as though

> you were, even though you're a very different person. Hmm. I'm going to have to think about this. I still feel swamped by the pool party, though."

And so on. The pool party may have been a real issue, and Mock Coven will have to deal with that. But real or not, that issue tied into a deeper issue: Thornbush felt like he was back in the position of an overworked middle child with a nagging father—and he cast Old Oak, the High Priest, in the father's role. If the discussion had focused only on the pool party, the other issues could never have been discovered or resolved. Thornbush would have gone on feeling resentful of Old Oak—without understanding why—and sooner or later the conflict would have erupted again. Now that Thornbush understands the underlying issue, hopefully he can relate differently to Old Oak and take responsibility for saying "no," one adult to another, when he feels overworked.

Of course, sometimes the issue *is* just the pool party. Don't go fishing for deeper issues unless conflict keeps popping up again and again between the same people, or there are intense emotional reactions that just can't be explained by the surface issue.

Remember that you don't have to solve these tangles alone. You can ask a neutral coven elder with good facilitation skills to lead the discussion. Sometimes you can get a respected elder from another coven to mediate. Sometimes the problem can only be resolved with professional therapy for one or both parties. Sometimes the people involved cannot, or will not, do the work required to solve it, and a parting of the ways is the only answer.

Decision-Making

Every coven has decisions to make, and most of them do it in one of four ways—or some combination of them. The four main methods are authoritarian, oligarchic, democratic, and consensual.

Let's suppose that Mock Coven has a High Priestess who runs the whole show: we'll call her Dominia. Perhaps other coveners are granted some power in their limited spheres, but she is the Ultimate Authority who can approve or disapprove any decision. She may be fairly restrained in her interventions, or she may micromanage to the nth degree ("Birdwing, my dear, rearrange the altar cloth so that it stops an inch short of the carpet, not touching it"). This system does have the advantage of clarity and simplicity. If the leader is fairly sensitive and intelligent, it may work well for a while, especially in a group where all are new to the Craft. The difficulty is that as members become more confident and empowered, they tend to resent the control and question the leadership. In time, if they are not allowed to share responsibility and authority, they will either begin a power struggle or leave the coven. The submissive or dependent personalities won't leave; but if Dominia survives the challenges to her authority, Mock Coven will end up filled with wimps.

An oligarchic system vests power in a small group of people, perhaps a Council of Elders. This approach can work if there are fair, objective qualifications for joining the council, and if council members are good communicators who care about the needs and wishes of the other members. Unfortunately, it can also turn into the worst of all possible systems, where a clique vies for control among themselves, uniting only to keep the "peasants" in their place.

Democracy is what we are used to. To be more precise, a democratic republic is one in which the citizens elect their decision-makers. In a large population, such as a nation-state, this may be the most workable balance between tyranny and chaos, but it does have drawbacks. We have all heard the phrase "the tyranny of the majority." Sometimes the majority can neglect the legitimate needs of the minority, or even actively persecute them. In the United States and many other countries, there is a Bill of Rights to protect individuals and minorities, but in smaller majority-rule groups, such a document may not exist.

In a coven that works democratically, the whole membership usually acts as a Coven Council. Decisions are made by majority vote after discussion, often using Robert's Rules of Order. Jade points out that "The basic purpose of Robert's Rules of Order is to allow people who don't agree to conduct business without killing one another." The problem is that there is no mechanism for making sure that the minority's needs are met. There is a tendency in all majority-rule systems to say "We've got 51 percent of the vote, that settles it." It is a lazy approach to decision-making, a shortcut that means you can avoid the hard work of finding a solution that fits everyone's needs. Decisions can be made fairly quickly and easily, but they are not always the best decisions possible. Group cohesion suffers because some members may feel that they were not heard, respected, or cared about.

This brings us to consensus decision-making. Here, the whole membership is the council and discussion continues until a decision is reached that *everyone* can accept. Not everyone has to love the decision, but everyone must be able to say "I can live with that."

Consensus has three advantages: it fosters mutual respect, community, and the "group mind" so important to magick; it avoids having an unhappy minority of "losers"; and it forces the group to be more creative in their decisions and solutions. When it's done right, everybody wins. The disadvantages are that it is harder work and more time-consuming.

Here is how it works. First, a specific proposal is stated. Then people bring up questions, concerns, or problems. The proposal can be amended at any time if everyone agrees. After further discussion, the chair can ask if there is consensus. If it's clear there is not, then discussion may continue, or the proposal can be referred to a committee for further research and refinement. If everyone agrees with the proposal (or most agree and a few abstain), you are done.

When the chair asks if there is consensus, individual members have three choices. They can consent, which means they support the proposal and are willing to help implement it. They can abstain or "stand aside," which means they don't particularly support it, but won't stop the rest of the group from proceeding with it. Or they can "block," which effectively kills the proposal unless someone (preferably the blocker) later can come up with a change that will satisfy them as well as the rest of the group. A block should only be used in extreme circumstances, and if the same individual repeatedly blocks otherwise well-supported proposals, then your coven may not be the best place for them.

Let's listen to the Mock Coven as they use the consensus method:

Puma: "Well, it's my turn to chair the Coven Council. Shall we get started? First item on the agenda is to choose a location for the coven retreat."

Milkweed: "I propose that we hold it at the Golden Cedar Resort. I checked prices, and it would cost about $230 apiece for the weekend."

Riverrun: "I love that place! They've got canoeing and tennis and really great food—like, you know, those fried cattail things. Let's do it."

Galaxy: "Uh . . . that's awfully expensive. Isn't there someplace less pricey?"

(Discussion continues for a while.)

Puma: "Can we take a straw poll here? How many in favor of Golden Cedar? Opposed? That's seven for and one against. Any suggestions?"

Galaxy: "Well, I think it's awfully expensive, but I won't block it. Maybe I can come up with the money."

Osiris: "I think we need to find an answer that Galaxy can be happier with. What if we go to Scraggly Pines Lodge instead? They're cheaper."

(Chorus of moans.)

Riverrun: "No way, man. Last time I was there I found a spider in my oatmeal, and wild marmots got into my luggage and chewed up my Adidas."

Foxwomon: "How about this? Most of us have good jobs and can afford Golden Cedar, and we all know it's nice. What if we just offer a stipend or "scholarship" to Galaxy, out of the coven treasury?"

Galaxy: "I'm not comfortable with that—too much like charity."

Milkweed: "Better still, let's pool our funds and make it a sliding scale for each member. If you can handle $230, that's what you give. If you can afford less, put in less. If you can afford more, then give more.

After we've all contributed what we can, we add it up. If we're short, we cover it out of the treasury."

Puma: "I like it. All in favor? Looks like we have consensus. Next item is the Community Pumpkin Roll scheduled for September . . . ."

The Mock Coven could have decided to operate by majority rule, and simply overridden Galaxy's objections early in the discussion. As a result, Galaxy might have missed the retreat, or paid more than her budget could easily handle and shown up feeling stressed and resentful. By choosing to seek consensus, everyone's needs were met. (Of course, this could result in a drain on the treasury and might not work on a continuing basis; but that's a future decision.)

No system has to be "purely" one thing or the other. A group may use different decision-making processes for different kinds of business. A coven could choose to give the High Priestess final authority in matters of ritual and magick, for example, if she were the only member experienced in these areas, but they might operate by consensus when it comes to social events, service projects, and coven finances. Or they might decide that new programs and policy changes require consensus, whereas a majority vote is sufficient to elect officers or set the budget. In this way, the essential business necessary for the survival of the coven cannot be blocked by one person; but policy or program changes will have the support of the whole group if enacted.

Another option is to work by consensus but have a "fail-safe system." In case of deadlock, the High Priest and High Priestess confer and decide, or the High Priestess decides alone.

Constellation Exercise

This exercise is designed to create a model of your coven and help members think about their relationships to other coveners. It is probably best done by individuals for their own education; sharing this exercise as a group could cause some hurt feelings.

Imagine your coven as a constellation of stars. Draw the constellation on a large sheet of paper, with a star to represent each coven member. Place each star nearer or distant from each other star according to the closeness of the relationship; partners would be very close, mere acquaintances quite distant from each other.

You will soon discover that it is easier to adjust relationships if the stars are moveable. Cut them out of colored paper, write a covener's name on each, and move them around. Then you may discover that it's difficult to make an accurate model in two dimensions; if you want to, you can make a three-dimensional model with balls of clay or styrofoam to represent the coven members, attached by lengths of stiff wire or slender dowel rods. Ideally every "star" should be in an accurate relationship, by distance, from every other.

Doing this exercise may surprise you, and will certainly make you think about coven relationships. Hopefully it will motivate you to strengthen your relationships with the more distant "stars." If you are a coven leader, you may want to create opportunities for the least-acquainted members to work together on projects, classes, or rituals. Thus the stars of your coven "constellation" become ever closer.

Scenarios for Discussion

These can be discussed or role-played with your coven. You can switch viewpoints and ask, "How would you handle this if you were a new Dedicant? If you were a coven Elder? If you were the High Priest/ess?" Every time you come up with a solution, think about the potential impact on the coven and the Craft. Have each covener write out their response, then discuss them as a group. Later you can compare your proposed resolution with the author's commentary provided.

A. A newcomer to town has contacted Cauldron Coven and wants to join. After meeting her a couple of times, all but one of the coveners like Ravenfeather and are inclined to offer her membership. But Cactus says, "I don't know exactly why, but I'm just not comfortable around her." What do you do?

B. Morning and Hawkwing are partners, and both are members of Coven Solstice. Their relationship seems to be very strained just now—they scarcely talk to each other at coven meetings, and sometimes only one or the other will come. When a covener gently brings up the subject, one of them replies shortly, "That's really our business, isn't it?" What do you do?

C. Your group, Pie-in-the-Sky Coven, seems happy enough, but is very loose when it comes to programs and schedules. Activities often aren't planned out in advance, people often show up late, and not a lot seems to get done. What do you do, if anything?

D. A local group, Fundamentalists for Religious Domination, has decided to launch a crusade against Paganism. Your coven has been attacked from the pulpit and in the press, one of your meetings was picketed by some very nasty and vocal folks, and there are rumors that the FRD is attempting to get a list of coven members and contact your employers. Some coveners are getting nervous and fearful, and there is dissension in the group as to how to handle the situation. What should you do?

E. Your group, the Puppy-Pile Coven, has been together for a long time, and members are very warm and affectionate toward one another. (It includes both couples and singles, as well as two people whose partners are not members.) One night you are all basking in the warm afterglow of a ritual, when one member says, "Hey, I've got a great idea! Let's rent Pinewood Cabin for the weekend and all explore our sexuality together. After all, we're adults, and we all love each other." How do you respond?

F. The Pond-of-Pine-Needles Coven has been doing fairly well since it was organized two years ago, but now one of the members, Redhawk, complains that "Regalia (the High Priestess) is getting kind of bossy. She thinks she knows it all and doesn't let the rest of us have any say." Some members point out that everyone has a chance to be heard in the planning meetings, but others wonder if Redhawk is right. Is Regalia just self-assured or maybe a little arrogant? Does she really take the opinions of the coveners seriously? What do you do?

G. One of the members of Panpipes Coven, Faunus, is a great guy but tends to drink a lot and ramble at coven meetings. His endless jokes and stories are entertaining, and occasionally he gets serious about coven business, but usually it's hard to plan or decide anything when he's around. When this is mentioned delicately, he replies that "Paganism is all about celebration! We're a joyous religion! 'Acts of love and pleasure!' Don't always be so serious!" What should the coven do?

H. Convolutia is a very dedicated and hard-working candidate, but clearly has some emotional difficulties. She is usually tense and anxious, and needs a great deal of attention and reassurance. Frequently coven meetings turn into long discussions of her problems and fears. She doesn't consciously try to always be the focus, but more time is spent on her concerns than those of any other four coveners. A couple of the members are getting impatient, but don't want to be unkind. What do you do?

I. Kingfisher seems always to be at the center of a controversy. Sometimes he's crusading against his employer, the local media, or the city government because he feels they discriminate against Pagans. Sometimes he is at odds with other covens or Pagan groups because of real or imagined slights. If no other battle is handy, he is on the Internet arguing, or bringing complaints against other members of his own coven. Frequently his original issue seems valid, but some feel his attitude is provocative and confrontational, and that he is addicted to drama and controversy. What do you do?

J. Deepwoods comes to your coven after two years in another coven of a different tradition, in another state. Although he is generally courteous and personable, he soon begins hinting that he doesn't like your coven's methods. His conversation is often loaded with references to "the way we did this back in . . .," and a couple of times he has told new students about "a better way" to do something, which happens to be at odds with your coven's tradition. Some of the dedicants are confused, and some of the elders are starting to get irritated with his attitude. What do you do?

K. Thoth studied on his own for three years before coming to Coven Greyfeather. He is placed in a class with three other new dedicants, all younger than him, but soon begins complaining that he "doesn't need all this basic stuff; after all, he did a lot of reading before he came here." His mentor replies that book knowledge is good, but not a substitute for practice in a group. Thoth counters that he could teach the classes blindfolded; the mentor retorts that Thoth's knowledge is all theoretical and that he "wouldn't know a Cone of Power if it bit him on the butt." You enter at this point. What do you do?

L. Greenleaf got involved in a Pagan study group at college and has been active in two covens (where he earned a first and second degree) before he moved to your city. At this point, he is twenty-five years old but has more experience in the Craft than some newer members in their forties. After a couple of months in your coven he begins hinting that he is ready for his third degree. Discussing it with the elders, you find that some think he's just too young. One says, "He's smart all right, and I'm glad he's with us, but people expect a third degree priest to have some maturity and wisdom. He should be patient for a few years." What do you do?

M. Jack-o-Lantern is a very likable, cheerful person, and is quickly welcomed into Coven Lumina. About a month after his Dedication ceremony he is at a summer festival with several coveners, when he invites you all to share some marijuana with him. You are aware that the festival rules forbid illegal drugs on site, but when you point this out to Jack, he replies, "Hey, I purposely set up my tent behind these trees; nobody can see us." What do you do?

N. Shadowlight is a workaholic. Because she enthusiastically volunteers for every coven project and does them well, it is easy to say "OK" when she volunteers for the next. But one day an elder of the coven draws you aside and points out two disturbing facts: some of the other coven members aren't taking any responsibility for the coven work; and if Shadowlight's energies became unavailable for any reason, half the coven's program would fall apart. What do you do?

O. Rubella comes to Morningmist Coven full of excitement, and is well liked by other members. However, she misses the third dedicants' class due to illness, and two weeks later isn't feeling well enough to attend the Full Moon esbat. From that point on her participation is very erratic; she will attend four or five events in a row, then be sick for a month. She seems to be vulnerable to a variety of illnesses and numerous visits to doctors and healers don't seem to help for long. She insists her commitment is as strong as ever, but you never know when you'll see her. What do you do?

P. Walden wants to help. He volunteers to chair the fundraising project for Hidden Glade Coven, and offers to take on the office of Bard, and promises to write an article on mead-making for the coven newsletter. Unfortunately, he rarely fulfills his promises. His constant refrain is, "Oh yeah, I've got to get to that," or "Gee, I'm sorry, it slipped my mind," or "Next week I'll take care of that for sure." He seems sincere in his desire to serve, and genuinely regretful when he can't deliver, but it's driving the coven crazy. What do you do?

Q. Rosetta Stone is the High Priestess of Small Unidentified Pond Creatures Coven. She is very capable and efficient, and somewhat lacking in trust that anyone else can do a project as well as she can. As a result she tries to do it all herself, rationalizing that "It'll be quicker and easier to do it myself than to try to explain it all to someone else, and besides they all have such busy lives." The coven jobs all get done, but clearly Rosetta is stressed and overworked and some of the other members' skills are underutilized. What do you do?

R. About a month after Numenides comes to Grassroots Coven, while you are all discussing an interfaith conference, he objects to working with a certain church in town. "They have a history of oppression and genocide against our people!" he cries. "We should be attacking them, not cooperating on a conference! Remember the Burning Times!" Grassroots has made a beginning toward being accepted as a valid religion by local clergy, and some coveners feel that Numenides' attitude could jeopardize that progress. Others seem to be wondering if he is right. What do you do?

Author's Commentary

It is not claimed that these comments represent Ultimate Wisdom, or that they are the right solutions for every coven. However, they may give you another perspective and promote fruitful discussion.

A. (New Member) Many covens require consensus in order to admit a new member. If any present member is uncomfortable, the new prospect is not admitted. However, before a final decision is made, Cactus should be encouraged to examine his feelings and get to know the candidate better.

   If your coven operates by majority rule, or if new members are admitted by decision of a Council of Elders, then Ravenfeather can be admitted. However, you would still be wise to consider Cactus' feelings carefully, and make sure he feels heard.

In either case, if you have a year-and-a-day rule before initiation, the decision is not irrevocable. If Cactus' concerns are well founded, the reasons will probably appear before Ravenfeather is initiated into full membership.

B. (Partners at Odds) For covens to be at their best magickally, they must develop close emotional and psychic bonds. Once this happens, tension between any two members will affect everyone. The High Priestess and High Priest, or Elders delegated by them, should talk to Morning and Hawkwing and discover what the problem is. Then they can be given support in resolving it or referred to resources such as a family counselor.

   If the tension is affecting the coven badly, then the couple can be offered a sabbatical from coven activities, to give them time and space to work through the situation. If this becomes necessary, make sure that individual members stay in touch with each partner, so they do not feel isolated or rejected.

C. (Unorganized Program) If your coven's priority is informal socializing and occasional celebration of esbats or sabbats, then this kind of non-structure may be all right. If you have other goals such as priest/ess training, environmental activism, sponsoring open sabbats, public education and so on, then it's necessary to get more organized. It's more work, but it pays off in better programs, more people getting more deeply involved, and less frustration for the Virgos in your group.

   If you have been operating very loosely for a while, there will be resistance to change. You can either proceed gradually and watch the congenitally unorganized fade away one at a time, or you can hive off with the most energetic and efficient members and start from scratch.

   Start with a calendar of events printed in advance, with the responsibility for each activity assigned to a team of members. Choose officers and make sure they know their duties. If necessary, publicize your existence and bring in new blood, then immediately put them to work according to their talents.

   Our coven has been called "the most organized coven in North America." I don't know if that's true, but it is well-organized and it's been worth the effort.

D. (Fundie Attack) There are two basic strategies your coven can follow when the fundamentalists hit the warpath. One is to fade away underground and become a "hidden path" again. Without visible targets, the fundies' energy will dissipate in time. The other is to take a very open, bold posture, claim your rights to religious freedom, and tell the public the truth about Witchcraft. This requires at least some coveners who are willing to be open as Witches; and it requires a lot of liaison work with the media, public officials, school administrators, law enforcement agencies, and local religious bodies.

This open strategy may not work in every region and community—you know your territory best. For my coven, it worked: most of the fundies shut up, and now we have public sabbats and full moon esbats, a weekly space in the "Church News" of the local paper, and a fairly high level of public awareness about Wicca.

Not recommended: having your coven half-in and half-out of the broom closet. Either get very quiet or very loud, but know that whispers will be misheard every time.

E. (Group Sexuality) Group sex, open relationships, polyamory, mate-swapping and such alternatives are very, very tricky emotionally. Whether this is inherent to the human animal or a result of our culture and socialization, I don't know. But any coven that encourages these practices, especially as part of the coven "program," is taking a huge risk on two levels. First, the emotional fallout may damage or destroy the coven. Second, if news leaks out to the cowan community, it provides fuel for attacks on the Craft. No matter how loving or serious the experiment may be, it can be touted as an example of Pagan "licentiousness."

The better part of wisdom: encourage members to actively celebrate their sexuality outside the context of coven activities.

F. (Complaint About Bossy High Priestess) Sometimes a complaint about the coven leaders comes from an immature member who cannot handle any kind of authority. Sometimes it is a natural reaction from a growing, empowered Witch who is ready to take more responsibility and hasn't had the chance. Sometimes the coven leaders really are domineering, authoritarian egomaniacs who should retire.

There are two questions to ask. First, does most of the coven agree with the complainant? "The wisdom of the community" sometimes fails, but if several people share the same opinion, it is at least worth exploring further. Second, is there any chance that a leader is being "scapegoated" for other problems within the coven? If a leader hears out the complaint and makes a serious and open-hearted attempt to address it, but the coven is still dissatisfied, there may be other deeper problems that are not being addressed.

The complainant should first take the issue directly to the leader with whom they have a problem. If they cannot reach an understanding, then they should call in a third party to facilitate or mediate. As a last resort, you may eventually have to discuss the situation as a group. This usually doesn't work; it takes an extremely skilled facilitator and a very mature group to work through such problems in a group context.

G. (Drinking and Rambling) Few Pagans object to partying, story-telling, and drinking (at least in moderation), *but* there's a time and a place. Classes, business meetings, and most parts of ritual aren't it. If Faunus can't confine his play time to the social hour afterward, sabbat celebrations, or parties, he should be disinvited from programs where serious work is happening. Wiccan priest/esses can become "Party Pagans" when the time is right, but we also have work to do. Perhaps your elders need to ask Faunus whether he really wants to take on the responsibilities of a Wiccan priest, or whether membership in the congregation would better suit his needs.

H. (Focus on One Covener) What is the purpose of a Witches' coven? It is not to provide therapy for one individual but opportunities for spiritual growth and celebration to several (or many). Every member of the coven needs occasional emotional support from their sisters and brothers, and that is expected and necessary. But if one person comes to dominate the attention of the group, you cannot achieve the coven's first priorities. Convolutia should take a leave of absence from the coven while she gets professional counseling. In the meantime, she can attend open events and socialize privately with coveners, but she should not attempt to continue regular priestess training until she can demand less energy from the group and contribute more.

I. (Confrontational Crusader) There are times when confrontation is necessary, either with those who would persecute us, or with Pagans who forget the Wiccan Rede. However, confrontation as a way of life is extremely destructive to a coven. Someone who constantly needs an enemy and a battle is wrestling with inner demons at the expense of everyone.

   If their anger is directed at an appropriate target, such as an oppressive right-wing religious group, such personalities may be welcomed at first. But what happens when the external target fades, or gives up, and the crusader turns their wrath against targets in the Pagan community or even within the coven?

   If you are coping with a person addicted to battle, you may have to either help them become conscious of the pattern and seek counseling, or disengage by asking them to leave the coven and refusing further contact. This will make you the new target, of course, but there may be no other option; and if you don't respond to the attacks, they may eventually go seek a more satisfying adversary.

J. (Not the Way We Did It) This might be solved simply by a candid conversation with the High Priestess or High Priest. Explain that you welcome occasional new ideas and different ways of doing things, as long as the coven's traditions are respected. Tell Deepwoods when it would be appropriate to bring up new approaches or share his former coven's traditions. Make sure he understands how confusing it is for students to hear two different ways of casting a circle when they are so new to the Craft; and be firm that you want them to learn this coven's methods well before they are too much exposed to a different system.

Make sure that Deepwoods is actively involved in planning and carrying out the coven program. If he is idle and bored, he will be more likely idealize his old coven and disrespect his current one.

K. (Don't Need This Basic Stuff) It is not strange if an older candidate who has studied a good deal on his own feels out of place working with younger and less well-read students. However, reading books on the Craft cannot provide the same experience as working in a group. Thoth should be advised to look for opportunities to put his book learning into practice with the other students and, perhaps, to share his academic knowledge with them. However, if he has an overblown estimate of his own skill and wants to skip the "practicum" part of a Witch's education, then he may not be an appropriate candidate for the Wiccan priesthood. A question to ask: is he willing to focus on the positive, joyous aspects of (finally) doing the Craft instead of reading about it? Or does he want to focus on the notion that he is somehow being underappreciated and "held back"? A negative focus and undue impatience are not good omens for his future in the Craft; and in the final analysis, the coven has the right to say, "This is our program, the best we can offer. If it is not what you want, you are free to leave."

L. (Young Third Degree Aspirant) There are no easy answers in this situation, but much depends on your coven's requirements for the third degree. If you have specific requirements (books read, knowledge gained, skills demonstrated) and the candidate has met them, then it is difficult to justify withholding the degree on account of age or the nebulous quality called "maturity." If your degree requirements are fuzzy and subjective—"The candidate is ready when the elders think he is"—then you can withhold the degree, but you're going to engender resentment among the coveners. After all, it is hard to earn a degree if you don't know what the requirements are.

Many covens have a combination of objective and subjective requirements: you must read the books, show the skills, and so forth, but the initiates, elders, High Priestess, and High Priest must still rule on the intangibles: a sense of ethics, a level of wisdom, a connection with the spirit of the Craft. If a candidate fails the intangibles, the Elders can try to come up with a program of learning experiences that will engender these qualities. Inevitably, some candidates will never "seem" like third-degree priest/esses, despite their best efforts and yours. In such a case, do not compromise your standards. They will do what they must, even if it is to leave and seek further advancement in another coven.

M. (Marijuana at Festival) Some people have no ethical qualms about breaking the drug laws and see no health hazard in certain drugs. These are decisions that individuals must make for themselves when they are acting in isolation.

However, when drug usage affects unwilling others, it is a different story. By coming to the festival, Jack has implied his willingness to follow the festival rules. If he violates them, he breaks trust with the festival sponsors and organizers. The Pagan community needs trust in order to survive, and that trust should never be broken lightly. Further, if it becomes known that illegal drugs were used at the event, it could lead to raids by law enforcement agencies, and/or a public perception that Pagans are "druggies" and "outlaws."

The old Laws say that no Witch may endanger the community by his or her actions. To do so for the momentary pleasures of a drug high is irresponsible and selfish. Jack's covenmates should discuss these issues with him, and should not tolerate illegal activity at the festival or at coven events.

N. (Workaholic Volunteer) Shadowlight needs some counsel from the High Priestess, High Priest, or a respected elder. First, because it is possible that she is neglecting other responsibilities (and pleasures) such as her family and/or career, if her life has begun to center completely on coven work. Second, because every coven project or office is a growth opportunity and a responsibility, if she does a great deal more than her share and the other members are doing less than theirs, the energy flow is unbalanced. Third, a coven that is too dependent on one individual is a weak coven and could collapse at any time.

In a kind way, and with much appreciation of her hard work, she needs to be counseled to rechannel some of her energies. Part of her efforts could go toward training others to do some of the work she has been doing.

O. (Recurring Illnesses) If a member's participation is erratic due to poor health, he or she should be encouraged to take a sabbatical from priest/ess training in order to focus their energies on getting well. Individual coven members can certainly keep in touch socially, and Rubella should be invited to attend open sabbats and esbats when she feels up to it, but she should act as a member of the congregation or outer grove until her health is restored.

It is probably best to set a clear length for the leave of absence from classes, perhaps three to six months. At the end of that time, the coven can review the situation and decide whether Rubella should reactivate.

If the member has a serious, chronic illness which is probably not going to go away, they the situation is different. In this case the coven can tailor priest/ess duties and responsibilities to the individual's capabilities.

P. (Volunteer Who Doesn't Deliver) You can start by refusing Walden's new offers of help until he fulfills some of his old promises. When he volunteers again, just say: "Thanks for offering, but I know you've got that fundraising project, and your Bard duties and so on. Bluebell, could you handle this activity?" Then one of the coven leaders needs to talk to Walden, pointing out in detail exactly what he has promised to do and did not complete. The approach should be matter-of-fact, not angry or accusing. The focus should be on finding ways that Walden can fulfill his commitments and learn not to undertake new ones unless he is sure he can handle them. He may require either some pastoral counseling by a coven elder or professional counseling from outside. Bottom line: his behavior is irresponsible, and must change if he is to be a priest of the Craft and member of the coven.

Q. (Control Freak Priestess) Doubtless Rosetta is very skilled and effective, but she needs to understand that in the long run she is not helping the coven or herself by hoarding the work. The coveners cannot grow without responsibility; they must share the work and if necessary be taught how to do it. Rosetta is headed for burnout if she keeps trying to do it all; and in making herself indispensable, she is risking the coven's very existence if she becomes unavailable for any reason. It is time for gentle but very firm guidance from the other coven elders; when they see her taking on too much they must redirect the work to other willing hands, and privately explain why.

R. (Won't Work With Other Church) Numenides' feelings are understandable, particularly if he has had a bad experience with the church in this life or former incarnations. However, attacking the local branch of that church for something done years ago by another one is poor survival strategy. If we perpetuate old enmities with an immensely larger and more powerful organization, we will be the losers. Better to forgive as best we can—without ever forgetting the Burning Times—and give the present members of that church an opportunity to start fresh in an atmosphere of mutual tolerance. Build bridges to individual members rather than treating the church as a faceless monolith.

If the present-day church members choose to renew the oppression, then let it be on their karma. We have recourse through legal channels, public education, and recruiting allies among the more liberal religions. And, if necessary, we can become hidden once again. But let it not be said that we renewed the hostilities; and if there is any chance of creating an accepting world where the Craft can flourish in the sunlight, let us seize it.

A note to readers: Have you encountered problems that are not covered here? If you would like to share them, along with your solutions and how they worked (or didn't work), write to me in care of the publisher. Possibly I can include them, suitably disguised to protect confidentiality, in future editions of this book. Please don't include actual names.

RESOURCES

Starhawk, *Dreaming the Dark: Magic, Sex and Politics.* Boston: Beacon, 1988.

Starhawk, *Truth or Dare: Encounters With Power, Authority & Mystery*

Dorcas and Ellyntari, "Amazing Grace's Guide to Consensus Process," Web of Oz, 1997.

19 Communications, Cooperation, Conflict

Groups work best when there is a shared sense of purpose, ground rules that everyone agrees on, clear and direct communication, and trust. Some examples:

Issues Around a Shared Sense of Purpose

Conflict

Nightsky: "I want to suggest that we take action as a group to help preserve threatened species of wildlife in our area. We're Pagans; we should be involved in stuff like that."

Tristan: "We can do those kinds of things in other organizations —Sierra Club, Audubon Society . . . personally I would rather be learning more ceremonial magick here."

Tigereye: "Wait a second, I joined this coven to celebrate the moons and sabbats. We're a nature religion; shamanic work is one thing, but what's this about ceremonial magick? That's not the point of this coven."

Nightsky: "What *is* the point of this coven? Personally, I think—"

Cooperation

Stoneoak: "You know, our coven charter says that one of our purposes is to 'protect and heal the Earth,' but we really haven't done anything directly on that in the past few months. Anyone have ideas?"

Primrose: "I'm glad you brought that up. That's one of the reasons I joined, and I've been feeling bad because we don't do more. How about we survey sources of water pollution in our water conservation district? I'm sure the state environmental agencies have some data to get us started."

Water Lily: "That's great, but isn't that a pretty big job for one coven? Maybe we should start with, like, a litter cleanup project. Or wait, what if we did the watershed thing with a couple of other covens?"

Issues of Ground Rules Everyone Agrees On

Conflict

Treebark: "Well, that's a majority in favor of an open Beltane celebration."

Moss: "Hold it, a majority doesn't mean anything. Don't we operate by consensus? We've never taken a vote before."

Treebark: "We haven't disagreed on anything before. This is only our third meeting. Anyway, where I grew up, we had something called democracy, which means majority rule . . . ."

Cooperation

Moonchild: "Most of the group seems to want an open Beltane, but Dormouse, you don't look so sure."

Dormouse: "Well, you do what you want, but I can't come if it's open. If I'm recognized at a public sabbat I could lose my job."

Moonchild: "Our bylaws say we operate by consensus. Let's see if we can find an answer that everybody can live with. What if we had an open sabbat that Saturday, then a private coven celebration on the actual date of Beltane so Dormouse could come . . . ."

Issues of Clear and Direct Communication

Conflict

Mountainsky: "You know, Muskrat, there are people in the coven who think you never listen to anybody's feelings but your own."

Muskrat: "I do too! Besides, what people? Are they afraid to speak up for themselves?"

Mountainsky: "I'd rather not say who; I don't want to betray any confidences. But it's a big issue, and we could lose some folks if you don't clean up your act."

Muskrat: "I work my butt off for this coven, and this is the thanks I get?"

Cooperation

Broomhandle: "That Muskrat! He never listens to anybody's feelings, just does things any way he wants to!"

Artemisia: "I'm not sure exactly what you mean. Can you give me an example where he didn't seem to pay attention to your feelings?"

Broomhandle: "Well, yes! Last week I suggested that we schedule the tarot classes for September, after I get back from my trip. Then tonight he announced that the classes would start in August! He just doesn't care."

Artemisia: "Perhaps. Or maybe there was some reason why he couldn't teach in September, and he forgot to talk it over with you. I think it's important that you tell him you're upset, and find out why he made that decision. He's downstairs; how about we go ask him right now?"

Issues of Trust

Conflict

Mugwort: "So tell me, Leaf, what did you think of Sunhawk's workshop on ritual skills?"

Leaf: "I could have done without the snide comments and veiled criticism."

Mugwort: "Uh... maybe I missed something. Did Sunhawk say something critical about you?"

Leaf: "You know, those cracks about people getting loud and flamboyant in rituals. I'm sure he meant me, at the esbat I led last week!"

Cooperation

Bearcat: "Wish I knew where Glowworm is. She promised to help me with this class and it's past time to start."

Ivory: "I wonder if she just blew it off and decided she'd rather go to the harp concert at the auditorium."

Bearcat: "I doubt that. If she doesn't make it, there's probably a good reason, and I can always call her and clear it up tomorrow. Hope she's OK, though."

Some Ways NOT to Communicate

The Mysterious "They"

There may be no more scary and frustrating form of criticism than the anonymous complaint delivered secondhand: "People are upset with you, but I can't tell you who . . . ." Coven members have a responsibility to their covenmates to communicate their own issues directly. Conversely, coven members have an obligation *not* to relay the criticisms of others, but to encourage the one voicing the complaint to take it directly to the person involved. (In the case of a new student facing a coven leader, it may be necessary for another coven elder to be present and supportive.)

Direct communication is part of assuming responsibility for one's own action. Done with courtesy and respect, it leads to honesty and trust in the coven. Backbiting promotes distrust and disharmony. Also, direct communication is likely to be more clear: any message delivered secondhand is likely to be distorted or at least have important nuances left out. You may remember the children's game "Telephone," where a message is whispered around a circle: the final result bears little resemblance to the original!

Sometimes what is apparently secondhand criticism is not secondhand at all: it is a way for a person to avoid taking responsibility for their own feelings by imputing them to unnamed third parties. "Well, a lot of people are upset with the way you handled that" may be translated as "I am upset with the way you handled that." The speaker may be afraid that his or her opinion won't have as much effect as if an unnamed "lot of people" have the same issue. In any case, every covener must be encouraged to take responsibility and speak for herself or himself.

Nastygrams

Occasionally a covener may decide that the best way to express negative opinions is to write a letter; and before you know it, written attacks are flying back and forth and everyone is becoming more and more alienated.

Critical letters have some inherent limitations as a communications medium. First, they lack the visual, auditory, and psychic nuances of face-to-face communications. "You are an idiot," said affectionately and with a smile and nudge, is very different from "You are an idiot" in black-and-white without any cues. When it's written, it's up to the reader to guess *how* it was meant, which is more important than what was actually said.

Second, many people are simply not very good writers. Something that seemed crystal clear in the mind of the author can seem vague or contradictory to the reader. And a word that has very little emotional import for the author might just "push all the buttons" of the reader.

Third, written letters are moments frozen in time, rather than part of a rapid, free-flowing process. In a face-to-face process, the participants can correct misunderstandings, ask questions, do synergistic brainstorming, and arrive at a solution much more rapidly and effectively. It is the difference between journeying down a river together in a canoe, versus standing on opposite banks and throwing ice cubes back and forth.

Of course, a person who is shy or less than articulate verbally may not have an easy time of it in an intense conversation. In such a case, a mediator may be important to make sure that both parties get their message across. This should preferably be a respected elder with good listening skills and the capacity to be objective.

"I Statements" vs. "You Statements"

Speaking *for* ourselves is generally more effective than speaking *about* someone else. If I say, "You are so rude and you make me so angry," two things happen. First, all your defensive shields go up, and the chance for constructive discussion is probably lost. Second, I abdicate responsibility for my feelings to you—it's up to you whether I become angry or not.

What if I say, "When I am interrupted like that, I really feel as though my opinions don't count"? First, I am talking about a specific action, rather than labeling you as an irremediably rude person. Chances of a constructive dialogue, are improved. Second, I am describing my feelings without necessarily putting them in your power. It is generally more positive and self-empowering to use "I Statements."

Absolutes

"You *never*. . ." and "You *always*. . . ." In the heat of an emotional discussion, it is easy to say things that aren't true in order to "score points." But it's a mistake. Don't say, "You *never* clean up after rituals" unless it is literally true; even then, it would be more accurate to say, "So far you have not cleaned up after any of the rituals." By using absolutes, you risk causing defensiveness and focusing the discussion on the accuracy of your comment instead of the real issue.

Better to say, "In the past year you've cleaned up after ritual twice that I've noticed; I would really appreciate it if you would take a turn more often so that I can get home early to my kids sometimes. Would it be easier for you to remember if we had assigned nights and posted a schedule?"

Faction Meetings

It may happen that one of the coveners has a gripe, and gets together with part of the coven to talk about it. This might happen spontaneously after a coven event, or by design. In either case, beware. Dealing with a coven issue with only part of the coven present can quickly polarize the group into factions.

If someone brings up a complaint and it's personal, that individual should be encouraged to take it directly to the offending party. Example:

Nightflower: "I am so mad at Hornbeam. Didn't he act like a jerk to me last Thursday?"

Maypole: "I think it would be best if you cool off and then tell him how you feel. I'd rather not talk about it before you've taken it up with him."

Nightflower: "Oh, he won't listen to me."

Maypole: "Nonetheless, he's your coven brother. You should at least give him the chance to work it out."

Nightflower: "Maybe I should talk it over with Oak and Star. They've both had problems with Hornbeam before."

Maypole: "That will only make the situation worse. Please hear me: talk to Hornbeam directly. If that doesn't help, then both of you should go to the High Priestess together and ask for mediation."

If it's an issue that affects the whole coven, it should still be taken to the person most directly involved. If that doesn't accomplish enough, then it should be put in the hands of the coven leaders. As a last resort, it should be brought up for discussion by the whole group.

Here's the kind of situation you want to avoid:

Nightflower: "Hornbeam, some of us had a meeting and were talking about your behavior lately, and we feel you should take some time off from the coven."

Hornbeam: "What do you mean 'some of us'? I really don't like people talking about me behind my back. If someone's got a problem with me, why didn't they bring it to me first?"

Onyx: "Hold on a second. Nobody told me about any meeting. I'm a member of this coven, too. What exactly is going on and why was I left out of it? Deirdre, did you know anything about a meeting?"

And so on. You get the picture.

Psychic Accusations

Most Witches are trained to use their psychic senses and trust their intuition. Usually that's good, but occasionally it gets us into trouble. A possible scenario:

Rosehip: "That's three times that I've had a terrible nightmare, and Pinebranch was in the last one! I wonder if he could be broadcasting negative energy into my dreams?"

Moonbubble: "Here he comes. Pinebranch, what's this about you sending negative thoughts into Rosehip's dreams?"

Pinebranch: "Uh... what? I don't know what you're talking about."

Moonbubble: "That's really unethical, you know—interfering with someone's dreams."

Rosehip: "Hold on, I didn't say it was done consciously and maliciously. It could have been a subconscious thing that happened because you were mad at me last month."

Pinebranch: "But I'm not mad anymore. And I would never mess with someone's dreams. Well, not intentionally. And I didn't do it subconsciously either. I don't think. I mean, wouldn't I know?"

Moonbubble: "Not necessarily. You may have done it on a deep level of your mind. Maybe you didn't intentionally violate the Rede, but . . . ."

You see where this can lead. No one can prove that a psychic event did not happen, and the accused is defenseless. Variations on this theme:

> "You're a powerful broadcasting empath. You were unhappy and were subconsciously radiating bad feelings to your covenmates."
>
> "I'm really exhausted. Remember that elemental spirit you created to bring you a new job? I think it got out of hand and is draining my aura."
>
> "Your rage at your abusive father is being unconsciously transferred to the High Priest, so that you mess up the energy every time he leads a ritual."
>
> "I know you're attracted to me, but you've got to stop sending energy cords that connect with my sexual chakra. It's harassment and I won't stand for it—and it probably caused that yeast infection last week."

Anything is possible, but a healthy Witch with a strong energy field should not be vulnerable to every negative thought or bit of psychic flotsam in the ether. Accusations such as those above smack of a need to blame others and avoid responsibility for one's own health and happiness. If a member of your coven is ill or unhappy, they should look first to their own behavior and attitude for the cause. Coveners should know that once such an accusation is made it is extremely hard to restore trust between the parties involved. Unless there is tangible evidence of wrongdoing on someone's part, accusations of psychic or magickal misdeeds should be treated with great skepticism.

Encouraging Cooperation

We spoke earlier of four basics necessary for cooperation: a shared sense of purpose, ground rules everyone can agree on, clear and direct communication, and trust. How can a coven encourage these?

First, the purpose of the coven and the ground rules should be reviewed by the whole membership from time to time. If these are summarized in written coven by-laws, then the by-laws can be reviewed yearly. Discussing by-laws should not be a continuous activity for the coven: a coven that spends all its time arguing about purpose and process will never accomplish much. To put it another way, check in on WHO (we are) and HOW (we do things), but spend most of your time on WHAT (we're doing).

If the purpose of the coven, its vision or mission, is reviewed each year just before the coming year's program is planned, then the activities of the coven can be designed to support its long-range purpose.

Both good communications and trust can be encouraged by making sure that every member has lots of opportunities to work with every other member. This can be done partly in group settings, by pairing people for teaching or ritual leadership, and changing the pairs frequently. For example, Aspen and Chalice might lead the New Moon ritual, and then Redwood and Moonglow a sabbat, and then Staghorn and Columbine the Full Moon. The following month perhaps Aspen could lead with Moonglow, and Redwood with Columbine.

Of course this requires that teaching and rituals not be monopolized by a couple of leaders. If that happens, then the coven members become mere parishioners rather than priests and priestesses in training, and might as well sit in rows in wooden pews.

Coveners can also work in rotating pairs outside a group context. They might have tasks that can be done in pairs, like researching a particular deity for a report, cleaning the coven candlesticks, or gathering materials for the Beltane maypole. Shared projects like these will usually lead to greater bonding and trust (or alert you to interpersonal problems). Here are some suggestions for pair-projects:

Creating or obtaining a coven tool (sword, pentacle, cauldron, etc.)
Reorganizing coven supplies
Cataloging the coven library
Setting up the altar for ritual
Cleaning coven ritual tools
Organizing a potluck
Supply-buying expedition (candles, altar cloths, etc.)
Decorating for a special event
Preparing a book report
Researching a deity
Publicizing open classes or sabbats
Planning a coven field trip
Coordinating festival participation
Planning community service
Publishing a coven newsletter
Organizing a fundraiser
Preparing a recommended reading list
Making a coven banner
Representing the coven at an intercoven regional meeting
Leading a festival workshop
Creating a coven brochure

There's always plenty of work to do in an active coven. The trick is to make sure it gets spread around and that work teams get remixed frequently. If too few people do all the work, you get burnout for some and boredom for others. If teams are not shuffled, then you will see tiny cliques forming. Treat your coven like a tossed salad and everyone will be happier. Communications will improve as well.

Communications work best when everyone works to speak from an honest and respectful place. Kathleen Killoran[1] lists the following principles and practices developed by an organization called ProcessWorks:

Principle . . . and Practice

Authenticity: Inquire from a genuine desire to know and understand. Listen fully, with the intent to truly hear. Speak your truth, from the heart, without attempting to make someone wrong.

Respect: Speak one at a time; do not interrupt. Avoid probing, giving advice, or attempting to change someone else's point of view.

Thoughtfulness: Speak only when moved to speak. Take time to reflect before speaking. Honor silence.

Inclusion: Speak through the center for all to hear. Allow time and space for every voice.

Openness: Seek meaning, not closure. Suspend assumptions.

This is very different from some of the communications models we are used to. Think about the grandstanding, filibusters, and competition in many legislative assemblies, where the effort is not to find solutions but to prove others wrong, assert power-over, and force acceptance of particular proposals. Surely priestesses and priests of the Craft of the Wise can do better.

NOTES

1. Kathleen Killoran, Article on the Womanshare program in *Albuquerque Woman*, July-August 1997.

20 Pastoral Counseling

Counseling is a process that helps people understand themselves, take responsibility for their lives, and solve their problems. It is not something you do to, or for, your clients; it's what you do *with* them, working together. Your responsibility is to act in a professional way, help the process along, and possibly refer them to other resources. Their responsibility is to be in charge of their lives and make their own decisions. You cannot, and should not, take the whole burden of responsibility for the outcome of counseling: that rests far more with the client than with you.

Does Counseling Really Work?

In November of 1995, *Consumer Reports* presented an article "Mental Health: Does Therapy Help?"[1] The highlights are worth repeating. Over 4,000 people were surveyed who had sought help from a family doctor, therapist, or self-help group. About nine out of ten people felt they were helped either "somewhat" or "a lot," with more being helped "a lot." Whether they went to a social worker, psychiatrist, psychologist, or self-help group didn't make much difference—all tended to be helpful. Seeing a marriage counselor or family doctor tended to help, but not as often.

Family doctors often fail to diagnose psychological problems and treat their clients for a shorter period, but prescribe psychiatric drugs more than four times as often as mental health specialists. However, they "sometimes prescribe psychiatric drugs for too short a time or at doses too low to work." In only one-fourth of the cases were patients referred to mental health specialists.

Therapy is not necessarily a quick fix. About half the clients "recovered" after eleven weekly sessions, and another quarter after a full year. A two-year stretch of counseling is not that uncommon.

Counseling in a Spiritual Context

The focus of pastoral counseling is to help people grow and cope with life's challenges in the context of their religious beliefs and resources. Most Wiccan priests and priestesses operate from certain assumptions when counseling:

- That clients contain the immanent God/dess, and thus have more inner strength and resources than they may realize;
- That some problems can be solved by a combination of magick and "acting in accord" on the physical plane;
- That seemingly negative situations usually contain positive elements or opportunities, which can be explored through divination;
- That nonmaterial entities such as plant devas, animal spirit allies, and deity aspects can help an individual heal, grow, or solve problems;
- That many of our experiences, challenges and behaviors are a karmic result of our own actions in the past (including past lives); and
- That the solution to any problem should ideally be "with harm toward none, for the greatest good of all."

As a Witch, a "wise one," people will come to you with their problems. It has been that way for thousands of years and it will be the same for you if you live up to the name.

What Problems Will You Encounter?

The problems they bring are often permutations on a few basic life issues:

- Relationships (dating, marriage, sexual problems, conflicts, children)
- Health (frequent sickness, alcohol or drug addictions, stress-related illnesses)
- Money (not enough, or poor planning and management)
- Jobs (performance, conflicts with bosses or co-workers, poor working conditions)
- Religion (choices, lack of support from family and friends)

You may get the occasional question about a business opportunity, someone's sexual orientation, or a UFO abduction. But the vast majority of situational problems will fall into one of the basic categories above.

Then there are chronic emotional and mental disorders, which are less directly related to a particular situation in the client's life. As a priest or priestess rather than a trained professional therapist, you are not expected to understand the causes and treatment for such disorders. But it is useful to be able to recognize the symptoms and make a tentative diagnosis, so you can wisely refer a client and can discuss the issue intelligently with professional therapists.

According to Kennedy and Charles,[2] the major classifications are as follows.

- Organic mental disorders: dementia, delirium, intoxication, drug withdrawal.
- Psychoactive substance use: dependence, abuse.

- Schizophrenia: delusions, hallucinations.
- Mood disorders: manic, depressive, bipolar.
- Anxiety disorders.
- Somatoform disorders: apparently physical, but with no known organic basis.
- Adjustment disorders: "maladaptive reaction to an identifiable psychosocial stressor," occurs after a traumatic event.
- Personality disorders: reactions of others causing subjective distress.

Be very careful about jumping to conclusions based on a little evidence, or—Goddess forbid—spreading your conclusions around without the client's express permission. What your client says to you in a professional relationship is confidential, and so are your conjectures about the nature of their illness. Diagnosis is not an intellectual exercise, nor is it a way to show off our psychological vocabulary. It is a powerful tool for good or ill, and if misused, can damage a client's reputation, self-image, and healing.

When you are first exploring a potential client's situation, remember that all emotional problems are directly related to the client's physical health. Sometimes emotional crises are the cause of physical problems, sometimes the result. Sometimes there is a deteriorating cycle of cause and effect that must be broken or end in death. Never can you deal with an emotional problem in isolation from the body. At the very least, things like proper rest, good nutrition, and exercise will help the client deal with their problems with fewer distractions and impediments. Issues which seemed out of control to a tired, stressed, physically ill person can miraculously diminish if their health improves.

Remember that some mental and emotional illnesses are partly or wholly caused by physical factors. An example is depression, which can be caused by a shortage of serotonin in the brain, and sometimes alleviated by the use of antidepressant drugs prescribed by a psychiatrist. You could counsel a depressed person 'till the cows come home, and if their problem is a chemical imbalance, you won't accomplish much. Whenever there is reason to suspect a physical cause or influence—for example, when the client's reactions don't change with their life situations, or when their emotional response seems all out of proportion to the obvious issues—then you must encourage the client to see a professional therapist or medical doctor.

In most crises, the challenge is for the client to make a decision or series of decisions, hopefully ones that are ethical, practical, and self-affirming. Your job as counselor is not to make choices for them, but to help them see the situation clearly so they can decide for themselves. Counseling can be defined as the art of helping a person grow to understand and solve their own problems. Pastoral counseling uses the beliefs, insights, and tools of religion to do this.

Are You Their Best (And Only) Resource?

When someone comes to you with a problem, there is an immediate question you must answer: should you work with this individual or should you refer them elsewhere?

When someone comes to us with their troubles, it is natural to feel both concern for them and also a certain amount of pride that we have been chosen as a source of help. In an overeager attempt to help and to prove ourselves, we may be tempted to say, "Sure, I'll be your counselor," even if the problem is one that we are not particularly equipped to deal with.

But sometimes the right answer must be: "Look, I'm not the best person to help with this issue. But I can help you find someone who is." Why? Maybe they have an eating disorder, and you know nothing about the subject. Maybe the problem is long-term depression, which may involve medical complications, and you're not trained in medicine. Maybe it's about someone's relationship, and you already are biased toward one party. Maybe the person is an emotional leech who will eat up massive amounts of your time and energy without solving anything. Maybe the timing is terrible, and you could help if you weren't up to your eyebrows coping with your own problems.

If one of the following situations exists, you should probably refer the individual to another resource.

1. **The situation requires specialized training that you don't have.**
2. **The individual is considering suicide.**
3. **The individual is potentially violent.**
4. **The individual is under the influence of drugs, legal or otherwise.**
5. **The individual does not seem to be interested in taking responsibility for his or her life.**
6. **The individual needs help on a long-term basis, and you cannot commit the time and energy without neglecting other responsibilities.**
7. **Your own needs and commitments make it impossible for you to counsel anyone effectively at the moment.**
8. **One of you is planning to move beyond commuting distance soon.**
9. **You have tried to work together and the relationship is simply not working out.**

The first six situations usually indicate that a professional therapist is needed. In the remaining cases, you will have to decide whether to refer to a therapist, or whether another priest/ess, friend, or relative might be able to help.

In most cases you can be supportive even if you do not become the person's primary counselor. Simply listening and showing that you care counts for a lot. It may be helpful simply to remind them of their resources within the Wiccan faith:

"The God/dess is within you, and that means that you can get through this. Have you talked with Her lately?" or "Do you think it's time for a ritual of self-blessing?" or "You have a community of friends in the coven; are you spending any time with them?" Granted, religious resources may not be the whole answer to a problem, but they are the resources you are best equipped to provide.

The individual may need counseling on two levels: spiritual and secular—or even three, if there is a medical component. In that case you may join the client's "team" or "staff," and use your special skills in tandem with a therapist and a psychiatrist or M.D. You will need to get the client's permission for communication to happen between you and the other specialists; and you will probably want to set up a joint meeting among everyone involved, to discuss strategies. Be careful not to disempower the client by talking *about* her with the specialists in front of her, or making plans for her as though she were not capable of making her own decisions. The client is not a lamb chop to be prepared according to your recipe. She is a human being with the authority and responsibility to guide her own life.

You will need to know your local resources: hospitals, clinics, drug units, self-help groups like Alcoholics Anonymous, suicide prevention services, psychologists, social workers, and of course other Wiccan clergy with specialized training or experience. When a new clinic opens or a new professional comes to town, you may wish to get acquainted: make an appointment for a visit, call, or send a note introducing yourself. Do expect an acknowledgment.

When you refer someone to another source for help, be sure the client makes contact, not you. The new counselor or specialist may need some information from you, but you should send only information requested, and only if the client agrees in writing.

What if you are referring the client not to an additional helper, but to one who will replace you as primary counselor? This may bring up some emotional issues for the client, such as feelings of rejection or abandonment. You can defuse these issues in a couple of ways. For one thing, make referral a possibility from the start, never letting the client assume that you are the only possible counselor for them. You can use phrases like: "Let's explore whether it might be useful for us to work together, at least for a while; and if we get to the point where it looks like someone else can help you more, then we'll talk about our options." If it begins to appear that referral is probable, then approach it gradually—don't hand the client any sudden surprises.

Of course you may have some emotional reactions of your own to deal with. Guilt? Inadequacy? Anger? Loss? Face your feelings honestly and work through them, with help from a colleague if necessary. Do not burden the departing client with them.

When it comes time for the change, act with assurance. End the relationship with clean edges. Once referral is made, stay clear of the process, even if the client pressures you to let them return. If you remain involved, even to the extent of letting the client call you and talk about their new counselor, you may muddy the waters and make it very difficult for the new person to establish a working relationship with the client.

If a referral seems necessary but you don't know of appropriate resources to which you can refer the client, you might ask your doctor for suggestions. You can also contact national professional associations or their local chapters. These include:

- American Psychiatric Association at (202) 682-6220;
- American Psychological Association at (202) 336-5800;
- National Association of Social Workers at (800) 638-8799, ext. 291;
- American Association for Marriage and Family Therapy at (800) 374-2638; and the
- American Psychiatric Nurses Association at (202) 857-1133.

Other possible sources of referral information are local universities, hospitals, and psychotherapy training centers. Don't forget to seek out peer support groups as well. For general information on mental illness, contact the National Alliance for the Mentally Ill at (800) 950-6264.

Power-Over Versus Empowerment

It should be clear by now that counseling is not the same as solving someone's problems for them, nor is it giving advice. Neither of these leaves the client stronger and more capable. Care-taking and advice-giving weaken and create dependence; counseling empowers and fosters self-reliance.

Counseling Styles

There are many kinds of counseling, each based on a "model" or theory about the nature and workings of the human mind. Some people respond better to certain methods. Many people hear "counseling" and think of Freudian psychoanalysis, stereotyped as the client lying on a couch discussing his or her childhood. Though some of Freud's work was obviously affected by his own Victorian upbringing, his three-part model of the self (id, ego, superego) is at least superficially similar to the psychological/spiritual models of Huna and Faery Wicca.

The work of C. G. Jung is popular with many Neopagans, with its focus on mythology and archetypes. The archetypes dovetail nicely with many Wiccans' understanding of the aspects of Goddess and God, and can be useful in ritual work aimed at mental or emotional healing.

Therapists such as Milton H. Erickson are known for their use of hypnosis—we might say trancework—in the illumination of problems and the creation of solutions. This approach is often used as part of Neuro-linguistic

Programming, a set of counseling and communications techniques that focuses on the link between sensory stimuli and mental states. Several Wiccan priest/esses have found that NLP training enhances magick and ritual, and it can be used in healing addictions, phobias, and other emotional problems.

Feminist counseling begins with the proposition that many personal problems are caused or aggravated by living in a sexist society, which limits and dehumanizes both women and men. Healing focuses on understanding this oppression, rebuilding self-worth, and reclaiming the power to make one's own decisions.

Co-counseling is a peer counseling technique that allows two non-professionals to help each other. It is not a substitute for professional counseling, or for pastoral counseling by an experienced priest/ess. But as a formalized and focused system of peer support, it can be valuable.

Rebirthing allows you to "start fresh" from Day One of this incarnation, and to do it with a degree of warmth and nurturance that you may not have enjoyed the first time through. It is a very "hands-on," kinesthetic, and emotional experience, at the opposite end of the spectrum from the intellectualized forms of psychoanalysis. It requires a trained and competent rebirther and a lot of trust on the client's part, and for certain people it can be very healing.

Correctly used, divination can be considered a counseling method. This option is discussed in some detail later on.

There are other types of counseling, of course; but these are some common ones you are likely to run into. When referring a client, it is important to try to match the client's needs to the counselor's method and style.

Looking At Yourself

When you look at yourself as a potential counselor, remember first that you are a priestess or priest: a Witch. For most of us, this mean: NOT a trained therapist, or a doctor, nor a psychoanalyst. It would be a huge mistake for you to set aside your unique skills and insights and try to act like a psychotherapist. As Kennedy and Charles say, "The minister who forsakes his own identity to act as a neutral and secular counselor does justice neither to his fundamental identity nor to the counseling in which he engages."[3] So BE a Witch, use your skills of inspiration and magick and divination and ritual, and if the client needs anything in addition, send them along to the appropriate professional.

There are some questions that can usefully be asked of any counselor, secular or religious. Ask yourself these:

- Do you want clients to like you? Fine, they probably will, either because they chose you in the first place or because you care enough to try to work with them. But do you want it too much? If you need to be liked so badly that you always agree, that you sacrifice honesty, that you avoid asking hard questions, or that you offer a kind or degree of support that crosses your professional boundaries—this is not good. Being liked is helpful, but, after all, it's not why you're here. The client did not come to you in order to boost your self-esteem, but to get your help.

- Do you tend to be judgmental? It should be obvious that you're not going to be much help if you are simply measuring the client by your own moral standards, instead of first trying to understand them and their standards. As a priest/ess you can help them understand their actions in the light of Wiccan ethics; but first, seek to understand.
- Do you enjoy asking questions? Questions can be very useful (more on this later), but ask only the minimum necessary to keep the client thinking and communicating. Sometimes it's better just to allow a fruitful silence, where the client's feelings and insights can slowly bubble to the surface.
- Are you a compulsive interpreter? Does this sound like something you might say? "Clearly a traumatic incident in your childhood has caused you to distrust all men with mustaches, and this is at the root of your arguments with John." Resist the temptation to be a combination of Sigmund Freud and Sherlock Holmes, or to create a simplistic psychological theory to explain your client to him or herself. This behavior may cause resentment and withdrawal.
- Are you distressed by displays of intense emotion? If a client gets angry, do you have an instinctive urge to calm them down? If a client cries, do you instantly reassure them and try to stop the tears? Emotional release is often a revealing and healing thing, and you do clients no favors by trying to get them to deny, hide or "stuff" their feelings. After all, if you can't show your feelings to your counselor, where can you show them?
- Are you curious and caring? Do you really, really want to know how others see the world, what they are feeling, and why they act as they do? Can you withhold judgment, interpretation, and explanation until you are ready for understanding? Kennedy and Charles suggest that a counselor must "Get on the inside of the world of another and . . . stand there without trampling on or confusing their meaning."[4]

A Clear "Contract"

When you first discuss the possibility of counseling someone, you want to develop an agreement or understanding as soon as possible. This does not have to be a written, legalistic document, but it does have to be clear. Initially, the agreement may be very simple: "Why don't you drop by at 7:00 Thursday evening? We'll talk over the problem for half an hour and decide where to go from there."

If you decide to work together, then the contract can get more detailed: "Let's make sure we both understand the arrangement. You're going to come over to my house every Thursday evening for an hour, from seven to eight P.M., and we'll work together on this problem. In return you're going to come over Saturday mornings and help me by weeding my garden for two hours. If something comes up and you can't make it on either day, you'll let me know as soon as you can, if possible the day before. We'll try this arrangement for four weeks, and then decide whether we both feel we should continue."

If either you or the client can't fulfill your part of the bargain, you should renegotiate the contract. If you can't agree on the contract, then you are probably not meant to work together as counselor and client.

You should begin by getting basic information, if you don't already have it:

1. Client's full name
2. Job, career goals
3. Living situation
4. Religious involvement
5. Medical or psychological treatment, past or present
6. Address
7. Telephone number and possibly e-mail address
8. Age
9. Marital status
10. Family information (partner and children, if any)
11. Information about parents, upbringing

Should you charge for counseling? Most clergy do not; pastoral counseling is considered part of their duties as a priest/ess, minister, or rabbi. Besides, taking payment would make counseling your profession, and you might need professional certification depending on which state you live in. (Even accepting services in exchange might affect your tax and professional status; your coven might want to check this with a tax lawyer.)

Nonetheless, it is usually a good idea to arrange some kind of energy exchange; the client might help with your house chores, organize the coven library, clean the ritual room, or trade some service in which they are skilled, like picture framing, computer work, or gardening. This increases the client's investment in the counseling process and may encourage them to work at it seriously. In addition, it helps you feel that there is an energy balance and that you are receiving something tangible for your efforts. If there is no energy-sharing arrangement, then you have a dependent and unequal relationship, and, in time, one or both of you may feel resentful.

Be very clear on your contract, including when you will begin and end the sessions. Warn the client a few minutes before time is up: "We have five minutes left. Before we start to wrap up for today, was there anything else you wanted to say about what happened with your husband?" At the very end, make sure you are both clear about your next meeting: "As I recall, you said you would be out of town next Thursday, so we'll meet again the following Thursday, April 14. And if you need to talk before then, you'll give me a call?"

One more thing about the contract: confidentiality. What happens during the session is private; that is implied in every client-counselor relationship. However, it is a good idea to make it explicit: "You should know that everything you say to me, all that happens in this room, is confidential." If there are exceptions, make them known up front: "Unless I have your written permission, I will not discuss our sessions with anyone but my supervisor (or 'High Priest,' or 'the priestess who does peer review on my counseling work'), who is also pledged to confidentiality." Be very clear in your own mind what your ethical obligations are, and honor them.

Time, Place, and Atmosphere

Counseling works best if the time and place are right. If possible, don't try to work with someone during the social hour after a coven ritual or any time you may be interrupted. Set aside a block of time when you will not be disturbed, turn on the telephone answering machine, and focus completely on your client.

You will probably be counseling coveners in your home or theirs, or possibly outdoors in a park or forest preserve. Whatever the location, make sure it is comfortable—not too hot or cold, without distracting background noises. The client should preferably have access to a restroom, and make sure there is a box of tissues at hand. Most counselors prefer a simply furnished room with few visual distractions.

If you are going to use divination or ritual as part of the process, then give it appropriate emphasis and engage Younger Self by wearing robes, using candles and incense, playing background music, setting up an altar if need be, and so on. In this case, a visually rich environment is appropriate, assuming the decor is focused toward a specific purpose.

The Client-Counselor Relationship

How can you best help your clients? First, by caring about them. Some people just don't like people very much, and are far happier with a book, a dog, or a computer. If that's you, don't try to counsel: your indifference or impatience will show.

Second, you need to be curious about people's feelings and motivations, needs and hopes, and enjoy exploring them. You may like people fine in a social context or while working together on a job and still not be interested in doing gut-level emotional work.

Third, you must be willing to set aside your own interests, ideas, stories, and desire for attention for a while. The client deserves your complete attention.

Fourth, you must be able to be friendly and concerned without getting emotionally involved. As a counselor you give the gifts of objectivity, calmness, and complete honesty. These are gifts you could not offer as a friend or lover. Remember also that it is not ethical to take advantage of a client's vulnerability by promoting a personal relationship they might not choose in calmer times. If you find yourself attracted on a personal level and cannot set your feelings aside, then you have only one choice: refer the person to another counselor, end the client-counselor relationship, and a few months later—if you still wish it—see if the individual wants to explore a potential personal relationship. Any other course of action can be painful, confusing, and damaging for both you and the client.

As you have gathered by now, a counselor must walk a fine line between two extremes: you cannot allow a deep personal involvement, nor can you be cold, impersonal, and distant. You may feel drawn toward one extreme or the other. The client might push you toward one extreme or the other. But you must be wise enough to know that the client needs neither love nor indifference from you—just counseling.

Some people would like to be all-powerful "fixers" or all-wise advisors. "There, there, you just leave everything to me and I'll take care of the problem." Or just as bad, "I know exactly what you should do to fix this." And we may want to say such things out of a genuine desire to be helpful. But even if we had such capabilities, we would do others no favor by assuming responsibility for their problems and control over their lives.

If we leave a client feeling a little more clear about his needs, a little stronger, a little more confident that they can handle life, then we have done well by them. This requires that we deal with the person, not the problem. If you solve a problem for your client, be certain that they will face another problem next month when you are not around to fix it for them. If you help empower a client, then they can solve the next one by themselves. The old proverb is true: "Give a man a fish, and he will eat for a day. Teach a man to fish, and he will eat for a lifetime."

How do you empower a client? First, by refusing to take responsibility for the client's decisions. If they ask, "What should I do?" then reply, "What are your choices?" or "What would you like to do?"

Second, by showing confidence that they can make tough decisions: "I guess you've faced some pretty tough choices before—in the war, in your job, deciding whether to move here. I have the feeling that you can handle this one, once you're clear on your options." Focus on their competence, strength, past successes, and network of resources.

Third, by reminding them that they have choices and helping them discover even more. Suppose the client says, "I don't have much choice. My boss would fire me if I told the customer about the shortfall." You can respond, "That's your boss' choice, and maybe he would fire you. But what are your choices? Can you sell honesty to your boss as a political necessity? For example, 'They're going to find out anyway; if we're up front now, and offer to fix it, we may keep them as a customer.' Can you appeal to the CEO if you get fired? Can you resign and go to work for your competitor? Can you inform the customer anonymously? Can you let your boss take responsibility on this one, and focus on redesigning the system so this never happens again?" Better still if the client comes up with alternatives, but the main point is that there are always choices, and that fact gives your client power in any life situation.

There is something very Wiccan about the whole notion of empowering others. If we really believe the statement "Thou art God/dess," can we then place a client in a position of childlike dependence? If we believe that Gaia is an interdependent whole, that we are all connected on a deep and primal level, can we do other than affirm, honor, and encourage the strength of our sisters and brothers—and thus ourselves?

Effective Listening

The first and primary skill required of a counselor is the ability to listen. This requires that you be concerned and curious about your client. You will listen intently and paraphrase the client's words back to them—the technique sometimes called "active listening" or "reflective listening." This reassures the client that you've heard them, checks whether you've understood accurately, and helps them clarify and refine their thoughts and feelings. If you are following well, they will tell you with words or body language. If you're just not getting it, they will correct you with words or with an eloquent silence.

Usually you don't have to pry the client open like a reluctant clam. They come to you to be heard and to be understood. If you don't understand, ask a question or simply give them a quizzical look. Then listen—not to the details, but to what their story tells us about how they experience life. Listen—not through your own filters, but through theirs. Listen—not to the stories, but to the client. What do they feel; where does it hurt; what are the themes that color their perspective and explain their universe; what is it like to live in their world? Listen and don't interrupt. Keep at it until both of you are sure you understand.

Part of you should pay attention to your reactions. Ask yourself, "What do I feel right now? How am I reacting to this person?" Try to discover if your feelings are your own baggage first; if not, are they triggered by something the client is saying or doing? Kennedy and Charles say that "What the clients do to us is just a sample of what they do all the time to the people in their everyday environment."[5]

Many professional therapists suggest that clergy should be generally supportive and help clients cope with immediate life crises, but avoid deep work with the subconscious or unconscious levels of the client's mind. This is probably good advice for most Wiccan priest/esses, but doesn't necessarily apply to those who are highly skilled in dealing with the shadow-self, past-life regression, certain kinds of trancework, and/or the three-level Huna or Faery Wicca models of the self. It is necessary to be very honest with yourself and avoid trespassing on the deepest and most intimate parts of the soul unless you really have the training and skills to be helpful. Far better to offer a cup of tea and an emotional Band-Aid, if that's what you have to give, than to risk upsetting a delicate mental balance that keeps the client alive and functioning.

How much of yourself should you share when you are counseling? Of course you will want to avoid the self-absorption of some would-be counselors: "So you're feeling suicidal? That reminds me of the time my dog was run over by a pick-up . . . boy, was I depressed! Well, I just felt like . . . ." But if your experiences or feelings are having a real impact on your counseling, it is certainly all right to be honest. For example, "I'm sorry if I seem distracted: my wife is ill, and I'm having a hard time thinking about anything else. Would you like to reschedule for Friday?" Or, "Your experience with your father is hitting really close to home, because of my own history. I'm not sure I can be objective about this . . . ." But unless your stuff is influencing your counseling, it's usually best to keep it to yourself. Focus on the client.

Asking the Right Questions

You will need to ask questions occasionally to keep the client communicating aloud, to clarify things you don't fully understand, and to suggest options. The main thing to remember is never to ask leading questions—that is, questions which by their wording or tone imply a preferred answer.

A Good Approach

Horned Owl: "How do you feel about the issue of space in your relationship? Do you each have time to be by yourself if you want to, to pursue your separate interests?"

Milfoil: "Well, I guess I haven't really worked on my frog collection lately. . . that would be fun . . . and I doubt that Rosithorn would mind."

A Not-So-Good Approach

Blue Toad: "Don't you often feel kind of confined in your relationship, like Rosithorn never gives you space to do fun things on your own?"

Milfoil: "Well, I guess I do feel that way sometimes. I miss working on my frog collection, but I'm always doing something with Rosi and she doesn't like frogs. I DO feel kind of cramped!"

This is a rather blatant example of a leading question, and sometimes they can be much more subtle but still prejudicial. Changing the tone of your voice, lifting an eyebrow, or emphasizing a single word can all slant a question unacceptably. If you are unsure whether the question you're about to ask is leading, ask yourself:

> "Why am I asking this? Am I simply trying to understand the client better—and help him understand himself? Am I open to any answer the client gives me? Or do I want/expect/hope for a particular answer that fits in with my thinking?"

Discovering Options

Once you and the client are clear exactly what the problem is, you can begin thinking about solutions. It's best if the client comes up with potential options—you may only need to ask, "What are some different ways you might deal with this?"

When the client has a list of possibilities, s/he can start evaluating them by whatever standards they have for an acceptable solution. Is this plan practical—can it be accomplished with available resources? A plan that costs too much or requires the manpower of the Chinese Army is not practical. Is this plan ethical? That is, can I get what I want without hurting someone else? Is this plan achievable in a reasonable time? There may be other criteria as well. Is this plan safe? Is this plan acceptable to other parties involved? Some of these questions may require research before they can be answered. Where answers are simply unknown and unguessable, even with research, you can resort to divination.

Once the client has a tentative solution that meets all the criteria, they can go ahead and implement it to see what happens. This of course is the scary part, especially when the stakes are high or when the client has only one shot at a solution. Here is where the client must ask, "Are the possible gains of the new solution worth the risk? Or does my heart say to try a different answer? Or do I have the option of doing nothing, letting time or other people work it out?"

We have been discussing counseling mainly as decision-making, and that is usually important. But human problems always have an emotional component, and all the logical effort in the world may not address the feelings involved.

Serious emotional problems may not be susceptible to rational or verbal approaches. The problem may have begun when the client was a baby, in a pre-rational, pre-verbal state, or in a past life which the client does not remember. The client may have feelings of fear, anxiety, depression, or self-contempt and have absolutely no idea where they came from.

Or, the client may have ideas and theories about the origin of the problem, and these theories may have nothing to do with the real problem. For example, Joe says, "Sure, I'm mad all the time, but it's because my boss won't get off my case." Some questioning may reveal that he has felt the same way about all his bosses, or that he feels angry even when he's nowhere near his boss. So we are led to believe that some deeper pattern is being played out, something that can't be solved by a change of supervisors.

Many counselors operate on the theory that simply understanding the origin of a problem will lead to healing and resolution. Others believe that understanding is less important than catharsis, the chance to release old feelings by screaming, weeping, pounding on pillows, or whatever. Some believe that emotional pain caused by a traumatic birth or parental neglect can be healed by replaying events with a totally supportive, unconditionally loving counselor—rebirthing or reparenting. Others suggest that looking at the problem from a different perspective or "reframing" can help: "I wasn't a bad kid. I was the family scapegoat for my parents' drinking problems." Sometimes this replaces self-destructive feelings like guilt and shame with "cleaner" feelings like anger, which may be easier to deal with.

The bottom line is that coping with feelings is part of counseling, and "head trips" which provide only intellectual answers are useful only for superficial problems. If you cannot be comfortable when a client shows deep emotion, and supportive even if they are weeping all over you or screaming in rage, then don't try to counsel. You can still be a teacher and an advisor where this seems appropriate.

A Plan of Action

If counseling results in self-understanding, it has accomplished a lot. But since Wiccans tend to be an activist lot—we do magick, after all—it is consistent if counseling also results in a plan of action: something to do based on our new feelings and insights. This is especially necessary if the client sought counseling because of a practical, decision-oriented problem ("How can I overcome an addiction? Should I pursue this relationship?"). But it is equally useful if they are dealing with long-term emotional issues such as self-esteem or phobias. A change in mental or emotional state should have effects in the "real" world outside the client's mind, and you can encourage this by helping the client create a plan of action.

This plan may well include ritual and magickal elements as well as tactics that are not special to our religion. For example, suppose you are counseling someone on their fear of cats. Some tactics might include the following.

- Regression to discover if the phobia began with a traumatic incident in a past life (". . . then the mountain lion knocked me down and ate me . . .").
- Placing pictures of cats all around the house (desensitization).
- Meeting a very gentle kitten owned by a friend, and putting a bit of its fur in an amulet bag.

- Performing a ritual in which the client aspects as Bast, the Egyptian cat goddess of joy, music, fertility, and sunlight.
- Writing an affirmation to be spoken five times daily ("I am calm and relaxed in the presence of cats").
- Having you, the counselor, holding a cat in your lap and petting it during a session.

This approach gives the client some active things to do outside the counseling sessions, and can be very confidence-building. It further removes the client from the passive role of "helpee" and gives the primary responsibility for solving their problems to them—where it belongs.

Using Divination

Divination may help in creating the plan of action. It takes many forms such as tarot, astrology, runes, I Ching, casting stones, and radiesthesia (pendulum work or dowsing). Depending on how these techniques are used, they can resemble counseling, prophecy, or advice-giving. As a counseling technique, divination can guide you in asking pertinent questions of the client, and guide the client in exploring feelings and options. Always remember, and remind your client, that divinatory "answers" are not carved in stone. As a prophetic tool, divination can only suggest trends, tendencies, and possibilities. It can never tell you what you "should" do. Its greatest value is as a tool for increased self-understanding—a glorified Rorschach Test.

Used in combination with discussion, common sense, and a clear set of values, divination can be very useful. But if your client shows a tendency to become dependent on it and you for making life's daily decisions, steer them back toward taking responsibility for their own life.

There are at least three general methods of "reading for" a querent or client. You can memorize traditional meanings from a book, and tell your client, for instance, that "We see here the Tower card and the King of Rods, which means there will be a cataclysmic change in your life involving a strong-willed man of fiery temper." Or, you can read psychically, according to your own intuition: "I sense that the Tower, in this case, refers to the emotional defenses you have erected; and the King represents your father who shielded himself in much the same way." Or, you can use what is sometimes called a "gestalt" method, where you ask questions and elicit the meanings from the querent's deep mind: in effect you prompt the client to read for themselves. An example:

Reader: "What is the first thing that you notice in the Tower card?"

Querent: "The lightning."

Reader: "And what does lightning feel like to you?"

Querent: "I don't know . . . well, high energy, in sudden bursts."

Reader: "Does that relate to anything in your life?"

Querent: "No, it's not my style... wait though, my boyfriend is like that. Bursts of enthusiasm, gets real busy at something, then suddenly it all goes away and he's a couch potato."

Reader: "How do you react to that?" And so on.

In such a method, the client comes up with the answers. The counselor/reader is a facilitator, asking questions and encouraging the client to "get into" the card and extract the meaning it has for that individual at this moment in life. Because the insights gained are their insights, not ill-fitting answers from a book or dependent on the reader's intuition, they are more immediately relevant and certainly more empowering.

Not every method of divination lends itself to this technique. But with any system, much depends on the reader's attitude. Ask yourself always: is divination a process of mutual exploration, or does it cast reader and querent in the roles of "Fount of Arcane Knowledge" versus "Ignorant Supplicant"? Does it support the goals of counseling?

Using Ritual

Ritual, and magick generally, are the stock in trade of Witches and can certainly be used as part of the plan. Here are just of few of the ways they can be used:

- Grounding and centering techniques can help stabilize a client as they pass through a crisis.
- Casting the circle can minimize outside distractions and provide the client with a safe and quiet space to work on their problems or to escape them for a while. A guided meditation or visit to an astral temple can do the same.
- Aspecting deity, or "assuming the god-form," can help the client tap into new sources of strength and clarity.
- A shamanic journey can put the client in contact with spirit allies.
- The creation of appropriate amulets or talismans can help the client keep in contact with specific energies necessary in their work.
- Daily meditation before an altar dedicated to a patron/matron deity can give the client comfort and support.
- A regular chakra cleansing exercise, such as the Middle Pillar, can prepare the client to better deal with stress.
- Candle spells and the like can help the client focus on their goals and progress toward them.

- Affirmations or words of power can keep the client strong and focused.
- Raising power through drumming, chanting, or dancing can be cathartic and empowering, and if properly directed can assist the healing process.
- Playing with Younger Self, perhaps embodied in a doll or stuffed animal, is very healing.
- A cord ritual can be used to bind certain qualities more closely to oneself, or to help release negative feelings and thought patterns.

If you are not adept in such magicks, you may want to enlist the help of a more experienced Witch to advise you and the client in these matters

Closure

The time will come when counseling has accomplished its purpose and the client is able to cope without your help, relying on themselves and their network of friends, family, and colleagues. It is often wise to gradually taper off your sessions as the client's life stabilizes and they become more confident of their ability to "fly free." You may move from weekly meetings to meetings every other week, then monthly, then schedule a couple of sessions at three-month intervals so the client can "check in." Hopefully you will both recognize when the time has come to end the counseling relationship.

It is natural for both of you to have mixed feelings about this. The client may be afraid, on a deep level, that their problems will reappear, and that they cannot cope "alone." You can help by emphasizing the progress they have made, how well they have been handling their affairs recently, and that they do have a "personal support network" of friends and/or family. You may also leave the door open for the client to contact you again if a crisis occurs; but don't leave the door too far open ("Call me anytime!"), lest you encourage the client to become dependent rather than independent.

Be clear about your own feelings. You may miss working with the client, and doubtless you will see many facets of the client's life that could use additional work—personal growth is a never-ending process. But counseling cannot be never-ending. Know when it's time to let go, and do it cleanly, clearly, respecting your own and your client's dignity. After all, there are other challenges waiting for you.

Pitfalls

When things go well, counseling can be a wonderful, life-transforming experience for the client and a source of deep satisfaction for the counselor. But there are pitfalls. Here are some to watch for.

Dependency

The client may come to rely on you too much for guidance, and even want you to take over decision-making for their daily life. As discussed earlier, you can avoid this by consistently putting the responsibility right back where it belongs—in their hands.

It is always a mistake to try to control or dominate the client's life. In its worst form this becomes the Pygmalion Complex, where the counselor attempts to remold the client in their own image or an idealized fantasy.

Emotional Attachment

The client may decide that they are in love with you. You may inadvertently set yourself up for this by being too warm, attentive, and helpful in ways that go beyond your role as counselor. Suddenly the relationship may be sexually charged. Responding to sexual overtures by a client—or initiating them!—is considered unethical, can do a lot of emotional damage, and must be avoided. The client is probably in a vulnerable and confused state, which is not the best time to begin a new relationship with anyone, especially their counselor. If you find yourself attracted to a client, and can no longer keep the relationship professional, then your only option is to refer the client to another counselor. At some later date, after a "cooling-off" period, you can each consider whether you want to explore a personal relationship further.

Losing Objectivity

You may very naturally have your own opinions in the situation under discussion (thinking to yourself, for example, Your friend said that? What a jerk!). But it is important that the client arrive at their own assessment of their situation and choose their own solution. Try not to ask leading questions ("Don't you think that was a nasty thing to say?"), much less offer your own flat pronouncements ("That was really nasty!"). Use neutral questions ("How did you feel when he said that?") that allow the client to examine their own feelings without your influence.

Occasionally it may be OK to insert a reality check ("Some people would feel that such behavior is really out of line, and would question whether they wanted to be friends with such a person. What do you think?").

Focusing on Yourself

The focus should almost always be on the client. Some counselors are inclined to gab on about themselves, under the impression that their own life can serve as a model for the client. But that story about what you did with Aunt Mabel's cat when you were nine, even though it seems quite relevant to you, is probably not what the client needs to hear. Avoid "That reminds me of the time when I . . ." or you will begin to sound self-indulgent, egotistic, and not at all concerned about your client.

Some counselors share too much of their own stuff not because they are egomaniacs, but because they feel it breaks the ice, puts them on equal footing with the client, or makes them just likable "folks" instead of a distant and forbidding figure. Perhaps they feel an urge to boast about an achievement or share their own problems with a handy captive audience. It may also be that the client reminds them of someone they know: trusted aunt, good friend, younger brother, whatever. But none of these are good reasons for focusing the session on themselves.

Criticizing

The client should be able to feel that you are always supportive of their growth and best interests. If you criticize the client or their actions, your rapport will be jeopardized. This does not mean that you have to endorse all of the actions of your client; but if a behavior or decision seems harmful to the client or someone else, then in a calm and neutral way help them explore the consequences and see for themselves that there is a problem.

The opposite end of the spectrum is appeasement, where the counselor becomes a "yes-man," saying what they think the client wants to hear, and never leading the client to confront difficult issues. This approach may please the client for a while—until they realize that they've made no progress in solving their problems.

Taking Sides in a Family Dispute

In one sense, of course, you are always on your client's side. But if that comes out as attacking the client's spouse or relatives, you will possibly do more harm than good. Try to support your client's feelings without putting down others involved in the situation. This can come across as competition, and your client may feel they have to choose between their spouse's support or yours. Never put a client in that position.

Money/Exchange Issues

If the client has agreed to exchange something for your counseling help, and gets behind or fails to live up to the agreement, it is likely to cause stress on your part and interfere with your effectiveness. If things start to go wrong, explore the problem very openly with the client, in a non-judgmental way. Maybe they have hit a temporary obstacle—or maybe there is a deeper problem. Perhaps they don't feel the counseling is useful and are reluctant to give anything in exchange. Perhaps you need to change the agreement, or perhaps you may decide to allow the client to defer payment. But scrapping the exchange agreement and offering your counseling services for free is probably not a good idea. That may cause the client to feel dependent and helpless, and can foster resentment on your part as well.

Resistance

Sometimes clients simply do not want to do the work involved in changing their lives. They may just want an affirmation that they are fine as they are, and it's the rest of the world that's messed up. They may get some "secondary gains" from being in counseling: sympathy, lowered expectations from their family, time off from a job they hate. They may be afraid of change, and secretly want to settle for a lifestyle that is self-defeating but at least familiar.

Resistance can take many forms, and some of them are subtle. It's pretty obvious if a client crosses his arms, clamps his mouth shut and glares at you. But it can also show up as conversational rambling that changes the subject whenever the discussion becomes intense. It can be minimizing the problem: "Well, it's no big deal, and I can handle it by myself." It might appear as tantrums and theatrics.

The client may present herself as very calm and controlled, and treat sessions as an academic exercise, intellectualizing, theorizing and generalizing, even competing to analyze herself better than you can, without ever expressing her feelings. If the session begins to feel like a consultation with a colleague of a psychology seminar, your client may be resisting—though totally unaware of her defenses.

Resistance can manifest in other ways: canceling appointments, seductive behavior, or getting competing "advice" from other people and challenging your approach with it. However it appears, you should help the client look at their behavior and the reasons for it, and not let yourself be distracted from the work that must be done.

Transference and Countertransference

Transference occurs when the client develops feelings toward the counselor that are based on other relationships they have had with parents, lovers, teachers, and so forth. Such feelings have nothing to do with you as an individual (though they will seem to be aimed at you), and everything to do with the client's history. If you remind the client of a stern father, they may treat you with the same sullen anger they felt toward their parent. If you remind them of a fickle lover, they may try constantly to win proof of your affection and respect; and so on. Countertransference is the reverse: feelings you may have toward your client based on your own history. Do not fall into the trap of relating to your client as you have related to your significant others. Build the relationship afresh, and treat your client as the unique individual they are, not as a ghost of your past.

Taking Care of Ourselves

At the same time that you are focusing on the client, you will need to keep in touch with your own feelings. If you find yourself becoming drawn into the client's emotional state, do what you must in order to maintain your center and keep your energy flowing.

Use empathy without getting overwhelmed. For very sensitive empaths, who are common in the Craft, this can be difficult. Fortunately there are many tools, mundane and magickal, which you can use.

First, be aware of your own emotional reactions. Scan your chakras (energy centers) from time to time, and see if any are agitated, constricted, or closed. Be sensitive to your body, since emotional stress manifests physically. Is your breathing shallow? Are your neck or shoulder muscles tense? Are you holding yourself in a cramped, closed posture? Is your speech rapid, tight, or higher-pitched? If you can, step aside from your body for a moment and observe yourself. If you are not aware of your own feelings, they will control you either blatantly or subtly, and your usefulness as a counselor will be lost.

You may need to shift focus away from an intense subject long enough for both of you to re-center. Or it may be useful to take a "stretch break," get a beverage for yourself and your client, or do some deep-breathing exercises.

A simple grounding exercise can work wonders: imagine yourself as a tree, put your roots deep into the Earth, and allow tension to flow out and calm energy to flow in. Or touch a large rock, kept by your chair for this purpose, and drain the excess nervous energy into it. Or excuse yourself and wash your hands: flowing water can be wonderfully restorative. Whether you perform these exercises by yourself, or invite your client to join you, will depend on the circumstances. An experienced Witch will join you readily; a novice may need instruction; a cowan may be confused and resist. In any case do not interrupt the session just because the client gets emotional. They may be making a breakthrough in understanding, or experiencing a healing catharsis. After the tears subside you can help the client ground and center.

Occasionally it may be wise to psychically shield yourself, particularly if you are a receiving empath and the client is emoting intensely. You can cast a personal circle about yourself with your mind alone (whipping out your athame and chanting "I conjure thee . . ." could be a bit distracting to the client). You can also use a snowplow visualization, where the emotional energy is diverted to both sides of you; or a "slow glass" visualization, where you imagine a thick pane of special glass between you, which slows and filters out the raw energy but not the meaning.

Yet another way to take care of yourself is by networking with other counselors frequently. At the very least you should consult with other Witches who are experienced in counseling, and you may wish to have your counseling work supervised by a priest/ess, a professional therapist, or both. This can be an informal peer-support arrangement or part of an effort to earn a degree in psychology or social work. This is important: DON'T GO IT ALONE. You are dealing with the hearts and souls of human beings, and whether you know it or not, you need supervision or at least feedback from other wise and experienced counselors.

Last but not least, know your limits and stick to them. If you find yourself feeling burdened and exhausted by too many clients, or especially demanding ones, start adjusting the energy exchange and/or referring clients elsewhere. A burned-out, brain-fried counselor isn't much use to your clients, your coven, or the Gods.

Expectations

It is the nature of those who want to help that they set high expectations for themselves. We see unhappy people who do not know how to function in the world, and we want to rescue them, remake them, transform them, and make their lives whole and joyous.

Rarely can we do so much; nor should we. It is the client's life and their responsibility to make of it what they can. Even if we could effect a miraculous transformation, it would be our triumph, not theirs, and therefore our failure.

What can we do? Kennedy and Charles explain that there is "no disgrace in not being able to remake people . . . (and) every honor . . . in helping people to move even a few inches closer to self-responsibility . . . to turn in a new and healthier direction in life."[5]

So keep your expectations of yourself reasonable. You won't always succeed in helping a client transform their life. There are clients you won't be able to help at all. But if, more often than not, you manage to help a client discover a little more strength, a single resource, a ray of hope—then you have done well.

Summary

Counseling is a way to help people with their problems, not by solving the problems for them, but by empowering them to take responsibility for their own lives. Studies show that counseling really does make a difference, especially when done by a trained therapist over an extended period of time. However, even a relatively untrained priestess or priest can help a lot, first by just being supportive, and second by helping the client use the special tools of magick.

A counselor may encounter a huge variety of problems over time, ranging from tough life choices to ongoing mental disorders. It is vitally important not to get in over your head, but to refer people to trained professionals when it's a situation you're not trained to handle. You may wind up as the religious part of a client's staff, along with a professional therapist and medical doctor. In any case, make sure that you have supervision or peer support when you counsel.

When you do counsel someone, start by making them comfortable and getting basic information. Together, put together a clear contract as to what each of you will do in the counseling relationship. Then listen a lot. Ask non-leading questions when necessary. Work very hard to understand the client. Discover options with them and put together a plan of action. Incorporate the tools of magick, divination, and ritual.

Beware of pitfalls such as fostering dependence instead of empowering the client; getting too emotionally attached; focusing on yourself; becoming critical; taking sides in a family dispute; exchange-of-energy issues; subtle forms of client resistance to counseling; and transference, as well as counter-transference.

Take care of your own needs during the process, so long as you don't infringe on the client's needs. Make sure you don't get burned out and that the client does not take advantage of you. Don't expect dazzling successes every time, and remind yourself that in times of emotional crisis, even a little help may mean a lot.

Now read this summary again; then read it before and after each counseling session, until you know it by heart. May the Lady and the Lord be with you every time you counsel another.

RESOURCE

Kennedy, Eugene, and Sara C. Charles, *On Becoming a Counselor: A Basic Guide for Nonprofessional Counselors*, New York: Crossroads Publishing, 1994.

NOTES

1. "Mental Health: Does Therapy Help?" *Consumer Reports*, November 1995.
2. Eugene Kennedy and Sara C. Charles, *On Becoming a Counselor: A Basic Guide for Nonprofessional Counselors,* New York: Crossroads Publishing, 1994.
3. Ibid.
4. Ibid.
5. Ibid.

21 Children and Young People

Probably someone in your coven has children. Here's a question: do they participate in your Wiccan religious life, and do you integrate your Wiccan beliefs into their lives? Or is Witchcraft an "adult hobby" that doesn't have anything to do with your children?

Should Your Children Be Raised Wiccan?

Part of the parenting equation for Wiccans is the question: "Should I raise my kids Wiccan, or leave them alone to choose their own spirituality?" Many Witches answer this by reacting against the religion of their childhood, if it was repressive or simply boring. They may recall dozing through boring church services on hard pews or attending Sunday School classes where they colored endless pictures of sheep and Middle Eastern patriarchs. Some recall being confused by preachers who spoke to them in foreign languages or yelled at them for being "sinners." Many vowed never to subject their own children to such experiences, and to this day scrupulously avoid "pushing" any organized religion on their offspring—even Wicca.

Their motives are excellent; they want never to foist upon their children the mind-numbing, pride-crushing versions of religion they themselves may have endured. And they want to allow their children the freedom to choose their spiritual paths.

Such parents forget two things. First, the Wiccan experience is not the same as what they knew as children. We don't make people sit in rows while an "authority" tells them that they are sinful, and tells them exactly how they must live in order to escape eternal punishment. Wiccan ritual empowers us rather than denigrates us; celebrates with our "Inner Children" rather than represses them; connects us with nature instead of asserting mastery over it. And so on.

Second, giving a young child a choice to participate in religious activities is the same as giving them no religion at all. A child is not mature and knowledgeable enough to make such a choice; and most are not interested in questions of belief and values at all except as they impinge directly on their lives. Would you give your child a choice whether to eat whatever they could scrounge from the refrigerator, the neighbors' house, or the candy machine at school? Or do you give them balanced, healthful meals? If children were equipped to make intelligent choices and structure their own lives, they wouldn't be children—they would be adults.

As parents, we have the responsibility to teach our children the best that we can and expose them to beliefs and activities that will help them grow into strong, loving, and wise women and men. When they become adults they will have the option to choose another religion or lifestyle. Until then, we do them a disservice if we leave them floundering without guidance or structure. Not to put it too crudely, but a spiritual vacuum sucks. Children need some kind of moral guidance and at least tentative answers to the Big Questions. If we give them nothing, they are vulnerable to the first religious charlatan or Bible-thumper they meet.

So the answer is: yes, if Wicca works for you, then give your children the gift of Wicca—but without strings. Give it to them in a simple, enjoyable, age-appropriate way, and give them more as they show interest. If they grow up to become wise, loving, and powerful Witches, wonderful. And if they do choose a different religion later in life, be sure that they will keep in their hearts much of what they learned from you. At the very least, you will have given them a yardstick by which they can measure other faiths. But your job is to continue to love and accept them as the precious beings they are.

Family Rituals at Home

You can involve children at home in ways that are suited to their ages. A baby can sometimes be brought into the room where the parents are doing magick (inside the circle, please), and at an early age feel what it is to be in the circle, to smell the incense, watch the candles, and hear the chanting.

With slightly older children you can hold a "candle circle" with the whole family. Sit in a circle, light a candle for the Goddess and one for the God, and then have each family member tell about their week, ask for what they need, and give thanks for their blessings. Then sing a song, share hugs all around, and put out the candles. You can also "say grace" Wiccan-style at meals, and give the Moon Lady's blessing at bedtime.

Of course the sabbats should be special times for the whole family, by decorating the house or table, having special meals, singing or playing music, and so forth. Look through the sabbat activities suggested in this book and see how many the children would enjoy. Celebrating at home is important whether or not you also participate in a coven or community sabbat.

Your family's home and lifestyle can reflect your Wiccan beliefs in many ways besides ritual. Set up a family altar and change it with the seasons. Eat healthful foods, and before each meal give thanks the the spirits of the plants and animals who provided your nourishment. Recycle. Decorate the house with goddess and god images, wildlife photos, and other Pagan pictures and ornaments. Create herb and vegetable gardens. Treat animal friends with kindness and respect. Enjoy nature walks and outdoor recreation as a family. Play Pagan music at home. Keep track of your kids' studies in school, and give them a Wiccan perspective. Use small magicks in daily life.

Sabbats and Esbats with the Family

Your coven may decide to have "members-only" sabbat celebrations, but increasingly many covens are opening their sabbats to coveners' families, a wider congregation, the whole Pagan community in the area, or even the public at large.

If you invite families with children, then be sure that the program is one that will appeal to all ages. Most children and young people will enjoy activities like decorating special candles, hunting Ostara eggs, dancing the maypole, feasting at a corn roast, carving jack-o-lanterns, and decorating a Yule tree. Rituals should be fairly short (less than an hour) and involve lots of music, dancing, and other participation. If you can focus some special attention on the young ones, so much the better. They might be invited to come to the center of the circle for a tale by a storyteller, or asked to help asperge the circle or hand out rattles and drums.

The Adults-Only Work of the Coven

Some covens open their esbats to children, and some do not. It depends in part whether your moon rituals are purely celebratory or whether you will be raising the cone of power to work magick. The former can easily include young ones; but they should normally not be present for any intensive magick-working. The energy can have an intense impact on a child, or anyone who doesn't know how to channel, ground, or shield; it can leave them feeling tense, nervous, and unable to sleep. Arrange child care if necessary for such rituals. Each family can do a brief moon ritual at home before the parents leave for the esbat.

There are other coven activities, such as classes, where children should not be present. Much of the work of a coven would not be interesting or understandable to a child. And of course children can be distracting, especially to adults who are not used to living with them. Behavior that a parent finds normal or even charming can be irritating to other adults.

Covens should have a clear policy about which events children are invited to, and be very wary about making exceptions. At large events you may be able to set up child care with a volunteer member or a teenager. Sometimes older children can come along to the event and amuse themselves in a different room with a book, toy, television, or computer. Occasionally families with children may be able to take turns providing care, or pool their resources to place all the kids at one house and hire one sitter.

On the other side of the coin, children and young people should be encouraged or expected to participate in all appropriate events such as sabbat celebrations, summer festivals, and community service projects.

Summer Festivals

The summer festivals are wonderful places for kids, especially those that have a Children's Pavilion with an organized program of classes, craft projects, and nature hikes. Often the children's program functions as a cooperative; that is, if you send your children to participate, then you are expected to help out there for a few hours sometime during the festival. Normally there will be a bulletin board where you can sign up to help during certain hours, your "work shift."

When your children are not at the Children's Pavilion, they are your responsibility as usual. If several of your coven are camping together, your covenmates may be glad to help keep an eye on the kids. Older children often roam free over the festival site, reporting in to their parents at meals. As long as they stay within the boundaries of the site, they should be quite safe; be sure that most other Pagans value children as much as you do, and will respond instantly if your kids have an accident.

You may want to give your child some pocket money (or a chance to earn it) to spend at the merchant booths. Some items like ritual tools or velvet capes will be beyond their means, but usually there are inexpensive trinkets or costume items as well. If there are food vendors, impose reasonable limits on what the children may buy and eat.

If your children are new to Pagan festivals, let them know that they will probably see skyclad (nude) or topless people here and there, unless the site contract forbids it. Nudity is no big thing to most Pagans and is simply a way to feel free and close to nature. If you show no concern, then your children will very soon think nothing of it.

There are some potential hazards in any outdoor camping experience. Plan ahead and you won't have to worry too much about them:

Sunburn. On sunny days, make sure that your children are slathered with a good sunblock lotion (SPF 30 or higher) three or four times a day. Wearing a hat or cap is also a good idea.

Dehydration. Be sure there's a good supply of clean water and other beverages on hand, and every time you see them, remind your kids to drink. They may want to carry light plastic canteens or water bottles as well.

Hypothermia. In some regions, especially in the mountains and at night, temperatures can drop suddenly and unpredictably. What feels a little chilly to you can be dangerous to someone with a smaller body who is fatigued and perspiring. Make sure your kids are dressed warmly in windy or cool conditions.

Constipation. This occurs all too often on camping trips. Giving your children fresh fruit two or three times a day will help.

Water Accidents. If the festival is held at a lake, river, or beach site, let your children swim or play by the water only if supervised by a lifeguard or adult swimmer.

Poisonous Plants. Remind your young ones not to taste anything they find growing wild, unless you have personally approved it first.

Wildlife. Some sites are in bear country, and many attract raccoons and other smaller creatures. Although most animals will avoid a busy area filled with people, your children should still be warned not to approach any wild animal.

Molesters. Child molestation is extremely rare in the Pagan community, but in any large gathering of people it becomes a possibility. Tell your children that if they are approached by anyone who acts strangely, asks them to go to a private place, or touches them in sexual ways, that they should yell and run straight to your camp. Then notify a festival organizer or security team member at once.

Of course any active child may encounter bruises, scrapes, and blisters in the normal course of play. Have a simple first aid kit with you and insist that even minor injuries be washed and treated. Any well-organized festival will have a first aid station in case you need supplies or more expert help. But doubtless your young ones will survive the festival with intact bodies and happy memories.

Young People from Non-Pagan Families

If your coven is open in your community, from time to time you may be approached by a teenager who is fascinated by the Craft and wants to learn more, but whose parents are not interested. Your first step should be to contact the parents or guardians, and if possible have a face-to-face discussion about Wicca and their child's interest. Never assume that it is all right to share information with a minor or invite them to events, even if the teenager says "They don't care" or "It's fine with them." Such comments may be based on a misunderstanding, wishful thinking, or outright deception; and if you interact with the young person without checking, then you may lay yourself open to charges of "recruiting."

If you have talked with the parents or guardians and they are genuinely supportive, then you may ask them to sign a permission slip and waiver of liability for their young person to participate in whatever programs you think are appropriate: open classes, sabbat celebrations, community service projects, and so on. You may wish to assign a coven member with parenting experience as a "big sister" or "big brother" to keep an eye on the young participant.

Young People and Dedication

What do you do if a minor wants to dedicate and study to become a priestess or priest? Many covens have a firm policy that no one under the age of eighteen may become a dedicant; first, because experience has shown that most young people are in a time of transition and cannot be expected to maintain the same interests and commitments for very long. The teen years are appropriately a time of learning, exploration, and experimentation, and expecting someone of that age to be sure about their spiritual beliefs is asking a lot.

Second, priesthood of any variety requires a level of maturity and life experience which most teens do not yet possess. Wiccan clergy may be called upon to organize, administer, counsel, teach, and design and lead ritual—activities that most seasoned adults find challenging. Also, remember that with initiation may come the task of representing Wicca in the community; and how many teenagers (or even adults) have the knowledge, personal presence, articulateness, and diplomacy to explain the Craft to outsiders?

Young people of high school age may be encouraged to explore the Craft in many ways: by reading, participating in open events, becoming active in environmental projects, and communicating with Pagan pen pals by letter or on the Net. As a general rule, however, they should probably not be accepted into formal training for the Wiccan priesthood.

Hart and Crescent Award

Young people who want to study Wicca in a systematic way, and be recognized for their achievements, may be interested in the Hart and Crescent Religious Award sponsored by the Covenant of the Goddess. This is similar in many ways to the religious awards offered by faiths connected with the Scouting programs: awards such as the Ad Altere Dei (Roman Catholic), God and Country (Protestant), Religion in Life (Unitarian), and Ner Tamid (Jewish) in Boy Scouting, and the Marian Medal (Roman Catholic), Liahona (Latter-Day Saints), Menorah Award (Jewish), and God and Community (Protestant) in Girl Scouting.

The Hart and Crescent Award is different from many of these because it may be earned by girls and boys whether they are involved in Scouting or not. In fact, as of this writing our award is not recognized for official wear on the uniform by either the Boy Scouts of America or the Girl Scouts of the U.S.A. The Covenant of the Goddess negotiated for years with both organizations to get the same status for the Hart and Crescent as other religions' awards, and was refused.

However, the Hart and Crescent award exists and may be earned whether or not the Scouting agencies recognize it. It is designed for young people ages eleven to eighteen who consider themselves members of Wicca or any other nature-oriented religion. They will need a local adult counselor (parent or religious advisor) to work with them on the award. Some of the requirements involve working to defend the Earth's environment and wildlife, learning about goddesses and gods, discussing ethics, helping with a sabbat celebration, and practicing simple skills like relaxation and grounding. However, the counselor has wide discretion to adapt the requirements to the young person and their specific faith.

The award itself is a medal depicting a stag leaping in front of a crescent moon, and is suspended from a green, white, and blue ribbon. When the candidate has completed the requirements, the counselor signs an application and sends it to COG with a modest fee. The medal is sent back to the counselor for presentation. You may wish to present the award at a meeting or ritual of your coven.

There is a related award for adults, the Distinguished Youth Service Award. This may be presented by any coven or equivalent group to an adult who has offered exceptional service to youth in their community. The pendant is identical to the youth award, but suspended from a long neck ribbon rather than in medal form.

For a detailed Hart and Crescent requirements booklet, send $4.00 to COG, P.O. Box 1226, Berkeley, CA 94701. For information on the adult award, send $1.00 to the same address. Mark "Hart and Crescent" on the outside of the envelope.

RESOURCES

O'Gaea, Ashleen. *The Family Wicca Book: The Craft for Parents and Children*, St. Paul: Llewellyn, 1993.

K, Amber. *Pagan Kids' Activity Book*, Victoria, BC: Horned Owl Publishing, 1998.

Carson, Anne, ed. *Spiritual Parenting in the New Age*, New York: Crossing Press, 1989.

"Resources for Children and Youth," Covenant of the Goddess, 1995.

Animal Town Toys, Games and Books mail order catalog (P.O. Box 485, Healdsburg, CA 95448), Telephone: 1-800-445-8642. Environmentally friendly, multicultural, cooperative, and educational.

22 The Coven Elders

Wicca is one of the few religions where a priest/ess can be considered an "elder" at a rather young age. Because the Craft is growing so fast, and has a shortage of experienced teachers at this stage, many people in their forties, thirties, and even twenties find themselves in the odd situation of being the most experienced priest or priestess in their local community.

So for our purposes, an elder can be regarded as an initiate who is among the most knowledgeable and experienced members of their coven or local community.

These people have special needs that are different in some respects from the newer coveners. A new dedicant is full of enthusiasm and has the challenge of mastering a whole range of magickal skills, usually under the guidance of someone more experienced. Their goals are often fairly simple and straightforward: read some good books on the Craft, learn how a ritual is put together, find or make the basic magickal tools, practice raising and directing energy, and so on.

A more experienced Witch is long past learning basics. They have read the Craft books, and find many of the newly published ones repetitive. They have mastered the skills of designing and presenting a meaningful ritual. They have closets full of magickal tools and paraphernalia, and possibly enough occult jewelry to equip a platoon of Witches. And perhaps they have met and conquered some of the personal challenges they faced: addictions, emotional problems, relationship traumas, whatever.

The Problems

Witches may face new problems at this point in their careers. Perhaps they have learned all they easily can from books and other local Witches, and they cannot find adepts sufficiently advanced to teach them.

Perhaps they have healed old wounds and outgrown some personal problems, but the ones remaining are the stubborn, deeply rooted challenges that cannot be solved with an affirmation or a candle spell.

They may be frankly bored with the coven program ("Another dream circle?"), and want something unusual, creative, and demanding to do.

And they may have been the teachers and organizers so long, and worked so hard for the Wiccan community, that they are simply burned out. The endless trickle or stream of seekers and new students; the unrelenting drudge work of answering letters, making phone calls, and meeting newsletter deadlines; the sometimes petty and pointless politics and personality clashes between covens all take their toll, and the wondrous, fresh, bright world discovered years before becomes a little tarnished and dim.

Spiritual Challenges

Elders should take a regular inventory of their lives and decide what issues they need to focus on in order to continue the spiritual quest that is part of the life of every priest/ess. I have listed some of the potential issues; some may not seem "spiritual" at first glance, but doesn't spirituality encompass every aspect of our lives?

What is our best possible vocation? Many people, Witches included, find themselves in jobs that disappoint them; either they continue from inertia in some field they thought they wanted back in high school, or they drift from job to job according to what is convenient and available at the time. There comes a time when it is necessary to take a fresh look at your work, and perhaps have the courage to fly free and aim for a career that is more meaningful and congruent with your needs and convictions. Maybe it's time for an old dream to revive; maybe you've become aware of possibilities you never knew existed in your youth. Maybe you just know that your present job is not what you want to be doing the rest of your life, and it's time to do some research and see what's out there. You might want the services of a career counselor, you might see what help your college alumni office can provide, or you might want to spend some time at your library or surfing the Web. But consider this: over the next ten years you will spend about 20,000 hours at your job. Do you want to do what you're doing now for 20,000 more hours (or 40,000 or 60,000)?

Parenting is something many of us do, but how well are we doing it? I don't wish to add to the guilt of many parents who live with the nagging feeling that they should be doing something better, or different, for their children. But it's probably true. After all, most of us get little or no training for being parents; we do what our parents did for or to us, while perhaps leaving out the bits we didn't like. And most of us haven't taken a lot of time to attend parenting seminars, read parenting books, or discuss parenting issues in depth with other parents. Mostly we muddle through. But if you have children, maybe now is the best time to review how you parent and make changes where necessary. You might be doing a great job, so that only a minor "tune-up" is needed: a little more time with your kids, a little more attention to good nutrition, a little less television and more outdoor recreation, an occasional visit to a museum or historic site, more hugs and smiles, some exposure to good music. Or maybe there are more serious concerns, and a parenting seminar isn't such a bad idea after all. Or maybe a visit to a family counselor is really essential.

Wiccans are no strangers to fear, but unlike many, we are expected to confront and heal our fears. Perhaps you have already done much of this work in your first years in the Craft; and perhaps there is more to do. What do you fear? Illness? Hunger? Pain? Being alone? Poverty? Homelessness? Disfigurement? Ostracism? Loss of job, status, or prestige? Death? What comes after death? Then there are all the common phobias like fear of heights, cats, dogs, fire, enclosed places, flying, spiders, or Greek markets. And for the really phobic, fear of flying cats and flaming spiders in high enclosed Greek markets.

Whatever your fears, perhaps you owe it to yourself to work on them—even if your life is functioning fairly well with them. Sure, you can take the train instead of a scary airplane to visit Aunt Eggnog, and you can avoid your girlfriend's cats and stay out of spidery places (most of the United States). But not only is your life restricted, your magickal power is dimmed by the deep awareness of those fears. The fewer fears you have, and the more courage, the fewer are the limits to your magick. You may not be able to heal your fears alone, but counselors and the resources of your coven sisters and brothers are available.

Fear is only one of the "shadow side" emotions we must face. Witches are well aware that we all have negative aspects to our personalities, dark places in the heart. Lest we be ruled by them, we acknowledge them, face them, and in time heal those that harm us or others. Do you carry within you jealousy, anger, hatred, the capacity to kill? Most of us do; it is part of the human heritage, though not the most powerful part. Our willingness to face the "Dark Side of the Force" within allows us to understand it and heal that part which is generated by pain and fear. We can take its energy and either use it carefully to destroy that which harms the world, or transform it into creation and growth. And we can acknowledge the hurt we have caused in the past, when we didn't know any better, and make amends for it by loving acts today.

This is dark and mysterious psychological territory, and though the final work is always done alone, you may take companions on the first part of the journey. Priestess-counselors, shamanic guides, goddess-aspects, and animal allies all stand ready to walk with you as far as they may; and professional therapy may have its uses as well. If you hesitate, remember that magick is a double-edged blade, and one you should not wield unless you have faced your shadow and emerged whole.

Estrangements are another category of spiritual challenge for elders. Perhaps you carry the pain and loss from a former relationship and need to find resolution. Are you alienated from your family of origin? From a former friend, lover, or spouse? Can you reach out to heal and renew the relationship, or if not, can you release it in love rather than anger? And what of estrangement from ourselves—our feelings, bodies, hopes, and dreams? If you have repressed your emotions, you may need help in rediscovering and expressing them. If you have become distanced from your physical self, you may want to embrace it again through sports, outdoor recreation, dance, or making love. If you have turned your back on early ambitions and desires, know that you can claim them again and make them real. Part of maturity is accepting and embracing the world, yourself included, rather than walling yourself away piecemeal from the parts that hurt you.

Hieros Gamos means the "Sacred Marriage." This concept exists on many levels, from the meeting of Goddess and God from which primal creation springs, to the inner marriage, which brings wholeness to an individual. On the latter level it has been explored by C. G. Jung: he believed that every man holds an inner feminine aspect, the *anima*; and that every woman contains an inner masculine side, the *animus*. Jung believed that no one could become a full human being until they had recognized and accepted and integrated their inner "other half."

This idea is reflected in the yin-yang symbol of Taoism. It is composed of a dark teardrop shape (the yin or feminine) and a light teardrop (the yang or masculine) curving around each other, together forming a perfect circle. However, there is more: the yin shape carries within it a small light circle, and the yang carries a dark one. Thus each polarity holds the seed or potential of the other.

So men and women each have a job to do, reclaiming that part that society encourages us to ignore. This does not mean that men have to eat quiche or that women have to drive trucks (though it's fine if they do). Nor does it mean that we should all become androgynous or asexual blends of both sexes. It means that males have a bit of the Goddess within, and that they become more fully, deeply, splendidly, wholly man and human by embracing Her, and the converse for women. It's a mystery worthy of an elder's quest.

Yet another spiritual challenge is to define our relationship to society and the planet and to accept responsibility for the future of both—to have a dream or vision for the world and act to bring it closer to reality. Of course we do shape what happens by our lifestyles: recycling, walking instead of driving, and voting for candidates who share our ideals are all little ways to create the future. Beyond this are other possibilities: we can choose to be educators and reformers, building on the foundation of our present culture and improving it. We can be rebels and outlaws, attacking the old corruption and injustices from outside society. We can be pioneers, creating new communities as alternative role models for the world. But it all begins with a vision of what could be (and how many of us have a clear and powerful vision?). And it continues by changing the one thing we all have power to change: ourselves. And in changing ourselves, we change our world.

A common thread that ties together all these spiritual challenges is the idea of legacy. An elder might wish to write down, in detail, what legacy they wish to leave and detailed steps to make it happen. At the close of this chapter in your book of lives, what will you leave for your children, physical or spiritual? Will it be an inspiring example of a life well lived? Memories of a loving parent and good provider? The story of a priestess or priest who dared confront the shadow, and emerged whole? Will it be a forest planted, wise laws enacted, artistic beauty created? Could it be a rare species saved, a law of nature revealed, or shelter built for the homeless? Might it be priestesses taught and magick done? You are planting and harvesting day by day. What will be the sum of your harvest for this incarnation?

Ongoing Learning

One thing that elders need is new learning experiences. Granted, one learns a great deal by teaching new students, but there comes a time when fresh input is needed. Some of this can be gained from workshops at festivals, but these are hit-or-miss propositions: almost anyone can sign up to present a workshop, and the teachers' skills and level of the material vary wildly from one program to the next.

A local Pagan association or COG Local Council may organize a Workshop Day where the best teachers from each coven teach at a day-long event, or exchange teachers for an evening or weekend to teach their specialties to a nearby coven. Perhaps Moonwhistle of Coven Agrimony is a respected tarot teacher and agrees to teach four evening classes at Coven Beebalm. In return, Suncatcher from Coven Beebalm agrees to present her famous weekend Walking Herbal Identification Tour for Coven Agrimony.

Some covens are willing to host an elders' exchange, where priest/esses get to become honorary members of a different coven for a few weeks or months. The chance to see a different tradition at work can be really stimulating, and they may return to the home coven with more energy and some new ideas.

There are also many opportunities to learn Pagan-related skills and knowledge at "Non-Pagan" events. There are conferences and seminars on mythology, ancient history, alternative healing methods, clinical hypnosis, pastoral counseling, organic gardening, environmental quality, and a myriad of other interesting topics. Local colleges, YMCAs, park districts, and clubs may offer classes in belly dancing, yoga, folk dancing, the Internet, jewelry-making, and other subjects which could be built into the coven program.

If there's no "official" program available and your elders would like to learn a new skill, invite an expert to share with you. Ask a professional therapist to train you in basic pastoral counseling skills. Ask a member of the Garden Club to help you start a coven herb garden. Ask a martial arts instructor to work with you in channeling *chi* energy. Ask a park ranger to bring you up to date on local wildlife habitats. Ask a blacksmith or amateur knife-maker to help you create new athames, bollines, or even a coven sword. Ask a priest, monk or shaman of another path to speak to you. An evening's brainstorming can yield a huge list of possibilities if you are near a city, or a respectable list even if you are in a rural area. Of course you may need to provide an honorarium to cover time and travel expenses, but if this is divided among the coven members it should be affordable.

It may be an extra little "motivator" if your coven has some way to recognize advanced achievement among your elders: perhaps a coven "Mistress of Arts" or "Master of Arts" degree developed between each elder and a peer or mentor. This should have specific requirements, a schedule or target date for completion, and some tangible symbol at the end of it: a new cord, badge, or emblem. As part of the program, the elder student should teach some basic workshops on the subject for the coven and perhaps other Pagans in the area.

Special Roles in the Coven

For some Witches, a new challenge comes when they assume the office of High Priestess or High Priest. Those who have held these positions know that it is extremely rewarding work: you are doing the work of the Triple Goddess and the Horned God, creating religious community and guiding priests and priestesses on an ancient and honorable spiritual path. These jobs are also time-consuming, energy-draining, frustrating, and crazy-making.

Not every experienced Witch gets to taste these joys; fortunately there are other creative and rewarding jobs within the coven, and one of the best ways to keep learning and growing is to change offices from time to time. If an elder seems stale, challenge them to try something new.

- Lead a drive to find and purchase land for a coven retreat cabin.
- Help some of the coven's young people to earn the Hart and Crescent Award sponsored by the Covenant of the Goddess.
- Organize a community service project: environmental education in the schools, litter clean-up, sponsoring a needy family at the holidays, a food or clothing drive, a park beautification project.
- Create a scrapbook of the coven's history.
- Supervise the next public Wicca 101 classes.
- Compile and publish a new coven Book of Shadows or songbook.
- Contact other covens in the area and organize the learning exchange mentioned earlier.
- Reorganize and redecorate the temple room at the covenstead.
- On private land, create an outdoor circle with a stone altar, statuary, herb gardens, and landscaping.
- Rewrite the coven's teaching curriculum, incorporating new books and research.
- Create a videotape introducing Wicca for public education and show it on the local public access television channel.

- Reorganize the coven library. Make a list of books you should acquire to bring it up to date and organize fundraising to purchase the new books.
- Organize or reorganize the coven's music collection (records, tapes, and CDs), get suggestions for new acquisitions from coveners, other covens, and Pagan periodicals, and start to build the collection.
- Organize a field trip for the coven—to Salem, Massachusetts, or to sacred sites in England.

And so much more that you can think of. Ask yourselves, "What would make our coven's program even more outstanding?"—then put your elders to work doing it!

In the Community

Some elders need a break from coven responsibilities and are ready for wider challenges in the Pagan community locally, regionally, or nationally. If your coven has been at all isolated from your neighbors, this is a good opportunity to make connections and enjoy the resources out there. Even if your High Priestess or High Priest has been quite active networking, it can be an exciting growth experience for your elders to explore the wider Pagan world and represent the coven at meetings and festivals.

Consider some ways to get involved beyond the coven.

- Take charge of the program for Pagan youth at a local festival.
- Coordinate an intercoven community service project.
- Present a workshop for local law enforcement officers: "Alternative Religions and the Law."
- Visit with local librarians and help them upgrade their alternative religions and occult collections.
- Present a short talk on Wicca at a local interfaith meeting.
- Visit a high school history or humanities class and discuss Wicca with the students.
- Help organize a pan-Pagan potluck, concert of Pagan music, workshops by guest speakers, regional festival, Renaissance faire, or psychic fair.
- Serve as advisor to a Pagan student association at your nearest college or university.
- Work with other Pagans and environmentalists to organize an All-Species Day, Arbor Day, or Earth Day event.
- Help sponsor a Halloween Party for local kids in your community center or public library.
- Publish a newsletter and calendar of events for your city, area, or state.

- Visit Wiccan prisoners, if any, at the nearest correctional facility.
- Trade visits and presentations with an area Buddhist temple, Jewish synagogue, Native American church, Christian church, or other religious organization.
- Appear on a radio talk show or interview with a local newspaper about Wicca.
- Compile a list of campgrounds, hiking trails, picnic areas, hot springs, retreat centers, and other outdoor resources and share it with covens and Pagan groups in your community.

National Networking

There are further challenges in national and international networking. For some, the Internet offers a chance to socialize with other Pagans here and abroad. Some use it as a way to keep up with news affecting Pagans worldwide, and some use it as an educational tool: doing surveys, collecting ritual ideas, or asking for contacts or information on a specialized field of study.

A few elders use their special experiences and skills to write books on magick or Paganism, preserving our heritage, and offering more resources to seekers and the Craft. Metaphysical and New Age publishers like Llewellyn and Samuel Weiser are well known in the United States, as are Hale and Aquarian Press in the United Kingdom. Other publishers who specialize in such material or are open to it are Beacon, Citadel, Harper and Row, HarperCollins, Delphi, and The Crossing Press.

Those who are highly respected as teachers locally may try sharing their knowledge away from home. An easy way to begin is to offer workshops at summer festivals. Each time you do so, you will refine your teaching skills, and in time you may wish to travel and lead weekend workshops or retreats. However, be aware that even apart from the ethical issues of charging for Craft teaching, this is not a practical way to earn a living. Many Pagans are not able to afford hefty workshop fees even if you felt comfortable about charging them (it's said that the difference between a Pagan event and a New Age event is two decimal points in the fee). So go afield to teach if you love to teach, travel, and meet new people.

Elders with excellent group skills, communications, and patience may become active as officers of national and international organizations such as the Covenant of the Goddess (primarily U.S. and Canada), the Covenant of Unitarian Universalist Pagans (U.S.), the Pagan Federation (mostly the United Kingdom), and the Pan-Pacific Pagan Alliance (Australia, New Zealand, and beyond). The Covenant of the Goddess has Local Councils which may cover part of a state or an entire state or more; they need officers each year to network in their areas. All three organizations require national officers to function. These are volunteer positions elected from the membership; all require large amounts of time and energy, but generally the terms are only a year or two. Being elected an officer of a large group can be stressful and frustrating (accomplishing anything is "like trying to herd cats," according to one elder), but there are long-term rewards as the Craft grows in cooperation, maturity, and respect.

A small but growing number of Craft elders are investing their energies in interfaith work. There are interfaith organizations on local, state, national, and international levels; many are open only to Christian churches, but others are interested in fostering understanding and cooperation among all religious communities. A few are semi-open; that is, you might have to educate them about Wicca so that they understand we are a serious religion and not some variant on the Church of Monday Night Football.

Wicca took a big step in 1993 when the Parliament of World's Religions met in Chicago for the second time in a century. The Covenant of the Goddess was one of many co-sponsors, and nature religions were also represented by Circle Sanctuary and the EarthSpirit Alliance. Not only did Witches host workshops and presentations on the Craft and modern Paganism, but we also maintained a hospitality suite and sponsored a public Full Moon ritual. With this event the Craft "came out of the broom closet" to the interfaith community in a major way. Not all the religions represented were friendly; in fact, because Wiccans were present a few delegates left—under the odd impression that we do not recognize a deity or deities. But the great majority of delegates seemed to have a genuine desire to understand, communicate, and explore common ground. One result of the Parliament was a statement, "Towards a Global Ethic," signed by delegates from a number of the world's faiths, including Wicca.

Interfaith efforts can be seen as one kind of specialized ministry. Other elders find themselves a vocation working with Wiccans in the prisons, hospital chaplaincies, law enforcement agencies, the military, the media, or even dictionary publishers. Because of their work, Wicca is slowly becoming recognized and accepted by professionals and community leaders.

Sabbaticals

Sometimes the best restorative for a tired elder is a vacation from coven activities—a leave of absence, or sabbatical. Then they can do something "re-creational":

- becoming a couch potato with videos of every Goldie Hawn movie ever made;
- hanging out at the local swimming pool or "Y" and getting in shape;
- visiting the Indy 500, the Kentucky Derby, or a favorite sports team;
- holing up in a home workshop and making furniture or jewelry;
- visiting friends or relatives in another part of the country;

- traveling and playing tourist;
- hiking, camping, and nature photography;
- taking classes and seminars;
- staying home and reading good books;
- remodeling or redecorating the house; or
- creating an herb, flower, or vegetable garden.

Find an activity that would be a restful change of pace for that individual. The sabbatical might take a month, three months, six months, or longer. If your coven is strong, you can spare one member for that length of time. If your coven relies on that one person for its continued health or existence, then it's time to reorganize anyway.

When the elder returns, some reintegration may be required. Make sure the returnee gets to visit and socialize individually with the other members, to tell their adventures and catch up on the news. A conference with the High Priestess and High Priest might be a good idea, to discuss whether the returning elder wants to take back the same coven jobs or try something new.

Hiving

Some elders may wish to stay with their home coven for many years, serving as teacher and counselor to succeeding generations of new students. Others may use their home coven as a base from which to do community organizing or regional and national networking. A few may succeed to the offices of High Priestess and High Priest of and carry on the traditions of the coven in their own style.

But many elders are ready for coven leadership before the High Priestess and High Priest of their home coven are ready to step aside. Then hiving becomes a natural alternative. According to tradition, hiving occurs when a second- or third-degree initiate, with the blessing of their coven leaders, leaves the coven to create a new offshoot. If others in the home coven want to go with them, they are free to do so. Traditionally, until they receive their third degree, a second-degree Witch still operates under the guidance of their home High Priestess and High Priest. Various traditions of the Craft differ as to how much fealty is owed to the original High Priestess, but practically speaking the new coven is its own entity.

Hiving works best when the home coven has grown large (thirteen or more), and when several members join the new coven, so that both of the resulting covens have a large enough core to function well from the beginning. But often only two or three members will choose to hive, and then they should open their doors to at least a couple of new members as soon as they are ready. There are exceptions, but in general a coven of fewer than five members has difficulty sustaining itself for long.

What happens if a dedicant or first-degree initiate chooses to leave and start their own coven? Of course they are free to do so, but considering that they have only minimal training, they may encounter problems due to lack of knowledge and experience; and they may or may not be recognized as a member of the same tradition.

Wise coven leaders will be sensitive to each covener's growth and will know if an elder is "chafing at the bit" and ready to lead their own coven. It is not unknown for such an elder to unconsciously manufacture or magnify differences with the coven leaders, making it emotionally easier to leave the group. This kind of situation has some similarities to the teenager who asserts his independence from his parents by creating a huge argument and then storming off to get his own apartment. There are issues of individuation and separation. Sometimes scenarios like this can be avoided if the coven leaders make it clear that hiving will be encouraged and supported.

Despite everyone's best efforts, members do not always leave under amicable circumstances. If a covener is stripped of membership or rejects the authority of the coven leadership and leaves, then any new coven formed in the aftermath is not a proper hive, meaning it cannot claim lineage in the tradition of the home coven. The members of the home coven must decide how they want to deal with the situation. Depending on the circumstances, they may make overtures of cooperation, adopt a very neutral posture and see what happens, or announce that all ties are severed and refuse to interact with the former member. It is not sensible to snub new members of the dissident's new coven when you encounter them at community events. Be courteous and friendly. After all, they were not part of the original dispute. Also, avoid verbal or other attacks on the dissident as this would only polarize the community. Allow the Lords of Karma and the Law of Return to deal with the situation and get on with your coven's work.

Summary

Elders have special needs, which differ from people who are newer to the coven. They require more advanced learning experiences, more challenging roles in the coven, and perhaps projects, offices, and resources outside the coven: in the community, the region, or nationally and internationally. Some elders succeed the High Priestess and High Priest who taught them, others may hive and found a new coven. And sometimes they just need a break—a leave of absence or sabbatical. Capable coven leaders will work to see that their elders are challenged, growing, and have opportunities for teaching, leadership, or advanced study.

Counsel to an Elder

If you don't know who you are by now,
then choose whom you desire to be.

Listen much, speak little.

When the teacher is ready to learn,
the students will come to teach.

You can affect the lives of others, but in the end
their lives are their responsibility.

Coyote has a standing invitation to your life,
issued by Himself.

You may live to be a hundred; but will you have lived a hundred years,
or the same year a hundred times?

Always have a rubber trout or its spiritual equivalent
on the altar.

We are by nature a young and frolicsome species.
Never consider yourself too old to play.

All that you have seen or sensed in every God/dess
is within you.

Bless all about you. Blessed be.

23 Customs and Traditions

Every coven has customs; some are common to the whole Craft, and have the force of law within our community. Others are unique to a single tradition or coven, and are part of what defines its identity and makes it special. Some are essential to Wicca, others are pleasant variations on a theme. Some customs "large and small" follow;[1] read them over with your coven. Those presented here are not dogma. However, I have put those in bold type which, in my opinion, are crucial to the existence of a strong Wiccan coven. Some you may wish to adopt; others may lead you to think about your own contrasting choices. After reading each, ask yourself what your coven will do.

Ritual Apparel and Tools

Long, green, hooded robes shall be worn for classes and open rituals. For Moon rituals and most magick, the coven shall commonly work skyclad, weather permitting. At Sabbats, robes or festive garb of any sort shall be worn.

Each person shall wear a cord, girdle, or cingulum of a color denoting their degree. Dedicants shall wear white, Initiates green, and Elders red. High Priestesses shall wear silver, High Priests gold.

Women may wear a necklace of stones, shells, seeds, or wood to symbolize the Great Circle of life, death, and rebirth. Men may wear a torc for the Lord of Life and Death. Both may wear such other jewelry as they desire.

A High Priestess may wear a garter of green suede and sky-blue silk, with a silver buckle for each coven started by her or hived from hers. A High Priestess, or female ritual leader acting in that role, may wear a silver or jeweled crescent tiara. A High Priest, or male ritual leader acting in that role, may wear a horned headdress.

Every initiate of the coven may wear a bracelet of silver with the sigil of the coven and his or her magickal name engraved in Theban script.

It is appropriate for each member to wear an image or token of their power animal, totem animal, or deep-self animal.

Each Initiate shall create or obtain these ritual tools: a black-handled athame (and better it be with a double-edged blade of silver, copper, or bronze); a white-handled bolline (with blade of any shape and metal); a chalice; a pentacle; and a wand. Tools shall be consecrated and may be marked with the owner's name.

Each member may have such other tools as she or he desires: a wand, runestones, tarot cards, broom, and so on. No member shall touch the tools of another without the owner's permission.

The Esbats and Sabbats

At each Full Moon there shall be held a ritual to honor the Lady and the Lord, and to do whatever magick is needful for the members or the Earth. Full Moon esbats should commonly be celebrated on the evening of the Full Moon; but may occasionally be celebrated on one of the weekends bracketing it, as close to the actual event as possible.

New Moon esbats shall be celebrated at Diana's Bow, when the new crescent is first visible, about three evenings after the actual New Moon.

Sabbats may be celebrated on the traditional night or on one of the weekends bracketing it; except **Samhain, which is celebrated on the night of October 31 and no other.**

At Sabbats, between the ritual and the feast the coven shall lift a toast to the Lady, the Lord, and our sacred selves.

Each year the coven shall hold a camping retreat to celebrate and bond more closely, usually over a long weekend. The location may vary but should always include some outstanding natural feature close by such as a cave, waterfall, mountain, or ancient forest.

At each Sabbat there shall be a feast held; everyone who is able shall contribute food or drink, and better it be healthful and prepared at home.

Ritual Etiquette

The altar shall normally be placed in the East, the direction of the dawn and new beginnings, from whence the Craft came in days of old. Ritual activities shall begin in the East and proceed deosil. In special magicks this may vary.

No covener shall come late to a ritual and ask entrance after the circle is cast; no one shall be admitted to a ritual after it has begun. A covener who is unavoidably detained and cannot call in may wait quietly in another room, study Craft books, or meditate until the ritual is ended.

Wine will normally be used in the ritual chalice. Members who do not partake of wine may symbolically touch the chalice to their lips in their turn. Other beverages shall be used occasionally. All consecrated wine shall be consumed within the circle or given to the Earth in libation before ending the ritual.

Common rituals will be done from memory. Coveners are expected to become familiar with traditional forms of casting the circle, making invoking and banishing pentagrams, and standard ritual phrasing used in the coven. Words and actions peculiar to a certain ritual may be read.

Except in need, no covener shall leave the circle until it is opened at the end of the ritual. If one must leave, they shall cut a doorway in the northeast and seal it again after passing through.

The coven altar shall normally have upon it images of the Lady and Lord so that They may smile upon our rituals, and a token of the Trickster (in our tradition, usually a rubber trout or small stuffed moose) so that S/he may intervene as little as possible.

Coven Relationships

Coveners shall support one another outside of formal coven activities; if a covener is ill, or hungry, or otherwise in need, they shall have the reasonable support of coven sisters and brothers.

All coveners shall strive to work and celebrate always in harmony with one another. However, if there should be conflict and the parties do not promptly work it out on their own, then they shall seek counsel and mediation from the High Priestess, High Priest, or other initiate. If mediation fails, they shall agree to arbitration by the High Priestess or High Priest, and willingly accept their decision. No dispute between coven members shall be taken outside the coven, except by consensus of the Coven Council.

It is natural that each member will form close personal relationships with other members and with the group as a whole. We encourage love and trust, openness, sharing of feelings, constructive criticism, and emotional support within the coven. Prospective participants whose partners are not joining must resolve any conflicts this may cause at home before being accepted for membership.

Touching and hugging are a natural part of emotional sharing and support and are encouraged to the extent that recipients welcome them. Sexual contact between members is not part of the usual affection shared within the coven. Members and Dedicants may not engage in unwelcome and repeated sexual requests, touching, or comments with others. Sexual relations between consenting members are not part of coven activities and should be kept private. Sexual relationships between Dedicants and those of significantly higher degree (i.e., in a position to influence their Craft advancement) are discouraged.

Other Customs and Guidelines

Coven meetings shall be held at the covenstead (the home of the High Priestess) or outdoors at a location chosen by the Coven Council. Or, at the invitation of a member and with the consent of the High Priestess, at other members' homes occasionally.

Each covener, upon Initiation or before, shall choose a Craft name that symbolizes her or his special attributes, or those they wish to enhance. This name may be used only within the coven or within the larger Pagan community, as the member wills. Or, the covener may have two magickal names, one for the coven and one for the wider community. Members may add or change names as their spiritual growth indicates.

Continuing growth is expected of each Initiate; and each shall continue to study and enhance their skills in a chosen field either through the coven and/or outside resources. An Initiate who achieves competence in a specialized field may be recognized as a Mistress of Arts or Master of Arts.

The coven shall have an astral temple, a place of peace and healing, joy and renewal, to which any Initiate may go when she or he chooses.

There shall be no money required of members to participate in the coven's regular program. When the coven has need, it shall be met by donations or special fundraising activities.

Members shall be encouraged to participate in the greater communities of the Craft and Paganism, and to visit other covens if invited and learn what they may. But no member shall hold membership in two covens at once, unless by consensus of the Coven Council.

Rites of passage of coveners and their families shall be recognized with appropriate ceremony, such as Birth/Wiccaning, Puberty, Adulthood, Handfasting/Marriage, Handparting, Cronehood/Sagehood, Death, Dedication, Initiation, Elder status, attainment of a Mistress/Master of Arts, and Ordination.

The privacy of each participant shall be respected. No one shall reveal to cowans the coven or Craft affiliation of another, except with that individual's consent.

The coven shall have a winter retreat once each year at a ski lodge in the mountains (or a summer retreat at a campground, or a fall retreat at a rented cabin, or whatever is appropriate).

The coven shall have refreshments at each esbat, and a potluck feast after every sabbat.

After each initiation, the coven leaders shall lead toasts to the Lady, the Lord, the coven, and the new Initiate.

At each initiation it shall be customary for the new Initiate to present a gift to the coven (a book, ritual tool, service, etc.) and for each member to present a small gift to them.

At Yule, the coven shall have a wassail bowl, caroling, and a gift exchange.

The coven shall keep a book of activities and events, and each person present shall sign in so that attendance can be tracked.

Dedicants shall be responsible for cleaning the coven tools and keeping coven supplies in order, under the supervision of the Maiden.

Upon each initiation, the new Initiate shall be presented with a certificate from the coven confirming their status.

Shoes shall not be worn in the temple (i.e., in any room used for ritual).

When a member of the coven must move out of town for personal or career reasons, the coven shall host a farewell party, and the remaining members shall be encouraged to keep in communication with the one who is leaving.

Once each year an appreciation banquet shall be held, to thank all those who have served the coven in any office.

Once each summer the coven will plan to attend a local or regional festival as a group, and camp together.

When in the company of Pagans who are not members of the coven, the High Priestess and High Priest shall be referred to with the titles "Lady" and "Lord" as a sign of respect. Within the coven, the titles shall not be used except during ritual.

As time goes on, your coven will evolve or adopt its own customs, some symbolic, some practical, some funny. Maybe you will impose a penalty for anyone who forgets their robe; for example, buying a book for the coven library or bringing an edible treat for the coven next time. Maybe you will begin each coven feast with a toast to "Maid Marian, Robin Hood, and his dog." Such traditions, solemn or silly, are worth cultivating; they strengthen the group's identity and each member's sense of belonging.

Other, more formal rules can be outlined in the coven by-laws (see the appendices for an example). In combination, the by-laws, customs, and most of all the Wiccan Rede and Law of Return should define the coven and give it clear guidance in a positive direction.

NOTES

1. Most of the customs listed are from the Coven of Our Lady of the Woods. They are offered only as examples and possibilities.

24 Serving a Congregation

One definition of a coven is a small community of priestesses and priests dedicated to preserving the Old Religion. If all Craft initiates are clergy, a logical question is, "Where are the lay people?"

There are two ways to look at this. One is to say that our congregations were converted, killed, or frightened away during the Burning Times. Another is to assert that there are not, nor should there be, any lay people. That every Wiccan should be empowered to find his or her own link to the Divine and not require an intermediary of any kind. We are all priestesses and priests, period. In a spiritual and thealogical sense, few Witches would disagree with this: everyone has the Divine within and has only to reach in and touch It.

There is a practical problem, however. Many people are Wiccan or Pagan at heart, but do not have the time, energy, skills, or desire to train as a priest/ess. Saying "Every Wiccan their own priest/ess" makes a great slogan, but is a little like saying "Everyone their own farmer" or "Everyone their own plumber." The fact is, human civilization has made its achievements through specialization. Not every person can be everything from an expert farmer to a registered pharmacist, but we can, and do, share our special talents and training and achieve more as a society of specialists than we ever could as a loose gang of generalists.

The same is true when it comes to the skills of a priest/ess, "the technology of the sacred." A Wiccan priest/ess is ideally a ritualist, counselor, teacher, magickian, group facilitator, and scholar of the heart and mind. Some people excel at designing and leading rituals; other people love to come together for a good ritual, but would have little clue how to plan one and no desire to lead it. Some people have a gift for spiritual counseling, and others would rather be nibbled to death by ducks than try it. In short, some people have great natural talents for religious work, others don't. Some have education and training in related skills, others don't. Some have a deep desire to help other people with their spiritual lives, others don't. We all may bear personal responsibility for our spirituality, but we don't all have the talent, training, or desire to make a good job of it without help.

So having a specialized clergy makes sense, at least among social animals like us. This does *not* mean that our clergy have to function just like the clergy of other faiths. We do not have to have a paid professional clergy, for example. We do not need to tell people (or imply) that they must obey our clergy in order to be "saved." We do not have to serve gods who are jealous, domineering, and sexist. We *can* have clergy who are dedicated to wisdom, love, power-with instead of power-over, and reverence for all beings.

And whom do these clergy serve? Only sister and brother initiates within their own covens? Or also those people who want to celebrate the sabbats, would like to have rites of passage for themselves and their families, need occasional resources like Wiccan spiritual counseling, want occasional workshops in magickal skills to improve their lives, and want both a Pagan community and the services of skilled priest/esses?

These are the people who potentially form local Pagan congregations. We might just as well call them "outer grove members," or "coven visitors," or "organized non-clerical coven affiliates," but congregation is simple, has pleasant associations for many, and is actually comprehensible to the non-Wiccan community.

A few paragraphs ago the question may have occurred to many readers: how can one priest or priestess be highly competent in all those priestly skills—counseling, rituals, and so on? Well, in general they can't. This is the beauty of having a coven full of priest/esses serving a congregation of Pagans, instead of paying one poor schmuck and expecting them to be "master of all religious skills." Within a coven there is likely to be at least one Witch who is better at leading sabbats, another who has a flair for pastoral counseling, and another who teaches really great classes. The sum of a coven's skills is greater than any individual's. Together they can share the work involved in serving a congregation and potentially do a better job than any lone paid clergyperson could.

A Congregation Structure

A congregation need not be as highly organized as a coven, for the simple reason that the coven officers can handle much of the congregation's business. In its simplest form, a congregation might have only one officer: a "Congregation Coordinator" (or other title of your choice) who acts as an all-purpose administrator and communications nexus.

A slightly more elaborate setup would include the following officers.

- A Program Officer, who meets with the congregation to solicit program ideas and then works with congregation and coven to set up a schedule of open rituals, classes, social and recreational events, and service projects.
- A Communications Officer, who is responsible for keeping the group informed about events through phone calls, media contacts and mailings.

This officer might also put sign-up sheets out at open events and maintain a database of congregation members and friends.

- A Facilities Officer, who rents meeting facilities, gets park permits, arrives early to make sure that things are set up, and supervises a volunteer clean-up crew afterwards. These duties could also be handled by a Pursewarden, if the congregation has funds of its own.

All these offices might be filled by volunteers or elected by members at an annual congregational business meeting. You will want to be sure that the officers get plenty of thanks and recognition for their hard work.

A Congregation Program

If it is to maintain interest and participation, the congregation program should include a varied menu of events at fairly regular intervals. You can begin with sabbat celebrations and Full Moon esbats, add classes and workshops, put in some social and recreational events, and perhaps add some community service projects. Then there will be special events such as rites of passage. A full congregation calendar might include the following:

Sabbats	Full Moon Esbats
Yule (about December 21)	Wolf Moon (January)
Imbolc (February 2)	Snow Moon (February)
Ostara (about March 21)	Seed Moon (March)
Beltane (May 1)	Grass Moon (April)
Litha (about June 21)	Flower Moon (May)
Lughnassad (August 2)	Strawberry Moon (June)
Mabon (about September 21)	Thunder Moon (July)
Samhain (October 31)	Green Corn Moon (August)
	Harvest Moon (September)
	Hunter's Moon (October)
	Beaver Moon (November)
	Cold Moon (December)
	Blue Moon (13th in the year)

(Note: the Moon names are chosen from "The Names of the Full Moons" chart in the appendices. Your coven or tradition may use other names.)

Class Ideas

What kind of classes would be appropriate for a congregation of Pagans? These might fall into the general categories of The Basics of Wicca, Mythology, Individual Spiritual Practices, Self-care and Healing, Pagan History, and Resources. Some ideas are listed below; you can think of many more.

The Basics of Wicca

The Sabbats and the Wheel of the Year
Wiccan Ethics: The Rede, the Law, and the Ordains
How Do You Experience the Goddess?
How Do You Experience the God?
Pantheism, Animism, and All Those Isms
The Evidence for Reincarnation
Ritual Etiquette and Symbolism
Living Wiccan 24 Hours a Day

Mythology

Goddesses and Gods of Old Europe
Celtic Mythology
Moon and Sun Goddesses Around the World
The Green Man
The Horned God
Harvest Gods, Death and Rebirth
The Goddess as Earth Mother
Warrior and Huntress Goddesses
The Deities of (choose one: Egypt, India, the Middle East, Africa, Mexico and Central America, Native North America, China, etc.)

Individual Spiritual Practices

Choosing a Magickal Name
Elements and Elementals
Tree Lore and Spirits
Animals and Magick
Making Amulets and Talismans
Tarot for Beginners
Chants for Fun and Ritual
How to Be an Environmental Activist
Creating a Home Altar
Choosing a God/dess Aspect to Work With
Making God and Goddess Statues
The Magickal Uses of Gemstones
Guidance from the Runes
An Introduction to Drumming
Ethical Love Spells and Aphrodisiacs

Self-Care and Healing

Herbal Home Remedies
Natural Remedies for Stress
Chakra Cleansing Exercises
Diet and Nutrition
Alternative Healing Choices for Pagans
You Can Plant an Herb Garden
Fasting for Cleansing and Health

Pagan History

Religion in the Paleolithic
The Celtic Culture
The Burning Times
Stone Circles and Sacred Sites in England
Robin Hood and the Old Religion
The Legends and Reality of King Arthur

The Lost Years: Wiccan Survival or Re-creation?
The Other Pagans: Druids, Asatru, and More
Gerald Gardner and Doreen Valiente
What the Religious Right Is Doing Today

Resources

A Look at Pagan Publications
Book Discussions
Pagan Summer Festivals: What, Where and How
Pagan Music Reviews
Sources for Magickal Supplies
Pagans on the Internet

The only subjects to avoid, at least in public classes, are any advanced magicks that could be twisted and used for harmful purposes. Restrict these to dedicants or initiates whose ethics you are sure of. Other subjects that might be of interest to the coven, but not necessarily the congregation, are priest/ess skills such as Ritual Design and Presentation, Pastoral Counseling, Coven Administration, or in-depth studies of Thealogy and Comparative Religions.

Congregation or open classes can be offered on a regular evening (such as the first Monday of each month), as a weekend workshop, or as part of a sabbat program, just prior to the ritual and potluck. One or two classes a month are sufficient, unless you want to offer an occasional weekly series, for example, a "Wicca 101" or "World Mythology."

Teachers can be recruited from among the congregation itself, from friends and relatives, from the coven, and by tracking down outside experts or professionals. Most teachers from the coven or congregation would be expected to donate their time and skills; outside experts may well require an honorarium, which can be covered from the treasury or free-will donations.

Social and Recreational Events

See the chapter on Special Activities for more of these. And remember, in Wicca "fun" is not a four-letter word.

Potluck dinners (possibly with ethnic themes)
Video nights ("Witchy" movies)
Game evenings (board games, cards, charades, etc.)
Arts and crafts evenings
Theater outings (or concerts, ballet, opera, etc.)
Movie-and-dinner outings
Museum visits
Picnics
Visits to historic or sacred sites
Hiking and camping trips
Wilderness trips (river rafting, backpacking, caving)
Ski trips or tobogganing

Weekend retreats
Softball, soccer, or volleyball tournaments
Amateur talent nights

Service Projects

Service projects can be undertaken by the coven and congregation together, or in cooperation with other covens and Pagan groups in the area, or even with other churches and service clubs. Your coven will have to decide whether to flaunt the fact that you are Wiccan or downplay it.

Food collection for needy families or pantries
Clothing collection
Coats and winter clothing for children
Highway cleanup (usually a one-mile section)
Litter pickup in parks and public areas
Blood drive donations (discreetly)
Landscaping or gardening a median strip
School educational programs on the environment
Wildlife habitat creation or cleanup
Tree-planting
Watershed studies and cleanup
Recycling campaigns
Voter registration drives
Assistance to public schools with special equipment needs
Youth career day program
Programs for disabled or special education children
Erosion control projects

A Sample Calendar

In putting together a calendar of events for a congregation, you must decide how much to schedule on traditional dates—according to moon phase and the old sabbat dates, and how much to schedule for convenience by the modern calendar. Below is a sample calendar that shows a compromise between tradition and convenience:

Mockingbird Coven's Congregational Calendar of Events for 1997

JANUARY

Mon. Jan. 6	Open Class
Jan. 18–19	Ski Trip/Retreat
Thu. Jan. 23	Full Moon Esbat

FEBRUARY	
Sat. Feb. 1	Imbolc Sabbat
Mon. Feb. 10	Open Class
Sun. Feb. 22	Full Moon Esbat
MARCH	
Sat. Mar. 1	Potluck/Video Night
Mon. Mar. 9	Open Class
Sun. Mar. 23	Ostara Sabbat/Full Moon Esbat
APRIL	
Mon. Apr. 6	Open Class
Sat. Apr. 19	Highway Cleanup
Tues. Apr. 22	Full Moon Esbat
MAY	
Sat. May 3	Beltane Sabbat
Mon. May 11	Open Class
Thu. May 22	Full Moon Esbat Project
JUNE	
Mon. June 9	Open Class
Sat. June 21	Litha Sabbat/Full Moon Esbat
Sat. June 28	Field Trip: Sacred Site
JULY	
Sun. July 6	Picnic
Mon. July 13	Open Class
Sun. July 20	Full Moon Esbat
AUGUST	
Sat. Aug. 2	Lughnassad Sabbat
Mon. Aug. 11	Open Class
Mon. Aug. 18	Full Moon Esbat
SEPTEMBER	
Mon. Sept. 8	Open Class
Tues. Sept. 16	Full Moon Esbat
Sat. Sept. 20	Mabon Sabbat
OCTOBER	
Sat.-Sun. Oct. 4–5	Festival
Mon. Oct. 13	Open Class
Thu. Oct. 16	Full Moon Esbat
Fri. Oct. 31	Samhain Sabbat
NOVEMBER	
Mon. Nov. 10	Open Class
Fri. Nov. 14	Full Moon Esbat
Sat. Nov. 22	Family Service Project

DECEMBER

Sat. Dec. 6	Family Service Project
Mon. Dec. 8	Open Class
Sun. Dec. 14	Full Moon Esbat
Sun. Dec. 21	Yule Sabbat

Please note that the coven will have special classes and rituals of its own in addition to these congregational events.

Here are the guidelines that Mockingbird Coven used to create their congregational calendar of events:

- Sabbats will be scheduled on the weekend nearest the traditional date, on either a Friday or a Saturday. This should make it easier for people to attend and stay late. The only exception is Samhain, which will be celebrated only on the traditional date: October 31.
- Full Moon esbats will be scheduled on whatever evening the full moon occurs. The only exceptions are when a full moon and a sabbat occur very close together. In this case, a combination sabbat/Full Moon esbat will be held, even if it's a night away from the actual full moon. This is to avoid having a sabbat celebration with an esbat only a day or two earlier or later.
- Open classes will normally be held on the second Monday of each month.
- Other events (social, recreational, service) will be placed wherever there is a gap in the calendar, so that we don't go for too many weeks without some kind of activity.

Mockingbird Coven will aim for about three congregational events per month. Fewer than that, we feel the program drags and people lose interest. More than that and life gets too hectic; they're not even sure they could handle a busier schedule than this, what with jobs, families, and additional coven-only events.

Please note that this is not "THE" right way to plan a calendar; it is only one way, which Mockingbird members happen to like. They could have chosen to do some things differently.

- They could have held the sabbats on the traditional dates, rather than the nearest weekend.
- They could have meetings on a regular weekly schedule, say every Wednesday evening, and celebrate the New and Full Moon esbats on the Wednesday closest to those dates. The other Wednesdays would be used for classes, business meetings, or other coven functions.
- They could celebrate Full Moons and sabbats on the actual dates, and on any week that doesn't have either, hold a class or social event on a standard day: Thursday evenings or whatever.

- They could have decided to aim for two open events per month, or four, or whatever works for them.

It is important to determine what the "right number" of events per month seems like, balancing between boredom and burnout; and to have a system everyone understands. Each group must decide for itself how important it is to meet according to moon phases and traditional dates as opposed to the convenience of meeting, for example, every other Wednesday. In regard to esbats, remember that if you are doing serious magick and using lunar energy, there is no getting around the fact that the energy peaks at the full moon, and that the dark or new moon is best for divination. Meeting on a convenient weekend "near" one or the other is not going to be the same, magickally speaking.

As far as the celebration of sabbats, there is certainly a nice feeling meeting on the actual "traditional" night (though the old Pagan villagers probably weren't exact in their dates) and knowing that hundreds of covens all over the world are gathering at the same time. But then you might get better attendance if you waited until the following Saturday. There is a trade-off between tradition and convenience, and only your members can make the choice.

Meeting Places for the Congregation

Although congregations start small, they grow; and it will not be long before you'll need someplace larger than a living room or ritual room. Public places are preferable anyway because they are usually easier to find, and because people who are new to Paganism may be more comfortable going there for their first visit. There are any number of possibilities.

- Outdoors in a public park. Sometimes permits are required, especially if you want to reserve a pavilion or other park facility.
- Outdoors in someone's backyard. Parking, privacy, and the noise level must be considered; you don't want the neighbors complaining to the police.
- Outdoors in a national forest or on Bureau of Land Management property. Call the office nearest you to find out what the resources and rules are.
- In a church. The Unitarians are often very willing to rent their facilities to Pagans, assuming your schedule doesn't conflict with their own programs. Another possibility is a Friends' (Quaker) meeting house. It may also be worthwhile checking with Jewish centers or even a nearby United church.
- In a community center. Many towns and cities have community recreation halls available for rental.

- In a library. Not all libraries will rent to religious groups, or have large enough meeting rooms, but it's worth checking. Remember that drumming and singing may not be welcome in a library, depending on the soundproofing.
- In a school. Many elementary schools, high schools, and colleges will rent space after hours.
- In a private club or organizational facility. A local service club, recreational facility or other group may rent out rooms to supplement their income. In some areas there may be a Grange Hall, a 4-H building, or a county fairground facility.
- In a local college and university. You may need a student affiliate group to make the arrangements.

When in doubt, call the local town hall or Chamber of Commerce and ask if they have a list of meeting rooms available for rent in town. Almost all indoor facilities will charge a fee for use, but often it's quite modest and you can cover the expense by "passing the hat" or putting out a "prosperity cauldron" during your event.

When renting a room, make doubly sure that you pick up a key in advance or that there will be someone there to let you in. It's rather embarrassing having your congregation standing about on the porch while you wander the city looking for the custodian with the building key.

Of course you will want to have someone there early to turn on the heat and arrange furniture, set up for the ritual or class, and welcome people as they arrive. You may want to put up a coven banner, literature table, and so forth to personalize the place a bit during your activity. Then make sure you have a volunteer cleanup crew to put the place back in pristine condition. It doesn't hurt to send a thank-you note to the owners afterward. In it, mention any problems you noticed with the facility (broken lights, graffiti, etc.), so they don't assume that you caused them. If you treat the property respectfully and cultivate a good relationship with the owners, you will probably be welcome to use the space again.

Communications

Unless your congregation has a very regular schedule—meeting every Sunday evening at the Unitarian Church, for example—you will need some reliable communications to let people know when and where events are happening. Most congregations will want at least to celebrate the full moons and the sabbats, which of course do not show up on easily remembered dates. There are several approaches to communications.

You may have a volunteer phone crew who call everyone on the sign-up list before each event. If your list is not very long, and there are no long-distance phone charges involved, this may work well. It has the advantage that your callers can also remind people of special needs for the ritual—for example, "Bring drums or rattles," "Bring something to symbolize your goals in life," or "Bring food for a potluck dinner."

You may distribute an annual calendar of events. This requires some careful long-range planning, and probably an initial mailing at the beginning of the year plus a mailing of changes and additions halfway through.

You may publish a congregation newsletter. This could be sent out quarterly or eight times a year just before the sabbats. It can be as simple as a one-page calendar of events, or it can run to several pages and include articles, artwork, rituals, recipes, chants, and so on, contributed by coven and congregation members.

Depending on your community, you may be able to list events in the church news section of your local newspaper. Some newspaper staffs may be uninformed about Wicca, and it may be necessary to talk with the editor and convince them that Wicca is a valid religion. It may help to point out that Wicca is recognized by the U.S. armed services chaplains, the IRS, and most state corporation commissions.

You may likewise be able to get community service announcements on your local radio station, especially if you are incorporated as a church or non-profit religious organization.

You should have a telephone number that people can call for information about congregation events. Obviously, it should be one with an answering machine or voice message service.

It will be more and more important to have an e-mail address as the computer revolution continues to explode. Hopefully you have at least one member who can lend an address for coven and congregation purposes, and doesn't mind checking and replying to e-mail at frequent intervals.

A Sample Open Sabbat

Let's look in on the Mockingbird Coven as they set up for an open sabbat. They have rented a large room in the Community Center. Half an hour early, several coven members arrive to get everything prepared. Rosalie is the Maiden, and begins setting up the altar with supplies she has brought. Dana and Hawkfeather will be priestess and priest for the evening's ritual, and are in the next room getting robed and going over the ritual. Tam is the Congregation Coordinator, and will be acting as "greeter" at the door.

Tam: "Say, Hermes, could you spread out these flyers and activity schedules on that table over there, and put out the little cauldron? Thank you! Andraste, I wonder if you would start organizing the potluck food on the big table? There are paper plates and stuff in the box."

(A couple of people enter.)

Tam: "Hi, are you here for the sabbat celebration? Your first visit? Welcome—my name's Tam, and I'm the Congregation Coordinator. We still have some time before the ritual; maybe you'd like to put your food over there and take your coats off. There's some literature on this other table. Let me introduce you to Sequoia, who's one of our priestesses. She can answer any questions you might have. Sequoia, perhaps you could introduce these folks around?"

(Gradually more people come in. Only a few are completely new to this, but everyone is greeted and Tam makes sure that the new people are introduced to someone experienced. Hawkfeather and Dana have finished their ritual preparations and re-entered the room.)

Dana: "Could I have your attention, please? Would you all please join us in a circle and sit down; if anyone isn't comfortable on the floor, we can pull up a couple of chairs . . . thank you. Welcome to this evening's Mabon sabbat celebration, sponsored by Mockingbird Coven. My name is Dana, and I will be leading this evening's ritual, together with Hawkfeather here. Let's begin by going around the circle and introducing ourselves. If you'd like to mention where you're from or anything else about yourself, feel free. Andraste, will you start?"

(Everyone introduces themselves.)

Dana: "I'm so glad you could all be here tonight. We do have an announcement or two, then Hawkfeather will tell us a little about Mabon and what it means, and briefly go over the outline of tonight's ritual. After the ritual, we'll have the potluck and a chance to socialize a bit. Hermes, did you have an announcement?"

Hermes: "Just wanted to mention that the schedule of events is on the table by the door. Please take one, and any of the flyers about Wicca and Mockingbird. Also, there's a Contact List there, and if you want to be notified of future activities, please sign up on it. And lastly, that little copper cauldron over there is our 'Prosperity Pot.' If you have a buck or two to spare, please feed the cauldron; we do have to pay to rent this space and your donations will be appreciated."

Hawkfeather: "Thanks, Hermes. Let's talk about Mabon for just a minute. Mabon happens at the autumnal equinox, when the days and nights are equal in length. We think of it as the second harvest celebration, a sort of Pagan Thanksgiving . . . ." (He continues for a minute or two.)

Dana: "Great. Now did you want to explain the ritual?"

Hawkfeather: "Sure. Most of you will be familiar with the general pattern, but if you're new to Wiccan ritual and I say something confusing, feel free to ask questions. Now first we're going to do an attunement, to get us all in harmony with one another . . . ." (He covers the ritual plan briefly.)

Dana: "It is time to begin." (Rosalie dims the lights, and Dana lights two candles, one white and one black.) "Please close your eyes, and clasp hands with the people on either side of you. Breathe deeply and slowly, and remember the summer . . . ."

(The ritual continues to the end.)

Dana: ". . . the circle is open yet never broken. May the peace of the Goddess go with you. Merry meet, and merry part, and merry meet again!"

Hawkfeather: "Thank you all. Well, there's food—let's eat!"

Hermes: "Don't forget the sign-up list and the Prosperity Pot!"

(Everyone moves toward the food and information tables, but there's still some more business to take care of.)

Dana: "Rosalie, when everyone has gotten some food, would you announce the Full Moon esbat next week, and ask Greenvale to announce the tree-planting project at the same time? Thanks. Tam, could you get a couple of volunteers for cleanup later?"

Hawkfeather: "I noticed a couple of new faces tonight. Dana, let's make sure we introduce ourselves and get to know them a little."

Dana: "Absolutely. But first I want some of that green chile chicken stew!"

Please notice that the responsibilities for the evening were shared among coven and congregation folks. This was not a one-person show. Also, new people were greeted and connections made as soon as they walked in the door; no one is going to leave the ritual feeling that the Witches were cold and aloof. At the same time, the logistics and business ends were not neglected; there were activity schedules for people, and a sign-up sheet, and a pot for contributions, and announcements of upcoming events. Yet because everyone pitched in to help, and because there was a clear understanding of what needed to be done, everything got done quite easily.

How the Coven and Congregation Interact

When you first form a congregation, most likely the coven will run the whole show, and provide most of the attendance at open events. But as soon as you get a couple of people attending events, you can begin to build the congregation's identity as a semi-independent entity. Obviously this is going to take some time and energy, and it's not going to feel like a group until you get several of the same people consistently showing up for events. Don't be surprised if it takes a year or more to make the transition from "coven and a couple of visitors" to "coven and congregation."

You can help the congregation grow and achieve its own identity in several ways.

- Hold open events every single month. There must be events happening often enough that enthusiasm and momentum can build. As an example, Our Lady of the Woods holds eight open sabbats, twelve to thirteen open Full Moon esbats, at least twelve open classes and a handful of special activities and service projects each year. That's an average of three events every month open to the congregation. It sounds like a huge amount of work, but remember that almost all of these events would be happening anyway if we had only the coven.
- Publicize the events well. We have already discussed this under "Communications," but it can't be emphasized too strongly.
- Make it clear that both congregation and coven are important; the coven is different because it is training priestesses and priests, but that doesn't make coveners a spiritual elite, just a group of people who have a vocation for priest work. So you will need to honor people for their participation and work in the congregation (with private thanks and public acclaim, certificates, titles, etc.), just as you honor people for their work in the coven (with degrees, colored cords, titles, etc.).
- Be very consistent with things like your sign-up sheet, literature table, and donation pot. Also consistently meet at the same time for all your evening events, and if possible, in the same place (or the same indoor place in winter and outdoor place in summer).
- Use the energies of your new congregants. It may be very tempting to have coveners do all the work because many of them are experienced and don't have to be trained or guided. But it is crucial to make a distinction between the work that requires a priest/ess and the work that can be done by a competent congregation member. Find and train congregation members to do the administration, phone calls, publications, program planning (except rituals and some classes), maintenance of mailing lists, finances, and so forth. Leave the coven members free to focus on ritual leadership, pastoral counseling, healing, interfaith networking, and classes on magick. By requiring your congregants to run most of their own organization, you allow them to build an investment and make their membership more meaningful.
- Let the membership of coven and congregation be fluid enough to serve individual needs. The congregation may be a source of coven dedicants,

and a community for those who have tried studying for the priesthood and find they do not have the calling or cannot commit the time required.

Potential Pitfalls

What can go wrong? Lots. But for every problem there's an answer: "Where there's a Witch there's a Way."

- Lack of interest in the community. Naturally there may be little interest at first, because you are probably an unknown factor. Many potential members still don't know what Wicca is. Others have heard of Wicca and Paganism, but don't know you and your coven. It requires a lot of public education, then a lot of trust-building.
- Perceived low status of congregation members. Many people who are attracted to the Craft will believe that the coven is the "in" group and the congregation is somehow not as (pick one): a. Spiritual; b. Powerful and Mysterious; or c. Fun. Most of the time you can explain the differences, tell them how much more time and energy the coven requires, and the expectations of service from coveners, and then let them decide. Meanwhile, honor the congregants and build the congregation so that any fool can see it's a great group to belong to.
- Stonewalling from the community. What if you go to rent a room for an open sabbat, and nobody in town will rent you space? You send an announcement to the local newspaper, and it never gets printed? You go to a copy shop to get flyers printed, and their photocopier is "down for repairs"—until you have left. If you run into obstacles everywhere, then you have some basic foundation-building to do. Set aside the idea of a congregation and start a long-term program of public education.
- Attacks from religious extremists. A visible congregation means that you are potentially a target for fundamentalists. In most areas, the attacks will be limited to letter-to-the-editor rantings and perhaps "Spiritual Warfare" prayer sessions. You can live with that. Answer the letters with very calm and informative letters of your own (see the sample in the appendices), and ignore the prayer meetings. If the hostility escalates to vandalism or assault, you had better have your ducks in a row with the local law enforcement authorities. Explain Wicca to the police chief before there's a cross burning on your lawn. Then use the law to protect your right of religious freedom. If you need an attorney and can't afford one, ask for help from the national Wiccan community (see Chapter 25, "Networking and Affiliation").
- Disruptive personalities in the congregation. Occasionally someone will start attending events who makes everyone else want to stay away. They might be negative, abrasive, sexually aggressive, or just more

"woo-woo" than people can deal with ("Did you known that I receive spiritual guidance from the Neptune High Space Command through my pocket comb?"). Unless a little straight-from-the-shoulder advice will fix the problem, you may have to "disinvite" the individual. As calmly and courteously as possible, tell them that this group is probably not the right group for them and that they should look elsewhere. This is a horrible thing to have to do, but if the alternative is that others stay away in droves, you may have no choice. And after all, it's your congregation, and you collectively have the right and responsibility to control who's allowed to participate.

These are simply a few of the common problems congregations face. You could probably talk to any minister, priest, or rabbi of any faith and hear horror stories of a hundred more. But if you face the difficulties with a united front, using all the wisdom, love, and strength the Lady and Lord have given you, you can handle just about anything.

Congregations in Wicca's Future

Are congregations served by covens a passing experiment, or the wave of the future for Wicca's structure? There are many in the Wiccan community who feel very attached to the coven structure and have little interest in working with larger and possibly less intense groups. They enjoy the intimate family feeling of their covens, and thrill to the harmonious magickal energies that a small, close-knit coven can achieve. On the other end of the spectrum are those who see the successes—at least in numbers—of mainstream churches with large congregations, and imagine new Pagan temples thronged with hundreds or thousands singing the praises of the God/dess.

For most Witches, numbers alone mean little. A wise priest of my acquaintance, Sparrow, says of the big mainstream churches: "Remember how they got that way and what they had to do to us and themselves. Fulfilling this image would fill our egos, but at what cost to our spirits? We may always be the minority for it has always been harder to listen to the voice within than the voices without that are so eager to define 'the truth' for whoever will listen. But what of that? Ultimately, spirit paths are walked alone, with only the God/dess for company."

Our challenge is to maintain the special blessings of the coven structure, yet serve the spiritual needs of Pagans who do not find coven membership workable for them, or who simply cannot find a congenial coven with room. The coven-congregation model attempts to do both, by using the coven priest/esses as a volunteer clergy team in service to a larger community of Pagans. This larger community may have to have its own sub-groups to achieve any sense of intimacy, just as mainstream churches do: committees, project teams, adult classes, potluck dinner groups and so on. Can a Pagan congregation maintain its identity even if it grows to the size of a mainstream church? It may work for your coven and community; it may not. But it is worth considering.

25 Networking and Affiliation

Networking, "an informal system whereby persons having common interests or concerns assist each other, as in the exchange of information . . . ." is something that was lost to the Craft for many years. When the remaining Witches went underground during the Burning Times, oral tradition says that there were individuals who linked the hidden covens, traveling from one to another and carrying news. Such an individual was variously known as the Man in Black, the Summoner, or the Walker, according to different accounts (though the first two titles have different duties imputed to them in other stories). Many surnames reflect an ancestor's role in the community; it is interesting to speculate that some people who have the surnames Black or Walker today may be descended from the Witch-officers who kept the community connected in a dangerous era.

It would seem that the system broke down almost completely over time, until most of the remaining covens and families were isolated from one another. The Witch community remained largely fragmented until roughly the 1970s, when two new phenomena appeared: summer festivals and regional/national associations.

The festivals provided a neutral ground where Witches and other Pagans of many traditions could come together and share workshops and ritual space, as well as spend time socializing informally around campfires or over the wares of artisans. Individuals became connected with covens, covens pledged exchanges of information or aid on projects of mutual interest, and barriers dissolved. For the first time, "the Wiccan community" began to be a reality.

During the same era, regional and national associations of Witches began to form. Some, like the Council of American Witches and the American Brotherhood of Witches, did not survive long. Others, such as the Covenant of the Goddess, Circle Network, the Re-formed Congregation of the Goddess, and the Pagan Federation (based in Great Britain) survived and flourished. Many city, state, and regional networks have sprung up; some continue.

Pagan Periodicals

In the meantime, Pagan periodicals have spread like wildfire; literally hundreds of newsletters and journals have come and gone, and there may be as many as 300 currently being published. Some of the most durable have been *The Green Egg* (oriented toward the Church of All Worlds), *Circle Network News* (Pagans in general), *Of A Like Mind* (Goddess Women and Dianic Witches), *SageWoman* (Pagan women), *The Green Man* (Pagan men), and the *COG. Newsletter* (Witches). Newer to the scene, but very polished and professional, are *Connections* (Pagans in general) and *The Lady Letter* (Witches); see the appendices for addresses. Most of these include seasonal material related to the upcoming sabbat, articles on Paganism and Witchcraft, book and music reviews, letters, special columns on astrology or herbs or whatever, calendars of festivals and workshops, ads for ritual tools and a hundred other things, and contact information for Pagan organizations in various areas.

Some covens will order subscriptions to the nearest regional newsletter and three or four of the best national ones, and make them available at the covenstead for members to read. When the next issue arrives, the old ones can be filed in looseleaf binders or library-style periodical boxes in the coven library. Back issues can be valuable resources, especially for material to use in planning your sabbat celebrations.

The Internet

The Pagan resources on the Internet have blossomed in the past few years, and more Witches are connected and communicating than you can imagine. Some of the better-known Pagan web sites and e-mail addresses are included in the appendices. No list can hope to keep current with all the web sites, listserves and chat rooms springing up, but this list will get you started. Once you are on the Net and have found even a few web sites, the links will lead you to others; and as you meet other Pagans on the Net, they can guide you to resources they have encountered. The Net is a wonderful source of information on Wiccan organizations and events, as well as helping you make social connections. As always, caution and common sense are advisable: not everyone on the net is well informed and ethical. Remember also that the World Wide Web can be a useful tool, but it is not the only tool, nor is it always accurate.

The Web is made up of millions of individual sites, each with its own address (the now familiar naming structure http://www.xxxxx.xxx.xxx). Each site/address/name is "owned," operated, and maintained by a different person or organization. There are no standards for minimal accuracy, updates, reliability, good grammar, or anything else. All that a site requires is that someone has paid the fee to register that site/address/name.

Some organizations are very efficient, having their data screens laid out in a way that is clear and easy to read, and updating their site on a regular basis, checking information before they post it on their site, letting people know how to contact them in case there is a problem or inaccuracy with their site, having their site stored on a reliable computer system so that it is available more often than not, and so forth.

Other sites may have been made just for fun ("Hey, everybody come see what I built at my own personal web site!"), or the owner doesn't have the resources to maintain it properly, or they may have their own agenda and only want to present their viewpoint. All this can be compared to going shopping. Some stores are very well laid out, are user-friendly, have helpful clerks, provide better parking, and are just easier to use than other stores. Some stores may have everything you want, while other stores have nothing you want. Some stores have closed down, but their old sign is still up. You won't know until you go and look.

A few notes about searching for different sites. If you want to learn more than is listed below I would suggest your local library, or bookstore, or an online FAQ (Frequently Asked Questions) file.

First, there are "web browsers," which usually have a built-in feature called "find" or "search." This only looks for words on the web page you are viewing at any given moment. But web browsers are able to use other "search engines" (some of which are Lycos, Alta Vista, InfoSeek, Excite, Yahoo, and other trademarked names). Search engines seek information on the web and return with the addresses of potentially useful sites so that you can go there. A search engine works through the following steps:

1. A web site administrator may choose one or more words as "key words" to describe that site. For example, a sporting goods company may use words such as "fishing, sports, outside, hiking," and so on. A site used to post information about nuclear waste would use a different set of key words. These words are placed in an electronic index, similar to the index in the back of a book, and the search engine looks through this index in order to find related topics and point you to that site.
2. The organizations that maintain these indexes use software "robots" to continually search web sites, strip out the words from the home page of a site or a site's key word listing, and update their index. So, the indexes receive information from different sources.
3. The search engine you choose looks through whichever index it uses and reports back to you on any matches it has found.
4. If a web administrator did not do a very good job of using key words to label and cross-reference that site, your search may not find it. If the web site was well made and well indexed, but the site was later

> discontinued, the site may still be listed in the index, but you won't be able to access it. This is similar to using the Yellow Pages. If a store has listed itself under several different subject areas it is easier for you to find. If a store goes out of business, it is still listed until you get a new Yellow Pages book next year.

Even though they all perform the same function, each search engine is built a little bit differently. Try those engines that are available to you and see which one you feel most comfortable using, and is most efficient in finding the information you want. Each of them will have a field where you enter the key word(s) you want to search for in a web site. Depending on the engine, these key words will be controlled by different operational commands (the + sign, or the use of certain words between your subject words). You will have to look in the help section of each engine to see how the commands are used in it.

For example, you may want to search for any site that has the word "Witch" in it. This will give you a lot of "hits" or potential sites to explore, though many of them probably won't be what you really want. If you set up your search to look for sites that have the words "Witch" AND/OR "Western Europe" AND/OR "Middle Ages" you will get back a listing of all sites that have any of those subjects in them.

If, however, you set up your search to look for sites that have the words "Witch" AND "Western Europe" AND "Middle Ages" you will only get back a listing of sites with all three of those subjects in them. If you try to make a search too specific you may not have any possibilities reported back to you. You may have to do a search several times using more and fewer key words in order to find what you're looking for while keeping the number of returns manageable.

Most people learn how to use one or two engines fairly well, until they are able to use that engine quickly and efficiently. Use whatever works for you.

The usenet newsgroups you may want to visit include alt.religion.wicca, alt.pagan, and alt.pagan.contacts. Most online services like America Online and Compuserve have a Wiccan/Pagan area; usually you search with the keyword "pagan."

Local Relationships

You may wonder if your coven should join, or create, an association or network in your city, state, or region. There may be a Local Council of the Covenant of the Goddess in your area; you can find out by contacting the COG National Office at P.O. Box 1226, Berkeley, CA 94701, or visiting their web site. A letter of introduction should get you an invitation to the next Local Council meeting, where you can meet the members in the area, find out about projects and programs, and decide if you would like to join. COG Local Councils vary a great deal in their programs; they may sponsor community sabbat celebrations, share workshops and classes, organize regional festivals, do public education, community service, and parties and social events. It is really up to the local members.

There may be an independent association in your area not connected with any national organization. Some of these are open to Pagans generally, others specifically to Witches. Some are moderately large and well organized, others are quite loose, even haphazard. Some do the same sorts of projects that COG does, others have a single pet project, such as sponsoring a festival or buying land for a Pagan center. You can usually find a contact by visiting the nearest metaphysical or occult bookstore; the owners will know who's who in the area. Then you need to get in touch and get invited to the next meeting. Once you're there, and have a firsthand glimpse of the organization, you can decide whether to get involved.

Local and regional associations are as good as the members are willing to make them. If you are willing to put in quality time and energy, they can be very valuable to your coven and provide a number of advantages.

- They give you a chance to socialize with other Witches and Pagans, and to feel less isolation and more community with like-minded people.
- You can exchange information, resources, and classes, enriching your program.
- You have a chance to see how others do ritual, organize their covens, etc.
- You can coordinate your efforts to educate the public and increase understanding and respect for the Craft.
- You can undertake community service projects that would not be possible for one coven to manage.
- You can put together events that your coven could not easily do alone, such as festivals, retreats, conferences, open houses, parties, concerts, or field trips.
- You can expand the horizons of your students by involving them in wider networking efforts.
- You can act with a united front in case of discrimination or persecution.

Working with others in the Pagan community can be a very good thing. But a couple of cautionary notes are in order. First, if you are a primary leader of your coven, don't offer your services as a primary leader in the association. Especially not if you have a day job or children. Share the wealth—there's plenty of work to go around. You can hand over your coven responsibilities to another member who would benefit by the experience, then take on the job with the association. Or you can encourage other coven members to put some energy into the association. Don't do it all yourself.

Second, be aware that not everyone in the Pagan world is easy to work with. Your local association may include its share of difficult or impossible personalities. If you encounter such, first make sure that your attitude or behavior is not contributing to the problem. Others may be a mirror or catalyst for your own, less than highly evolved qualities. Then remind yourself that you don't have to marry them in order to work constructively with them at an occasional meeting. See if you can focus on their positive qualities and encourage appropriate behavior by example.

But, if the individual is incorrigibly disruptive, or has a poor sense of ethics, you may have to make a tough choice: either leave the association or try to get them out. Beyond a certain point, severing the connection is the only wise option. Only you can decide what you must do to preserve your integrity and emotional balance. However, in terms of the impact on the local Pagan community, you do not have to decide or act in a vacuum. Consult with the most respected elders in the community in confidence; check what your heart says, then act.

Most Witches find that there is much to be gained by networking with others near and far; sometimes it's challenging, but in the end, you must make connections or be a hermit.

National Organizations

There are several organizations that work on a national or international level, and your coven may want to affiliate with one or more. This is by no means a complete listing, simply some of the more well-known and durable organizations with histories that promise they will be around for a while.

For the most part, these are volunteer-run and have very limited budgets. So when writing to any of these organizations, it is courteous to enclose a stamped, self-addressed envelope and a dollar for copying costs.

Aquarian Tabernacle Church (ATC)

ATC is an umbrella organization for several covens, with a center in Washington State. Like COG (see below), ATC is very interested in achieving recognition and acceptance of the Craft as a legitimate religion. ATC publishes *Panegyria* newsletter and hosts a Spring Mysteries festival in Washington as well as open sabbats and other events. Contact:

Aquarian Tabernacle Church
P.O. Box 409
Index, WA 98256

Their telephone number is (206) 793-1945. Their net address is BBS AquaTabCh@aol.com.

Circle

Circle publishes *Circle Network News* and other Pagan resources including the very useful *Guide to Wiccan/Pagan Resources*. It sponsors the Pagan Spirit Gathering each summer in the Midwest and hosts numerous workshops and open sabbats there throughout the year. Circle is open to Pagans generally. Contact:

Circle Sanctuary
P.O. Box 219
Mt. Horeb, WI 53572

Their telephone is (608) 924-2216, but it is probably better to write with your questions.

Covenant of the Goddess

COG is an international (but largely U.S.A.-based) federation of Witches' covens and solitaries—the largest organization specifically for Witches in the world. It is divided into Local Councils, which decide what programs they want to organize, though there are many at-large members who do not live near a Local Council or choose not to participate in local activities. COG includes well over a hundred covens from varying traditions.

COG makes ministerial credentials available to qualified priests and priestesses; does a great deal of media contact and public information about the Craft; publishes *The COG Newsletter*; sponsors an annual festival, Merrymeet, which moves around the U.S.; sponsors a listserve and web page on the Internet; publishes resource guides; sponsors the Hart and Crescent Award, which can be earned by Pagan Scouts and other Pagan youth; and often intervenes to assist Witches who are being harassed or persecuted.

Individuals can join COG through covens or as associates or solitary elders. To join COG, a coven must fulfill the following.

- Worship the Goddess and the Old Gods (or the Goddess alone).
- Accept the Wiccan Rede and a Code of Ethics compatible with COG's.
- Have been active six months or more.
- Have three or more members who have been formally accepted into training for the clergy.
- Have at least one member eligible to receive Elder Priest/ess credentials.
- Be a cohesive, self-perpetuating group.

Prospective members apply through their Local Councils, or at the National level if there is no Local Council in their area. For more information, write to:

The Covenant of the Goddess
P.O. Box 1226
Berkeley, CA 94701

Their Internet address is netco@cog.org. Their web page address is http://www.cog.org/cog/.

Covenant of Unitarian Universalist Pagans

Not actually a Wiccan organization, CUUPS is home to many Pagans who also feel an affinity to the Unitarian-Universalist Church (or vice versa). There are local chapters at many UU churches all over the United States, and in many conservative communities, joining CUUPS is the safest way to meet kindred spirits.

Re-Formed Congregation of the Goddess

RCG is a network focused on the Goddess and women's spirituality, with a strong emphasis on Dianic Wicca. It publishes *Of A Like Mind* newspaper and other resources, and sponsors conferences in Wisconsin and at several branches elsewhere around the country. RCG offers the Cella training program for priestesses, with several specialized "tracks": Healer, Ritualist, Artist, Scholar/Teacher, Earthwalker, and Organizer. A long-term project is the creation of The Grove (near Madison, Wisconsin), a rural center for Goddess-oriented programs and events. Contact:

Re-formed Congregation of the Goddess
P.O. Box 6677
Madison, WI 53716

Wiccan/Pagan Press Alliance

The WPPA suggests standards for Pagan publications and helps them network among each other. Contact:

Wiccan/Pagan Press Alliance
℅ Black Forest Publishing
P.O. Box 1392
Mechanicsburg, PA 17055-1392

Witches Anti-Defamation League

WADL gathers information on cases where Witches encounter discrimination in employment, the court system, the military, and elsewhere, and works to assure fair treatment for all of us. Contact: same as WPPA above.

Witches League for Public Awareness

WLPA does much the same work as WADL, with an emphasis on educating the public through the media. Contact:

Witches League for Public Awareness
P.O. Box 8736
Salem, MA 01971-8736

Festivals

As mentioned earlier, festivals are a great way to connect with other Witches and Pagans. Larry Cornett, who publishes the National Calendar of Pagan Events, has graphed the growth in Pagan festivals, and says they are growing exponentially—doubling in number every five years. There is probably at least one major festival within driving range of almost every state in the United States, and often several to choose from.

Most of these events last from two to five days and occur during the summer months. However, there are a few major festivals in the spring and autumn as well. For most Pagans, the outdoor camping festival is the favorite kind; however, some events are held at retreat centers with cabin or bunkhouse accommodations in addition to tent space. A few conferences are held in large hotels.

The typical Pagan festival, if there is such a thing, is sponsored by a Pagan organization or association of groups, and draws strongly from the region where it is held (though the bigger ones draw participants from all over North America, as well as the occasional visitor from overseas). Frequently, preregistration is required, though some festivals will allow registration at the gate or even sell day passes. The cost might be in the range of $25–$200 per person (less for children), depending on whether meals or indoor accommodations are included. Admission is restricted to Pagans and Pagan-friendly folk. On the average, festivals last three or four days (a long weekend), and will have a printed program of activities. These usually include workshops on many different areas of magick and Paganism; rituals of several kinds (an opening, an evening "main ritual," men's, women's, closing, and a few special-interest rituals); singing, drumming, and bardic circles around a fire at night; vendors (merchants and artisans) selling things like ritual tools, pottery, books, or jewelry; concerts of Pagan music or amateur talent shows; and more.

Who attends? The diversity is impressive. You will see very small children and elderly folk; Witches, shamans, Asatru (Norse-tradition Pagans), Druids, and generic Pagans; straights, bisexuals, lesbians and gays; people dressed in ceremonial robes, jeans and tees, or nothing but jewelry; seasoned teachers and complete newcomers; bards, healers, artisans, and musicians; and others who cannot be easily described.

Festivals are usually run by volunteer staffs and are often well organized. There will be crews in charge of site preparation and clean-up, registration, a Healing Pavilion (first aid and alternative healing resources), adult programs, children's programs, registration, security and safety, the "Merchant Area," supply runs, sometimes a centering tent (counseling for the emotionally stressed), and other logistics. At many festivals, every participant is expected to put in a few hours of volunteer work to help keep them running.

Common rules and customs include the following.

- Honor the Earth: no digging, chopping live plants, littering (including cigarette butts), or anything else that might hurt the environment. Pagan campsites are invariably cleaner afterwards than they were when the Pagans arrived.
- Build fires only in designated firepits, and practice fire safety.
- Be courteous to others at all times. Respect others of differing traditions and lifestyles.
- No illegal substances.
- Alcohol is usually permitted, though obnoxious drunkenness and underage drinking are not.
- Firearms are forbidden; swords and knives are okay.
- Private sexual activity between consenting adults is up to you. But nudity is neither an invitation nor license for harassment.
- Do not interrupt rituals or workshops.
- If you sign up for a workshift or volunteer to help, honor your commitment.
- Be on time for scheduled events.
- Many sites do not allow animal friends, except seeing-eye dogs.

Many covens arrange to attend a festival as a group. They can cook, camp, or bunk together, and go their separate ways to visit the various workshops, then come together again to share what they have learned. If the coven wants to set up a merchanting booth as a fundraiser, the coveners can take turns attending the booth. Playing merchant is not an arduous job; in fact, it's an opportunity to meet new people and chat with them, as well as make a little money for the coven treasury. If you plan to do a group outing, make sure you get the dates and cost well in advance, so your members can plan ahead. Register early, since some festivals have size limits and fill up quickly.

There will also probably be coveners going off to other festivals in ones and twos, and they should be encouraged to bring back goodies for the coven—workshop notes, new songs and chants, and interesting resources or contacts in the Pagan world.

Most Pagan periodicals carry listings of some festivals, but probably the most complete source is the *National Calendar of Pagan Events* published by Larry Cornett. He lists the date, cost, location, a description, and the contact information for each event. You can get a hardcopy subscription (six issues a year), or check his web site at http://www.io.com/~cookec/pagan.d/calendar.htm. To list events (two days or longer), contact lcorncalen@aol.com.

A Special Note: The Ardantane Project

Our Lady of the Woods, a coven, congregation, and incorporated tax-exempt church centered in Los Alamos, New Mexico, is creating Ardantane, a Wiccan learning center/theological seminary. "Ardantane" is an Anglicized version of "Ardh an teinne," meaning "the light of the fire."

At present Ardantane seminars and workshops are offered periodically in rented facilities in New Mexico, though occasionally Ardantane instructors go "on the road" and present seminars in other cities. Subjects include ritual, coven organization and leadership, magick, divination, Pagan lifestyles, environmental sustainability, and other topics of interest to Wiccan priests and priestesses.

We hope that the Ardantane-accredited faculty will grow, so that it can offer programs all over the United States. Eventually it will have a central campus on land in New Mexico. This campus will be a model of alternative building techniques and sustainable resources and will offer evening classes and weekend seminars, as well as week-long, summer, and year-long educational programs.

OLW and the Ardantane Project publish a quarterly journal, The Lady Letter, which includes articles of interest to Wiccan clergy and progress reports on Ardantane. To subscribe or get more information, write to Lady Letter, c/o OLW, P.O. Box 1107, Los Alamos, NM 87544, or e-mail LadyLettr@aol.com.

You can help Ardantane grow. If the project interests you, you can:

- Subscribe to Lady Letter;
- Attend Ardantane classes and seminars;
- Nominate an experienced Craft teacher to be accredited by Ardantane;
- Organize an Ardantane seminar in your area (we'll send the teachers);
- Join the "Blessed Bees," the volunteer work force that will build and maintain the main campus; and/or
- Make a tax-deductible contribution in any amount.

Contact us at the address above to offer help or learn more.

26 The Coven in the Community

Had this book been written in the 1950s or 60s, our discussion would have been how to hide from the community. Virtually no covens had any public presence because coven leaders everywhere knew that they would be regarded as crazies or devil-worshippers if they came "out of the broom closet." Granted, the Witchcraft Act had been repealed in England, and the United States technically endorsed freedom of religion, but public Witches could still easily lose their jobs, have their property vandalized, and be shunned by their neighbors.

The situation has changed drastically in many areas. Wicca has been recognized by the U.S. federal government through tax-exempt church status, by military chaplains' offices, and by many media representatives and law enforcement personnel who have some basic knowledge of who we are and are not. Pagan participation in the 1993 Parliament of World Religions exposed thousands of religious leaders from all over the world to Witchcraft as a religion and, with one or two exceptions, the various delegates were quite tolerant and even respectful.

The world is still not always a safe place for the Craft, as many can testify. But the fact that there are any safe places is due to the courage, faith, and determination of those who have "come out" in recent years—and due to the public education efforts of organizations like The Covenant of the Goddess, the Pagan Federation, the Fellowship of Isis and Circle Network.

This changing social climate means that many covens have had to reassess their relationship to their home communities. If a community accepts its responsibility to allow our free and open worship, then what are our responsibilities to the community?

It seems that community participation and community service have become options for many covens. Many Witches believe that "Perfect Love and Perfect Trust" are ideals that do not end at the boundary of the coven circle but should be pursued in the wider community.

One avenue is through interfaith councils. These vary widely in their openness to minority faiths. One large council in the Pacific Northwest has a Wiccan as chairperson, at this writing. Berkeley Area Interfaith Council has had Wiccan participation for many years. Others may limit participation to Christian churches, or to the "major" faiths, which vary according to who's counting. But where Witches are allowed in, they can actively support the educational and charitable programs of the councils side by side with everyone else. If you are interested in "testing the waters" to see if your local interfaith council will be friendly, and if there is a Unitarian (or other liberal) church in town, start by talking to that minister. Chances are he or she can tell you what's happening with interfaith organizations, and how you are likely to be received if you approach them.

Of course there are an infinite number of other ways to serve a community. One coven runs a "Koats for Kids" program, gathering used winter clothing and distributing it to needy children. Another sponsors a needy family in the local "Christmas" charity, sending boxes of food, clothing, and gifts to them during the holiday season. Still others do environmental protection projects. You may want to contact local ecology, peace, feminist, or wildlife organizations, or children's programs, and ask if your Wiccan group can help out on some special project, or volunteer individual time for a stated time period. Sure, you could (and do) volunteer individually, but why not let them know that it is Wiccans who are in there working? Here's a list of some community service projects your coven could try:

Create a wildlife habitat
Clean up graffiti
Collect for a food pantry
Clean up a creek or riverbank
Sponsor a holiday toy drive
Hold a voter registration drive
Refurbish a playground
Plant trees (with permission)
Build a picnic pavilion
Assist at a retirement home
Adopt a highway
Adopt a park or roadway median
Volunteer at a state park
Entertain children in a hospital
Donate Pagan books to a library
Do a soil erosion control project
Provide prison chaplain services
Help create a teen center

And here are some projects oriented toward political and social change:

Ban the Nukes: Get together a letter-writing campaign urging the government to continue its efforts toward multilateral disarmament. Do some research so you can speak intelligently about treaties now in force or under consideration. Also write to each foreign government with a nuclear capability; your local peace groups can supply detailed information.

Working With Environmental Organizations: A high priority for most covens is helping organizations which protect and heal the Earth and Her creatures. Contact local chapters and see how you can help. Or how about an "Honor Thy Mother" display on the environment, with lots of information on environmental groups and how to support them or become involved? Some groups that may share information:

- The Sierra Club
- The Audubon Society
- The Nature Conservancy
- Greenpeace
- The Wilderness Society
- Earth First
- Arbor Day Foundation
- Bat Conservation International
- Friends of the Earth
- International Wildlife Federation
- Local Forest Council or Trust
- American Cetacean Society
- Rainforest projects
- National Parks and Conservation Association

Minister Visits: If you're really out of the closet, make social calls on area ministers—or visit the local interfaith council—and tell them about the Craft. Naturally this kind of openness will depend on your personal situation and how tolerant the community is. In some areas, it can move the Craft toward acceptance. In the wrong place, it could simply give local fundamentalists ammunition for a Witch hunt.

If you do this, you will have to explain very carefully why you're visiting, that is, to provide information and avoid potential misunderstandings. Otherwise many ministers will assume you're trying to convert them (that's what they want to do to you), or that you are asking for a "seal of approval" so you can look legitimate in the community (which you already are).

Some ministers will be friendly and curious, some polite but tense, and some might be downright antagonistic. Don't argue—you can't win an argument with someone who believes the Bible is the literal Word of Yahweh, and anyway you're not there to convert anybody. Stay friendly and relaxed, be informative, and don't stay too long. Will it help? Maybe.

Educational Slide Presentation or Video: Do you have someone in the coven who's handy with a camera? Put together a presentation. Some of the material can be shot from books, including art books showing Goddess and God statues and paintings. Someone else can provide the narration and another covener may tape background music. Then you can present the show to the public. Your local metaphysical bookstore might sponsor a showing or perhaps you could show it at the library. Your members can have a good time and exercise a lot of creativity on this.

Suggestion: go easy on depicting the horrors of the Burning Times, and emphasize the positive—especially our love for the Goddess/Nature.

Educating the Law: Ready for more challenges? Set up a seminar to orient law enforcement officers, social workers, and family court judges regarding the Craft. First you will need to talk individually to some of these people, explaining that there have been legal problems in some areas because law and court personnel just weren't informed about Wicca as a legitimate religion. Then if you find one person who is open-minded and fairly sympathetic, they can help you network with all the right people and set up a seminar on "Alternative Religions and the Law." Better still, a law enforcement agency might invite you as a speaker as part of their training programs—which will guarantee a better attendance than if you set up something "off campus," as it were.

This means a lot of study and research so that you can speak knowledgeably about state and local ordinances involving the occult—such as laws against "fortune-telling." Primarily, you can inform them about the Craft and remind them that Wicca is a religion covered under the Bill of Rights, so that it is entirely legal to practice Witchcraft. Don't forget informational flyers for the audience. An excellent resource is *The Law Enforcement Guide to Wicca*, by Kerr Cuhulain (Horned Owl Publishing, 1997).

And by the way, if you have any lawyers in your coven who are willing to represent Witches in custody battles, sue employers who fired them on the grounds of religion, or similar discrimination, please ask them to contact the Covenant of the Goddess so they can be added to a "legal resources" list.

Pollution Map: More environmental activism: research and prepare a map of your township, city, county, or state, showing by name the major sources of air and water "emissions" and toxic waste. Governmental environmental monitoring agencies can provide the data. Make sure everything is well documented and footnoted, and have an attorney check it over, otherwise the media may not touch it. When it's ready, print up a bunch and send them simultaneously to the polluters and all the news media. Send other copies to every political organization, service club, and environmental group you can think of. Be aware; if you do it well enough to sting the polluters, they will fight back. Don't try this project on your own unless you have a strong position in the community; you can always work as part of a coalition of environmental organizations.

Library Survey: Visit each local library and see what books they have on the Craft. If any are defamatory, show them to the head librarian and tell him or her some facts about Wicca, or show them the press packet available from COG. Gently ask them if they would carry anti-Semitic or anti-Christian books on the shelves, and suggest that in fairness they should not have anti-Wiccan propaganda. Then present a list of factual books (by Adler, Starhawk, Weinstein, etc.) and ask that they be added to the list of planned acquisitions. Stay courteous, and demand nothing. If the librarian seems prejudiced, you can always go the library board, then the city council, then court. Also be aware that

Witchcraft books often "walk," and consider offering to replace them if they disappear (using coven funds).

Public Education Classes

Many covens now offer "Wicca 101" classes to the public as an introduction to Witchcraft. Some participants stay to join the coven or congregation, others simply go away better informed: it's a win-win proposition. Generally the courses meet one evening a week for between four to thirteen weeks, and charge few or no fees but accept donations toward expenses. They may be held in a public facility on neutral ground. The classes inform, but do not proselytize; no one is pressured into "converting." Topics covered might include the History of Witchcraft; the Wheel of the Year; Wiccan Ethics; The Goddess and the God; the Earth as Sacred; Coven Customs and Traditions; and Wiccan Lifestyles. There is a more complete suggested outline in the chapter on Education and Training. Usually magick is not taught in a public class: participants are not pledged to the Wiccan Rede and could potentially misuse what they learn.

Such classes are often advertised by word of mouth, but you can also put notices on the local newspaper's Calendar of Events; submit news releases to the print media, television, and radio stations; and put up posters or flyers on public bulletin boards, especially in metaphysical bookstores.

Occasionally, covens may have the chance to talk to school classes about Wicca—not to make converts of course, but to educate students as part of a course in social studies, humanities, history, or comparative religions. You can check with your local school district and see if any of the schools routinely invite speakers from different faiths as part of their program. If so, and if you have coveners who are willing to be that open, then volunteer to add a new perspective to the program. Our coven has done this four years running at the local high school, and the young people have been courteous and attentive. Some simply have a few myths dispelled; others find they are not alone in their spiritual beliefs. The following is an outline of the sort of program we do in a two-hour time slot.

High School Presentation on Wicca

Set up altar, tools display, literature table (books and handouts)
Welcome and introductions
Preview of the program; and hand out 3"x5" cards for students
to write anonymous questions
The history of the Craft in brief
Paleolithic times
Pagan Europe and the Roman Empire
Paganism and the early Christian Church
The Burning Times

The Craft underground
The 20th-century Renaissance
The beliefs and ethics of the Craft
Immanent Deity
Goddess and God
The sacredness of Nature
Reincarnation
The Wiccan Rede and Law of Return
The practices of the Craft; show-and-tell altar
Esbats and sabbats
Magick and ritual
Traditional healing
Collect 3"x5" cards
Short ritual demonstration: an Earth Blessing
Panel answers questions on cards
Final question and answer period
Where to look for more information; mention literature table
Thanks and farewell

This same outline could be used for an adult program addressing an interfaith group, a conference, or similar gathering. It should be mentioned that we usually have three people do the presentation; varying the speakers adds interest. Most often we have one speaker dressed very conservatively (suit and tie), one dressed casually, and one in full ritual regalia. The last is possible because we are known and established in town; it may not be advisable everywhere. If possible, have at least one male present, to dispel the idea that Witchcraft is an all-girl club.

Open Communications

A few covens have a weekly listing in the "Religious News" or "Church Announcements" section of their local newspaper, mentioning open sabbats or full moon esbats, as well as classes and service projects. Some covens have been listed in the Yellow Pages of the telephone directory. A couple of covens have even set up dial-a-message phone lines, with announcements of events each week. And of course, posting information in local alternative, New Age, or occult bookstores is a good idea. Some bookstores even have classrooms for rent, and these can be ideal for a "Wicca 101" series.

The Covenant of the Goddess publishes a fine press packet about the Craft, which explains something about our history, ethics, thealogy/theology, holidays, and terminology. Your coven could hand-deliver a copy to the editor of each newspaper, and the news managers of each television and radio station in your area. Then the next time there is an "occult" story in the news, they will have accurate information on file and a contact (your coven) in case they have questions. In some cases, this contact may lead to feature stories on the Craft as represented by your coven; you will have to be careful if some of your members are "in the broom closet." To obtain press packets, write to the COG Public Information Officer, P.O. Box 1226, Berkeley, CA 94701. Enclose a small donation for each copy requested.

Note: It has been our experience that printed features are more susceptible to error than live radio or television interviews. On the air you're speaking for yourself; in print, a semi-informed (at best) reporter is trying to explain you second-hand, and you won't know what they misunderstood until you see it in print. Of course, don't go on the air unless you can be relaxed and articulate, and don't dress like Broomhilda.

If your community has parades, fairs, or festivals, you might consider getting involved. One Iowa coven (and Pagan friends) marches in the Independence Day parade each year with costumes and banners. You might sell baked goods or other refreshments as a fundraiser. You could set up an information table; if you need general brochures on Witchcraft, you can copy the ones in the appendices. In short, if it is safe to be "out" at all, you can consider doing the same sorts of things that any other religious group in town does.

Dealing With Negativity

What happens if you decide to be public and get a negative response? First, keep calm. There is a natural tendency to go into "fight or flight" mode and respond too quickly. Think about who is attacking you. A couple of letters to the editor from fundamentalist fanatics do not mean the Inquisition has returned. Chances are you are hearing from either a noisy individual, or at worst a handful of "religious warriors" from a small church, who have been whipped up by an ignorant minister.

If they have attacked your reputation in public, or spread lies about Witchcraft and your coven, then respond calmly and factually through the media. You may offer to meet with them and share information about your spiritual path. They probably won't take you up on it, but if they do then stay calm and expect nothing. This is simply an exercise in assertiveness and a demonstration that you do not fear them and will not give up your religious freedoms.

One thing you don't want to do is to get in an endless argument with fundamentalists. If someone writes a letter to the editor or makes a comment on a radio show, respond and then drop it (unless they have violated the law). If the squabble goes back and forth too long, the public is liable to decide that both groups are fringe fanatics and not worth listening to. And don't ever assume that you will open the mind of a fundamentalist or get them to accept the facts; their emotional investment in their dogmas is too great to allow room for the truth. Rather than waste your energies fighting them, focus on building your coven.

There are exceptions to the "reply and drop it" rule. There could be an instance of slander, vandalism, trespass, harassment, or even assault. If your critics or attackers cross the line and commit an act you believe to be illegal, then consult an attorney immediately about filing a civil suit or criminal complaint. Use the law and the media to protect yourself from further problems. Use your magick too, but only to defend yourself. And call on the Pagan community, the liberal churches or other minority religions, and even the American Civil Liberties Union for support.

What if it doesn't feel safe to be open as a coven, or you just don't want to risk this kind of conflict? Then don't. But if you are going to stay in the "broom closet," stay all the way in. You can survive through strict secrecy. You may be able to survive by putting on a bold face, as public Witches openly claiming your right to religious freedom. But if you are half in and half out—if the community knows that "something" is going on at your house during full moons, but not what—then you are in danger. It is too easy for people to take rumors, a stray fact or two, and vivid imagination, and come up with spine-chilling notions of devil worship and sacrifice. So give them all the facts, or nothing.

To be "in the broom closet" means requiring vows of secrecy and confidentiality from each person before they join the coven. It means appointing a "Watcher" or coven security officer who is strict and competent. It means that you cannot drop hints to friends or relatives. It means getting coven mail at a post office box in another town. It means that every covener keeps their Witchcraft books, robes, and ritual tools hidden, lest a neighbor's child or landlord see something and tell the town. And it means living your lives as exemplary citizens and forging networks of non-Pagan friends in the community, so that if secrecy fails and you are forced into the public eye, you have a chance of being heard and accepted because people respect you as a friend and neighbor.

Whether you are secret or open about your spiritual path, it is wise to be a contributing part of the community. Live with honor and treat each member of the community, as well as the environment, with love and respect; after all, we are *all* part of the Goddess, and She deserves no less.

Resource

Kerr Cuhulain. *The Law Enforcement Guide to Wicca.* Victoria, BC, Canada: Horned Owl Publishing, 1989, 1997.

27 The Life Cycle of the Coven

by Alane Crowomyn with Amber K

Covens, like other groups, go through certain stages in their development. While no two covens are alike, there is still a pattern that can be discerned in most of them. A leader who knows generally what to expect is more likely to respond wisely when the coven enters a new stage and can design coven rituals or activities to recognize and address group needs and issues.

For those who like cute mnemonic devices, the five stages of group life have been called Forming, Storming, Norming, Performing, and Adjourning. This and many of the concepts of this chapter are drawn from Susan Wheelan's work on training groups, itself derived from decades of psychological research on group dynamics. Alane, a social psychologist, has adapted Wheelan's ideas and applied them to group development in covens.

Stage One: Forming

When a group is new, people are cautious because they don't know "the rules," formal or unspoken. (If there are any who've been in the group longer, or had experience in a similar group, the rules are taken for granted; they may be invisible and unspoken.) People are curious about the other members and are very polite to one another while they get acquainted. As in childhood, there is great dependence on the leaders. Leaders are treated like parents and may be idolized or at least idealized. They are also expected to do most of the work, because they know what's going on.

New members may have some fears. They may be wondering if they will be safe, especially if they are new to Wicca and have misconceptions about the Craft fostered by movies and folklore. Fortunately, realizing that the High Priestess is an accountant with a silly sense of humor, or that the High Priest is an environmental restoration specialist who loves cats, can usually dissipate those fears.

Some issues on people's minds at this stage are: "Am I really accepted as part of the group?", "Am I behaving appropriately?", and "What do the leaders think of me?"

But the main sentiment felt by all is that of celebration at having found such wonderful kindred spirits. Members think: We're so alike!

Stage Two: Storming

This is the adolescence of the group. Issues of dependency versus counter-dependency arise. Members are getting empowered, developing identities within the group, feeling the need to express themselves, assert themselves, and even rebel. Folks are not very good at listening during this time, but they are stating their issues.

People may shoot off in different directions. Some may find the emotional work of building the coven too threatening or difficult, and avoid it by staying superficial or joking around a lot, taking on a "jester" role. Others may react to the tension by quarreling over trivial issues. It's hard to get things done; organizing the simplest coven activity may feel like trying to get a bunch of teenagers ready to leave the house on time. There is likely to be cliquing: one group standing by the old leaders, others wanting to take over.

Some groups move through this stage easily, and some get stuck here for a long time. If leaders find it hard to give up the parent/teacher role, it can be hard to move through this stage. If the issues are ignored or dealt with superficially, they will remain underneath and come up again later.

Questions that members face are: "Is my voice being heard?", "Aren't I just as important as the leaders?", and "Why is it done this way, instead of another?" "Can't anyone else see that our leaders are flawed?" As people know each other better and discover differences of opinion, they are shocked to realize: We're not totally alike!

Stage Three: Norming

This is a transition stage, the coven's early adulthood. The group is solidifying. Most issues of power and leadership have been decided, although some members have probably been lost in the process. The task of "assertively striving for a place in the group" is largely finished. People don't want to fight anymore. Now the coven is moving on to other issues: norms, rules, how to do things.

At this stage, members talk everything to death. Enormous amounts of time may be devoted to discussion of by-laws and procedures. Because they don't want more conflict, everyone is extremely careful about including and listening to one another. There is more facilitating and sharing.

Members are just learning to trust each other. The comfort level is increasing. Gradually there is more structure, more agreed-upon process and procedure. More people are involved in leadership. During this stage and the next, members will begin to have the confidence and encouragement to show their hidden talents. It would not be unusual to discover, for example, that one member can make wonderful ritual masks or that another can play the lute. Now that the struggles have subsided, people begin to blossom. And as the ground rules become more clear, there is more experimentation.

The questions at hand are: "How can we operate in a way that's acceptable to everyone?", "How can we avoid conflict and get on with our work?", and "Now that I have the basics down, what variations can I try?" The underlying sentiment is, "We're different individuals, but it looks like we can work together."

Stage Four: Performing

This is the coven's adulthood. There is relative stability; the rules are established, much has been hammered out. The members find themselves in deeper interpersonal relationships—people understand, appreciate, and love one another.

Stage Four feels good. There is a sense of effortlessness. People just take care of things. The mood shifts easily between fun and seriousness. Most members can switch roles easily as necessary. Issues are dealt with in a straightforward way because there are fewer hidden agendas. If a group encounters a conflict at this stage, it is much less threatening than it would have been before; people know the group can handle a disagreement without falling apart. This trust allows for more honest communication, and problems are solved more creatively.

The questions here are: "What can we tackle next, now that we have our act together?" and "Shall we share our expertise and competence with the wider Craft community?" The sentiment is, "We are a team; we can handle anything we choose to."

Stage Five: Adjourning

Eventually the group begins moving toward closure. Members focus on other interests and drift away or leave to start their own covens. Hopefully people share what they have meant to one another and thank each other. They talk about the group's history. It's good to openly acknowledge the group's ending, though some people will have trouble admitting the reality.

The questions encountered may be: "What shall I do next?", "How will my relationships change once the coven is gone?", and even "How can I make the coven stay together?" or "If it has to end, how can I duplicate the experience with a new group?" The sentiments range from bittersweet ("I gained a lot, I'll miss it") to unaccepting ("No, I need it and I won't let it die!").

A major external challenge can cause a group to revert to an earlier stage. So can instability in membership. If there is a trickle of new members, the group may experience all the stages in a mixed way: this is the cost of having an open group. People leaving will also mean shifts in stages.

Each stage can be facilitated by interventions tailored to deal with the issues that are being raised. An intervention is any action taken deliberately in order to guide the group's healthy development. There are three broad categories of interventions: conceptual, experiential, and structural.

Conceptual Interventions

You can use a conceptual intervention to help someone understand intellectually why events are playing out as they are in the group. A conceptual intervention could take place during an informal conversation, or it can take the form of more formal instruction. It may be part of a class or workshop. Conceptual interventions help coveners gain a broader perspective; they are helpful when you want to balance too much emotionality with some analytical thinking: more Air, less Water.

As the group goes through growing pains, people tend to think that the challenges are unique to their coven, or that they are caused by particular group members. Conceptual interventions can show that what is going on is a perfectly normal aspect of group process. A conceptual intervention may involve looking at the problem at an abstract, theoretical level. Having a discussion of this chapter would be a good example. Or, you might look at how the coven's issues reflect the broader social context. For example, Storming Stage gender battles may have more to do with larger issues of gender roles in our society, rather than individual motives.

When you run into a situation, think whether it would be helpful for people to see how this particular problem is an example of a normal group dynamic. It can be very empowering to give coveners this understanding of the "why." Then they can recognize for themselves when similar dynamics emerge, and make informed choices of their own.

Of course simply explaining a problem on an intellectual level may not be enough to make the emotions go away. Coven leaders will still have to listen to people's feelings and validate them. The following are examples of how you might approach a situation:

A Bad Approach

Juniper: "Dammit, look at this mess! Can't anyone pick up after themselves? I've mentioned this a thousand times!"

Windcloud: "Well, it's understandable that you should be upset. At this stage in a coven's development, people often blow up over trivial issues because they find the emotional challenges of group-building too threatening or difficult."

Juniper: "#**!%##!!!"

A Better Approach

Juniper: "This place is a pigsty! I've told people and told people to clean up when they're done here!"

Graywillow: "You're really mad, aren't you? Here, I can help—"

Juniper: "Oh, it's not the work. It's that keeping the place clean is important to me, and nobody seems to listen when I bring it up."

Graywillow: "So you think nobody's listening, or else nobody cares about your feelings on this?"

Juniper: "Exactly. And it's driving me crazy."

Graywillow: "I don't blame you. But please remember that the coven's still new, and right now people are more interested in finding their own niche in the coven than in hearing what everyone else needs. I guess we're not very good at listening yet. But that will change as we get more comfortable with each other."

Juniper: "Maybe you're right. But meanwhile the place is a mess."

Graywillow: "It's almost time for announcements; let's bring this up and get some volunteers to help clean up."

Experiential Interventions

Experiential interventions are just mindful interactions. You use your communication skills to share your awareness of the group's dynamics. Like families, covens can be good at keeping silent about problems. It is very powerful to simply speak the truth about what is happening. For example, if there is an inconsistency between the group's goals and what is actually happening, you can point that out. If the group seems stuck, you can point out the impasse. If the coven is in the Forming stage, you can verbalize your own self-consciousness so others can talk about theirs. For example:

Ariadne: "...so we need to decide if we're going to be a skyclad coven or make robes, or what. Any ideas?"

Foxfur: "I don't know about anyone else, but I'm feeling really self-conscious. I mean, you all seem really nice, but I still don't really know some of you very well. And I'm wondering what you'll think of me if I speak honestly."

Sandy: "Oh God, me too. I'm sitting here thinking, What would they say if they knew I walk around naked in my house all the time? Oops, guess I'll find out."

Ariadne: "How many other people are feeling kind of awkward discussing this? Well, that's pretty natural at this point. So how do we get past this shyness? We could write down our ideas and have one person read them all anonymously . . . ."

An experiential intervention may involve not speaking, too. If there is too much dependence on you as Great Mother or Father, then your silence can encourage others to begin to take responsibility. When the issues are particularly threatening, as can be the case with Storming stage power struggles, a paradoxical intervention may work well. If you say something outrageous, like "You seem really comfortable with letting the leaders make all of the decisions," this might stimulate disagreement and open a discussion.

Experiential interventions are very helpful for setting positive group norms. If counterproductive trends are left unchecked, they can become entrenched. Noticing aloud keeps the group self-aware. When you do speak up, guard against the temptation to offer an instant solution. After you illuminate the group's dynamics, you may have to wait and give people time to process what you have said. They may not respond immediately, but before long the subject will resurface so that the group can work with it. If the solution is the result of group discussion rather than handed down by leadership, the coven as a whole will be more likely to "own" the solution and make it work. By the time a coven is firmly in the Performing stage, everyone will likely have gained confidence in using experiential interventions. An example:

Mudbunny: "So does beef stew sound good for Saturday night? Then for breakfast, how about eggs and sausage . . . ."

Wild Celery: "But I'm a vegetarian. Everything you've mentioned includes meat!"

Aolus: "Yeah, but most of us are carnivore types. You can pick the meat out of yours. What's planned for lunch?"

Cypress: "Hold on. We decided long ago to work by consensus, and try to meet everybody's needs. I think Wild Celery's concerns just got brushed aside. Shall we try again?"

(Silence.)

Aolus: "Sorry, Cel. Guess I wasn't thinking."

Mudbunny: "Me too. What if we plan all vegetarian meals, then have some meat on the side for those that want to add it?"

Structural Interventions

Structural interventions involve planned activities. Many people find that they learn best when they "do." Rather than telling the group what it needs to understand, you craft an experience that allows them to discover the answers for themselves. Wiccan ritual provides a rich environment for structural interventions. If people need to learn about one another in the Forming stage, a self-disclosure activity can be built into ritual. Working with a strong goddess like Athena or Durga may help the group to find the sacred side of the Storming stage. A vision quest may be of help in the Norming stage. After all, the cycles of the group are all part of the sacred cycle of life and of the Earth, and can be honored as we honor the changes of the seasons and our lives.

Structural interventions are very useful for establishing healthy norms by having everyone interact in the desired way. Instead of talking about the value of loving one another, simply design an activity that tends to bring out love. Even something as simple as offering bread to one another and saying "May Mother Earth nourish you" can help to establish a caring coven. Helping a group member cope with a life crisis through a supportive ritual develops group closeness while making good magick.

Many of the activities that you use in training can do double duty, teaching magickal skills while facilitating group growth. You can use role playing to practice both ritual procedures and the interpersonal processes that are always part of ritual. Most good workshops alternate between explaining and giving participants a chance to discover, process, and practice.

A group that gathers for several days will go through the same stages of development, even if it is in a rather vague and messy way. So when you plan a long event such as a coven retreat or a regional festival, you can think of the structured events as interventions into predictable developmental issues. The focus of rituals and workshops can be planned accordingly.

Ritual and Activity Ideas

Each stage can be facilitated by certain coven programs or rituals tailored to deal with the issues that are being raised. A few ideas follow.

Forming

Sharing circle: How did you come here, what was your first experience with Wicca?

Sharing life stories: Each member in turn can tell their story, either during an esbat or at the beginning of the "social hour" afterwards. This may work best if only one person does it at a time; otherwise all the information starts to blur together. Alternatively, at a weekend coven retreat, ask one person to tell about their life at the end of each meal.

Self-empowerment: This ritual might begin with a self-blessing, continue with stories of people's successes, and end with raising energy to empower coveners to accomplish their goals.

Orientation: Before a ritual where there will be several first-timers, go over the outline of the ritual, explaining what will happen and why. This can reduce anxiety about the unfamiliar. If there is just one new person, assign a "buddy" to answer their questions.

Storming

Mixing cliques: If factions have started to form, assign people from different cliques to work together in ritual or on other coven projects.

Empowerment: If individuals are feeling "out of the power loop" for any reason, it may be helpful to give them extra responsibilities in such areas as teaching, ritual leadership, and coordination of events. In other words, put them in charge of something important.

"Celebrating diversity" ritual: Acknowledge individual differences, speak of the positive elements in each, and end with the whole coven affirming the value of each person.

Leadership change: Sometimes the best way to defuse tension is for the leaders to volunteer for a temporary sabbatical or vacation, or to suggest a system of trading or rotating roles or offices.

Norming

Tarot exercise: A deck is spread out in the middle of the floor, cards face up. Each person picks a card to represent each other person. Then the group picks an individual and goes round-robin, with everyone explaining why they chose particular cards for that person. Then each person picks a card to represent the energy or gestalt of the entire group, and explains it.

Leadership discussion: Ask everyone to share their honest feelings about leadership in the coven—how it's handled, what's OK, what isn't. This only works if the coven leaders are well grounded and able to handle constructive criticism. Note: if done at the "forming" stage, no one will have enough information, and comments will likely be vague and "peachy-keen" in tone. If done during the "storming" stage, there may be lots of not-so-constructive criticism and the group may be further polarized.

Sharing needs: In the circle, let each covener talk about the needs and expectations they had when they first joined, and how these are—or are not—being fulfilled. Make an action plan for a more fulfilling coven.

"Who we are": Explore questions of coven identity, describe the tradition of which you are a part, and write down a "vision" and "mission" for the group.

Performing

Community events: The coven may wish to host or sponsor open sabbat rituals or a major community service project.

Area events: The coven might sponsor an area festival, or workshops or rituals at a large regional festival.

National events: A coven can organize a national project or event, such as a fundraising drive within the Pagan community for an environmental cause, a national seminar, or a resource guide or other Pagan-oriented publication.

Recognition dinner: Reserve space at a local restaurant and, after dessert, present tokens of appreciation or gag gifts to those who have served the coven as officers—hopefully everyone.

Bragfest: Hold an old-fashioned Celtic feast where each person tells stories (in a grandiose manner) of their skills and accomplishments. Follow with body-painting to honor and celebrate individuals.

Adjourning

Parting ritual: Hold a farewell ceremony at which members share memories round-robin. Hold a cord-cutting (of the ties which bind the group, not individual relationships). Write notes about your coven experiences on parchment: toss them in a cauldron if they're things that you want to release, keep them if they're things you want to remember.

Parting Letter: If it is difficult to gather everyone, then have a leader write a good-bye letter. Send it around for each person to add to, then copy the final product and send it to each participant.

"Pagan Potlatch": Invite area covens to a potluck dinner and disperse the coven's belongings. If there is one special object that symbolized the group, which it would not be appropriate to share, then burn it or bury it in the woods.

Whether it is a conceptual, experiential, or structural type, each intervention is a learning experience. People have different learning styles, so it is helpful to tailor your plans to the people involved. While some people will immediately click into a conceptual intervention, less analytic types may become restless. Some people love role playing, others freeze up when asked to perform in front of a group. In the earlier developmental stages, it is helpful to stay within the comfort zone of the people you are working with. As the coven develops and trust builds, you can ask the members to stretch more.

Remember that interventions needn't be covert; your goal is to lead, not to manipulate. It is quite appropriate to discuss possible interventions together and encourage the group to identify its own issues and choose its own strategies.

When selecting an intervention strategy, above all listen to your intuition. If you have a bad feeling about trying something, don't do it. Your feel for what the group is ready for is surely based on many signals that you read without even being aware you are doing so. Trust your instincts.

Remembering Basic Needs

In an open group, where members come and go, there will not be clear group stages because individuals are going through different stages at different times. And of course some people will have worked through many issues in other groups, or will be especially sensitive to some issues and not others. Therefore, it is wise to look always to individual needs and how well they are being met, and never assume that one "answer" will serve the needs of all.

Although we all share the same basic human needs, different motives will be more or less central for different people. For example, try rating yourself on the following needs. For each, assess whether it is unimportant, important, or very important to you.

- **Desire for belonging, to be involved, to be part of the group, to be accepted.**
- **Desire to lead, to persuade, to dominate, to be in control, to be influential.**
- **Desire to be intimate, to form close attachments, express warmth, be loved.**
- **Desire to excel, to achieve, to create, to be respected.**

These four needs can be labeled inclusion, power, intimacy, and achievement. Although you could probably identify other needs that the coven meets for its members, these needs influence the group's dynamics as it evolves. People who have strong needs for inclusion will be prominent in the group's emotional life during the Forming stage. Their needs will help move the coven through this stage, because they will be motivated to make sure that group membership issues are dealt with.

As the group enters the Storming stage, those with stronger power motivation will move to the foreground of the group.

Later, in the Norming and Performing stages, those whose needs focus on intimacy will take on emotional leadership and help the coven to nurture "Perfect Love and Perfect Trust." Achievement motivation can surface at any time but may be very obvious in the Performing stage, when the coven is likely to consider larger scale projects such as leading a major ritual at a regional festival.

Understanding your own needs as a coven leader can be helpful. For example, if you don't have strong power needs, some of the interpersonal dynamics in the Storming stage may go right over your head. Because you don't share the needs of those who are concerned with power issues, you may feel that there is a lot of fuss being made over nothing. On the other hand, if your power needs are strong, you may see issues of control as being more important than many of your coveners do. Either way, it is essential to keep in mind how diverse individual viewpoints can be.

You can design a structural intervention if you want to explore needs issues as a group. For example, designate different directions for each of the needs. You might place achievement in the east, power in the south, intimacy in the west, and belonging in the north. Then have everyone go to the direction that represents their strongest need. Look at who is where and talk about it. Then have everyone go to their second strongest need, their third, and then their last. You might want to notice which needs are strongest or weakest in the group as a whole, which can be an interesting way to think about the "personality" of your coven.

RESOURCES

Wheelan, Susan. *Facilitating Training Groups*. (n.p., n.d.).

Starhawk, *Dreaming the Dark: Magic, Sex and Politics* (Boston: Beacon Press, 1982).

"Group Cycles in Wiccan Circles," a workshop by Alane Crowomyn. If you are interested in having Alane present this workshop, contact her at P.O. Box 742, Durango, CO 81302.

Conclusion

We—the Goddess- and Horned-God-worshipping magickal peoples—existed long before the word *Wicca* was coined, and long before covens came into being. We have continued to survive by virtue of our adaptability; indeed, the formation of covens during the Burning Times was one expression of our flexibility. We will continue to survive if and when covens are no longer the common, or only, mode of Witch organization. The heart of our religion is not the way we structure our groups, but our reverence for Nature, our love of the immanent God/dess, and our understanding of magick. As long as we know that, we can afford to experiment with organizational structures and still call ourselves Witches.

Yet covens have served us well in the past centuries and have advantages that I do not think we will find in any other structure. They allow for a great deal of focus on individual needs and individual growth. They make possible the warmth and love of a chosen extended family. And they are large enough to be an effective force in a community without being totally unwieldy.

A coven is a collection of extreme individualists packed tightly into a circle and pressure-cooked by magick. Certainly membership in a coven can be demanding, frustrating, even crazy-making at times. The understatement of the century is that leading a coven is like herding cats. But for all its challenges, there is no better place to find out who you are, and if you choose, to transform yourself into something more.

"Necessity is the mother of invention." Though we were forced to create the coven in order to escape the displeasure of kings and survive the Burning Times, I doubt that many Witches would be glad to see the coven be replaced today. If it did not exist, we might be forced to invent it simply as an antidote to sitting in rows of pews in mainstream churches. Whatever Witchcraft of the future looks like, I hope it keeps the coven. And I hope your coven is filled with love and laughter. Blessèd be!

Appendix A: Coven Organization

A-1

Common Beliefs and Practices of Witchcraft

Not every Witch or Wiccan will subscribe to all of these points, but generally they are representative.

1. The divine Spirit is present in all creatures and things: people, animals, plants, stones, and so on.
2. Because the Earth and all of Nature are divine, we should treat them with reverence and respect.
3. The ultimate creative force manifests in both feminine and masculine modes; therefore, it is often symbolized as the Goddess and the God. In some covens, both are celebrated equally. In others, the Goddess is given precedence or even celebrated without reference to the God.
4. All goddesses and gods are aspects of The Goddess and The God. The aspects most traditional in the Craft are the Triple Goddess of the Moon (Maiden, Mother and Crone); the Earth Mother; and the Horned God of wildlife, death and rebirth.
5. We evolve spiritually over the course of many lifetimes. Upon death one goes to the Summerland, a state of rest and reflection, and eventually chooses where and when they will be reborn.
6. We can influence ourselves and our environment through magick, which should be practiced only for positive purposes such as spiritual development, healing, guidance, and safety.
7. Rituals are generally performed according to the phases of the Moon and at Sabbat festivals that mark the progression of the seasons. Witches prefer to celebrate outdoors when possible.
8. Witches work, study, and celebrate in small groups called covens—usually three to thirteen in number—and sometimes in larger groves or congregations. These may be associated with a tradition or federation, but are usually autonomous. There is no central church authority.

9. Individuals have access to the divine and do not require an intermediary. Every initiate is regarded as priest/ess. There is no revealed scripture, prophet, or messiah.
10. The central ethic is "An ye harm none, do as ye will." This is reinforced by The Law of Return, the understanding that whatever energy you send out returns to you threefold.
11. Though Witchcraft is most commonly associated with Europe, it has its roots in the earliest spiritual expressions of humanity. The gods, myths and customs of many cultures can be harmoniously blended with its beliefs and practices.
12. Witchcraft welcomes all those whose hearts are drawn to the Old Religion, regardless of race, ethnic heritage, gender, sexual orientation, physical handicap, or age (providing they have attained their majority).
13. Witchcraft or Wicca is not the only valid spiritual path, and people should be free to choose the religion that best fits their needs.

A-2
The Laws of the Craft

The Laws, Ordains, or Ardaynes are an important part of many Wiccan traditions, although no one is certain of their origin. They may be centuries old, originating in the Burning Times; or they may have appeared much later; or they may be a mixture of old and new. There are several versions in existence; one of the most popular updated versions is *The New Wiccan Book of the Law* by Lady Galadriel, Grove of the Unicorn, Moonstone Publications, P.O. Box 13384, Athens, GA 30324, U.S.A.

What follows is an updated version, without archaic language and with obsolete sections dropped (such as the rule that most Witches are not allowed to know where other covens meet). It is not as eloquent or extensive as *The New Wiccan Book of the Law*, but conveys the gist of the material. Note that the numbers will not correspond to other versions.

Personal Standards

1. An ye harm none, do as ye will.
2. If you know the Rede is being broken, you must work strongly against it.
3. Watch, listen, and withhold judgment; in debate, let your silences be long, your thoughts clear, and your words carefully chosen.
4. Never boast, or threaten, or speak ill of anyone.
5. Be truthful always, save when speaking would lead to a great harm.
6. Do not haggle over the price of your ritual tools.
7. Keep clean your body, your clothes, and your house.
8. Should you take a task upon yourself, work hard and well to accomplish it properly and in good time.

Relationships with Others

9. Revere, honor, tend, and heal the Earth.
10. Of that which you grow, make, or use, let as much as possible return to the Earth as an offering to Her, as a way to nourish the cycle of life.
11. Do not judge those of other paths, but offer them love and aid.
12. Do not steal from human, animal, or spirit; if you have needs you cannot meet, turn to our community.
13. Offer friendship and hospitality to strangers who visit among you.
14. You shall never handfast or wed someone you do not love.
15. Honor the relationships and commitments of others, and do not couple together if it will cause pain to another.

16. Raise your children with kindness; feed, clothe, and house them as well as you can. Show them love and affection; teach them strength and wisdom.
17. You may not own slaves, or willingly be part of any nation, community, or organization which allows this practice.
18. Deal fairly and honestly in all your transactions with others, following the letter and spirit of any contract you agree to.

Within the Coven

19. The High Priestess shall rule her coven as a representative of the Goddess.
20. The High Priestess shall choose whom she will have as High Priest, providing he have sufficient rank.
21. The High Priest shall support her as a representative of the God.
22. In the circle, the commands and wishes of the High Priestess are law.
23. The High Priest commands the respect due a magus, counselor, and father.
24. If there are disputes among you, let the High Priestess convene the Elders. They shall hear both sides, alone, then together, and make a just decision.
25. If the High Priestess and High Priest find it necessary to correct, rebuke, or punish a covener, this should be done in private and accepted with good grace by the recipient.
26. Any who will not work under the High Priestess may found a new coven, if they are third degree. They and any members who choose to go with them must avoid the old coven for a time, until the new coven has bonded and harmonious relations can be established between the covens.
27. If a High Priestess leaves her coven, but returns within a year and a day, she shall be taken back and all be as before. Meanwhile, her Maiden or chief deputy shall act as High Priestess. If the High Priestess does not return within the allotted time, then a new High Priestess shall be elected: the one who has been acting in that role, unless there is powerful reason to the contrary.
28. The High Priestess shall gracefully retire in favor of a new High Priestess, should the coven so decide in Council.
29. You must immediately depose any High Priestess who consents to the breaking of the Rede.
30. Before the coven uses magick, let them debate at length; only if all are satisfied that none will be harmed may magick be used.

31. The circle must be duly cast and purified. The Wicca should be prepared and purified to enter the circle.
32. No one may tell outsiders where the covenstead is, or the meetings, without the consent of the coven.

Within the Craft

33. Do not gossip or speak evil of others of the Wicca.
34. Never lie to the Elders or to any of the Wicca.
35. None but the Wicca may see our inner mysteries; but with the consent of the coven, friends and relatives may be invited to the ordinary rituals.
36. No one shall reveal to outsiders who is Wiccan, or give names or addresses, or anything which can betray any of us. No one may do anything which will endanger any of the Craft, or bring them into contact with the law of the land, or any of our persecutors.
37. Keep within your Book of Shadows the teachings of your coven, and also a record of your own rites and learning.
38. None may come to meetings with those with whom they are at odds. In any disputes among Wiccans, no one may invoke any laws but those of the Craft, nor any court but that of the Priest, Priestess, and Elders.
39. It is all right to accept money for the work of your hands, but not for work done within the circle. Never accept money for the use of magick, or for the teaching of the Craft within the Circle.
40. Never use magick for show, pride, or vainglory.
41. Give of your skills, your work and your earnings to your coven, to the Craft, to priests and priestesses who do Her work, and to worthy causes which honor the Lady and the Lord. Honor those others who work willingly for the good of the Craft without pay.
42. Never do anything to disgrace the Goddess or the Wicca.

A-3
Recommended Reading List

Witchcraft in General

Adler, Margot. *Drawing Down the Moon: Witches, Druids, Goddess Worshippers and Other Pagans in America Today*. Boston: Beacon, 1986, revised 1997.

Buckland, Raymond. *Buckland's Complete Book of Witchcraft*. St. Paul, MN: Llewellyn, 1990.

———. *Witchcraft from the Inside*. St. Paul, MN: Llewellyn, 1995.

Cabot, Laurie. *Power of the Witch: The Earth, the Moon, and the Magical Path to Enlightenment*. New York: Delta, 1989.

Campanelli, Pauline and Dan. *Ancient Ways*. St. Paul, MN: Llewellyn, 1991.

———. *Wheel of the Year: Living the Magical Life*. St. Paul, MN: Llewellyn, 1989.

Clifton, Charles, ed. *Witchcraft Today, Book One: The Modern Craft Movement*. St. Paul, MN: Llewellyn, 1992.

———. *Witchcraft Today, Book Two: Modern Rites of Passage*. St. Paul, MN: Llewellyn, 1993.

———. *Witchcraft Today, Book Three: Witchcraft and Shamanism*. St. Paul, MN: Llewellyn, 1994.

———. *Living Between Two Worlds: Challenges of the Modern Witch*. St. Paul, MN: Llewellyn, 1996.

Crowley, Vivianne. *The Phoenix from the Flame*. London: Aquarian Press, 1994.

———. *Wicca*. London: Aquarian Press, 1989.

Cuhulain, Kerr. *The Law Enforcement Guide to Wicca*. Victoria, BC, Canada: Horned Owl Publishing, 1989, 1997.

Cunningham, Scott. *The Truth About Witchcraft Today*. St. Paul, MN: Llewellyn, 1988.

———. *Wicca: A Guide for the Solitary Practitioner*. St. Paul, MN: Llewellyn, 1990.

———. *Living Wicca: A Further Guide for the Solitary Practitioner*. St. Paul, MN: Llewellyn, 1993.

Donovan, Frank. *Never on a Broomstick*. New York: Bell Publishing, 1971.

Dunwich, Gerina. *Wicca Source Book*. New York: Citadel, 1996.

Ehrenreich, Barbara and Deirdre English. *Witches, Midwives and Nurses: A History of Woman Healers*. New York: The Feminist Press, 1973.

Farrar, Janet and Stewart. *What Witches Do*. Custer, WA: Phoenix, 1983.

———. *Eight Sabbats for Witches*. London: Robert Hale, 1981.

Farrar, Janet, Stewart Farrar, and Gavin Bone. *The Pagan Path*. Custer, WA: Phoenix, 1995.

Gardner, Gerald. *Witchcraft Today.* New York: Citadel, 1954.

———. *The Meaning of Witchcraft.* London: Aquarian Press, 1959.

Glass, Justin. *Witchcraft: The Sixth Sense.* Wilshire, 1965.

Green, Marian. *A Calendar of Festivals: Traditional Celebrations, Songs, Seasonal Recipes and Things to Make.* Shaftesbury, Dorset: Element, 1991.

Guiley, Rosemary Ellen. *The Encyclopedia of Witches and Witchcraft.* New York: Facts on File, 1989.

Harrison, Michael. *The Roots of Witchcraft.* New York: Tandem, 1973.

Hughes, Pennethorne. *Witchcraft.* New York: Pelican, 1965.

Leek, Sybil. *The Complete Art of Witchcraft.* New York: New American Library, 1973.

Lethbridge, T. C. *Witches: Investigating an Ancient Religion.* New York: Citadel, 1962, 1968.

McCoy, Edain. *The Sabbats: A New Approach to Living the Old Ways.* St. Paul, MN: Llewellyn, 1994.

Murray, Margaret. *The Witch Cult in Western Europe.* Oxford: Oxford University Press, 1921, 1971.

———. *The God of the Witches.* Oxford: Oxford University Press, 1931, 1970.

O'Gaea, Ashleen. *The Family Wicca Book: The Craft for Parents and Children.* St. Paul, MN: Llewellyn, 1993.

Orion, Loretta. *Never Again the Burning: Paganism Revived.* Prospect Heights, IL: Waveland Press, 1995.

RavenWolf, Silver. *To Ride a Silver Broomstick: New Generation Witchcraft.* St. Paul, MN: Llewellyn, 1993.

———. *To Stir a Magick Cauldron.* St. Paul, MN: Llewellyn, 1995.

Sheba. *The Grimoire of Lady Sheba.* St. Paul, MN: Llewellyn, 1974.

Starhawk. *The Spiral Dance: A Rebirth of the Ancient Religion of the Great Goddess.* New York: Harper & Row, 1979, rev. 1989.

———. *Dreaming the Dark: Magic, Sex and Politics.* Boston: Beacon Press, 1982.

———. *Truth or Dare: Encounters With Power, Authority and Magic.* New York: Harper & Row, 1987.

Valiente, Doreen. *Where Witchcraft Lives.*†

———. *Witchcraft for Tomorrow.* London: Robert Hale, 1978.

———. *The ABC of Witchcraft: Past and Present.* London: St. Martin's Press, 1973.

———. *The Rebirth of Witchcraft.* London: Robert Hale, 1989.

Valiente, Doreen, and Evan Jones. *Witchcraft: A Tradition Renewed.* Custer, WA: Phoenix, 1990.

Warren-Clarke, Ly. *The Way of the Goddess: A Manual for Wiccan Initiation.* Prism Press, 1987.

Traditions of Witchcraft

Buckland, Raymond. *The Tree: The Complete Book of Saxon Wicca*. York Beach, ME: Samuel Weiser, 1978.

———. *Scottish Witchcraft: The History and Magick of the Picts*. St. Paul, MN: Llewellyn, 1991.

Budapest, Z. *The Holy Book of Women's Mysteries* (2 vols.). Susan B. Anthony Coven No. 1, 1979.

Farrar, Janet and Stewart. *The Witches' Way: Principles, Rituals and Beliefs of Modern Witchcraft*. London: Robert Hale, 1984.

Fitch, Ed. *A Grimoire of Shadows: Witchcraft, Paganism and Magick*. St. Paul, MN: Llewellyn, 1996.

Grimassi, Raven. *Ways of the Strega: Italian Witchcraft: Its Legends, Lore and Spells*. St. Paul, MN: Llewellyn, 1995.

Jade. *To Know: A Guide to Women's Magic and Spirituality*. New York: Delphi, 1991.

K, Amber. *Moonrise: Welcome to Dianic Wicca*. Madison, WI: Re-formed Congregation of the Goddess, 1992.

Leland, Charles, ed. *Aradia: Gospel of the Witches*. York Beach, ME: Samuel Weiser, 1974.

McCoy, Edain. *Witta: An Irish Pagan Tradition*. St. Paul, MN: Llewellyn, 1993.

Ryall, Rhiannon. *West Country Wicca: A Journal of the Old Religion*. Custer, WA: Phoenix, 1989.

Stepanich, Kisma. *Faery Wicca Book One: Theory and Magick*. St. Paul, MN: Llewellyn, 1994.

———. *Faery Wicca Book Two: Shamanic Practices of the Cunning Arts*. St. Paul, MN: Llewellyn, 1995

Weinstein, Marion. *Earth Magic: A Dianic Book of Shadows*. New York: Earth Magic Productions, 1994.

Goddess Lore

Eisler, Riane. *The Chalice and the Blade*. New York: Harper & Row, 1987.

Farrar, Janet and Stewart. *The Witches' Goddess*. Custer, WA: Phoenix, 1987.

Campbell, Joseph. *In All Her Names*. San Francisco: HarperSanFrancisco, 1991.

Condren, Mary. *The Serpent and the Goddess: Women, Religion and Power in Celtic Ireland*. New York: HarperCollins, 1989.

Gimbutas, Marija. *Goddesses and Gods of Ancient Europe*. Berkeley, CA: University of California Press, 1982.

Graves, Robert. *The White Goddess*. New York: Farrar, Straus & Giroux, 1966.

Monaghan, Patricia. *The New Book of Goddesses and Heroines*. St. Paul, MN: Llewellyn, 1997.

Muten, Burleigh, ed. *Return of the Great Goddess*. Boston: Shambhala, 1994.

Neuman, Erich. *The Great Mother*. Princeton, NJ: Princeton University Press, 1955, 1963.

Olson, Carl, ed. *The Book of the Goddess, Past and Present*. New York: Crossroad, 1986.

Pattai, Raphael. *The Hebrew Goddess*. New York: Avon/Discus, 1967, 1978.

Reed, Ellen Cannon. *The Goddess and the Tree*. York Beach, ME: Samuel Weiser, 1997.

Rush, Anne Kent. *Moon, Moon*. Moon Books, 1976.

Sjoo, Monica and Mor, Barbara. *The Ancient Religion of the Great Cosmic Mother of All*. New York: Harper & Row, 1982.

Spretnak, Charlene. *Lost Goddesses of Early Greece*. Boston: Beacon Press, 1992.

Stone, Merlin. *When God Was A Woman*. New York: Harvest/HBJ, 1976.

———. *Ancient Mirrors of Womanhood* (2 vols.). New Sibylline Books, 1979.

Walker, Barbara. *Woman's Encyclopedia of Myths & Secrets*. New York: Harper & Row, 1983.

God Lore

Campbell, Joseph. *The Hero With a Thousand Faces*. Princeton, NJ: Princeton University Press, 1990.

Conway, D. J. *Lord of Light and Shadow: The Many Faces of the God*. St. Paul, MN: Llewellyn, 1997.

Farrar, Janet and Stewart. *The Witches' God*. Custer, WA: Phoenix, 1990.

Gimbutas, Marija. *Goddesses and Gods of Ancient Europe*. Berkeley: University of California Press, 1982.

Klein, Kenny. *The Flowering Rod: Men, Sex and Spirituality*. New York: Delphi, 1993.

Richardson. *Earth God Rising: Return of the Male Mysteries*. St. Paul, MN: Llewellyn, 1990.

Magick and Psychic Work

Bias, Clifford, ed. *Ritual Book of Magic*. York Beach, ME: Samuel Weiser, 1981.

Butler, W. E. *Magic: Its Ritual, Power and Purpose*. York Beach, ME: Samuel Weiser.†

———. *The Magician: His Training and Work*. York Beach, ME: Samuel Weiser.†

Campanelli, Pauline. *Rites of Passage: The Pagan Wheel of Life*. St. Paul, MN: Llewellyn, 1994.

Cunningham, Scott. *Earth Power: Techniques of Natural Magic*. St. Paul, MN: Llewellyn, 1987.

———. *Earth, Air, Fire and Water: More Techniques of Natural Magic*. St. Paul, MN: Llewellyn, 1991.

Fitch, Ed. *A Book of Pagan Rituals*. York Beach, ME: Samuel Weiser, 1978.

Gray, William. *Inner Traditions of Magic*. York Beach, ME: Samuel Weiser, 1970.

Harner, Michael. *The Way of the Shaman*. San Francisco: HarperSanFrancisco, 1990.

K, Amber. *True Magick: A Beginner's Guide*. St. Paul, MN: Llewellyn, 1990.

Leek, Sybil. *Cast Your Own Spells*. Bee-Line Books, 1970.

Mariechild, Diane. *Mother Wit: A Feminist Guide to Psychic Development*. London: Crossing, 1981.

Regardie, Israel. *The Art and Meaning of Magic*.†

Skinner, S., and F. King. *The Techniques of High Magic*. Destiny Books, 1976.

Strachan, Francoise. *Natural Magic*. Black Watch, 1974.

Teish, Luisah. *Jambalaya: The Natural Women's Book of Personal Charms and Practical Rituals*. New York: Harper and Row, 1985.

Valiente, Doreen. *Natural Magic*. London: St. Martin's Press, 1975.

Weinstein, Marion. *Positive Magic*. New York: Pocket Books, 1978.

Fiction

Abbey, Lynn. *Daughter of the Bright Moon*. New York: Ace, 1979.

———. *The Black Flame*. New York: Ace, 1980.

Auel, Jean. *Earth's Children* (series)

———. *The Clan of the Cave Bear*. New York: Bantam, 1980.

———. *The Valley of Horses* New York: Bantam, 1991.

———. *The Mammoth Hunters*. New York: Bantam, 1991.

———. *The Plains of Passage*. New York: Bantam, 1991.

Baudino, Gael. *Gossamer Axe*. New York: ROC Penguin, 1990.

———. *Strands of Starlight*. New York: Signet, 1989.

———. *Maze of Moonlight*. New York: ROC Penguin, 1993.

———. *Shroud of Shadow*. New York: ROC Penguin, 1993.

Bradley, Marion Zimmer. *The Mists of Avalon*. New York: Ballantine, 1982.

———. *The Forest House*. New York: Penguin, 1993.

Clayton, Jo. *Moongather*.†

———. *Moonscatter*.†

———. *Changer's Moon*.†

Fallingstar, Cerridwen. *The Heart of the Fire*. Cauldron Publications, 1990.

Farrar, Stewart. *The Twelve Maidens*.†

———. *Omega*. New York: Times Books, 1980.†

Fortune, Dion. *Moon Magic*. York Beach, ME: Samuel Weiser, 1979.

———. *Sea Priestess*. York Beach, ME: Samuel Weiser, 1978.

Gardner, Gerald. *High Magic's Aid*. Hinton, WV: Godolphin House, 1996.

Gear, Kathleen. *People of the Lakes*. Forge, 1994.

Godwin, Parke. *The Last Rainbow*. New York: Bantam, 1985.

Kaye, Marvin. and Parke Godwin. *Masters of Solitude*†

———. *Wintermind**

Kurtz, Katherine. *Lammas Night*. New York: Ballantine, 1983.

———. *The Adept*. New York: Ace, 1991.

———. *The Adept: Lodge of the Lynx*. New York: Ace, 1992.

———. *The Adept: Dagger Magic*. New York: Ace, 1995.

Paxson, Diane. *Westria* (series)

Shwartz, Susan, ed. *Hecate's Cauldron*†

Speare, Elizabeth Gorge. *The Witch of Blackbird Pond*. New York: Dell, 1958, 1997.

Starhawk. *The Fifth Sacred Thing*. New York: Bantam, 1994.

Strieber, Whitley. *Catmagic*. New York: Tor, 1987.

Thomas, Elizabeth Marshall. *Reindeer Moon*. New York: Pocket Books, 1991.

———. *Animal Wife*. New York: Houghton Mifflin, 1990.

Other Feminist Spirituality

Andrews, Lynn V. *Medicine Woman*. New York: HarperCollins, 1983.

———. *Flight of the Seventh Moon*. New York: HarperCollins, 1985.

———. *Jaguar Woman*. New York: HarperCollins, 1986.

———. *Star Woman*. New York: HarperCollins, 1987.

———. *Crystal Woman*. New York: HarperCollins, 1988.

———. *Windhorse Woman*. New York: HarperCollins, 1990.

———. *Shakkai*. New York: HarperCollins, 1993.

———. *Woman at the Edge of Two Worlds*. New York: HarperCollins, 1994.

———. *The Dark Sister.* New York: HarperCollins, 1996.

Iglehart, Hallie. *Womanspirit: A Guide to Women's Wisdom*. New York: Harper & Row, 1983.

Harding, M. Esther. *Woman's Mysteries, Ancient and Modern*. New York: Harper/Colophon, 1971.

Bolen, Jean Shinoda. *Goddesses in Everywoman*. New York: Harper & Row, 1984.

Starhawk. *Dreaming the Dark: Magic, Sex and Politics*. Boston: Beacon, 1982.

Walker, Barbara G. *The Crone: Woman of Age, Wisdom and Power*. New York: Harper & Row, 1985.

†These and possibly others may be out of print, but worth seeking in libraries or used bookstores.

A-4

Elements of Coven Names

If you are organizing a new coven and need a name, try mixing and matching to find a name that fits.

General for Covens

Coven, Circle, Grove, Temple, Assembly, Ring, Order, Pool, Web, Company, Sisterhood, Brotherhood, Fellowship, Children, Daughters, Companions, Mages, Guardians, Seekers, Pilgrims, Maidens, Mothers, Crones, Amazons.

Nature

Light, Shadows, Stars, Forest, Earth, Sea, Sky, Lake, Mountain, Rainbow, Ocean, Land, Country, Tree, Cave, Path, Stones, River, Hill, Feather, Air, Flame, Fire, Water, Wind, Wings, Stream, Spring, Herbs, Flowers, Island, Spring, Summer, Autumn, Winter, Seasons, Tor, Shore, Mesa, Peak, Desert, Field, Meadow.

Planets and Space

Moon, Sun, Mercury, Venus, Mars, Jupiter, Saturn, Uranus, Neptune, Pluto, Ceres, Vesta, Comet, Morning Star, Evening Star, Galaxy.

Colors

Black, Sable, Dark; Red, Scarlet, Crimson, Gules; Green, Verdant, Emerald, Vert; Violet, Lavender, Purple; Blue, Cerulean, Azure, Sapphire; Ivory, White, Snowy; Yellow, Topaz; Brown, Russet, Umber, Sienna; Silver, Argent; Golden; Copper; Bronze; Grey, Dove-grey, Iron.

Adjectives

Sacred, Holy, Everlasting, Immortal, Endless, Eternal, Boundless, Radiant, Shining, First (through Ninth, plus Thirteenth), Merry, Laughing, Magickal, Wiccan, Healing, Solar, Lunar, Universal, Hidden, Horned, Rising, Deep, Earthy, Airy, Fiery, Watery.

Magickal Beasts

Unicorn, Dragon, Griffin/Gryphon, Serpent, Sphinx, Cockatrice, Basilisk, Cameleopard, Winged Horse, Flying Snake, Feathered Serpent, Phoenix, Minotaur, Wyvern, Harpy, Medusa, Aurochs, Chimera, Firedrake.

Animals

Cat, Lion, Panther, Tiger, Leopard, Lynx, Dog, Hound, Talbot, Horse, Mare, Stallion, Deer, Hart, Stag, Doe, Fawn, Bull, Cow, Ram, Ewe, Hare, Dolphin, Whale, Goat, Fish, Wolf, Otter, Wolverine, Fox, Seahorse, Snake.

Birds

Falcon, Cormorant, Albatross, Seagull, Eagle, Hawk, Raven, Songbird, Robin, Heron, Cock, Swan, Swallow, Owl, Peacock, Nightingale, Dove.

Trees

Birch, Rowan, Ash, Alder, Willow, Hawthorn, Oak, Holly, Hazel, Vine, Ivy, Reed, Elder, Silver Fir, Aspen, Yew, Furze, Heather, Pine, Tamarack, Spruce, Sequoia, Redwood, Elm, Cedar, Magnolia, Hickory, Apple, Mahogany, Ebony, Maple, Rosewood, Ironwood, Madrone, Cherry, Walnut.

Herbs

Chamomile, Cherrybark, Willowbark, Catnip, Coltsfoot, Plantain, Ginger, Cayenne, Comfrey, Garlic, Lobelia, Motherwort, Damiana, Aloe Vera, Ginseng.

Stones and Gems

Granite, Bedrock, Stone, Gem, Jewel, Diamond, Sapphire, Ruby, Emerald, Topaz, Amethyst, Amber, Jet, Tiger's Eye, Carnelian, Obsidian, Agate, Jasper, Crystal, Turquoise, Citrine, Moonstone, Rose Quartz, Lapis Lazuli, Holy Stone, Aquamarine, Pearl, Onyx, Jade.

Magickal Beings

Gnomes, Sylphs, Salamanders, Undines, Faeries, Sidhe, Elves, Sprites, Devas, Mermaids, Naiads, Nereids, Oreads, Dryads, Nymphs, Fauns, Satyrs, Leprechauns, Centaurs, Pookas, Silkies, Familiars.

Goddesses and Gods

See lists in appropriate books from Recommended Reading List (A-3, page 360).

Magickal Tools

Staff, Athame, Bolline, Chalice, Cup, Bell, Book, Candle, Wand, Sword, Pentacle, Mirror, Showstone, Talisman, Amulet, Robe, Altar, Tarot, Ring, Garter, Thurible, Cauldron, Broom, Besom, Tiara, Necklace, Torc, Cord.

Other Nouns

Magick, Life, Darkness, Light, Witchery, Spell, Enchantment, Song, Smoke, Mist, Love, Laughter, Mystery, Birth, Path, Way, Rede, Rune, Sigil, Delight, Earth, World, Goddess, Maiden, Mother, Crone, Dolmen, Trilithon, Menhir, Garden, Art, Scroll, Tree of Life, Shrine, Pentagram, Seal, Glyph, Spirit, Greenwood.

Suggestion

Keep it simple. It's hard to design letterhead for "The Sacred Azure Coven of the Forest Moon of Endor Shrine of the Emerald Wyvern and Ebony Pentacle in the Crimson Bubinga Grove by the Chamomile Circle."

A-5

Coven Sigils

A coven sigil should be simple enough that any member can draw it easily. It can be inscribed on ritual tools and silver bracelets, or used on a banner that accompanies the coven to festivals, drawn after signatures on Craft documents, and so on. Some examples are shown below. These are intended to be fictional, and any resemblance to actual coven names or sigils is coincidental.

A-6
Sample Articles of Incorporation

The document below is an actual sample of a coven that incorporated in the state of Wisconsin, although the individuals' names have been changed. Although the procedures and fees will vary somewhat from state to state, and are very different in Canada and other nations, the wording of this example may be useful to some covens who wish to have legal recognition.

Executed by the undersigned for the purpose of forming a Wisconsin corporation under Chapter 181 of the Wisconsin statutes, WITHOUT STOCK AND NOT FOR PROFIT.

Article 1. The name of the corporation is The Church of Our Lady of the Woods, Incorporated.

Article 2. The period of existence shall be perpetual.

Article 3. The purposes shall be to support, publicize, research and teach the religious traditions, practices, beliefs and values of Wicca.

In addition to, and support of, the above, the corporation shall have further general purposes and powers as follows:

A. To sue and be sued.

B. To publicize, publish, teach, research and explore the religious traditions, practices, beliefs and values of Wicca; and to exercise any, all, and every power which an establishment of religion is entitled to.

C. To create, establish, modify or dissolve branches; schools; religious orders, sororities and fraternities; research and experimental organizations, and other subsidiary organizations as the Board may direct.

D. To authorize, bestow, convey, grant or issue: certificates, charters, credentials, degrees, diplomas, franchises, licenses, memberships; ordinations; or to do otherwise, as the Board may direct.

E. To act as responsible party or custodian for: licenses, permits, bonds, tax matters, and contracts; or to do otherwise as the Board may direct.

F. To receive property by devise or bequest, subject to the laws regulating the transfer of property by will; and otherwise acquire and hold all property, real or personal, including shares of stocks, bonds and securities of other corporations; to act as trustee under any trust incidental to the principal objects of the corporation; and receive, hold, administer and expend funds and property subject to such trust.

G. To borrow money; contract debts; issue bonds, notes and debentures; and to secure, pay interest on, and redeem same.

H. To enroll, expel, fire, hire, recruit or train persons; establish various and diverse classes of membership, employees, volunteers, or otherwise as the Board may direct.

I. To keep accounts, files, inventories and records, as the Board may direct.

J. To do all other acts necessary or expedient for the administration of the affairs and attainment of the purposes of the corporation, within the scope of activities authorized by Chapter 181 of the Wisconsin Statutes.

K. Notwithstanding any of the above statements of purposes and powers, this corporation shall not, except to an insubstantial degree, engage in any activities or exercise any powers which are not in furtherance of the primary purpose of this corporation.

L. No substantial part of the activities of this corporation shall consist of carrying on political propaganda, or otherwise attempting to influence specific legislation, and the corporation shall not participate or intervene in any political campaign on behalf of any candidate for public office.

Article 4. The principal office is located in Dane County, Wisconsin, and the address of such principal office is: Our Lady of the Woods, 333 Artemis Street, Madison, Wisconsin 53716.

Article 5. The name of the initial registered agent is Tabitha Anne Spellcaster.

Article 6. The address of the initial registered agent is: 333 Artemis Street, Madison, Wisconsin 53716.

Article 7. These articles may be amended in the manner authorized by law at the time of amendment.

Article 8. The number of directors shall be fixed by by-law, but shall not be less than three.

Article 9. The names and addresses of the initial Board of Directors are:

Arthur Tiberius Rex, P.O. Box 13, Camelot, Wisconsin 53617.

Tabitha Anne Spellcaster, 333 Artemis Street, Madison, Wisconsin 53716.

Wayland Theodore Smith, 192 Forge Lane, Village Smithy, Wisconsin 53713.

Article 10. Membership provisions will be set forth in the by-laws.

Article 11. Other provisions:

A. The property of this corporation is irrevocably dedicated to religious, and charitable or scientific as they apply to religious purposes; and upon liquidation, dissolution or abandonment by the Board of Directors, and after providing for the debts and obligations thereof, the remaining assets shall not inure to the benefit of any private person, but will be distributed to a nonprofit fund, foundation or corporation which is organized and operated exclusively for religious, charitable or scientific purposes and which has established its tax-exempt status under Section 501 (c)(3) of the Internal Revenue Code of the United States of America.

B. The by-laws of this corporation may be adopted by the Board of Directors, and may thereafter be amended or repealed as therein provided.

C. The Board of Directors will issue no stock, voting or non-voting.

D. The order in which various items or activities appear listed herein establishes no system of priorities.

E. This corporation is being formed as a new organization and a new establishment of religion and no existing unincorporated religion is being incorporated.

Article 12. The name and address of incorporator (or incorporators) are:

Arthur Tiberius Rex, P.O. Box 13, Camelot, Wisconsin 53617.

Tabitha Anne Spellcaster, 333 Artemis Street, Madison, Wisconsin 53716.

Wayland Theodore Smith, 192 Forge Lane, Village Smithy, Wisconsin 53713.

Executed in duplicate on the 11th day of April, 1984.

All incorporators sign here:
STATE OF WISCONSIN, County of Dane } ss.

Personally came before me this 11th day of April, A.D. 1984, the aforenamed incorporator(s): ______________________

____

____

to me known to be the person(s) who executed the foregoing instrument, and acknowledged the same.

____

Notary Public

[Notarial Seal]

My commission expires ______________

This document was drafted by Tabitha Anne Spellcaster.

____

Instructions and Suggestions

Content of the Form

A. Article 1. The name must contain "Corporation", "Incorporated", or "Limited" or the abbreviation of one of those words.

B. Article 2. Insert "perpetual" or insert any limitation desired, but not "indefinite".

C. Article 3. May show definite purposes or may use language to the effect that the corporation may engage in any lawful activities authorized by Chapter 181 of the Wisconsin Statutes. (The statute expressly states that it is not necessary to enumerate the powers.)

D. Article 4. Give complete mailing address of the corporation's principal office in Wisconsin, including street name and number, city and ZIP code, and the COUNTY within which the office is located. P.O. Box addresses may be used.

E. Article 5 and 6. The corporation must have a registered agent in Wisconsin. Be sure to show a complete address, including street and number, city and ZIP code for the registered agent. A P.O. Box address may be included, in addition, for mailing purposes.

F. Article 9. Section 181.20(2) Wisconsin Statutes provides that the initial board of directors shall be named in the articles of incorporation. The number of directors shall not be less than three. Please give complete addresses, including street and number, city and ZIP code for all directors.

G. Article 10. If the membership provisions are set forth in the articles of incorporation (rather than in the by-laws) provide for A) method of accepting and discharging members; B) any denial or restriction of voting rights; and C) any classification of members, including the distinguishing features of each class.

   If the corporation is to have NO MEMBERS, strike out both imprinted Articles 10 and substitute the remark that "The corporation is to have no members", and further set forth the manner of election or appointment of directors.

H. Article 12. Have the INCORPORATOR SIGN before a Notary Public. The number of incorporators may be one or more, but all the incorporators listed in the articles must sign. Make sure that both of the copies have ORIGINAL SIGNATURES. Carbon copy, photocopy, or rubber stamp signatures are not acceptable.

I. Notary Public must SIGN AND AFFIX SEAL on both copies of the articles, and complete their statement in the area provided. Make sure that original signatures and seal impressions appear on both copies.

J. If the document is executed or acknowledged in Wisconsin, Sec. 14.38(14) of the Wis. Statutes provides that it shall not be filed unless the name of the person (individual) who, or the government agency which, drafted it is printed, typewritten, stamped or written thereon in a legible manner.

Preparation, Fees, and Transmittal

K. Prepare document in DUPLICATE ORIGINAL. Furnish the Secretary of State two identical copies of the articles of incorporation. (MAILING ADDRESS: Corporation Division, Secretary of State, P.O. Box 7846, Madison WI 53707). One copy will be retained (filed) by the Secretary of State and the other copy transmitted directly to the Register of Deeds of the county within which the corporation's principal office is located, together with your check for the recording fee. When the recording has been accomplished, the document will be returned to the address you furnish on the back of the form.

L. Two SEPARATE REMITTANCES are required.

1) Send a FILING FEE of $35 payable to SECRETARY OF STATE with the articles of incorporation. Your cancelled check is your receipt for fee payment.

2) Send a RECORDING FEE of $10 (or more) payable to REGISTER OF DEEDS OF ____________ COUNTY, WISCONSIN with the articles of incorporation. Name the county within which the corporation's principal office is located. Recording fee for this standard form is $10. If you append additional pages, add $2 more recording fee for each additional page. Please furnish the fee for the REGISTER OF DEEDS in check form to this office and we will transmit it to the Register of Deeds with the document for recording.

Note: All of these instructions are for a 1984 Wisconsin filing. Check with your state's Secretary of State or other appropriate office for instructions for incorporating in your state.

A-7

Sample Coven By-Laws

The Coven of the Inner Moon

I. Statement of Purpose

A. Our purposes are to:

1. Live in a manner which honors the Lady and the Lord, following the Wiccan Rede;
2. Explore and practice Wiccan beliefs and traditions, with a primary focus on the traditions of the British Isles;
3. Support one another within the coven in our healing, growth, and aspirations;
4. Hold Wiccan rituals on the Sabbats and Esbats and other special occasions, in order to celebrate the seasons, work magick, recognize rites of passage, and honor the Lady and Lord;
5. Honor the Earth and all Her creatures as sacred, and work to heal and protect the environment within our community, throughout our nation, and across the world;
6. Teach Wiccan beliefs and traditional skills to members and students, and sisters and brothers in the Craft and kindred spiritual paths; and
7. Where appropriate, to educate the general public about Wicca.

B. Commitment: All members of this coven must have fully committed themselves to this purpose in their beliefs, their activities, and their lives.

II. Membership

A. Qualifications: Membership shall be offered to individuals upon recommendation of the High Priestess and High Priest, and consensus of all Initiates (full members) of the coven. No person shall be denied access to membership on the basis of gender, race, ethnic background, sexual preference, physical handicap, or age providing they have attained their majority.

B. Degrees of Participation and Membership: Participants in the programs sponsored by this coven may include the following:

1. Guests: Interested parties who may attend all open activities, and coven-only activities in the company of an Initiate, with the consent of all other Initiates in attendance.
2. Congregants: Persons who consider themselves Wiccan and participate in and support the open activities of the congregation.

3. Dedicants: Persons who have dedicated themselves to study the path of Wicca and who, with the approval of all active Initiates, are following the prescribed course of study in this coven. After one year and a day of participation, a Dedicant may be asked to state her/his intention to qualify for initiation into the priesthood or to withdraw from the coven.
4. Membership in the coven itself shall be limited to:
   a. Initiates: Persons who have been active in the Craft, and preferably this coven, for at least a year and a day, and have met all requirements for initiation as defined by the Coven Council.
   b. Second Degree Initiates: Persons who have been active in the Craft, and preferably this coven, for at least two years and two days, and have met all requirements for Second Degree status as defined by the Coven; and have been recommended by the High Priestess and High Priest, and approved by a consensus of Initiates.
   c. Third Degree Initiates: Persons who have attained Second Degree status; have demonstrated proficiency in ritual design and leadership, teaching, counseling, group process and administration; and have been recommended by the High Priestess and High Priest, and approved by a consensus of Initiates.

C. Additional Titles of Recognition: The titles Mistress of Arts or Master of Arts shall be granted by this coven in recognition of special achievement. Initiates who have attained proficiency in the appropriate field and have been approved by a committee of all active Second and Third Degree initiates may be designated Mistress or Master of:
   1. Divinatory Arts (general, or specializing in Tarot, astrology, scrying, I Ching, runes, lithomancy, dreamcraft, radiesthesia, etc.)
   2. Herbalism (for healing, amulets/talismans, incenses, oils, etc.)
   3. Healing Arts (specializing in herbal healing, nutrition, energy work, aromatherapy, flower remedies, psychic healing, rebirthing, color therapy, music therapy, stones, or other healing modality)
   4. Familiar Arts (animal magick, totems, shapeshifting, etc.)
   5. Talismanic Arts (creating amulets and talismans)
   6. Ritual Toolcraft (the crafting of ritual tools in metal, wood, etc.)
   7. Psychic Skills (specializing in astral travel, telepathy, telempathy, clairvoyance, clairsentience, clairaudience, psychometry, etc.)
   8. Incantation (words of power, charms, chants, mantras)

9. Fascination (trancework, meditation, hypnosis)
10. Bardic Arts (music, storytelling, drama)

    Additional titles may be created by the Coven Council as desired.

D. Membership Status: Any person's membership or participation may be curtailed, suspended, or terminated by decision of the Coven Council, either for lack of attendance and/or participation, or violation of the Wiccan Rede.

III. Administration and Operation

A. Coven Council: This body shall handle the ordinary business of the coven.

1. Membership: The Coven Council shall consist of all Initiates (full members) of the coven. Dedicants may be invited to attend and participate in Council meetings as well.
2. Scope: The Council shall discuss all matters of:
    a. Program planning and activities;
    b. Dedication, initiation, and membership generally;
    c. Finance and budget; and
    d. Outreach, networking, and affiliations.
3. Facilitation: The High Priestess shall ordinarily chair meetings of the Council. Where she is absent, or chooses to delegate this responsibility, the High Priest shall chair the meeting.
4. Method of operation: The Coven Council shall make decisions by consensus. When consensus cannot be reached, the Council may refer the decision to the High Priestess (or in her absence, the High Priest), who shall consider all that has been discussed and make the decision.
5. Meetings: The Council shall meet at least quarterly on a regular basis, or as called by any Initiate.
6. Quorum: A quorum shall consist of the active members present at a regularly scheduled meeting of the Coven Council, or three-quarters of the active membership at any specially called meeting.

B. Offices and Duties: The following offices shall be filled by the Coven Council whenever a vacancy occurs.

1. High Priestess: Chairs the Coven Council; coordinates the teaching program; provides counseling as necessary; leads the rituals or provides resources to those doing so; supervises the work of other Officers; directs the initiation of candidates to the priesthood; supervises the work of candidates for second and third degree status; represents the coven to the Craft and

the public; enhances the inner strength and harmony of the coven; provides overall guidance to the work of the coven; and exercises final authority regarding ritual, initiation, ordination, and other religious matters.

2. High Priest: Chairs the Coven Council in the absence, or at the request of, the High Priestess; teaches; provides counseling as necessary; helps to lead the rituals or provide resources to those doing so; assists in supervising the work of the other officers; shares the responsibility for initiating candidates to the priesthood; assists in the preparation of candidates for second and third degree status; represents the coven to the Craft and the public; leads in the defense of the coven where worldly dangers threaten it; and supports and encourages the High Priestess in the performance of her duties.
3. Maiden: Assists the High Priestess with rituals and her other responsibilities, and assumes the duties of the High Priestess in her absence.
4. Summoner: Assists the High Priest with rituals and his other responsibilities; notifies coveners of meetings and other important information; and assumes the duties of the High Priest in his absence.
5. Bard: Collects songs and chants; teaches and leads the coven in music, and provides accompaniment; collects lore and legends; preserves and passes on the old lore, coven history, and traditions.
6. Scribe: Keeps minutes of Council meetings, handles correspondence as requested. Keeps records of coven projects, rituals, and activities.
7. Pursewarden: Collects money, keeps accounts, makes purchases or reimburses others for authorized purchases, coordinates fundraising projects, and keeps files of records related to the church's legal status.
8. Watcher: Handles safety and security at coven events. Indoors, checks locks and closes curtains, etc. Outdoors, finds safe places for ritual work, posts sentries, and sets wards. Knows laws regarding freedom of religion and assembly, etc.; serves as liaison with law enforcement officers. May teach self-defense.
9. Ritual Leaders, Project Leaders, and Trip Leaders: Coordinate design, logistics, and implementation of coven events. These positions are vacated at the conclusion of each event. A team may share responsibility for any given event.

10. Additional, temporary offices may be created and filled as the Coven Council deems necessary.

C. Guidelines for Conduct: All Dedicants and members shall be guided in their conduct by the Wiccan Rede, the Law of Return, A New Wiccan Book of the Law, and by the Goddess and God within each person.

IV. Meeting Schedule

A. Rituals

1. Esbats shall normally be held on the evening of the New Moon and the Full Moon.
2. Sabbats may be held on their actual date or on the weekend nearest, as determined by the Coven Council, except that Samhain shall always be celebrated on the night of October 31.
3. Once scheduled, a date shall not be changed unless two or more members request it, and unless the entire membership can attend on the proposed alternative date.
4. During clement weather, rituals shall normally be held outdoors at a site established by the Council. During inclement weather, rituals shall normally be held in the covenstead, at other members' homes, or in a public place selected by the Coven Council.

B. Classes

1. Introductory seminars and other classes open to the public shall be offered at such times and places as the Council decides.
2. Classes for Dedicants and members shall be held at least twice each month, on a schedule determined by the Council.
3. The curricula shall be established by the Coven Council.
4. Special classes which are part of an M.A. or ordination program shall be arranged according to the needs of those involved.
5. Classes shall be held at the covenstead, or such other location as the High Priestess designates.
6. No fees shall be charged for classes that are part of the regular curriculum of the coven and congregation.

C. Field trips and special events shall be held at such times and place as the Council decides.

V. Attendance

A. New Moon esbats shall be open only to Dedicants, Initiates, and approved guests. Full Moon esbats shall be open to the community.

B. Sabbats shall be open to all who are friendly to the Craft; except that the Coven Council may schedule a second, coven-only celebration on or near selected sabbats.

C. Classes shall be designated open only to Dedicants and Initiates of this coven, or open to all within the community, by the Coven Council.

D. Dedicants and Initiates are expected to participate in Esbats, Sabbats, and classes. If any attends fewer than 75% of these events, their status shall be subject to review by the Council. Second and third-degree Initiates are excused from the 75% rule in recognition of the work they are expected to perform for the wider Pagan community.

VI. Finances

A. Coven income shall include donations, profits from fundraising projects, and interest from banking accounts, if any, established by the Council.

B. The budget shall be established and disbursements approved by the Council.

C. The Pursewarden shall make a full quarterly report of income and expenses to the Council.

D. All required forms and reports shall be filed with the state and federal governments as required to maintain the church's legal status.

VII. Privacy of Members

A. The names, addresses, telephone numbers, and other information relating to individual members shall be considered confidential and may not be disclosed to non-members without the permission of the individual involved.

B. Disclosure of confidential information may, at the discretion of the Council, be considered a violation of the Wiccan Rede and grounds for expulsion from membership.

VIII. Revising the By-Laws

A. Any part of these By-laws may be amended by consensus of the Coven Council.

____

High Priestess (President)

____

Scribe (Secretary)

A-8

IRS 501(c)(3) Questions

The following questions were asked by the IRS in the course of a 501(c)(3) application by a Wiccan church. There is no guarantee that the questions will be the same for every application, but this should provide an idea of the information the IRS needs.

I. Is your organization in any way connected with any other religious order or church; have you paid a fee for a church charter or ordination papers? If so, please furnish the name and address of the organization and a copy of the document.

   Note: If you have a parent organization, you may be exempt as part of a group ruling. Normally, a parent organization that is covered under a group ruling will automatically add new or subordinate units to the group rulings. We suggest you contact your parent organization for guidance in this matter before you answer the following questions.

II. Describe the religious training of your deacons, minister or pastor. Include in your explanation the following information:

   a. Is there a prescribed course of study and/or a formalized method of ordination?
   b. Please explain, in detail, the education and experience requirements necessary to become one of your deacons, ministers, or pastor.
   c. Provide a copy, if applicable, of any certificates of ordination issued to them.
   d. Will your organization issue licenses or otherwise ordain ministers and/or charter churches? If so, please explain in detail the requirements needed to be so licensed, ordained or chartered by your organization.

III. Describe fully and in detail the requirements for membership in your organization. Include in your explanation the following information:

   a. How many active members are currently enrolled in your church?
   b. Is the general public admitted to your services?
   c. State whether an individual who is a member of another religion may become a member of your church. If so, on what basis?
   d. Is renunciation of prior religious beliefs a prerequisite for membership? If not, please explain.
   e. Does your organization impose a formal code or doctrine on your members? If so, is there any form of discipline and/or censure employed?

IV. Does your church have a distinct religious history? If so, please describe in detail.

V. Describe fully the manner in which your religion is practiced. Include the following information:

a. A brief description of your services and/or rituals.

b. Describe the religious significance of the dates and/or events commemorated by your church.

c. Does your organization have Sunday schools for religious instruction?

d. What is your regular schedule of services; what is the average attendance?

VI. Describe in detail all properties, excluding your church facility, owned by the organization and indicate how these properties are used.

a. State amount of income generated from each property.

b. Indicate if any properties are used, leased or rented by anyone other than the organization.

c. Provide copies of all leases, contracts, loans and financing agreements.

VII. Does your organization have an established place of worship? If so,

a. Provide the name and address of the owner or lessor.

b. Provide a description of the site, including the address.

c. Provide copies of any rental or lease agreements. If property is owned by the organization, provide a copy of the Title. If not, state where your services are held; if the site is variable, describe the procedure used to select the sites.

VIII. Does your organization pay or contemplate paying any salary or other compensation? If so, provide a schedule of salaries and/or compensation for the circled individuals listed below and describe their duties.

a. Deacons

b. Ministers

c. Pastor

d. Officers, elders, or directors

e. Office and/or maintenance staff

IX. Provide representative copies of literature, bulletins, brochures which describe your organization.

X. Will any of the funds or property of your organization be used by any director, officer or employee (other than your pastor) for their personal needs or convenience? If so, describe the nature and circumstances of such use.

XI. Describe your ecclesiastical government: i.e.: Archbishop, Elders, Deacons, etc.

XII. If you have received any contributions in excess of 1% of your gross contributions, please furnish the name and amount of each donor in the past year.

A-9

U.S. Armed Forces Chaplain's Handbook on Wicca

Following is an excerpt from the *Religious Requirements and Practices of Certain Selected Groups: A Handbook for Chaplains*, pgs. 231–236, published by the Department of the Army, Office of the Chief of Chaplains. The page headers read "Wicca, Witchcraft" on odd-numbered pages, and "Religious Requirements and Practices" on even-numbered pages.

Wicca

Address

No central address. Wiccan worship groups, called covens, are essentially autonomous. Many, but far from all, have affiliated with:

Covenant of the Goddess
P.O. Box 1226
Berkeley, CA 94704

Other Names By Which Known

Witchcraft, Goddess worshippers; Neo-Paganism; Paganism; Norse (or any other ethnic designation) Paganism; Earth Religion; Old Religion; Druidism; Shamanism. Note: All of these groups have some basic similarities and many surface differences of expression with Wicca.

Leadership

No central leadership. The Covenant of the Goddess annually elects a First Officer and there is a constitutional limit of two consecutive terms, but in practice officers have almost always served for one year only. In 1991, there are two co-First Officers, Phoenix Whitebirch and Brandy Williams.

Membership

Because of the complete autonomy of covens, this cannot be determined. There are an estimated 50,000 Wiccans in the United States.

Historical Origin

Wicca is a reconstruction of the Nature worship of tribal Europe, strongly influenced by the living Nature worship traditions of tribal peoples in other parts of the world. The works of such early twentieth century writers as Margaret Murray, Robert Graves and Gerald B. Gardner began the renewal of interest in the Old Religion. After the repeal of the anti-Witchcraft laws in Britain in 1951, Gardner publicly declared himself a Witch and began to gather a group of students and worshippers.

In 1962, two of his students, Raymond and Rosemary Buckland (religious names: Lady Rowen and Robat), emigrated to the United States and began teaching Gardnerian Witchcraft here. At the same time, other groups of people became interested through reading books by Gardner and others. Many covens were spontaneously formed, using rituals created from a combination of research and individual inspiration. These self-created covens are today regarded as just as valid as those who can trace a "lineage" of teaching back to England.

In 1975, a very diverse group of covens who wanted to secure the legal protections and benefits of church status formed Covenant of the Goddess (CoG), which is incorporated in the State of California and recognized by the Internal Revenue Service. CoG does not represent all, or even a majority of Wiccans. A coven or an individual need not be affiliated with CoG in order to validly practice the religion. But CoG is the largest single public Wiccan organization, and it is cross-Traditional (i.e., non-denominational).

Basic Beliefs

Wiccans worship the sacred as immanent in Nature, often personified as Mother Earth and Father Sky. As polytheists, they may use many other names for Deity. Individuals will often choose Goddesses or Gods from any of the world's pantheons whose stories are particularly inspiring and use those Deities as a focus for personal devotions. Similarly, covens will use particular Deity names as a group focus, and these are often held secret by the groups.

It is very important to be aware that Wiccans do not in any way worship or believe in "Satan," "the Devil," or any similar entities. They point out that "Satan" is a symbol of rebellion against and inversion of the Christian and Jewish traditions. Wiccans do not revile the Bible. They simply regard it as one among many of the world's mythic systems, less applicable than some to their core values, but still deserving just as much respect as any of the others.

Most Wiccan groups also practice magic, by which they mean the direction and use of "psychic energy," those natural but invisible forces which surround all living things. Some members spell the word "magick," to distinguish it from sleight of hand entertainments. Wiccans employ such means as dance, chant, creative visualization, and hypnosis to focus and direct psychic energy for the purpose of healing, protecting, and aiding members in various endeavors. Such assistance is also extended to non-members upon request.

Many, but not all, Wiccans believe in reincarnation. Some take this as a literal description of what happens to people when they die. For others, it is a symbolic model that helps them deal with the cycles and changes within this life. Neither reincarnation nor any other literal belief can be used as a test of an individual's validity as a member of the Old Religion.

Most groups have a handwritten collection of rituals and lore, known as a Book of Shadows. Part of the religious education of a new member will be to hand-copy this book for him- or herself. Over the years, as inspiration provides, new material will be added. Normally, access to these books is limited to initiated members of the religion.

Practices and Behavioral Standards

The core ethical statement of Wicca, called the "Wiccan Rede" states "an it harm none, do what you will." The rede fulfills the same function as does the "Golden Rule" for Jews and Christians; all other ethical teachings are considered to be elaborations and applications of the Rede. It is a statement of situational ethics, emphasizing at once the individual's responsibility to avoid harm to others and the widest range of personal autonomy in "victimless" activities. Wicca has been described as having a "high-choice" ethic.

Because of the basic Nature orientation of the religion, many Wiccans will regard all living things as sacred, and show a special concern for ecological issues. For this reason, individual conscience will lead some to take a pacifist position. Some are vegetarians. Others will feel that, as Nature's Way includes self-defense, they should participate in wars that they conscientiously consider to be just. The religion does not dictate either position, but requires each member to thoughtfully and meditatively examine her or his own conscience and to live by it.

Social forces generally do not yet allow Witches to publicly declare their religious faith without fear of reprisals such as loss of job, child-custody challenges, ridicule, etc. Prejudice against Wiccans is the result of public confusion between Witchcraft and Satanism. Wiccans in the military, especially those who may be posted in countries perceived to be particularly intolerant, will often have their dogtags read "No Religious Preference." Concealment is a traditional Wiccan defense against persecution, so non-denominational dogtags should not contravene a member's request for religious services.

Wiccans celebrate eight festivals, called "Sabbats," as a means of attunement to the seasonal rhythms of Nature. These are January 31 (called Oimelc, Brigit, or February Eve), March 21 (Ostara or Spring Equinox), April 30 (Beltane or May Eve), June 22 (Midsummer, Litha or Summer Solstice), July 31 (Lunasa or Lammas), September 21 (Harvest, Mabon or Autumn Equinox), October 31 (Samhain, Sowyn or Hallows), and December 21 (Yule or Winter Solstice). Some groups find meetings within a few days of those dates to be acceptable, others require the precise date. In addition, most groups will meet for worship at each Full Moon, and many will also meet on the New Moon. Meetings for religious study will often be scheduled at any time convenient to the members, and rituals can be scheduled whenever there is a need (i.e. for a healing).

Ritual jewelry is particularly important to many Wiccans. In addition to being a symbol of religious dedication, these talismans are often blessed by the coven back home and felt to carry the coven's protective and healing energy.

Organizational Structure

Most Wiccans meet with a coven, a small group of people. Each coven is autonomous. Most are headed by a High Priestess, often with the assistance of a High Priest. Some are headed by a High Priestess or a High Priest without a partner, and some regard themselves as a gathering of equals. Covens can be of mixed gender, or all female or male, depending on the preferences of the members. Every initiate is considered to be a priestess or a priest. Most covens are small. Thirteen is the traditional maximum number of members, although not an absolute limit. At that size covens form a close bond, so Wiccans in the military are likely to maintain a strong affiliation with their covens back home.

There are many distinct "Traditions" of Wicca, just as there are many denominations within Christianity. The spectrum of Wiccan practice can be described as ranging from "traditional" to "eclectic," with Traditions, Covens and individuals fitting anywhere within that range. A typical difference would be that more traditional groups would tend to follow a set liturgy, whereas eclectic groups would emphasize immediate inspiration in worship.

These distinctions are not particularly important to the military chaplain, since it is unlikely that enough members of any one Tradition would be at the same base. Worship circles at military facilities are likely to be ad hoc cross-Traditional groups, working out compromise styles of worship for themselves and constantly adapting them to a changing membership. Therefore, the lack of strict adherence to the patterns of any one Tradition is not an indicator of invalidity.

While many Wiccans meet in a coven, there are also a number of solitaries. These are individuals who choose to practice their faith alone. They may have been initiated in a coven or self-initiated. They will join with other Wiccans to celebrate the festivals or to attend the various regional events organized by the larger community.

Role of Ministers

Within a traditional coven, the High Priestess, usually assisted by her High Priest, serves both as leader in the rituals and as teacher and counselor for coven members and unaffiliated Pagans. Eclectic covens tend to share leadership more equally.

Worship

Wiccans usually worship in groups. Individuals who are currently not affiliated with a coven, or are away from their home coven, may choose to worship privately or may form ad hoc groups to mark religious occasions. Non-participating observers are generally not welcome at Wiccan rituals.

Some, but not all, Wiccan covens worship in the nude ("skyclad") as a sign of attunement with Nature. Most, but not all, Wiccan covens bless and share a cup of wine as part of the ritual. Almost all Wiccans use an individual ritual knife (an "athame") to focus and direct personal energy. Covens often also have ritual swords to direct the energy of the group. These tools, like all other rituals tools, are highly personal and should never leave the possession of the owner.

Other commonly used ritual tools include a bowl of water, a bowl of salt, a censer with incense, a disk with symbols engraved on it (a "pentacle"), statues or artwork representing the Goddess and God, and candles. Most groups will bless and share bread or cookies along with the wine. All of these items are used in individual, private worship as well as in congregate rituals.

Dietary Laws or Restrictions

None.

Funeral and Burial Requirements

None. Recognition of the death of a member takes place within the coven, apart from the body of the deceased. Ritual tools, materials, or writings found among the effects of the deceased should be returned to their home coven (typically a member will designate a person to whom ritual materials should be sent).

It is desirable for a Wiccan priest or priestess to be present at the time of death, but not strictly necessary. If not possible, the best assistance would be to make the member as comfortable as possible, listen to whatever they have to say, honor any possible requests, and otherwise leave them as quiet and private as possible.

Medical Treatment

No medical restrictions. Wiccans generally believe in the efficacy of spiritual or psychic healing when done in tandem with standard medical treatment. Therefore, at the request of the patient, other Wiccan personnel should be allowed visiting privileges as though they were immediate family, including access to Intensive Care Units. Most Wiccans believe that healing energy can be sent from great distances, so, if possible, in the case of any serious medical condition, the member's home coven should be notified.

Other

With respect to attitude toward military service, Wiccans range from career military personnel to conscientious objectors.

Wiccans do not proselytize and generally resent those who do. They believe that no one Path to the Sacred is right for all people, and see their own religious pattern as only one among many that are equally worthy. Wiccans respect all religions that foster honor and compassion in their adherents, and expect the same respect. Members are encouraged to learn about all faiths, and are permitted to attend the services of other religions, should they desire to do so.

General Sourcebooks

The best general survey of the Wiccan and neo-Pagan movement is:

Adler, Margot. *Drawing Down the Moon.* Boston: Beacon Press, 1986. 595 pp.

For more specific information about eclectic Wicca, see:

Starhawk. *The Spiral Dance.* New York: Harper & Row, 1979.

For more specific information about traditional Wicca, see:

Farrar, Janet, and Stewart Farrar. *Eight Sabbats for Witches.* London: Robert Hale, 1981. 192 pp.

———. *The Witches' Way.* London: Robert Hale, 1984. 394 pp.

For More Information, Contact:

Pagan Military Newsletter
℅ Terri Morgan, Editor
829 Lynnhaven Parkway 114-198
Virginia Beach, VA 23452

Because of the autonomy of each coven and wide variance of specific ritual practices, the best contact person would be the High Priestess or other leader of the member's home coven.

End Transcription.

A-10
Dedicant Agreement

I wish to join the Wiccan Coven of _____________. As a Dedicant I will:

1. Work hard to learn the Craft for as long as I am associated with the coven;
2. Participate in at least 75% of the classes, rituals, and other required coven activities;
3. Meet on a regular basis with my Mentor to discuss my learning and growth within the coven;
4. Cultivate relationships of cooperation, friendship, and respect with other coven members;
5. Follow the Wiccan Rede: "An ye harm none, do as ye will";
6. Honor the Goddess and the God;
7. Work to protect and heal the Earth and Her creatures;
8. Use magick affecting other individuals only with their express consent;
9. Support my sisters and brothers within the coven in their learning, growth and aspirations;
10. Keep the identity of other coven members and friends confidential, except with their permission; and
11. Support the work of the coven with energy, money, or other resources, while giving first priority to the needs of my family and livelihood.

Signed ______________________________ Date ________________

NOTE: This document is confidential and will not be shared outside the leadership of ______________________. However, you may sign with your magickal/Craft name if you wish.

Mailing Name ____

Mailing Address ____

City, State, Zip ____

Home Phone ____

Work Phone ____

E-mail Address ____

A-11

Congregation Member's Agreement

The Congregation of ______________________________

I wish to join the Wiccan congregation of __________. As a member I will:

1. Follow the Wiccan Rede: "An ye harm none, do as ye will";
2. Honor the Goddess and the God;
3. Work to protect and heal the Earth and Her creatures;
4. Support my sisters and brothers within the congregation in their learning, growth, and honorable aspirations;
5. Keep the identity of other congregation members and friends confidential, except with their permission;
6. Support the work of the congregation with energy, money, or other resources, while giving first priority to the needs of my family and livelihood;
7. Help make decisions within the congregation by cooperation and consensus;
8. Use magick affecting other individuals only with their express consent; and
9. Respect the beliefs of others which may differ from my own.

Signed ______________________________

Date ______________________________

NOTE: This document is confidential and will not be shared outside the leadership of ______________. However, you may sign with your magickal/Craft name if you wish.

Mailing Name ______________________________

Mailing Address ______________________________

City, State, Zip ______________________________

Home Phone ______________________________

Work Phone ______________________________

E-mail address ______________________________

A-12

Degrees of Initiation: A Three-Level Plan

Most Wiccan traditions use a three-degree system to recognize the growth, learning, and experience of their members, but the meaning of those three degrees varies according to the coven and their tradition. The outline presented here is based on the Coven of Our Lady of the Woods, and a comparison may help you analyze and clarify your own coven's system.

Dedicant (first year student, white cord)

In the first year of study, and before any initiations take place, the student is known as a dedicant. The dedicant's first task is to learn the basics of the Craft; they will probably be given a "Wicca 101" introduction to Craft history, ethics, cosmology and thealogy, and the wheel of the year. Then they may read a few introductory books, be introduced to the customs and practices of the coven's tradition, and learn simple ritual skills. Following this, they will spend the rest of their first year or so working on the First Degree. It is generally expected that each following degree will require at least a year and a day of additional work, depending on individual strengths and challenges.

First Degree (in the Ladywood tradition, a green cord)

A. Learn to take care of your physical health through proper diet, exercise, releasing addictions, and so forth.

B. Learn and use skills to earn a livelihood and support yourself and your family in reasonable health, safety, and comfort.

C. Perform a cleansing and blessing ceremony in your home, ward it properly, and create a home altar.

D. Learn basic first aid and begin to study a healing technique of your choice (herbcraft, massage, reiki, etc.).

E. Discover and work with an animal ally, familiar, or totem spirit.

F. Create your own Book of Shadows and keep it current with notes and descriptions of classes, rituals, and personal magickal workings.

G. Read at least six books from the reading list, and discuss them with coveners.

H. Accept an office within the coven and perform its duties to the satisfaction of the Coven Council.

I. Learn the meaning and magickal uses of the basic ritual tools: athame, wand, chalice, and pentacle.

J. In partnership with a more experienced priest/ess, design and lead at least one New Moon or Diana's Bow esbat, a Full Moon esbat, and a sabbat celebration.

K. Participate in at least 75% of the required classes (see list), rituals and other coven activities.

L. Be active with the coven for a period of at least a year and a day (this requirement may be modified if the Dedicant comes to the coven with prior Craft training and experience).

M. Receive the endorsement of the High Priestess and High Priest of the coven that you are ready to be initiated in the First Degree.

N. Earn the unanimous agreement of your coven that you live according to the Wiccan Rede, that your participation brings the coven closer to perfect love and perfect trust, and that your life in general honors the Lady and the Lord, and exemplifies the ideals of Wicca.

O. In an interview with the Coven Council, satisfy the coven that you have met all the requirements above.

P. Be willing to take the required oaths (see First Degree initiation ritual, B-5, page 433).

Second Degree (in the Ladywood tradition, a red cord)

A. Continue or repeat A–H as listed above, plus L.

B. Learn to evaluate, cleanse, energize, and heal your chakras and energy body.

C. Continue to design and lead New Moon or Diana's Bow esbats, Full Moon esbats, and sabbat celebrations.

D. Assist with at least three rites of passage (house blessings as well as personal rites).

E. Learn the magickal uses of several additional ritual tools, such as the staff, cauldron, cord, candles, amulets, and talismans.

F. Learn to use at least one system of divination skillfully. Do readings for others within your coven or Pagan community.

G. Develop and demonstrate at least one psychic skill such as telepathy, clairvoyance, remote healing, astral projection or telekinesis.

H. Enhance your relationships with your Lower/Younger Self and your Higher/God/dess Self.

I. Develop a special relationship with at least one goddess-aspect and one god-aspect.

J. Learn to take responsibility for your emotions, and how you express and transform them. Confront and heal at least one of your "dark side" issues, related to your pain, anger, hatred, or other negative emotions.

K. Learn basic counseling skills, and use them with positive results with a member of your coven or Pagan community.

L. Teach at least three different Craft-related subjects, with positive evaluations from your students.

M. Choose a very significant personal goal and achieve it.

N. Organize an important project or event for your coven, motivating and leading others to complete it.

O. Participate in at least 75% of the required classes, rituals and other coven activities.

P. Receive the endorsement of the High Priestess and High Priest of the coven that you are ready to be initiated in the Second Degree.

Q. Earn the unanimous agreement of your coven that you live according to the Wiccan Rede, that your participation brings the coven closer to perfect love and perfect trust, and that your life in general honors the Lady and the Lord, and exemplifies the ideals of Wicca.

R. In an interview with the Coven Council, satisfy the coven that you have met all the requirements above.

Third Degree (in the Ladywood tradition, a silver cord for women or a gold cord for men)

A. Continue or repeat each of the requirements as listed above.

B. Discover and define your True Will.

C. Explain your understanding of your spiritual development over several incarnations, and the important spiritual challenges before you now.

D. Explain what legacy you plan to leave when you pass from this incarnation, and what you are doing to manifest it.

E. Lead at least three rites of passage.

F. Design and lead a large-group ritual at a community sabbat or festival.

G. Learn and practice at least five magickal techniques that can be performed without ritual tools.

H. Organize and help teach a Wicca 101 series of introductory classes on Witchcraft.

I. Serve your local, regional or national Pagan community in a leadership capacity.

J. Are excused from participation in at least 75% of the required classes, rituals and other coven activities by their service to the local, regional, or national Pagan community. However, they are encouraged to attend often as teachers and role models for the newer students.

K. Receive the endorsement of the High Priestess and High Priest of the coven that you are skilled in the areas of ritual design and leadership, teaching, group process, counseling and coven administration, and are ready to be initiated in the Third Degree.

L. Earn the unanimous agreement of your coven that you live according to the Wiccan Rede, that your participation brings the coven closer to perfect love and perfect trust, and that your life in general honors the Lady and the Lord, and exemplifies the ideals of Wicca.

M. In an interview with the Coven Council, satisfy the coven that you have met all the requirements above.

A-13

Degrees of Initiation: An Elemental Plan

Though most Wiccan traditions use a three-degree system to recognize the growth, learning and experience of their members, some use a five-degree system based on the elements. The following system is loosely based on the Pagan Way tradition.

Dedicant (first year student, white cord)

In the first year of study, and before any initiations take place, the student is known as a dedicant. The dedicant's first task is to learn the basics of the Craft; they may read a few introductory books, be introduced to the customs and practices of their coven's tradition, and learn simple ritual skills. They will probably be given a "Wicca 101" introduction to Craft history, ethics, cosmology and thealogy, and the wheel of the year. Following this, they will spend the rest of their first year or so working on the Earth Degree. It is generally expected that each following degree will require at least a year of additional work, depending on individual strengths and challenges.

Earth Degree (first degree initiate, yellow cord)

A. Learn to take care of your physical health through proper diet, exercise, releasing addictions, etc.

B. Learn and use skills to earn a livelihood and support yourself and your family in reasonable comfort.

C. Perform a cleansing and blessing ceremony in your home, ward it properly, and create a home altar.

D. Understand the basics of ecology and learn about the environment in which you live: its geology, plant and animal communities, watershed, weather, and more.

E. Learn basic first aid and simple healing techniques, especially with herbcraft and stones.

F. Discover and work with an animal ally, familiar or totem spirit.

G. Learn the meaning and magickal uses of the pentacle, amulets and talismans.

Water Degree (second degree initiate, green cord)

A. Learn to take responsibility for your emotions, and how you express and transform them.

B. Enhance your empathy and learn to respond constructively to the feelings of others.

C. Establish and maintain warm, positive relationships with others in your family and coven.

D. Demonstrate that you can work in harmony and cooperation with others, and resolve conflicts constructively.
E. Learn basic co-counseling skills, and use them with positive results with a member of your coven or Pagan community.
F. Learn to use at least two systems of divination skillfully. Do readings for others within your coven or Pagan community.
G. Understand the cycles of the moon and basic lunar magick, including "drawing down the moon."
H. Learn the meaning and magickal uses of the chalice and cauldron.

Fire Degree (third degree initiate, red cord)

A. Learn to discover your True Will.
B. Learn to evaluate, cleanse, energize and heal your chakras and energy body.
C. Show that you can channel energy strongly and clearly, in both ritual and mundane contexts.
D. Choose a very significant personal goal and achieve it.
E. Organize an important project or event for your coven or Pagan community, and motivate and lead others to complete it.
F. Learn the meaning and magickal uses of the athame and the sword, as well as candle magick.

Air Degree (fourth degree initiate, blue cord)

A. Research, write and present a significant scholarly addition to the history of the Craft or the literature of magick.
B. Create a work of fictional literature (story, novel, myth, poem, epic, play) or art (painting, sculpture, stained glass panel, dance, song, symphony, etc.) related to Wicca. Present this at a Pagan gathering.
C. Teach at least three different Craft-related subjects to at least three different groups, with positive evaluations from your students.
D. Memorize a long poem, song, or teaching story, and present it to the coven or other Pagan gathering.
E. Demonstrate the use of three breathing techniques useful in magick or mundane life.
F. Learn the meaning and magickal uses of the wand and staff, as well as incense magick or aromatherapy.

Spirit Degree (fifth degree initiate, purple cord)

A. Write a paper on the meaning of the Wiccan Rede, and present it orally or have it accepted for publication.

B. Serve your coven or Pagan community in a leadership capacity.

C. Strengthen and demonstrate at least one psychic skill such as telepathy, clairvoyance, remote healing, astral projection or telekinesis.

D. Enhance your relationships with your Lower/Younger Self and your Higher/God/dess Self.

E. Develop a special relationship with at least one goddess-aspect and one god-aspect. Show that you can aspect Them (invoke Them into yourself).

F Explain your understanding of your spiritual development over several incarnations and the important spiritual challenges before you now.

G. Explain what legacy you plan to leave when you pass from this incarnation and what you are doing to manifest it.

H. Learn and practice at least five magickal techniques that can be performed without ritual tools.

I. Earn the unanimous agreement of your coven that you live according to the Wiccan Rede, that your participation brings the coven closer to perfect love and perfect trust, and that your life in general honors the Lady and the Lord and exemplifies the ideals of Wicca.

The coven may determine which of these degrees corresponds to third degree ("High Priest/ess") in the other system. Or, you may decide to use the title "High Priest/ess" only for the person occupying that office, instead of linking it to a degree. Or, you may establish a separate "ordination track," as the Temple of the Pagan Way did, in which a candidate follows an individualized study program and demonstrates proficiency in five areas: teaching, counseling, group process, administration, and ritual leadership.

A-14

Mistress and Master of Arts Specialties

The titles Mistress of Arts or Master of Arts may be granted within a coven in recognition of special achievement. Initiates should attain a certain standard of proficiency in their chosen field and be approved by the appropriate authority (the Coven Council may designate a mentor or committee of mentors, not necessarily limited to coven members). The most common major fields of study include:

- **Bardic Arts:** teaching and magick through music, storytelling, drama
- **Divinatory Arts:** tarot, astrology, scrying, I Ching, runes, lithomancy, dreamcraft, radiesthesia, etc.
- **Familiar Arts:** animal magick, totems, shapeshifting, etc.
- **Fascination:** consciousness-altering by natural means: trancework, meditation, hypnosis
- **Healing Arts:** With one or more specialties: counseling, herbal healing, nutrition, energy work, aromatherapy, flower remedies, psychic healing, rebirthing, color therapy, music therapy, crystals and stones, massage therapy, etc.
- **Herbalism:** healing, amulets/talismans, incenses, oils, etc.
- **Incantatory Arts:** words of power, charms, chants, mantras
- **Psychic Studies:** astral travel, telepathy, telempathy, clairvoyance, clairsentience, clairaudience, telekinesis, teleportation, levitation, etc.
- **Ritual Smithcraft:** creating ritual tools: design, metalwork, woodcarving, ceramics, etc.
- **Talismanic Arts:** creating amulets and talismans

Additional titles may be created by the Elders as desired. These courses of study may be especially appropriate for those who have attained third degree and wish to continue their education within a structured format. In covens where third degree work is basically preparation for group leadership, an M.A. may be a useful alternative for second degree members who do not feel called to that role.

A-15

A Sample Budget

Scarlet Oak Coven - Annual Budget and Actual

	Budgeted	Actual
Carried over from last year:		$ 124
Income:		
Donations	$ 600	$ 705
T-shirt sales (at festivals)	$ 500	$ 530
Coven yard sales (2)	$ 400	$ 762
Interest on bank accounts	$ 60	$ 85
Total Projected Carryover + Income	$ 1684	$ 2206
Expenses:		
T-shirts and silkscreen materials	$ 275	$ 318
Garage sale advertising	$ 20	$ 20
Altar supplies and open sabbats (Candles, incense, flowers)	$ 300	$ 355
Books for coven library	$ 120	$ 156
Coven retreat (gas, cabin rental)	$ 250	$ 223
Wicca 101 classes (room rental, ads, etc.)	$ 60	$ 45
Community Service (seedlings, Yule food box)	$ 125	$ 162
Newsletter (printing, postage)	$ 400	$ 374
COG national dues	$ 90	$ 90
Cords for initiations	$ 30	$ 30
Total Projected Expenses	$ 1645	$ 1773
Estimated Remaining in Treasury at Year's End	$ 39	
Actual Remaining in Treasury at Year's End	$ 433	

A-16

A Sample Letter to the Editor

P.O. Box 13
Besom Village, MA 02137

October 10, ——

Dear Editor:

Halloween is coming, and already the stores are full of costumes and decorations: monsters and devils, goblins and black cats . . . .

And "witches."

Everybody is familiar with the image of the cackling, snaggle-toothed hag on her broomstick. The "Wicked Witch of the West" in Oz. The nasty woman with the candy cottage in "Hansel and Gretel." But not too many people know where the stereotype came from.

In medieval Europe the old nature religions were practiced before and alongside Christianity. There were Druids, and Norse Odinists, and the Wicca (Witches) who were the healers, priestesses, and wise elders in many country villages. When the Inquisition was launched, all these groups came under attack; and in order to feed the frenzy, the Inquisitors pictured the Witches as evil, ugly devil-worshippers. It was propaganda in a religious hate war.

Over a period of five centuries, several hundred thousand, and possibly millions, of women, children, and men were accused of Witchcraft and killed. Many were not Witches, but elderly eccentrics or wealthy or attractive people with jealous neighbors. The real Witches went underground and practiced their religion in secret.

The Witch stereotype was false centuries ago, and it is false now. This hateful image connects women, old age, and power (magic) with ugliness and evil. It is a disservice to elderly women everywhere, especially strong, old women. And it is a slander on a living religion, called Wicca or Witchcraft.

Wicca exists today. It is a benevolent nature religion which teaches respect for the Earth and worships the Creator as both feminine and masculine (Goddess and God). It has nothing to do with Satanism, warts, or hexes.

I know, because I am a Wiccan priestess—a real Witch, not the fairy-tale stereotype. And as October 31 approaches, it saddens me to see the ugly images in store windows and advertising as part of the Halloween "fun." Putting down any group of people—whether Blacks, Jews, Catholics, old women, or Wiccans—is a poor way to celebrate a holiday.

So here's a request from a neighbor. Decorate your house or store with goblins and spooks if you like—they're not real. And black cats and pumpkins—they won't care. But skip the ugly "witch" pictures—I'm real, and I do care.

Blessed Be,

Robin Silvertongue
(My Witch name)

NOT FOR PUBLICATION, PLEASE:
Darlene Falworth
1214 Oak Street
Arlesville, MA 02136
Tel. (212) 555-9846

A-17

The Invoking and Banishing Pentagrams

When you call the Quarters or Elemental Powers during ritual, face the appropriate direction and draw a pentagram in the air using an athame. If no athame is available, you can use a wand or hand. The Quarters are called or invoked near the beginning of the ritual, and banished or released near the end. As you trace the pentagram, imagine a line of glowing light in the appropriate color.

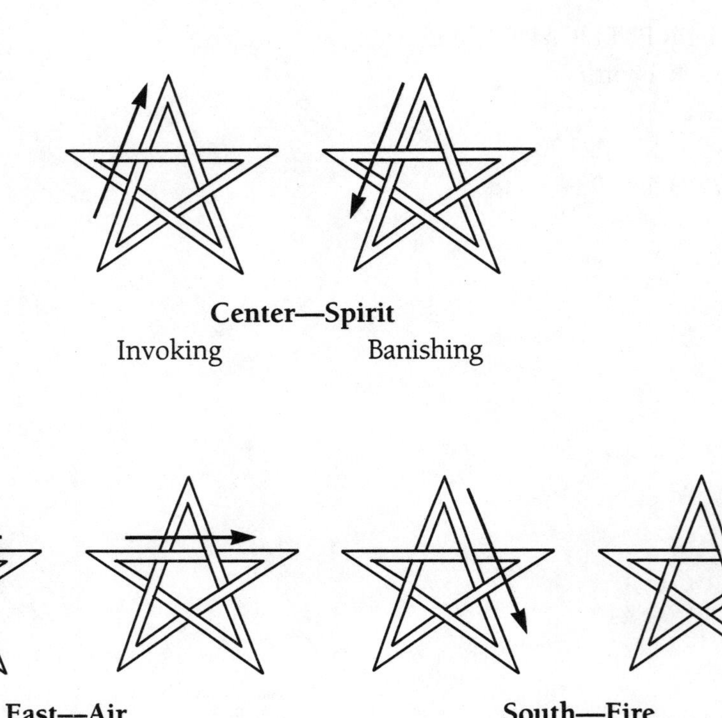

Center—Spirit
Invoking Banishing

East—Air
Invoking Banishing

South—Fire
Invoking Banishing

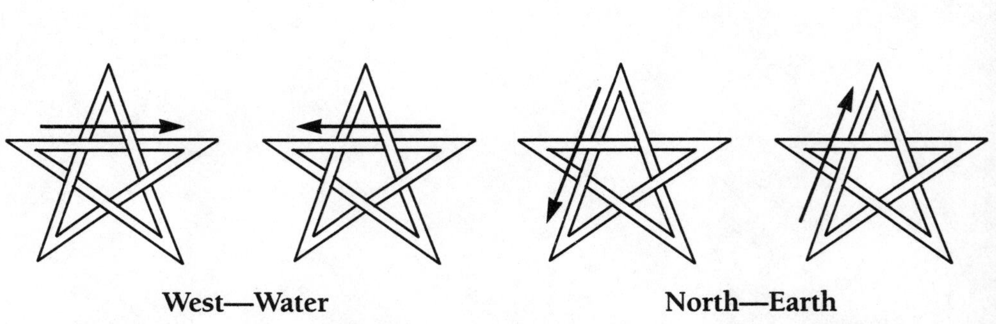

West—Water
Invoking Banishing

North—Earth
Invoking Banishing

A-18

Problem Personalities

Not all candidates are appropriate for your coven. Some of these will be immediately obvious: the alcoholic who arrives pickled and barfs on your carpet during her first ritual, the psychopathic ax murderer with blood on his clothes, the leering Lothario who pinches the High Priestess when they're introduced. Most are difficult in more subtle ways therefore you need time to get acquainted, hence the "year-and-a-day" rule before initiation.

Many of the stereotypes listed here will be familiar to anyone who has been a member of a group. I have purposely exaggerated their characteristics for clarity; but remember that people can have one or more of these traits to a lesser degree and still be valuable members of the group. The question is: Are they willing to look at themselves honestly, acknowledge their problems, and work at growth and change?

The Adoring Acolyte

Description and M.O.: Believes the coven leader(s) can do no wrong, and is embarrassingly fulsome in praising and complimenting them.

The Strategy for Coping: Focus on behaviors; quietly draw them aside and ask them to cool it on the praise. Try to disillusion them gently, but don't be shocked if your image crumbles suddenly one day in the harsh light of reality, and they react bitterly. Meanwhile, do all you can to empower them.

The Adversary

Description and M.O. This one is never happy without an enemy, and glories in the crusade. Unfortunately if they lack an obvious external threat to the coven, they will find enemies within the coven or Pagan community. Your basic loose cannon, and you never know where the barrel will point next.

The Strategy for Coping: The marginal benefit you gain while they're focused on real threats is not worth the damage you will sustain later. Cut the hawsers and let them roll off the ship.

The Bag Lady/Bag Man

Description and M.O.: This person is carrying an enormous load of emotional stuff centering around their parents, partners, and other authority figures in their life. They tend to reenact the same problems in the coven, with the coven leaders standing in for the parents.

The Strategy for Coping: Serious counseling is indicated. Don't let them train for the priesthood until they have addressed their earlier issues and shed some of the load.

The Black Hole of Neediness

Description and M.O.: This person has many needs, and somehow the conversation in the coven will always turn to their emotional problems. After a while, most of the coven's energy goes toward propping them up, counseling them, and nurturing them.

The Strategy for Coping: You can't fill their needs. Serious counseling is indicated. Don't let them train for the priesthood until they have addressed their earlier issues and learned some independence. Sound familiar?

The Blamer

Description and M.O.: Their motto is, "It wasn't me. I didn't do it. Tommy must have done it!" This individual is incapable of accepting responsibility for their actions, admitting error, or looking at their own shadow side.

The Strategy for Coping: Strong counseling within the coven may help them understand that taking responsibility is an essential quality for a priest/ess. Meanwhile, every single time they evade the truth, make them face it squarely. They will either shape up or leave.

The Center of All Things

Description and M.O.: This is simply an egotist who wants constant attention. They usually dominate any given conversation, and usually talk about themselves. Their knowledge and experience is apparently limitless, and if anyone else speaks, it is obviously an interruption to the main event.

The Strategy for Coping: A coven leader can counsel them privately, guiding them to keep the silence, listen, and care about others. In the meantime you can use a talking stick round-robin in discussion, to ensure that other members have an opportunity to speak. But don't endure the situation too long unless this person has some really special, redeeming qualities, or you'll lose the rest of the coven.

The Drama Addict

Description and M.O.: This person loves conflict, suffering, excitement, storms of passion, great struggles; in short, they are living in a soap opera, and your coveners will be cast as leading characters. Every decision is a crisis, and nothing can ever be resolved quietly or simply. Some common themes: "I stand alone against injustice," and "I see the danger that all have overlooked."

The Strategy for Coping: Be calm and matter-of-fact, and refuse to play the crisis game. When they point out a problem, either redefine it as a non-problem or deal with it quickly and decisively. Help them learn to ground and center, and the virtues of silence and minimal intervention. Counsel them about reframing their reality. And watch your back, because if you won't play the game, you may be recast as the blind fool or the enemy. If that happens, move swiftly to get them out of the coven.

The Eternal Volunteer

Description and M.O.: Some people are so eager to help, or so intent on proving themselves, that they will volunteer to do everything. If they are extremely capable they may actually accomplish it all—leaving nothing for other coveners to do. If they are normally competent, they won't be able to do all that they've committed to. Either way the coven suffers.

The Strategy for Coping: When they start to bite off too much, just thank them and suggest another person for the job. Make sure they follow up on old projects. Gentle pastoral counseling may help them see that their place in the coven is secure without being a superhero, and why it's important for all the coveners to contribute.

The Grand High Pooh-Bah

Description and M.O.: Such people love titles and authority, even if they have to be a huge frog in a tiny pond. They want to lead all the rituals, and insist on being addressed as "My Lord" or "My Lady." They focus on maintaining their prestige rather than empowering coven members (funny how it took Ravenwing eight years to reach Second Degree).

The Strategy for Coping: If they founded the coven and you are a regular member, get out. Find a coven where your strengths will be recognized and nourished. If they are new to the coven and show Pooh-Bah tendencies, refuse to elevate them until they get past such nonsense.

Here Come De Judge

Description and M.O.: A highly critical personality, who finds fault with everyone except whomever they are speaking with at the moment. If they are speaking with you, be sure that you will not be immune in their next conversation elsewhere.

The Strategy for Coping: Agree among the coven that none of you will listen to negative comments about the others, or indeed about anyone unless it serves some immediate and urgent purpose. An elder may wish to remind "the judge" that the Laws of Witchcraft forbid speaking ill of another Witch.

The Hermit

Description and M.O.: They come to meetings, they participate as requested, but they reveal nothing personal and scarcely talk to anyone. They are self-isolated in the midst of the group.

The Strategy for Coping: Make sure it's a safe environment. Make friends. Be there. Encourage them every time they open up or share a bit of themselves. Discover their interests, their passions, and ask about them. Encourage others to do the same. And privately explain that they too have an obligation to reach out.

The Kidder With a Shiv

Description and M.O.: What a clever tongue! This person always has a witticism ready—usually with a hidden barb, put-down, or sarcastic twist. "Hey, just kidding around; we're all adults, right, can't you take a joke?"

The Strategy for Coping: Edged humor can be very destructive; in no time at all the coven may be bleeding from a thousand tiny wounds. A paper cut is no big deal, right? But you don't want one, much less a dozen. Speak privately with the kidder; then when they attack next, call them on it. Do it every single time, until the kidding stops.

The New Age Dabbler

Description and M.O.: The dabbler is interested in any sort of unusual spiritual path, trendy self-help product, or metaphysical quick fix. They invented the term "eclectic." Their interest may fade when the next fad comes along ("Can't make the esbat—there's a seminar on "Channeling Angels with Crystal-charged Organic Vegetables").

The Strategy for Coping: Emphasize to them the profound responsibilities involved in becoming a Wiccan priest/ess, and that it is a lifelong commitment. Chances are they'll flutter on to the next flower; if not, maybe they're ready to get serious.

The Overwhelmed

Description and M.O.: This individual just can't seem to deal with life's ordinary demands, much less training as a Witch. They have one personal crisis after another: illness, depression, losing a job, family problems, huge debts, and so on. Studying the occult may be an escape from coping with normal life.

The Strategy for Coping: Some people are just not ready to work with a coven, no matter how appealing it seems to them. It is reasonable to expect that they get their mundane life in some semblance of order before training for the priesthood. Otherwise, Wicca is just another excuse not to do life well.

The Paranoid

Description and M.O.: All Witches—smart ones—are cautious, living in this society. Some go so far past cautious that fear rules their lives. The ones who are obviously terrified and obviously have a Secret are the ones that often draw persecution to them. Their very aura screams "VICTIM!" They certainly aren't having fun, and it makes the Witches around them edgy.

The Strategy for Coping: You can try some "What if . . .?" pastoral counseling, and help them see that even the possibility of exposure can be intelligently considered and planned for. Clearly they need work on empowerment and self-confidence to get past the fear. Strong, calm role models in the coven can help.

The Party Dude/tte

Description and M.O.: Though this person may be quiet and respectful during class and ritual, it probably means they are asleep. Their only real interest is party time—food, drink, sex, dancing, loud music, and seconds of everything, please. They are conspicuously absent when it comes to community service, teaching, or organizational work.

The Strategy for Coping: Most Pagans love to party. Most Pagans can also work their tails off for something important. Anyone who avoids the work and shows up for the parties needs to be given work assignments and expected to perform them or move on.

The Rainbows-and-Bunnies Child of Light

Description and M.O.: This darling creature makes Positive Thinking look like suicidal depression. Fiercely interested in promulgating Life, Light, Sweetness, and Love, they will never admit to having a shadow side and can deal with pain or anger only by pretending it doesn't exist.

The Strategy for Coping: An early step is to help them admit their negative emotions, and express them honestly and constructively. Their training must help them meet the Dark Goddess and the Lord of Death, and learn to face Them unflinchingly. If they are young, time and life experience may help them find a balance.

The Sex God/dess

Description and M.O.: This one wants your body. Not that you're special, they want everybody's body. Their thealogy, career interest, hobby, and avocation is sex; and they value others based on how sexy and available they are.

The Strategy for Coping: A healthy interest in sex is great, and Wicca is very sex-friendly—at least toward ethical safe sex between consenting adults. But monomania about sex or any other single facet of life is unbalanced. This individual should get help in exploring other kinds of relationships and perspectives, or just accept being a Party Pagan rather than aspiring priest/ess.

The Waffle

Description and M.O.: Maybe they don't want to offend anyone. Maybe it's too much trouble to choose and defend a set of values. Whatever the reason, this person has no opinions and is always squarely on the fence. This makes other Witches crazy, because most of us have the courage of our convictions and want to know who'll stand up if the Inquisition comes again.

The Strategy for Coping: Before they reach initiation, they should be required to think out and express their ethics, values, and beliefs, and affirm them through action. Someone who can never risk taking a stand is not ready to be a Witch.

The Witchy-In-The-Night Witch

Description and M.O.: Such people love the aura of dark mystery surrounding the Craft, and squeeze it like a lemon. You can recognize them by their dark clothing, excessive eye make-up (or goatee), and conversation hinting at dark secrets. They look like vampires-in-training.

The Strategy for Coping: If it's a member of your coven, point out that they are supporting a stereotype and suggest they lighten up. If it's someone else, grin and ignore it, as long as they don't do anything unethical or directly dangerous to the Craft.

Using This Information

Coping with difficult personalities requires wisdom and a sensitive touch. The focus should be on helping individuals grow in maturity, or if that is beyond the resources of your coven, getting them to move on with a minimum of trauma. The aim of this list is to help coven leaders recognize potential problems before they reach a crisis, and perhaps to help all members take an honest, direct look at their own challenges—not to provide ammunition for "Witch Wars." So please, use it for positive purposes, and carefully.

A-19

Pagan Periodicals

The following is a partial listing of Wiccan/Pagan periodicals. It has been estimated that there are about 300 such publications, and titles are born and disappear every year. I have selected periodicals for this list because they have a Wiccan/Pagan emphasis, are national or international in scope, have existed for several years, have a high-quality content, or have a special focus (for women, men, Pagan parents, etc.).

For more extensive lists, see *The Circle Guide to Pagan Groups* (available from Circle, P.O. Box 219, Mt. Horeb, WI 53572), and *The Wicca Source Book* by Gerina Dunwich, Citadel Press, 1996 (available through most bookstores).

Acorns: Wicca and Paganism. Quarterly. Sample $2.50, subscription $12.00. Lady Amethyst, ed., P.O. Box 6006, Athens, GA 30604.

Bridge Between the Worlds: Witchcraft, international contacts. Quarterly. Sample $3.00, sub. $10.00. 10 Royal Orchard Blvd., Box 53067, Thornhill, Ontario L3T 7R9, Canada.

Calendar of Events: Festivals and other Pagan events. Sub. $4.50, $5.00 in Canada. Larry Cornett, ed., 9355 Sibelius Drive, Vienna, VA 22182.

The Cauldron: Wicca and Earth Mysteries. Sub. $20.00 cash. Mike Howard, ed., Caemorgan Cottage, Caemorgan Road, Cardigan, Dyfed, SA43 1QU, Wales, United Kingdom.

Circle Network News: Paganism, contacts. Quarterly. Sample free, sub. $15.00, $20.00 in Canada. Dennis Carpenter, ed., P.O. Box 219, Mt. Horeb, WI 53572. Call (608) 924-2216.

Connections: Community, Philosophy and Magick. Quarterly. Sub. $14.80. 1705 14th street #181, Boulder, CO 80302.

Covenant of the Goddess Newsletter: Witchcraft, COG business. Eight times yearly. Sample $3.00, sub. $20.00. P.O. Box 1226, Berkeley, CA 94704.

Earth Circle News: Wicca, Paganism. Quarterly. Sample free, sub. $15.00. P.O. Box 1938, Sebastapol, CA 95473.

Golden Isis: Wicca, Paganism and positive magick. Quarterly. Sample $2.95, sub. $10.00 U.S., $15.00 in Canada and elsewhere. Gerina Dunwich, ed., P.O. Box 525, Fort Covington, NY 12937.

Green Egg: Neopaganism, environment, psychic development, Church of All Worlds. Quarterly. Sample $6.00, sub. $24.00, outside U.S., $36.00. P.O. Box 1542, Ukiah, CA 95482. E-mail: 5878037@mcimail.com.

Green Man: For Pagan men. Sample $4.00, sub. $13.00, Canada $18.00. Diana Darling, ed., P.O. Box 641, Point Arena, CA 95468.

H.A.M. (How About Magick?): For Pagan youth. Nemeton, P.O. Box 488, Laytonville, CA 95454.

Heartsong Review: Pagan and spiritual music reviews. Sample $5.00, sub. $8.00, Canada $10.00. Sampler tape with each issue. Wahaba Heartsun, ed., P.O. Box 5716, Eugene, OR 97405.

Hecate's Loom: Paganism in Canada and beyond. Quarterly. Sample $3.95 Canadian. Sub. $13–18.00 U.S., $11–15.00 Canadian (sliding scale), $18–24.00 overseas. P.O. Box 5206, Station B, Victoria, British Columbia V8R 6N4, Canada.

Hole in the Stone: A Journal of the Wiccan Life: Paganism. Quarterly. Sample $2.00, sub. $12.00, Canada $17.00. Rhiannon Asher and George Moyer, eds., 2125 W. Evans, Denver, CO 80223.

Isian News: International Goddess-oriented Paganism, members only. Quarterly. Sample $2.50, sub. $20.00. Lord Strathlock and Hon. Olivia Robertson, eds., Fellowship of Isis, Foundation Centre, Clonegal Castle, Clonegal Enniscorthy, Ireland.

The Lady Letter: Wicca, especially priest/ess skills, and the Ardantane Project to create a Wiccan residential seminary. Quarterly. Sub. $13.00. Our Lady of the Woods, P.O. Box 1107, Los Alamos, NM 87544.

New Worlds: Llewellyn book catalog, articles on Wicca, astrology, metaphysics. Six times a year. Sample $2.95, sub. $7.00. P.O. Box 64383, St. Paul, MN 55164.

North Star: Pagan/Wiccan families, home schooling. Six issues. Sample $1.00, sub. $12.00, Canada and Mexico $18.00. P.O. Box 878-887, Wasilla, AK 99687.

Of A Like Mind: Goddess womyn, feminist spirituality, Dianic Wicca. Quarterly. Sample $4.00, sub. $15–35.00 (sliding scale). Lynn Levy, ed., P.O. Box 6677, Madison, WI 53716.

Pagan Dawn: British Wicca, Paganism, Druidism. Quarterly. Sample $7.00, sub. $25.00 cash. Pagan Federation, BM Box 7097, London WC1N 3XX, England.

Pagan Nuus: Covenant of Unitarian Universalist Pagans. Sample $1-2.00 (sliding scale). P.O. Box 640, Cambridge, MA 02140.

Pagans for Peace Newsletter: Pagan theology and political networking. Six issues a year. Sample free, sub. $10.00. Samuel Wagar, ed., P.O. Box 2205, Clearbrook, British Columbia, Canada V2T 3X8.

Panegyria: Paganism, Aquarian Tabernacle Church. Eight issues. Sample, three stamps. Pete Pathfinder, ed., P.O. Box 409, Index, WA 98256.

Quest: Natural and ritual magick. Quarterly. Sample $4.00, sub. $20.00. Marian Green, ed., BCM-SCL Quest, London WC1N 3XX, England.

Reclaiming: Spirit and politics. Quarterly. Sample $2.00, sub. $6-25.00 (sliding scale). P.O. Box 14404, San Francisco, CA 94114.

Sage Woman: Goddess women's spirituality. Quarterly. Sample free. Sub. $18.00. Anne Newkirk Niven, ed., P.O. Box 641, Point Arena, CA 95468.

Solitary, By Choice or By Chance: For solitary Wiccans and Pagans. Quarterly. Sample $3.50, sub. $15–36.00 (sliding scale). De-Anna Alba, ed., P.O. Box 6091, Madison, WI 53716.

Thesmophoria: Voice of the new women's religion. Sample free, send self-addressed stamped envelope. P.O. Box 11363, Oakland, CA 94611.

T.I.P. (Teens Into Paganism): Networking for Pagan teens (12 to 18). 8–12 issues per year. Sample $1.00, sub. $5.00. c/o EarthSpirit, P.O. Box 365, Medford, MA 02155.

Unicorn: Wicca. Eight times a year. Sub. $10.00. Rev. Paul V. Beyerl, ed., P.O. Box 0691, Kirkland, WA 98083.

Voice of the Anvil: Pagan and Wiccan networking. Monthly. Sample free. Sub. $6.00. P.O. Box 060672, Palm Bay, FL 32906.

The Wiccan: Pagan Federation Journal: Quarterly. Sample $6.00 cash, sub. $18.00. BM Box 7097, London WC1N 3XX, England.

Witches' Almanac: Occult lore and legend, Moon calendar, astrology, etc. Annual. $7.45, $8.45 Canada. P.O. Box 348, Cambridge, MA 02238.

A-20
Wiccan/Pagan Networks

There are several organizations that work on a national or international level, and your coven may want to affiliate with one or more. This is by no means a complete listing—simply some of the more well-known and durable organizations with histories that promise they will be around for a while. They are listed alphabetically. For the most part, these groups are volunteer-run and have very limited budgets. So when writing to any of these organizations, it is courteous to enclose a stamped, self-addressed envelope and a dollar for copying costs.

Aquarian Tabernacle Church

ATC is an umbrella organization for several covens, with a center in Washington State. Like COG (see below), ATC is very interested in achieving recognition and acceptance of the Craft as a legitimate religion. Two of their strengths are interfaith work and ministry to Pagans in the correctional system. ATC publishes *Panegyria* newsletter and a Spring Mysteries festival in Washington as well as open sabbats and other events. Contact: Aquarian Tabernacle Church, P.O. Box 409, Index, WA 98256. Their telephone is (206) 793-1945, and the net address is BBS AquaTabCh@aol.com.

Circle

Circle publishes *Circle Network News* and other Pagan resources including the very useful *Guide to Wiccan/Pagan Resources*. It sponsors the Pagan Spirit Gathering each summer in the Midwest, and hosts numerous workshops and open sabbats in Wisconsin throughout the year. Circle is open to Pagans generally, and sponsors the Pagan Spirit Alliance and Lady Liberty League. Contact: Circle Sanctuary, P.O. Box 219, Mt. Horeb, WI 53572. Their telephone is (608) 924-2216, but it is probably better to write with your questions or e-mail circle@mhtc.net.

Covenant of the Goddess

COG is an international (but largely U.S.A.-based) federation of Witches' covens and solitaries, and probably the largest organization of Witches in the world. It is divided into Local Councils, which decide what programs they want to organize, though there are many at-large members who do not live near a Local Council or choose not to participate in LC activities. COG includes well over a hundred covens from varying traditions.

COG makes ministerial credentials available to qualified priests and priestesses; does a great deal of media contact and public information about the Craft; publishes *The COG Newsletter*; provides referrals to local or area covens; sponsors an annual festival, Merrymeet, which moves around the U.S.; sponsors a listserve and web page on the Internet; publishes resource guides; sponsors the Hart and Crescent Award, which can be earned by Pagan youth;

networks with other religions; and often intervenes to assist Witches who are being harassed or persecuted.

To join COG, a coven must fulfill the following:

1. Worship the Goddess and the Old Gods (or the Goddess alone)
2. Accept the Wiccan Rede and a Code of Ethics compatible with COG's
3. Have been active six months or more;
4. Have three or more members who have been formally accepted into training for the clergy
5. Have at least one member eligible to receive Elder Priest/ess credentials
6. Be a cohesive, self-perpetuating group

Prospective members apply through their Local Councils, or at the National level if there is no LC in their area. For more information, write to: The Covenant of the Goddess, P.O. Box 1226, Berkeley, CA 94701. Please enclose $2.00 for postage and handling. Internet address: netco@cog.org. Web page: URL: http://www.cog.org/cog/.

Earth Religions Assistance List

ERAL exists to network among religious rights activists and support religious freedom. For more information see http://205.226.66.2/~rowanf/ERAL/eral.html. A directory of contacts by state can be viewed on the Web at: http://ddi.digital.net/~billk/rights.htm.

Pagan Educational Network

This organization is "devoted to disseminating correct and factual information about Wicca/Paganism" and supporting religious freedom. For a sample newsletter and information, send $3.00. Write PEN, P.O. Box 1364, Bloomington, IN 47402-1364.

The Pagan Federation

This is a British and European network of Witches and other Pagans. It publishes Pagan Dawn and can be reached at BM Box 7097, London WC1N 3XX, United Kingdom, Europe. Their web site: http://sunacm.swan.ac.uk/~paganfed.

Re-formed Congregation of the Goddess

RCG is a network focused on the Goddess and women's spirituality, with a strong emphasis on Dianic Wicca. It publishes *Of A Like Mind* newspaper and other resources, and sponsors conferences in Wisconsin and at several branches elsewhere around the country. RCG offers the Cella training program for priestesses, with several specialized "tracks": Healer, Ritualist, Artist, Scholar/Teacher, Earthwalker, and Organizer. A long-term project is the creation of The Grove (near Madison, Wisconsin), a rural center for Goddess-oriented programs and events. Contact: Re-formed Congregation of the Goddess, P.O. Box 6677, Madison, WI 53716.

Wiccan/Pagan Press Alliance

The WPPA helps Pagan publications network among each other. Their monthly newsletter, *The Midnight Drive*, discusses "news and trends from the Pagan publishing industry." Contact: Wiccan/Pagan Press Alliance, c/o Black Forest Publishing, P.O. Box 1392, Mechanicsburg, PA 17055-1392.

Witches Anti-Discrimination Lobby

WADL gathers information on cases where Witches encounter discrimination in employment, the court system, the military, etc., and works to assure fair treatment for all of us. Contact: same as WPPA above.

Witches League for Public Awareness

WLPA does much the same work as WADL, with an emphasis on educating the public through the media. Contact: WLPA, P.O. Box 8736, Salem, MA 01971-8736.

A-21

Internet Resources

Following is a list of e-mail addresses and web sites. Most have been up and maintained for some time, but there is no guarantee that they will remain so in the future. We, the author and publisher(s), do not have any personal or monetary interest in any of these sites. We have looked at many of the sites that are listed below, though we cannot guarantee the accuracy of all of them. They are only presented to give you a place to begin your researches or make contacts.

E-Mail Addresses

The Aquarian Tabernacle Church: BBS: AquaTabCh@aol.com.

Circle Sanctuary: circle@mhtc.net.

The Covenant of the Goddess: netco@cog.org.

The Covenant of Unitarian-Universalist Pagans: cuupshq@efn.org.

The Green Egg, a well-known Pagan periodical: 5878037@mcimail.com.

The PagaNet News: nurien@aol.com.

Web sites

National Calendar of Pagan Events lists dates, costs, locations, descriptions, and contact information for festivals and gatherings across the United States and internationally: http://members.aol.com/lcorncalen/CALENDAR.htm. To list events (two days or longer), contact lcorncalen@aol.com. For topic-specific web pages (for finding help), contact: http://members.aol.com/lcorncalen/helplink.htm.

Earth Religions Assistance List: http://205.226.66.2/~rowanf/ERAL/eral.html. A directory of contacts by state: http://ddi.digital.net/~billk/rights.htm. To subscribe, send an e-mail to eral-request@dreksys.com with the single word "subscribe."

The Covenant of the Goddess: http://www.cog.org/cog/. COG is a federation of about 120 covens (at this writing) throughout the U.S., with a few international members.

A **"Help-yourself Guide for Finding Help/Giving Help,"** in case of legal problems related to your religion: http://www.nfx.net/~firespring/eral. Also check the Links site: http://members.aol.com/lcorncalen/helplink.htm.

The Pagan Federation, headquartered in London, England: http://sunacm.swan.ac.uk/~paganfed.

The following sites are listed by name only, but can be found with a search engine and a little time, or by following links. Many are from the "Pagan Best of the Web" site, and I have added others.

Alaine's Circle of Wicca
Arachne's Web
Auramooth's Wiccan Page
Avalon
Azure's Gateway to Wicca
Catala's Wicca Page
Covenant of Gaia (Canada)
The Craft
Daemon Child's Witch Resource
The Denver Pentagram
Farrar and Bone Homepage
Francesca's Wiccan... Grimoire
The Green Pages
Heckate's Broom
Joan's Witch Directory
Living Wicca Foundation
Manor House for Wiccan Studies
Moonleaf's Witchcraft Page
Outer Gate Wicca
Paganism, Wicca and Witchcraft
Sid's Wicca Page
SpiritDancer's Wiccan Web
Triple Goddess WebPlace
Wiccan Grove
Witches' Book of Days
Witches Central
Witches' League for Public Awareness
The Witching Hours
Witchsight
Witch Way
Witch Worlds
Witches' Hearth
Witches' League Virginia
Witches' World Homepage
Witches' Voice

A-22

Festivals

Most Pagan festivals bring together 100-500 people from many different traditions, usually for a long weekend (two to four days). The majority involve camping, some have cabins or bunkhouse accommodations, and a very few are held in hotels. The cost can range from nominal ($25) to $200 or more, depending on the lodging and whether meals are provided. Preregistration is ordinarily required. The program usually includes rituals, a variety of workshops, and concerts, talent shows, or bardic circles. Dress ranges from ceremonial to casual to none at any given event. DO: respect the land, be tolerant of differing traditions and lifestyles, bring alcoholic beverages if you like, take "no" for an answer. DO NOT: bring drugs, firearms, or animal friends; litter or harm the land in any way; get drunk and obnoxious; expect orgies or free sex.

Festivals change from year to year: new ones are created, while some disappear. Rather than list every festival known at this time, I have chosen to list some of the larger and more durable events. It is very likely that there are others scheduled in your state or region. For a more extensive list, see *The Circle Guide to Pagan Groups* (available from Circle, P.O. Box 219, Mt. Horeb, WI 53572).

Also, most Pagan periodicals carry listings of some festivals, but probably the most complete source is the *International Calendar of Pagan Events* published by Larry Cornett. He lists the date, cost, location, a description, and the contact information for each event. You can get a hardcopy subscription (six issues a year), or check the Web at:

http://www.io.com/~cookec/pagan/calendar.html

or, http://www/members/aol.com/lcorncalen/CALENDAR.htm.

To list events (two days or longer), contact lcorncalen@aol.com.

Mixed Festivals (Men and Women Welcome)

Ancient Ways Festival: May; California. Ancient Ways, 4075 Telegraph Ave., Oakland, CA 94609.

Dragonfest: August; Colorado. Dragonfest, P.O. Box 6927, Denver, CO 80206.

Earth Magick Gathering: September;, Indiana. Elf Lore Family, P.O. Box 1082, Bloomington, IN 47402-1082.

Free Spirit Festival: June; Maryland. Free Spirit Alliance, P.O. Box 5358, Laurel, MD 20726.

Goddess Gathering: June; Ohio. Temple of Wicca and others, P.O. Box 2281, Lancaster, OH 43130.

Heartland Spirit Festival: May; Kansas. Heartland Spirit Alliance, P.O. Box 3407, Kansas City, KS 66103.

High Desert Midsummer Gathering: June; Arizona. The Sacred Grove, 16845 N. 29th Ave., Phoenix, AZ 85023.

Highlands of Tennessee Samhain Gathering: October; Tennessee. Avalon Isle, P.O. Box 6006, Athens, GA 30604.

Merrymeet: August or September; location varies. Covenant of the Goddess, P.O. Box 1226, Berkeley, CA 94701.

Magickal Mountain Mabon: September; New Mexico. Chamisa Local Council of COG, P.O. Box 1107, Los Alamos, NM 87544.

Pagan Federation Annual Conference: November; England. Pagan Federation, BM 7097, London, WC1N 3XX, England.

Pagan Kith and Kin: June; Wisconsin. The Earth Conclave, P.O. Box 14377, Madison, WI 53714.

Pagan Spirit Gathering: June; Ohio. Circle, P.O. Box 219, Mt. Horeb, WI 53572.

Pan Pagan Festival: August; Illinois. Midwest Pagan Council, P.O. Box 160, Western Springs, IL 60558-0160.

Rites of Spring: May; Massachusetts. EarthSpirit and CCR, P.O. Box 365, Medford, MA 02155.

Samhain Freedom Festival: November; Florida. Church of Iron Oak, P.O. Box 060672, Palm Bay, FL 32906.

Spiral: September; Georgia. Wyrd Sisters, P.O. Box 658, Dahlonega, GA 30533.

Spring Mysteries: April; Washington State. Aquarian Tabernacle Church, P.O. Box 409, Index, WA 98256.

Starwood: July; New York. ACE, 1643 Lee Rd. #9, Cleveland Heights, OH 44118.

United Earth Assembly: September; Texas, Oklahoma, New Mexico (migrates). UEA, P.O. Box 10161, Enid, OK 73706.

Wic-Can Festival: June; Ontario Canada. Wic-Can Fest, P.O. Box 125, 3090 Danforth Ave., Scarborough, Ontario, Canada M1L 1B1.

Women's Festivals

Gathering of Priestesses: May; Wisconsin. RCG, P.O. Box 6677, Madison, WI 53716.

Gulf Coast Womyn's Festival: May; Mississippi. Henson Productions, P.O. Box 12, Ovett, MS 39464.

Hallows Gathering: October; Wisconsin. RCG, P.O. Box 6677, Madison, WI 53716.

Michigan Womyn's Music Festival: August; Michigan. WWTMF. Michigan Womyn's Music Festival, P.O. Box 22, Walhalla, MI 49458.

National Women's Music Festival-Spirituality Conference: June; Indiana. Women in the Arts, P.O. Box 1427, Indianapolis, IN 46206.

Northern California Woman's Goddess Festival: June; California. Milk and Honey, (707) 824-1155.

Summer Solstice: A Women's Event: June; New Mexico. New Mexico REEF, P.O. Box 7726, Albuquerque, NM 87194-7726.

Womynspirit Festival: October; Ontario, Canada. Womynspirit Collective, 62 Hayes Ave., Guelph, Ontario, Canada N1E 5V8.

A-23

Checklist for a Healthy Coven

1. We are clear about out goals and how we intend to achieve them. We work hard on the material plane as well as the astral.
2. Our membership is clearly defined, as are the responsibilities and privileges of membership.
3. We know, like, and respect each other well enough to feel very comfortable working together.
4. Our magick is ethical—used only for those who request help, and never to harm.
5. Our friendship extends outside the group; we see one another socially and support one another through difficulties.
6. We share the responsibilities of making the coven work; every individual's talents are used and every individual's contribution is important.
7. We enjoy one another. There is play, fun, laughter, and affection at our meetings.
8. We work at learning magick. We dig deep, compare different sources, try new techniques, practice old ones, ask pointed questions, and do it again until we get it right.
9. We do not make a virtue of authority or obedience, but treat one another as respected equals regardless of the formal structure of the coven.
10. We keep ourselves healthy and fit in order to more readily receive insight and channel power.
11. We constantly seek knowledge from many sources: people, books, workshops, other paths—and especially nature.
12. We keep our ritual areas, clothing, and tools orderly and clean.
13. We raise genuine power and channel it. Our rituals are not tame readings or rote gestures, but filled with energy, vitality, will, and purpose.

A-24
Sample Press Release

The Coven of the Bright Moon
P.O. Box 39 • Basilton, New York 20307

NEWS RELEASE

TO: R.A. Smithers, Religion Editor, Basilton Herald-Tribune

DATE: April 6, 1997

SUBJECT: May Day Celebration

TEXT:

On Saturday, May 3 a May Day/Beltane celebration will be held at Greenwood Park in Basilton. The festivities will begin at 6:00 p.m. with a maypole dance and short ceremony to honor the season of warmth, life and growth. A potluck supper will follow at approximately 7:30 p.m. The event is open to the public, and families are welcome. A special children's maypole dance will be offered for little ones.

The celebration is sponsored by The Coven of the Bright Moon, a Wiccan church serving the greater Basilton-Ferndale area. Wicca is a nature religion with roots in ancient Europe, focusing on deity as Goddess as well as God.

For further information, call Daphne at 555-1313, or write to Bright Moon, P.O. Box 39, Basilton NY 20307.

CONTACT PERSON: Daphne Bolline PHONE: 555-1313

SUGGESTED RELEASE DATE April 12, 1997

APPROVAL NAME/DATE Catherine Crescenthorn *Catherine Crescenthorn* April 6, 1997

Appendix B: Rituals

B-1

A Basic Ritual Outline

Preparation

Prepare the ritual space, cleaning the room or altar. Set up the altar; most often it is placed in the East, though some traditions prefer the North or the center of the circle. Place on it the altar cloth (if desired), lamps of art, the tools or symbols of the Elements (including a small dish of salt and a bowl of water), statuettes of the Lady and Lord if you wish, and any special supplies needed. Prepare yourself by cleansing your body and clearing your mind of all but the work ahead. Put on your robe and/or cord and jewels.

Attunement

Have the coveners sit quietly in the circle and center. After a couple of minutes, hold hands and breathe, hum, chant, or sing quietly together.

Asperging

Purify the ritual area with salt and water. Point your athame at each in turn, visualizing them glowing with a pure light and saying:

> I exorcise thee, O Spirit of salt, casting out all impurities which may lie within. Likewise do I exorcise thee, O Spirit of water, casting out all impurities which may lie within.

Place three athame-tips worth of salt in the water and mix them deosil (sunwise, clockwise). Asperge (sprinkle the salt water) the area and participants, walking deosil around the circle. Some covens purify with fire and air as well, circling with a thurible of incense.

Casting the Circle

Cast the circle, walking deosil around the circle with your athame or sword, visualizing a line of blue fire growing at the edge, and saying:

> I conjure thee, O Circle of power, that thou beist a boundary between the world of humanity and the realms of the Mighty Ones, a guardian and a protection to preserve and contain the power we shall raise within. Wherefore, do I bless and consecrate thee.

Calling the Quarters

Now the HP (Air and Fire) and the HPs (Water and Earth) call the quarters; or, four volunteers from the coven may do so. They draw the appropriate invoking pentagram (see A-17, page 402) with their athames and say, for example:

> **AIR**: Guardians of the Watchtowers of the East, Powers of Air, I call upon Thee. Thou Who art the breezes, winds and zephyrs . . . and Who art also mind, intellect, and imagination . . . grace our circle with Your Presence this night. Great Eagle of the Eastern Skies, I summon, stir, and call Thee up!
>
> **FIRE**: Guardians of the Watchtowers of the South, Powers of Fire, I call upon Thee. Thou Who art the fiery rays of the sun, the dancing flames of the hearthfire, and the deep heat within the Earth's core . . . and Who art also energy, will, and passion . . . grace our circle with Your Presence this night. Red Lion of the Southern Desert, I summon, stir, and call Thee up!
>
> **WATER**: Guardians of the Watchtowers of the West, Powers of Water, I call upon Thee. Thou Who art the mountain streamlets, the mighty rivers, and the vast oceans . . . and Who art also feeling, emotion, and intuition . . . grace our circle with Your Presence this night. Sweet Dolphin of the Western Seas, I summon, stir, and call Thee up!
>
> **EARTH**: Guardians of the Watchtowers of the North, Powers of Earth, I call upon Thee. Thou Who art the towering mountains, the fertile plains, and the enduring bedrock . . . and Who art also our bodies and all things material . . . grace our circle with Your Presence this night. Black Bear of the Northern Forest, I summon, stir, and call Thee up!

Calling the God

Invite the god-aspect you wish to be present for the ritual. For example, if you choose Cernunnos, saying:

> Cernunnos, Horned One, God of the Wilds, we call You to our circle! Let your energy, your joy, your passion fill us as we launch our new coven! Show us Your paths through the wilderness and guide us on our journey. Grant that we may celebrate in Your forests and fields, protect Your creatures, and feel Your presence as the Old Ways live again within our circle!

If you have been trained to do so, you may also invoke the god into yourself and speak as Him.

Calling the Goddess

Invite the goddess-aspect Who is to be present for the work. If you were to choose Cerridwen, for example, saying:

> Cerridwen, Great Mother, Mistress of the Magicks of Rebirth, we call You to our circle! Let Your wisdom, Your love, and Your power fill us as we begin our new coven! Teach us the arts of magick, healing, and transformation. Grant that we may come forth from Aven, Your cauldron of rebirth, to celebrate and honor You! Let the Old Ways live again within our circle!

If you have been trained to do so, you may also invoke the goddess into yourself and speak as Her.

Stating the Purpose

State the purpose of the ritual:

> We are gathered here this night to celebrate the full moon, in which is the sign and presence of the Triple Goddess; to honor the Horned Lord, Her consort; and to work such magicks of protection, healing, and blessing as we have need of. Welcome to this circle!

Magickal Work or Celebration

This will vary according to whether you are performing a rite of passage, doing various magicks at an esbat, or celebrating a sabbat. Examples can be found in the chapters on esbats and sabbats, and in the ritual outlines which follow.

Cakes and Wine

Then the coven shares "cakes and wine," or cookies and juice, bread and mead, or whatever your coven chooses. Usually before the ritual begins, the beverage is poured into a large goblet or chalice, and the cakes placed on a platter or pentacle. The High Priest blesses the beverage, saying for example:

> We thank the gods of wine for the nourishment and pleasure which flows from the fruits of the Earth. Blessed be this wine.

Likewise the High Priestess blesses the cakes, saying:

> We thank the goddesses of the grain for the nourishment and strength which comes from the harvest of the Earth. Blessed be these cakes.

Following this, the chalice and platter are taken or passed deosil around the circle, and offered to each covener with good wishes or blessings such as the following:

> May you drink deep of life.
>
> May your cup overflow with love and friendship. May you always have enough for yourself and a friend.
>
> May the bounty of the earth fill your table.

(I prefer the positive statements, rather than the reverse negative, "May you never hunger . . .", because the mind skips over negatives—"none," "never," "can't"—and connects only with the "May you ___ hunger" message. Say what you want, and the message remains clear.)

Farewell to the Goddess

When the time is right, begin the closing. Say farewell to the Goddess in your own words. Or if you have invoked the Goddess and aspected as Her, She will say farewell to the coven.

Farewell to the God

Say farewell to the God in your own words. Or if you have invoked the God and aspected as Him, He will say farewell to the coven.

Dismissing the Quarters

Say farewell to the quarters starting in the North and moving widdershins (counterclockwise), saying for example:

> Guardians of the Watchtowers of the North, Powers of Earth, we thank Thee for attending. If go ye must, we say: Hail and Farewell!

Others (echo): Hail and Farewell! And so on for the West, South and East.

Opening the Circle

Open the circle, starting in the East and moving widdershins with your athame or sword. Upon returning to the East, replace the athame on the altar and say:

> By the Earth that is Her body, by the Air that is Her breath, by the Fire of Her bright spirit, by the living Waters of Her womb, may the peace of the Goddess go in your hearts. By His hoof and His horn, blessed be. The circle is open but never broken.
>
> (Here all join in.) Merry meet, and merry part, and merry meet again!

Refreshments, Socializing, Singing, Etc.

NOTE: The ritual outlines which follow will not repeat every step in detail, but simply list, for example, "Calling the Quarters." If there is a different wording suggested for a particular ritual, that will be spelled out. In most cases refer back to this outline for details, or use your own tradition's forms. The abbreviation HP indicates the High Priest; HPs indicates the High Priestess.

B-2
Ritual Birthing for a Coven

Preparation

Attunement

Asperging

Casting the Circle

Calling the Quarters

As usual but with appropriate changes in wording. For example:

> **EAST:** I call the Guardians of Air, asking the gifts of intelligence, imagination, and inspiration for the coven to be born!
>
> **SOUTH:** We call the Guardians of Fire, asking the gifts of energy, will and passion, for the coven to be born!
>
> **WEST:** We call the Guardians of Water, asking the gifts of love and empathy for the coven to be born.
>
> **NORTH:** We call the Guardians of Earth, asking the gifts of health, strength, and prosperity for the coven to be born!

Calling the God

Then invoke the god-aspect you wish to be patron of your coven.

Inviting the Goddess

Invoke the goddess-aspect Who is to be the coven's special protector.

Stating the Purpose

For example:

> We gather tonight to celebrate the birth of a new coven of Witches, who shall gather to honor the Goddess and the God, to celebrate the wheel of the year, to work magick in accord with the Wiccan Rede, and in all ways to serve as priestesses and priests of the Old Religion.

Divination

Now if you have any skills at divination, explore the future for the new coven with Tarot, pendulum, runestones, scrying, or whatever. You may want to ask such questions as:

> Is (date) appropriate for an organizational meeting?
>
> What is the best role for each of us in the group?
>
> What qualities must we cultivate in ourselves in order to help the group succeed?

Meditation and Sharing Goals

Meditate to discover what are the most important actions you can take during the coming month to help the coven thrive. Set goals which you can accomplish before the Moon's next cycle, and write them on a parchment slip. When you are done, fold the paper and place it in the cauldron.

Now in great clarity and detail, visualize yourselves accomplishing those goals. Allow yourselves to feel the satisfaction, strength, and self-confidence you will feel when they are done. As you do so, touch your Third Eye. And in the month to come, whenever you touch that place again, the energy and joy will return to help you move on toward your goals.

Then each person shares their goals. The rest of the group should encourage them with applause and expressions of support.

Symbolic Planting

If you want to, perform a symbolic act such as planting a seed in a pot (choose a perennial herb or flower which has the energies you want for the coven), then place the pots in the cauldron with the papers.

Charging the Goals

Then raise power—for example, by chanting, dancing, or drumming—and release it toward the cauldron when it peaks. Earth any excess energy into the ground, or remove the pots and earth the energy into them.

Self-Blessing

(Adapted from *Book of Pagan Ritual*) Bring forth a silver chalice, half filled with water and half with white wine. Dip your fingers within, and say:

> (Touching forehead) **Bless me, Maiden, now and forever.**
>
> (Touching eyelids) **Blessed be my eyes, that I may see Thy path.**
>
> (Touching nose) **Blessed be my nose, that I may breathe Thy essence.**
>
> (Touching lips) **Blessed be my lips, that I may speak of Thee.**
>
> (Touching breast) **Blessed be my heart, that I may be faithful in Thy works.**
>
> (Touching loins) **Blessed be my loins, that create life as You have brought forth the universe.**
>
> (Touching feet) **Blessed be my feet, that I may walk ever in Thy ways.**

Cakes and Wine

(With appropriate changes in wording)

> **As we partake of these cakes and this wine, let it be a sign that what is above shall be made manifest below; that we act on this**

plane to achieve our aims, as well as placing our intentions on the astral level. The coven is born.

Farewell to God

Dismissing the Quarters

Guardians of the Watchtowers of the North, Powers of Earth, we thank Thee for attending, and bringing to our new coven your strength, health, and prosperity! If go ye must, we say: Hail and Farewell!

Others (echo): Hail and Farewell!

Repeat similar for Water, Fire, and Air.

Opening the Circle

Celebration

Socialize, feast, or sing as you wish.

Acting in Accord

Plant the seeds outdoors when the weather is right.

B-3

The Charge of the Goddess

"The Charge of the Goddess" is probably the best-loved writing in the liturgy of Witchcraft. In its original, simpler form it was given to folklorist Charles Leland by a strega, or northern Italian Witch, named Maddalena. Since then it has been published in several modified forms; the best known recent version is by Starhawk, and was published in *The Spiral Dance*. This version is nearly identical to Starhawk's.

"Listen to the words of the Great Mother, Who of old was called Artemis, Astarte, Dione, Melusine, Aphrodite, Ceridwen, Diana, Arianrhod, Brigid, and by many other names:

> Whenever you have need of anything, once in the month, and better it be when the moon is full, you shall assemble in some secret place and adore the spirit of Me Who is Queen of all the Wise.
>
> You shall be free from slavery, and as a sign that you be free you shall be naked in your rites. Sing, feast, dance, make music and love, all in My presence, for Mine is the ecstasy of the spirit and Mine also is joy on earth. For my law is love unto all beings. Mine is the secret that opens upon the door of youth, and Mine is the cup of the wine of life that is the Cauldron of Cerridwen that is the holy grail of immortality.
>
> I give the knowledge of the spirit eternal and beyond death I give peace and freedom and reunion with those that have gone before. Nor do I demand aught of sacrifice, for behold, I am the mother of all things and My love is poured out upon the earth.

Hear also the words of the Star Goddess, the dust of Whose feet are the hosts of heaven, Whose body encircles the universe:

> I Who am the beauty of the green earth and the white moon among the stars and the mysteries of the waters, I call upon your soul to arise and come unto Me. For I am the soul of nature that gives life to the universe. From Me all things proceed and unto Me they must return.
>
> Let My worship be in the heart that rejoices, for behold—all acts of love and pleasure are My rituals. Let there be beauty and strength, power and compassion, honor and humility, mirth and reverence within you.
>
> And you who seek to know Me, know that your seeking and yearning will avail you not, unless you know the Mystery: for if that which you seek, you find not within yourself, you will never find it without. For behold, I have been with you from the beginning, and I am that which is attained at the end of desire."

From *The Spiral Dance* by Starhawk, adapted from the version by Doreen Valiente, adapted and expanded from the version given to Charles Leland by Maddalena in 1897 and published in *Aradia: The Gospel of the Witches.*

B-4
Dedication Ritual

Preparation

Attunement

Asperging

Casting the Circle

Calling the Quarters

Inviting the God

Inviting the Goddess

Stating the Purpose

HP: The Coven of ________ is gathered tonight to honor the Lady and the Lord and to dedicate a new student, our friend ________, to the study of the Craft. Welcome.

The Questions

The Summoner leads the Dedicant to the center of the circle, facing the High Priestess and High Priest who stand before the altar.

HPs: Have you come to this circle to learn the Craft of the Wise?

Dedicant: Yes, I have.

HP: By what name shall you be known within this circle?

Dedicant: I will be known as ________ (gives new Craft name, if any; otherwise, mundane name).

HPs: (name of dedicant), the hand of the Goddess will be upon you, and She changes everything She touches. Are you ready to begin the transformation?

Dedicant: I am ready.

HP: Do you promise and swear to live your life by the Wiccan Rede, 'An ye harm none, do as ye will?' And do you promise to use the Craft only when it harms none, as long as you shall live?

Dedicant: I promise.

HPs: Never shall you reveal outside the circle any personal information about other coveners, without their express permission. Never shall you teach the secrets of the Craft except to those who have made these promises. Do you promise and swear to keep the secrets of the circle?

Dedicant: I do so promise.

HP: Do you commit yourself to work diligently at the study of the Craft for so long as you are a Dedicant of this circle?

Dedicant: Yes, I do.

HPs: Bearing in mind that family and job responsibilities come first, will you share some of your time and energy to help do the necessary work of the coven?

Dedicant: Yes, I will.

Presentation of the Cord

HP or HPs: A white cord (or whatever your tradition dictates) is the sign of a Dedicant within this circle. (Ties it around Dedicant's waist.) Whenever you wear this cord, remember this night and the promises you have made." (Standing in the center with the Dedicant, slowly turns her or him around to view each member of the circle.) Sisters and brothers, ________ has come to this circle to learn the Craft of the Wise. ________ has promised to live by the Wiccan Rede, and to keep the secrets. Now welcome ________ to our midst!

All: Welcome! (Hugs, handshakes, etc.)

Other Work

The Dedicant rejoins the circle. Then proceed with a self-blessing or other ritual work, followed by the customary closing steps.

Cakes and Wine

Farewell to the Goddess

Farewell to the God

Dismissing the Quarters

Opening the Circle

Feasting and Social Hour

B-5
Ritual of First Degree Initiation

Most covens and traditions have a First Degree initiation ritual which they traditionally use; but if you do not, or if you are not satisfied with the ritual passed on to you, this outline may be helpful. It is adapted from the Gardnerian-Alexandrian format presented in *The Witches' Way* by Janet and Stewart Farrar. If you choose to adopt this outline, I would recommend that you change and add elements to make it unique to your coven. The addition of music or singing is also recommended.

The ritual below is written as though for a male Candidate, and in a tradition where cross-gender initiation is practiced, the High Priestess would have the major role. With a female Candidate the High Priest would be the primary Initiator. If you have a single-sex coven, or a tradition which does not emphasize physical polarity, you may do it differently.

Preparation

Candidate chooses a new magickal or Craft name, if this is part of your tradition. You may ask that the Candidate fast for a certain period before the ritual. Just before leaving home, the Candidate takes a purifying ritual bath. Upon arrival at the covenstead or ritual site, the Candidate is led to a secluded area or room. You may decide to make this barely within hearing range, so the candidate can hear the first part of the ritual. They are to stay until the guide returns for them. Before leaving, the guide asks whether they have chosen a new Craft name and coaches them as to correct responses in the ritual.

Meanwhile, those participating in the ritual (usually First Degree initiates and above) prepare the temple, indoors or out, and set up the altar. Coveners who are not yet First Degree may prepare refreshments for later, in another place where the ritual cannot be heard.

Attunement

Those participating in the ritual attune with whatever chant or exercise you prefer.

Asperging

Casting the Circle

Calling the Quarters

Invocation of the God Cernunnos

Invocation of the Goddess Aradia

The Summoning of the Candidate

The guide leaves to fetch the Candidate, and has him disrobe. Then he is blindfolded, and the guide leads him to approach the circle from the Northeast (if possible).

The Charge of the Goddess

This is presented by the High Priest and High Priestess. See Appendix B-3.

The Challenge

(The guide brings the Candidate forward, but the Summoner bars the way with athame):

Summoner: You who stand on the threshold between the world or humanity and the realms of the Mighty Ones, have you the courage to proceed?

Candidate: I do.

Summoner: That is good . . . for truly I say to you, it were better that you should rush upon this blade and perish (touches athame to breast) than to make the attempt with fear or falseness in your heart. Yet still, we await the passwords.

Candidate: I have two: Perfect Love and Perfect Trust.

HPs: All who have these are doubly welcome in this circle. Now I give you a third, to pass you through this sacred portal.

She moves around behind the Candidate, embraces him from there, and presses him into the circle with her body. The Summoner closes the gateway with his sword or athame.

Introduction to the Watchtowers

The Candidate is led to each of the cardinal directions in turn. The Summoner strikes a drum or gong three times and calls loudly:

> Take heed, O Guardians of the Watchtower of the (East, South, West, North), that (name) is properly prepared to be initiated as Priest/ess and Witch!

The Candidate is then led to the center of the circle.

Channeling Power

Dance in a circle around the Candidate, chanting:

> EKO, EKO, AZARAK! EKO, EKO, ZOMELAK,
>
> EKO, EKO, CERNUNNOS! EKO, EKO, ARADIA!

(This is a very old chant, and no one is certain of the meaning. In *The Roots of Witchcraft* Michael Harrison suggests that it may be corrupted Basque, part of a chant celebrating the November Eve or Samhain sabbat. If you wish, you may choose another power-raising chant in English or your native language.) When sufficient power has been raised, it is sent into the Candidate by laying on of hands.

The Fivefold Kiss

The HPs performs the Fivefold Kiss:

> Blessed be thy feet, which have brought thee in these ways. (Kiss feet.) Blessed be thy knees, which shall kneel before the sacred

altar. (Kiss knees.) Blessed be thy womb (phallus), without which we would not be. (Kiss just above pubic hair.) Blessed be thy breast, formed in beauty and in strength. (Kiss chest or breasts.) Blessed be thy lips, that shall utter the Sacred Names. (Kiss lips.)

Taking the Measure

The HPs or HP measures a length of cord from the Candidate's feet to the top of his head and cuts the cord; then measures around the forehead, the heart, and the hips, tying a knot in each place. The cord is placed on the altar. (It may be kept by the coven, as a symbol of the Candidate's commitment to the group; or given back to the Candidate, as a sign of the coven's trust in him. In earlier times it might have been used to work magick against the individual if he betrayed the coven to its persecutors.)

The Ordeal

HPs: Before you are sworn, are you ready to pass the ordeal and be purified?

Dedicant: I am.

The Candidate is put through a symbolic ordeal; in the Gardnerian and Alexandrian traditions, this involves tying the Candidate's feet and lightly whipping him with a scourge. (Details can be found in *The Witches' Way* by Janet and Stewart Farrar.) Other traditions may replace the scourging with another test of courage and trust, leave the ordeal out, or employ a symbolic rebirth instead. Whatever your coven chooses, make sure it is safe and dignified.

The Oath

The Candidate is led to face the altar.

HPs: You have passed the test. Are you ready to swear fealty to the Craft?

Dedicant: I am.

HPs: Then say after me: 'I, (Candidate's name), in the presence of the Lady and Lord, the Mighty Ones, and the Guardians of the Watchtowers, do freely and solemnly swear that I will ever be true to the Craft of the Wise; that I shall follow the Rede to the best of my ability; that I will never reveal the secrets of the Art, except to a proper person well-prepared; and that I will help, protect, and defend my sisters and brothers of the Craft. All this I swear by my hopes of a future life; and may my tools turn against me if I break this, my solemn oath.'

The Candidate repeats each phrase after her.

Consecration With the Triple Sign

A container of oil and a chalice of wine are brought forth. (The oil may be specially prepared and used only for initiations.)

HPs: I mark you with this Triple Sign.

She draws a delta triangle, sign of the Goddess and the First degree, on the third eye chakra (between the eyebrows) with ritual oil; or, marks the Candidate just above the groin, at their right breast, left breast, and back at the first spot.

HPs: I anoint you with wine.

She dips her fingers in the chalice and draws the same sign again.

HPs: I consecrate you with my lips.

She kisses him in the same place(s), then adds:

> By this sign shall you be recognized as Priest/ess and Witch, by all those who have eyes to see.

The Initiate's blindfold is removed.

Presentation of the Ritual Tools

Now the HPs and HP bring forth the Initiate's magickal tools. Though the Initiate may have been working with some or all of them for months, in the ceremony he is now recognized as having the skill and full right to use them.

HPs: I present the chalice, the womb of the Mother, the cauldron of Cerridwen, the holy grail of immortality. From this we drink in Her honor, in celebration, and for healing and transformation.

HP: I present the athame, with which you may form the magick circle between the worlds, and rule the energies within.

HPs: I present the pentacle, which may be used to call spirits, to keep your connections with the Earth, and to shield yourself and your companions from all negative forces.

HP: I present the wand, which you may use to attract and repel, and direct all energies in accord with your true will and the Wiccan Rede.

HPs: Next I present the Cord, which may be used to bind and to loose the sigils of the Art, and (if a girdle or cingulum) to symbolize your degree in our tradition. (This can be simply a cord or set of cords used in magick often 9' long, the diameter of magick circles; or it may be the girdle or cingulum tied around the waist to hold one's robe. If the latter, its color may be symbolic of one's degree or rank.)

If you wish, the new Initiate may now consecrate his tools.

Congratulations and Gifts

At this time the Dedicants may be invited to join the celebration. All hug the Initiate and offer congratulations, and give any personal gifts they have ready. Then everyone may sing, feast, and make merry.

Farewells to the Goddess and God

Dismissing the Quarters

Opening the Circle

B-6

Ritual of Second Degree Initiation

Preparation

The site and Candidate are prepared as in the first degree initiation. Ask the Candidate whether they wish to choose a new Craft name, and what God- and Goddess-aspect they wish invoked. Coach them as to correct responses in the ritual.

Attunement

Asperging

Casting the Circle

Calling the Quarters

Inviting the God (Candidate's choice)

Inviting the Goddess (Candidate's choice)

The Summoning

Summoner brings the blindfolded Candidate to the circle.

The Challenge

HP: Who comes to this sacred place?

Candidate: (States Craft name; this may be a new name if they wish.)

HP: Only a Wiccan Priest or Priestess may enter this circle tonight. By what right do you seek entrance?

Candidate: I am a Wiccan Priestess.

HP: But still, you must speak the password.

Candidate: Perfect Love and Perfect Trust.

A portal is opened; the Candidate enters.

Presentation to the Quarters

The HP or HPs leads the Candidate to each of the quarters and says:

> Guardians of the Watchtowers of the East (South, West, North) I present to you ________, a consecrated Priest/ess and Witch, who is properly prepared to receive the Second Degree. Grant her your blessings!

The Question

HPs or HP: You have come to Craft and this coven to learn, but often learning involves suffering. (Lifts from the altar a scourge, and holds it before the Candidate.) Are you willing to suffer to learn?

Candidate: I am.

HPs or HP: And you have. It is not necessary that we add to your suffering with this (gestures with scourge), because life itself gives you pain as well as joy, and the opportunity to learn from both. Instead we offer you a few moments of silence, in which to remember the painful events of your life, and what you have learned from them. (All bow their heads, and are silent for three minutes.)

HPs or HP: Remember well the lessons you have learned, and offer your compassion and understanding to those who have each suffered in their own way.

(The next part is used only if the initiators know that the Candidate has chosen a new name.)

The Naming

HP or HPs: Now let us turn our minds to a thing of wonder and joy, for you come among us changed, and new, and it is appropriate that you should be named anew. Have you chosen a new name?

Candidate: I have.

HP or HPs: Then we ask you to share with your coven brethren your new name and its meaning.

Candidate: (Tells their new name and its meaning.)

HP or HPs: Tell us again, what is your name? (Here the candidate repeats it, and all those present ask in turn, **What is your name?** in gradually louder voices, making the Candidate repeat it in a stronger and stronger voice.)

HP or HPs: (Makes a sweeping gesture with both hands.) **Enough! You ARE** (new name). **So mote it be!** (All coveners echo.)

The Oath

The Candidate is led to face the altar.

HPs: Are you ready to swear fealty to the Craft again, as you have done once before?

Dedicant: I am.

HPs or HP: Then say after me, using your new name: 'I, (Candidate's name), in the presence of the Lady and Lord, the Mighty Ones, and the Guardians of the Watchtowers, do freely and solemnly swear that I will ever be true to the Craft of the Wise; that I shall follow the Rede to the best of my ability; that I will never reveal the secrets of the Art, except to a proper person well prepared; and that I will help, protect, and defend my sisters and brothers of the Craft. All this I swear by my hopes of a future life; and may my tools turn against me if I break this, my solemn oath.'

The Candidate repeats each phrase after her.

The Empowering

HP: All power comes from within you, and from the Lady and the Lord, who are within and all around us. Yet we may share our powers with one another, for the good of the Craft. I will my power into you.

(The HP places his left hand under Candidate's knee, and his right hand on her head, and channels his energy into her.)

Consecration With the Pentagram Sigil

A container of oil and a chalice of wine are brought forth. (The oil may be specially prepared and used only for initiations.)

HP: I mark you with this sign.

He draws a pentagram, sign of the Second Degree, on the Candidate with ritual oil; at the throat, right hip, left breast, right breast, left hip, and back at the throat.

I anoint you with wine.

He dips his fingers in the chalice and draws the same sign again.

I consecrate you with my lips.

He kisses her in the same places.

By this sign shall you be recognized as Priestess and Witch of the Second Degree.

The new Second Degree Initiate's blindfold is removed.

Presentation of the Tools

HPs or HP: Do you have tools of the Art to be consecrated, which have come into your possession since your first initiation? If the new Second degree Initiate has such, they are consecrated and placed on the altar.

Presentation to the Quarters

The HP or HPs again leads the Initiate to each of the quarters and says:

Guardians of the Watchtowers of the East (South, West, North) I present to you ________, who has been consecrated Priestess and Witch of the Second Degree. Guard her, guide her, and protect her!

The Legend of the Descent

Here a mystery play is read or, better still, enacted by the participants. Most often the story of the descent of Inanna into the underworld is used. A short version is given in *The Witches' Way* by Janet and Stewart Farrar, and other, longer versions can be found in books on Inanna or Sumerian myth.

HPs: In your journeys through darkness and into the light, remember the courage of the Goddess, and know that She is with you and within you. Welcome to the circle of the Second Degree.

Congratulations and Gifts

All hug the Initiate and offer congratulations, and give any personal gifts they have ready. This may be a good time for the Dedicants and First Degree Initiates to arrive; they should not see the ritual, but they may join in the celebration afterwards.

Farewells to the Goddess and God

Dismissing the Quarters

Opening the Circle

Celebration

Toasts are made and a feast is enjoyed.

B-7

Ritual of Third Degree Initiation

This ritual may be used as is, if you have an eclectic coven, or adapted to fit the thealogy and liturgy of your tradition. It is adapted from the Gardnerian/Alexandrian Third Degree Initiation as written by Janet and Stewart Farrar.

Preparation

The site and Candidate are prepared as in the earlier initiations. Ask the Candidate whether they wish to choose a new Craft name, and what God- and Goddess-aspect they wish invoked. Coach them as to correct responses in the ritual.

Attunement

Asperging

Casting the Circle

Calling the Quarters

Inviting the God (Candidate's choice)

Inviting the Goddess (Candidate's choice)

HPs seats herself on the altar or a throne (a draped high-backed chair), with HP to her right and the Maiden to her left.

The Summoning

Summoner brings the blindfolded Candidate, but stops at the edge of the circle.

The Challenge

HP bars the way with hand or staff, touches athame to neck or breast and says:

> STOP! Only a Wiccan Priest or Priestess may enter this sacred circle tonight. By what right do you seek entrance?

Candidate: I am a priestess of the Craft.

HP: But still, you must speak the password.

Candidate: Perfect love and perfect trust.

Summoner: That is good. For truly I say to you, it were better that you should rush upon this blade than enter this circle with fear or falseness in your heart.

Removes athame from neck or breast, cuts a gate into the circle, leads the Candidate within, closes the gate, then removes the blindfold.

HPs: Bring the Candidate to me.

Summoner calls the Candidate forth, and directs them to kneel before the HPs.

HPs: Why have you come?

Candidate: To serve the Lady and honor the Lord as a Priestess of the Third Degree, if it be your will to recognize me.

HPs: It is . . . but first you must remember and renew your vows. Say after me: 'I, (Candidate's name), in the presence of the Lady and Lord, the Mighty Ones, and the Guardians of the Watchtowers, do freely and solemnly swear that I will ever be true to the Craft of the Wise; that I shall follow the Rede to the best of my ability; that I will never reveal the secrets of the Art, except to a proper person well prepared; and that I will help, protect, and defend my sisters and brothers of the Craft. All this I swear by my hopes of a future life; and may my tools turn against me if I break this, my solemn oath.'

The Candidate repeats each phrase after her.

The Cakes and Wine

The HP brings forth a platter of cakes, and presents it to the HPs, who touches each cake with the wine-moistened tip of her athame.

HP: O Queen of Life, bless this food which has come forth from Your Earth, and with it grant us health, strength, and abundance. They each partake, then pass the platter round with a kiss.

The HPs holds forth the wand, and HP holds forth the chalice of wine. The HPs lowers the point of the athame into the chalice, and they say:

HPs: As the wand is to the God . . .

HP: . . . so the cup is to the Goddess . . .

HPs: . . . and conjoined within . . .

HP: . . . they are the Sacred Marriage.

HP and HPs together: Blessed be. The chalice is shared round with a kiss.

The Naming

This part is used only if the initiators know that the Candidate has chosen a new name.

HP or HPs: Now let us turn our minds to a thing of wonder and joy, for you come among us changed, and new, and it is appropriate that you should be named anew. Have you chosen a new name?

Candidate: I have.

HP or HPs: Then we ask you to share with your coven brethren your new name and its meaning.

Candidate: (Tells their new name and its meaning.)

Note: The remaining sections of the ritual are written as for a female Candidate; if the Candidate is male, the HPs becomes the altar, and the Candidate assists the HP, and the rest of the ritual is adapted accordingly.

The Great Rite

The HP leads the Candidate to the center, where she lies down. He says:

Now I must reveal a great mystery.
Assist me to erect the ancient altar,
at which in days past all worshipped,
The Great Altar of all things;
For in ancient times, Woman was the altar,
And the sacred point was the point within the center of the circle.
Which is not simply the womb, but the mind and imagination,
the heart and the hands. These are the origin of all things;
Therefore should we adore you, and whom we adore we also invoke.

The **HPs** says:

Hear my invocation: O Circle of Stars,
Marvel beyond imagination, soul of infinite space,
Not unto thee may we attain unless thy image be love.
Therefore, by seed and root, by stem and bud,
By leaf and flower and fruit do we invoke thee,
O Queen of space, O spiral of being
You are the continuous One, the source of all beauty and strength,
The fount of life without which we would not be,
She Who makes the universe anew, to the wonder and glory of all.

(If the HP and Candidate are married to each other or are established lovers, all other coveners now leave the room, and they may make love as God and Goddess. In all other cases the Rite is symbolic; the HP may kneel and kiss her, and no one need leave.)

O Secret of Secrets,
That art hidden in the being of all lives,
I am the flame that burns in the heart of every man,
And in the core of every star.
I am life and the giver of life,
And, therefore, also the Lord of death and rebirth.
I am Who I am, and I am in you,
And my name is Mystery of Mysteries.

Consecration With the Pentagram Sigil

HP assists Candidate in rising. A container of oil and a chalice of wine are brought forth. (The oil may be specially prepared and used only for initiations.)

HP: I mark you with this sign.

He draws a pentagram with a fire triangle on top, sigil of the Third Degree, on the Candidate with ritual oil (above the groin, right foot, left knee, right knee, left foot, above the groin once more; then lips, right breast, left breast, lips).

HP: I anoint you with wine. He dips his fingers in the chalice and draws the same sign again.

HP: I consecrate you with my lips.

He kisses her in the same places, then adds:

By this sign shall you be recognized as Priestess and Witch of the Third Degree.

Then the HP says:

O Sacred Priestess,
In the great and holy name of (Goddess),
And by the sacred name of (God),
Let the Lady and the Lord be as one in you;
Let the starlight crystallize in your blood,
And may you know life and death and life again,
For there is no part of you that is not of the gods.

Presentation to the Quarters

HP and HPs (or whoever called the quarters): One by one, take the Initiate to each quarter and present them to the Watchtowers: Air, Fire, Water, Earth:

Guardians of the Watchtowers of the ________, Powers of ________, I present to you (name), who, duly trained and consecrated, takes up the silver cord as a High Priestess of Wicca. Grant her your wisdom, love and power, now and forever!

Congratulations and Gifts

All hug the Initiate and offer congratulations, and give any personal gifts they have ready. This may be a good time for the Dedicants and First and Second Degree initiates to arrive; they should not see the ritual, but they may join in the celebration afterwards.

Farewells to the Goddess and God

Dismissing the Quarters

Opening the Circle

Celebration

Toasts are made and a feast is enjoyed.

B-8

New Moon or Diana's Bow Esbat

Preparation

As usual; plus if indoors, a large lunar crescent symbol is placed on the altar or the wall behind it.

Attunement

Hold hands and chant:

Evo, Evo, Evohe, Saluté Diana....

(pronounced AY-voh AY-voh AY-voh-ay, SAL-yoo-tay Di-AH-na).

Asperging

By the Priest with salt and water, or Priestess with a handcrafted broom.

Casting the Circle

By the Priestess or Priest, with athame or the coven sword.

Calling the Quarters

Saying, for example:

EAST: We call the Guardians of Air, through which Diana's shining rays descend!

SOUTH: We call the Guardians of Fire, reflected in Her cool and silver light!

WEST: We call the Guardians of Water, for She holds dominion over the ebb and flow of the seas.

NORTH: We call the Guardians of Earth, on which the crescent Moon shall shine (now shines)!

Inviting the God

(Adapted from Lady Sheba) The Priest invokes the God, saying:

By the flame that burneth bright,
O Horned One!
We call Thy Name into the night,
Awake young Pan!
Thee we invoke, by the moonlit lake,
By the standing tower and the coiled snake;
Come where the round of the dance is trod,
Horn and Hoof of the goat-foot God!
Come to the charm of the chanted prayer,
As the new Moon rides the evening air;

Through the stars to the heaven's height,
We hear Thy hoofs on the wind of night!
As candle flames now tremble and sigh,
By joy and passion we know Thee nigh!

Inviting the Goddess

The Priestess invokes the Goddess, saying:

Come, radiant princess of the sky,
Thou shining cup of splendor!
Diana, Whose silver arrows fly
So swift and sure and tender!
We draw Your gleaming crescent down:
From out of darkness, bring the light!
Our circle's cast, we've gathered 'round,
The cauldron's fire is burning bright.
We sound the conch, now comes the tide,
Your wild, sweet music fills our blood;
It wakens passion, power, and pride
In surging, swelling, moonlit flood!
Wax strong, O Maiden, and soon, but soon,
We'll feel the waves of joy arise
As we lift to the ever-changing Moon
Our ever-changing eyes.

(By Amber K, with last two lines adapted from W .B. Yeats)

Stating the Purpose

The Priest states the purpose of the ritual, for example:

The Coven of ________ is gathered tonight to celebrate the New Moon (or Diana's Bow), to honor the Lady and the Lord, and to work magick for the healing of ________, and such other work as any of us may bring to the circle. Welcome.

Self-Blessing

The Priestess brings forth a silver chalice, half filled with water and half with white wine. Coveners dip their fingers within, then repeat her gestures and words:

(Touching forehead) Bless me, Maiden, now and forever.

(Touching eyelids) Blessed be my eyes, that I may see Thy path.

(Touching nose) Blessed be my nose, that I may breathe Thy essence.

(Touching lips) Blessed be my lips, that I may speak of Thee.

(Touching breast) Blessed be my heart, that I may be faithful in Thy works.

(Touching loins) Blessed be my loins, that create life as You have brought forth the universe.

(Touching feet) Blessed be my feet, that I may walk ever in Thy ways.

(From *Book of Pagan Ritual*, adapted)

Allow a moment of silence. Then move into planning for the coming month.

Knowing Your Will

Priestess: As the dark moon holds the potential of the full moon, so we have within us the seeds of the lives we will someday live, the spirit of the persons we shall become.

Priest: Meditate now, to know your True Will. Go deep, and know what it is that you truly desire. Then discover what is the most important action you can take during the coming month to achieve that desire. Set a goal which you can accomplish before the Moon's next cycle, and write it on this parchment (distributes paper and pens). When you are done, fold the paper and place it next to the cauldron.

All meditate to quiet music. When all have completed their papers:

Priestess: Now visualize, in great clarity and detail, yourself accomplishing that goal. Allow yourself to feel the satisfaction, strength, and self-confidence you will feel when it is done. As you do so, touch your Third Eye. And in the month to come, whenever you touch that place again, the energy and joy will return to help you move on toward your goal.

Each covener reads their goals, if they wish, and places the paper in the cauldron. The rest of the coven encourages them with applause and expressions of support.

Magickal Work

This may include messages of thanks to the Lady and Lord for blessings received, petitions for help, healings, consecration of ritual tools, short divinations, safe travel spells, etc. The Priestess has the coveners state their needs. Then power is raised—for example, by chanting, dancing, or drumming—and is released toward its goal on the signal of the Priestess. Coveners then earth any excess energy into the ground.

Cakes and Wine

Priestess We have charged also these cakes of light and this lunar wine. As we partake of them, let it be a sign that what is above shall be made manifest below; that we act on this plane to achieve our aims, as well as placing our intentions on the astral level.

Priestess and Priest serve each other, then pass cakes and wine. When the time is right, the Priest begins the closing.

Farewell to the Goddess

Farewell to the God

Dismissing the Quarters

Opening the Circle

Feasting and Social Hour

B-9

Full Moon Esbat

Preparation

As usual, then sit for a moment in meditation before beginning the work. If outdoors, feel the light of the moon upon you; if indoors, imagine it.

Attunement

Asperging

Casting the Circle

Calling the Quarters

Inviting the God

The Priest invokes the God, saying:

> Now do I call You to this our circle, Great Lord of all. I call You by Your many names and faces: the Good Father, the Green Man, the Horned One, the Clever Trickster, the Gentle Brother, the Passionate Lover, the Mighty Warrior, the Strong Defender, the Wise Sage. Let Your spirit now descend on me! Harrahya!

Inviting the Goddess

Then the Priest kneels in the West and calls upon the Goddess:

> I invoke and call upon Thee,
> O Mighty Mother of us all,
> Bringer of all fruitfulness.
> By seed and root, by bud and stem,
> By leaf and flower and fruit,
> By life and love,
> Do I invoke Thee to descend upon
> Her who is here in Your Name.

Priestess: Draws the power of the moon into her.

Priest: Listen to the words of the Great Mother,
Who of old was called among men
Artemis, Astarte, Diana, Aphrodite, Cerridwen,
And by many other names.

Priestess: At my altars the youth of most distant ages
Gave love and made due sacrifice.
Once in the month, at the time of the full moon,
Gather and adore Me.
Lead My dance in greenwood shade,
By the light of the full moon.

In a place wild and lone,
Dance about My altar stone.
Work the holy mystery, ye who are fain to sorcery.
I will teach you the mystery of rebirth.
Work ye My mysteries in mirth!
No other law but love I know;
By naught but love may I be known.
All things living are Mine own;
From Me they come—to Me they go.

All: Raise hands to the moon and say:
Great Mother, Giver of all Life,
I invoke You into this blessed circle,
That Your Presence here
May fill me with joy and understanding.
Triple moon, Ever-Changing One,
I invoke and call upon Thee.

Stating the Purpose

For example:

Priest: The Coven of ________ is gathered tonight to celebrate the Full moon, to honor the Lady and the Lord, to bring fruition to the magicks we began at the new moon (Diana's Bow), and to perform such other work as any of us may bring to the circle. Welcome.

Magickal Work

The Priestess has polled the coven prior to the ritual to discover their needs. Now divination is performed if necessary. Then power is raised—for example, by chanting, dancing, or drumming—and is released toward its goal on the signal of the Priestess. Coveners then earth any excess energy into the ground.

Cakes and Wine

The Priestess holds the cakes while the Priest blesses them. He takes them from her and walks the circle with the cakes, saying:

Priest: Horned One! Horned One! God of forest, field and sun;
These our offerings, Lord, to Thee, Who givest Life to all we see.
Half a man and half a beast, come to us and share our feast.
Accept these cakes I offer Thee, God of all fertility.

He turns and offers the cakes to the High Priestess, who says:

Priestess: Lo, I receive the gifts Thou bringest Me—
Life, and more life, in fullest ecstasy.
I am the moon, the moon that draweth Thee.

I am the waiting Earth that needest Thee.
Come unto Me, Great God, come unto Me.

She returns the cakes to the altar and blesses the cup which the Priest holds out to Her. Holding up the wine, she says:

Priestess: Great Goddess! Holiest of the Holy,
Perpetual comfort of humankind,
Natural Mother of all things, Mistress of all the elements,
Great Lady, God Mother, accept this self I offer Thee.

She turns and offers the wine to the High Priest, who says:

Priest: O first-begotten love, come unto Me,
And let the worlds be formed of Me and Thee.
I receive the gifts Thou bringest Me—
Life, and more Life, in fullest ecstasy.

The cakes and wine are shared by all.

Farewell to the Goddess

Farewell to the God

Dismissing the Quarters

Opening the Circle

Feasting and Social Hour

(Ritual adapted from The Temple of the Pagan Way)

B-10

Sabbat Celebration Outline

Preparation

Preparation as usual, plus potluck tables, literature table (if an open sabbat), special decorations appropriate to the season.

Welcome Participants

Show them where to put coats and potluck dishes and where to change into robes. While they are waiting, introduce them around; if they are new, socialize, teach chants that will be used in the ritual. Meanwhile the Priestess and Priest are reviewing the ritual and preparing themselves in another room.

Activity

If appropriate, have a pre-ritual activity: making candles for an Imbolg ritual, decorating eggs for Ostara, erecting the maypole for Beltane, discussing Samhain traditions, etc.

When all are ready, call everyone to the circle. All sit for a moment in silent meditation before beginning the work.

Attunement

Asperging

Casting the Circle

Calling the Quarters

Inviting the God

By the Priest, in whatever form is appropriate to the season: Sun Child, Holly King, Winter King, Pan, Sun Lord. Oak King, Lugh, Harvest Lord, etc.

Inviting the Goddess

By the Priestess, in whatever form is appropriate: Sun Goddess, Brigid, Ostara, Maiden, Mother, Crone.

Welcome and Statement of Purpose

If an open ritual and not too large, go around the circle and let the participants introduce themselves. Otherwise, introduce only the presiding Priestess and Priest, and the sponsoring organization. Then say a little about the sabbat's meaning and the rest of the ritual.

Song or Chant

Choose one appropriate to the holiday: "The Holly and the Ivy" for Yule, "The Shepherd and the Lady" for Beltane, etc. This is for celebration, not to raise power.

Activity
Select one which will involve everyone. This could include decorating a tree for Yule, consecrating magickal candles for Imbolg, a egg hunt for Ostara, the maypole dance at Beltane, a Catherine Wheel at Litha, "sacrificing" the Sun God/corn dolly at Lughnassad, a squash roll at Mabon, or communing with departed spirits at Samhain. See Chapter 14, "The Sabbats," for additional ideas.

Song or Chant
Possibly with a circle dance.

Cakes and Wine
The Priest and Priestess bless them, and they are shared by all. The cakes can be special to the season: "Sun Cookies," roast corn, etc. If wine is used for the beverage, have a non-alcoholic alternative such as juice. If the group is large, have more than one chalice and platter circulating (A rule of thumb: have one chalice and platter for each twenty participants). Give people the choice of saluting with the chalice or pouring a libation if they don't wish to drink from a common chalice.

Song or Chant

Farewell to the God

Farewell to the Goddess

Dismissal of the Quarters
Either individually or with a single chant such as" "The Earth, the Water, the Fire, the Air, return, return, return, return . . . ."

Opening the Circle
Or, you may choose to expand the circle and leave it in place during feasting, allowing it to dissipate gradually. This is only done at sabbat celebrations, not at rituals where serious magick is performed.

Feasting and Social Hour
And possibly a bardic circle later.

Announcements
During the feasting: literature table, donations, clean-up volunteers, future events.

Clean-Up

B-11
Ritual of Parting for a Coven

Not every coven lives forever; there may come a time when it seems right or necessary to dissolve the coven so that the members may follow their life paths in different directions. If so, the coven's passing should be marked.

In advance of the ritual, the group should decide how the coven property (if any) should be disposed of. Many of the ritual tools, etc., used by the coven may actually be the personal property of the High Priestess and High Priest; if so, that simplifies matters. If the coven owns anything as a group, and you are a tax-exempt 501(c)(3) church, it must go to another tax-exempt organization—possibly a local coven you are friendly with, or a larger organization like the Covenant of the Goddess. Otherwise you can divide up the items, except for a few (like a coven banner?) which you may want to burn or bury as part of the ritual.

You must also decide what to do about the coven's name. In many traditions the name "goes with" the High Priestess, in case she decides to re-create the coven later on. She may choose to release the name to another coven elder, or you may all agree that none of you will use it again. Of course some other outside party may come up with the name independently, and there's nothing you can do about that unless you have the name legally registered as a trademark.

Now to the ritual. Prepare the ritual space, cleaning and setting up the altar. Any symbolic items to be burned or buried should be placed on it.

Attunement

Asperging

Casting the Circle

Calling the Quarters

Inviting the God
Call the god-aspect Who is most special to your coven (if you are very eclectic and have no single favorite, you may invoke a god of endings such as Shiva).

Inviting the Goddess
Then call the goddess-aspect Who was the coven's special protector (or a goddess of endings such as Kali or another Crone).

Stating the Purpose
For example:

> We gather tonight to say farewell to (name of coven). We do not say good-bye to our friends within the coven, whom we shall see again. We keep ever with us the memories, the growth, the learning and healing we have experienced here. We hold to our vows

as priestesses and priests of the Old Religion. We cherish and preserve our bonds of love and loyalty to the Goddess and the God. But the time has come that this coven, this unique group, should pass on, and so we are here to honor its life and its passing.

Sharing Circle

Be seated in a circle, and go round-robin so that each covener speaks in turn. Share what you have learned from the coven, and how you have changed and grown. Share memories of favorite rituals or other events, former members who have moved on, and good work the coven has done. Keep going around until no one has anything more to add.

Burning or Burial of the Token

If you have been indoors, move outside to a prepared place. Take the coven banner or other symbol of the group, and either burn it in a ritual fire, or bury it. Speak words such as these:

Burning: We consign this symbol of (name of coven) to the flames. Let its energy rise to the astral plane, and there be transformed, to manifest again in the proper time and place. Farewell (name of coven), and blessed be.

Burying: We place this symbol of (name of coven) in the womb of Mother Earth, there to rest and be transformed, and to nourish the fertile Earth so that a new entity shall sprout and grow in its season. Farewell (name of coven), and blessed be. (If you wish, plant a tree seedling at this time.)

Blessings

Return to the circle and be seated. Each person should meditate silently for a little while, then write a blessing or good wish for the future on a slip of parchment. When all are ready, each person reads their goals aloud, and places their paper in a cauldron in the center of the circle.

Raising Power

Then raise power by chanting, dancing, singing or drumming—and release it into the cauldron when it peaks. Light the papers and let the wishes ascend to the astral plane. Earth any excess energy into the ground.

Cakes and Wine

The ritual leaders bless the cakes and wine (or whatever substitutes you prefer), and say:

As we partake of these cakes and this wine, let it be a sign that what is above shall be made manifest below; that the blessings, hopes and dreams we have sent to the astral will return to us threefold. Now, for the last time as a coven, let us share the bounty of the Lady and the Lord together.

Farewell to the God and Goddess

When the time is right, begin the closing. Say farewell to the God and the Goddess in your own words. If they are the coven's special deities, add something like this:

> For all your blessings to us, we thank you. For your guidance, your protection, your love and power and wisdom, we thank you. Though this coven exists no longer, each of us carries You with us in our hearts as we walk our separate paths. Be with us always.

If you invoked deities of ending, you may say:

> Thank you for Your presence. Grant that this ending may be peaceful, and that the love and wisdom we have experienced may continue even though the coven is no more. Let the old depart, and make way for the seeds of the new growth to come. Blessed be.

Farewell to the Quarters

Dismiss the quarters starting in the North and moving widdershins (counterclockwise), saying:

> Guardians of the Watchtowers of the North, Powers of Earth, we thank Thee for your presence and power at all the rituals we have performed. Until we meet again, in a new place and time, we say: Hail and Farewell!

Opening the Circle

Open the circle with words such as these:

> This circle is open for the last time, but in our hearts, it is never broken. With sadness, but also with hope and faith, let us say: Merry meet, and merry part, and merry meet again!

Refreshments and Social Hour

B-12

Wiccaning or Child Blessing Ritual

Note: For simplicity's sake, the following ceremony is written as for a girl child. For a boy, it would be the same except for the pronouns. Note also that nowhere in the ritual is the child committed to the Wiccan path; it is a point of honor among Wiccan parents that their child be free to choose their spiritual path when they are of age.

All: Sit for a moment in meditation before beginning the work. If outdoors, feel the light of the sun or moon upon you. Consider the bright prospects and hopeful possibilities which lie before the child.

Attunement

Asperging

Casting the Circle

HPs: Bring forth the child. What shall she be named?

Parent(s): Her name shall be ________.

HPs: Daughter of ________ and ________, your name shall be ________. Blessed be.

HP: We are gathered here to welcome this child, ________, into our community and to ask the blessings of the Elemental Powers and the Goddess and God upon her. We shall also hear the pledges of those who would stand as god- and goddessparents to her, and we will plant a special tree in commemoration of the new life among us. Welcome.

Now the HP (Air and Fire) and the HPs (Water and Earth) bring the child to each of the quarters and ask their blessing, or four friends of the family may do so. They may say, for example:

> **AIR:** Guardians of the Watchtowers of the East, Powers of Air, I call upon Thee. Thou Who art the breezes, winds and zephyrs . . . and Who art also mind, intellect, and imagination . . . grace our circle with Your Presence. Grant this child, ________, a keen intellect, a vivid imagination, and that she may be inspired by the gods. Great Eagle of the Eastern Skies, I summon, stir, and call Thee up! (Breathe gently on the child, or brush a feather across her.)
>
> **FIRE:** Guardians of the Watchtowers of the South, Powers of Fire, I call upon Thee. Thou Who art the fiery rays of the sun, the dancing flames of the hearthfire, and the deep heat within the Earth's core . . . and Who art also energy, will, and passion . . . grace our circle with Your Presence. Grant this child, ________, a strong

will, high energy, and a passionate nature tempered by wisdom. Red Lion of the Southern Desert, I summon, stir, and call Thee up! (Present the child before a red candle.)

WATER: Guardians of the Watchtowers of the West, Powers of Water, I call upon Thee. Thou Who art the mountain streams, the mighty rivers, and the vast oceans . . . and Who art also feeling, emotion, and intuition . . . grace our circle with Your Presence. Grant that this child, ________, may love and be loved, and know her emotions, and have a powerful intuitive sense. Sweet Dolphin of the Western Seas, I summon, stir, and call Thee up! (Touch the child's forehead with pure water.)

EARTH: Guardians of the Watchtowers of the North, Powers of Earth, I call upon Thee. Thou Who art the towering mountains, the fertile plains, and the enduring bedrock . . . and Who art also our bodies and all things material . . . grace our circle with Your Presence this night. Grant this child, ________, a healthy body, long life, and prosperity in all things. Black Bear of the Northern Forest, I summon, stir, and call Thee up! (Touch the child's forehead with a bit of salt.)

HPs: Shall this child have a magickal name as well?

Parent(s): Yes. Her magickal name shall be ________, until she chooses another.

The High Priest invokes the God, saying:

Now do I call You to this our circle, Great Lord of all. I call You by Your many names and faces: the Green Man, the Horned One, the Clever Trickster, the Gentle Brother, the Passionate Lover, the Mighty Warrior, the Strong Defender, the Wise Sage. But as we meet to welcome and bless this child, I call You especially as the Good Father. Let Your spirit now descend on me and those of our circle!

Turns to the child, who is being held by a parent.

________, in the name of the Good Father I welcome you to this world. May He bless you, guide you, protect you, and grant you wisdom, love, and strength.

The High Priestess invokes the Goddess, saying:

Great Mother, Giver of all Life, I invoke You into this blessed circle. You are the Virgin Huntress, the Earth Mother, the Bringer of the Arts of Civilization, the Dear Sister, the Goddess of Love, the Amazon Warrior, the Wise Crone. But as we meet to welcome and bless this child, I call You especially as the Mother of All Things. Triple Moon, Ever-Changing One, I invoke and call upon Thee.

High Priestess turns to the child.

________, in the name of the Great Mother I welcome you to this world. May She bless you, guide you, protect you, and grant you wisdom, love, and strength.

HP: Are there those among us who will stand forth as god- or goddess-parents to this child?

God/dessparent(s): (Stepping forward.) I will.

HP: Do you promise in the names of the Lord and Lady, and by the Powers of the Elements, that you will ever stand as a friend, protector, and advisor to ________, and even as parent should the need arise?

God/dessparent(s): I do so promise. (Each kisses the child.)

HP: So mote it be.

(The next part is optional. If the weather is good and the moon is in the right phase and sign, the entire ceremony can be held at the place where the tree will be planted. Otherwise, this part can be postponed until good weather or the appropriate time.)

HPs: Now it is time to plant a special tree for ________, as was the custom of our ancestors. May this tree stand a symbol of ________'s connection to the world of nature; in years to come, may she visit it often, and find in it a true friend and companion. Lady and Lord, bless this young tree as you bless this child. (Parents plant tree. They may, if they wish, place the baby's umbilical cord beneath it. Others water it and place small charms, amulets, and talismans on its branches, representing their good wishes for the child.)

HP: If any have gifts for ________, bring them forth! (Gifts are opened. Following this, toasts to the child and parents are offered.)

Farewells to the Goddess and the God

HPs and HP (or other Quarter-callers) dismiss the quarters starting in the North and moving widdershins, saying:

Guardians of the Watchtowers of the North, Powers of Earth, we thank Thee for attending, and for your blessings on this child. If go ye must, we say: Hail and Farewell!

All (echo): Hail and Farewell!

Opening the Circle

Feasting and Social Hour

Parts adapted from the Wiccaning ritual in *Eight Sabbats for Witches* by Janet and Stewart Farrar; and from *Rites of Passage: The Pagan Wheel of Life*, by Dan and Pauline Campanelli.

B-13

Ritual of Womanhood

This can be offered by a young woman's female family and friends when she reaches puberty, or adapted for the time when she is ready to leave home, or anytime in between. Though the ritual is all female, male relatives and friends can be invited for the celebration and feasting afterward.

Preparation of the State

The altar should be decorated in red (for moon blood) and white (for purity), and decorated with fresh flowers and herbs. On it the young woman should place tokens or symbols of her life goals, and the women present should place gifts. In particular, one of the gifts should be a piece of jewelry with a red stone (red jasper, garnet, ruby) to symbolize her moon cycles, and one should be jewelry or an altar piece representing the chosen goddess-aspect Who will be invoked during the ritual.

Preparation of the Young Woman

She should take a ritual bath, by candlelight or moonlight, with soft music playing. If indoors, the water should be scented with fragrant herbs and oils. If outdoors, she may bathe in a pool, hot spring, lake, stream or the sea. When she is ready, she should be escorted from the water, dried with soft towels, and robed in red and white.

Attunement

After she is brought to the ritual site, all hold hands and sing Goddess chants softly for a while.

Asperging

The site is swept with a broom, and participants cleansed with salt water and incense.

Casting the Circle

One of the women casts the circle using a wooden staff entwined with flowers (they can be real or silk), saying:

> I conjure thee, O Circle of power, to be a boundary between the world of humanity and the realms of the Goddess, a guardian and a protection for the women within, and a vessel to contain the power we shall raise within. Wherefore, by Her many Names do I bless and consecrate thee.

Calling the Quarters

Now have four women call the quarters, if possible. Ideally, have a young woman call the East as Maiden; another young woman call the South as Warrior; a mature woman call the West as Mother; and an older woman call the North as Crone. Draw the appropriate invoking pentagrams with appropriate tools or symbols: a flower for East, an athame, sword or labrys for South; a wand, cornucopia or large seashell for West; and a cauldron or staff for North.

> **EAST:** I am the Maiden, and I face the dawn to call the Guardians of Air, asking the gifts of intelligence, imagination, and inspiration for our sister (name)!
>
> **SOUTH:** I am the Warrior, and I stand beneath the noonday sun to call the Guardians of Fire, asking the gifts of energy, will, and passion for our sister (name)!
>
> **WEST:** I am the Mother, and I face the sunset to call the Guardians of Water, asking the gifts of love and empathy for our sister (name).
>
> **NORTH:** I am the Crone, and I face the night to call the Guardians of Earth, asking the gifts of health, strength, and prosperity for our sister (name)!

Invocation of the Goddess

Then invoke the goddess-aspect Who is to be the young woman's special guide and protector. If she were to choose Artemis, for example, you might say:

> Artemis, Maiden Huntress, Silver Crescent, Forest Guardian, Wild Woman! Let Your wisdom, Your love and Your power fill (name) as she begins her life as a woman! Teach her the magick of the Moon and to speak with Your wild creatures. Run with (name) as she hunts her dreams, and share with her Your strength and freedom!

Statement of Purpose

State the purpose of the ritual, for example:

> We gather tonight to celebrate (name), whose Moon cycles have begun, and who now begins the journey from girlhood to womanhood. Let all the company of women welcome her, love her, help her and guide her.

Chant

Choose an appropriate Goddess chant or women's chant.

Circle of Women

A bright red ribbon is tied loosely around the young woman's wrist, and then the wrist of the woman to her left, and so on around the circle. The Crone says:

> As women we are linked together always; welcome to this circle of women.

The ribbons are cut, but left on each woman's wrist. Then the circle is expanded, so that participants are several yards apart (or in different rooms), and the young woman goes in turn to each of the other women. In turn they share with her their experience of womanhood, and answer questions. Each woman can speak generally to this theme, or one woman can speak of love, another of sex, another of children, another of career, another of identity, another of spirituality, and so on. Each woman should have her prepared comments written out, so they can be given to the young woman at the end of the ritual. When each has shared her wisdom, the circle contracts again.

Self-Blessing

Bring forth a silver chalice, filled half and half with red wine and water. The young woman dips her fingers within and performs the Self-blessing Rite described in the New Moon/Diana's Bow Esbat ritual.

Song

Favorite song of the young woman's choice, sung live or taped.

The Statement of Goals

One of the women says:

> You are a young woman now, and before very long will be a full adult, responsible for your own choices as you make your way in the world. Who will you choose to be—a healer, a priestess, a mother, a pilot, a scientist, a secretary, a computer programmer, a forester . . . ? All doors are open to you, all things are possible. You can be anything and anyone you choose. Please, share with us now your goals and dreams.

The young woman now speaks. She can talk about specific career goals, lifestyle wishes, or more general comments about the kind of woman she wants to be. She should show the tokens she placed on the altar and explain what each symbolizes. When she is done, one of the women may say:

> Now visualize, in great clarity and detail, yourself accomplishing those goals. Allow yourself to feel the satisfaction, strength and self-confidence you will feel as you achieve them. As you do so, touch your Third Eye. And in the years to come, whenever you touch that place again, the energy and joy will return to help you move on toward your goals.

The rest of the group should encourage her with applause and expressions of support.

Raising Power

The circle may raise power to share with the young woman, and charge the tokens and gifts, in any way they wish: dancing, singing, chanting, drumming, etc. Make sure that excess energy is earthed after the power is channeled.

Divination

Here the Crone (or woman most adept at divination) does a reading with the young woman, regarding the path she will take in life. Though challenges should not be ignored or minimized, the emphasis should be on the positive, including the young woman's strengths, resources, and network of support.

Cakes and Wine

Red wine and moon cakes are shared around the circle, with each woman offering a blessing to the woman on her left. Then the two key gifts are given to the young woman, and their significance explained.

The Planting

If you want to perform a symbolic act such as planting a tree seedling (choose a variety which has the energies desired for the young woman), you may do so at this time, or after the circle is opened.

Thanks to the Goddess

Say thank you to the Goddess in your own words, and ask that She guide and protect the young woman all her life.

Dismissing the Quarters

Dismiss the quarters starting in the North and moving widdershins (counter-clockwise), saying for example:

> Guardians of the Watchtowers of the North, Powers of Earth, we thank Thee for attending, and for your gifts of strength, health, and prosperity to (name). If go ye must, we say: Hail and Farewell!

Others (echo): Hail and Farewell!

Opening the Circle

Open the circle, saying:

> This circle of women is open but never broken. Merry meet, and merry part, and merry meet again!

Celebration and Feasting

Socialize, present more gifts, feast, or sing as you wish. At this point male family and friends may be invited to join the celebration.

B-14

Ritual of Manhood

This can be offered by a young man's male family and friends when he reaches puberty, or adapted for the time when he is ready to leave home, or anytime in between. Though the ritual is all male, female relatives and friends can be invited for the celebration and feasting afterward.

Preparation of the Space

The altar should be decorated in green and brown, and decorated with stag horns and greenery. On it the young man should place tokens or symbols of his life goals, and the men present should place gifts. In particular, one of the gifts should be a piece of jewelry of bronze, steel, iron or gold, perhaps with horn or bone, to symbolize either the Horned God or an animal ally, and one should be jewelry or an altar piece representing the chosen god-aspect Who will be invoked during the ritual.

Preparation of the Young Man

He should take a ritual bath, by candlelight or sunlight, with stirring music playing. If indoors, the water should be scented with herbs and oils. If outdoors, he may bathe in a pool, hot spring, lake, stream or the sea. When he is ready, he should be escorted from the water, dried with soft towels, and robed in green and brown.

Attunement

After he is brought to the ritual site, all hold hands and sing God chants or drum together.

Asperging

Casting the Circle

One of the men casts the circle using a wooden staff entwined with leaves (they can be real or silk), or sword or athame, saying:

> I conjure thee, O Circle of power, to be a boundary between the world of humanity and the realms of the Gods, a guardian and a protection for the men within, and a ring of fire to contain the power we shall raise here. Wherefore, by His many Names do I bless and consecrate thee.

Calling the Quarters

Now have four men call the quarters, if possible. Ideally, have a young man call the East as Youth; another young man call the South as Warrior; a mature man call the West as Father; and an older man call the North as Sage. Draw the appropriate invoking pentagrams with appropriate tools or symbols: a feather or athame for East, a wand or torch for South; a trident or large seashell for West; and a stone or shield for North.

EAST: I am the Young Hero, and I face the dawn to call the Guardians of Air, asking the gifts of intelligence, imagination, and inspiration for our brother (name)!

SOUTH: I am the Warrior, and I stand beneath the noonday sun to call the Guardians of Fire, asking the gifts of energy, will, and passion for our brother (name)!

WEST: I am the Father, and I face the sunset to call the Guardians of Water, asking the gifts of love and empathy for our brother (name).

NORTH: I am the Sage, and I face the night to call the Guardians of Earth, asking the gifts of health, strength, and prosperity for our brother (name)!

Invocation of the God

Then invoke the god-aspect Who is to be the young man's special guide and protector. If he were to choose Cernunnos, for example, you might say:

> Cernunnos, Horned Hunter, Holder of the Bronze Torc, Forest Guardian, Wild Man! Let Your wisdom, Your love and Your power fill (name) as he begins his life as a man! Teach him the magick of the woods and to speak with Your wild creatures. Run with (name) as he hunts his dreams and share with him Your strength and freedom!

Statement of Purpose

State the purpose of the ritual, for example:

> We gather tonight to celebrate (name), who now begins the journey from boyhood to manhood. Let all the company of men welcome him, love him, help him and guide him.

Chant

Choose an appropriate God chant or men's chant.

Circle of Men

A leather thong is tied loosely around the young man's wrist, and then the wrist of the man to his left, and so on around the circle. The Sage says:

> As men we are linked together always; welcome to this circle of men.

The thongs are cut, but left on each man's wrist. Then the circle is expanded, so that participants are several yards apart (or in different rooms), and the young man goes in turn to each of the other men. In turn they share with him their experience of manhood, and answer questions. Each man can speak generally to this theme, or one man can speak of love, another of sex, another of children, another of career, another of identity, another of spirituality, and so on. Each man should have his prepared comments written out, so they can be given to the young man at the end of the ritual. When each has shared his wisdom, the circle contracts again.

Self-Blessing

Bring forth a silver chalice, filled half and half with white wine and water. The young man dips his fingers within and performs the Self-blessing Rite described in the New Moon/Diana's Bow Esbat ritual (Appendix B-8, page 445).

Song

Favorite song of the young man's choice, sung live or taped.

The Statement of Goals

One of the men says:

> You are a young man now, and before very long will be a full adult, responsible for your own choices as you make your way in the world. Who will you choose to be—a healer, a priest, a father, a pilot, a scientist, a secretary, a computer programmer, a forester . . . ? All doors are open to you, all things are possible. You can be anything and anyone you choose. Please, share with us now your goals and dreams.

The young man now speaks. He can talk about specific career goals, lifestyle wishes, or more general comments about the kind of man he wants to be. He should show the tokens he placed on the altar and explain what each symbolizes. When he is done, one of the men may say:

> Now visualize, in great clarity and detail, yourself accomplishing those goals. Allow yourself to feel the satisfaction, strength and self-confidence you will feel as you achieve them. As you do so, touch your Third Eye. And in the years to come, whenever you touch that place again, the energy and joy will return to help you move on toward your goals.

The rest of the group should encourage him with applause and expressions of support.

Raising Power

The circle may raise power to share with the young man, and charge the tokens and gifts, in any way they wish: dancing, singing, chanting, drumming, etc. Make sure that excess energy is earthed after the power is channeled.

Divination

Here the Sage (or man most adept at divination) does a reading with the young man, regarding the path he will take in life. Though challenges should not be ignored or minimized, the emphasis should be on the positive, including the young man's strengths, resources, and network of support.

Cakes and Wine

White wine and cakes are shared around the circle, with each man offering a blessing to the man on his left. Then the two key gifts are given to the young man, and their significance explained.

The Planting

If you want to perform a symbolic act such as planting a tree seedling (choose a variety which has the energies desired for the young man), you may do so at this time, or after the circle is opened.

Thanks to the God

Say thank you to the God in your own words, and ask that He guide and protect the young man all his life.

Farewell to the Quarters

Dismiss the quarters starting in the North and moving widdershins (counterclockwise), saying for example:

> **Guardians of the Watchtowers of the North, Powers of Earth, we thank Thee for attending, and for your gifts of strength, health, and prosperity to (name). If go ye must, we say: Hail and Farewell!**

Others (echo): **Hail and Farewell!**

Opening the Circle

Celebration and Feasting

Socialize, present more gifts, feast, or sing as you wish. At this point female family and friends may be invited to join the celebration.

B-15

A Handfasting Ritual

Handfasting is the Wiccan equivalent of marriage, with one important difference. By tradition handfasting may be for a year and a day, or for life. The couple who choose the year and a day may, at the end of that time, either make a commitment for life or go their separate ways in peace. (If they were handfasted in a legally binding ceremony, they will need a legal divorce should they part.) Note that Wiccan priest/esses may officiate over a legal marriage ceremony just as well as the clergy of other faiths, but some local or state jurisdictions may require them to register as clergy prior to the event. Check with your county clerk for the requirements in your area.

Preparation

The altar is set up, the circle decorated, and the guests seated. The couple wait at a distance with their escorts, on opposite sides of the circle but within sight of each other.

Welcome

(Ring chimes.)

HP: Dear friends—welcome! Out of affection for ________ and ________ we have gathered together to witness and bless their vows which will unite them in marriage. To this moment they bring their loving hearts, the dreams which inspire their lives, and two unique personalities and spirits. We have been asked as a community of loving friends to share their joy with them, and to pledge ourselves to support and honor their love. No matter how strong their love for each other, they will need our support. I ask each of you present today to do all in your power to sustain and encourage ________ and ________ in their commitment to each other. We rejoice with them for this union of hearts, a union created by friendship, respect, and love.

HPs: ________ and ________ have chosen each other as partners and lovers, and the choice seems obvious and right to those who know them both. It is clear that they share so much: love and laughter, passion and curiosity, a sense of adventure and play, and their deep commitment to the same spiritual path. Their love, like any love between committed and responsible adults, is a reflection of that infinite, divine love which embraces us all. They have chosen to name their love and to honor it. Your support and sharing of their love, and their life together, will make their journey together fuller and richer. For this, they and we thank you.

Get Acquainted

HP: We are a community who share the bond of loving ________ and ________. But they have an advantage on us. They know all of us, but since we have been drawn from different parts of ________'s life and ________'s life, we don't all know one another. We want you to have a chance to get to know one another a little better. So I will ask you to mingle for a couple of minutes, and introduce yourselves to someone you don't know, by saying how you know ________ or ________.

(Pause for a few minutes, then ring chimes.) We hope that was a good start and that your conversations can continue at the reception.

Attunement

HPs or Bard: Let us join in song:

Weave, weave, weave me the sunshine, out of the falling rain;
Weave me the hope of a new tomorrow and fill my cup again.

Asperging

Casting the Circle

Calling the Quarters

Inviting the God

The High Priest invokes the god-aspect most special to the couple.

Inviting the Goddess

The High Priestess invokes the goddess-aspect most special to the couple.

Processional

(Continuous chimes) The couple are escorted by two chosen friends, from opposite directions. They meet before the altar.

Reading

Written or selected by the couple, to express their feeling about loving relationships and what they mean.

Songs

Dedicated to each other by the couple. They may be taped or sung live if you have talented voices.

Lighting of the Candles

During the songs, lighting of three candles: each lights their own candle, and from these they light a central candle representing their relationship.

Stories and Blessings by Congregants

The High Priest invites the congregants to step forward one at a time to share stories about ________ and ________, wishes for their future together, or blessings. It is wise to prepare a few volunteers beforehand, so they can get the ball rolling.

The Charge of the Goddess

(chimes)

HP: Now we would like to share with all of you some words which are very important to our faith. This is called 'The Charge of the Goddess.' (Pause, lift arms to congregation.) Listen to the words of the Great Mother . . . .' (Make sure you include the name of the goddess invoked at the beginning of the ritual.) And so on, with the High Priestess speaking as the Great Mother and the Star Goddess.

The Charge to the Witness

HP: To all of you who are here to witness this ceremony: You have shown your love and support for ________ and for ________ as individuals. I charge you now to love them also as a couple, to honor and support their marriage, to rejoice with them in their successes and to help them through times of hardship. I know they will do the same for you, and together we create a loving community.

The Charges to the Couple

These should be personalized statements of wisdom and counsel from both the High Priestess and High Priest.

The Vows

HP: Trials will come, and tests, for there is much in this world that would long to pull you apart. Do you bring strength and vision to your relationship, courage and understanding?

Response: I do (in unison).

HPs: Joys will come, graces and blessings will warm your souls and give you wonder. Do you bring thanksgiving and rejoicing to this relationship, laughter and abandon?

Response: I do (in unison).

PRIEST: Do you, ________, take ________ to be your beloved partner, to love, honor and cherish?

Response: I do.

HP: Do you, ________, take ________ to be your beloved partner, to love, honor and cherish?

Response: I do.

HP: You may now speak your vows.

Each of the couple now speaks the vows they have written, together or individually.

Promise to Children (if any)

Here the new stepparent makes appropriate promises to the children their partner brings to the marriage, then adds:

Please accept this as a token of my love and respect for you.

(The stepparent then hands the child or children appropriate tokens—perhaps pendants.)

Exchange of Rings

A Child or Friend brings forth the rings on a wand and gives them to the High Priest. He blesses the rings and gives them to the couple, who place them on each other's fingers.

________, then ________: In the name of the Goddess; Maiden, Mother and Crone; and in the name of the God, with this ring, I thee wed.

The Handfasting

A Friend brings the ribbon. The couple clasp hands.

HPs: With this ribbon I will join ________'s hand with ________'s, as a symbol of the joining of their lives. This is the actual act of handfasting. She entwines the ribbon around the couple's joined hands.

By the powers of Earth and Air, Fire and Water, may your lives ever be joined together in love. (Traditionally the couple stays bound by the ribbon until the handfasting has been consummated.)

Jumping the Broom

A Friend brings the broom.

HPs: Jumping the broom is a very ancient custom. The broom, or besom as it once was called, symbolizes the creation of a hearth and home together (She places the broom on the earth and invites the couple to jump over it, then leads applause.)

Pronouncement

(Chimes.)

HPs: ________ and ________, in the presence of this company and of the Goddess and the God, you have spoken the vows and performed the rites which unite your lives. Therefore do we pronounce you joined together as partners in life, love and the spirit. (Pause) **May**

your lives together be as sweet as this honey, a gift of the Goddess. (Place a little honey on the couple's lips. They kiss, then offer each other the chalice.)

Affirmation by the Community

HP: ________ and ________, you have proclaimed your commitment in this sacred circle before your community of family and friends. I now invite everyone to join me in the confirmation of this marriage.

HP (To congregation): Please repeat after me:

In the presence of this good company (pause)
By the power of your love (pause)
You have exchanged vows of commitment (pause)
And we recognize, honor, and celebrate your marriage. (pause)

Blessing

HP: To (God's Name), we thank You for Your presence, and invite You to stay for the celebration. To ________ and ________,

May your lives together be joyful and content,
And may your love be bright as the stars,
Warm as the sun, accepting as the ocean,
And enduring as the mountains.

Benediction

HPs: To (Goddess' Name), we thank You for Your presence, and invite You to feast with us. We come now to the close of this event, and for ________ and ________, the beginning of a new life together. We offer to them and to each of you, this blessing:

By the earth that is Her body,
By the air that is Her breath,
By the fire that is Her bright spirit,
By the living waters of Her womb,
The circle is open, but unbroken.
The peace of the Goddess and the God go in our hearts.
Merry meet, and merry part, and merry meet again.
Blessed be!

Recessional

Rose petals are tossed on the couple as they leave the altar, and music plays.

Reception

Music, toasts, cutting the wedding cake, and so on.

Signing of the License

At this point the High Priest and High Priestess may sign the necessary documents and have them witnessed, to make the marriage legal.

B-16

Ritual of Handparting

If a married or handfasted couple decides they must part ways, much more than a ritual is required. There are legal procedures involved (if it was a state-recognized marriage), possibly child custody issues, the division of property, and emotional stresses which may require counseling. These issues are beyond the scope of this book. Here we offer only a ritual which might be the culmination of all these other processes. It is assumed here that both parties are willing and able to participate in the ritual. If not, it can be performed with only one of the former couple present, with perhaps a photograph on the altar to "stand in" for the other party.

Preparation

As usual. Any symbolic items to be released or destroyed should be placed on the altar: for example, a wedding ring and photo (or any picture of the couple together).

Attunement

Asperging

Casting the Circle

Calling the Quarters

Invoking the God

Invoke a god of endings such as Shiva or Osiris; a god of healing like Apollo; or a loving god such as the Dagda, depending on your needs.

Invoking the Goddesses

Invoke a goddess of endings such as Kali or another Crone; or a goddess of healing such as Brigid; or a goddess of compassion such as Kwan-Yin, depending on your needs.

Stating the Purpose

For example:

> We gather tonight to recognize the handparting of (name) and (name). We trust that they will keep the memories, the growth, learning and healing they have experienced during their marriage (partnership). We hope that they may be able to keep a bond of friendship, understanding and compassion between them. But the time has come that they must travel different paths, and so we are here to honor their decision.

Sharing Circle

Be seated in a circle, and allow each former partner to speak. They should share what they have learned from the marriage, and how they have changed and grown. Share memories of favorite events, of their children if any, and their achievements during their time together. Keep going back and forth until neither has anything more to add. (It may be useful to have a facilitator for this part of the ritual.)

Burning or Burial of the Token

If you have been indoors, move outside to a prepared place. Take the photo of the couple, cut it in half, and either burn it in a ritual fire, or bury it. If you wish, bury the wedding rings. Speak words such as these:

> **Burning:** We consign this photograph of (names) to the flames. Let its energy rise to the astral plane, and there be transformed, to manifest again in the proper time and place. Farewell, and blessed be.
>
> **Burying:** We place this symbol of (names) in the womb of Mother Earth, there to rest and be transformed, and to nourish the fertile Earth so that something new shall sprout and grow in its season. Farewell, and blessed be.

Plans for the Future

Let each former partner now tell something of their plans for the future; the friends within the circle should feel free to offer help, support or encouragement.

Cakes, Wine, and Blessings

Each former partner should meditate silently for a little while, and as the cakes and wine are shared, speak aloud a blessing or good wish for the future for the other.

Farewell to the Goddess

Farewell to the God

Farewell to the Quarters

Opening the Circle

Open the circle with words such as these:

> This circle is open. The marriage is ended, may you each go forth in peace and freedom to create new lives with the love and support of your friends. With sadness, but also with hope and faith, I say: Merry did you meet, now must you part; and when you meet again may it be with healed hearts, and as friends. So mote it be.

Refreshments and Social Hour

If desired.

B-17

Ritual of Croning or Sagehood

NOTE: For simplicity, this is written as a Croning ritual; however, a few changes in language will make it suitable for Sagehood instead. Only the individual involved can choose the appropriate time for such a rite of passage. For some, it may be when children leave home, for others the arrival of menopause; some may choose the second Saturn Return (fifty-sixth birthday); and others, when it "feels right."

Preparation

Invite your friends well in advance; make sure they know to bring your favorite foods and beverages for the potluck. If you are shy about asking this, have an extroverted friend make the calls.

Prepare the ritual space, cleaning and setting up the altar. If possible, include a chart of your family tree and photographs of elders in your family near the center of the altar. You can also put photographs of crones or sages you admire, whether or not they are related to you. On the left side, add mementos of the major events and achievements in your life so far. On the right, put pictures and written descriptions of things you hope to do in the years to come. The pictures can be drawn or cut out of magazines.

Before your friends and covenmates arrive, take a luxurious bubble bath by candlelight, playing soft music.

Attunement

Have everyone sit quietly and center. Hold hands in a circle and chant your favorite chant, or sing your favorite song.

Asperging

Casting the Circle

Calling the Quarters

If you have four friends present, each may call one. Draw the appropriate invoking pentagrams with your athames and say, for example:

> **EAST:** I call the Guardians of Air, to thank you for your gifts of intelligence, imagination and inspiration to (name), as she approaches the honored state of cronehood!
>
> **SOUTH:** We call the Guardians of Fire, to thank you for your gifts of energy, will and passion to (name), as she approaches the honored state of cronehood!
>
> **WEST:** We call the Guardians of Water, to thank you for your gifts of love and empathy to (name), as she approaches the honored state of cronehood!

> **NORTH:** We call the Guardians of Earth, to thank you for your gifts of health, strength and prosperity to (name), as she approaches the honored state of cronehood!

Inviting the God

This may be a favorite aspect with Whom you have worked in the past, or one you would like to guide and bless you in your cronehood. If you wish to call a Sage-god, you might choose from among these: Dagda, Odin, Thoth, Temu or Atum-Ra, Sin, Cronus, Janus, Saturn, or Merlin.

Inviting the Goddess

Again, this may be a favorite aspect with Whom you have worked in the past, or one you would like to guide and bless you in your cronehood. If you want to invoke a Crone-goddess, consider the following possibilities: Rhea Kronia, Cerridwen, Macha, Hecate, Ereshkigal, Morgan, Minerva, Nuit, Neith, Athena, Persephone, Asase Yaa, Metis, or Sophia.

Stating the Purpose

Have a priestess from the coven, or the HPs state the purpose:

> **We gather tonight to celebrate a transition, as our beloved (name) accepts the mantle of cronehood. During the stage of her life which now passes, she has given her friends and family much that is rich and wonderful. In her new life as a crone, she has much more to share with us, and we with her.**

A Personal Bardic Sharing

The group is seated. Now the new crone tells the story of her life up to this point, illustrating highlights with the photographs and mementos on the left side of the altar. She may wish to pass them around the circle. Her friends and family may ask questions. When she is done, chalices should be filled and toasts made to the important people and events of her past.

Song

Here the group may sing one of the crone's favorite songs, or all may listen to it on tape or disc.

Dreams of the Future

Now the crone shares the items on the right side of the altar, telling about her plans, dreams, and wishes for the years ahead. These might include career goals in her present job, a new career, travel, creative projects, leadership positions, classes she wants to take or teach, home remodeling, recreation plans, etc. The group should ask questions, share their enthusiasm, and offer resources to help. When she is done, chalices should be filled and toasts made to her dreams.

Planting a Seed

If she wants to perform a symbolic act such as planting a seed (choose an herb, flower or tree which has the energies you want), then she can do so now. Then raise power—for example, by chanting, dancing or drumming—and release it toward the pot or seedling when it peaks. Earth any excess energy into the ground.

Divination

If the new crone desires, a friend or family member may explore the energies for her future with tarot, pendulum, runestones, scrying, etc. You may want to ask such questions as:

> What are the energies surrounding this plan (project, new career, etc.)?
>
> Which card has the most to teach me right now?
>
> What qualities should I cultivate in myself in the years ahead?

Self-Blessing

Bring forth a silver chalice, filled half and half with white wine and water. The crone dips her fingers within and performs the Self-blessing Rite described in the New Moon/Diana's Bow Esbat ritual.

Tribute and Gifts

Here the group should be seated again. Going around the circle, each person speaks their admiration and respect of the new crone, and presents a gift.

Farewell to the Goddess

Farewell to the God

Dismissing the Quarters

Chant:

> The Earth, the Water, the Fire, the Air, return, return, return, return . . . .

Opening the Circle

Feasting and Social Hour

Enjoy a feast of the crone's favorite foods and beverages.

B-18

Passing Over or Requiem

Attunement

Softly chant:

> We all come from the Goddess, and to Her we shall return,
> Like a drop of rain, flowing to the ocean.

Asperging

Casting

Calling the Quarters

Inviting the God

The High Priest says:

> Now do I call You to this our circle, Great God. I call You as Lord of the Harvest, Lord of Death, Holder of the Keys, Lord of the Underworld; and I call you as the Comforter and Consoler, the Compassionate One Who leads us all to the Cauldron from which we are reborn. Give welcome now to ________, who comes to you in honor and humility to visit Your other lands for a while.

Inviting the Goddess

Then the High Priest kneels in the West and calls upon the Goddess:

> I invoke and call upon Thee,
> O Mighty Mother of us all.
> By seed and root, by bud and stem,
> By leaf and flower and fruit,
> By life and love,
> Do I invoke Thee to join
> Those gathered here in Your Name.

HPs: I call upon the Lady as Crone, She Who harvests all that lives, Who has taken ________ by the hand and led (him) into the Summerland, there to rest and reflect and joy in the company of the Goddess and the God until it is time for (him) to be born again to the circle. For She is also the Mother of all things and the Lady of rebirth, and She shall surely grant ________ the gift of life again when the Wheel has turned.

Stating the Purpose

HP: We are gathered to celebrate the life of our friend ________ and to say farewell until we meet in the Summerland or in another life. Some of you have expressed your desire to share a story about ________, or just to give your thanks for having known him/her. ________, would you like to begin?

Sharing Our Stories

Family and friends come forward one at a time to share memories and gratitude.

HP: Let us think on these things and on the good times we have shared with ________, in silence for a moment. (Musical interlude.)

Gifts and Memorials

HPs: I know that some of us have gifts we would like to send with ________ on the journey to Summerland, or memorials we would like to make. I'll begin by offering this....

Family and friends come forward and offer gifts or memorials. If the body is to be interred, these might include items of sentimental or symbolic value to be placed in the grave. Memorial gifts might include contributions to the deceased's favorite charities, or trees planted in his/her name, sponsorship of children or endangered animals, and the like. The family may wish to offer suggestions well in advance of the ritual.

Interment or Scattering of Ashes

HPs: ________'s body was the gift of Mother Earth, and now it is time to return that body to the Earth, as part of the eternal cycle.

Here the body is interred or the ashes scattered if there has been a cremation. If on private land,† the High Priestess may wish to say a few words explaining why this place was special to the deceased.

Planting the Seeds

HP: All die, but in the fullness of time all are reborn. As a sign of that rebirth, we plant these seeds. They will rest quietly in the earth for a time, as ________ rests in Summerland. But then, as they sprout and blossom, let us be reminded that one day our beloved ________ will return—in a new form, but with the same beauty and strength of spirit. Like the self-sowing perennial, our bodies are not everlasting; but our spirits, the very core of our being, are; and like the perennial, we shall return again and again.

Here the High Priest plants some seeds (or explains where they will be planted), preferably of evergreen or perennial plants or flowers.

The Charge of the Goddess

Thanks to Allies

The High Priest says a special thank you to the familiar, spirit guide, animal totem, patron or matron god/dess aspect, and other creatures and spirits associated with the deceased.

†Check local ordinances for legal requirements and restrictions for interment on private land.

The Mystery

HPs: All creatures die, but first they live and love. To fulfill love, one must meet, and remember, and love again. But in order to meet again, one must be born. Before one can be born, there must be love. And that is all the mystery. May ________ be born again to the circle.

Farewell to the God

HP: Lord, thank you for the life and joy you have shared with our friend. Let (him) find reunion with those who have gone before, and walk with ________ in the Summerland until it is time for (him) to return to this world.

Farewell to the Goddess

HPs: Lady, thank you for the presence of ________ in our lives. Hold (him) close to you, love (him), heal (him), and walk with (him) in the Summerland until it is time for (him) to be born again.

Dismissing the Quarters

Say, for example:

> Guardian of the Watchtowers of the North, Spirit of Earth, guide and protect the spirit of ________ as they journey to the Summerland. Hail and farewell!

Opening the Circle

The High Priestess opens the circle. Upon returning to the East, she replaces the sword or athame on the altar and says:

> The circle is open but never broken. To one another and especially to ________, we say: "Merry did we meet, and merry did we part, and merry shall we meet again!

Toasts and Refreshments

If there are toasts, a glass should be filled for the deceased and placed on the altar. Later the wine can be returned to the Earth as a libation.

Glossary

Following are some important terms related to Wicca. Different traditions might emphasize different terms, but the following would probably be on most lists:

Air—In many Wiccan traditions, the element corresponding to the East, the color light blue, mind, intellect, and imagination.

Altar—A flat surface holding ritual tools and symbols. In many magickal traditions, it is placed in the East; others prefer it in the North or Center.

Amulet—A natural object worn or carried for its protective powers; e.g., a seashell, stone, seed, or animal claw.

Animism—The belief that natural objects, and Nature itself, are alive and conscious; or the belief that an immaterial force animates the universe. Many Witches are comfortable with this theory.

Ardaynes—See "Laws of Witchcraft."

Aspect—A form, facet, or persona of Deity. A manifestation of the Goddess or the God having its own name, appearance, qualities, attributes, and mythology. For example, Persephone, Kore and Artemis are maiden aspects of The Goddess. Helios, Ra and Apollo are solar aspects of The God.

Asperger—A ritual tool used to sprinkle water for purification purposes. It can be a crafted artifact or something as simple as a pinecone or a twig with leaves or needles.

Athame—A black-handled, double-edged, knifelike tool used by Witches to channel energy, but never to cut anything material. It may be marked with the owner's name and other symbols, and may symbolize Fire or Air depending on the owner's tradition.

Attunement—An activity which brings the minds, emotions, and psyches of a group into harmony prior to ritual: chanting, singing, guided meditation, and breathing exercises are common ways to attune.

Aura—The energy field of the human body, and especially that radiant portion visible to the "third eye" or psychic vision. The aura can reveal information about an individual's health and emotional state.

Bell—In some traditions, a bell is rung to "alert the quarters" prior to invoking the elemental powers. It is usually a small hand bell.

Besom—The old name for a broom. In medieval days a Witch might disguise her staff as a broom to escape persecution. Some Witches use a broom to sweep and symbolically cleanse the area where the circle is to be cast.

Blessed Be—An all-purpose greeting, response and farewell among Witches. It reminds us that everything and everyone is sacred.

Bolline—A white-handled Witch's knife used to carve or cut materials necessary for ritual or healing. Sometimes a bolline used to harvest herbs will have a small, silver, sickle-shaped blade.

Book of Shadows—A personal journal in which Witches keep their notes on ritual and magick, and perhaps records of dreams, herbal recipes, class notes, and so forth. Also, the guidelines, beliefs and common rituals of a given coven or tradition. Thus there is a distinction between, say, "Samantha's Book of Shadows" and "the Gardnerian Book of Shadows." Today, frequently a "Disk of Shadows."

Burning Times—The period of European history roughly between 1200 and 1700 C.E., during which the Church of Rome launched the Inquisition, an organized campaign of extermination against Jews, heretics, Pagans, and homosexuals. The most conservative estimate is that 90,000 may have been killed; estimates range as high as 9 million.

Candles—See "Lamps of Art." In addition to illuminating the altar, candles are sometimes used to mark each of the four quarters, and can also be used for spellworking. They may be anointed with oils and inscribed with runes.

Casting Stones—Several systems of divination call for small stones to be cast upon the ground, or a special board or cloth. The stones may be marked with runes, or their color may indicate their meaning.

Casting the Circle—The psychic creation of a sphere of energy around the area where ritual is to be performed, both to concentrate and focus the power raised, and to keep out unwanted influences or distractions. The space enclosed exists outside ordinary space and time.

Cauldron—The cauldron represents the womb of the Goddess, as in Cerridwen's cauldron named Aven, or the source of all plenty, as in the Dagda's cauldron. Modern Witches use a cauldron either as a symbol, or to cook in for sabbat feasts, or to burn things in as part of a spell.

Centering—The process of moving one's consciousness to one's spiritual center, leading to a feeling of great peace, calmness, strength, clarity and stability.

Chakras—The nexi or focal points of the human energy field. There are traditionally seven major chakras in a line from the top of the head to the base of the spine, as well as many smaller ones. Being able to sense and influence the chakras is an important form of healing.

Chalice—The chalice or cup usually holds wine that is shared around the circle in Wiccan ritual. It is a symbol both of Water and the womb.

Charge of the Goddess—A Witches' liturgical writing in which the Goddess addresses Her followers, first obtained by Charles Leland from an Italian strega named Maddelena around 1886, and published in *Aradia: Gospel of the Witches*. It was rewritten and expanded by Doreen Valiente, probably in the 1950s, and then again by Starhawk in *The Spiral Dance*, 1979. See the appendices.

Circle—See "casting the circle." Also a term for a coven or other magickal group, and also a verb meaning "to gather together for ritual."

Cone of Power—The energy raised during magick is imaged as a cone, which at its peak is released toward a specific goal.

Cord—The Witch's cord is also called a girdle or cingulum; in many traditions the color signifies the Witch's degree. However, the cord can also be used in knot magick and binding and loosing spells.

Correspondences—A system of symbolic equivalences used in magick. For example, a red candle may correspond to the element of Fire, which in turn corresponds to energy and will.

Coven—A group of Witches who gather regularly to celebrate their faith and work magick. They range in size from three to twenty or more, though most covens limit their size to thirteen or fewer. Covens are self-governing and vary widely in their styles and interests. Some covens are affiliated with a particular tradition (denomination) of the Craft, while others are eclectic.

Cowan—Anyone who is not a Witch.

Craft—Another name for Wicca or Witchcraft; not to be confused with the Masonic "craft."

Dedicant—A non-initiated student of Wicca; sometimes called a neophyte, seeker, student or candidate.

Degrees—Levels of initiation representing spiritual development and Craft skill, knowledge, and experience. Most Wiccan traditions have three degrees: first, second and third, with third being the highest.

Deosil—Clockwise or "sunwise." This is the direction the priestess or priest moves when casting the circle, calling Quarters and raising power; it is the movement of attraction, creation and growth. See "widdershins" for the opposite.

Divination—The art and practice of foreseeing trends and discovering hidden knowledge, using such tools as the tarot, I Ching, runes, casting stones, or a showstone. Divination is highly useful prior to working ritual magick.

Drum—Drums are used by many covens as a means of raising power during ritual, as well as for trancework and entertainment. Many different sizes and kinds of drums are used, from the bodhran to the tambour; it is a matter of individual preference.

Earth—In many Wiccan traditions, the element corresponding to the North; the colors black, yellow or forest green; and foundations, stability, the human body, all solid material things, and prosperity.

Earthing—Sending excess energy into the Earth; done in ritual after power has been raised and sent to its goal.

Elder—One who is recognized as an experienced leader, teacher, and counselor within the Craft.

Element—In classical magick, Earth, Air, Fire or Water, each representing a class of energies in the universe, and all of which together make up Spirit and the reality we know. See listings for each element.

Esbat—A gathering of Witches to celebrate a certain phase of the moon (most commonly the full moon), work magick, and socialize; from a French word meaning "to frolic."

Familiar—An animal companion trained to assist in magickal workings. Little is known about the original functions of familiars, though the Inquisitors had their own warped ideas. Nowadays most Witches have animal friends or pets, but few are trained as familiars.

Fire—In many Wiccan traditions, the element corresponding to the South, the color red, energy, will, passion, determination, purpose, and ambition.

Full Moon—That phase in the lunar cycle when the moon is at Her brightest and appears perfectly round; a high point of lunar power when Witches traditionally gather to work magick for healing and abundance, and to celebrate the Goddess. In "The Charge of the Goddess," She says, "Once in every month, and better it be when the Moon is full, gather and adore Me . . . ."

God—The male personification of Deity. In Wicca, His most celebrated aspect is the Horned God of the Wilds.

Goddess—The female personification of Deity. In Wicca, Her most celebrated aspects are the Triple Goddess of the Moon, and the Earth Mother.

Grounding—Psychically reinforcing one's connections with the Earth, by reopening an energy channel between your aura and the Earth.

Grove—An organized group of Pagans. In Witchcraft, a congregation is sometimes called the outer grove to distinguish it from the coven, which is composed of priestesses, priests, and those studying for the priesthood.

Healing—The goal of a great deal of magick, especially among healing-oriented spiritual traditions such as Wicca. Some alternative forms of healing in use among Witches include chakra/energy work, visualization, herbcraft, spirit journeys, and crystal healing. Many Witches are professionals in the fields of health and medicine.

Heathen—A non-Christian, from "one who dwells on the heath." See "Pagan."

Herbs—Wiccan priest/esses often use herbs in simples, extracts, oils, etc., for healing; and in amulets, talismans, and incenses.

High Priest—The primary male leader within a coven. Very often he is a third-degree initiate who either helped found the coven, was chosen by the High Priestess, or was elected by the membership.

High Priestess—The primary female leader within a coven. Very often she is a third-degree initiate who either founded the coven or was elected by the membership.

I Ching—A Chinese system of divination in which yarrow stalks or coins are cast to create hexagrams, which are then interpreted from a standard I Ching book. The I Ching is used by many Witches.

Immanence—The belief that Deity exists within all things, including people, and cannot be separated from them.

Incense—These are often burned in ritual magick, for purification and as a symbol of Fire and Air. They may be in the form of sticks, cones, resins, or dried herbs. The incense chosen will depend on the nature of the magick being performed.

Initiation—A profound spiritual experience in which one's unity with Deity is realized. Also, the ritual by which such an experience is celebrated, and/or one is welcomed as a full member of a particular religious tradition or group.

Karma—The total effect of a person's actions during their successive incarnations, which determines their destiny. A Hindu concept that many Witches find congruent with the Law of Return.

Lamps of Art—Candles used to illuminate the altar at a ritual; they may be white, or colored to correspond with the sabbat being celebrated or the magickal work being done.

Law of Return—Whatever energy is sent out returns to the sender multiplied. Some traditions say it is multiplied by three, and therefore call this principle the "Threefold Law."

Laws of Witchcraft—A list of rules for Witches, focusing on individual conduct and coven operation. They are sometimes called the "Ordains" or "Ardaynes." Several versions exist. Their origin is unclear: they may be from the Burning Times, or recent, or a pastiche of ancient and modern.

Library—Most Witches collect books on the Craft, ancient religions, mythology, nature magick, ceremonial magick, the Qabalah, and related subjects. See the Recommended Reading list in the appendices. Be careful in your selections, as there is still a great deal of nonsense about the Craft in print.

Lunar Cycle—The roughly 29-day cycle during which the visible phase of the moon waxes from dark to full and wanes to dark again. Much magick is geared to the energies present at certain phases.

Magick—The "art of changing consciousness at will." Also the psychic direction of natural energies, using the symbolic language of correspondences, to achieve a goal. Magick is often spelled with a "k" to distinguish it from staged illusions or fantasy magic.

Magick Mirror—A specially constructed dark "mirror" into which the seeker gazes, looking for divinatory images. This art is called scrying, and the mirror is also sometimes called a speculum.

Moon—Symbol of the Triple Goddess (Maiden, Mother, and Crone) in the Wiccan faith, and of feminine powers of intuition and magick, and of female physiological cycles which are attuned to Her.

Mortar and Pestle—A stone bowl and grinding implement used to prepare herbs or other materials for healing or magick.

Name—Many (though not all) Witches take a "coven name" or "magickal" name when they first become involved in the Craft or upon initiation. The name may symbolize their strongest qualities, or qualities they hope to enhance in themselves. Names from nature or mythology are most popular.

Natural Objects—Many Wiccan altars hold an assortment of stones, shells, antlers, pinecones, and other objects, either to symbolize the Goddess, God, and Elements, or just because they're pretty or unusual.

Occult—Knowledge which is supposedly hidden from the eyes or understanding of anyone but adepts, usually referring to techniques or principles of magick. In fact, information formerly considered to be "occult" is freely available to anyone dedicated enough to seek it out from books or teachers.

Oils—These can be homemade or purchased at an occult supply store; they are often used on oneself or one's tools for blessing or consecration.

Ordains—See "Laws of Witchcraft."

Pagan—A follower of any nature-based religion, especially those with European roots such as Wicca, Druidism, and Asatru. From the Latin *paganus* or "country-dweller," a member of the community or resident of the district.

Pantheism—A doctrine that identifies Deity with the universe and its phenomena; or, the worship of all gods. Many Witches consider the God/dess and the universe to be identical, and all gods to be valid facets or aspects of Deity.

Pen of Art—A pen used especially for magickal work or recording information in one's Book of Shadows; some Witches use a quill pen, while others prefer a ballpoint or a computer keyboard.

Pendulum—A divinatory tool consisting of a small weight on a thread or fine chain. It can be made of crystal, stone, wood, or other materials. Its use is called radiesthesia or dowsing.

Pentacle—A disc of metal, ceramic, or wood with a pentagram and other symbols inscribed on it. It is a symbol of the element Earth, and sometimes salt or cakes are placed on it.

Pentagram—A starlike, five-pointed figure of very ancient origin, used magickally for blessing, protection, and balance. The five points stand for Earth, Air, Fire, Water, and Spirit. Witches often wear a silver pentagram encircled, with one point up to symbolize Spirit guiding and balancing the elements. Also called *pentalpha*, "the endless knot," and other names.

Perfect Love and Perfect Trust—A Wiccan ideal; we begin by working to create them within the coven, and expand from there.

Polarity—The interaction of two differing polarity-energies can raise enormous amounts of magickal energy, and this insight is incorporated into most traditions of Wicca, as well as alchemy and other philosophies. The female-male polarity is most commonly discussed, but of course there are others as well: Fire/Water, Yin/Yang, Darkness/Light, and so on.

Polytheism—A belief in many gods. Witches are polytheists to the extent that they believe in many aspects or facets of Deity. However, they could as well be called dualists or monotheists. A saying popular among many Witches is: "All goddesses are one Goddess; all gods are one God; Goddess and God are one."

Power—Energy drawn from natural sources, then concentrated and directed within a ritual for magickal purposes.

Priest—*The American Heritage Dictionary* defines "priest" as "a person having the authority to perform and administer religious rites." We could say that a Wiccan priest is one who performs Wiccan religious rites at will, authority be damned. However, the definition of *shaman* from the same dictionary also fits: one who "acts as a medium between the visible world and an invisible spirit world and who practices magic . . . for healing, divination and control over natural events." A Wiccan priest is also a spiritual teacher and counselor.

Priestess—The same dictionary defines "priestess" as "a woman who presides over especially pagan rites." Add the functions of a priest as defined above, and that seems accurate enough.

Quarters—A shorthand term for the four Elemental powers and the directions they correspond to. Quarters are "called" and "dismissed" during ritual. See also *Elements*.

Reincarnation—The belief that an individual soul or spirit is born more than once, each time into a new body. Most Witches believe in reincarnation, and many practice past life recall or regression.

Ritual—A planned series of activities leading to the accomplishment of a goal through magickal means. The steps or components are described in the chapter on ritual.

Ritual Tools—Implements used in ritual magick. The basic tools for most Witches are the athame, wand, chalice and pentacle, although there are many others which can be made or purchased.

Robe—Some covens wear robes to ritual, others go skyclad. Robes are usually floor-length, long-sleeved, hooded, and held at the waist with a cord. The color may symbolize the season, the Witch's degree, or membership in a particular coven.

Runes—Letters used in the old Norse and Teutonic cultures, both for normal inscriptions and for magick. Each letter is believed to have a special symbolic meaning and power. Casting the runes (carved or painted on wood, stone or ceramic markers) is one form of divination popular among Witches.

Sabbat—One of the holy days of the Wiccan religion, celebrating themes such as birth, fertility and death, related to the turning of the seasons. Most Wiccan traditions celebrate eight sabbats. They have more than one name each, but one set goes as follows: Yule, Imbolg, Ostara, Beltane, Litha, Lughnassad, Mabon and Samhain.

Salt—In ritual, salt is both a symbolic element of Earth and a cleansing agent, especially when mixed with water.

Scourge—This consists of several strands of light cord attached to a handle; some traditions require a token scourging as part of initiation, to ritually purify the candidate or induce trance.

Show Stone—A crystal ball or other polished stone used for scrying; see *Magick Mirror*.

Skyclad—Clothed by the sky; i.e., naked. Some Wiccan traditions practice occasionally or regularly in the nude, while others wear robes. By tradition, nudity deemphasizes socio-economic differences, recognizes the sanctity of the human body, and allows the free flow of psychic energy. It is not an invitation to sexual advances or orgies.

Spell—A pattern or series of words and/or actions performed with magickal intent; or sometimes simply a spoken incantation. A spell may be part of a ritual, but may also be performed without the usual ritual steps: casting the circle, calling the Quarters, invoking Deity and so on.

Staff—A Witch's staff can be a ritual tool of Fire or Air, or symbolize the masculine energy of the God. They are sometimes used as hiking sticks, and sometimes in ritual. The kind of wood used and the carvings and decorations are usually symbolic of energies important to the owner.

Stang—A forked stick placed in the center of the circle, as a primitive symbol of the Horned God or other deity being invoked.

Stones—Rocks and gems are used for healing, divination, talismans, and other magickal purposes. Lodestone (magnetite) and quartz crystals are two commonly used stones, but many others are used as well.

Summerland—The Wiccan concept of the afterlife, where spirits rest in the company of the Lady and Lord, reflect on what they have learned in their most recent incarnation, and prepare for the next one. Witches do not believe in heaven, hell, or purgatory, but only the Summerland.

Sword—A ritual tool of Air or Fire, used in ritual to cast the circle. Most often individual Witches will own athames, and the coven may own a sword. It is also a masculine symbol; a priestess who wears a sword may take the part of a priest, in some traditions.

Talisman—A constructed magickal object, usually with inscribed symbols, intended to attract certain specialized energies (clarity, wealth, health, safety, etc.) and worn as a piece of jewelry.

Tarot—A set of images on cards, traditionally 78, probably first developed in Europe in the late fourteenth century. The pictures represent different stages in the lives and spiritual journey of humankind. The tarot is extremely popular as a tool of divination and self-understanding among modern Witches.

Thaumaturgy—"Low magick" used to influence things and events in everyday life: to protect your house, heal a cold, get a job, travel safely, etc.

Theurgy—"High magick" employed to connect with Deity and foster spiritual growth or transformation.

Three Levels of Self—Some Wiccan traditions use a model of the Self which has three parts: Younger or Lower Self, "Talking Head" or Middle Self, and God/dess or Higher Self. The model is similar to that of Huna, or in some ways Freudian psychology.

Threefold Law—See "Law of Return."

Thurible—A metal incense burner, sometimes suspended from a triple chain, used for cleansing and as a symbol of Air in ritual.

Tradition—A division or denomination of the Wiccan religion. Some of the best-known traditions are the Gardnerian, Alexandrian, Georgian, Faery, Dianic, Pagan Way, and New Reformed Order of the Golden Dawn (NROOGD). Many covens are eclectic and draw from more than one tradition.

Wand—A ritual tool of Fire or Air, traditionally of fruitwood and about seventeen inches long, which can be used in magick to attract or repel. Modern wands are sometimes made of glass, copper, crystal, or other materials.

Warlock—Not a term for a male Witch. Warlock means "oath breaker." A male Witch is called a Witch.

Water—The Element corresponding in some traditions to the West, light green, medium blue, and silver, emotions and intuition.

Wheel of the Year—The cycle of seasons extending throughout the year. For most Witches, the year ends and begins at Samhain, or ends at Samhain and begins at Yule.

Wicca—A beneficent and magickal Earth religion which celebrates the immanent Triple Goddess of the Moon and the Horned God of Nature; also called the Old Religion, the Craft, or Witchcraft. Also, the old term for a male Witch. From the Anglo-Saxon "holy or consecrated"; possibly related to "wise" or "to bend or shape."

Wicce—A female Witch.

Wiccan Rede—The ethical core of the Craft, summed up in eight words: "An ye harm none, do as ye will." In modern language: "As long as you do not harm anyone, follow your inner guidance, your True Will."

Widdershins—Counterclockwise; the direction a magician moves when she or he wishes to banish, remove or release energy. See *deosil* for the opposite term.

Witch—A priestess or priest of the Old Religion, Wicca.

Witchcraft—See *Wicca*. From the Anglo-Saxon *wiccacraeft*, related to the words for magick, divination, wisdom, and bending or shaping. The term has been misused by the Inquisition and careless anthropologists to indicate devil worship, evil magick, or magick generally from any culture.

Witches' Pyramid—A symbolic depiction of the qualities necessary to practice magick. The four sides of the pyramid are imagination, will, secrecy or silence, and faith. The pyramid is filled with love and rests on a foundation of knowledge.

Witch Jewels—Female Witches wear necklaces of gemstones or other natural materials, and some males wear a metal torc. The High Priestess may wear a crescent tiara, necklace of amber and jet, and special garter; the High Priest may wear a horned headdress. Witches of both sexes may wear an inscribed silver bracelet, rings, amulets, and talismans.

Bibliography

Adler, Margot. *Drawing Down the Moon: Witches, Druids, Goddess-Worshippers and Other Pagans in America Today*. Boston: Beacon Press, 1986, 1996.

Butler, W. E. *The Magician: His Training and Work*. York Beach, ME: Samuel Weiser, 1969

Campanelli, Dan and Pauline. *Rites of Passage: The Pagan Wheel of Life*. St. Paul, MN: Llewellyn Publications, 1994.

Campanelli, Pauline. *Wheel of the Year: Living the Magical Life*. St. Paul, MN: Llewellyn Publications, 1990.

Circle. *Circle Guide to Wiccan/Pagan Resources*. Circle Publications, annual.

Conway, D. J. *The Ancient & Shining Ones: World Myth, Magic & Religion*. St. Paul, MN: Llewellyn Publications, 1994.

Cuhulain, Kerr. *The Law Enforcement Guide to Wicca*. Victoria, BC, Canada: Horned Owl Publishing, 1997.

Dunwich, Gerina. *The Wicca Source Book: A Complete Guide for the Modern Witch*. Secaucus, NJ: Citadel Press, 1996.

Farrar, Janet and Stewart. *Eight Sabbats for Witches*. London: Robert Hale, 1981.

Farrar, Janet and Stewart. *The Witches' Way: Principles, Rituals, and Beliefs of Modern Witchcraft*. London: Robert Hale, 1984.

Galadriel, Lady. *The New Wiccan Book of the Law. Grove of the Unicorn*. P.O. Box 13384, Athens, GA 30324: Moonstone Publications, 1992.

Green, Marian. *A Calendar of Festivals: Traditional Celebrations, Songs, Seasonal Recipes and Things to Make*. Rockport, MA: Element, 1991.

Hughes, Pennethorne. *Witchcraft. Longmans, Green, England, 1952*. Baltimore: Penguin Books, 1965.

Huson, Paul. *Mastering Witchcraft: A Practical Guide for Witches, Warlocks & Covens*. New York: Berkeley Publishing, 1970.

Jade. *To Know: A Guide to Women's Magic and Spirituality*. Oak Park, IL: Delphi, 1991.

Jones, Evan and Valiente, Doreen. *Witchcraft: A Tradition Renewed.* Custer, WA: Phoenix Publishing, 1990.

K, Amber. *How to Organize a Coven or Magickal Study Group.* Blue Mounds, WI: Nine Candles, 1984 (incorporated in its entirety into this book).

K, Amber. *A Treasury of Coven Activities.* Blue Mounds, WI: Nine Candles, 1986 (incorporated in its entirety into this book).

Kennedy, Eugene and Charles, Sara C. *On Becoming a Counselor: A Basic Guide for Nonprofessional Counselors.* New York: Crossroads Publishing, 1994.

Leek, Sybil. *The Complete Art of Witchcraft.* New York: New American Library, 1971.

Rush, Anne Kent. *Moon, Moon.* New York: Random House; Berkeley, CA: Moon Books; 1976.

Starhawk. *The Spiral Dance: A Rebirth of the Ancient Religion of the Great Goddess.* San Francisco: Harper & Row, 1979.

Weinstein, Marion. *Positive Magic.* New York: Pocket Books, 1978.

Index

F

G

H

Q

R

U

V

W

Y

Z

New Worlds
of Mind & Spirit
Women's Spirituality

True Magick

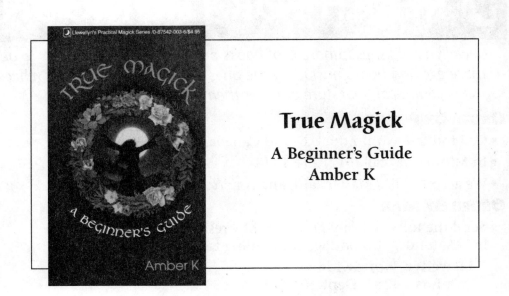

A Beginner's Guide
Amber K

True Magick can change your life. With magick's aid, you can have vibrant health, prosperity or a new career. You can enhance your relationships or bring new ones into your life. With magick, you can reach deep inside yourself to find confidence, courage, tranquility, faith, compassion, understanding or humor. If you're curious about magick, you will find answers in this book. Amber K, a High Priestess of the Wiccan religion and experienced practitioner of magick, explains not only the history and lore of magick, but also its major varieties in the world today. And if you want to practice magick, then this book will start you on the path.

0-87542-003-6, 272 pp., mass market, illus. $4.95

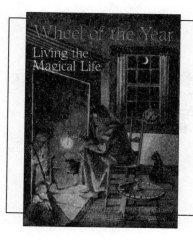

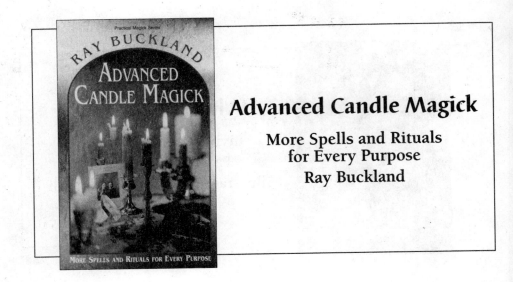